This book was donated
to honor
the birthday of

Tommy Martin

by

Thomas Martin Sr + Cynthia Phillips

2002
DATE

Cassell's Humorous Quotations

Cassell's Humorous Quotations

NIGEL REES

CASSELL&CO

First published in the United Kingdom in 2001 by Cassell & Co

Distributed in the United States of America by
Sterling Publishing Co., Inc.
387 Park Avenue South, New York, NY 10016-8810

A CIP catalogue record for this book is available from the British Library

ISBN 0-304-35720-0

Printed and bound in Finland

Cassell & Co, Wellington House, 125 Strand, London WC2R 0BB

Contents

Introduction

The first move any compiler of a dictionary of humorous quotations makes is to take a look at the work of those who have attempted the task before him. That done, he exclaims, 'But that's not humorous!'

So what exactly is a humorous quotation? Does it have to raise a laugh or even a smile to qualify?

On the whole, I think, yes. The quotations selected should not just be pithy observations or critical barbs, but things said with either the warmth of humour or the cleverness of wit. But I am perfectly aware that the same test will be made of the quotations in my collection and, on occasions, I, too, am found wanting.

Nevertheless, I should be surprised if the majority of quotations in this volume did not produce a reaction in the reader somewhere on the scale from wry amusement to outright glee, as was their authors' intention. There are also some remarks included because they are themselves risible, in the sense of being laughed *at* rather than *with*, and not because their speakers intended them to be so received.

In addition there is a selection of quotations not necessarily humorous in themselves but on the subject of humour, comedy and wit.

As in all my books – and, if I may say so, unlike most other compilers of dictionaries of humorous quotations – I have tried to provide some sort of source for the quotations and not just plonk down the quote with an 'attributed to …', though, alas, there are occasions when this has been necessary. There is, again somewhat unusually, a comprehensive index, which should make it the simplest matter to find any half-remembered line that the reader might be interested in.

I have encountered the majority of quotations in this book during the more than twenty-five years I have spent writing and presenting the BBC Radio programme *Quote ... Unquote*. My thanks to Radio 4 and the World Service for maintaining their faith over what is, by anybody's standards, a very long time in broadcasting.

My thanks are also due to the many faithful readers of *The 'Quote ... Unquote' Newsletter* around the world. In asking about and contributing humorous quotations, they have kept me up to date on the sayings that have amused them or about which they have sought sources or further information. In particular, I should like to acknowledge the help and interest of: Dr J.K. Aronson; H.E. Bell; John Campbell; Jonathan Cecil; Barry Day; Philip Eden; Jaap Engelsman; Mark English; John Fletcher; Charles G. Francis; Ian Gillies; John Gray; W. Eric Gustafson; Raymond Harris; Donald Hickling; Roy Hudd; W.W. Keen James; Sir Antony Jay; Justin Kaplan; Miles Kington; Oonagh Lahr; Michael R. Lewis; R.P.W. Lewis; Leonard Miall; Professor Wolfgang Mieder; the late Frank Muir; Michael and Valerie Grosvenor Myer; Denis Norden; John Julius Norwich; John O'Byrne; Derek Parker; Philip Purser; Steve Race; Claire Rayner; Tony Ring, P.G. Wodehouse Society; Brian Robinson; Jeffery L. Yablon; and many, many others.

Those who have read my *Cassell Dictionary of Humorous Quotations* (1998) may well be wondering how this new *Cassell's Humorous Quotations* differs from it. The answer is simple: it contains more than twice the number of quotations as the earlier book and is of more than twice the extent.

Nigel Rees

LONDON, 2001

The Dictionary

Aardvark

1 It's aardvark, but it pays well.

Anonymous. Quoted in John S. Crosbie, *Crosbie's Dictionary of Puns* (1977). Compare: 'Aardvarks never killed anybody' from 'The Lost Emperor' in BBC Radio's *The Goon Show* (4 October 1955), script by Spike Milligan. The same sort of pun is also made in BBC Radio's *Round the Horne* (25 February 1968).

2 In the beginning was the word. And the word was 'Aardvark'.

Anonymous (graffito). Included in my book *Graffiti 2* (1980).

Abdication

Within days of the abdication of King Edward VIII in December 1936 schoolchildren were singing:

3 Hark the herald angels sing
Mrs Simpson's pinched our king.

Anonymous (British). Quoted in Kenneth Harris, *Attlee* (1982). Also in Cleveland Amory, *Who Killed Society?* (1960).

Aberdeen, Scotland

4 Bleakness, not meanness or jollity, is the keynote to Aberdonian character ... For anyone passing their nights and days in The Silver City by the Sea ... it is comparable to passing one's existence in a refrigerator.

Lewis Grassic Gibbon, Scottish novelist and journalist (1901–35). *Scottish Scene, or the Intelligent Man's Guide to Albyn*, 'Aberdeen' (1934).

Abilities

To H.G. Wells:

5 It is all very well to be able to write books, but can you waggle your ears?

(Sir) J(ames) M. Barrie, Scottish playwright (1860–1937). Quoted in J. A. Hammerton, *Barrie: The Story of a Genius* (1929).

Abortion

6 One doctor consulted another because he wished to have the other doctor's opinion on the termination of a pregnancy. The circumstances were as follows. The father was syphilitic, and the mother tuberculous. Of the children that had already been born the first was blind, the second had died, the third was deaf and dumb, the fourth was tuberculous. 'What would you have done?' the first doctor asked his colleague. 'I would have ended the pregnancy,' replied the second. Said the first: 'Then you would have murdered Beethoven.'

Anonymous. Quoted by Enid Bagnold in *The Times* (14 November 1962). She had it from Maurice Baring when she was his neighbour at Rottingdean in Sussex.

Absence

7 What is better than Presence of Mind in a Railway accident? Absence of Body.

Anonymous. *Punch* Magazine, Vol. 16 (9 June 1849).

1 I was … court-martialled in my absence, sentenced to death in my absence. So I said, right, you can shoot me in my absence.

Brendan Behan, Irish playwright (1923–64). *The Hostage* (1962 version).

2 The more he looked inside, the more Piglet wasn't there.

A.A. Milne, English children's writer (1882–1956). *The House at Pooh Corner*, Chap. 1 (1928).

Absentmindedness

3 Archbishop Chenevix Trench retired from the see of Dublin and spent his last two years in London. On returning to visit his successor Lord Plunkett, in Dublin, his memory lapsed and he forgot that he was no longer host, remarking to his wife: 'I'm afraid, my love, that we must put this cook down among our failures.'

Richard Chenevix Trench (1807–86), English Anglican Archbishop of Dublin (1864–84). Quoted in *The Monarch Book of Christian Wisdom*, ed. Robert Paterson (1997).

Telegram to wife:

4 Am in Market Harborough. Where ought I to be?

G.K. Chesterton, English poet, novelist and critic (1874–1936). *Autobiography*, Chap. 16 (1936): 'Of those days the tale is told that I once sent a telegram to my wife in London, which ran: "Am in Market Harborough. Where ought I to be?" I cannot remember whether this story is true; but it is not unlikely or, I think, unreasonable.' Maisie Ward, in *Return to Chesterton (*1944), says that a hundred different places have been substituted for 'Market Harborough' in the telling of this story. Chesterton's wife, Frances, on this occasion cabled the answer 'Home' – because, as she explained, it was easier to get him home and start him off again.

5 The utterly distinguished Justice Wendell Holmes once boarded a train in Washington DC but soon found out that he had lost his ticket. The conductor recognized him and said, 'Don't worry about it, sir. I'm sure when you find it, you'll send it in.' Justice Holmes replied: 'Young man, the question is not, Where is my ticket?, but rather, without it, how am I supposed to know where I am going?'

Oliver Wendell Holmes Jnr, American lawyer (1841–1935). Source untraced. The story is also told about Ambassador Dwight Morrow and William Cecil, Bishop of Exeter (1863–1936) – of the latter in John Train, *True Remarkable Occurrences* (1978).

6 Michael Ramsey was, as a young man, on the staff of Boston Parish Church in Lincolnshire. On one occasion he went out of his lodgings without his door key. When he came back, he rang the doorbell, but his landlady was nervous of strangers and called out through the door, 'I'm sorry, Mr Ramsey is out.' Ramsey replied, 'I'll return later.'

Michael Ramsey (1904–88), English Anglican Archbishop of Canterbury. Quoted in Owen Chadwick, *Michael Ramsey, A Life* (1991). Chadwick says of this story that 'there is excellent evidence of its truth'. Compare one of several *Punch* cartoons based on this kind of incident: G.L. Stampa's 'ABSENCE' (1 February 1899) has the caption: *Mr Brownrigg (an absent-minded old Gent):* 'Let me see – does Mr Brownrigg live here?' *New servant (not recognizing her master):* 'Yes, Sir; but he's not in at present.' *Mr B.:* 'Oh, well, never mind, I'll call again.'

Absinthe

7 Ladies and gentlemen, I give you a toast; it is: Absinthe makes the tart grow fonder.

Hugh Drummond, British aristocrat. Quoted in Sir Seymour Hicks, *The Vintage Years* (1943).

8 Absinthe makes the heart grow fonder.

Oliver Herford, American humorist (1863–1935), and Addison Mizner, American architect (1872–1933). *The Cynic's Calendar* (1902).

9 Absinthe makes the parts grow stronger.

Jack Hibberd. *Odyssey of a Prostitute* (1983).

1 After the first glass of absinthe you see things as you wish they were. After the second you see them as they are not. Finally you see things as they really are, and that is the most horrible thing in the world.

Oscar Wilde, Irish playwright, poet and wit (1854–1900). Quoted in Jonathon Green, *Consuming Passions* (1985).

Abstinence

2 Abstinence is the thin end of the pledge.

Anonymous (graffito). Quoted in my book *Graffiti Lives OK* (1979).

3 A teetotaller is the very worst sort of drunkard.

E.F. Benson, English novelist (1867–1940). *The House of Defence* (1906).

4 Abstainer: a weak person who yields to the temptation of denying himself a pleasure.

Ambrose Bierce, American journalist (1842–?1914). *The Cynic's Word Book* (later retitled *The Devil's Dictionary*) (1906).

5 There should be asylums for habitual teetotallers, but they would probably relapse into teetotalism as soon as they came out.

Samuel Butler, English novelist and writer (1835–1902). *Notebooks* (1902).

6 There is nothing wrong with sobriety in moderation.

John Ciardi, American poet and critic (1916–86). In *The Saturday Review* (1966).

7 There was once a man who learnt to mind his own business. He went to heaven. I hope the teetotallers will remember that.

T.W.H. Crosland, English poet (1865–1924). *The Beautiful Teetotaller* (1907).

8 If you resolve to give up smoking, drinking and loving, you don't actually live longer; it just seems longer.

(Sir) Clement Freud, English humorist and politician (1924–). Quoted in *The Observer* (27 December 1964) and ascribed to 'a third-rate comedian in Sloane Square'.

9 Abstinence is as easy to me as temperance would be difficult.

(Dr) Samuel Johnson, English writer and lexicographer (1709–84). Quoted in *The Treasury of Humorous Quotations*, eds Evan Esar & Nicolas Bentley (1951). Possibly an expansion of 'He could practise abstinence, but not temperance' in James Boswell, *The Life of Samuel Johnson* (1791) – for March 1781.

10 I'd hate to be a teetotaller. Imagine getting up in the morning and knowing that's as good as you're going to feel all day.

Dean Martin, American actor and singer (1917–95). Attributed remark.

11 I'm only a beer teetotaller, not a champagne teetotaller.

Bernard Shaw, Irish playwright and critic (1856–1950). *Candida*, Act 3 (1895).

12 He never touches water: it goes to his head at once.

Oscar Wilde, Irish playwright, poet and wit (1854–1900). In *The Letters of Oscar Wilde*, ed. Rupert Hart-Davis (1962).

Abuse

Of Lord John Russell:

13 If a traveller were informed that such a man was Leader of the House of Commons, he might begin to comprehend how the Egyptians worshipped – AN INSECT.

Benjamin Disraeli (1st Earl of Beaconsfield), British Conservative Prime Minister and writer (1804–81). Pseudonymously in 'The Letters of Runnymede' in *The Times* (January–May 1836).

When a man attacked him with coarse raillery:

14 Sir, your wife, under pretence of keeping a bawdy-house, is a receiver of stolen goods.

(Dr) Samuel Johnson, English writer and lexicographer

(1709–84). Quoted in James Boswell, *The Life of Samuel Johnson* (1791) – for 1780. Here Boswell reproduces some Johnsoniana collected by Bennet Langton. When the 'contests' in abusive language conducted between passers-by on the River Thames are mentioned, this example is adduced, though it is not clear whether Johnson himself was on the river when he uttered the squelch.

French sentry (to King Arthur):

1 I fart in your general direction! Your mother was a hamster and your father smelt of elderberries.

Line from film *Monty Python and the Holy Grail* (UK 1975). Written and performed by the Monty Python team.

See also INSULTS.

Academics

2 The reason academic politics are so bitter is that so little is at stake.

Anonymous – though variously attributed to Woodrow Wilson, Wallace Sayre and others, but principally to Henry Kissinger, who has commented that he does not recall saying it but that it 'sounded' like him. In fact, the most likely progenitor is Wallace Stanley Sayre (1905–72), professor of political science at Columbia University. 'Sayre's Law' is sometimes cited by political scientists, and one version of it is: 'The politics of the university are so intense because the stakes are so low.' Another version goes: 'In any dispute, the intensity of feeling is inversely proportional to the value of the stakes at issue. That is why academic politics are so bitter' – quoted in Charles Philip Issawi, *Issawi's Laws of Social Motion* (1973).

3 No academic person is ever voted into the chair until he has reached an age at which he has forgotten the meaning of the word 'irrelevant'.

Francis M. Cornford, English academic (1874–1943). *Microcosmographia Academica* (1908).

Accents

4 The Morningside accent is one of the glories of Edinburgh: it is what the posh people use. And yet there are many recollections of a Morningside lady whose tones you could cut with a knife, remarking, 'People talk of an Edinburgh accent, but I've never heard it.'

Anonymous. Quoted by Dr Eric Anderson on BBC Radio *Quote ... Unquote* (9 July 1986). On the same show, Robert Stephens recalled (24 March 1992) how his then wife Maggie Smith had been complimented on her Edinburgh accent when playing the title role in the film *The Prime of Miss Jean Brodie*. A woman speaking in pure Morningside said, 'But there is no Edinburgh accent ...'

5 One of the people I hung out with in the small hours was Walter Winchell. He'd often print remarks of mine. One that he paraphrased years later was my comment on the composer Vernon Duke, with his English accent: 'You speak with a monocle in your throat.'

Oscar Levant, American pianist and actor (1906–72). *Memoirs of an Amnesiac* (1965).

6 In a Lancashire cotton-town you could probably go for months on end without once hearing an 'educated' accent, whereas there can hardly be a town in the South of England where you could throw a brick without hitting the niece of a bishop.

George Orwell, English novelist and journalist (1903–50). *The Road to Wigan Pier* (1937).

7 I have traveled more than any one else, and I have noticed that even the angels speak English with an accent.

Mark Twain, American writer (1835–1910). *Following the Equator*, 'Conclusion' (1897).

Accordions

8 A gentleman knows how to play the accordion, but doesn't.

Al Cohn, American saxophonist (1925–88). Attributed remark.

Accountancy

1 [Accountancy is] a profession whose idea of excitement is sharpening a bundle of No. 2 pencils …

Anonymous. Quoted in *Time* Magazine (19 April 1993).

2 Your report here says that you are an extremely dull person. You see, our experts describe you as an appallingly dull fellow, unimaginative, timid, lacking in initiative, spineless, easily dominated, no sense of humour, tedious company and irrepressibly drab and awful. And whereas in most professions these would be considered drawbacks, in chartered accountancy they are a positive boon.

Lines from BBC TV *Monty Python's Flying Circus*, First Series, Episode 10 (21 December 1969). Script by the Monty Python team.

3 Bloom, do me a favour. Move a few decimal points around. You can do it. You're an accountant. You're in a noble profession. The word count is part of your title.

Line from film *The Producers* (US 1967). Screenwriter: Mel Brooks. Spoken by Zero Mostel (Max Bialystock) to Gene Wilder (Leo Bloom).

Achievement

4 Every man who is high up loves to feel that he has done it himself; and the wife smiles, and let's it go at that. It's our only joke. Every woman knows that.

(Sir) J(ames) M. Barrie, Scottish playwright (1860–1937). *What Every Woman Knows*, Act 4 (1908). Maggie speaking.

5 It is a sobering thought … that when Mozart was my age he had been dead for two years.

Tom Lehrer, American songwriter and entertainer (1928–). On record album *That Was the Year That Was* (1965).

Acquaintances

6 Acquaintance: a person whom we know well enough to borrow from, but not well enough to lend to.

Ambrose Bierce, American journalist (1842–?1914). *The Cynic's Word Book* (later retitled *The Devil's Dictionary*) (1906).

When Algernon is to be sent back to London, Cecily says:

7 It is always painful to part from people whom one has known for a very brief space of time. The absence of old friends one can endure with equanimity. But even a momentary separation from anyone to whom one has just been introduced is almost unbearable.

Oscar Wilde, Irish playwright, poet and wit (1854–1900). *The Importance of Being Earnest*, Act 2 (1895).

Acting and actors

8 Do actors need brains? If they can act, no. If they can't, yes

James Agate, English dramatic critic (1877–1947). *The Later Ego* (1951).

Of Sir Seymour Hicks, English actor-manager (1871–1949):

9 It was said that whereas Irving and Garrick had been *tours de force*, Hicks had been forced to tour.

Anonymous. Quoted by Sheridan Morley on BBC Radio *Quote … Unquote* (1989). Peter Hay, in *Theatrical Anecdotes* (1987), also finds both 'Olivier is a *tour de force* but Wolfit is forced to tour' *and* Mrs Patrick Campbell saying to Lilian Braithwaite, 'You are a perfect *tour de force* and here I am forced to tour.' Ned Sherrin in *Theatrical Anecdotes* (1991) has the Campbell version (reported by Emlyn Williams), said when Braithwaite was playing a role based on Campbell in Ivor Novello's *Party* (1932), and when Braithwaite was in the West End but the real Campbell off to the provinces. And Sherrin has the Olivier version as a recycling by Hermione Gingold's writers for a revue in the 1940s.

Of a certain actor:

1 He has delusions of adequacy.

Anonymous. Quoted in my book *A Year of Stings and Squelches* (1985).

Of the English actor Denholm Elliott (1922–92):

2 Never work with children, dogs, or Denholm Elliott.

Anonymous. Quoted in *The Guardian* (29 April 1989). This view has also been attributed to Gabriel Byrne.

Of John Hurt in the film 1984:

3 As usual he looked just like Joan of bloody Arc – *after* she's been burnt at the stake.

Anonymous. Quoted in my book *A Year of Stings and Squelches* (1985).

Producing one of his own plays, the author was approached by a young actor who was having difficulty interpreting his part. He told him:

4 Try and look as if you had a younger brother in Shropshire.

(Sir) J(ames) M. Barrie, Scottish playwright (1860–1937). Quoted in Lady Cynthia Asquith, *Diaries* 1915–18 (1968) – entry for 6 January 1918. The story also occurs in John Aye, *Humour in the Theatre* (1932), where the advice is, 'I should like you to convey that the man you portray has a brother in Shropshire who drinks port.' From about the same period there is said to have been a stage direction (from another dramatist): 'Sir Henry turns his back to the audience and conveys that he has a son' (quoted in Michael Holroyd, *Bernard Shaw, Vol. 3: 1918–1950*, 1991).

5 For an actress to succeed, she must have the face of a Venus, the brains of a Minerva, the grace of Terpsichore, the memory of a Macaulay, the figure of Juno, and the hide of a rhinoceros.

Ethel Barrymore, American actress (1879–1959). Quoted in George Jean Nathan, *The Theatre in the Fifties* (1953).

6 Sarah Bernhardt was one of the first actors whose aversion to performing with animals or children was made apparent. When asked to appear on the music-hall stage in a scene from *L'Aiglon*, she declined, saying: 'Between monkeys, not.'

Sarah Bernhardt, French actress (1844–1923). Quoted in Michael Billington, *Peggy Ashcroft* (1988).

Of Peter O'Toole's Macbeth *at the Old Vic:*

7 He delivers every line with a monotonous bark as if addressing an audience of Eskimos who have never heard of Shakespeare.

Michael Billington, English theatre critic (1939–). In *The Guardian* (1980). Quoted in Ned Sherrin, *Cutting Edge* (1984).

8 An actor's a guy who, if you ain't talking about him, ain't listening.

Marlon Brando, American film actor (1924–). Quoted in *The Observer* (January 1956). In fact, according to Bob Thomas in *Brando* (1973), Brando appears to have been quoting George Glass (1910–84).

Of working with a dull actor:

9 Like acting with 210 pounds of condemned veal.

Coral Browne, Australian-born actress (1913–91). Attributed remark.

10 The secret of acting is sincerity – and if you can fake that, you've got it made.

George Burns, American comedian (1896–1996). Quoted in Michael York, *Travelling Player* (1991). Fred Metcalf in *The Penguin Dictionary of Modern Humorous Quotations* (1987) has Burns saying, rather: 'Acting is about honesty. If you can fake that, you've got it made.' However, Kingsley Amis in a devastating piece about Leo Rosten in his *Memoirs* (1991) has the humorist relating 'at some stage in the 1970s' how he had given a Commencement address including the line: 'Sincerity. If you can *fake that* ... you'll have the world at your feet.' So perhaps the saying was circulating even before Burns received the credit. Or perhaps Rosten took it from him? An advertisement in *Rolling Stone*, *c.* 1982, offered a T-shirt with the slogan (anonymous): 'The secret of success is sincerity. Once you can fake that you've got it made.' Fred MacMurray was quoted in *Variety* (15 April 1987): 'I once asked Barbara Stanwyck the secret of acting. She said: "Just be truthful – and if you can fake that, you've got it made".'

Of Jeanette MacDonald and Nelson Eddy:

1 An affair between a mad rockinghorse and a rawhide suitcase.

(Sir) Noël Coward, English entertainer and writer (1899–1973). Quoted in my book *A Year of Stings and Squelches* (1985).

Of an actress unable to elicit comedy from his lines:

2 She couldn't get a laugh if she pulled a kipper out of her cunt.

(Sir) Noël Coward. Quoted in *The Sayings of Noël Coward*, ed. Philip Hoare (1997). When the said actress got a laugh: 'She's pulled it out' – quoted in Richard Briers, *Coward and Company* (1987).

To a limp-wristed actor who was turning in a less than convincing martial performance as a soldier:

3 A little more Marshall and rather less Snelgrove, if you please!

(Sir) Noël Coward. Quoted in my book *A Year of Stings and Squelches* (1985). Marshall & Snelgrove was the name of a prominent London store.

Reviewing Robert Mitchum's performance in the TV mini-series The Winds of War:

4 Nowadays Mitchum doesn't so much act as point his suit at people.

Russell Davies, Welsh journalist (1946–). *The Sunday Times* (18 September 1983).

Of Ingrid Bergman:

5 Dear Ingrid – speaks five languages and can't act in any of them.

(Sir) John Gielgud, English actor (1904–2000). Quoted in Ronald Harwood, *The Ages of Gielgud* (1984).

6 Somebody once asked W.S. Gilbert whether he had been to see the great Sir Henry Irving, who was appearing on the London stage at that time in *Faust*. He had not. 'I go to the pantomime,' replied Gilbert, 'only at Christmas.'

(Sir) W.S. Gilbert, English writer and lyricist (1836–1911). Quoted in Leslie Ayre, *The Gilbert and Sullivan Companion* (1972).

On being told by a fellow actor, 'I'm a smash hit. Why, yesterday I had the audience glued to their seats':

7 Clever of you to think of it.

Charles Herford, American actor. Attributed remark.

8 Actresses will happen in the best-regulated families.

Oliver Herford, American humorist (1863–1935). Quoted in *The Treasury of Humorous Quotations*, eds Evan Esar & Nicolas Bentley (1951).

9 Actors are cattle.

(Sir) Alfred Hitchcock, English film director (1899–1980). Quoted in the *Saturday Evening Post* (22 May 1943). Later: 'I deny I ever said that actors are cattle. What I said was "actors should be *treated* like cattle"' – quoted in *The Home Book of Humorous Quotations*, ed. A.K. Adams (1969). In François Truffaut, *Hitchcock* (English version), Chap. 6 (1968), Hitchcock more seriously commented: 'A few years prior to my arrival in Hollywood I had been quoted as saying that all actors are cattle. I'm not quite sure in what context I might have made such a statement. It may have been made in the early days of the talkies in England, when we used actors who were simultaneously performing in stage plays [who did not have much commitment and regarded films as slumming] ... I had no use for that kind of actor.'

Of Raymond Massey's continuing his interpretation of Abraham Lincoln off-stage:

10 Massey won't be satisfied until somebody assassinates him.

George S. Kaufman, American playwright (1889–1961). Quoted in Howard Teichman, *George S. Kaufman* (1973).

Visiting the set of the 1941 remake of Dr Jekyll and Mr Hyde *with Spencer Tracy in the title roles:*

11 Which is he playing now?

W. Somerset Maugham, English novelist, playwright and writer (1874–1965). Quoted in Leslie Halliwell, *The Filmgoer's Book of Quotes* (1978). The point of this story is that Tracy did not use any shock make-up, other than a pair of false teeth, to show the transformation from Dr Jekyll to Mr Hyde. The effect was rather subtle – obviously too much so for Maugham. Discussed in John Sutherland, *Can Jane Eyre Be Happy?* (1997).

To Dustin Hoffman during the filming of Marathon Man *(c. 1975) – Hoffman having stayed up for three nights in order to portray a sleepless character:*

1 Dear boy, why not try acting?

Laurence Olivier (Lord Olivier), English actor (1907–89). Quoted in *The Times* (17 May 1982).

2 Scratch an actor and you'll find an actress.

Dorothy Parker, American writer (1893–1967). Quoted in Leslie Halliwell, *The Filmgoer's Book of Quotes* (1973), but unverified.

To an actor with a large nose and no chin to speak of, who told her of his hopes in Hollywood:

3 Oh, they've been searching for a new Cary Grant.

Dorothy Parker. Quoted in *The Sayings of Dorothy Parker*, ed. S.T. Brownlow (1992).

Of an elderly actress who was acting in Camelot:

4 Playing a battlement, no doubt.

Dorothy Parker. Attributed in the same book as above.

Leo (on Max's suggestion that the actors be shot to close the play):

5 Have you lost your mind? How can you kill the actors? ... Actors are not animals. They're human beings.
Max:
They are? Have you ever eaten with one?

Lines from film *The Producers* (US 1967). Screenwriter: Mel Brooks. Spoken by Zero Mostel (Max Bialystock) and Gene Wilder (Leo Bloom).

On Crossroads:

6 The TV soap opera whose acting gives trees a bad name.

Tim Satchell, English critic (1946–). In the *Daily Mail* and quoted in my book *A Year of Stings and Squelches* (1985).

To an actor who wailed, 'Who do I have to fuck to get out of this show?':

7 The same person you fucked to get in!

Stephen Sondheim, American songwriter (1930–). To Larry Kert during a technical rehearsal for the London production of *Company* (1972). Quoted in Ned Sherrin, *Cutting Edge* (1984).

8 *Ehrhardt (to Tura, in disguise):*

What he [Tura] did to Shakespeare, we are doing now to Poland.

Line from film *To Be Or Not To Be* (US 1942). Screenwriter: Edwin Justus Mayer. Spoken by Jack Benny (Joseph Tura) to Sig Rumann (Colonel Ehrhardt).

9 English actors act quite well, but they act between the lines.

Oscar Wilde, Irish playwright, poet and wit (1854–1900). Quoted in *The Treasury of Humorous Quotations*, eds Evan Esar & Nicolas Bentley (1951).

On the Burton-Taylor Private Lives *in 1964:*

10 He's miscast and she's Miss Taylor.

Emlyn Williams, Welsh actor and playwright (1905–87). Quoted in James Harding, *Emlyn Williams* (1987).

See also THEATRICAL CRITICISM.

Activity

A vicar's wife is talking to an old, somewhat rustic gentleman who has been laid up with an injured foot. She is sympathizing with him and saying: 'Now that you can't get about, and are not able to read, how do you manage to occupy the time?' He replies:

11 Well, mum, sometimes I sits and thinks and then again I just sits.

Gunning-King, English cartoonist. Caption to cartoon in *Punch* Magazine, Vol. 131 (24 October 1906).

Adam and Eve

12 When Eve upon the first of Men
The apple press'd with specious cant,
Oh! what a thousand pities then
That Adam was not Adamant!

Thomas Hood, English poet and humorist (1799–1845). 'A Reflection' (1842).

Adaptations

On adapting Middlemarch *for television:*

1 Like getting an elephant into a suitcase.

Andrew Davies, English TV playwright and adapter (1936–). Quoted by Sue Birtwhistle in *The Guardian* (13 October 1995).

Addiction

2 Cocaine habit-forming? Of course not. I ought to know. I've been using it for years.

Tallulah Bankhead, American actress (1903–68). *Tallulah* (1952). Compare: 'Typhoid is a terrible disease; it can kill you or damage your brain. I know what I'm talking about, I've had typhoid' – Comte Maurice de MacMahon, French soldier and statesman (1808–93). Quoted in Bechtel & Carrière, *Dictionnaire de la Bêtise* (1983).

3 Giving up smoking is easy. I've done it hundreds of times.

Mark Twain, American writer (1835–1910). Attributed but not verified. Quoted in *The Sayings of Mark Twain*, ed. James Munson (1992). *Reader's Digest* (December 1945) ascribed this saying to Twain, giving *Coronet* magazine as its source.

Adjectives

4 As to the Adjective: when in doubt strike it out.

Mark Twain, American writer (1835–1910). *Pudd'nhead Wilson*, Chap. 11 (1894).

Adolescence

5 Adolescence is the stage between puberty and adultery.

Anonymous. Quoted in John S. Crosbie, *Crosbie's Dictionary of Puns* (1977).

Adultery

6 Do not adultery commit;
Advantage rarely comes of it.

Arthur Hugh Clough, English poet (1819–61). 'The Latest Decalogue' (1862).

7 Adultery is the application of democracy to love.

H.L. Mencken, American journalist and linguist (1880–1956). 'Sententiae' (1921–48)

Adulthood

8 Was it for this I uttered prayers,
And sobbed and cursed and kicked the stairs,
That now, domestic as a plate,
I should retire at half-past eight?

Edna St Vincent Millay, American poet (1892–1950). 'Grown-Up' in *A Few Figs from Thistles* (1920).

Adventure

9 [Eating] an egg is always an adventure: it may be different.

Oscar Wilde, Irish playwright, poet and wit (1854–1900). Quoted in Herbert V. Prochnow, Snr & Jnr, *A Treasury of Humorous Quotations* (1969). Sometimes remembered as 'Eating a boiled egg is an adventure.'

Advertising

10 Advertising is 85 percent confusion and 15 percent commission.

Fred Allen, American comedian (1894–1956). Quoted in Herbert V. Prochnow, Snr & Jnr, *A Treasury of Humorous Quotations* (1969).

Two women are being served in a chemist's shop and one called 'Sweet Simplicity' says:

11 And I'll have a bottle of that Dentifrine – I must try some of that. All the advertisements speak so well of it.

Anonymous (cartoonist). *Punch Almanack* (1911).

12 The codfish lays ten thousand eggs
The homely hen lays one.
The codfish never cackles
To tell you that she's done.
And so we scorn the codfish,
While the humble hen we prize,

Which only goes to show you
That it pays to advertise.

Anonymous. Quoted in *Bartlett's Familiar Quotations* (1980 edn).

1 When the client moans and sighs
Make his logo twice the size.
If he still should prove refractory,
Show a picture of a factory.
Only in the gravest cases
Should you show the clients' faces.

Anonymous. Quoted in David Ogilvy, *Ogilvy on Advertising* (1983). Another version of this is: 'When your client's hopping mad, / Put his picture in the ad. / If he still should prove refractory / Add a picture of his factory.'

Suggested all-purpose advertising line:

2 It's what it's not that makes it what it is.

Anonymous. Quoted in my book *Slogans* (1982). In 1997, the Guernsey Tourist Board actually ran advertisements with the slogan, 'It's what it isn't that makes it what it is.'

Suggesting a slogan:

3 Everybody sat around thinking about Panasonic, the Japanese electronics account. Finally I decided what the hell, I'll throw a line to loosen them up … 'The headline is, the headline is: From Those Wonderful Folks Who Gave You Pearl Harbor.' Complete silence.

Jerry Della Femina, American advertising executive (1936–). *From Those Wonderful Folks Who Gave You Pearl Harbor* (1970).

4 Advertising is the most fun you can have with your clothes on.

Jerry Della Femina, in the same book as above.

A grubby tramp is writing a testimonial:

5 GOOD ADVERTISEMENT. I used your soap two years ago; since then I have used no other.

Harry Furniss, Irish cartoonist (1854–1925). *Punch* Magazine, Vol. 86 (26 April 1884). This cartoon caption was taken up, with permission, by Pears' Soap and widely used in advertisements during the 1880s and 1890s. The slogan was changed slightly to: 'Two years ago I used your soap *since when* I have used no other!'

6 Doing business without advertising is like winking at a girl in the dark: you know what you are doing, but nobody else does.

Edgar Watson Howe, American journalist and author (1853–1937). Quoted in *The Penguin Dictionary of Modern Humorous Quotations*, ed. Fred Metcalf (1987).

7 Advertisements contain the only truths to be relied on in a newspaper.

Thomas Jefferson, American President and polymath (1743–1826). Letter (1819).

8 Advertising may be described as the science of arresting the human intelligence long enough to get money from it.

Stephen Leacock, Canadian humorist (1869–1944). *The Garden of Folly*, 'The Perfect Salesman' (1924).

9 Half the money I spend on advertising is wasted, and the trouble is I don't know which half.

1st Viscount Leverhulme (William Hesketh Lever), English soapmaker and philanthropist (1851–1925). Quoted by David Ogilvy *in Confessions of an Advertising Man* (1963). This observation has also been fathered on John Wanamaker and, indeed, on Ogilvy himself. Ogilvy puts it like this: 'As the first Lord Leverhulme (and John Wanamaker after him) complained … ' Leverhulme remains the most likely originator – he made his fortune through the manufacture of soap from vegetable oils instead of from tallow. Ogilvy had Lever Brothers as a client and could presumably have picked up the remark that way. However, Wanamaker, who more or less invented the modern department store in the US, was active by the 1860s and so could possibly have said it first.

10 I think that I shall never see
A billboard lovely as a tree.
Perhaps unless the billboards fall,
I'll never see a tree at all.

Ogden Nash, American poet (1902–71). *Happy Days*, 'Song of the Open Road' (1933).

1 It is a mistake to use highfalutin language when you advertise to uneducated people. I once used the word *obsolete* in a headline, only to discover that 43 per cent of the housewives had no idea what it meant. In another headline, I used the word *ineffable*, only to discover that I didn't know what it meant myself.

David Ogilvy, British-born advertising executive (1911–99). *Confessions of an Advertising Man*, Chap. 6 (1963).

Advice to advertising copywriters:

2 The consumer isn't a moron; she is your wife.

David Ogilvy. From the same book, though the advice was being quoted in 1956.

3 Advertising is the rattling of a stick inside a swill bucket.

George Orwell, English novelist and journalist (1903–50). Quoted in Laurence J. Peter, *Quotations for Our Time* (1977), but original source not traced.

See also PUBLIC RELATIONS, PUBLICITY.

Advice

4 Never eat at a place called Mom's. Never play cards with a man called Doc. Never go to bed with a woman whose troubles are greater than your own.

Nelson Algren, American novelist and short-story writer (1909–81). *A Walk on the Wild Side*, 'What Every Young Man Should Know' (1956). Algren states that he had it from a convict in prison. But *Bartlett's Familiar Quotations* (1992 edn) finds it only in H.E.F. Donahue, *Conversations with Nelson Algren* (1964) where Algren says he was taught it by 'a nice old Negro lady'. The wording varies.

5 Approach a mule the way a porcupine makes love: Slow 'n keerful.

Anonymous. Quoted in *Savvy Sayin's*, ed. Ken Alstad (1986).

6 When in danger or in doubt,
Run in circles, scream and shout.

Anonymous. Quoted in *The Norton Book of Light Verse*, ed. Russell Baker (1986).

7 1. Never hunt south of the Thames.
2. Never drink port after champagne.
3. Never have your wife in the morning lest something better should turn up during the day.

Anonymous (British). Quoted in Laurence Olivier, *Confessions of an Actor* (1982).

8 The advice of a wife is worthless, but woe to the man who does not take it.

Anonymous (Welsh proverb).

9 Samuel Johnson recalled some harsh but sensible advice once given him by his college tutor at Oxford. 'Read over your compositions,' he said, 'and where ever you meet with a passage which you think is particularly fine, strike it out.'

Anonymous. Quoted in James Boswell, *The Life of Samuel Johnson* (1791) – for 30 April 1773. Compare Quiller-Couch below.

10 Treat every woman as if you have slept with her and you soon will.

Anonymous. Quoted in the author's diary (17 April 1966).

11 No man has ever yet discovered the way to give friendly advice to any woman, not even to his own wife.

Honoré de Balzac. French novelist (1799–1850). *Petites misères de la vie conjugales* (1846). Translated.

12 1. Never drink claret in an East wind.
2. Take your pleasures singly, one by one.
3. Never sit on a hard chair after drinking port.

(Revd) H.J. Bidder, English clergyman. Quoted in *Geoffrey Madan's Notebooks* (1981): 'Three pieces of earnest advice from the Revd H.J. Bidder, aged 86, after sitting silent, with a crumpled face, all through dinner.'

13 Advice is like castor oil, easy enough to give but dreadful uneasy to take.

'Josh Billings' (Henry Wheeler Shaw), American humorist

(1818–85). Quoted in *The Home Book of Humorous Quotations*, ed. A.K. Adams (1969).

1 When a man comes to me for advice, I find out the kind of advice he wants, and I give it to him.

'Josh Billings' (Henry Wheeler Shaw). Quoted in *The Treasury of Humorous Quotations*, eds Evan Esar & Nicolas Bentley (1951).

2 Never go to a doctor whose office plants have died.

Erma Bombeck, American humorous columnist (1927–96). Quoted in *Hammer and Tongues*, eds Michèle Brown & Ann O'Connor (1986).

3 When Maurice Bowra was Warden of Wadham College, Oxford, he was interviewing a young man for a place at the college. He eventually came to the conclusion that the young man would not do. Helpfully, however, he let him down gently by advising the young man, 'I think you would be happier in a larger – or a smaller – college.'

(Sir) Maurice Bowra, English academic (1898–1971). Quoted by Sir Claus Moser (a later Warden of Wadham) in a speech at Oxford (28 June 1998).

4 Of all the horrid, hideous notes of woe,
Sadder than owl-songs or the midnight blast,
Is that portentous phrase, 'I told you so.'

Lord Byron, English poet (1788–1824). *Don Juan*, Canto 14, St. 50 (1819–24).

5 She generally gave herself very good advice (though she very seldom followed it).

Lewis Carroll, English writer (1832–98). *Alice's Adventures in Wonderland*, Chap. 1 (1865).

6 Be wiser than other people if you can, but do not tell them so.

4th Earl of Chesterfield (Philip Dormer Stanhope), English politician and writer (1694–1773). *Letters to His Son* (1774) – letter dated 19 November 1745.

7 Advice is seldom welcome; and those who want it the most always like it the least.

4th Earl of Chesterfield. In the same book as above – letter dated 29 January 1748.

8 Never trust men with short legs. Brains too near their bottoms.

(Sir) Noël Coward, English entertainer and writer (1899–1973). Attributed remark.

Advice to actors:

9 Just know your lines and don't bump into the furniture.

(Sir) Noël Coward. This was attributed to Spencer Tracy in *Bartlett's Familiar Quotations* (1980 edn) but to Coward in the 1992 edition. In *H. Allen Smith's Almanac* (1965), Alfred Lunt is credited with the line: 'The secret of my success? I speak in a loud, clear voice and try not to bump into the furniture'. In *Time* Magazine (16 June 1986), it was reported that President Reagan had offered a few hints on appearing before the cameras to a White House breakfast for Senators: 'Don't bump into the furniture,' he said, 'and in the kissing scenes, keep your mouth closed.' Coward seems to be the originator and Dick Richards in *The Wit of Noël Coward* (1968) has that he said it during the run of his play *Nude With Violin* (1956–7). *The Sayings of Noel Coward*, ed. Philip Hoare (1997) has this from a 'speech to the Gallery First-Nighter's Club, 1962': 'Speak clearly, don't bump into people, and if you must have motivation think of your pay packet on Friday.'

10 Love your country, tell the truth and don't dawdle.

1st Earl of Cromer (Evelyn Baring), English colonial administrator (1841–1917). The agent and consul-general in Egypt (1883–1907) offered this philosophy of life to the boys of the Leys School, Cambridge. Quoted in James Morris, *Farewell the Trumpets* (1978). John G. Murray, *A Gentleman Publisher's Commonplace Book* (1996) has, rather: 'Field Marshal Sir William Robertson after the First World War made a speech at a school prize-giving: "Boys, I have a great deal to say to you but it won't take long: so remember it. Speak the truth. Think of others. Don't dawdle."'

11 If your head is wax, don't walk in the sun.

Benjamin Franklin, American politician and scientist (1706–90). *Poor Richard's Almanack* (July 1749).

1 Never miss an opportunity to relieve yourself; never miss a chance to sit down and rest your feet.

George V, British King (1865–1936). His son, the Duke of Windsor, was later to ascribe this remark to 'an old courtier' – quoted in Herbert V. Prochnow, Snr & Jnr, *A Treasury of Humorous Quotations* (1969) – but it seems likely that it was said by George V himself. A correspondent who wished to remain anonymous wrote in 1981 that a naval officer of her acquaintance who was about to accompany Prince George, Duke of Kent, on a cruise was asked by George V to make sure that the Prince was properly dressed before going ashore. He also advised: 'Always take an opportunity to relieve yourselves.' Another correspondent suggests that it was an equerry's first advice to the new King George V; yet another that Edward VII was the first to say this when he was Prince of Wales. On the other hand, more than a century earlier, the Duke of Wellington had said: 'Always make water when you can.' Compare Mencken below.

Advice to all actors:

2 Always remember before going on stage, wipe your nose and check your flies.

(Sir) Alec Guinness, English actor (1914–2000). This may have originated when he was interviewed on BBC TV *Parkinson* around the time of the first *Star Wars* film. He said he had been given the advice by Sir John Gielgud … Quoted in *Time* Magazine (11 May 1987) as: 'Blow your nose and check your fly.' Michael Freedland in *Kenneth Williams* (1990) has it as a comment to Williams after Guinness had apparently tried to jostle Williams out of public view and behind a potted palm during *Hotel Paradiso* (Williams's flies being undone). As this incident is not recorded in *The Kenneth Williams Diaries* (1993), it may not be true.

3 When you have got an elephant by the hind legs and he is trying to run away, it's best to let him.

Abraham Lincoln, American Republican President (1809–65). Quoted in *The Treasury of Humorous Quotations*, eds Evan Esar & Nicolas Bentley (1951).

4 It's not that I'm prudish. It's just that my mother told me never to enter any man's room in months ending in 'R'.

Line from film *Love Affair* (US 1939). Screenwriters: Delmer Daves, Donald Ogden Stewart. Spoken by Irene Dunne (Terry McKay) to Charles Boyer (Michel Marnet). Repeated almost verbatim in the re-make *An Affair to Remember* (1957).

5 Never trust a member [of the US House of Representatives] who quotes the Bible, the Internal Revenue Code or the Rules of the House.

Eugene McCarthy, American Democratic politician (1916–). Attributed remark.

6 Few of the many wise apothegms which have been uttered have prevented a single foolish action.

Thomas Babington Macaulay (Lord Macaulay), English historian and poet (1800–59). Quoted in *The Treasury of Humorous Quotations*, eds Evan Esar & Nicolas Bentley (1951).

7 I long ago associated with the Chinese doctrine that it is foolish to do anything standing up that can be done sitting down, or anything sitting down that can be done lying down.

H.L. Mencken, American journalist and linguist (1880–1956). *Happy Days* (1940). Compare these other versions: Claire Rayner, the British 'agony aunt', has a longer version according to the Sister Tutor who trained her as a nurse back in the 1950s: 'Nurse, never stand when you can sit, never sit when you can lie down, and never lie if there's any chance they might find you out' – quoted in *The 'Quote … Unquote' Newsletter* (October 1993). Samuel Freeman, American jurist (*fl.* 1862–90) served in the US Supreme Court and reputedly said: 'Never walk when you can ride, never sit when you can lie down.' The poet Coleridge wrote to John Thelwall (14 October 1797): '… at other times I adopt the Brahman Creed, & say – It is better to sit than to stand, it is better to lie than to sit, it is better to sleep than to wake – but Death is the best of all!' (in E.L. Griggs, *Collected Letters of Samuel Taylor Coleridge*, Vol.1, 1956).

Notes & Queries (5th Series, 7; 1877) printed a query along the lines: 'It is better to be sitting than standing, / It is better to be in bed than sitting, / It is better to be dead than in bed.' This produced a reply that, 'The lines asked for are, I believe, an imperfect version of a Hindoo proverb which runs thus: "It is better to walk than to run: it is better to stand than to walk: it is better to sit than to stand: it is better to lie than to sit"." Compare George V above.

1 Treat a whore like a lady and a lady like a whore.

Wilson Mizner, American playwright (1876–1933). Quoted in Bob Chieger, *Was It Good For You Too?* (1983).

2 A man with a bristling grey beard [a yachtsman], said: 'I made up my mind, when I bought my first boat, never to learn to swim ... When you're in a spot of trouble, if you can swim you try to strike out for the shore. You invariably drown. As I can't swim, I cling to the wreckage and they send a helicopter out for me. That's my tip, if you ever find yourself in trouble, cling to the wreckage!'

(Sir) John Mortimer, English author, playwright and lawyer (1923–). Quoted as the epigraph to his autobiography *Clinging to the Wreckage* (1982). Mortimer concludes: 'It was advice that I thought I'd been taking for most of my life.'

3 Whenever you feel an impulse to perpetuate a piece of exceptionally fine writing, obey it – wholeheartedly – and delete it before sending your manuscript to press. *Murder your darlings.*

(Sir) Arthur Quiller-Couch, English academic and critic (1863–1944). In the twelfth and final lecture 'On Style', given at Cambridge on 28 January 1914 in a series published as 'On the Art of Writing'. Hence: 'Kill your darlings' or 'throw away your babies', advice often given to aspiring journalists (and certainly in use by the 1960s). It means 'get rid of obviously impressive writing to which you may become unreasonably attached'. Hence, also, the title of Terence Blacker's novel *Kill Your Darlings* (2000). Quiller-Couch may, however, have been quoting an earlier source, and not just Johnson above.

4 While grace is saying after meat, do you and your brethren take the chairs from behind the company, so that when they go to sit again, they may fall backwards, which will make them all merry; but be you so discreet as to hold your laughter till you get to the kitchen, and then divert your fellow-servants.

Jonathan Swift, Anglo-Irish writer and clergyman (1667–1745). *Directions to Servants* (1745).

To a man struggling under the weight of a grandfather clock:

5 My poor fellow, why not carry a watch?

(Sir) Herbert Beerbohm Tree, English actor-manager (1853–1917). Quoted in Hesketh Pearson, *Beerbohm Tree* (1956). Coincidentally or not, there is a cartoon in Punch (27 March 1907) that shows a man struggling with a large clock (the sort, however, that would fit on a mantelpiece). A bystander, characterized in the caption as 'Funny Man', says to him: 'PARDON ME, SIR, BUT WOULDN'T YOU FIND IT MORE CONVENIENT TO CARRY A WATCH?'

6 I have found that the best way to give advice to your children is to find out what they want and then advise them to do it.

Harry S. Truman, American Democratic President (1884–1972). Interviewed by his daughter, Margaret, on CBS TV *Person to Person* (27 May 1955).

7 Never refuse to do a kindness unless the act would work great injury to yourself, and never refuse to take a drink – under any circumstances.

Mark Twain, American writer (1835–1910). *Mark Twain's Notebook*, ed. A.B. Paine (1935).

On being asked by Queen Victoria how hundreds of sparrows could be removed from the Glass Palace of the Great Exhibition (1851):

8 Try sparrow-hawks, Ma'am.

1st Duke of Wellington (Arthur Wellesley), Irish-born soldier and politician (1769–1852). Quoted in Elizabeth Longford, *Wellington: Pillar of State* (1972).

Advice to a new member of Parliament at Westminster:

9 Don't quote Latin; say what you have to say, and then sit down.

1st Duke of Wellington (Arthur Wellesley). Quoted in *The Frank Muir Book* (1976).

1 There are three rules for writing plays. The first rule is not to write like Henry Arthur Jones; the second and third rules are the same.

Oscar Wilde, Irish playwright, poet and wit (1854–1900). Quoted in Hesketh Pearson, *The Life of Oscar Wilde* (1946). On another occasion, when Wilde's *A Woman of No Importance* was being rehearsed at a theatre where a Jones play was in its last week, a terrific crash was heard. Wilde spoke: 'Pray do not be alarmed ladies and gentlemen. The crash you have just heard is merely some of Mr Jones's dialogue that has fallen flat.'

2 It is always a silly thing to give advice, but to give good advice is absolutely fatal.

Oscar Wilde. *The Portrait of Mr W.H.* (1889).

3 *Lord Goring:*

I always pass on good advice. It is the only thing to do with it. It is never of any use to oneself.

Oscar Wilde, *An Ideal Husband*, Act 1 (1895).

Afternoons

4 In the posteriors of this day, which the rude multitude call the afternoon.

William Shakespeare, English playwright and poet (1564–1616). *Love's Labour's Lost*, V.i.81 (1592–3). Don Armado speaking.

Age and ageing

5 Was she old? When they lit all the candles on her birthday cake, six people were overcome with the heat.

Fred Allen, American comedian (1894–1956). *Much Ado About Me* (1956).

Accepting an award:

6 I recently turned sixty. Practically a third of my life is over.

Woody Allen, American film actor, writer and director (1937–). Quoted in *The Observer*, 'Sayings of the Week' (10 March 1996).

The distinguished actress had been so impressed by the flattering work of this particular photographer that she engaged him again to take her picture. 'Oh dear,' she remarked, looking at the new prints when they were finished, 'you make me look older than last time.' The photographer was the quintessence of tact. Said he:

7 Ah yes, but I was much younger in those days.

Anonymous. Who were the original participants? Possibly Marlene Dietrich and the cinematographer Hal Mohr. When they were working together on the film *Rancho Notorious* (US 1952), Dietrich asked why she wasn't looking as good on the film as when the same cinematographer had shot her in *Destry Rides Again* 13 years before. Mohr replied that he was, of course, 13 years older.

8 Just because there's snow on the roof, it doesn't mean the boiler has gone out.

Anonymous (by 1993).

9 I am 46, and have been for some time past.

Anita Brookner, English novelist (1928–). Letter to *The Times* (5 November 1984) when she considered it had drawn too much attention to her actual age. In *Hotel du Lac*, Chap. 4 (published that same year), she had written: 'She was a handsome woman of forty-five and would remain so for many years.' Compare No. 99 in the original *Joe Miller's Jests* (1739): 'A Lady's Age happening to be questioned, she affirmed, she was but *Forty*, and call'd upon a Gentleman that was in Company for his Opinion; Cousin, said she, do you believe I am in the Right, when I say I am but *Forty?* I ought not to dispute it, Madam, reply'd he, for I have heard you say so *these ten Years.*'

10 A lady of a 'certain age', which means Certainly aged.

Lord Byron, English poet (1788–1824). *Don Juan*, Canto 6, St. 69 (1819–24).

11 A man is as old as he's feeling, a woman as old as she looks.

Mortimer Collins, English writer (1827–76). *The Unknown Quantity*.

1 The years between fifty and seventy are the hardest. You are always being asked to do things, and yet you are not decrepit enough to turn them down.

T.S. Eliot, American-born poet, playwright and critic (1888–1965). Remark (23 October 1950). Quoted in *The Oxford Book of Ages* (1985).

2 At sixty-six I am entering … the last phase of my active physical life. My body, on the move, resembles in sight and sound nothing so much as a bin-liner full of yoghourt.

Stephen Fry, English writer and actor (1957–). *The Hippopotamus*, Chap. 3 (1994).

3 She may very well pass for forty-three
In the dusk with a light behind her!

(Sir) W.S. Gilbert, English writer and lyricist (1836–1911). *Trial by Jury* (1875). Ian Bradley writes in *The Annotated Gilbert and Sullivan*, Vol. 2 (1984): 'Gilbert had a thing about women in their forties. Poor Ruth in *The Pirates of Penzance* is mocked by Frederic for being forty-seven … while Marco is warned by Gianetta in *The Gondoliers* not to address any lady less than forty-five.'

4 We do not necessarily improve with age: for better or worse we become more like ourselves.

(Sir) Peter Hall, English theatre director (1930–). Quoted in *The Observer* (c. 1988). Almost a proverbial expression by this time. In my *Eavesdroppings* (1981), I quoted this from Miss Bernice Hanison of Haywards Heath: 'On the London Underground, I heard one of those carrying, well-bred, female voices saying to her companion: "I don't know about you, but as we get older I always find we get more and more like ourselves".'

At the age of 76:

5 Three things happen when you get to my age. First your memory starts to go … and I have forgotten the other two.

Denis Healey (Lord Healey), English politician (1917–). Quoted in *The Independent*, 'Quote Unquote' (23 July 1994).

6 Men are like wine – some turn to vinegar, but the best improve with age.

John XXIII, Italian Pope (1881–1963). Quoted in Gerald Brenan, *Thoughts In a Dry Season* (1978).

On being asked his age when he was 77:

7 I am just turning forty and taking my time about it.

Harold Lloyd, American film comedian (1893–1971). Quoted in *The Times* that same year (1970).

8 They say a man is as old as the woman he feels. In that case I'm eighty-five.

Groucho Marx, American comedian (1895–1977). *The Secret Word Is Groucho* (1976).

On his challenger, Walter Mondale, during the 1984 election:

9 I will not make age an issue of this campaign. I am not going to exploit for political purposes my opponent's youth and inexperience.

Ronald Reagan, American actor and President (1911–). TV debate (22 October 1984). At that time, Reagan was 73 and Mondale 56.

10 The years that a woman subtracts from her age are not lost. They are added to the ages of other women.

Diane de Poitiers, French mistress of Henri II (1499–1566). Quoted in *The Home Book of Humorous Quotations*, ed. A.K. Adams (1969).

11 Nowadays most women grow old gracefully; most men, disgracefully.

Helen Rowland, American humorist (1875–1950). Quoted in *The Treasury of Humorous Quotations*, eds Evan Esar & Nicolas Bentley (1951).

12 'Someone who Must Not be Contradicted said that a man must be a success by the time he's thirty, or never.'
'To have reached thirty,' said Reginald, 'is to have failed in life.'

Saki (H.H. Munro), English writer (1870–1916). 'Reginald on the Academy', *Reginald* (1904).

1 When I was young, I was told: 'You'll see, when you're fifty.' I am fifty and I haven't seen a thing.

Erik Satie, French composer (1866–1925). In a letter to his brother, quoted in Pierre-Daniel Templier, *Erik Satie* (1932).

2 One should never trust a woman who tells one her real age. A woman who would tell one that, would tell one anything.

Oscar Wilde, Irish playwright, poet and wit (1854–1900). *A Woman of No Importance*, Act 1 (1893).

3 The old believe everything: the middle-aged suspect everything: the young know everything.

Oscar Wilde. 'Phrases and Philosophies for the Use of the Young', in *The Chameleon* (December 1894).

4 No woman should ever be quite accurate about her age. It looks so calculating.

Oscar Wilde. *The Importance of Being Earnest*, Act 3 (1895).

5 *Lady Bracknell:*
Thirty-five is a very attractive age. London society is full of women of the very highest birth who have, of their own free choice, remained thirty-five for years.

Oscar Wilde. In the same act of the same play.

At age eighty-seven:

6 I'm very uncomfortable living in a world where the Pope is twenty-five years younger than I am.

Billy Wilder, American film director and writer (1906–). Quoted in *The Independent*, 'Quote Unquote' (17 July 1993).

Agents

7 Then there was the actor who put in his will that he wanted to be cremated and ten per cent of his ashes thrown in his agent's face.

Anonymous. Quoted by Larry Adler on BBC Radio *Quote ... Unquote* (25 January 1976).

8 Hollywood is bounded on the north, south, east, and west by agents.

William Fadiman, American writer and producer (1909–). *Hollywood Now* (1972).

9 The trouble with this business is that the stars keep 90% of the money.

Lew Grade (Lord Grade), Russian-born British media tycoon (1906–98). Quoted in A. Andrews, *Quotations for Speaker's and Writers* (1969).

When a Hollywood agent told him how he had been swimming unscathed in shark-infested waters:

10 I think that's what they call professional courtesy.

Herman J. Mankiewicz, American screenwriter (1897–1953). Quoted by Dick Vosburgh on BBC Radio *Quote ... Unquote* (31 July 1979).

11 Mrs Morland very wittily defined an agent as someone whom you pay to make bad blood between yourself and your publisher.

Angela Thirkell, English novelist (1890–1961). *Pomfret Towers* ([illegible]).

Agreement

12 We're not quarrelling! We're in complete agreement! We hate each other!

Line from film *The Band Wagon* (US 1953). Screenwriters: Adolph Green, Betty Comden. Spoken by Nanette Fabray (Lily Marton) to Oscar Levant (Lester Marton).

13 My idea of an agreeable person is a person who agrees with me.

Benjamin Disraeli (1st Earl of Beaconsfield), English politician and writer (1804–81). *Lothair*, Chap. 41 (1870). Hugo Bohun speaking. This has also been ascribed to Samuel Johnson.

Alimony

14 Alimony is the screwing you get for the screwing you got.

Anonymous (graffito). Included in my book *Graffiti 4* (1982). From Australia. Compare Lana Turner's comment on her lover Johnny Stompanato's use of her money in 1958: 'I wonder if the screwing I'm getting is worth the screwing I'm getting' – quoted in Bob Chieger, *Was It Good For You Too?* (1983).

1 Alimony is like buying oats for a dead horse.

Arthur ('Bugs') Baer, American columnist and writer (1897?–1969). Quoted in *The Treasury of Humorous Quotations*, eds Evan Esar & Nicolas Bentley (1951). The line also occurs in the Eddie Cantor film *Kid Millions* (US 1934).

On reading ex-husband Roger Vadim's memoirs:

2 If he needed the money so badly, I'd have given him alimony.

Jane Fonda, American actress (1937–). Quoted in *Sunday Today*, 'Quotes of the Week' (17 August 1986).

Amateurs

3 The Arts Council doesn't believe in supporting amateurs, except in its own ranks.

(Sir) John Drummond, English arts administrator (1934–). Quoted in *The Observer* (29 March 1998).

4 Hell is full of musical amateurs: music is the brandy of the damned.

Bernard Shaw, Irish playwright and critic (1856–1950). *Man and Superman* (1903).

Ambitions

To the Comte d'Orsay who had said he was born French, had lived French and would die French:

5 Have you no ambition, man?

Benjamin Disraeli (1st Earl of Beaconsfield), English politician and writer (1804–81). Attributed by Miles Kington on BBC Radio *Quote ... Unquote* (13 September 1999). Alfred, Comte d'Orsay lived and married in England and was a friend of Disraeli's youth.

When a child:

6 I should like to be a horse.

Elizabeth II, British Queen (1926–). Quoted in *Handbook of 20th Century Quotations*, ed. Frank S. Pepper (1984).

7 What is my loftiest ambition? I've always wanted to throw an egg into an electric fan.

Oliver Herford, American humorist (1863–1935). Quoted in *The Treasury of Humorous Quotations*, eds Evan Esar & Nicolas Bentley (1951).

8 Everybody sets out to do something, and everybody does something, but no one does what he sets out to do.

George Moore, Irish novelist (1852–1933). Quoted in the same collection as above.

At the time of the Profumo scandal in 1963:

9 I want to be another Emma Hamilton. I'm looking for another Lord Nelson, only taller.

Mandy Rice-Davies, English 'model and showgirl' (1944–). Quoted in *Handbook of 20th Century Quotations*, ed. Frank S. Pepper (1984).

10 Ambition is the last refuge of the failure.

Oscar Wilde, Irish playwright, poet and wit (1854–1900). 'Phrases and Philosophies for the Use of the Young', in *The Chameleon* (December 1894).

America and the Americans

On society people leaving the opera:

11 It was widely known in New York, but never acknowledged, that Americans want to get away from amusement even more quickly than they want to get to it.

Line from film *The Age of Innocence* (US 1993). Screenwriters: Jay Cocks, Martin Scorsese (from Edith Wharton novel). Spoken by Joanne Woodward (Narrator).

12 Now ain't that great, Myrtle? – a gen-u-yne Bed-oo-yne Ay-rab!

Anonymous (cartoonist). *Punch* (11 March 1936). Caption to cartoon of American couple in Arab country.

13 Instead of the Pilgrim Fathers landing on the Plymouth Rock, the Plymouth Rock should have landed on the Pilgrim Fathers.

Anonymous. H.L. Mencken in his *Dictionary of Quotations* (1942) has this in the form, 'How much better it would have been if the Plymouth Rock had landed on the Pilgrim Fathers' – and ascribes it to an 'Author unidentified'. Cole Porter's verse to the song 'Anything Goes' also contains the idea (1934).

1 God protects fools, drunks and the United States of America.

Otto von Bismarck, Prusso-German statesman (1815–98). Attributed remark. *Compare* HEAVEN 204:2.

2 America is the only country in history which miraculously has gone directly from barbarism to degeneration without the usual interval of civilization.

Georges Clemenceau, French Prime Minister (1841–1929). So ascribed by Hans Bendix in *The Saturday Review of Literature* (1 December 1945). No more substantial attribution appears to exist.

3 There are some things in every country that you must be born to endure; and another hundred years of general satisfaction with Americans and America could not reconcile this expatriate to cranberry sauce, peanut butter and drum majorettes.

Alistair Cooke, English-born American journalist and broadcaster (1908–). Quoted in *The Observer* (5 September 1999).

4 I've roamed the Spanish Main
Eaten sugar-cane
But I never tasted cellophane
Till I struck the U.S.A.

(Sir) Noël Coward, English entertainer and writer (1899–1973). Song, 'I Like America' in *Ace of Clubs* (1949).

5 I am willing to love all mankind, *except an American*.

(Dr) Samuel Johnson, English writer and lexicographer (1709–84). Quoted in James Boswell, *The Life of Samuel Johnson* (1791) – for 15 April 1778. Johnson was not a supporter of the American Revolution – the Declaration of Independence had been signed less than two years previously. He went on characterize Americans as 'Rascals – Robbers – Pirates'.

6 No one ever went broke underestimating the intelligence of the American people.

H.L. Mencken, American journalist and linguist (1880–1956). What, in fact, he said on the subject of journalism in the *Chicago Tribune* (19 September 1926), was: 'No one in this world, so far as I know – and I have searched the records for years, and employed agents to help me – has ever lost money by underestimating the intelligence of the great masses of the plain people. Nor has anyone ever lost public office thereby.'

7 America is a nation that conceives many odd inventions for getting somewhere but can think of nothing to do when it gets there.

Will Rogers, American humorist (1879–1935). Quoted in *The Treasury of Humorous Quotations*, eds Evan Esar & Nicolas Bentley (1951).

8 The United States never lost a war or won a conference.

Will Rogers. Quoted in the same collection as above.

9 America is a large, friendly dog in a very small room. Every time it wags its tail it knocks over a chair.

Arnold Toynbee, English historian (1889–1975). Quoted in broadcast news summary (14 July 1954).

10 *October 12, the Discovery*. It was wonderful to find America, but it would have been more wonderful to miss it.

Mark Twain, American writer (1835–1910). *Following the Equator*, 'Conclusion' (1897).

11 Of course America had often been discovered before Columbus, but it had always been hushed up.

Oscar Wilde, Irish playwright, poet and wit (1854–1900). *Personal Impressions of America* (1883).

12 Perhaps, after all, America never has been discovered ... I myself would say that it had merely been detected.

Oscar Wilde. *The Picture of Dorian Gray*, Chap. 3 (1891).

1 If one had the money to go to America, one would not go.

Oscar Wilde. Quoted in Hesketh Pearson, *The Life of Oscar Wilde* (1946).

2 *Mrs Allonby:*
They say, Lady Hunstanton, that when good Americans die they go to Paris.
Lady Hunstanton:
Indeed? And when bad Americans die, where do they go to?
Lord Illingworth:
Oh, they go to America.

Oscar Wilde. *A Woman of No Importance*, Act 1 (1893). Earlier, this exchange had appeared in *The Picture of Dorian Gray*, Chap. 3 (1891). The originator of the remark 'Good Americans, when they die, go to Paris' was Thomas Gold Appleton (1812–84). He was so quoted by Oliver Wendell Homes in *The Autocrat of the Breakfast Table* (1858).

3 All Americans lecture, I believe. I suppose it is something in their climate.

Oscar Wilde. *A Woman of No Importance*, Act 2.

4 It is absurd to say that there are neither ruins nor curiosities in America when they have their mothers and their manners.

Oscar Wilde. Attributed remark.

5 In America the President reigns for four years, and Journalism governs for ever and ever.

Oscar Wilde. 'The Soul of Man Under Socialism' (1895).

6 In America the young are always ready to give those who are older than themselves the full benefits of their inexperience.

Oscar Wilde. Quoted in *The Uncollected Oscar Wilde*, ed. John Wyse Jackson (1995).

7 There at any rate is a country that has no trappings, no pageantry, and no gorgeous ceremonies. I saw only two processions – one was the Fire Brigade preceded by the Police, the other was the Police preceded by the Fire Brigade.

Oscar Wilde. *Impressions of America* (pub. 1906).

Amity

8 The lion and the calf shall lie down together, but the calf won't get much sleep.

Woody Allen, American film actor, writer and director (1937–). In *The New Republic* (31 August 1974).

Amnesty

9 Amnesty, *n*. The state's magnanimity towards those offenders whom it would be too expensive to punish.

Ambrose Bierce, American journalist (1842–?1914). *The Cynic's Word Book* (later retitled *The Devil's Dictionary*) (1906).

An

10 As soon as the Jubilee [of 1897] was over we went to what is called in England 'an hotel'. If we could have afforded an horse and an hackney cab we could have had an heavenly time flitting around.

Mark Twain, American writer (1835–1910). In *Europe and Elsewhere*, ed. James Brander (1923).

Anarchy and anarchists

11 We started off trying to set up a small anarchist community, but people wouldn't obey the rules.

Alan Bennett, English actor and playwright (1934–). *Getting On*, Act 1 (1972).

Ancestry

On Pitt the Younger's first speech (February 1781):

12 Not merely a chip off the old 'block', but the old block itself.

Edmund Burke, Irish-born politician and philosopher (1729–97). Quoted in N. W. Wraxall, *Historical Memoirs of My Own Time* (1904 edn).

1 I cannot help reflecting that if my father had been American and my mother British, instead of the other way round, I might have got here on my own.

(Sir) Winston S. Churchill, British Conservative Prime Minister and writer (1874–1965). Speech to US Congress (26 December 1941).

2 I can trace my ancestry back to a protoplasmal primordial atomic globule. Consequently, my family pride is something inconceivable. I can't help it. I was born sneering.

(Sir) W.S. Gilbert, English writer and lyricist (1836–1911). *The Mikado*, Act 1 (1885). Spoken by Pooh-Bah, the corrupt official, who – contrary to the view of anti-evolutionists who think that such a descent is undignified – glories in it.

3 My folks didn't come over on the *Mayflower*, but they were there to meet the boat.

Will Rogers, American humorist (1879–1935). Quoted in *The Treasury of Humorous Quotations*, eds Evan Esar & Nicolas Bentley (1951).

Andrews, (Dame) Julie

ENGLISH BORN ACTRESS AND SINGER (1935–)

After her great stage success as Eliza Doolittle in My Fair Lady, *Julie Andrews was rejected in favour of Audrey Hepburn in the Warner Bros. film version of the musical. And this despite the fact that Hepburn's singing voice had to be dubbed. Andrews was thus available to go on and star in* Mary Poppins *for which she duly won an Academy Award in 1964. Collecting her Oscar she said:*

4 I'd like to thank all those who made this possible – especially Jack L. Warner.

Julie Andrews. Quoted in Leslie Halliwell, *The Filmgoer's Book of Quotes* (1973).

5 Julie Andrews is like a nun with a switchblade.

Anonymous. Quoted in the same book as above.

After they had made The Sound of Music *(1965):*

6 Working with her is like being hit over the head by a Valentine's Day card.

Christopher Plummer, Canadian actor (1927–). Quoted in the same book as above.

Anecdotage

7 When a man fell into his anecdotage it was a sign for him to retire from the world.

Benjamin Disraeli (1st Earl of Beaconsfield), English politician and writer (1804–81). *Lothair*, Chap. 28 (1870). Earlier, however, his father, Isaac Disraeli, had noted in *Curiosities of Literature* (1839): 'Among my earliest literary friends, two distinguished themselves by their anecdotical literature: James Petit Andrews, by his "Anecdotes, Ancient and Modern", and William Seward, by his "Anecdotes of Distinguished Persons". These volumes were favourably received, and to such a degree, that a wit of that day, and who is still a wit as well as poet, considered that we were far gone in our "Anecdotage".' The word 'anecdotage' in a less critical sense had been used by De Quincey in 1823 simply to describe anecdotes collectively.

Anglo-Irishness

8 *Pat:*

He was an Anglo-Irishman.

Meg:

In the blessed name of God what's that?

Pat:

A Protestant with a horse.

Brendan Behan, Irish playwright (1923–64). *The Hostage* (1958).

Animals

9 The giraffe must get up at six in the morning if it wants to have its breakfast in its stomach by nine.

Samuel Butler, English novelist and writer (1835–1902). Quoted in *The Treasury of Humorous Quotations*, eds Evan Esar & Nicolas Bentley (1951).

10 Odd things animals. All dogs look up at you. All cats look down at you. Only a pig looks at you as an equal.

(Sir) Winston S. Churchill, British Conservative Prime

Minister and writer (1874–1965). Quoted in *The Sayings of Winston Churchill*, ed. J. A. Sutcliffe (1992). Martin Gilbert, in *Never Despair* (1988), has the version: 'I am fond of pigs. Dogs look up to us. Cats look down on us. Pigs treat us as equals', reported by Churchill's son-in-law Lord Soames, as the great man scratched a pig in the piggery at Chartwell Farm. According to Churchill's Private Secretary 1952–65, Anthony Montague Brown (speech to the International Churchill Societies, 25 September 1986), what he said was: 'I like pigs. Cats look down on you; dogs look up to you: but pigs treat you like an equal.'

1 A mule has neither pride of ancestry nor hope of posterity.

Robert Green Ingersoll, American lawyer and writer (1833–99). Quoted in *The Treasury of Humorous Quotations*, eds Evan Esar & Nicolas Bentley (1951). The remark has also been ascribed to Ignatius Donnelly, American politician (1831–1901), in a speech at Minnesota Legislature.

2 Some reptiles are helpful to man by eating harmful bugs and little animals. Some other reptiles are harmful to man by eating him.

Art Linkletter, American writer (1912–). *A Child's Garden of Misinformation* (1965).

Anniversaries

3 Sent a complimentary (sic) copy of Waterstone's Literary Diary which records the birthdays of various contemporary figures. Here is Dennis Potter on 17 May, Michael Frayn on 8 September, Edna O'Brien on 15 December, so naturally I turn to my own birthday. May 9 is blank except for the note: first British Launderette is opened on Queensway, London 1949.

Alan Bennett, English playwright and actor (1934–). Published diary entry for 2 January 1977, quoted in *The Oxford Dictionary of Literary Quotations*, ed. Peter Kemp (1997).

Anomalies

When asked if, in view of certain anomalies, he would examine alternatives:

4 We are examining alternative anomalies.

William Whitelaw (1st Viscount Whitelaw), English politician (1918–99). Speaking in the House of Commons (1 December 1981).

Answers

5 If you need an answer today, the answer's 'No'.

Lew Grade (Lord Grade), Russian-born British media tycoon (1906–99). Or, at least, it was a Grade family motto, according to Michael Grade on BBC Radio *Quote … Unquote* (28 February 2000).

6 To the recent query, 'If you could ask one question about life, what would the answer be?' Eugène Ionesco responded, 'No.'

Eugène Ionesco, Romanian-born playwright (1912–94). Quoted in *Esquire* (December 1974).

7 She has the answer to everything and the solution to nothing.

Oscar Levant, American pianist and actor (1906–72). *Memoirs of an Amnesiac* (1965).

8 *Calvera:*
What I don't understand is why a man like you took the job in the first place. Why?
Chris:
I wonder myself.
Calvera:
No, come on, come on: tell me why.
Vin:
Like a fellow I once knew in El Paso. One day he just took all his clothes off and jumped into a mess of cactus. I asked him the same question, Why?
Calvera:
And?
Vin:
He said it seemed to be a good idea at the time.

Lines from film *The Magnificent Seven* (US 1960). Screenwriters: William Roberts, Walter Newman, Walter Bernstein (based on the film *The Seven Samurai*). Spoken by Steve McQueen (Vin), Yul Brynner (Chris) and Eli Wallach (Calvera).

Anthologists

1 Most anthologists of poetry or quotations are like those who eat cherries or oysters, first picking the best and winding up by eating everything.

Nicolas-Sébastien Chamfort, French writer (1741–94). Quoted in Herbert V. Prochnow, Snr & Jnr, *A Treasury of Humorous Quotations* (1969).

Anthropology

2 Anthropology is the science which tells us that people are the same the world over – except when they are different.

Nancy Banks-Smith, English journalist and critic (1929–). In *The Guardian* (21 July 1988).

Anticipation

3 What we anticipate seldom occurs; what we least expected generally happens.

Benjamin Disraeli (1st Earl of Beaconsfield), English politician and writer (1804–81). *Henrietta Temple* (1837).

Anticlimax

A crossword clue in The New York Times *for one word of nine letters was a quote from Yale University's song 'For God, for Country, and for Yale'. The answer:*

4 Anticlimax.

Anonymous. Quoted in my book *A Year of Stings and Squelches* (1985). Compare this from *Time* Magazine (11 June 1951): 'Waggish non-Yale men never seem to weary of calling "For God, for Country and for Yale," the outstanding single anti-climax in the English language.'

Apathy

Of the British Prime Minister during the 1970 General Election:

5 Harold Wilson is going around the country stirring up apathy.

William Whitelaw (1st Viscount Whitelaw), English politician (1918–99). Discussed by him in *The Independent* (14 July 1992).

Aphorisms

6 Aphorisms are salted and not sugared almonds at Reason's feast.

Logan Pearsall Smith, American writer (1865–1946). Quoted in Herbert V. Prochnow, Snr & Jnr, *A Treasury of Humorous Quotations* (1969).

Aphrodisiacs

7 Oysters is amorous,
Lobsters is lecherous,
But shrrrimps, Chrrrist,
When my old man came 'ome last night …

Anonymous recitation. Denny Desoutter commented (1999): 'I think of it as one of the indelicate military monologues which I heard fifty years ago in army entertainments, performed by the men. [The woman's] "old man" seems to have had his hopes realised, until she had had enough. Then, in his courteous way, for the umpteenth time, "'Says 'e,' Mrs Haitch,'your haperture if you please.' / 'Haperture, nuffink' says I, stuffin me ankie up it." A memorable line, and I can't remember more.' Peter Brooks recalled that the Mrs H., so evoked, may have been 'Missus 'Oskins'.

Apologies

8 Randolph Churchill, famous for his drunken and boorish behaviour at social events, once wrote apologetically to a hostess whose dinner party he had ruined with one of his displays of drunken rudeness: 'I should never be allowed out in private.'

Randolph Churchill, English journalist and politician (1911–68). Quoted in Brian Roberts, *Randolph* (1984). Writing a letter to his father (Winston) (16 October 1952), Churchill called this a 'mot' he had coined about himself.

Appearance

9 When I appear in public, people expect me to neigh, grind my teeth, paw the ground and swish my tail – none of which is easy.

Anne, British Princess Royal (1950–). Quoted in *The Observer* (22 May 1977).

10 In June 1855, when the poet Tennyson entered the Sheldonian Theatre in Oxford to receive

an honorary degree of doctor of civil laws, his long hair was in disorder, dishevelled and unkempt. A voice cried out to him from the gallery, 'Did your mother call you early, dear?'

Anonymous. Quoted in Julian Charles Young, *A Memoir of Charles Mayne Young* (1871) and based on his son's diary note (8 November 1863). The allusion is to Tennyson's poem 'The May Queen' (1832): 'You must wake and call me early, call me early, mother dear; / Tomorrow'll be the happiest time of all the glad New-year; / Of all the glad New-year, mother, the maddest merriest day; / For I'm to be Queen o' the May, mother, I'm to be Queen o' the May.'

Of a fellow female:

1 Her heart's in the right place – what a pity the other thirteen stone aren't!

Anonymous. Quoted in my book *A Year of Stings and Squelches* (1985).

Of the poet A.E. Housman:

2 He looked as though he was descended from a long line of maiden aunts.

Anonymous. Quoted by Alan Bennett on audiotape *Poetry in Motion* (1990). However, J.A. Cross's *Sir Samuel Hoare, a Political Biography*, Chap. 1 (1977) suggests that the description has also been applied to others: 'Hoare later recalled that, according to the contemporary gossip, [historian Reginald] Lane-Poole was thought to have "descended through a long line of maiden aunts". Perhaps some of the scholar's passion for academic precision rubbed off on to Hoare for this was the very phrase which was applied to him by a ministerial colleague of the 1920s, Lord Birkenhead (F.E. Smith) ... Hoare, with becoming modesty, later admitted that he thought the maiden aunt gibe "not inaptly applied to me".'

But the matter doesn't end there. From John Farrow, *The Story of Thomas More*, Chap. 4 (1954): 'Holbein shows [More] long-nosed and thin-lipped, cadaverous, and somewhat bland in expression ... He had pale blue eyes and, as Lindsay in his famed book on the Reformation remarks, "the dainty hands, and general primness of his appearance" suggested descent "from a long line of maiden aunts".' This presumably refers to Thomas M. Lindsay's noted book, *The Reformation* (1907). The only trouble is, I cannot find this passage in it ...

Of an American general:

3 An imitation rough diamond.

Margot Asquith (Countess of Oxford and Asquith) (1864–1945). Quoted by her stepdaughter Baroness Asquith on BBC TV programme *As I Remember* (30 April 1967).

On Sir Arthur Wing Pinero's eyebrows:

4 [Like] the skins of some small mammal just not large enough to be used as mats.

(Sir) Max Beerbohm, English writer and caricaturist (1872–1956). Quoted in Christopher Hassall, *Edward Marsh* (1959).

When told by Lord Berners that Lady Cunard, whom he had not seen for years, had not changed at all and was exactly the same:

5 I am very sorry to hear that.

(Sir) Max Beerbohm. Quoted in David Cecil, *Max* (1964). Also in Mark Amory, *Lord Berners* (1998). David Cecil heard this put-down being administered and commented that it was 'the best-timed remark I had ever heard'.

6 [Georgie] arrayed himself in ... a mauve tie with an amethyst pin in it, [and] socks, tightly braced up, of precisely the same colour as the tie, so that an imaginative beholder might have conjectured that on this warm day the end of his tie had melted and run down his legs.

E.F. Benson, English novelist (1867–1940). *Queen Lucia*, Chap. 6 (1920).

To choreographer about male dancer with unsightly bulge:

7 For God's sake, go and tell that young man to take the Rockingham tea service out of his tights.

(Sir) Noël Coward, English entertainer and writer (1899–1973). Quoted in *Noël Coward: A Life in Quotes*, ed. Barry Day (1999). The dancer was playing Harlequin in Coward's *Sigh No More* (1945) and the choreographer was Wendy Toye.

On Edith Evans in the 1964 revival of Hay Fever:

1 She took her curtain calls as though she had just been un-nailed from the cross.

(Sir) Noël Coward, quoted in the same book as above.

On Claudette Colbert's appearance in the 1956 TV version of Blithe Spirit:

2 I'd wring her neck – if I could find it.

(Sir) Noël Coward, quoted in the same book as above.

Of himself:

3 Looking like a balding salmon.

Philip Larkin, English poet (1922–85). Quoted in *The Times* (3 December 1985). On another occasion he told Andrew Motion, author of Philip Larkin: *A Writer's Life* (1993), that a photograph showed him like 'an intellectual Eric Morecambe' rather than a 'bald, pregnant salmon'.

4 Underneath all this drag, I'm really a librarian, you know.

Bette Midler, American actress and singer (1945–). Attributed remark.

Of Evelyn Waugh:

5 He looked, I decided, like a letter delivered to the wrong address.

Malcolm Muggeridge, English writer and broadcaster (1903–90). *Tread Softly For You Tread on My Jokes*, 'My Fair Gentleman' (1966).

6 *One woman in society to another:*

You're looking nicer than usual, but that's so easy for you.

Saki (H.H. Munro), English writer (1870–1916). Quoted in my book *A Year of Stings and Squelches* (1985).

7 Last week I saw a woman flayed, and you will hardly believe, how much it altered her person for the worst.

Jonathan Swift, Anglo-Irish writer and clergyman (1667–1745). *A Tale of a Tub*, Chap. 9 (1704).

8 Twenty-four years ago, Madam, I was incredibly handsome. The remains of it are still visible through the rift of time. I was so handsome that women became spellbound when I came in view. In San Francisco, in rainy seasons, I was frequently mistaken for a cloudless day.

Mark Twain, American writer (1835–1910). From a letter written towards the end of his life.

9 As long as a woman can look ten years younger than her own daughter, she is perfectly satisfied.

Oscar Wilde, Irish playwright, poet and wit (1854–1900). Quoted in *The Treasury of Humorous Quotations*, eds Evan Esar & Nicolas Bentley (1951).

10 It is only shallow people who do not judge by appearances.

Oscar Wilde. *The Picture of Dorian Gray*, Chap. 2 (1891).

11 It is better to be beautiful than to be good. But … it is better to be good than to be ugly.

Oscar Wilde. In the same work, Chap. 17.

Appeasement

12 An infallible method of conciliating a tiger is to allow oneself to be devoured.

Konrad Adenauer, West German Chancellor (1876–1967). Quoted in Bennett Cerf, *The Laugh's On Me* (1961).

13 An appeaser is one who feeds a crocodile hoping it will eat him last.

(Sir) Winston S. Churchill, British Conservative Prime Minister and writer (1874–1965). Speech, House of Commons (January 1940).

Appetite

14 On the bus the other day a woman with a baby sat opposite, the baby bawled, and the woman at once began to unlace herself, exposing a large red udder, which she swung into the baby's face. The infant, however, continued to cry and the woman said, 'Come on, there's a good boy – if you don't, I shall give it to the gentleman opposite.'

W.N.P. Barbellion, English essayist and diarist (1889–1919). *The Journal of a Disappointed Man* (1919). Compare, however, a cartoon caption from *Punch* Magazine, Vol. 126 (11 May 1904). 'THE UNPROTECTED MALE' shows a man in an omnibus being addressed thus: *'Mother (after vainly offering a bottle to refractory infant)* "'ERE, TIKE IT, WILL YER! IF YER DON'T 'URRY UP, I'LL GIVE IT TO THE GENTLEMAN OPPOSITE!"'

Applause

1 Don't clap too hard – it's a very old building.

John Osborne, English playwright (1929–94). *The Entertainer* (1957) – but an old music-hall joke.

Arabs

2 I come from a land, from a faraway place
Where the caravan camels roam.
Where they cut off your ear if they don't like
  your face.
It's barbaric, but – hey – it's home.

Lyric from film *Aladdin* (US 1992). Lyrics/music: Howard Ashman, Alan Menken. From the opening song 'Arabian Nights' in the Disney cartoon. When the film opened in Britain, in order not to offend Arab sensibilities, the lyrics had become: 'Where it's flat and immense and the heat is intense / It's barbaric but – hey – it's home.' The amendment was written by Peter Schneider.

3 The Arabs are only Jews upon horseback.

Benjamin Disraeli (1st Earl of Beaconsfield), English politician and writer (1804–81). *Tancred*, Bk 4, Chap. 3 (1847).

Archaeologists

4 An archaeologist is the best husband any woman can have; the older she gets, the more interested he is in her.

(Dame) Agatha Christie, English detective novelist (1890–1976). She was married to the archaeologist Sir Max Mallowan, and so it seemed quite feasible when she was quoted as saying this in a news report (8 March 1954), also in *The Observer* (2 January 1955). However, according to G.C. Ramsey, *Agatha Christie: Mistress of Mystery* (1967), she vehemently denied having said it, insisting that it would have been a very silly remark for anyone to make, and neither complimentary nor amusing.

Archer, Jeffrey (Lord Archer)

ENGLISH NOVELIST AND POLITICIAN (1940–)

To Jeffrey Archer:

5 Is there no beginning to your talents?

Clive Anderson, English broadcaster (1952–). On Channel 4 TV series *Clive Anderson Talks Back*. Quoted in *The Independent* (1 December 1991).

Architects

6 An architect is defined as someone who forgets to put in the staircase.

Gustave Flaubert, French novelist (1821–80). *Dictionnaire des idées reçues* (1881).

7 The physician can bury his mistakes, but the architect can only advise his client to plant vines.

Frank Lloyd Wright, American architect (1867–1959). Quoted in *The New York Times* (4 October 1953).

Architectural criticism

On the Shakespeare Memorial Theatre at Stratford-upon-Avon:

8 Hideous place on a Sunday. What needs my Shakespeare for his honoured bones? Certainly not a theatre looking like a barracks-cum-roadhouse.

James Agate, English dramatic critic (1877–1947). *Ego* (1935) – entry for 3 September 1933, writing shortly after the new building had been opened. It has also been referred to as 'The Jam Factory'. The earlier Victorian Gothic theatre had mostly been destroyed by fire in 1926.

Of Chiswick House, London – a Palladian villa built by the 3rd Earl of Burlington in 1725–9:

9 Too small to live in and too large to hang on a watch-chain.

Anonymous. Quoted in Cecil Roberts, *And So to Bath* (1940). In Richard Hewlings, *Chiswick House and Gardens* (1989), the version 'too little to live in and too large to hang to one's watch' is ascribed to Lord Hervey.

Of London's National Theatre building:

1 The best view of London is from the National Theatre, because from there you can't see the National Theatre.

Anonymous. Quoted in my book *A Year of Stings and Squelches* (1985). Compare: 'During William Morris's last visit to Paris, he spent much of his time in the restaurant of the Eiffel Tower, either eating or writing. When a friend observed that he must be very impressed by the tower to spend so much time there, Morris snorted, "Impressed! I remain here because it's the only place in Paris where I can avoid seeing the damn thing"' – quoted in Lewis & Faye Copeland, *10,000 Jokes, Toasts and Stories* (1939). This comment has also been attributed to the writer Guy de Maupassant (in Roland Barthes, *The Eiffel Tower and other Mythologies* (1979).

Compare also: 'Political anecdotes are rife, like the one about the monstrous Palace of Culture, Stalin's gift in the middle of Warsaw: the best view of Warsaw, they say, is the one from the Palace, because it is the only place in Warsaw from which you can't see the Palace' – Adlai Stevenson, *Friends and Enemies* (1959).

Of the clock over the entrance to Worcester College, Oxford:

2 C'est magnifique mais ce n'est pas la gare [It is magnificent, but it isn't the station].

Anonymous. 'Oh, I thought that was the railway station' is quoted as said by a 'bright young man' in a 'novel' in Dacre Balsdon, *Oxford Life* (1957). It had earlier been applied to Waterhouse Tree Court at Caius College, Cambridge, so it may be a very old critical format indeed.

Of the Albert Memorial, London:

3 It has all the earmarks of an eyesore.

Anonymous (American tourist). Quoted in *Handbook of 20th Century Quotations*, ed. Frank S. Pepper (1984).

4 In my experience, if you have to keep the lavatory door shut by extending your left leg, it's modern architecture.

Nancy Banks-Smith, English journalist and critic (1929–). In *The Guardian* (20 February 1979).

On the Gilbert Scott belfry at Christ Church, Oxford:

5 The advantage of having been born in the reign of Queen Anne, and of having died in that or the subsequent reign, has never been so painfully apparent as it is now.

Lewis Carroll (Revd C.L. Dodgson), English writer (1832–98). Quoted in *The Works of Lewis Carroll* (1965).

Describing the proposed design for a new wing of the National Gallery in London:

6 A kind of vast municipal fire station ... I would understand better this type of high-tech approach if you demolished the whole of Trafalgar Square, but what is proposed is like a monstrous carbuncle on the face of a much-loved and elegant friend.

Charles, British Prince of Wales (1948–). Speech to the Royal Institute of British Architects (30 May 1984). It had an effect: the design was scrapped and replaced by another one.

7 You have to give this much to the Luftwaffe – when it knocked down our buildings it didn't replace them with anything more offensive than rubble. We did that.

Prince Charles. Speech to the Corporation of London Planning and Communications Committee (2 December 1987).

8 Look at the National Theatre! It seems like a clever way of building a nuclear power station in the middle of London without anyone objecting.

Prince Charles. TV film, *A Vision of Britain* (October 1988).

Of the Royal Pavilion at Brighton:

9 As if St Paul's had come down and littered.

(Revd) Sydney Smith, English clergyman, essayist and wit (1771–1845). Quoted in Peter Virgin, *Sydney Smith* (1994). 'It was as though St Paul's had gone down to the sea and pupped' is another version.

On being shown round Moss Hart's elegant country house and grounds:

10 Just what God would have done if he had the money.

Alexander Woollcott, American writer and critic (1887–

1943). Quoted in Moss Hart, *Act One* (1959). Also attributed to George S. Kaufman (visiting the Rockefeller family's Hudson River estate) in Michael Kramer and Sam Roberts, *I Never Wanted to be Vice-President of Anything!* (1976).

Argument

1 There are three sides to every argument: my side, your side and the truth.

Anonymous. Modern proverbial saying, variously ascribed: a version that goes '... There are three sides to every case' is said to be spoken by 'an old lawyer' advising his pupil; the version with '... to every argument' was said to be 'a quote from a bloke in the pub'; from the *Financial Times* (25 October 1986): 'As everyone knows there are always three sides to the story of any marriage: His, Hers and the Truth. Here we have Hers [Dylan Thomas's widow's] with nothing kept back this time.'

2 When you have no basis for an argument, abuse the plaintiff.

Marcus Tullius Cicero, Roman orator and philosopher (106–43 BC). Quoted in *The Treasury of Humorous Quotations*, eds Evan Esar & Nicolas Bentley (1951).

Of Stephen Douglas:

3 His argument is as thin as the homeopathic soup that was made by boiling the shadow of a pigeon that had been starved to death.

Abraham Lincoln, American Republican President (1809–65). Quoted in Keith W. Jennison, *The Humorous Mr Lincoln* (1965).

4 I am not arguing with you – I am telling you.

James McNeill Whistler, American painter (1834–1903). *The Gentle Art of Making Enemies* (1890).

5 The man who sees both sides of a question is a man who sees absolutely nothing at all.

Oscar Wilde, Irish playwright, poet and wit (1854–1900). 'The Critic as Artist' (1890).

6 Ah, don't say that you agree with me. When people agree with me I always feel that I must be wrong.

Oscar Wilde. In the same work as above, also in *Lady Windermere's Fan*, Act 2 (1892).

7 Arguments are to be avoided; they are always vulgar, and often convincing.

Oscar Wilde. Quoted in *The Treasury of Humorous Quotations*, eds Evan Esar & Nicolas Bentley (1951).

Aristocracy

8 *Lord Illingworth:*
A title is really rather a nuisance in these democratic days. As George Harford I had everything I wanted. Now I have merely everything that other people want.

Oscar Wilde, Irish playwright, poet and wit (1854–1900). *A Woman of No Importance*, Act 4 (1893).

Army

9 Join the army, meet interesting people, and kill them.

Anonymous (graffito). Included in my book *Graffiti Lives, OK* (1979). From Bromley, Kent.

10 Military Intelligence is a contradiction in terms.

Anonymous. Quoted in my book *Graffiti Lives, OK* (1979). Said to come from a Ministry of Defence building in London (where it remained briefly). Attributed to Groucho Marx in Art Spiegelman and Bob Schneider, *Whole Grains* (1973).

11 The Army works like this: if a man dies when you hang him, keep hanging until he gets used to it.

Spike Milligan, Irish entertainer and writer (1918–). Quoted by Richard Ingrams on BBC Radio *Quote ... Unquote* (4 May 1977).

12 I don't know what effect these men will have upon the enemy, but, by God, they frighten me.

1st Duke of Wellington (Arthur Wellesley), Irish-born soldier and British Prime Minister (1769–1852). Popular summary of a despatch to Sir Colonel Torrens, military secretary at the Horse Guards (29 August 1810). This referred to some of his generals, and not to his regimental officers or to the rank and file, as is made clear from the full text. Wellington in fact wrote: 'As Lord Chesterfield said of the generals of his day, "I only hope that when the enemy reads the list of their names, he trembles as I do".'

1 The General was essentially a man of peace, except in his domestic life.

Oscar Wilde, Irish playwright, poet and wit (1854–1900). *The Importance of Being Earnest*, Act 3 (1895).

Art and art criticism

On being presented with pair of nude statues for his town hall:

2 Art is art, and nothing can be done to prevent it. But there is the Mayoress's decency to be considered.

Anonymous (Mayor of Lancashire town). Quoted in James Agate, *Ego* (1935).

3 All the arts in America are a gigantic racket run by unscrupulous men for unhealthy women.

(Sir) Thomas Beecham, English conductor (1879–1961). Quoted in *The Frank Muir Book* (1976).

Replying to criticism of his work, that 'any child could do better':

4 Yes, but it takes courage for an adult to draw as badly as that.

Mel Calman, English cartoonist (1931–94). Quoted in his obituary in *The Independent* (12 February 1994).

On his portrait painted by Graham Sutherland:

5 The portrait is a remarkable example of modern art. It certainly combines force and candour. These are qualities which no active member of either House can do without or should fear to meet.

(Sir) Winston S. Churchill, British Conservative Prime Minister and writer (1874–1965). Speech, Westminster Hall, London (30 November 1954). For his birthday, both Houses of Parliament presented Churchill with the portrait. He did not like it but accepted the picture with a gracefully double-edged compliment. Lady Churchill's dislike of the portrait took a more practical form: she had it destroyed.

6 I look as if I was having a difficult stool.

(Sir) Winston S. Churchill. Remark on the same portrait, quoted in *The Lyttelton Hart-Davis Letters* (1978) – for 20 November 1955. Other versions of this criticism are: 'How do they paint one today? Sitting on a lavatory!' (said to Charles Doughty, secretary of the committee which organized the tribute), and 'Here sits an old man on his stool, pressing and pressing.'

7 I hate all Boets and Bainters.

George I, British King (1660–1727). Quoted in Lord Campbell, *Lives of the Chief Justices* (1849). However, as it is said that George I never learned to speak English (even German-accented), a more believable account is that George II (1683–1760), who did speak English, said it. As it is given that he was discussing Hogarth's picture *The March to Finchley* at the time – and this was not published until 1750/1, this would square better with the dates. John Ireland's *Hogarth Illustrated* (1790) recounts that when the picture was brought to George II for approval, he asked who Hogarth was. On being told that he was a painter, the King exclaimed: 'I hate *bainting* and *boetry* too! neither the one nor the other ever did any good!'

8 Have you seen that bloody Leonardo da Vinci cartoon? I couldn't see the bloody joke ... The sense of humour must have changed over the years. I bet when that da Vinci cartoon first came out, I bet people were killing themselves. I bet old da Vinci had an accident when he done it ... Apart from that, Pete, it's a different culture. It's Italian y'see, we don't understand it. For instance, *The Mousetrap* did terribly in Pakistan.

Lines from BBC TV *Not Only But Also*, 'Art Gallery' sketch (23 January 1965). Written and performed by Peter Cook and Dudley Moore. The Leonardo cartoon of the Virgin and Child with St Anne and the Infant St John had been purchased for the National Gallery a year or two before this. Originally a cartoon was a full-size drawing made to facilitate the painting of a large work. The term came to be applied to humorous sketches through *Punch* in the mid-19th century.

At the unveiling of an unlifelike statue of Nurse Edith Cavell outside the National Portrait Gallery in London (1920):

1 My god, they've shot the wrong person!

James Pryde, English artist (1866–1941). Quoted on BBC Radio *Quote ... Unquote* (6 July 1977).

2 The first duty of an art critic is to hold his tongue at all times and upon all occasions.

Oscar Wilde, Irish playwright, poet and wit (1854–1900). Lecture, 'The English Renaissance of Art', New York (9 January 1882).

3 The unfortunate aphorism about Art holding the mirror up to Nature is deliberately said by Hamlet in order to convince the bystanders of his absolute insanity in all art-matters.

Oscar Wilde. 'The Decay of Lying', in *Nineteenth Century* (January 1889).

4 The English public, as a mass, takes no interest in a work of art until it is told that the work in question is immoral.

Oscar Wilde. Quoted in *The Fireworks of Oscar Wilde*, ed. Owen Dudley Edwards (1989).

5 It is only an auctioneer who should admire all schools of art.

Oscar Wilde. Quoted in *The Treasury of Humorous Quotations*, eds Evan Esar & Nicolas Bentley (1951).

Art and artists

6 Donatello's interest in the female nude made him the father of the Renaissance.

Anonymous (schoolboy/student). Quoted in Louis Untermeyer, *A Treasury of Laughter* (1946).

7 Of course we all know that [William] Morris was a wonderful all-round man, but the act of walking round him has always tired me.

(Sir) Max Beerbohm, English writer and caricaturist (1872–1956). Quoted in S.N. Behrman, *Conversations with Max* (1960).

8 What were they going to do with the Grail when they found it, Mr Rossetti?

(Sir) Max Beerbohm. Caption to cartoon showing the Pre-Raphaelite D.G. Rossetti being quizzed as to the subject of one of his paintings. The remark was allegedly made by Benjamin Jowett, Master of Balliol, about the murals in the Oxford Union (1916).

9 Any fool can paint a picture, but it takes a wise man to be able to sell it.

Samuel Butler, English author (1835–1902). Quoted in *The Treasury of Humorous Quotations*, eds Evan Esar & Nicolas Bentley (1951).

10 Art, like morality, consists of drawing the line somewhere.

G.K. Chesterton, English poet, novelist and critic (1874–1936). Quoted in *The Treasury of Humorous Quotations*, eds Evan Esar & Nicolas Bentley (1951).

11 We must remember that art is art. Still, on the other hand, water is water – and east is east and west is west, and if you take cranberries and stew them like apple sauce, they taste much more like prunes than rhubarb does.

Line from film *Animal Crackers* (US 1930). Screenwriters: Morrie Ryskind, George S. Kaufman. Spoken by Groucho Marx (Capt. Spaulding).

12 I paint with my prick.

Pierre Auguste Renoir, French painter (1841–1919). *The Oxford Dictionary of Quotations* (1992) suggests that it is possibly an inversion of 'It's with my brush that I make love', from A. André, *Renoir* (1919). D.H. Lawrence, *Lady Chatterley's Lover*, Chap. 4 (1928) has: 'Renoir said he painted his pictures with his penis ... he did too, lovely pictures! I wish I did something with mine.'

13 What garlic is to salad, insanity is to art.

Augustus Homer Saint-Gaudens, Irish-born American sculptor (1848–1907). *Reminiscences* (1913).

14 How often my Soul visits the National Gallery, and how seldom I go there myself!

Logan Pearsall Smith, American writer (1865–1946). *Afterthoughts* (1931).

Of Turner's The Slave Ship:

15 A tortoise-shell cat having a fit in a platter of tomatoes.

Mark Twain, American writer (1835–1910). Quoted in *The Frank Muir Book* (1976).

To a woman who told him a landscape reminded her of his work:

1 Yes, madam, Nature is creeping up.

James McNeill Whistler, American painter (1834–1903). Quoted in D.C. Seitz, *Whistler Stories* (1913).

To enthusiast who said she knew of only two painters in the world, himself and Velasquez:

2 Why drag in Velasquez?

James McNeill Whistler. Quoted in the same book as above.

3 All that I desire to point out is the general principle that Life imitates Art far more than Art imitates Life.

Oscar Wilde, Irish playwright, poet and wit (1854–1900). 'The Decay of Lying', in *Nineteenth Century* (January 1889).

4 One should either be a work of art, or wear a work of art.

Oscar Wilde. 'Phrases and Philosophies for the Use of the Young', in *The Chameleon* (December 1894).

5 There are moments when art attains almost to the dignity of manual labour.

Oscar Wilde. Quoted in *The Treasury of Humorous Quotations*, eds Evan Esar & Nicolas Bentley (1951).

6 I hate views – they are only made for bad painters.

Oscar Wilde. Quoted in Richard Ellman, *Oscar Wilde* (1987).

Aspirates

When J.H. Thomas, the Labour MP, complained he ''ad a 'eadache':

7 Try taking a couple of aspirates.

F.E. Smith (1st Earl of Birkenhead), English politician and lawyer (1872–1930). Quoted in John Campbell, *F.E. Smith, First Earl of Birkenhead* (1983), in a form which has Thomas saying, 'Ooh, Fred, I've got an 'ell of an 'eadache' (told to the author by Lady Gaselee).

Aspiration

8 We are all in the gutter, but some of us are looking at the stars.

Oscar Wilde, Irish playwright, poet and wit (1854–1900). *Lady Windermere's Fan*, Act 3 (1892).

Assassination

Of an attempt on his life:

9 It is one of the incidents of the profession.

Umberto I, Italian King (1844–1900). Attributed in A. Andrews, *Quotations for Speakers and Writers* (1969).

Assumptions

One elderly person was overheard saying to another:

10 If anything should happen to either of us, you may take it that I'm definitely going to live in Bournemouth.

Anonymous. Quoted in *Pass the Port Again* (1980). In my book *Eavesdroppings* (1981), it is given as said on a park bench: 'When one of us passes on, I shall move south to live with my daughter.' There is nothing new, etc.: in *Samuel Butler's Notebooks* (which covered the years 1874–1902) there appeared the entry: 'Warburg's old friend ... said to Warburg one day, talking about his wife, who was ill, "If God were to take one or other of us, I should go and live in Paris".'

Astrology

11 I don't believe in astrology; I'm a Sagittarian and we're sceptical.

(Sir) Arthur C. Clarke, English science fiction writer (1917–). Quoted by Paul Heskett in *Astronomy Now* Magazine.

Atheists

12 An atheist is a man who has no invisible means of support.

John Buchan (Lord Tweedsmuir), Scottish politician and writer (1875–1940). Quoted in H.E. Fosdick, *On Being a Real Person* (1943).

13 I am still an atheist, thank God.

Luis Buñuel, Spanish film director (1900–83). Quoted in *Le Monde* (16 December 1959).

1 God can stand being told by Professor Ayer and Marghanita Laski that he doesn't exist.

J.B. Priestley, English novelist and playwright (1894–1984). Quoted in *The Listener* (1 July 1965).

Attention

2 It's most dangerous nowadays for a husband to pay any attention to his wife in public. It always makes people think that he beats her when they are alone.

Oscar Wilde, Irish playwright, poet and wit (1854–1900). *Lady Windermere's Fan*, Act 2 (1892).

Attlee, Clement (1st Earl Attlee)

BRITISH LABOUR PRIME MINISTER (1883-1967)

Of himself:

3 Few thought he was even a starter
There were many who thought themselves
  smarter
But he ended PM, CH and OM
An Earl and a Knight of the Garter.

Clement Attlee. Lines written by him on 8 April 1956. Quoted in Kenneth Harris, *Attlee* (1982).

On Clement Attlee's reluctance to fly to Moscow and speak plainly to Stalin:

4 He dare not absent himself from his Cabinet at home. He knows full well that when the mouse is away the cats will play.

(Sir) Winston S. Churchill, British Conservative Prime Minister and writer (1874–1965). Quoted in Harold Nicolson, *Diaries and Letters* (1968) – entry for 12 December 1946.

5 A sheep in sheep's clothing.

(Sir) Winston S. Churchill. Quoted in Willans & Roetter, *The Wit of Winston Churchill* (1954). However, according to William Safire, in *Safire's Political Dictionary* (1980), Churchill told Sir Denis Brogan that he had said it not about Attlee but about Ramsay MacDonald, with rather more point. If so, it would appear that he was quoting a joke made by the humorous columnist Beachcomber *c.* 1936. Aneurin Bevan alluded to this same source *c.* 1937 – 'Beachcomber once described Mr Ramsay MacDonald as ... It applies to many of the front-bench men with whom the Parliamentary Labour Party is cursed' (quoted in Michael Foot, *Aneurin Bevan*, Vol. 1, 1962). Sir Edmund Gosse is supposed to have said the same of T. Sturge Moore, the 'woolly-bearded poet', *c.* 1906 – and was quoted so doing by Ferris Greenslet in *Under the Bridge* (1943).

6 An empty taxi arrived at 10 Downing Street, and when the door was opened Attlee got out.

(Sir) Winston S. Churchill. When John Colville told Churchill this remark was being attributed to him, he commented gravely, 'after an awful pause': 'Mr Attlee is an honourable and gallant gentleman, and a faithful colleague who served his country well at the time of her greatest need. I should be obliged if you would make it clear whenever an occasion arises that I never would make such a remark about him, and that I strongly disapprove of anybody who does.' This denial was reported in Kenneth Harris, *Attlee* (1982). Compare: 'An empty cab drove up, and Sarah Bernhardt got out' – Arthur ('Bugs') Baer, American humorist (1897?–1969), quoted in *The Treasury of Humorous Quotations*, eds Evan Esar & Nicolas Bentley (1951).

7 A modest man who has a good deal to be modest about.

(Sir) Winston S. Churchill. Quoted in the *Chicago Sunday Tribune Magazine of Books* (27 June 1954) – perhaps in a review of Willans & Roetter, *The Wit of Winston Churchill* (1954).

8 He never used one syllable where none would do.

Douglas Jay (Lord Jay), English Labour politician (1907–96). Quoted in Peter Hennessy, *Muddling Through* (1996). Jay was Attlee's personal assistant in the 1945 Labour Government.

9 Reminds me of nothing so much as a recently dead fish before it has had time to stiffen.

George Orwell, English novelist and journalist (1903–50). Diary entry for 19 May 1942, quoted in *The Collected Essays, Journalism and Letters of George Orwell*, Vol. 2 (1968).

Attraction

1 She was short on intellect, but long on shape.

George Ade, American humorist and playwright (1866–1944). Quoted in *The Treasury of Humorous Quotations*, eds Evan Esar & Nicolas Bentley (1951).

2 To the Theatre, where I saw again *The Lost Lady*, which doth now please me better than before. And here, I sitting behind in a dark place, a lady spat backward on me by mistake, not seeing me. But after seeing her to be a very pretty lady, I was not troubled at it at all.

Samuel Pepys, English civil servant and diarist (1633–1703). Diary entry for 28 January 1661.

3 *Mae:*
How tall are you, son?
Man:
Ma-am, I'm six feet seven inches.
Mae:
Let's forget the six feet and talk about the seven inches.

Mae West, American vaudeville and film actress (1893–1980). Quoted in Leslie Halliwell, *The Filmgoer's Book of Quotes* (1973). Famously indelicate exchange, possibly inserted by West in Mike Sarne's screenplay of Gore Vidal's *Myra Breckinridge* (US 1970). She delivered the lines in the film. It is a very old exchange: In Harriette Wilson's *Memoirs* (1825) (the book that supposedly gave rise to the Duke of Wellington's response, 'Publish and be damned!') a stranger says to her, 'A name is not important. I stand before you, an upright man of five feet nine inches.' Lord Alvanley then quips, also in French, 'The lady knows about your five feet, but she's not sure of your nine inches.'

4 Is that a gun in your pocket or are you just pleased to see me?

Mae West. Quoted in Joseph Weintraub, *Peel Me a Grape* (1975). Sometimes remembered as 'pistol' and also in connection with her play *Catherine Was Great* (1944) in the form: 'Lieutenant, is that your sword, or are you just glad to see me?' Leslie Halliwell in *The Filmgoer's Book of Quotes* (1978 edn), has this last as West's reaction in a Broadway costume play, when the romantic lead got his sword tangled in his braid so that it stuck up at an unfortunate angle.

Auden, W.H.

ANGLO-AMERICAN POET (1907–73)

5 He didn't love God, he just fancied him.

Anonymous. Quoted in my book *Quote ... Unquote* 3 (1983). Also in John Mortimer, *In Character* (1983).

Of his face:

6 If a fly walked over it, it would break its leg.

Anonymous. Quoted on BBC Radio *Quote ... Unquote* (5 June 1980).

Of himself:

7 My face looks like a wedding-cake left out in the rain.

W.H. Auden. No, it was not said by someone else about Auden (as stated, for example, in L. Levinson, *Bartlett's Unfamiliar Quotations*, 1972). The poet himself said to a reporter: 'Your cameraman might enjoy himself, because my face looks like a wedding cake left out in the rain' (cited in Humphrey Carpenter, *W.H. Auden*, 1981). However, according to Noël Annan in *Maurice Bowra: a celebration* (1974), Bowra once referred to E.M. Forster's *work* as a wedding-cake left out in the rain.

Audiences

8 Long experience has taught me that in England nobody goes to the theatre unless he or she has bronchitis.

James Agate, English dramatic critic (1877–1947). *Ego* 6 (1944).

9 The best audience is one that is intelligent, well-educated – and a little drunk.

Alben W. Barkley, American Democratic politician (1877–1956). Quoted by Adlai Stevenson in *The New York Times* (15 February 1965).

Throwing a sea bass to a noisily coughing audience:

10 Busy yourselves with *this*, you damned walruses, while the rest of us proceed with the libretto.

John Barrymore, American actor (1882–1942). Quoted in Bennett Cerf, *Try and Stop Me* (1944). Cerf has it that the incident occurred when Barrymore was playing Fedor in *The Living Corpse*, a version of Tolstoy's *Redemption*, in 1918.

On playing to matinée audiences at Bridlington:

1 You could see the dampness rising from the wet raincoats like mist on the marshes.

Les Dawson, English comedian (1934–93). Quoted in *The Independent on Sunday* (10 July 1993).

2 Would the people in the cheaper seats clap your hands. And the rest of you – if you'd just rattle your jewellery.

John Lennon, English singer and songwriter (1940–80). To audience at the Royal Variety Performance (4 November 1963). From the soundtrack of the TV recording.

To audience at Carnegie Hall:

3 A painter paints his picture on canvas. But musicians paint their pictures on silence. We provide the music, and you provide the silence.

Leopold Stokowski, American conductor (1882–1977). Quoted in *The Home Book of Humorous Quotations*, ed. A.K. Adams (1969).

On being asked by a friend how his latest play had gone:

4 It was a great success but the audience was a total failure.

Oscar Wilde, Irish playwright, poet and wit (1854–1900). Quoted in Edmund Fuller, *Thesaurus of Anecdotes* (1942). The play was *Lady Windermere's Fan* (1892).

5 The audience strummed their catarrhs.

Alexander Woollcott, American writer and critic (1887–1943). Quoted in Herbert V. Prochnow, Snr & Jnr, *A Treasury of Humorous Quotations* (1969).

Aunts

6 When Aunt is calling to Aunt like mastodons bellowing across primeval swamps.

(Sir) P(elham) G. Wodehouse, English-born novelist and lyricist (1881–1975). *The Inimitable Jeeves*, Chap. 16 (1923).

Austen, Jane

ENGLISH NOVELIST (1775–1817)

Accepting an Oscar for her screenplay of Sense and Sensibility *(1995):*

7 I hope she knows how big she is in Uruguay.

Emma Thompson, English actress and writer (1959–). Speech in Los Angeles (26 March 1996).

8 To me his [Edgar Allan Poe's] prose is unreadable – like Jane Austen's. No, there is a difference. I could read his prose on a salary, but not Jane's.

Mark Twain, American writer (1835–1910). In *Mark Twain's Letters*, ed. A.B. Paine (1917).

Austerity

On the National Health Service and continuing austerity:

9 Here is a pretty prospect – an endless vista of free false teeth with nothing to bite.

Robert Boothby (Lord Boothby), English Conservative politician (1900–86). Quoted in Herbert V. Prochnow, Snr & Jnr, *A Treasury of Humorous Quotations* (1969).

Australia and the Australians

10 God made the harbour, and that's all right, but Satan made Sydney.

Anonymous (citizen of Sydney). Quoted by Mark Twain in *More Tramps Abroad* (1897).

11 We had intended you to be
The next Prime Minister but three:
The stocks were sold; the Press was squared;
The Middle Class was quite prepared.
But as it is! ... My language fails!
Go out and govern New South Wales!

Hilaire Belloc, French-born English poet and writer (1870–1953). *Cautionary Tales*, 'Lord Lundy' (1907).

12 Australia is a huge rest home, where no unwelcome news is ever wafted on to the pages of the worst newspapers in the world.

Germaine Greer, Australian-born feminist writer (1939–). In *The Observer* (1 August 1982).

1 In Australia
Inter alia,
Mediocrities
Think they're Socrates.

Peter Porter, Australian-born poet (1929–). Unpublished clerihew, quoted in *The Dictionary of Australian* Quotations (1984). Porter commented on BBC Radio *Quote ... Unquote* (28 November 1989) that writing these lines meant he had recently been denied a grant by the Australian government.

Of Australia:

2 It must be so pretty with all the dear little kangaroos flying about. Agatha has found it on the map. What a curious shape it is! Just like a large packing case.

Oscar Wilde, Irish playwright, poet and wit (1854–1900). *Lady Windermere's Fan*, Act 2 (1892). Later the Duchess of Berwick calls it 'that dreadful vulgar place'.

Autobiography

3 Autobiography is now as common as adultery and hardly less reprehensible.

John Grigg (formerly Lord Altrincham), English writer (1924–). In *The Sunday Times* (28 February 1962).

4 Autobiography is an unrivalled vehicle for telling the truth about other people.

Philip Guedalla, English biographer and historian (1889–1944). *Supers and Supermen* (1920).

5 If you really want to hear about it, the first thing you'll probably want to know is where I was born and what my lousy childhood was like, and how my parents were occupied and all before they had me, and all that David Copperfield kind of crap.

J.D. Salinger, *The Catcher in the Rye*, Chap. 1 (1951). Opening words.

Autographs

On Neville Chamberlain and the Munich agreement (1938):

6 Well, he seemed such a nice old gentleman, I thought I would give him my autograph as a souvenir.

Adolf Hitler, German Nazi leader (1889–1945). Attributed remark in the *The Penguin Dictionary of Modern Quotations* (1971).

Said to an imposing gentleman, after bowing low to him:

7 I beg your pardon, sir, are you anyone in particular?

Theodore Hook, English writer, hoaxer and joker (1788–1841). Quoted in W.D. Adams, *Treasury of Modern Anecdote* (1886). Hook or not, 'Please, are you anybody?' was the caption to a cartoon by Lewis Baumer in *Punch* Magazine (16 February 1938). It showed a little girl with an autograph book approaching an impressive gentleman.

8 Gather ye autographs while ye may.

Cole Porter, American composer and lyricist (1891–1964). Title of song in *Jubilee* (1935), but dropped from the show.

9 I stopped believing in Santa Claus when I was six. Mother took me to see him in a department store and he asked for my autograph.

Shirley Temple, American child actor and diplomat (1928–). Attributed remark.

Awards

On receiving an award:

10 I don't deserve this, but I have arthritis, and I don't deserve that either.

Jack Benny, American comedian (1894–1974). Quoted in *Quote and Unquote*, ed. Peter and Josie Holtom (1973).

B

Babes and sucklings

Definition of a baby:

1 A loud voice at one end and no sense of responsibility at the other.

Ronald Knox, English priest and writer (1888–1957). So ascribed in A. Andrews, *Quotations for Speakers and Writers* (1969) and also in the 1976 BBC Reith Lectures, though Frank S. Pepper's *Handbook of 20th Century Quotations* (1984) gives it to 'E. Adamson'. *Bartlett's Familiar Quotations* (16th edn, 1992) ascribes 'Government is like a big baby – an alimentary canal with a big appetite at one end and no responsibility at the other' to Ronald Reagan 'while campaigning for governor of California (1965).' It was so ascribed by Stewart Alsop in *The Saturday Evening Post* (20 November 1965).

On being asked who made her:

2 I s'pect I growed. Don't think nobody ever made me.

Harriet Beecher Stowe, American novelist (1811–96). *Uncle Tom's Cabin* (1852). The little slave girl, Topsy, asserts that she has no mother or father. Hence, the rephrased expression: 'Like Topsy – she just growed.'

Bachelors

3 A bachelor is one who enjoys the chase but does not eat the game.

Anonymous. Quoted in Herbert V. Prochnow, Snr & Jnr, *A Treasury of Humorous Quotations* (1969).

4 'Home, Sweet Home' must surely have been written by a bachelor.

Samuel Butler, English author (1835–1902). Quoted in *The Treasury of Humorous Quotations*, eds Evan Esar & Nicolas Bentley (1951).

5 A single man has not nearly the value he would have in a state of union. He is an incomplete animal. He resembles the odd half of a pair of scissors.

Benjamin Franklin, American politician and scientist (1706–90). *Advice to a Young Man on the Choice of a Mistress* (25 June 1745).

6 Somehow a bachelor never quite gets over the idea that he is a thing of beauty and a boy forever.

Helen Rowland, American columnist and writer (1875–1950). *A Guide to Men* (1922).

7 A bachelor gets tangled up with a lot of women in order to avoid getting tied up by one.

Helen Rowland. Quoted in *The Treasury of Humorous Quotations*, eds Evan Esar & Nicolas Bentley (1951).

8 A Bachelor of Arts is one who makes love to a lot of women, and yet has the art to remain a bachelor.

Helen Rowland. Quoted in the same collection as above.

9 Bachelors should be heavily taxed. It is not fair that some men should be happier than others.

Oscar Wilde, Irish playwright, poet and wit (1854–1900). Attributed remark.

1 By persistently remaining single a man converts himself into a permanent public temptation.

Oscar Wilde. *The Importance of Being Earnest*, Act 2 (1895).

Bacon, Francis (1st Lord Verulam and Viscount St Albans)

ENGLISH PHILOSOPHER AND POLITICIAN (1561–1626)

2 Sir Francis Bacon
Is sometimes mistaken
For another old codger
Called Rodger.

'P.C.C.', in *New Statesman Competitions*, ed. Arthur Marshall (1955).

Bad

3 The reason Michael Jackson entitled his album *Bad* was because he couldn't spell *Indescribable*.

Anonymous – shortly after the album was released in 1987.

Of an inn at Bristol:

4 Describe it, Sir? – Why, it was so bad that Boswell wished to be in Scotland.

(Dr) Samuel Johnson, English writer and lexicographer (1709–84). In James Boswell, *The Life of Samuel Johnson* (1791) – for 29 April 1776.

Bagpipes

5 A true gentleman is a man who knows how to play the bagpipes – but doesn't.

Anonymous. Quoted in *Reader's Digest* (March 1976) as from *The Wall Street Journal*. This has also been ascribed to G.K. Chesterton. Compare the quip: 'The best place to be to listen to bagpipes being played in Scotland, is London.'

6 The bagpipes sound exactly the same when you have finished learning them as when you start.

(Sir) Thomas Beecham, English conductor (1879–1961). Quoted in Harold Atkins & Archie Newman, *Beecham Stories* (1978).

Baldness

7 The most delightful advantage of being bald – one can *hear* snowflakes.

R.G. Daniels, English magistrate (1916–). Quoted in *The Observer* (11 July 1976).

8 A hair in the head is worth two in the brush.

Oliver Herford, American humorist (1863–1935). Quoted in *The Treasury of Humorous Quotations*, eds Evan Esar & Nicolas Bentley (1951).

9 He used to cut his hair, but now his hair has cut him.

Theodore Hook, English novelist and wit (1788–1841). Quoted in the same collection as above.

10 He was not bald: for on his shining cranium
Remained one hair, it's colour pink geranium.
Oh how he idolised that single hair
That, last of loved ones, grew luxuriant there.

Lines from song 'The Man With the Single Hair'. Written by Robert Ganthony & Arthur H. Wood (1902) and performed by Mel B. Spurr.

11 There is more felicity on the far side of baldness than young men can possibly imagine.

Logan Pearsall Smith, American writer (1865–1946). *Afterthoughts* (1931).

12 Balding is God's way of showing you are only human ... he takes the hair off your head and sticks it in your ears.

Bruce Willis, American actor (1955–). Quoted in *The Observer* (3 March 1996).

Baldwin, Stanley (1st Earl Baldwin of Bewdley)

BRITISH CONSERVATIVE PRIME MINISTER (1867–1947)

13 Stanley Baldwin always hits the nail on the head, but it doesn't go in any further.

G.M. Young, English historian (1882–1959). Attributed remark.

Ballet

1 My own personal reaction is that most ballets would be perfectly delightful if it were not for the dancing.

Anonymous. Quoted in Michael Bateman, *This England: Selections from the New Statesman column 1934–1968*, Pt 1 (1969).

Banana republics

On the state of Britain in 1978:

2 If you subtracted the North Sea oil revenues you would realise that present policies are leading us to the status of a banana republic that has run out of bananas.

Richard Marsh (Lord Marsh), English politician (1928–). Quoted in *The Daily Telegraph* (6 September 1978).

3 Had the Conservative elite of the immediate post-war era shown half the energy and enterprise in peacetime as it had in war, it is hard to believe that Britain would have been reduced to her present stature of Italy with rockets.

Andrew Roberts, English historian (1963–). *Eminent Churchillians*, Introduction (1994).

Bananas

When asked whether he thought Mrs Thatcher would face any more banana skins:

4 I think there will be banana skins as long as there are bananas.

William Whitelaw (1st Viscount Whitelaw), English politician (1918–99). Quoted in *The Observer* (22 April 1984).

Bankers

5 A banker is a fellow who lends you his umbrella when the sun is shining and wants it back the minute it begins to rain.

Mark Twain, American author (1835–1910). Quoted in *The Treasury of Humorous Quotations*, eds Evan Esar & Nicolas Bentley (1951). Has also been ascribed to Robert Frost.

Bankhead, Tallulah

AMERICAN ACTRESS (1903–68)

When asked towards the end of her life if she was the famous Tallulah, the actress replied:

6 What's left of her.

Tallulah Bankhead. Quoted in Leslie Halliwell, *The Filmgoer's Book of Quotes* (1973).

7 Watching Tallullah on stage is like watching somebody skating on thin ice. Everyone wants to be there when it breaks.

Mrs Patrick Campbell, English actress (1865–1940). Quoted in Bankhead's obituary in *The Times* (13 December 1968).

8 A day away from Tallulah is like a month in the country.

Howard Dietz, American writer and film executive (1896–1983). Recalled in his book *Dancing in the Dark* (1974). This remark has also been attributed to all the usual suspects – Parker, Ace, Kaufman, Woollcott and Benchley – but Dietz claimed he said it and Bankhead herself wrote in *Tallulah* (1952): 'How Dietz once remarked, "A day away from Tallulah is like a month in the country." Ever since he's enjoyed the reputation of a great wit.' Ouch.

9 I've just spent an hour talking to Tallulah for a few minutes.

Fred Keating. Quoted in Ned Sherrin, *Cutting Edge* (1984).

Banquets

10 A Banquet is probably the most fatiguing thing in the world except ditch digging. It is the insanest of all recreations. The inventor of it overlooked no detail that could furnish weariness, distress, harassment, and acute and long-sustained misery of mind and body.

Mark Twain, American writer (1835–1910). Quoted in *Mark Twain in Eruption*, ed. Bernard de Vote (1940).

Barrie, (Sir) J(ames) M.

SCOTTISH PLAYWRIGHT (1860–1937)

11 The cheerful clatter of Sir James Barrie's

cans as he went round with the milk of human kindness.

Philip Guedalla, English writer (1889–1944). *Supers and Supermen*, 'Some Critics' (1920).

Basingstoke

1 *Mad Margaret:*
When I am lying awake at night, and the pale moonlight streams through the latticed casement, strange fancies crowd upon my poor mad brain, and I sometimes think that if we could hit upon some word for you to use whenever I am about to relapse – some word that teems with hidden meaning – like 'Basingstoke' – it might recall me to my saner self.

(Sir) W.S. Gilbert, English writer and lyricist (1836–1911). *Ruddigore* (1887).

Bathing

2 My grandmother took a bath every year, whether she was dirty or not.

Brendan Behan, Irish playwright (1923–64). *Brendan Behan's Island* (1962).

3 Two Jews were conversing about bathing. 'I take a bath once a year,' said one, 'whether I need one or not.'

Sigmund Freud, Austrian psychiatrist (1856–1939). Discussing an anti-Semitic joke in *Jokes and their Relation to the Unconscious* (1905), Freud adds, helpfully, 'It is clear that this boastful assurance of his cleanliness only betrays his sense of uncleanliness.' Sometimes told concerning Queen Elizabeth I – that she would take a bath once a month 'whether she need it or no.' For example, from Walter Rye's *Some Historical Essays Chiefly Relating to Norfolk*, Pt 6 (1928): 'In a lecture given at the Castle Museum, in March last, by a gentleman … he is reported to have caused great amusement, not to say surprise, to many of his hearers by stating that the modern idea of changing one's clothes was distinctly modern. Queen Elizabeth only had a bath once a year, when she really changed the garment next her skin. Except on that occasion she did not … ' Rye goes on to rubbish this idea.

Bavarians

4 A Bavarian is half-way between an Austrian and a human being.

Otto von Bismarck, Prusso-German statesman (1815–98). Attributed remark. R.P.W. Lewis recalled this, however, from Edward Teller's obituary of the physicist Werner Heisenberg – a Bavarian – in *Nature* (15 April 1976): 'On the 800th anniversary of the Bavarian state, he appeared on television and said, "The Bavarian unites the discipline of the Austrian with the charm of the Prussian".'

BBC (British Broadcasting Corporation)

5 The BBC does itself untold harm by its excessive sensitivity. At the first breath of criticism the Corporation adopts a posture of a hedgehog at bay.

Noël Annan (Lord Annan), English academic and writer (1916–2000). *Report of the Committee on the Future of Broadcasting* (1977). This British official inquiry was chaired by Annan who, although he may not have written this passage, was certainly responsible for the overall tone of the piece and its unusual readability.

6 Its atmosphere is something halfway between a girls' school and a lunatic asylum.

George Orwell, English novelist and journalist (1903–50). Diary entry for 14 March 1942, quoted in *The Collected Essays, Journalism and Letters of George Orwell*, Vol. 2 (1968).

Beards

7 Christlike in my behaviour,
Like every good believer,
I imitate the Saviour,
And cultivate a beaver.

Aldous Huxley, English novelist and writer (1894–1963). *Antic Hay* (1923).

8 There was an old man with a beard,
Who said, 'It is just as I feared!
Two Owls and a Hen,
Four Larks and a Wren
Have all built their nests in my beard.

Edward Lear, English poet and artist (1812–88). *A Book of Nonsense* (1846).

Beauty

1 Every woman who is not absolutely ugly thinks herself handsome.

4th Earl of Chesterfield (Philip Dormer Stanhope), English politician and writer (1694–1773). *Letters to His Son* (1774) – for 5 September 1748.

2 Women's beauty, like men's wit, is generally fatal to the owners.

4th Earl of Chesterfield. *Miscellaneous Works*, Vol. 2 (1778).

Beckett, Samuel

IRISH PLAYWRIGHT (1906–89)

3 He's a great skin, and he kept me going with occasional hand-outs when my readies were low. I don't understand his plays, but so what? I go for swims in the ocean, and I don't understand that either.

Brendan Behan, Irish playwright (1923–64). Quoted in Peter Arthurs, *With Brendan Behan* (1981).

Bede, The Venerable

ENGLISH HISTORIAN AND SCHOLAR (673–735)

4 The Venerable Bede
Omitted half the Creed;
And also two-thirds
Of the Comfortable Words.

Anonymous (clerihew).

5 The Venerable Bede
Could read.
It's a pity he couldn't spel
As wel.

Lakon (*nom de plume*). In *New Statesman Competitions*, ed. Arthur Marshall (1955).

6 'This', said the Venerable Bede,
'Is a very important matter indeed.
Would it be uncanonical
To contribute to the Anglo-Saxon
Chronicle?'

Barry G. Smallman, in the same book as above.

Beds

7 It's not the wild, ecstatic leap across that I deplore. It is the weary trudge home.

Anonymous. 'Double Beds versus Single Beds', quoted in *The Penguin Dictionary of Modern Quotations* (1971). Derek Parker recalled (1996) the comedian Derek Roy saying something similar in his act at the Palace Theatre, Plymouth, in 1957: 'It's not the quick dash over – it's the slow drag back.'

8 Let the saints be joyful in glory: let them sing aloud upon their beds.

The Bible. Psalms 149:5.

9 Believe me, you have to get up early if you want to get out of bed.

Line from film *The Cocoanuts* (US 1929). Screenwriters: George S. Kaufman, Morrie Ryskind. Spoken by Groucho Marx (Hammer). Possibly an allusion to J.R. Lowell, *The Biglow Papers*, First series, No. 1 (1848): 'An' you've gut to git up airly / Ef you want to take in God.'

10 Many are called but few get up.

Oliver Herford, American humorist (1863–1935), and Addison Mizner, American architect (1872–1933). *The Cynic's Calendar* (1902).

11 I always feel so selfish sleeping alone in a double bed, when there are people in China sleeping on the ground.

Line from film *The Owl and the Pussycat* (US 1970). Screenwriter: Buck Henry (from a play by Bill Manhoff). Spoken by Barbara Streisand (Doris) to George Segal (Felix).

Beethoven, Ludwig van

GERMAN COMPOSER (1770–1827)

12 Beethoven was so deaf, he thought he was a painter.

Anonymous (graffito) on Intercity train between Newcastle and Sheffield. Contributed to BBC Radio *Quote … Unquote* (19 February 1979) by Pete and Kathy Weslowski of South Gosforth.

On the third movement of the 7th Symphony:

1 What can you do with it? – it's like a lot of yaks jumping about.

(Sir) Thomas Beecham, English conductor (1879–1961). Quoted in Harold Atkins & Archie Newman, *Beecham Stories* (1978).

On being asked what he thought of Beethoven:

2 I love him, especially his poems.

Ringo Starr, English pop musician (1940–). Quoted in Hunter Davies, *The Beatles* (1968). At a press conference during The Beatles' first American tour in 1964.

Beggars

When asked why he constantly gave money to beggars:

3 Madam, to enable them to beg on.

(Dr) Samuel Johnson, English writer and lexicographer (1709–84). Quoted in *Johnsonian Miscellanies*, ed. Hill (1897).

Beginning

4 'Where shall I begin, please, your Majesty?' he [the White Rabbit] asked. 'Begin at the beginning,' the King said, gravely, 'and go on till you come to the end: then stop.'

Lewis Carroll, English writer (1832–98). *Alice's Adventures in Wonderland*, Chap. 12 (1865).

Behaviour

5 Be good (if you can't be good, be careful).

Anonymous saying. Quoted in *H.L. Mencken's Dictionary of Quotations* (1942), where it is described as an American proverb, though its pedigree in *The Concise Oxford Dictionary of Proverbs* (1982) is mostly British – the first proper citation here being in 1903 (from A.M. Binstead, *Pitcher in Paradise*). In 1907, there was an American song called 'Be Good! If You Can't Be Good, Be Careful!' written by Harrington Tate. All in all, it is mostly used as a nudging farewell, sometimes completed with 'and if you can't be careful, name it after me' – or 'buy a pram'. The same sort of farewell remark as 'Don't do anything I wouldn't do!'

6 'Do you mean to say,' he joshed, 'that the Union Club has come to a day when a man can bring his mistress to the club?' Along with the great club revolution, the doorman remembered the great club tradition. 'You may, Sir,' he replied stiffly, 'if the lady is the wife of one of the members.'

Cleveland Amory, American writer (1907–). *Who Killed Society?* (1960).

7 'It is always best on these occasions to do what the mob do.' 'But suppose there are two mobs?' suggested Mr Snodgrass. 'Shout with the largest,' replied Mr Pickwick.

Charles Dickens, English novelist (1812–70). *The Pickwick Papers*, Chap. 13 (1837).

An Admonition. Bridget:

8 Now then, Miss Effie, you must behave yourself properly, or not at all!

(Sir) Bernard Partridge, English cartoonist and artist (1861–1945). Caption to cartoon in *Punch* (24 April 1897). A similar caption also appeared in a cartoon by George Belcher on 27 April 1932: *'Indignant Young Lady*. "If you can't behave properly, you'd better not behave at all".'

Belief

Of the actress Diane Keaton:

9 In real life, Keaton believes in God. But she also believes that the radio works because there are tiny people inside it.

Woody Allen, American film actor, writer and director (1937–). Attributed remark.

10 Believe only half of what you see and nothing that you hear.

Anonymous. Quoted in Mrs (Dinah) Craik, *A Woman's Thoughts* (1858).

11 Believe nothing until it has been officially denied.

Anonymous. Quoted in Claud Cockburn, *In Time of Trouble* (1956), as advice frequently given to him as a young man.

1 All in all there is much to suggest that the Established Church is in a state of bewilderment and has lost its way. As a wag put it when writing to *The Times*: 'There doesn't seem very much left for us agnostics not to believe in.'

Anonymous. Quoted in *Faith and Heritage* (Summer 1995).

2 There are three statements that you should never believe: (1) 'A cheque is in the post'; (2) 'I am from the Government and I am here to help you'; (3) 'Of course, darling, I will still respect you in the morning.'

Anonymous. Quoted by Robin Oakley on BBC Radio *Quote ... Unquote* (9 September 2000).

Asked whether he believed in God:

3 We've never been intimate – but maybe we do have a few things in common.

(Sir) Noël Coward, English entertainer and writer (1899–1973). In TV interview with David Frost on LWT *Frost on Saturday* (28 December 1968).

4 Lord, I do not believe; help thou my unbelief.

Samuel Butler, English author (1835–1902). Quoted in *The Treasury of Humorous Quotations*, eds Evan Esar & Nicolas Bentley (1951).

5 Why, sometimes I've believed as many as six impossible things before breakfast.

Lewis Carroll, English writer (1832–98). *Through the Looking-Glass and What Alice Found There*, Chap. 5 (1872). Alice has asserted, 'One can't believe impossible things' and the White Queen tells her she can't have had much practice: 'When I was your age, I always did it for half-an-hour a day...'

6 When men cease to believe in God, they will not believe in nothing, they will believe in anything.

G.K. Chesterton, English poet, novelist and critic (1874–1936). Attributed remark. The earliest citation appears in Emile Cammaerts, *Chesterton: The Laughing Prophet* (1937), where, in the middle of some direct quotation, there is the paraphrase, 'The first effect of not believing in God is to believe in anything.'

When asked by a child from the Commonwealth whether she believed in Father Christmas:

7 I like to believe in Father Christmas.

Elizabeth II, British Queen (1926–). In Christmas TV broadcast (25 December 1989).

8 My dear child, you must believe in God in spite of what the clergy tell you.

Benjamin Jowett, English scholar (1817–93). Quoted in Margot Asquith, *Autobiography* (1920–2).

Of W.E. Gladstone:

9 I don't object to the Old Man's always having the ace of trumps up his sleeve, but merely to his belief that God Almighty put it there.

Henry Labouchère, English journalist and politician (1831–1912). Quoted in Hesketh Pearson, *Lives of the Wits* (1962).

10 I must believe in the Apostolic succession, there being no other way of accounting for the descent of the Bishop of Exeter from Judas Iscariot.

(Revd) Sydney Smith, English clergyman, essayist and wit (1771–1845). Letter (1818), quoted in *The Sayings of Sydney Smith*, ed. Alan Bell (1993).

Replying to a minor government official who had accosted him in Pall Mall with the words: 'Mr Jones, I believe':

11 If you believe that, you will believe anything.

1st Duke of Wellington (Arthur Wellesley), Irish-born soldier and British Prime Minister (1769–1852). The earliest source I have for this story is Elizabeth Longford, *Wellington: Pillar of State* (1972). It is said that there was a Mr Jones who bore a striking resemblance to Wellington – George Jones RA (1786–1869), a military painter. This likeness is referred to by W.P. Frith in *My Autobiography and Reminiscences*, Vol. 1 (1887), together with Wellington's comment on hearing that Jones was sometimes taken for him: 'Mistaken for me, is he? That's strange, for no one ever mistakes me for Mr Jones.'

In 1993, George Andrews of Lisbellaw, Co. Fermanagh, commented reasonably, 'Even on [Wellington's] lips ['if you believe that ... '] has always sounded to be like a quotation; is it possible that he was quoting from somebody even earlier?'

Well, a cartoon that appeared in *Punch* (9 April 1864) [Wellington had died in 1852] has this curious caption:

Polite Oxbridge tradesman (in quest of little Nibbs of S. Boniface, and walking by mistake into the rooms of long Nobbs, who 'keeps' on the same staircase). 'Mr. Nibbs, I believe?'

Nobbs (who is six feet one, and rowed a trifle over twelve stone at Putney, the other day). 'Then, my good fellow, you'll believe anything!'

Now, it was not unknown for *Punch* cartoonists to take existing jokes and make something quite new of them, but is that what has happened here? Or was the Wellington anecdote based on the cartoon situation? Note in passing that Mr Nobbs has something of a resemblance in the nose area to the Great Duke and the (anonymous) cartoonist has shaded it in quite noticeably.

1 I can believe in anything, provided that it is quite incredible.

Oscar Wilde, Irish playwright, poet and wit (1854–1900). *The Picture of Dorian Gray*, Chap. 1 (1891).

2 Where will it all end? Half the world does not believe in God, and the other half does not believe in me.

Oscar Wilde. Quoted in E.H. Mikhail, *Oscar Wilde: Interviews and Recollections* (1979).

Benn, Tony

ENGLISH LABOUR POLITICIAN (1925–)

3 Tony Benn is the Bertie Wooster of Marxism.

Anonymous. Quoted in Matthew Parris, *Scorn* (1995). This remark was contributed by Malcolm Bradbury to BBC Radio *Quote ... Unquote* (11 September 1979) and might well have been of his own manufacture.

4 He immatures with age.

Harold Wilson (Lord Wilson), British Labour Prime Minister (1916–95). In 1981. Quoted in Anthony Sampson, *The Changing Anatomy of Britain* (1982).

Best

5 It is a funny thing about life: if you refuse to accept anything but the best you very often get it.

W. Somerset Maugham, English writer (1874–1965). Quoted in *The Treasury of Humorous Quotations*, eds Evan Esar & Nicolas Bentley (1951).

Best-sellers

6 A best-seller was a book which somehow sold well simply because it was selling well.

Daniel J. Boorstin, American writer (1914–). *Images* (1961).

7 A best-seller is the gilded tomb of a mediocre talent.

Logan Pearsall Smith, American writer (1865–1946). *Afterthoughts*, Chap. 5 (1931).

Betjeman, (Sir) John

ENGLISH POET LAUREATE (1906–84)

8 We naturally define the Betjeman genius as an infinite capacity for taking trains.

(Sir) Peter Parker, English industrialist (1924–). In a speech at the opening of the Betjeman restaurant at Charing Cross station, London. He was Chairman of British Rail at the time. Quoted on BBC Radio *Quote ... Unquote* (17 May 1978).

Bewilderment

9 There were two things that would always bewilder her, she said: how a zipper worked and the exact function of Bernard Baruch.

Dorothy Parker, American writer (1893–1967). Quoted in *The Sayings of Dorothy Parker*, ed. S.T. Brownlow (1992).

The Bible

10 The Bible was a consolation to a fellow alone in the old cell. The lovely thin paper and a bit of mattress in it – if you could get a match – was as good a smoke as ever tasted.

Brendan Behan, Irish playwright (1923–64). *The Quare Fellow* (1956).

1 There came forth little children out of the city, and mocked him, and said unto him, Go up, thou bald head; go up, thou bald head.

The Bible. 2 Kings 2:23.

2 He swalloweth the ground with fierceness and rage: neither believeth he that it is the sound of the trumpet. He saith among the trumpets, Ha, ha; and he smelleth the battle afar off, the thunder of the captains, and the shouting.

The Bible. Job 39:24–25. It is a *horse* that is being talked about.

3 Moab is my washpot; over Edom will I cast out my shoe.

The Bible. Psalms 60:8. One of the strangest sentences in the Bible. The New English Bible translation may make it clearer: (God speaks from his sanctuary) 'Gilead and Manasseh are mine; Ephraim is my helmet, Judah my sceptre; Moab is my wash-bowl, I fling my shoes at Edom; Philistia is the target of my anger.' In other words, God is talking about useful objects to throw, in his anger. (Moab was an ancient region of Jordan.) The actor and writer Stephen Fry entitled his memoirs *Moab Is My Washpot* (1997). In *The Independent* (18 August 1999) he explained his choice of title as having more to do with the following sentence ('Philistia, triumph thou because of me') – which he interprets as concerning 'vanquishing the Philistines. My adolescent self saw life as a war between the athlete and the aesthete, the inner life and the outer life. But then, I was something of a wanker.'

4 My beloved put his hand in by the hole of the door, and my bowels were moved for him.

The Bible. Song of Solomon 5:4.

The actor Thomas Mitchell visited W.C. Fields in a sanatorium during his last illness and was amazed to see the comedian thumbing through the Bible. When he asked, 'What are you doing?', Fields replied:

5 Looking for loopholes.

W.C. Fields, American comedian (1879–1946). Quoted in my book *Quote ... Unquote* (1978) – source unknown.

6 The total absence of humour from the Bible is one of the most singular things in all literature.

Alfred North Whitehead, English philosopher and mathematician (1861–1947). Quoted in Laurence J. Peter, *Quotations for Our Time* (1977).

7 When I think of all the harm that book [the Bible] has done, I despair of ever writing anything to equal it.

Oscar Wilde, Irish playwright, poet and wit (1854–1900). Quoted in E.H. Mikhail, *Oscar Wilde: Interviews and Recollections* (1979).

8 *Lord Illingworth:*
The Book of Life begins with a man and a woman in a garden.
Mrs Allonby:
It ends with Revelations.

Oscar Wilde. *A Woman of No Importance*, Act 1 (1893).

Bicycling

9 I think the most ridiculous sight in the world is a man on a bicycle, working away with his feet as hard as he possibly can, and believing that his horse is carrying him, instead of, as anyone can see, he carrying the horse.

Bernard Shaw, Irish playwright and critic (1856–1950). *An Unsocialist Socialist*, Chap. 11 (1881).

Bidets

Cabled response to his wife's complaint from Paris just after the Second World War that her accommodation did not have a bidet and would he send her one:

10 UNABLE OBTAIN BIDET. SUGGEST HANDSTAND IN SHOWER.

Billy Wilder, American film director and writer (1906–). Originally quoted in Tom Wood, *The Bright Side of Billy Wilder, Primarily* (1969), where the message begins: 'Charvet ties on way but impossible to obtain bidet. Suggest ... '

Bigamy

1 *Spaulding:*
Are we all going to get married?
Teasdale:
… But that's bigamy.
Spaulding:
Yes, and it's bigame too.

Lines from film *Animal Crackers* (US 1930). Screenwriters: Morrie Ryskind, George S. Kaufman. Spoken by Groucho Marx (Capt. Spaulding) to Margaret Dumont (Mrs Teasdale).

2 There was an old party of Lyme,
Who married three wives at one time.
When asked, 'Why the third?'
He replied, 'One's absurd,
And bigamy, sir, is a crime!'

William Cosmo Monkhouse, English art critic and poet (1840–1901). Quoted in *The Faber Book of Comic Verse*, ed. Michael Roberts (1974 edn) – though not ascribed to Monkhouse.

3 Bigamy is having one wife too many. Monogamy is the same.

Oscar Wilde, Irish playwright, poet and wit (1854–1900). Quoted in Herbert V. Prochnow, Snr & Jnr, *A Treasury of Humorous Quotations* (1969).

Billiards

4 To play billiards well is the sign of an ill-spent youth.

Charles Roupell, legal official. Attributed in David Duncan, *Life of Herbert Spencer* (1908). Often misascribed to Herbert Spencer and to Robert Louis Stevenson. Under Spencer, the *Oxford Dictionary of Quotations* (1979) had: 'It was remarked to me by the late Mr Charles Roupell … that to play billiards was a sign of an ill-spent youth.' On the other hand, in the archives of the Savile Club in London it is recorded that Robert Louis Stevenson, who was a member from 1874 to 1894, propounded to Spencer that 'proficiency in this game [note: probably billiards, because it was said in the Savile billiards room] is a sign of a misspent youth' (mentioned in 'Words', *The Observer*, 4 May 1986).

Other clubs also claim the honour and some people would supply the words 'snooker', 'bridge' and 'misspent youth'. A keen billiards player, Spencer was displeased when the saying kept being ascribed to him in newspapers. He had quoted it from someone else. So he dictated a denial to Dr David Duncan, who edited his *Life and Letters* (1908) from which the *ODQ* quotation was taken. *ODQ* (1992) puts the remark under Roupell and describes him as an 'official referee of the British High Court of Justice'.

Benham's Dictionary of Quotations (1948) notes that a similar view had earlier appeared in *Noctes Ambrosianae* in March 1827.

Biography

5 The Art of Biography
Is different from Geography.
Geography is about Maps,
But Biography is about Chaps.

E.C. Bentley, English journalist and novelist (1875–1956). *Biography for Beginners* (1905).

6 It adds a new terror to death.

Lord Brougham, Scottish jurist and politician (1778–1868). Hesketh Pearson, *Common Misquotations* (1937), insists that what Brougham said in a 'speech on an ex-chancellor' was 'Death was now armed with a new terror', but he gives no source for the remark. What was being talked about? In particular what Lord Campbell wrote in *Lives of the Lord Chancellors* (1845–7) without the consent of the subjects' heirs or executors. Lord Lyndhurst (three times Lord Chancellor, d.1863) said, 'Campbell has added another terror to death' (quoted 1924).

On the other hand, the lawyer and politician Sir Charles Wetherell (d.1846) is also quoted as having said of Lord Campbell: 'Then there is my noble and biographical friend who has added a new terror to death' – quoted in Lord St Leonards, *Mispresentation in Campbell's Lives of Lyndhurst and Brougham* (1869). So everyone seems to have been saying it.

Pearson adds that before all this, the view had been expressed when bookseller Edmund Curll (1683–1747) used to churn out cheap lives of famous people as soon as they were dead. John Arbuthnot had called him, 'One of the new terrors of death' (in a letter to Jonathan Swift, 13 January 1733).

7 A great American need not fear the hand of his assassin; his real demise begins only

when a friend like Mr Sorensen closes the mouth of his tomb with a stone.

Nigel Dennis, English writer (1912–89). Reviewing Theodore C. Sorensen's *Kennedy* (1965) in *The Sunday Telegraph*. Quoted in A. Andrews, *Quotations for Speakers and Writers* (1969).

1 Biography is a very definite region bordered on the north by history, on the south by fiction, on the east by obituary, and on the west by tedium.

Philip Guedalla, English biographer and historian (1889–1944). Quoted in *The Observer,*' Sayings of the Week' (3 March 1929).

2 Every great man nowadays has his disciples, and it is always Judas who writes the biography.

Oscar Wilde, Irish playwright, poet and wit (1854–1900). 'The Critic as Artist' (1890).

Birds

3 Der spring is sprung
Der grass is riz
I wonder where dem boidies is?

Der little boids is on der wing,
Ain't dat absoid?
Der little wings is on der boid!

Anonymous (New York). 'The Budding Bronx', quoted in Arnold Silcock, *Verse and Worse* (1952).

Birmingham (England)

4 They came from Birmingham, which is not a place to promise much, you know … One has not great hopes from Birmingham. I always say there is something direful in the sound.

Jane Austen, English novelist (1775–1817). *Emma*, Chap. 36 (1816). Mrs Elton speaking.

Birth

5 If men bore the children, there would be only one born in each family.

Anonymous. *Reflections of a Bachelor* (1903).

6 *Kath:*
Can he be present at the birth of his child? …
Ed:
It's all any reasonable child can expect if the dad is present at the conception.

Joe Orton, English playwright (1933–67). *Entertaining Mr Sloane* (1964).

7 It occurred to me that I would like to be a poet. The chief qualification, I understand, is that you must be born. Well, I hunted up my birth certificate, and found that I was all right on that score.

Saki (H.H. Munro), English writer (1870–1916). *Reginald*, 'Reginald's Rubaiyat' (1904).

8 Why is it that we rejoice at a birth and grieve at a funeral? It is because we are not the person involved.

Mark Twain, American writer (1835–1910). *Pudd'nhead Wilson*, Chap. 9 (1894).

On being chaffed for being an Irishman:

9 Because a man is born in a stable that does not make him a horse.

1st Duke of Wellington (Arthur Wellesley), Irish-born soldier and politician (1769–1852). Quoted in Elizabeth Longford, *Wellington: The Years of the Sword* (1969). Compare the proverbial 'The man who is born in a stable is a horse' (known by 1833).

When asked why he had been born in such an unfashionable place as Lowell, Massachusetts:

10 The explanation is quite simple. I wished to be near my mother.

James McNeill Whistler, American painter (1834–1903). Quoted in *Medical Quotations* (1989). A similar line was attributed to the British comedian Max Wall in his obituary in *The Guardian* (23 May 1990): 'I was born there because I wanted to be near my parents.' Note how the idea behind both these versions ended up as the caption to a cartoon in *Punch* (14 August 1935): 'What made them build the station such a long way from the town?' 'They 'ad to, M'm, so as to be near the railway.' Compare also William Powell's line to Myrna Loy in the film *Manhattan*

Melodrama (US 1934): 'I was born at home because I wanted to be near my mother ...'

1 *Jack:*
I don't actually know who I am by birth. I was, well, I was found ...
Lady Bracknell:
Found! ... Where did the charitable gentleman ... find you?
Jack:
In a hand-bag.
Lady Bracknell:
A hand-bag?

Oscar Wilde, Irish playwright, poet and wit (1854–1900). *The Importance of Being Earnest*, Act 1 (1895).

Birth control

2 Whenever I hear people discussing birth control, I always remember that I was the fifth.

Clarence Darrow, American lawyer (1857–1938). *The Story of My Life* (1932).

3 My views on birth control are somewhat distorted by the fact that I was the seventh of nine children.

Robert F. Kennedy, American politician (1925–68). Quoted in Bill Adler, *The Robert F. Kennedy Wit* (1968).

Bisexuality

4 It immediately doubles your chances for a date on Saturday night.

Woody Allen, American film actor, writer and director (1937–). Quoted in *The New York Times* (1 December 1975).

Bishops

On being told by a bishop that his palace had no less than forty bedrooms in it:

5 Oh dear – and only Thirty-Nine Articles to put in them.

(Sir) Winston S. Churchill, British Conservative Prime Minister and writer (1874–1965). Quoted on BBC Radio *Quote ... Unquote* (1979).

6 Archbishop: a Christian ecclesiastic of a rank superior to that attained by Christ.

H.L. Mencken, American journalist and linguist (1880–1956). 'Sententiae' (1912–48).

7 How can a bishop marry? How can he flirt? The most he can say is, 'I will see you in the vestry after service.'

(Revd) Sydney Smith, English clergyman, essayist and wit (1771–1845). Quoted in Lady Holland, *A Memoir of Sydney Smith* (1855).

8 A bishop keeps on saying at the age of eighty what he was told to say when he was a boy of eighteen, and as a natural consequence he always looks absolutely delightful.

Oscar Wilde, Irish playwright, poet and wit (1854–1900). *The Picture of Dorian Gray*, Chap. 19 (1891).

Bitchery

The film actress Jean Harlow inquired whether the name Margot was pronounced 'Margo' or 'Margott':

9 'Margo' – the 'T' is silent – as in 'Harlow'.

Margot Asquith (Countess of Oxford and Asquith) (1864–1945). This story did not appear in print until T.S. Matthews' *Great Tom* in 1973. Then, in about 1983, a much more convincing version of its origin was given. Margot *Grahame* (1911–82) was an English actress who, after stage appearances in Johannesburg and London, went to Hollywood in 1934. Her comparatively brief career as a film star included appearances in *The Informer, The Buccaneer* and *The Three Musketeers* in the mid-1930s. It was when she was being built up as a rival to the likes of Harlow (who died in 1937) that Grahame herself claimed the celebrated exchange had occurred. She added that it was not intended as a put-down. She did not realize what she had said until afterwards. Grahame seems a convincing candidate for speaker of the famous line. When her star waned people attributed the remark to the other, better known and more quotable source.

Of Edith Sitwell and her two brothers, Osbert and Sacheverell:

10 Two wiseacres and a cow.

(Sir) Noël Coward, English entertainer and writer (1899–1973). Quoted in John Pearson, *Façades* (1978).

Passing a Leicester Square movie poster which proclaimed 'Michael Redgrave and Dirk Bogarde in The Sea Shall Not Have Them*':*

1 I don't see why not: everyone else has.

(Sir) Noël Coward. Quoted by Sheridan Morley in *The Independent on Sunday* Magazine (12 November 1995). The film was released in 1954.

On a starlet:

2 I see – she's the original good time that was had by all.

Bette Davis, American film actress (1908–89). Quoted in Leslie Halliwell, *The Filmgoer's Book of Quotes* (1973). In the form, 'There, standing at the piano, was the original good time who had been had by all', it has also been attributed to Kenneth Tynan at an Oxford Union debate in the late 1940s.

To another woman:

3 Oh, what a pretty dress – and so cheap!

Zsa Zsa Gabor, Hungarian-born film actress (1919–). Quoted in John Robert Colombo, *Wit and Wisdom of the Moviemakers* (1979).

To Judy, wife of Liberal politician David Steel:

4 Tell me the history of that frock, Judy. It's obviously an old favourite. You were wise to remove the curtain rings.

Barry Humphries, Australian entertainer (1934–). As 'Dame Edna Everage' in LWT TV show, *Another Audience with Dame Edna* (1984).

When asked of Eleanor Roosevelt's whereabouts at a White House reception:

5 She's upstairs filing her teeth.

Groucho Marx, American comedian (1895–1977). Quoted on BBC Radio *Quote ... Unquote* (10 September 1983) by John Lahr whose father, Bert Lahr, was present when Marx said it.

On her husband, Harold Pinter, when he left her for Lady Antonia Fraser:

6 He didn't need to take a change of shoes; he can always wear hers; she has very big feet you know.

Vivien Merchant, English actress (1929–83). Quoted in *The Observer* (21 December 1975).

Of a London actress who had broken a leg:

7 Oh, how terrible. She must have done it sliding down a barrister.

Dorothy Parker, American writer (1893–1967). Quoted in *The Sayings of Dorothy Parker*, ed. S.T. Brownlow (1992).

On novelist Ethel Mannin:

8 I do not want Miss Mannin's feelings to be hurt by the fact that I have never heard of her ... At the moment I am debarred from the pleasure of putting her in her place by the fact that she has not got one.

(Dame) Edith Sitwell, English poet (1887–1964). Quoted in John Pearson, *Façades* (1978) after a report in *The Yorkshire Evening News* (8 August 1930). By 13 March 1940, James Agate appears to have been reascribing this (in his *Ego 4*): 'About an American woman novelist [Mannin was English] who had been rude to her in print, Lady Oxford [i.e. Margot Asquith] is reported to have said, "I would put Miss B. in her place if she had a place".'

On Virginia Woolf:

9 I enjoyed talking to her, but thought *nothing* of her writing. I considered her 'a beautiful little knitter'.

(Dame) Edith Sitwell. Letter to G. Singleton (11 July 1955).

10 Glenn Close is not an actress – she's an address.

(Dame) Maggie Smith, English actress (1934–). Quoted in Michael Coveney, *Cats On a Chandelier*, Chap. 10 (1999).

Of a woman journalist he disliked:

11 She missed the last lobby briefing, I hear. At the vet's with hardpad, no doubt.

Harold Wilson (Lord Wilson of Rievaulx), British Labour Prime Minister (1916–95). Quoted in James Margach, *The Abuse of Power* (1981).

Blame

1 This is a story about four people: Everybody, Somebody, Anybody, and Nobody. There was an important job to be done, and Everybody was asked to do it. Everybody was sure Somebody would do it. Anybody could have done it, but Nobody did it. Somebody got angry about that because it was Everybody's job. Everybody thought Anybody could do it. Nobody realized Everybody wouldn't do it. In the end, Everybody blamed Somebody when actually Nobody asked Anybody.

Anonymous. This story appeared in a letter to the editor (headed 'Successful Administration is Invisible – Poor Administration Is All Too Apparent') in the *Financial Times* (9 July 1988). Probably an example of 'office graffiti' and its original source never likely to be known.

Blessings

On his defeat in the 1945 General Election, to his wife who had told him it might be a blessing in disguise:

2 At the moment it seems quite effectively disguised.

(Sir) Winston S. Churchill, British Conservative Prime Minister and writer (1874–1965). Quoted in his *The Second World War*, Vol. 6 (1954).

Blindness

3 In the country of the blind the one-eyed man is king.

Anonymous. This saying has become associated with H.G. Wells because of its use by him in the story he wrote with the title 'The Country of the Blind' (1904) – though he quite clearly labelled it as an 'old proverb'. Indeed, it is that and occurs in the proverbs of many languages (as shown by the *Concise Oxford Dictionary of Proverbs*, 1982.) An early appearance is in a book of *Adages* by Erasmus (d. 1536): *'In regione caecorum rex est luscus.'* Other 16th-century uses of the saying include John Palsgrave's translation of Fullmin's *Comedy of Acolastus* and John Skelton's 'An one eyed man is Well syghted when he is amonge blynde men' (1522).

Blondes

4 She was a brunette by birth but a blonde by habit.

Arthur ('Bugs') Baer, American humorist (1897?–1969). Quoted in *The Treasury of Humorous Quotations*, eds Evan Esar & Nicolas Bentley (1951).

5 It was a blonde. A blonde to make a bishop kick a hole in a stained-glass window.

Raymond Chandler, American novelist (1888–1959). *Farewell, My Lovely* (1940).

6 She was a blonde – with a brunette past.

Gwyn Thomas, Welsh novelist, playwright and humorist (1913–81). In BBC2 TV *Line-Up* (25 October 1969).

7 It's also possible that blondes prefer gentlemen.

Mamie van Doren, American actress. Attributed remark.

Blood

8 I came in here in all good faith to help my country. I don't mind giving a reasonable amount, but a pint ... why that's very nearly an armful. I'm sorry. I'm not walking around with an empty arm for anybody.

Tony Hancock, English comedian (1924–68). In BBC TV *Hancock*, 'The Blood Donor' (23 June 1961). Script by Alan Simpson and Ray Galton.

Blurbs

9 There is something about a blurb-writer paying his respects to a funny book which puts one in mind of a short-sighted lord mayor raising his hat to a hippopotamus.

Michael Frayn, English playwright and novelist (1933–). Introduction to *The Best of Beachcomber* (1963).

Bogart, Humphrey

AMERICAN FILM ACTOR (1899–1957)

10 Bogart's a helluva nice guy till 11.30 p.m. After that he thinks he's Bogart.

Dave Chasen, American restaurateur (1899–1973). Quoted in Leslie Halliwell, *The Filmgoer's Book of Quotes* (1973).

Booing

Responding to a solitary boo amongst the mid-act applause at the first performance of Arms and the Man *(1894):*

1 I quite agree with you, sir, but what can two do against so many?

Bernard Shaw, Irish playwright and critic (1856–1950). Quoted in St John Irvine, *Bernard Shaw: His Life, Work and Friends* (1956).

Books

2 Of a certain author it was said, 'A first edition of his work is a rarity but a second is rarer still.'

Franklin P. Adams, American humorist (1881–1960). Quoted in *The Treasury of Humorous Quotations*, eds Evan Esar & Nicolas Bentley (1951). However, R.E. Drennan, *Wit's End* (1973), has it that when Alexander Woollcott was asked to sign a first edition of his book *Shouts and Murmurs*, he inquired rhetorically, 'What is rarer than a Woollcott first edition?' F.P. Adams produced the answer: 'A Woollcott *second* edition.' Also told of other people. As is often the case, Oscar Wilde seems to have got there first: 'While the first editions of most classical authors are those coveted by the bibliophiles, it is the second editions of my books that are the true rarities, and even the British Museum has not been able to secure copies of most of them' – in Hesketh Pearson, *The Life of Oscar Wilde*, Chap. 14 (1946).

3 Child, do not throw this book about;
Refrain from the unholy pleasure
Of cutting all the pictures out!
Preserve it as your chiefest treasure.

Hilaire Belloc, French-born English poet and writer (1870–1953). *A Bad Child's Book of Beasts*, Dedication (1896).

4 There is a good saying to the effect that when a new book appears one should read an old one. As an author I would not recommend too strict adherence to this saying.

(Sir) Winston S. Churchill, British Conservative Prime Minister and writer (1874–1965). Quoted in *The Sayings of Winston Churchill*, ed. J.A. Sutcliffe (1992).

5 The books that everybody admires are those that nobody reads.

Anatole France, French writer (1844–1924). Quoted in *The Treasury of Humorous Quotations*, eds Evan Esar & Nicolas Bentley (1951).

6 The proper study of mankind is books.

Aldous Huxley, English novelist and writer (1894–1963). *Crome Yellow* (1921).

On his hobby of growing trees:

7 I'm replacing some of the timber used up by my books. Books are just trees with squiggles on them.

Hammond Innes, English novelist (1913–98). Interview, *Radio Times* (18–24 August 1984).

8 Book – what they make a movie out of for television.

Leonard Louis Levinson, American writer (1904–74). Quoted in Laurence J. Peter, *Quotations for Our Time* (1977).

9 In the main, there are two sorts of books: those that no one reads and those that no one ought to read.

H.L. Mencken, American journalist and linguist (1880–1956). Quoted in *The Treasury of Humorous Quotations*, eds Evan Esar & Nicolas Bentley (1951).

10 I have known her pass the whole evening without mentioning a single book, or *in fact anything unpleasant*, at all.

Henry Reed, English poet and playwright (1914–86). Radio play, *A Very Great Man Indeed* (1953).

11 No furniture so charming as books, even if you never open them, or read a single word.

(Revd) Sydney Smith, English clergyman, essayist and wit (1771–1845). Quoted in Lady Holland, *A Memoir of Sydney Smith* (1855).

1 Never lend a book; never give a book away; never read a book.

John Sparrow, English scholar (1906–92). The 'book collector's caveat', which Sparrow was fond of quoting, according to his obituary in *The Independent* (4 February 1992).

When Sir Telford Waugh published a book on the history and prospects of Turkey, with the title Turkey: Yesterday, Today, and Tomorrow, *his cousin commented:*

2 Sounds like Boxing Day …

Arthur Waugh, English publisher (1866–1943) – and father of Evelyn Waugh, the novelist. Attributed remark.

3 In old days books were written by men of letters and read by the public. Nowadays books are written by the public and read by nobody.

Oscar Wilde. In *Saturday Review* (17 November 1894).

Bores and boring

A patrician lady in her country house invited an extremely boring and loquacious gentleman to come and pay her a visit. He ended up trapping her in a corner and talking and talking and talking to her. After a while, she said:

4 How very interesting, my dear. Why don't you go away and *write it all down*?

Anonymous. Quoted by Dr John Rae on BBC Radio *Quote … Unquote* (30 July 1983).

Of Arianna Stassinopoulos, Greek-born writer and socialite:

5 So boring you fall asleep halfway through her name.

Alan Bennett, English playwright and actor (1934–). Quoted in *The Observer* (18 September 1983). (Heaven knows what he would have said when marriage led to the woman being known as 'Arianna Stassinopoulos Huffington'.)

6 Bore, n. A person who talks when you wish him to listen.

Ambrose Bierce, American journalist (1842–?1914). *The Cynic's Word Book* (later retitled *The Devil's Dictionary*) (1906).

7 Society is now one polish'd horde,
Form'd of two mighty tribes, the *Bores* and
Bored.

Lord Byron, English poet (1788–1824). *Don Juan*, Canto 13, St. 95 (1819–24).

8 The age of chivalry is past. Bores have succeeded to dragons.

Benjamin Disraeli (1st Earl of Beaconsfield), English politician and writer (1804–81). *The Young Duke*, Bk 2, Chap. 5 (1831).

9 Why can we remember the tiniest detail that has happened to us, and not remember how many times we have told it to the same persons?

François, Duc de La Rochefoucauld, French writer (1613–80). Quoted in *The Treasury of Humorous Quotations*, eds Evan Esar & Nicolas Bentley (1951).

10 Make him [the reader] laugh and he will think you a trivial fellow, but bore him in the right way and your reputation is assured.

W. Somerset Maugham, English writer (1874–1965). *The Gentleman in the Parlour* (1930).

On Sir Anthony Eden:

11 He was not only a bore; he bored for England.

Malcolm Muggeridge, English writer and broadcaster (1903–90). *Tread Softly For You Tread on My Jokes*, 'Boring for England' (1966).

12 To be a bore is to have halitosis of the mind, as someone should probably have said before me.

Nigel Rees, English writer and broadcaster (1944–). *Best Behaviour* (1992). *Compare* INTELLECT 225:1.

13 I am one of those unhappy persons who inspires bores to the highest flights of art.

(Dame) Edith Sitwell, English poet (1887–1964). Quoted in *The Observer* (8 March 1998).

1 Sydney Smith's daughter describes in her memoir of him his reaction to the one-time reigning bore of Edinburgh, whose favourite subject was the North Pole: 'It mattered not how far south you began, you found yourself transported to the north pole before you could take breath; no one escaped him.' Francis Jeffrey (Lord Jeffrey), the critic, avoided this bore whenever possible, but one day the 'arch-tormentor' met him in a narrow lane and immediately began on his favourite subject. Jeffrey brushed past him, saying, 'Damn the North Pole!'

Smith encountered the bore himself shortly after this incident. The bore was boiling with indignation at Jeffrey's contempt for the North Pole. 'Oh, my dear fellow,' Smith soothed. 'No one minds what Jeffrey says, you know; he is a privileged person; he respects nothing, absolutely nothing. Why, you will scarcely believe it, but it is not more than a week ago that I heard him speak disrespectfully of the Equator!'

(Revd) Sydney Smith, English clergyman, essayist and wit (1771–1845). Quoted in Saba, Lady Holland, *A Memoir of Sydney Smith* (1855).

2 A bore is a man who, when you ask him how he is, tells you.

Bert Leston Taylor, American journalist (1866–1921). *The So-Called Human Race* (1922). Compare: 'Look, a bore is someone when you ask them how they are, they tell you' – line from film *Otley* (UK 1968). Screenwriters: Ian La Frenais, Dick Clement. Spoken by James Bolam (Albert). An almost traditional observation.

3 Someone's boring me. I think it's me.

Dylan Thomas, Welsh poet (1914–53). Quoted in Rayner Heppenstall, *Four Absentees* (1960).

Of Israel Zangwill:

4 He is an old bore; even the grave yawns for him.

(Sir) Herbert Beerbohm Tree, English actor-manager (1853–1917). Quoted in Max Beerbohm, *Herbert Beerbohm Tree* (1920).

5 Bore: a man who is never unintentionally rude.

Oscar Wilde, Irish playwright, poet and wit (1854–1900). Quoted in Herbert V. Prochnow, Snr & Jnr, *A Treasury of Humorous Quotations* (1969).

6 One should never take sides in anything ... Taking sides is the beginning of sincerity, and earnestness follows shortly afterward, and the human being becomes a bore.

Oscar Wilde. *A Woman of No Importance*, Act 1 (1893).

Boston (Massachussetts)

Of Shakespeare:

7 A great man! Why, I doubt if there are six his equal in the whole of Boston.

Anonymous. Said to W.E. Gladstone by an unnamed Bostonian. Quoted in my book *Quote ... Unquote* (1978). *H.L. Mencken's Dictionary of Quotations* (1942) has it that Gladstone got it from Lionel A. Tollemache (23 December 1897) as, 'There are not ten men in Boston equal to Shakespeare.'

8 And this is good old Boston,
The home of the bean and the cod,
Where the Lowells talk only to Cabots,
And the Cabots talk only to God.

John Collins Bossidy, American oculist (1860–1928). Toast at a Harvard dinner (1910).

9 Boston State-House is the hub of the solar system. You couldn't pry that out of a Boston man, if you had the tire of all creation straightened out for a crow-bar.

Oliver Wendell Holmes Sr, American physician and writer (1809–94). *The Autocrat at the Breakfast-table* (1858). Bostonians are said to refer to their city as 'The Hub', alluding to its self-proclaimed status as 'The hub of the universe'.

See also QUESTIONS 362:5.

Bottoms

1 I do most of my work sitting down; that's where I shine.

Robert Benchley, American humorist (1889–1945). Quoted in R.E. Drennan, *Algonquin Wits* (1968). However, in Herbert V. Prochnow, Snr & Jnr, *A Treasury of Humorous Quotations* (1969), this is ascribed to Robert Bushby.

2 The woman had a bottom of good sense.

(Dr) Samuel Johnson, English writer and lexicographer (1709–84). Quoted in James Boswell, *The Life of Samuel Johnson* (1791) – for 20 April 1781. Johnson was not without a sense of humour, though Boswell does describe one occasion when a joke seriously passed him by. Johnson had started the whole thing off by saying, 'The woman had a bottom of good sense.' Boswell comments: 'The word *bottom* thus introduced, was so ludicrous when contrasted with his gravity, that most of us could not forbear tittering and laughing.' Johnson did not take kindly to this and demanded, 'Where's the merriment? ... I say the woman was *fundamentally* sensible.' Then, Boswell adds, 'We all sat composed as at a funeral.'

3 *Quand je regarde mon derrière, je vois qu'il est divisé en deux parties* [When I look at my backside, I see that it is divided into two parts.]

(Sir) Winston S. Churchill, British Conservative Prime Minister and writer (1874–1965). Quoted on BBC Radio *Quote ... Unquote* (29 January 1979). From an alleged speech in Paris just after the Second World War. He meant to tell his audience that, looking back, he saw his career divided into two distinct and separate periods. So what he meant by his 'derrière' was not his backside but his past.

When a colleague ran a hand over Longworth's bald head and pronounced, 'It feels just like my wife's behind':

4 Why so it does.

Nicholas Longworth, American politician (1869–1931). Quoted in James Brough, *Princess Alice* (1975).

5 *Au plus élevé trône du monde, si ne sommes assis que sur notre cul* [Perched on the loftiest throne in the world, we are still sitting on our own behind].

Michel de Montaigne, French essayist (1533–92). *Essais*, Bk 3, Chap. 9 (1580).

Bourne

6 Gone to that country from whose Bourne no Hollingsworth returns.

J.B. Morton (Beachcomber), English humorous writer (1893–1979). *Gallimaufry*, 'Another True Story' (1936).

Boys

7 I like a girlish girl, a womanly woman and a manly man, but I cannot abide a boyly boy.

Anonymous.

8 Little boys should be obscene and not heard.

Oscar Wilde, Irish playwright, poet and wit (1854–1900). Quoted in H. Montgomery Hyde, *Oscar Wilde* (1976).

Brains

On F.E. Smith (1st Earl of Birkenhead):

9 He's very clever, but sometimes his brains go to his head.

Margot Asquith (Countess of Oxford and Asquith) (1864–1945). Quoted by Lady Violet Bonham Carter in 'Margot Oxford', *The Listener* (11 June 1953).

10 I have finally come to the conclusion that a good reliable set of bowels is worth more to a man than any quantity of brains.

Josh Billings (Henry Wheeler Shaw), American humorist (1818–85). Attributed remark.

11 The brain is a wonderful organ. It starts working the moment you get up in the morning, and does not stop until you get into the office.

Robert Frost, American poet (1874–1963). Quoted in *The Treasury of Humorous Quotations*, eds Evan Esar & Nicolas Bentley (1951). Sometimes rendered as '... until you get up to make a speech.'

12 Brahms is just like Tennyson, an extraordinary musician, with the brains of a third rate village policeman.

Bernard Shaw, Irish playwright and critic (1856–1950). Letter to Packenham Beatty (4 April 1893).

Brandy

1 A cordial composed of one part thunder-and-lightning, one part remorse, two parts bloody murder, one part death-hell-and-the-grave, two parts clarified Satan and four parts holy Moses!

Ambrose Bierce, American journalist (1842–?1914). *The Cynic's Word Book* (later retitled *The Devil's Dictionary*) (1906).

2 A mixture of brandy and water spoils two good things.

Charles Lamb, English essayist (1775–1834). Quoted in *The Treasury of Humorous Quotations*, eds Evan Esar & Nicolas Bentley (1951).

Brassières

3 What the brassière said to the top hat: 'You go on ahead while I give these two a lift.'

Anonymous. Quoted in John G. Murray, *A Gentleman Publisher's Commonplace Book* (1996). Murray adds that when the travel writer Freya Stark told this to the ambassador in Cairo in 1942, it shocked him.

Brazil

4 I'm Charley's aunt from Brazil – where the nuts come from.

Brandon Thomas, English playwright (1856–1914). *Charley's Aunt*, Act 1 (1892).

Breakfast

5 All happiness depends on a leisurely breakfast.

John Gunther, American journalist and writer (1901–70). Quoted in *Newsweek* Magazine (14 April 1958).

6 He that looketh on a plate of ham and eggs to lust after it, hath already committed breakfast with it in his heart.

C.S. Lewis, English scholar, religious writer and novelist (1898–1963). Letter of 10 March 1954.

7 To eat well in England, all you have to do is take breakfast three times a day.

W. Somerset Maugham, English writer (1874–1965). Quoted in Ted Morgan, *Somerset Maugham* (1980) as the response to a friend's statement that he 'hated the food in England': 'What rubbish. All you have to do is eat breakfast three times a day.'

8 In England people actually try to be brilliant at breakfast. That is so dreadful of them! Only dull people are brilliant at breakfast.

Oscar Wilde, Irish playwright, poet and wit (1854–1900). *An Ideal Husband*, Act 1 (1895).

Breasts

9 I must, I must, I must improve my bust.

Anonymous chant. Jennifer I. Brand of the University of Nebraska recalled (1999): 'In 1967 or 1968, an exercise group in an undergraduate girl's dorm at the University of Michigan used the chant while doing a standard arm and shoulder exercise, known informally as the "Sweater Filler". The chant, in full, was:

I must, I must, I must,
I must increase my bust.
I'd better, I'd better, I'd better,
I'd better fill out this sweater.

Note it is 'increase' here rather than 'improve'. I have also heard of a 'develop' version. Whatever the case, I was encouraged to do a bit more digging on this one and was directed to a reminiscence by the actress Jane Birkin of her short-lived marriage to the composer John Barry: 'I met John when we did a rather jolly musical called *Passion Flower Hotel* ... He got me to sing a song called "I must, I must improve my bust". That would have been in 1965. The musical, written with Trevor Peacock, was a disastrous flop, and the song is not included on the cast album. But was it the start of the chant or merely a picking up of something that was around already? We should, we should be told. The musical was based on a novel by 'Rosalind Erskine' (Roger Longrigg) (1962) but that book does not contain the line.

Pat Byfield recalled (1999) from her schooldays (it would be impolite to speculate when these were): 'I must, I must, / I must improve my bust. / The bigger the sweater, The tighter the better, / The boys depend on us.' David Rogers relayed the version he acquired from a postgraduate student of his from the University of Tulsa who had been a cheerleader: 'We must, we must, we must improve our bust. / The boys, the boys, the boys depend on us.'

Robert Rosenberg reported his sister's variation from the early 1960s: 'I must, I must, I must improve my bust / Oh dear, I fear, I have overdeveloped my rear!' Meanwhile, Celia Haddon bared all: 'I was doing "I must, I must, I must increase my bust" at the age of twelve at Queen Anne's School, upper fourth form, in the dorm at night. In those days I needed the mantra. It must have been 1957. And it must go back further.' Indeed, Rosalie Maggio recalled 'my friends and I were chanting "I must, I must, I must" in 1956' and concludes, 'I think it's another of those orphaned expressions one finds everywhere and nowhere.'

Turning to bikini-clad secretary and finding he is faced with her cleavage:

1 Hello boys. Have a good night's rest? I missed you.

Line from film *Blazing Saddles* (US 1974). Screenwriters: Mel Brooks and others. Spoken by Mel Brooks (Governor William J. Le Petomane).

On the films of Victor Mature:

2 I never go to movies where the hero's bust is bigger than the heroine's.

Groucho Marx, American comedian (1895–1977). Quoted in Leslie Halliwell, *The Filmgoer's Book of Quotes* (1978). Probably regarding Mature's appearance in *Samson and Delilah* (1949).

Breeding

When told by the Mayor of Boston, 'Of course, up in Boston, we think breeding is everything!':

3 Well, down here in New York, we think it's quite fun, too, but we don't think it's everything.

Alfred E. Smith, American politician (1873–1944) – when Governor of New York. Attributed remark.

4 Good breeding consists in concealing how much we think of ourselves and how little we think of the other person.

Mark Twain, American writer (1835–1910). *Mark Twain's Notebook*, ed. A.B. Paine (1935).

Brighton, England

5 [Brighton has] the perennial air of being in a position to help the police with their inquiries.

Keith Waterhouse, English writer, playwright and journalist (1929–). Quoted in *The Observer* (28 April 1991).

6 It is a town that looks as if it has been out on the tiles all night.

Keith Waterhouse. Quoted in the same article.

Britain and the British

7 The British, as usual, will fight to the last Frenchman.

Anonymous (German propagandist). From Anthony Rhodes, *Propaganda: The Art of Persuasion in World War II* (1976): 'Already in the "phony war" of 1939–40 the [German] Propaganda Ministry was organizing broadcasts to France, sowing discord between the Western Allies. The French were told that the British had sent only 6 divisions, and that the 80 French divisions would have to bear the brunt of the fighting. The British, as usual, would fight "to the last Frenchman".' Note how in the film *Passage to Marseilles* (US 1943), Sydney Greenstreet as a Nazi sympathizer gets to say: 'The British will fight to the very last drop of French blood.'

Broccoli

8 Broccoli,
Though not exoccoli,
Is within an inch
Of being spininch.

Anonymous.

9 I do not like broccoli and I haven't liked it since I was a little kid. I am President of the United States and I am not going to eat it any more.

George Bush, American Republican President (1924–). Statement (March 1990). Accordingly Bush banned broccoli from his plane, *Air Force One*. Outraged California farmers unloaded a 10-ton juggernaut of broccoli on the White House doorstep. Bush also said, 'I can't stand broccoli', and when this caused ructions among America's broccoli growers, he added: 'Wait till the country hears how I feel about cauliflower.' He also denounced carrots as 'orange broccoli'.

Bureaucracy

1 Guidelines for bureaucrats: (1) When in charge, ponder. (2) When in trouble, delegate. (3) When in doubt, mumble.

James H. Boren, American business executive (1925–). In *The New York Times* (8 November 1970).

Buses

On his first trip by bus:

2 This omnibus business is not what it is reported to be. I hailed one at the bottom of Whitehall and told the man to take me to Carlton House Terrace. But the fellow flatly refused!

George Curzon (1st Marquess Curzon), English Conservative politician (1859–1925). Quoted in *The Oxford Book of Political Anecdotes* (1986), without source. However, the origin of the tale could lie in *Punch* (10 April 1901) in which there was a cartoon by Everard Hopkins with this caption: 'A GIRLISH IGNORANCE. *Lady Hildegarde, who is studying the habits of the democracy, determines to travel by Omnibus. Lady Hildegarde.* "CONDUCTOR, TELL THE DRIVER TO GO TO No. 104, BERKELEY SQUARE, AND THEN HOME!"'

3 What is this that roareth thus?
Can it be a motor bus?

A.D. Godley, English classicist (1856–1925). There are many versions of Godley's macaronic which beginneth thus. *The Oxford Dictionary of Quotations* (1992), which prints only part of it, gives the source as a letter Godley sent to C.R.L. Fletcher on 10 January 1914, reprinted in *Reliquiae* (1926). The magazine *Oxford Today* (Michaelmas, 1992) took the trouble to find a complete, definitive version:

What is this that roareth thus?
Can it be a Motor Bus?
Yes, the smell and hideous hum
Indicat Motorem Bum!
Implet in the Corn and High
Terror me Motoris Bi:
Bo Motori clamitabo
Ne Motore caedar a Bo –
Dative be or Ablative
So thou only let us live:
Whither shall thy victims flee?
Spare us, spare us, Motor Be!
Thus I sang; and still anigh
Came in hordes Motores Bi,
Et complebat omne forum
Copia Motorum Borum.
How shall wretches live like us
Cincti Bis Motoribus?
Domine, defende nos
Contra hos Motores Bos!

The references to the Corn and High locate the poet in Oxford, where Godley taught for most of his life. Motor buses were first introduced to Oxford by William Morris and Frank Gray in 1912, so Godley would seem to have developed a rapid dislike of them.

Bush, George

AMERICAN REPUBLICAN PRESIDENT (1924–)

4 George Bush reminds every woman of her first husband.

Jane O'Reilly, American writer and editor (1936–). In *GQ* Magazine (1984).

5 Poor George, he can't help it – he was born with a silver foot in his mouth.

Ann Richards, American Democratic politician (1933–). In keynote speech at the Democratic convention, quoted in *The Independent* (20 July 1988).

Business

6 She was 'honeychile' in New Orleans,
The hottest of the bunch;
But on the old expense account,
She was gas, cigars, and lunch.

Anonymous. Quoted in *More Playboy's Party Jokes* (1965).

On how to succeed in the jewellery business:

7 We even sell a pair of earrings for under £1, which is cheaper than a prawn sandwich from Marks & Spencers. But I have to say the earrings probably won't last as long.

Gerald Ratner, English businessman (1949–). Speech to

the Institute of Directors, Albert Hall, London (23 April 1991). At the time he was Chairman of Ratners Group plc. The company's fortunes took a dive and Ratner resigned in 1992. In *The Independent* Saturday Magazine (14 February 1998), Ratner explained: 'It was a joke to make the speech more interesting. It was a dig at people who say "Our products are so cheap because we cut out the middleman" ... It's all bollocks ... we all buy our stuff the same way. So I said: "How can we sell this [decanter] at such a low price? Because it is total crap." It was just a joke that had nothing to do with what else I was saying.'

1 It is very vulgar to talk about one's own business. Only people like stockbrokers do that, and then merely at dinner parties.

Oscar Wilde, Irish playwright, poet and wit (1854–1900). *The Importance of Being Earnest*, Act 3 (1895).

Butlers

On the 17th Duke of Norfolk – among whose titles is 'Chief Butler of England':

2 And he's only just learned how to stack the dishwasher.

Anne, Duchess of Norfolk, in *c.* 1984. Quoted in my book *A Year of Stings and Squelches* (1985).

Byron, Lord

ENGLISH POET (1788–1824)

3 Byron! – he would be all forgotten today if he had lived to be a florid old gentleman with iron-grey whiskers, writing very long, very able letters to *The Times* about the repeal of the Corn Laws.

(Sir) Max Beerbohm, English writer and caricaturist (1872–1956). *Zuleika Dobson*, Chap. 18 (1911).

4 From Byron [people] drew a system of ethics in which the two great commandments were to hate your neighbour and to love your neighbour's wife.

Thomas Babington Macaulay (Lord Macaulay), English historian and poet (1800–59). Quoted in *The Treasury of Humorous Quotations*, eds Evan Esar & Nicolas Bentley (1951).

C

Caesar's wife

1 A newly elected mayor said that he felt, during his year of office, he should lay aside all his political prepossessions and be, like Caesar's wife, 'all things to all men'.

Anonymous. Quoted in G.W.E. Russell, *Collections and Recollections* (1898).

California

2 California is a fine place to live – if you happen to be an orange.

Fred Allen, American comedian (1894–1956). In *American Magazine* (December 1945).

Callaghan, James (Lord Callaghan)

BRITISH LABOUR PRIME MINISTER (1912–)

3 Now, now, little lady, you don't want to believe all those things you read in the newspaper about crisis and upheavals, and the end of civilization as we know it. Dearie me, not at all.

John O'Sullivan, English journalist. In *The Daily Telegraph* (10 June 1976). This example of Callaghan's patronizing style when dealing, as Prime Minister, with the then Leader of the Opposition, Margaret Thatcher, was quoted in all seriousness by *Newsweek* Magazine. It was, in fact, a parody written by O'Sullivan.

Callousness

4 Shortly after this, the cruel Queen, Broody Mary, died and a post-mortem examination revealed the word 'CALLOUS' engraved on her heart.

W.C. Sellar and R.J. Yeatman, English humorists (1898–1951) and (1897–1968). *1066 and All That*, Chap. 32 (1930).

Cambridge (England)

5 Oxford is on the whole more attractive than Cambridge to the ordinary visitor; and the traveller is therefore recommended to visit Cambridge first, or to omit it altogether if he cannot visit both.

Karl Baedeker, German publisher (1801–59). *Baedeker's Great Britain*, Route 30 'From London to Oxford' (1887).

6 For Cambridge people rarely smile,
Being urban, squat, and packed with guile.

Rupert Brooke, English poet (1887–1915). 'The Old Vicarage, Grantchester' (1912).

7 He glanced with disdain at the big centre table where the famous faces of the Cambridge theatre were eating a loud meal. 'So this is the city of dreaming spires,' Sheila said. 'Theoretically speaking that's Oxford,' Adam said. 'This is the city of perspiring dreams.'

Frederic Raphael, English novelist and screenwriter (1931–). *The Glittering Prizes* (1976).

Canada and the Canadians

8 You have to know a man awfully well in Canada to know his surname.

John Buchan (Lord Tweedsmuir), Scottish politician and writer (1875–1940). Quoted in *The Observer*, 'Sayings of the Week' (21 May 1950).

1 I don't even know what street Canada is on.

Al Capone, American gangster (1899–1947). Remark (1931), quoted in Roy Greenaway, *The News Game* (1966).

2 Canada could have enjoyed:
English government,
French culture,
And American know-how.
Instead it ended up with:
English know-how,
French government,
And American culture.

John Robert Colombo, Canadian writer (1936–) 'O Canada', in *The New Romans*, ed. Al Purdy (1968).

3 Canada is a country so square that even the female impersonators are women.

Line from film *Outrageous!* (Canada, 1977). Screenwriter/director: Richard Benner. Quoted in *The Guardian* (21 September 1978).

4 'I'm world-famous,' Dr Parks said, 'all over Canada.'

Mordecai Richler, Canadian novelist (1931–). *The Incomparable Auk*, Chap. 4 (1963).

Candour

5 On an occasion of this kind it becomes more than a moral duty to speak one's mind. It becomes a pleasure.

Oscar Wilde, Irish playwright, poet and wit (1854–1900). *The Importance of Being Earnest*, Act 2 (1895). Lady Bracknell speaking.

6 Whenever one has anything unpleasant to say, one should always be quite candid.

Oscar Wilde. Quoted in *The Treasury of Humorous Quotations*, eds Evan Esar & Nicolas Bentley (1951).

Canned goods

7 Carnation milk is the best in the land,
Here I sit with a can in my hand.
No tits to pull, no hay to pitch,
Just punch a hole in the son-of-a-bitch.

Anonymous. Quoted in David Ogilvy, *Confessions of an Advertising Man* (1963).

Cannibalism

When asked who the man was riding in a carriage with the portly Queen of Tonga at the 1953 Coronation:

8 Her lunch.

(Sir) Noël Coward, English entertainer and writer (1899–1973). In fact, it was the Sultan of Kelantan. This famous story made an early appearance in Dick Richards, *The Wit of Noël Coward* (1968). It is often told differently and may well be apocryphal. About the only thing to be said for certain is that Coward *did* spend most of Coronation Day watching TV – he says so in his diaries. According to Ned Sherrin, *Theatrical Anecdotes* (1991), Coward always denied the story, 'not least because she [Queen Salote] was a personal friend and would have been very upset'. Sherrin suggests that Emlyn Williams was the perpetrator and, curiously, casts Emperor Haile Selassie in the role of 'the lunch' (he did not even attend the Coronation).

In his diary entry for Coronation Day, James Lees-Milne has the Coward story and wrongly identifies the man as Queen Salote's husband. The passage is included in his published diaries, *A Mingled Measure* (1994), but seems probably to have been inserted at a later date. In *The Sayings of Noel Coward* (1997), Philip Hoare reveals that 'Coward disowned the line, ceding credit to David Niven.'

9 Eating people is wrong.

Michael Flanders, English writer and entertainer (1922–75). Song, 'The Reluctant Cannibal' (with music by Donald Swann), in *At the Drop of a Hat* (1957). Used as the title of a novel by Malcolm Bradbury (1959).

Capital

10 Spending one's own capital is feeding a dog on his own tail.

Mark Twain, American writer (1835–1910). *Mark Twain's Notebook*, ed. A.B. Paine (1935).

Capitalism

1 Capitalism, it is said, is a system wherein man exploits man. And communism – is vice versa.

Daniel Bell, American sociologist (1919–). *The End of Ideology* (1960). Note the 'it is said'. Laurence J. Peter in *Quotations for Our Time* (1977) describes it as a 'Polish proverb' and another source has it 'reported from Warsaw'.

Careers

2 His was the sort of career that made the Recording Angel think seriously about taking up shorthand.

Nicolas Bentley, English cartoonist and writer (1907–78). Quoted in *The Treasury of Humorous Quotations*, eds Evan Esar & Nicolas Bentley (1951).

Caricature

3 Caricature is the tribute which mediocrity pays to genius.

Oscar Wilde, Irish playwright, poet and wit (1854–1900). Quoted in Lloyd Lewis & Henry Justin Smith, *Oscar Wilde Discovers America* (1936).

Caroline of Brunswick

ESTRANGED WIFE AND QUEEN OF GEORGE IV (1768–1821)

4 Most Gracious Queen, we thee implore
To go away and sin no more,
But if that effort be too great,
To go away at any rate.

Anonymous. Quoted in *The Diary and Correspondence of Lord Colchester* (1861) – letter from Francis Burton (15 November 1820).

5 Fate wrote her a most tremendous tragedy, and she played it in tights.

(Sir) Max Beerbohm, English writer and caricaturist (1872–1956). In *The Yellow Book* (1894).

On her behaviour with the dey (governor) of Algiers:

6 She was happy as the dey was long.

Lord Norbury in 1820. Attributed remark.

Carter, Jimmy

AMERICAN DEMOCRATIC PRESIDENT (1924–)

7 Jimmy's basic problem is that he's super cautious. He looks before and after he leaps.

Joey Adams, American writer (1911–). In *New York Post* (1978).

8 I would not want Jimmy Carter and his men put in charge of snake control in Ireland.

Eugene McCarthy, American politician (1916–). Attributed remark in 1976.

9 Jimmy Carter had the air of a man who had never taken any decisions in his life. They had always taken him.

Guy Simon, English writer (1944–). In *The Sunday Times* (5 June 1978). Compare: from A.A. Milne, *The House at Pooh Corner*, Chap. 9 (1928): '[Pooh speaking] Because Poetry and Hums aren't things which you get, they're things which get *you*. And all you can do is to go where they can find you'; from Aneurin Bevan, quoted in Michael Foot, *Aneurin Bevan* (1962/1973): '[*As It Happened*] is a good title [for Clement Attlee's autobiography]. Things happened to him. He never *did* anything'; a letter (4 April 1864) from Abraham Lincoln to A.G. Hodges: 'I claim not to have controlled events, but confess plainly that events have controlled me.'

Cartland, (Dame) Barbara

ENGLISH ROMANTIC NOVELIST (1902–2000)

10 The animated meringue.

Arthur Marshall, English writer and entertainer (1910–89). Recalled by him on BBC Radio *Quote ... Unquote* (25 December 1979). Apparently, far from taking offence, Miss Cartland sent him a telegram of thanks.

Catch-22

Defining 'Catch-22':

11 There was only one catch and that was Catch-22, which specified that a concern for one's own safety in the face of dangers that were real and immediate was the process of a rational mind ... Orr would be crazy to fly

more missions and sane if he didn't, but if he was sane he had to fly them. If he flew them he was crazy and didn't have to; but if he didn't want to he was sane and had to.

Joseph Heller, American novelist (1923–99). *Catch-22*, Chap. 5 (1961). The title of Heller's novel about a group of US fliers in the Second World War has become a widely-used catchphrase. 'It was a Catch-22 situation,' people will say, as if resorting to a quasi-proverbial expression like 'Heads you win, tails I lose' or 'Damned if you do, damned if you don't'. What Heller did was to affix a name to the popular view that 'there's always a catch', some underlying law that defeats people by its brutal, ubiquitous logic. Oddly, Heller had originally called it 'Catch-18'. Robert Gottlieb, his publishers' editor, advised that this would clash with Leon Uris's *Mila 18*, being put out by the same house that season. 'I thought of *Catch-Eleven*, because it's the only other number to start with an open vowel sound,' Heller is quoted as saying, in *Something Like Fire: Peter Cook Remembered* (1996). 'I guess we doubled that.'

Cats

1 Alfred de Musset
Used to call his cat Pusset.
His accent was affected.
That was only to be expected.

Maurice Evan Hare, English writer (1886–1967). 'Byways in Biography' in *The Week-End Book* (1958 edn).

2 The thing that astonished him was that cats should have two holes cut in their coat, exactly at the place where their eyes are.

George Christoph Lichtenberg, German scientist and drama critic (1742–99). Attributed remark.

To a friend who was upset at having to get rid of his cat:

3 Have you tried curiosity?

Dorothy Parker, American writer (1893–1967). Quoted in *The Sayings of Dorothy Parker*, ed. S.T. Brownlow (1992).

Catsup *See* KETCHUP

Cauliflower

4 Training is everything. The peach was once a bitter almond; cauliflower is nothing but cabbage with a college education.

Mark Twain, American writer (1835–1910). *Pudd'nhead Wilson* (1894).

Caution

When asked in the 1970s/80s what he thought had been the effect of the French Revolution:

5 It's too soon to tell.

Anonymous (Chinese leader). A look at a British newspapers database turned up numerous ascriptions to Chou En-Lai (Zhou Enlai). However, the earliest citation (in a 1984 *Guardian* review) awarded the palm to Chairman Mao (who died in 1976).

Cavaliers and Roundheads

6 The Cavaliers (Wrong but Wromantic) and the Roundheads (Right but Repulsive).

W.C. Sellar and R.J. Yeatman, English humorists (1898–1951) and (1897–1968). *1066 and All That*, Chap. 35 (1930). A characterization of the opposing forces in the English Civil War which is worthy of being taken seriously.

Celebrity

7 A celebrity is one who works hard all his life to become well-known and then goes through back streets wearing dark glasses so he won't be recognized.

Fred Allen, American comedian (1894–1956). *Treadmill to Oblivion* (1956). Has also been attributed to Jane Powell, the American film actress (1929–) and to Dudley Murphy – so quoted in Bennett Cerf, *The Laugh's On Me* (1961).

8 I was photographed and interviewed and photographed again. In the street. In the park. In my dressing-room. At my piano. With my dear old mother. Without my dear old mother and on one occasion sitting up in an over-elaborate bed looking like a heavily-doped Chinese illusionist.

(Sir) Noël Coward, English entertainer and writer (1899–1973). Quoted in Dick Richards, *The Wit of Noël Coward* (1968), but otherwise untraced.

Censorship

1 A censor is a man who knows more than he thinks you ought to.

Laurence J. Peter, Canadian writer (1919–90). In *Quotations for Our Time* (1977).

2 Assassination is the extreme form of censorship.

Bernard Shaw, Irish playwright and critic (1856–1950). *The Shewing-Up of Blanco Posnet* (1911).

Censure

3 Censure is the tax a man pays to the public for being eminent.

Jonathan Swift, Anglo-Irish writer and clergyman (1667–1745). *Thoughts on Various Subjects* (1706).

Centipedes

4 A centipede was happy quite,
Until a frog in fun
Said, 'Pray, which leg comes after which?'
This raised her mind to such a pitch,
She lay distracted in a ditch
Considering how to run.

Mrs Edmund Craster, English poet (d. 1874). 'The Puzzled Centipede', quoted in *The Penguin Dictionary of Quotations* (1960).

Certainty

5 I'd know her with my eyes closed, down the bottom of a coal mine during an eclipse of the sun.

Line from film *Butterfield 8* (US 1960). Screenwriters: Charles Schnee, John Michael Hayes (from John O'Hara novel). Spoken by Tom Ahearne (Bartender) about Elizabeth Taylor (Gloria Wandrous).

6 Our new Constitution is now established, and has an appearance that promises permanency; but in this world nothing can be said to be certain, except death and taxes.

Benjamin Franklin, American politician and scientist (1706–90). Quoted in *Writings of Benjamin Franklin*, ed. A.H. Smyth (1905) – Letter to M. Leroy (13 November 1789). Earlier, the phrase 'Things as certain as death and taxes' was used by Daniel Defoe in *The History of the Devil*, Bk 2, Chap. 6 (1726).

Chamberlain, Neville

BRITISH CONSERVATIVE PRIME MINISTER (1869–1940)

7 Listening to a speech by Chamberlain is like paying a visit to Woolworths; everything in its place and nothing over sixpence.

Aneurin Bevan, Welsh Labour politician (1897–1960). In *Tribune* (1937).

8 A good mayor of Birmingham in an off-year.

David Lloyd George (1st Earl Lloyd George of Dwyfor), British Liberal Prime Minister (1863–1945). Quoted in A.J.P. Taylor, *English History 1914–1945* (1965). Chamberlain came to national politics after long experience in local government. Also, in the form: 'He might make an adequate Lord Mayor of Birmingham in a lean year', quoted in Leon Harris, *The Fine Art of Political Wit* (1965). In *Future Indefinite* (1954), Noël Coward ascribes to Lord Birkenhead (F.E. Smith), 'The most we can hope for from dear Neville is that he should be a good Lord Mayor of Birmingham in a lean year.' Also attributed (and possibly more correctly) to Lord Hugh Cecil in the form 'He is no better than a Mayor of Birmingham, and in a lean year at that. Furthermore he is too old. He thinks he understands the modern world. What should an old hunk like him know of the modern world?' Quoted in Lord David Cecil, *The Cecils of Hatfield House* (1973).

Champagne

9 Real pain for your sham friends, champagne for your real friends.

Anonymous. An Edwardian toast that the Irish-born British painter Francis Bacon (1909–92) acquired from his father, according to Daniel Farson, *The Gilded Gutter Life of Francis Bacon* (1993). 'Here's champagne to our real friends, / And real pain to our sham friends' is quoted in *Toasts for All Occasions*, ed. Lewis C. Henry (1949).

10 Between the revolution and the firing squad there is always time for a bottle of champagne.

Anonymous Russian prince, according to *The Sunday Times* (2 June 1996). But who? When? This interesting parallel was produced by Derek Robinson (1998): he remembered the following passage from Claud Cockburn's autobiography *In Time of Trouble* (1956), where the old rogue is describing Washington DC in June 1931 when President Hoover announced a one-year suspension of payment of debts between governments (because of the spread of the Depression to Europe). 'Violent wrangling' broke out over the exact terms of the moratorium between Washington and Paris. 'When "agreement in principle" was finally reached, M. Paul Claudel invited a number of American officials and others to the French Embassy to celebrate the event … In the drawing-room at the Embassy M. Claudel greeted them. "Gentlemen," he said simply, "in the little moment that remains to us between the crisis and the catastrophe, we may as well take a glass of champagne".' Claudel, though a diplomat, is now remembered as a poet, playwright and essayist. Then at the time of Munich (1938), Cockburn recalls that a Russian journalist Mikhail Koltzov quoted the Claudel story back at him (Cockburn). Could this be the original of the 'Russian prince'?

Derek Robinson adds: 'I'm sure I recall a French general being quoted as saying something similar when Dien Bien Phu – which was where he was in command – was about to fall [1954]. In his case, I think it was more like: "Gentlemen, in the short time we have between the crisis and the calamity, we might as well drink a glass of champagne".'

1 I drink it when I'm happy and when I'm sad. Sometimes, I drink it when I'm alone. When I have company, I consider it obligatory. I trifle with it when I'm not hungry and drink it when I am. Otherwise, I never touch it – unless I'm thirsty.

Lily Bollinger, French champagne producer (1899–1977). Attributed remark, quoted in the *Financial Times* (3 November 1999). Mme Bollinger was the wife of Jacques Bollinger, grandson of the firm's founder. Following his death in 1941, she became a great ambassadress for the product.

When asked why he drank champagne for breakfast:

2 Doesn't everyone?

(Sir) Noël Coward, English entertainer and writer (1899–1973). Quoted on BBC Radio *Quote … Unquote* (29 June 1977).

3 Champagne! I love it. It tastes like your foot's asleep.

Line from film *George White's Scandals* (US 1945). Screenwriters: Hugh Wedlock and others. Spoken by Joan Davis (Joan Mason).

4 In victory you deserve it: in defeat you need it.

Napoleon I, French Emperor (1769–1821). Attributed remark. On the other hand, 'Aid is … like champagne: in success you deserve it, in failure you need it' is ascribed to Lord Bauer (b. 1915), English economist, in Graham Hancock, *Lords of Poverty* (1989).

Change

5 The less things change, the more they remain the same.

Anonymous (Sicilian proverb). Quoted in Richard Condon, *Prizzi's Honour* (1982).

6 *Se vogliamo che tutto rimanga come è, bisogna che tutto cambi* [If we want everything to remain as it is, it will be necessary for everything to change].

Giuseppe Di Lampedusa, Italian novelist (1896–1957). *The Leopard* (1957). In the film, this comes out as: 'Things will have to change in order that they can remain the same.'

Changes

Refusing to accept any more changes when Irving Berlin was still fiddling with a song lyric just prior to the opening of a show:

7 Call me Miss Birds Eye, this show is frozen.

Ethel Merman, American actress and singer (1909–84). Quoted in *The Times* (13 July 1985). The song may have been from *Annie Get Your Gun* or *Call Me Madam*.

Character

8 Underneath this flabby exterior is an enormous lack of character.

Oscar Levant, American pianist and actor (1906–72). *Memoirs of an Amnesiac* (1965).

1 In my last movie I played an unsympathetic character – myself.

Oscar Levant. Quoted in *The Treasury of Humorous Quotations*, eds Evan Esar & Nicolas Bentley (1951).

2 I am afraid that he has one of those weak natures that are not susceptible to influence.

Oscar Wilde, Irish playwright, poet and wit (1854–1900). *An Ideal Husband*, Act 4 (1895). Mabel Chilton speaking of Lord Goring.

Charisma

Concerning a Texas gubernatorial primary:

3 When Loeffler started the campaign, his name recognition was well under 10% … Part of the problem, according to one Republican consultant, is his rather plodding nature. 'The guy is in desperate need of a charisma bypass,' said the consultant. 'But if he gets into the runoff against Clements, he might get some charisma in a hurry.'

Anonymous (consultant). Quoted in *The Washington Post* (2 May 1986).

Charity

Encountering a group from the Salvation Army and dropping a $50 bill into one of their tambourines:

4 Don't bother to thank me. I know what a perfectly ghastly season it's been for you Spanish dancers.

Tallulah Bankhead, American actress (1903–68). Quoted in Dorothy Herrmann, *With Malice Towards All* (1980).

5 It is better to give than to lend, and it costs about the same.

Philip Gibbs, English journalist (1877–1962). Quoted in *The Treasury of Humorous Quotations*, eds Evan Esar & Nicolas Bentley (1951).

6 If you pick up a starving dog and make him prosperous, he will not bite you. This is the principal difference between a dog and a man.

Mark Twain, American writer (1835–1910). *Pudd'nhead Wilson*, Chap. 16 (1894).

Charm

7 Unless one is wealthy there is no use in being a charming fellow.

Oscar Wilde, Irish playwright, poet and wit (1854–1900). Quoted in Herbert V. Prochnow, Snr & Jnr, *A Treasury of Humorous Quotations* (1969).

8 All charming people, I fancy, are spoiled. It is the secret of their attraction.

Oscar Wilde. *The Portrait of Mr W.H.* (1889).

Chastity

9 *Da mihi castitatem et continentiam, sed noli modo* [Give me chastity and continence – but not yet].

Augustine of Hippo, North African Christian theologian and saint (354–430). *Confessions* (397–8).

10 Of all sexual aberrations, perhaps the most peculiar is chastity.

Rémy de Gourmont, French writer (1858–1915). Quoted in *The Treasury of Humorous Quotations*, eds Evan Esar & Nicolas Bentley (1951).

11 Chastity: the most unnatural of the sexual perversions.

Aldous Huxley, English novelist and writer (1894–1963). *Eyeless in Gaza* (1936).

12 I may not be exactly what some people consider a virgin, but I've been chaste. Chased by every man.

Line from film *I Am a Camera* (UK 1955). Screenwriter: John Collier (from John van Druten's play based on Christopher Isherwood's stories). Spoken by Julie Harris (Sally Bowles).

Chatter

13 Every time a sheep bleats it misses a nibble.

Anonymous saying. Quoted on BBC Radio *Quote … Unquote* (25 August 1984). Sometimes rendered as 'Every time a sheep ba's it loses a bite'. H.L. *Mencken's Dictionary of Quotations* (1942) has 'Every time the sheep bleats it loses a mouthful' as an English proverb 'apparently borrowed from the Italian and familiar since the 17th century'. In this form it certainly appears in Thomas Fuller's *Gnomologia* (1732).

1 When the eagles are silent, the parrots begin to jabber.

(Sir) Winston S. Churchill, British Conservative Prime Minister and writer (1874–1965). Quoted in Sykes & Sproat, *The Wit of Sir Winston* (1965). A sort of proverb, possibly original to Churchill.

Chatting up

2 If I said you had a nice body would you hold it against me?

Anonymous (graffito). Included in my book *Graffiti 3* (1981). Taken, presumably, from the Bellamy Brothers song 'If I Said You Have a Beautiful Body Would You Hold It Against Me' (in turn from an old chat-up line). Among a selection of jokes by Max Miller, the English comedian (1895–1963), published in the *Sunday Dispatch* (no date) and collected in Benny Green, *Last Empires* (1986) is: 'I saw a girl who was proud of her figure. Just to make conversation I asked her, 'What would you do if a chap criticised your figure?' 'Well,' she said, 'I wouldn't hold it against him.'

3 There was the one about this doctor, you see. He was examining a girl's knee and he said, 'What's a joint like this doing in a pretty girl like you?'

Line from film *Kiss Me Stupid* (US 1964). Screenwriters: Billy Wilder, I.A.L. Diamond. Spoken by Dean Martin (Dino). 'Reducing the age-old seducer's spiel, while telling the same old story', as Walter Redfern comments in *Puns* (1984).

See also FLIRTING.

Chauvinism

To Adam Smith who was boasting about the charms of Glasgow:

4 Pray, Sir, have you ever seen Brentford?

(Dr) Samuel Johnson, English writer and lexicographer (1709–84). In James Boswell, *The Life of Samuel Johnson* (1791) – for 1783.

5 She said that all the sights in Rome were called after London cinemas.

Nancy Mitford, English author (1904–73). *Pigeon Pie* (1940). Compare the caption to a cartoon by Bert Thomas in *Punch* (12 January 1921): 'The Profiteer's Lady (in Rome): "Wot *was* the Coliseum, 'Enry? A cinema?"'

Cheating

6 Thou shalt not steal: an empty feat,
When it's so lucrative to cheat.

Arthur Hugh Clough, English poet (1819–61). 'The Latest Decalogue' (1862).

Cheerfulness

7 'What great cause is he identified with?'
'He's identified … with the great cause of cheering us all up.'

Arnold Bennett, English novelist (1867–1931). *The Card* (1911). Referring to the title character, Denry Machin.

8 I have tried too in my time to be a philosopher; but I don't know, cheerfulness was always breaking in.

Oliver Edwards, English lawyer (1711–91). Quoted in James Boswell, *The Life of Samuel Johnson* (1791) – for 17 April 1778.

9 It's being so cheerful as keeps me going.

Joan Harben, English actress (1909–53) – as the character Mona Lott, a gloomy laundrywoman with a dreary, flat voice, in *ITMA*, the BBC's immensely popular radio comedy show (1939–49). When told to 'keep her pecker up' by the star of the show, Tommy Handley, she would reply, 'I always do, sir, it's being so cheerful as keeps me going.' Her family was always running into bad luck, so she had plenty upon which to exercise her cheerfulness. Scripts for the show were by Ted Kavanagh and Handley himself. The catchphrase had earlier appeared in a *Punch* cartoon during the First World War (27 September 1916): 'Wot a life. No rest, no beer, no nuffin. It's only us keeping so cheerful as pulls us through.'

1 I went out to Charing Cross, to see Major-General Harrison hanged, drawn and quartered; which was done there, he looking as cheerful as any man could do in that condition.

Samuel Pepys, English civil servant and diarist (1633–1703). Diary entry for 13 October 1660. Thomas Harrison was one of the regicides. Pepys reflects that not only had he seen King Charles I beheaded but now he had seen 'the first blood shed in revenge for the blood of the King'.

Cheese

2 Milk is rendered immortal in cheese.

Enoch Powell, English Conservative then Ulster Unionist politician (1912–98). In a broadcast talk in 1967, I quoted Powell as having said this but have no idea where I got it from. If, indeed, Powell did say it, he had been anticipated by Clifton Fadiman (1904–) in *Any Number Can Play* (1957), where he wrote of: 'Cheese, milk's leap toward immortality.'

Cheques

3 We have come to an arrangement with our bankers. They have agreed not to sell drink. We, on our part, have agreed not to cash cheques.

Anonymous. Quoted in Flann O'Brien's column for the *Irish Times* (early 1940s).

Cherubim and seraphim

On the difference between a cherubim and a seraphim:

4 I have always believed that a cherubim was a seraphim beneath the age of consent.

Anonymous (professor). Quoted by Sir Huw Wheldon on BBC Radio *Quote ... Unquote* (1 December 1981).

Children

5 Why can't they be like we were? Perfect in every way!
What's the matter with kids today?

Lee Adams, American lyricist. Song, 'Kids', to music by Charles Strouse, from the musical *Bye Bye Birdie* (1960, filmed 1963).

6 It was no wonder that people were so horrible when they started life as children.

(Sir) Kingsley Amis, English novelist, poet and critic (1922–95). *One Fat Englishman*, Chap. 14 (1963).

7 *Mother (to Bobbie, who has made many feeble efforts to persuade her to stay with him):*
I must really go; I've got visitors downstairs.
Bobbie:
Oh, but that's all right. Why not tell them to come up here? I might bring out one of my 'quaint little sayings'.

Treyer Evans, British cartoonist. Caption to cartoon in *Punch* (19 November 1924).

When asked whether he liked children:

8 Boiled or fried?

W.C. Fields, American comedian (1879–1946). Quoted on BBC Radio *Quote ... Unquote* (22 June 1977), but unverified. Perhaps based on *Fields for President* (ed. Michael M. Taylor, 1971), in which the answer to the question whether he liked children is, 'I do if they're properly cooked.' Compare Charles Lamb's response to a woman who asked, 'Mr Lamb, how do you like babies?' 'B-b-boiled, ma'am.' Quoted in Frank Muir, *The Oxford Book of Humorous Prose* (1992).

9 Ah, the patter of little feet around the house. There's nothing like having a midget for a butler.

W.C. Fields. Attributed remark.

10 There's not a man in America who at one time or another hasn't had a secret desire to boot a child in the ass.

W.C. Fields. Attributed remark.

11 Father heard his children scream,
So he threw them in the stream,
Saying as he drowned the third,
'Children should be seen, not heard!'

Harry Graham, English writer and journalist (1874–1936). *Ruthless Rhymes for Heartless Homes*, 'The Stern Parent' (1899).

1 I love children, especially when they cry, for then someone takes them away.

Nancy Mitford, English author (1904–73). 'The Tourist' (short story) in *The Water Beetle* (1962).

Of W.C. Fields:

2 The only thing I can say about W.C. Fields, whom I have admired since the day he advanced upon Baby LeRoy with an ice pick, is this: any man who hates dogs and babies can't be all bad.

Leo Rosten, American writer (1908–97). Or 'Anybody who hates dogs and babies can't be all bad.' This view has often been ascribed to Fields himself (as, for example, by *Radio Times*, 12 August 1965), but it was, in fact, said *about* Fields by Rosten at a Masquer's Club dinner (16 February 1939).

A woman who thought herself to be a fine physical specimen once approached Bernard Shaw suggesting that they combine to make a baby, saying: 'You have the greatest brain in the world and I have the most beautiful body; so we ought to produce the most perfect child.' He replied:

3 What if the child inherits my beauty and your brains?

Bernard Shaw, Irish playwright and critic (1856–1950). Alas, this was not said to Isadora Duncan or any of the other women who have been woven into the tale. Hesketh Pearson in *Bernard Shaw* (1942) said the request came from 'a woman in Zurich', though no trace of a letter containing it has ever been found.

4 Parents are the bones on which children sharpen their teeth.

(Sir) Peter Ustinov, Russian-born actor and writer (1921–). Attributed remark.

China

5 The Great Wall, I've been told, is the only man-made structure on earth that is visible from the moon. For the life of me I cannot see why anyone would go to the moon to look at it, when, with almost the same difficulty, it can be viewed in China.

John Kenneth Galbraith, Canadian-born economist (1908–). In *The Sunday Times* Magazine (23 October 1977) – a prime example of Galbraith's laconic style. At the time, China had not opened itself up to tourism. The idea of 'the Wall of China' being 'the only work of man visible from the moon' was current by August 1939 when it was mentioned in the *Fortnightly Review*.

Chivalry

6 Definition of chivalry: 'going about releasing beautiful maidens from other men's castles, and taking them to your own castle'.

Henry W. Nevinson, English journalist and essayist (1856–1941). Quoted in *The Treasury of Humorous Quotations*, eds Evan Esar & Nicolas Bentley (1951).

Choice

7 More than any other time in history, mankind faces a crossroads. One path leads to despair and utter hopelessness. The other to total extinction. Let us pray we have the wisdom to choose correctly.

Woody Allen, American film actor, writer and director (1937–). *Side Effects* (1980).

8 Any customer can have a car painted any colour that he wants so long as it is black.

Henry Ford, American industrialist (1863–1947). This expression originated with Ford – to convey that there was no choice. He is supposed to have said it about the Model T Ford, which came out in 1909. Quoted in his *My Life and Work* (written with Henry Crowther, 1922). Hill and Nevins in *Ford: Expansion and Challenge* (1957) have him saying: 'People can have it any colour – so long as it's black.' However, in 1925, the company had to bow to the inevitable and offer a choice of colours. Dr Harry Corbett of Bayswater, Australia, commented (1996): 'Initially, the T model was available in several colours but when Ford changed to a different painting technique the product used was only available in the colour black. The early finishing technique was a carryover from the carriage industry and resulted in curing times of up to four weeks. This meant that huge numbers of cars had to be stored during the finishing process. From what I can gather, Ford changed to a faster-drying product – which was only available in black – to rid himself of the warehousing difficulties.'

1 Between two evils, I always pick the one I haven't tried before.

Line from film *Go West Young Man* (US 1936). Screenwriter: Mae West. Spoken by Mae West (Mavis Arden). The proverb, 'Of two evils choose the least' can be found in Chaucer (about 1340) and also in Cicero.

Pointing at stamp in middle of sheet, at Post Office:

2 I'll have that one, please.

(Sir) Herbert Beerbohm Tree, English actor-manager (1853–1917). Quoted in Hesketh Pearson, *Beerbohm Tree* (1956).

A woman, having just witnessed Sally faking an orgasm in the middle of a crowded restaurant, is asked by a waiter what she would like to order. She replies:

3 I'll have what she's having.

Line from film *When Harry Met Sally* (US 1989). Screenwriter: Nora Ephron. Spoken by Estelle Reiner (Woman in Restaurant).

Christianity

In a debate on the Middle East question, a US delegate to the United Nations exhorted warring Jews and Arabs to:

4 Sit down and settle their differences like Christians.

Warren Austin, American diplomat (1877–1962). Quoted in Fadiman & Van Doren, *The American Treasury* (1955).

To Frank Harris, who had claimed that Christianity and journalism were the two main curses of civilization:

5 Christianity, yes, but why journalism?

Arthur Balfour (1st Earl of Balfour), British Conservative Prime Minister (1848–1930). Quoted in Margot Asquith, *The Autobiography of Margot Asquith*, Chap. 10 (1920–22).

6 Christianity has not been tried and found wanting; it has been found difficult and not tried.

G.K. Chesterton, English poet, novelist and critic (1874–1936). Quoted in *The Treasury of Humorous Quotations*, eds Evan Esar & Nicolas Bentley (1951).

Christmas

7 I have often thought, says Sir Roger, it happens very well that Christmas should fall out in the Middle of Winter.

Joseph Addison, English essayist and politician (1672–1719). In *The Spectator*, No. 269 (8 January 1712).

8 The little Strangs say the 'good words,' as they call them, before going to bed, aloud and at their father's knee, or rather in the pit of his stomach. One of them was lately heard to say 'Forgive us our Christmasses, as we forgive them that Christmas against us.'

Samuel Butler, English author (1835–1902). *Notebooks* (1912) – for *c.* 1890.

9 I'm walking backwards for Christmas
Across the Irish sea.
I'm walking backwards for Christmas
It's the only thing for me.

Spike Milligan, Irish entertainer and writer (1918–). Song, 'I'm Walking Backwards for Christmas' (1956).

Chronology

Of his wife, Mary Anne:

10 She is an excellent creature, but she never can remember which came first, the Greeks or the Romans.

Benjamin Disraeli (1st Earl of Beaconsfield), English politician and writer (1804–81). Quoted in G.W.E. Russell, *Collections and Recollections*, Chap. 1 (1898).

Church of England

11 The Church of England is the Tory Party at prayer.

Anonymous. This description is often attributed to Benjamin Disraeli. However, Robert Blake, the historian and author of *Disraeli* (1966), told *The Observer* (14 April 1985) that he could not say who had said it first and that a correspondence in *The Times* some years before had failed to find an answer. According to Robert Stewart's

Penguin Dictionary of Political Quotations (1984), Agnes Maude Royden, the social reformer and preacher, said in an address at the City Temple, London (1917): 'The Church should no longer be satisfied to represent only the Conservative Party at prayer' – but even this sounds as though it was alluding to an already established saying.

On the Church of England:

1 I see it as an elderly lady, who mutters away to herself in a corner, ignored most of the time.

George Carey, English Archbishop of Canterbury (1935–). Interview, *Readers Digest* (UK edn, March 1991).

2 The hippopotamus's day
Is passed in sleep; at night he hunts;
God works in a mysterious way –
The Church can feed and sleep at once.

T.S. Eliot, American-born English poet, playwright and critic (1888–1965). 'The Hippopotamus' (1920).

3 The Catholic Church is for saints and sinners alone. For respectable people the Anglican Church will do.

Oscar Wilde, Irish playwright, poet and wit (1854–1900). Quoted in Richard Ellman, *Oscar Wilde* (1987).

4 The growth of common sense in the English Church is a thing very much to be regretted.

Oscar Wilde. 'The Decay of Lying', in *Nineteenth Century* (January 1889).

Church-going

5 As for the British churchman, he goes to church as he goes to the bathroom, with the minimum of fuss and no explanation if he can help it.

Ronald Blythe, English writer (1922–). *The Age of Illusion* (1963).

6 I am not a pillar of the church but a buttress – I support it from the outside.

(Sir) Winston S. Churchill, British Conservative Prime Minister and writer (1874–1965). Quoted by Montague Browne in a speech to the International Churchill Society, London (25 September 1985). Note, however, that it was earlier said of John Scott, Lord Eldon (1751–1838): 'He may be one of its [the Church's] buttresses, but certainly not one of its pillars, for he is never found within it' (H. Twiss, *Public and Private Life of Lord Eldon*, 1844). *The Home Book of Humorous Quotations*, ed. A.K. Adams (1969), has the remark attributed to 2nd Viscount Melbourne as: 'While I can not be regarded as a pillar, I must be regarded as a buttress of the church, because I support from the outside.'

7 A church is a place in which gentlemen who have never been to heaven brag about it to persons who will never get there.

H.L. Mencken, American journalist and linguist (1880–1956). Quoted in *The Treasury of Humorous Quotations*, eds Evan Esar & Nicolas Bentley (1951).

8 It is my aim to get the violence off the streets and into the churches where it belongs.

Jonathan Miller, English entertainer, writer and director (1934–). Spoken as a trendy vicar in 'Man Bites God', *Beyond the Fringe* (1961) – script credited to whole cast. Compare: 'Get Bingo out of the supermarkets and into the churches where it really belongs' – performed on CBS TV *Rowan and Martin's Laugh-In* and included on the record album *Laugh-In '69* (1969).

Churchill, Randolph

ENGLISH JOURNALIST AND POLITICIAN (1911–68)

9 Dear Randolph, utterly unspoiled by failure.

(Sir) Noël Coward, English entertainer and writer (1899–1973). Attributed by Leslie Thomas on BBC Radio *Quote … Unquote* (31 May 1978). Dick Richards, *The Wit of Noël Coward* (1968) has the remark aimed at an unnamed playwright.

Churchill, (Sir) Winston S.

BRITISH CONSERVATIVE PRIME MINISTER AND WRITER (1874–1965)

10 I thought he was a young man of promise, but it appears he is a young man of promises.

Arthur James Balfour (1st Earl of Balfour), British Conservative Prime Minister (1848–1930). Quoted by Churchill in *My Early Life* (1930).

1 He would make a drum out of the skin of his mother the louder to sing his own praises.

David Lloyd George (1st Earl Lloyd George of Dwyfor), British Liberal Prime Minister (1863–1945). Quoted by Peter Kellner on BBC Radio *Quote … Unquote* (15 August 1987).

2 Winston has devoted the best years of his life to preparing his impromptu speeches.

F.E. Smith (1st Earl of Birkenhead), English politician and lawyer (1872–1930). Quoted in my book *Quote … Unquote* (1978), but otherwise unverified.

Chutzpah

Defending his taste for alcohol:

3 I'm so holy that when I touch wine, it turns into water.

Aga Khan III, Muslim leader (1877–1957). Quoted in John Colville, *Footprints in Time* (1976).

4 The classic definition of chutzpa … is that quality enshrined in a man who, having killed his mother and father, [threw] himself on the mercy of the court because he is an orphan.

Leo Rosten, *The Joys of Yiddish* (1968). The story may have originated in 'A Hard Case' by Artemus Ward in the early 1860s. On the other hand, Anthony Gross, *Lincoln's Own Stories* (1912), has honest Abe saying: 'He reminds me of the man who murdered both his parents, and then, when sentence was about to be pronounced, pleaded for mercy on the grounds that he was an orphan.'

Circumlocution

To Queen Elizabeth II, when she asked him about his accommodation as Ambassador to the Court of St James (1969):

5 We're in the Embassy residence, subject, of course, to some of the discomfiture as a result of a need for, uh, elements of refurbishment and rehabilitation.

Walter Annenberg, American publisher and diplomat (1908–). Unfortunately, when he went to present his credentials to the Queen, a TV crew was hovering at his elbow making the film *Royal Family*. So millions were able to hear the peculiarly orotund remarks he thought appropriate for the occasion.

6 Indicate the way to my habitual abode
I am fatigued and I wish to retire.
I partook of a little liquor sixty minutes ago.
Wherever I may perambulate,
On land or sea or atmospheric vapour,
You will always hear me harmonise this
  melody:
'Indicate the way to my habitual abode.'

Anonymous. Quoted in 1998.

Cities

7 A city is a place where you're least likely to get a bite from a wild sheep.

Brendan Behan, Irish playwright (1923–64). *Brendan Behan's Island* (1962).

Civil servants

A minister making a speech in the House of Lords inadvertently read out an annotation which a civil servant had scrawled on his brief:

8 This is a rotten argument but it should be enough for their Lordships on a hot summer afternoon.

Anonymous. Quoted in Lord Home, *The Way the Wind Blows* (1976).

Civilization

When asked what he thought of modern civilization:

9 That would be a good idea.

Mahatma Gandhi, Indian politician (1869–1948). Quoted in E.F. Schumacher, *Good Work* (1979), where Schumacher describes seeing a newsreel film of Gandhi's visit to England in 1930. Disembarking at Southampton, Gandhi was swamped by journalists, one of whom put this question to him (sometimes reported as 'What do you think of *Western* civilization?') and got this reply.

On being asked why he was not fighting to defend civilization in the First World War:

1 Madam, I am the civilization they are fighting to defend.

Heathcote William Garrod, English academic (1878–1960). Quoted in Dacre Balsdon, *Oxford Then and Now* (1970). Hugh MacDiarmid squeezed the notion into a poem, 'At the Cenotaph' (1935): 'Keep going to your wars, you fools, as of yore; / I'm the civilisation you're fighting for.'

Clarity

In the revival of his play Hay Fever, *which Coward directed at the National Theatre in 1964, Edith Evans always said one line wrong. 'On a clear day you can see Marlow' was invariably changed by her to: 'On a very clear day ... ' Coward would not let her get away with it. Said he:*

2 Edith, dear, the line is 'On a clear day you can see Marlow.' On a *very* clear day you can see Marlowe and Beaumont *and* Fletcher as well ... '

(Sir) Noël Coward, English entertainer and writer (1899–1973). The earliest showing of this story would appear to be in Dick Richards, *The Wit of Noël Coward* (1968).

3 Pinero always said that the only way to get anything across to an English audience was first to say, 'I'm going to hit this man on the head', then 'I'm hitting this man on the head', and finally 'I *have* hit this man on the head'.

(Sir) Arthur Wing Pinero, English playwright (1855–1934). Recounted in *The Lyttelton Hart-Davis Letters* for 5 May 1957. Compare Hilaire Belloc's description of his lecturing method, as told to and reported by Hesketh Pearson in *Lives of the Wits* (1962): 'First I tell them what I am going to tell them; then I tell them; and then I tell them what I've told them.' And compare Irwin Edman, *Philosopher's Quest* (1973 edn): 'A country preacher was once asked to explain his success in preaching. "First," he said, "I tell them what I am going to tell them. Then I tell it to them. Then I tell them what I've just told them".'

Class

4 Like many of the Upper Class
He liked the Sound of Broken Glass.

Hilaire Belloc, French-born English poet and writer (1870–1953). *New Cautionary Tales*, 'About John who Lost a Fortune Throwing Stones' (1930).

When asked by a radio interviewer whether she thought British class barriers had come down:

5 Of course they have, or I wouldn't be sitting here talking to someone like you.

(Dame) Barbara Cartland, English romantic novelist (1902–2000). Quoted in Jilly Cooper, *Class* (1979). The interviewer was Sandra Harris of the BBC Radio *Today* programme.

6 The stately homes of England
How beautiful they stand,
To prove the upper classes
Have still the upper hand.

(Sir) Noël Coward, English entertainer and writer (1899–1973). Song, 'The Stately Homes of England' in *Operette*, Act 1 (1937).

7 He [Sir Alec Douglas-Home] is used to dealing with estate workers. I cannot see how anyone can say he is out of touch.

Caroline Douglas-Home, daughter of the British Prime Minister (1937–). Quoted in the *Daily Herald* (21 October 1963).

8 We of the sinking middle class ... may sink without further struggles into the working class where we belong, and probably when we get there it will not be so dreadful as we feared, for, after all, we have nothing to lose but our aitches.

George Orwell, English novelist and journalist (1903–50). *The Road to Wigan Pier*, Chap. 13 (1937).

9 Hickety, pickety, my red hen,
She lays eggs for gentlemen;
But you cannot persuade her with a gun
  or lariat
To come across for the proletariat.

Dorothy Parker, American writer (1893–1967). Quoted in *The Sayings of Dorothy Parker*, ed. S.T. Brownlow (1992).

Parody of nursery rhyme, at a dinner with G.K. Chesterton or at a party with Somerset Maugham, where the guests were asked to complete nursery rhymes.

1 *Algernon:*
Really, if the lower orders don't set us a good example, what on earth is the use of them?

Oscar Wilde, Irish playwright, poet and wit (1854–1900). *The Importance of Being Earnest*, Act 1 (1895).

Classics

2 '*Classic.*' A book which people praise and don't read.

Mark Twain, American writer (1835–1910). Epigraph to *Following the Equator: A Journey Around the World* (1897).

3 I don't believe any of you have ever read *Paradise Lost*, and you don't want to. That's something that you just want to take on trust. It's a classic ... something that everybody wants to have read and nobody wants to read.

Mark Twain. Speech at dinner of the Nineteenth Century Club, New York (20 November 1900). Twain appears to credit the line to a Professor Winchester who was present. Quoted in *Mark Twain's Speeches*, ed. A.B. Paine (1910).

Classification

Railway porter to Old Lady travelling with a Menagerie of Pets:

4 Station Master says, Mum, as Cats is 'Dogs', and Rabbits is 'Dogs', so's Parrots; but this 'ere 'Tortis' is a insect, so there ain't no charge for it!

Charles Keene, English cartoonist and illustrator (1823–91). Caption to cartoon in *Punch* (6 March 1869).

Cleanliness

5 Cleanliness is next to Godliness – only in an Irish dictionary.

Anonymous (graffito). Included in my book *Graffiti 2* (1980).

6 *Arthur:*
I'm going to take a bath.
Hobson (butler):
I'll alert the media.

Line from film *Arthur* (US 1981). Screenwriter: Steve Gordon. Spoken by Dudley Moore (Arthur Bach) and John Gielgud (Hobson).

7 Geoffrey Chaucer
Took a bath (in a saucer)
In consequence of certain hints
Dropped by the Black Prince.

E. Clerihew Bentley, English novelist, journalist and poet (1875–1956). Attributed remark.

8 Cleanliness is almost as bad as godliness.

Samuel Butler, English novelist and writer (1835–1902). Quoted in *The Treasury of Humorous Quotations*, eds Evan Esar & Nicolas Bentley (1951).

On the establishment of the 'Hays Office' in 1922 to monitor the Hollywood film industry:

9 Will Hays is my shepherd, I shall not want,
He maketh me to lie down in clean postures.

Gene Fowler, American screenwriter (1890–1960). Quoted in Clive Marsh & Gaye Ortiz (eds), *Explorations in Theology and Film* (1997).

10 If only he'd wash his neck, I'd wring it.

John Sparrow, English scholar (1906–92). Attributed remark.

Cleopatra

11 How different – how very different from the home life of our own dear Queen!

Anonymous. Quoted by Irvin S. Cobb in *A Laugh a Day Keeps the Doctor Away* ... (1921). During a London season some time in the reign of Queen Victoria, Sarah Bernhardt (1844–1923) essayed the role of Cleopatra in Shakespeare's *Antony and Cleopatra*. In the scene where Cleopatra receives the news of Mark Antony's defeat at the battle of Actium, she stabbed the messenger who brought her the news, 'stormed, raved, frothed at the mouth, wrecked some of the scenery in her frenzy and finally, as the curtain fell, dropped in a shuddering convulsive heap'.

As the applause died down, an American visitor overheard a middle-aged British matron saying the above to her friend in the next seat.

Clergy

1 Of late years an abundant shower of curates has fallen upon the North of England.

Charlotte Brontë, English novelist (1816–55). *Shirley*, Chap. 2 (1849).

2 Would you, my dear young friends, like to be inside with the five wise virgins or outside, alone, and in the dark, with the five foolish ones?

Henry Montagu Butler, English academic (1833–1918). Quoted in Edward Marsh and Christopher Hassall, *Ambrosia and Small Beer* (1964). A favourite story, to be taken with a pinch of salt, but if true, coming in the category of Sermons One Would Like To Have Heard Preached. Dr Butler, who was Headmaster of Harrow, then, from 1886, Master of Trinity College, Cambridge, was preaching a sermon in the college chapel when he is supposed to have put this misguided rhetorical question.

3 Don't you know, as the French say, there are three sexes – men, women, and clergymen.

(Revd) Sydney Smith, English clergyman, essayist and wit (1771–1845). Quoted in Lady Holland, *A Memoir of Sydney Smith* (1855).

When it was proposed that St Paul's Cathedral be surrounded by a wooden pavement:

4 Let the Dean and Canons lay their heads together and the thing will be done.

(Revd) Sydney Smith. Quoted in *The Home Book of Humorous Quotations*, ed. A.K. Adams (1969).

5 What bishops like best in their clergy is a dropping-down-deadness of manner.

(Revd) Sydney Smith. 'First Letter to Archdeacon Singleton' (1837) in *Works*, Vol. 2 (1859).

6 Some ministers would make good martyrs: they are so dry they would burn well.

(Revd) C.H. Spurgeon, English Baptist preacher (1834–92). Quoted in *The Home Book of Humorous Quotations*, ed. A.K. Adams (1969).

7 To all things clergic
I am allergic.

Alexander Woollcott, American writer and critic (1887–1943). Quoted in Samuel Hopkins Adams, *A. Woollcott, His Life and His World* (1945).

Clerihews

8 When questioned, E. Clerihew Bentley
Smiled gently.
Said those who can write a good clerihew
Are very few.

Peter Jeffrey, English actor (1929–99). Contributed to BBC Radio *Quote ... Unquote* (7 June 1978).

Cleverness

Of Dr Jonathan Miller, the English polymath, in the mid-1970s, it was said:

9 He's too clever by three-quarters.

Anonymous. Quoted on BBC Radio *Quote ... Unquote* (13 July 1977). I find this phrase used in my diary about Keith Kyle, the writer and broadcaster, on 12 November 1971, so perhaps this expression was fairly widely used in the 1970s.

Clichés

On the cliché-ridden content of a speech by another politician (possibly Anthony Eden):

10 It was clitch after clitch after clitch.

Ernest Bevin, English Labour politician (1881–1951). Quoted in Willard R. Espy, *An Almanac of Words at Play* (1975) – where it is said by Bevin of Aneurin Bevan.

On a long-winded memorandum by Anthony Eden:

11 As far as I can see, you have used every cliché except 'God is love' and 'Please adjust your dress before leaving'.

(Sir) Winston S. Churchill, British Conservative Prime Minister and writer (1874–1965). This is quoted in Maurice Edelman, *The Mirror: A Political History* (1966), together with Churchill's comment: 'This offensive story is wholly devoid of foundation.' In 1941, Churchill took the unusual course of writing to Cecil King of the *Daily Mirror* about the matter. The columnist 'Cassandra' had used the story, though labelling it apocryphal and saying he had taken it from *Life* Magazine. *Reader's Digest* in August 1943 certainly carried this version by Allan A. Michie: 'Asked once to look over a draft of one of Anthony Eden's vague speeches on the post-war world, he sent it back to the Foreign Minister with this curt note: "I have read your speech and find that you have used every cliché known to the English language except 'Please adjust your dress before leaving'."'

1 I had always assumed that cliché was a suburb of Paris, until I discovered it to be a street in Oxford.

Philip Guedalla, English biographer and historian (1889–1944). *Supers and Supermen*, 'Some Historians' (1920).

2 A Foreign Secretary – and this applies also to a prospective Foreign Secretary – is always faced with this cruel dilemma. Nothing he can say can do very much good, and almost anything he may say may do a great deal of harm. Anything he says that is not obvious is dangerous; whatever is not trite is risky. He is forever poised between the cliché and the indiscretion.

Harold Macmillan (1st Earl of Stockton), British Conservative Prime Minister (1894–1986). Speech, House of Commons (27 July 1955). In *Newsweek* Magazine (30 April 1956), Macmillan was also quoted as having said that his life as Foreign Secretary was 'forever poised between a cliché and an indiscretion'.

3 I realize that one man's cliché can be another man's conviction.

Adlai Stevenson, American Democratic politician (1900–65). Speech, Harvard Business School (6 June 1959).

Climate

4 What men call gallantry, and gods adultery,
Is much more common where the climate's sultry.

Lord Byron, English poet (1788–1824). *Don Juan*, Canto 1, St. 63 (1819–24).

Clocks

5 When a clock strikes thirteen, not only do you know it is wrong now, but you have a suspicion it has never been right before.

(Sir) A(lan) P. Herbert, English writer and politician (1890–1971). Quoted on BBC Radio *Quote ... Unquote* (1 June 1977).

Closeness

6 *Flo:*

Oh, hold me closer! Closer! Closer!

Hackenbush:

If I hold you any closer, I'll be in back of you!

Line from film *A Day at the Races* (US 1937). Screenwriters: Robert Pirosh, George Seaton, George Oppenheimer. Spoken by Groucho Marx (Dr Hackenbush) and Esther Muir (Flo).

Clothing

7 The sense of being well-dressed gives a feeling of inward tranquillity which religion is powerless to bestow.

Miss C.F. Forbes, English writer (1817–1911). Quoted in R.W. Emerson, *Letters and Social Aims* (1876).

8 Only men who are not interested in women are interested in women's clothes; men who like women never notice what they wear.

Anatole France, French writer (1844–1924). Quoted in *The Treasury of Humorous Quotations*, eds Evan Esar & Nicolas Bentley (1951).

9 When a woman is wearing shorts her charms are enlarged without being enhanced.

Beverley Nichols, English journalist and writer (1898–1983). Quoted in the same collection as above.

10 Clothes make the man. Naked people have little or no influence in society.

Mark Twain, American writer (1835–1910). *More Maxims of Mark Twain*, ed. Merle Johnson (1927).

1 With an evening coat and a white tie, anybody, even a stockbroker, can gain a reputation for being civilized.

Oscar Wilde, Irish playwright, poet and wit (1854–1900). *The Picture of Dorian Gray*, Chap. 21 (1891).

Clubs

2 Please accept my resignation. I don't care to belong to any club that will have me as a member.

Groucho Marx, American comedian (1895–1977). Quoted in Arthur Sheekman's introduction to *The Groucho Letters* (1967). Zeppo Marx recalled that this was about The Friars Club, a theatrical organization, for which his brother did not have much time. Hector Arce added that Groucho had some misgivings about the quality of the members – 'doubts verified a few years later when an infamous card-cheating scandal erupted there'. The actual letter unfortunately does not survive. In *Groucho and Me* (1959), the man himself supplied the version: 'PLEASE ACCEPT MY RESIGNATION. I DON'T WANT TO BELONG TO ANY CLUB THAT WILL ACCEPT ME AS A MEMBER.' Woody Allen in *Annie Hall* (1977) wryly suggests that the joke first appeared in Freud. An intriguing precursor occurs in a letter that Abraham Lincoln sent to Mrs O.H. Browning (1 April 1838). In it, Lincoln relates how he had felt obliged to propose marriage to an ugly woman – who turned him down. 'I have now come to the conclusion never again to think of marrying, and for a reason; I can never be satisfied with any one who would be block-headed enough to have me.' *Compare* LENDING 249:4.

Clues

Crossword clue:

3 Listen carefully, or a sexual perversion (5,2,4,4).

Anonymous. In *The Financial Times*, *c.* 1974. (Answer: Prick up your ears).

Clumsiness

To Vivien Leigh, who as Lavinia in Shakespeare's Titus Andronicus *had both her hands cut off and consequently dropped something:*

4 Butter stumps!

(Sir) Noël Coward, English entertainer and writer (1899–1973). Attributed remark – related by David Bamber on BBC Radio *Quote ... Unquote* (20 September 1999).

Coffee

5 English coffee tastes like water that has been squeezed out of a wet sleeve.

Fred Allen, American comedian (1894–1956). *Treadmill to Oblivion* (1956).

6 Coffee has two virtues; it is wet and warm.

Anonymous (Dutch proverb). Quoted in *H.L. Mencken's Dictionary of Quotations* (1942).

7 Coffee should be as black as Hell, strong as death and sweet as love.

Anonymous (Turkish proverb). Quoted in the same book as above. However, Representative Hale Boggs, of Louisiana, said during a debate on the free tariff list of 1960: 'We prefer our coffee as strong as love, as black as sin, and as hot as Hades.'

8 Coffee in England is just toasted milk.

Christopher Fry, English playwright (1907–). Quoted in the *New York Post* (29 November 1962).

Cold

9 Many are cold, but few are frozen.

Anonymous. On the service sheet at Frank Muir's funeral on a wintry day in January 1998 was inscribed, 'Many are cold but few are frozen: F. Muir.' I am sure this attribution is correct – although it does not appear to be the concluding line to any of his published *My Word* stories, as might be expected, and I have no idea when he produced the pun. Just a footnote, though: the line occurs in (the American) Howard Engel's thriller *Death on Location* (1983); it was available on a T-shirt printed in the US (1982); and also, it was listed under 'whimsy' in Reisner & Wechlser's *The Encyclopedia of Graffiti* (1974). So, probably, Muir was not the first to come up with the line.

10 Better the chill blast of winter than the hot breath of a pursuing elephant.

Anonymous ('Chinese saying'). Quoted in *Livres Sans Nom*, five anonymous pamphlets (1929–33) by Geoffrey

Madan (though it is not in all versions). As with most such sayings, authenticity is in doubt. In any case, might not Madan have invented it himself? The matter is discussed in *The Lyttelton Hart-Davis Letters*, Vol. 4 (1982).

Colonialism

1 Originally, the Africans had the land and the English had the Bible. Then the missionaries came to Africa and got the Africans to close their eyes and fold their hands and pray. And when they opened their eyes, the English had the land and the Africans had the Bible.

Jomo Kenyatta, Kenyan President (*c.* 1889–1978). This saying was attributed to Kenyatta on BBC Radio *Quote ... Unquote* (13 October 1984), but later *The Observer*, 'Sayings of the Week' (16 December 1984), had Desmond Tutu, Bishop of Johannesburg, saying it. A version relating to the Native North Americans had earlier been said by Chief Dan George (d. 1982): 'When the white man came we had the land and they had the Bibles; now they have the land and we have the Bibles' – *Bloomsbury Dictionary of Quotations* (1987).

Columbus, Christopher

GENOESE EXPLORER (1451–1506)

2 It is said that when Columbus started out from Spain, he did not know where he was going; when he got there, he did not know where he was; and when he got back, he didn't know where he had been.

Anonymous. Quoted in *H.L. Mencken's Dictionary of Quotations* (1942). It is sometimes also added that the chief thing was, the whole trip was done on someone else's money.

Columnists

3 Give someone half a page in a newspaper and they think they own the world.

Jeffrey Bernard, English journalist (1932–97). Quoted in *The Observer*, 'Sayings of the Week' (1 June 1986).

4 A daily column is a grave two inches wide and twenty inches deep.

Don Marquis, American writer (1878–1937). Quoted in Mae West, *Goodness Had Nothing To Do With It*, Chap. 14 (1959).

Comedians

5 The test of a real comedian is whether you laugh at him before he opens his mouth.

George Jean Nathan, American drama critic (1882–1958). In *The American Mercury* (September 1929).

Comedy

On Freud's theory that a good joke will lead to great relief and elation:

6 The trouble with Freud is that he never played the Glasgow Empire Saturday night.

Ken Dodd, English comedian and singer (1927–). In the ATV programme *The Laughter Makers* (and so quoted in *The Times*, 7 August 1965). Dodd's remark has appeared in several versions since that date. For example, with the addition of 'after Rangers and Celtic had both lost' in *The Guardian* (30 April 1991).

7 The most difficult character in comedy is the fool, and he must be no fool who plays that part.

Miguel de Cervantes, Spanish novelist (1547–1616). *Don Quixote*, Pt 2, Chap. 3 (1615).

8 People think that if you're directing comedy you've got to be funny. On the contrary, you've got to be serious.

Charles Crichton, English film director (1910–99). Quoted in *The Independent* (15 September 1999). Apparently, this was said to the cast during the making of *A Fish Called Wanda*.

9 Comedy, like sodomy, is an unnatural act.

Marty Feldman, English comedian and writer (1933–83). In *The Times* (9 June 1969).

10 Any fool can play tragedy, but comedy, sir, is a damned serious business.

David Garrick, English actor (1717–79). Attributed, also in the form 'Comedy is a very serious thing', in conversation with the actor Jack Bannister. The date 1778 was applied to this by Richard Briers. Hence, *A Damned Serious Business*, title of the later memoirs (1990) of Sir Rex Harrison – who does not, however, give a source for the observation. Probably a more accurate rendering occurs in *Garrick and His Circle* (1906) by Mrs Clement Parsons, in which it is related that when *Charles* Bannister tired of tragic parts and begged to be allowed to do comedy, Garrick told him: 'No, no! You may humbug the town some time longer as a tragedian, but comedy is a serious thing.'

1 Comedy is simply a funny way of being serious.

(Sir) Peter Ustinov, Russian-born actor and writer (1921–). Quoted in John Robert Colombo, *Wit and Wisdom of the Moviemakers* (1979).

Comfort

2 The duty of a newspaper is to comfort the afflicted and afflict the comfortable.

Anonymous. Quoted in *H.L. Mencken's Dictionary of Quotations* (1942). However, in John K. Winkler, *W.R. Hearst: An American Phenomenon* (1928), is this: 'For forty years he has carried out, rather literally, the dictum of Mr Dooley [i.e. the creation of Finley Peter Dunne] that the mission of a modern newspaper is to "comfort the afflicted and afflict the comfortable".' In the film *Inherit the Wind* (1960), Gene Kelly gets to say to Fredric March: 'Mr Brady, it's the duty of a newspaper to comfort the afflicted and to flick the comfortable.' To Michael Ramsey, the former Archbishop of Canterbury (1904–88), has been attributed the version: 'The duty of the church is to comfort the disturbed and to disturb the comfortable.' Clare Booth Luce introduced Eleanor Roosevelt at a 1950 dinner, saying: 'No woman has ever so comforted the distressed – or so distressed the comfortable.'

3 It is better to dwell in a corner of the housetop than with a brawling woman in a wide house.

The Bible (Authorized Version). Proverbs 21:9.

4 You will recall what Senator Dirksen said about the rocking chair – it gives you a sense of motion without any sense of danger.

John F. Kennedy, American Democratic President (1917–63). In note to Arthur Hays Sulzberger (1 May 1961).

Commandments

5 The eleventh commandment: mind your own business.

Anonymous. Quoted in *H.L. Mencken's Dictionary of Quotations* (1942), where the remark is said to be 'borrowed from Cervantes, *Don Quixote*, 1605'. Indeed, it is to be found there (in Pt 1, Chap. 8), although it is not described as the 'eleventh commandment'. But Mencken also records, 'The Eleventh Commandment: Thou shalt not be found out – George Whyte-Melville, *Holmby House*, 1860', and this is certainly the more usual version. The *OED2* adds from the *Pall Mall Gazette* (10 September 1884): 'The new and great commandment that nothing succeeds like success'; and from *Paston Carew* (1886) by Mrs Lynn Lynton, that the eleventh commandment was 'do not tell tales out of school'. Unverified is Charles Kingsley's 1850 observation that it is, 'Buy cheap, sell dear'. William Safire, *Safire's Political Dictionary* (1978) reports that 'Thou Shalt Not Speak Ill of Fellow Republicans' was the eleventh commandment advanced by Dr Gaylord E. Parkinson, California State Republican Chairman, in the run-up to the 1966 governorship elections. The 1981 re-make of the film *The Postman Always Rings Twice* was promoted with the slogan: 'If there was an 11th Commandment, they would have broken that too.'

6 Say what you like about the Ten Commandments, you must always come back to the pleasant fact that there are only ten of them.

H.L. Mencken, American journalist and linguist (1880–1956). 'Sententiae' (1916).

Comment

7 I don't believe in all that 'no comment' business. I always have a comment.

Martha Mitchell, American wife of John Mitchell, President Nixon's Attorney General (1918–76). Quoted in Barbara Rowes, *The Book of Quotes* (1979). Martha 'The Mouth' Mitchell was always sounding off to the press but finally helped blow the whistle on what was going on in the White House over Watergate.

Committees

1 A committee is a group of men who, individually, can do nothing, but collectively can meet and decide that nothing can be done.

Anonymous. Quoted in Herbert V. Prochnow, Snr & Jnr, *A Treasury of Humorous Quotations* (1969). Compare: 'A conference is a gathering of important people who singly can do nothing, but together can decide that nothing can be done' – Fred Allen, American comedian (1894–1956). Quoted in *The Treasury of Humorous Quotations*, eds Evan Esar & Nicolas Bentley (1951).

2 The refreshing definition of a camel: a horse designed by a committee.

Anonymous. Quoted in American *Vogue* (July 1958).

3 A committee is a cul de sac down which ideas are lured and then quietly strangled.

(Sir) Barnett Cocks, English parliamentary official (1907–89). Quoted in the *New Scientist* (8 November 1973). Also attributed to John A. Lincoln in Herbert W. Prochnow, Snr & Jnr, *A Treasury of Humorous Quotations* (1969).

4 What is a committee? A group of the unwilling, picked from the unfit, to do the unnecessary.

Richard Harkness. Quoted in *The New York Herald Tribune* (15 June 1960). Also ascribed to Carl C. Byerss.

5 If Moses had been a committee, the Israelites would still be in Egypt.

J.B. Hughes. Quoted in Herbert V. Prochnow, Snr & Jnr, *A Treasury of Humorous Quotations* (1969). Or: ' ... never would have got across the Red Sea' in a remark attributed in 1965 to General William Booth (1829–1912), founder of the Salvation Army.

6 A committee is an animal with four back legs.

John Le Carré, English novelist (1931–). *Tinker, Tailor, Soldier, Spy* (1974).

7 The number one book of the ages was written by a committee, and it was called the Bible.

Louis B. Mayer, American film producer (1885–1957). Quoted in the *Oxford Dictionary of Literary Quotations*, ed. Peter Kemp (1997).

8 A committee should consist of three men, two of whom are absent.

(Sir) Herbert Beerbohm Tree, English actor-manager (1853–1917). Quoted in Hesketh Pearson, *Beerbohm Tree* (1956). Also attributed to Lord Mancroft (1914–87) in some anthologies. *The Treasury of Humorous Quotations*, eds Evan Esar & Nicolas Bentley (1951), has E.V. Lucas (1868–1938) saying, 'The best committee is a committee of two when one is absent.' Compare: 'Nothing is ever accomplished by a committee unless it consists of three members, one of whom happens to be sick and the other absent' – Hendrik Van Loon, Dutch-born American writer (1882–1944). *America* (1927).

Common people

9 The Lord prefers common-looking people. That is why He makes so many of them.

Abraham Lincoln, American Republican President (1809–65). There is no evidence that Lincoln said this. James Morgan in a book called *Our Presidents* (1928) was the first to put it in his mouth. Also quoted as: 'God must have loved the plain people; he made so many of them.'

Communism

10 Communist: one who has nothing, and is eager to share it with others.

Anonymous. Quoted in *The Home Book of Humorous Quotations*, ed. A.K. Adams (1969).

11 If we could have the revolution over again, we would carry it out more sensibly and with smaller losses. But history does not repeat itself. The situation is favourable for us. If God existed, we would thank him.

Nikita Khruschev, Soviet Communist leader (1894–1971). Speech to Western ambassadors, Moscow (18 November 1956).

12 If it looks like a duck, walks like a duck and quacks like a duck, then it just may be a duck.

Walter Reuther, American labour leader (1907–70). Usually ascribed to Reuther during the McCarthyite witch-hunts of the 1950s. He came up with it as a test of whether someone was a Communist. Then it came to be applied elsewhere – but usually in politics: 'Mr Richard Darman, the new [US] Budget director, explained the other day what "no new taxes" means. He will apply the duck test. "If it looks like a duck, walks like a duck and quacks like a duck, it's a duck"' – *The Guardian* (25 January 1989). Curiously, it has also been attributed to Richard, Cardinal Cushing, who, commenting on the propriety of calling Fidel Castro a Communist, said: 'When I see a bird that walks like a duck and swims like a duck and quacks like duck, I call that bird a duck' – quoted in *The New York Times* (1 March 1964).

1 It is hard to make Communists out of Poles: they are too Catholic and they have a sense of humour.

Adlai Stevenson, American Democratic politician (1900–65). *Friends and Enemies* (1959).

Company

2 He that lies down with dogs shall rise up with fleas.

Benjamin Franklin, American politician and scientist (1706–90). *Poor Richard's Almanack* (July 1733) – a work in which Franklin often revised already existing sayings.

Comparisons

3 Fighting for peace is like fucking for virginity.

Anonymous (graffito). Included in my book *Graffiti Lives, OK* (1979) and said to have been observed in Covent Garden, London, in 1978.

Of Reykjavik:

4 About as exciting as Aberdeen on a Sunday night.

Anonymous. Quoted in my book *A Year of Stings and Squelches* (1985).

On a highly idiosyncratic TV commentator:

5 Eddie Waring has done for Rugby League what Cyril Smith has done for hang-gliding.

Reggie Bowden – a Rugby League player, captain of the successful Widnes team of the 1970s and the original captain and coach of the Fulham Rugby League team. Quoted in the same book as above.

6 Reading a fan magazine is similar to eating a banana under water.

Ezra Goodman, American writer. *The Fifty Year Decline and Fall of Hollywood* (1961).

7 As busy as a one-armed man with the nettle-rash pasting on wall-paper.

O. Henry, American writer (1862–1910). *The Gentle Grafter*, 'The Ethics of Pig' (1908).

8 Then Petra flashed by in a wink.
It looked like Eaton Square – but pink.

(Sir) Charles Johnston, English diplomat, poet and translator (1912–86). *Poems and Journeys*, 'Air Travel in Arabia' (1979).

Of Henry Cabot Lodge at the Republican National Convention in Chicago:

9 He was as cool as an undertaker at a hanging.

H.L. Mencken, American journalist and linguist (1880–1956). In the Baltimore *Evening Sun* (15 June 1920).

Of Liberal leader David Steel's rap record 'I Feel Liberal':

10 If he's going to take up pop singing, I'm going to take up belly dancing.

(Sir) Cyril Smith, Liberal politician (1928–). Quoted in *The Guardian* (24 September 1982).

11 I looked as out of place as a Presbyterian in hell.

Mark Twain, American writer (1835–1910). A.B. Paine, *Mark Twain: A Biography* (1912).

Compensation

On dealing with adverse criticism:

12 I cried all the way to the bank.

Liberace, American pianist and entertainer (1919–87). *Autobiography* (1973): 'I think the people around me are more apt to become elated about good reviews (or depressed by bad ones) than I am. If they're good I just tell them, "Don't let success go to your head." When the reviews are bad I tell my staff that they can join me as I cry all the way to the bank.' Liberace was using the expression by 1954. In Alfred Hitchcock's film *North by Northwest* (US 1959), the Cary Grant character gets to say: '... while we cry about it all the way to the bank'.

Compliments (backhanded and direct)

1 Why, you're one of the most beautiful women I've ever seen, and that's not saying much for you.

Line from film *Animal Crackers* (US 1930). Screenwriters: Morrie Ryskind, George S. Kaufman. Spoken by Groucho Marx (Capt. Spaulding) to Margaret Dumont (Mrs Teasdale).

2 Age shall not wither her, nor iron bars a cage.

Anonymous. Quoted in letter from Kenneth Williams to John Hussey (2 October 1971) in *The Kenneth Williams Letters* (1994). It has been ascribed to the BBC radio show *Much Binding in the Marsh* (1947–53).

Spoken to a father by someone looking at his children:

3 Are these *your* children? what darlings! and – er – what a very pretty woman your wife *must* be!

Anonymous. Caption to cartoon, *Punch*, Vol. 127 (3 August 1904).

4 *Mrs Teasdale (gushingly):*
Oh, your Excellency!
Firefly:
You're not so bad yourself.

Lines from film *Duck Soup* (US 1933). Screenwriters: Bert Kalmar, Harry Ruby, Arthur Sheekman, Nat Perrin. Spoken by Groucho Marx (Rufus T. Firefly) and Margaret Dumont (Mrs Teasdale).

Referring to his wife:

5 I am leaving tonight; Hannah and the rest of the heavy baggage will follow later.

5th Earl of Rosebery (Archibald Philip Primrose), British Liberal Prime Minister (1847–1929). Quoted in Robert Rhodes James, *Rosebery* (1963) – where it is given as one of Rosebery's 'alleged *mots*'.

6 Compliments always embarrass a man. You do not know anything to say. It does not inspire you with words ... I have been complimented myself a great many times, and they always embarrass me – I always feel that they have not said enough.

Mark Twain, American writer (1835–1910). Speech on Fulton Day, at Jamestown (23 September 1907). In *Mark Twain's Speeches*, ed. A.B. Paine (1923).

7 Women are never disarmed by compliments. Men always are. That is the difference between the two sexes.

Oscar Wilde, Irish playwright, poet and wit (1854–1900). *An Ideal Husband*, Act 3 (1895).

Composure

8 As someone pointed out recently, if you can keep your head when all about you are losing theirs, it's just possible you haven't grasped the situation.

Jean Kerr, American writer (1923–). *Please Don't Eat the Daisies*, Introduction (1958).

Computers

9 To err is human but to really foul things up requires a computer.

Anonymous. Quoted in *Farmers' Almanac for 1978* and on Granada TV *Cabbages and Kings* (11 August 1979).

10 We used to have lots of questions to which there were no answers. Now, with the computer, there are lots of answers to which we haven't thought up the questions.

(Sir) Peter Ustinov, English actor and writer (1921–). Quoted in *Illustrated London News* (1968).

Conceit

Referring to The World Crisis *(1923–9):*

1 Winston [Churchill] has written a book about himself and called it the world crisis.

Arthur Balfour (1st Earl of Balfour), British Conservative Prime Minister (1848–1930). Quoted in the revised bibliography to A.J.P. Taylor, *English History 1914–1945* (originally published in 1965). However, Anthony Montague Brown, Churchill's Private Secretary 1952–65, gave a different attribution in a speech to the International Churchill Societies in 1986. He ascribes 'Winston has written a huge book all about himself and called it The World Crisis' to Sir Samuel Hoare.

2 What a dust have I rais'd! quoth the fly upon the coach.

Thomas Fuller, English writer and physician (1654–1734). *Gnomologia*, No. 5476 (1732), quoting a much earlier source. Bacon said in his essay 'On Vain Glory' (1612): 'It was prettily devised by Aesop: The fly sat upon the axle-tree of the chariot-wheel and said, what a dust I do raise!'

Concentration

3 Depend upon it, Sir, when a man knows he is to be hanged in a fortnight, it concentrates his mind wonderfully.

(Dr) Samuel Johnson, English writer and lexicographer (1709–84). In James Boswell, *The Life of Samuel Johnson* (1791) – for 19 September 1777.

Conception

When a brigadier in the Indian Army asked his servant why, although many years married, he had had no children, the servant replied:

4 Ah, my wife, sir: she's inconceivable and impregnable.

Anonymous, and told to me anonymously (1999).

5 Oh, what a tangled web we weave when first we practise to conceive.

Don Herold, American humorist and artist (1889–1966). Quoted in *The Treasury of Humorous Quotations*, eds Evan Esar & Nicolas Bentley (1951).

In the early 1960s, Dr Edith Summerskill took part in an Oxford Union debate on contraception or abortion. Her opening words were:

6 Mr President, I cannot conceive …

Edith Summerskill (Baroness Summerskill), English Labour politician and doctor (1901–80). She never got any further. I think I was told this in about 1963, at the Oxford Union. (It wasn't true, of course – she had a lovely daughter.)

Conclusions

7 When a naked man is chasing a woman through an alley with a butcher's knife and a hard-on, I figure he isn't out collecting for the Red Cross.

Line from film *Dirty Harry* (US 1971). Screenwriters: Harry Julian Fink and others. Spoken by Clint Eastwood (Harry Callahan).

Conduct

8 The husband was a teetotaller, there was no other woman, and the conduct complained of was that he had drifted into the habit of winding up every meal by taking out his false teeth and hurling them at his wife.

(Sir) Arthur Conan Doyle, Scottish-born novelist (1859–1930). *The Adventures of Sherlock Holmes*, 'A Case of Identity' (1892).

Confidence

9 He had the supreme confidence which a Christian feels in four aces.

Mark Twain, American writer (1835–1910). *The Washoe Giant in San Francisco*, 'Washoe, Information Wanted' (1938).

10 All you need in this life is ignorance and confidence; then success is sure.

Mark Twain. Quoted in *When Huck Finn Went Highbrow*, ed. Benjamin de Carseres (1934).

Confusion

1 If you're not confused you're misinformed.

Anonymous (graffito). Included in my book *Graffiti 2* (1980). From the Bartlett School of Architecture, University of London.

Conscience

2 Conscience: the inner voice which warns us that somebody may be looking.

H.L. Mencken, American journalist and linguist (1880–1956). *A Little Book in C Major* (1916).

3 An uneasy conscience is a hair in the mouth.

Mark Twain, American writer (1835–1910). *Mark Twain's Notebook*, ed. A.B. Paine (1935).

4 Good friends, good books and a sleepy conscience: this is the ideal life.

Mark Twain, in the same book as above.

5 Conscience does make egoists of us all.

Oscar Wilde, Irish playwright, poet and wit (1854–1900). *The Picture of Dorian Gray*, Chap. 8 (1891).

6 There is nothing in the world so unbecoming to a woman as a Nonconformist conscience.

Oscar Wilde. *Lady Windermere's Fan*, Act 3 (1892).

Conservatives

7 A conservative is a man who will not look at the new moon, out of respect for that ancient institution, the old one.

Douglas Jerrold, English humorist and editor (1803–57). Quoted in *The Treasury of Humorous Quotations*, eds Evan Esar & Nicolas Bentley (1951).

8 A conservative is a man who just sits and thinks, mostly sits.

Woodrow Wilson, American Democratic President (1856–1924). Quoted in the same collection as above.

Consistency

9 A foolish consistency is the hobgoblin of little minds, adored by little statesmen and philosophers and divines. With consistency a great soul has simply nothing to do.

Ralph Waldo Emerson, American philosopher and poet (1803–82). *Essays*, 'Self-Reliance' (1841).

10 Inconsistency is the only thing in which men are consistent.

Horace Smith, English parodist (1779–1849). Quoted in *The Treasury of Humorous Quotations*, eds Evan Esar & Nicolas Bentley (1951).

11 Consistency is the last refuge of the unimaginative.

Oscar Wilde, Irish playwright, poet and wit (1854–1900). Quoted in Hesketh Pearson, *The Life of Oscar Wilde* (1946).

12 Consistency is the last refuge of the failure.

Oscar Wilde. Quoted in *The Uncollected Oscar Wilde*, ed. John Wyse Jackson (1995).

13 We are never more true to ourselves than when we are inconsistent.

Oscar Wilde. 'The Critic As Artist' (1890).

Contemporaries

14 Why was I born with such contemporaries?

Bernard Shaw, Irish playwright and critic (1856–1950). Quoted in *The Treasury of Humorous Quotations*, eds Evan Esar & Nicolas Bentley (1951).

Contraception

15 The best contraceptive is a glass of cold water: not before or after, but instead.

Anonymous Pakistani delegate at the International Planned Parenthood Federation Conference. Quoted in *The Penguin Dictionary of Modern Quotations* (1971).

16 A fast word about oral contraception. I asked a girl to go to bed with me and she said 'no'.

Woody Allen, American film actor, writer and director (1937–). In monologue on record album *Woody Allen Volume Two* (1965).

1 Contraceptives should be used on every conceivable occasion.

Spike Milligan, Irish entertainer and writer (1918–). He spoke the line in BBC Radio's *The Last Goon Show of All* (1972), for which he wrote the script.

Contracts

2 God is love – but get it in writing.

Gypsy Rose Lee, American striptease entertainer (1913–1970). Quoted in *The Guardian* (24 June 1975).

3 You can't fool me. There ain't no Sanity Clause!

Line from film *A Night at the Opera* (US 1935). Screenwriters: Joseph Fields, Roland Kibbee. Spoken by Chico Marx (Fiorello), the manager of a tenor whom Groucho Marx (Otis B. Driftwood) would like to sing with the New York Opera Company. They go through the contract in this fashion, Chico replying thus when Groucho says: 'If any of the parties participating in this contract is shown not to be in their right mind, the entire agreement is automatically nullified. That's what they call a sanity clause.'

Convenience

On his preference for flying Concorde:

4 I cannot get in and out of aircraft toilets but on three and a half hour flights I can hold out.

Luciano Pavarotti, Italian tenor (1935–). Quoted in *The Observer*, 'Sayings of the Week' (2 August 1987).

Conversation

Of Winston Churchill:

5 He never spares himself in conversation. He gives himself so generously that hardly anybody else is permitted to give anything in his presence.

Aneurin Bevan, Welsh Labour politician (1897–1960). Quoted in news summaries (26 April 1954).

6 Although there exist many thousand subjects for elegant conversation, there are persons who cannot meet a cripple without talking about feet.

Ernest Bramah, English writer (1868–1942). *The Wallet of Kai Lung* (1900). Compare: 'I cried because I had no shoes, until I met a man who had no feet' – ascribed to Confucius in Patricia Houghton, *A World of Proverbs* (1981), but unverified. Has also been described as a 'Zen saying'. 'There was the man who complained because he had no shoes, until he met a man who had no feet' (quoted in Jacob M. Braude, *Speakers' Encyclopedia*, 1955); 'I had no shoes, and I murmured, till I met a man who had no feet' (described as 'Arabic' in Viscount Samuel, *A Book of Quotations*, 1947). It has also been attributed to R.W. Emerson. But, rather, Emerson's source may be the first appearance of the saying. In the *Rose Garden* or *Gulistani*, Sheikh Muslih'ud-Din Sadi of Shiraz, who featured in 13th-century Persian classics, wrote: 'I had never complained of the vicissitudes of fortune, nor murmured at the ordinances of heaven, excepting on one occasion, that my feet were bare, and I had not wherewithal to shoe them. In this desponding state I entered the metropolitan mosque of Kufah, and there I beheld a man that had no feet. I offered up praise and thanksgiving for God's goodness to myself, and submitted with patience to my want of shoes.'

To a lady at dinner who wanted action against Russia and asked him what was he waiting for:

7 Potatoes at the moment, Madam.

Benjamin Disraeli (1st Earl of Beaconsfield), British Conservative Prime Minister and writer (1804–81). Quoted in Wilfrid Meynell, *The Man Disraeli* (1927 edn).

To Boswell:

8 Sir, you have but two topics, yourself and me. I am sick of both.

(Dr) Samuel Johnson, English writer and lexicographer (1709–84). Quoted in James Boswell, *The Life of Samuel Johnson* (1791) – for May 1776.

A 'blocking phrase' to say when putting down experts while in conversation with them:

9 'Yes, but not in the South', with slight adjustments will do for any argument about any place, if not about any person.

Stephen Potter, English humorist (1900–69). *Lifemanship* (1950). In a footnote, he remarks: 'I am required to state that World Copyright of this phrase is owned by its brilliant inventor, Mr Pound' – though which 'Pound' he does not reveal. Indeed, the blocking move was known before this. Richard Usborne wrote of it in a piece called 'Not in the South' included in *The Pick of 'Punch'* (1941). He introduced a character called Eustace who had found a formula 'for appearing to be a European, and world, pundit. It was a formula that let me off the boredom of finding out facts and retaining knowledge.' It was to remark, 'Not in the South.'

1 Yes, 'e come up to me an' I sez, 'Oh!' – an' 'e sez, 'Oh, it's "Oh," is it?' – an' I sez 'yes, it is "oh"!'

Frank Reynolds, English cartoonist. Caption to cartoon, *Punch* (30 March 1921).

2 *Mr Binks:*
One of my ancestors fell at Waterloo.
Lady Clare:
Ah? Which platform?

F.H. Townsend, English cartoonist. Caption to cartoon, *Punch*, Vol. 129 (1 November 1905). To this joke is often added the further response, 'Ha, ha! As if it mattered which platform!' Shamelessly misattributed over the years. *The Best of Myles* reprints as an overheard remark this from Flann O'Brien's Dublin newspaper column (early 1940s): 'D'you know that my great-grandfather was killed at Waterloo ... Which platform?' A.L. Rowse writes of Lord David Cecil in *Friends and Contemporaries* (1989): 'Anything for a laugh – simplest of jokes. I think of him now coming into my room [at Christ Church in the early 1920s], giggling and sputtering with fun. Someone had said, "My grandfather was killed at Waterloo." "I'm so sorry – which platform?"'

3 Talk to every woman as if you loved her, and to every man as if he bored you, and at the end of your first season you will have the reputation of possessing the most perfect social tact.

Oscar Wilde, Irish playwright, poet and wit (1854–1900). *A Woman of No Importance*, Act 3 (1893).

4 'What ho!' I said.
'What ho!' said Motty.
'What ho! What ho!'
'What ho! What ho! What ho!'

After that it seemed rather difficult to go on with the conversation.

(Sir) P(elham) G. Wodehouse, English-born novelist and lyricist (1881–1975). *Carry on, Jeeves!*, 'Jeeves and the Unbidden Guest' (1925).

Conversational gambits

During an audience with the Pope:

5 I expect you know my friend, Evelyn Waugh, who, like you, your holiness, is a Roman Catholic.

Randolph Churchill, English journalist and politician (1911–68). Quoted in *The Penguin Dictionary of Modern Quotations* (1971).

On being told that the person sitting next to him at a dinner party was 'writing a book':

6 Neither am I.

Peter Cook, English humorist (1937–95). Quoted by Richard Ingrams on BBC Radio *Quote ... Unquote* (25 August 1984), though Cook declined to claim it as original.

7 How's the old complaint?

Benjamin Disraeli (1st Earl of Beaconsfield), British Conservative Prime Minister and writer (1804–81). 'How careful Lord Beaconsfield was, in the great days of his political struggles, to flatter every one who came within his reach. To the same effect is the story that when he was accosted by any one who claimed acquaintance but whose face he had forgotten he always used to enquire, in a tone of affectionate solicitude, "And how is the old complaint?"' – G.W.E. Russell, *Collections and Recollections*, Chap. 24 (1898).

At the end of the First World War, General Nivelle, hero of Verdun, made a tour of the United States. When he reached Los Angeles, a big public reception was held so that he could meet members of the movie colony. Among those invited were Charles Chaplin and Will Rogers. Chaplin was oddly nervous about meeting this great war hero and confided in Rogers that he had absolutely no idea how he would start up a conversation. Advised Rogers:

1 Well, you might ask him if he was in the war, and which side he was on ...

Will Rogers, American humorist (1879–1935). Quoted in Irvin S. Cobb, *A Laugh a Day Keeps the Doctor Away* (1921). This turns up later in the caption to a *Punch* cartoon (4 July 1934): (Two bored people) 'My grandfather fought in the Zulu War.' 'On which side?'

Cooking and cooks

2 Even an old boot tastes good if it is cooked over charcoal.

Anonymous (Italian proverb).

3 Fish should swim thrice ... it should swim in the Sea; ... then it should swim in Butter; and at last, Sirrah, it should swim in good Claret.

Anonymous (proverbial saying). The first recorded use of this was in 1611 – 'We say, fish must ever swimme twice [in water and in wine]' – but by 1620, this had become: 'Fish ... never doth digest well ... except it swimme twice after it comes forth the water: that is, first in butter, so to be eaten: then in wine or beere after it is eaten.' Quoted in Jonathan Swift, *Polite Conversation* (1738) in the above form.

4 Boiled cabbage *à l'Anglaise* is something compared with which steamed coarse newsprint bought from bankrupt Finnish salvage dealers and heated over smoky oil stoves is an exquisite delicacy. Boiled British cabbage is something lower than ex-Army blankets stolen by dispossessed Goanese doss-house-keepers who used them to cover busted-down hen houses in the slum district of Karachi.

Cassandra (Sir William Connor), English journalist (1909–67), In *Daily Mirror* (30 June 1950).

Of Ian Fleming's hospitality:

5 The food was so abominable that I used to cross myself before taking a mouthful ... I used to say, 'Ian, it tastes like armpits.'

(Sir) Noël Coward, English entertainer and writer (1899–1973). Quoted in John Pearson, *The Life of Ian Fleming* (1966).

6 There is one thing more exasperating than a wife who can cook and won't, and that's the wife who can't cook and will.

Robert Frost, American poet (1874–1963). Quoted in *The Treasury of Humorous Quotations*, eds Evan Esar & Nicolas Bentley (1951).

7 Housewarming at Zola's. Very tasty dinner, including some grouse whose scented flesh Daudet compared to an old courtesan's flesh marinated in a bidet.

Edmond de Goncourt, French novelist (1822–96). *Journal* – for 3 April 1878.

8 I thought my mother was a bad cook but at least her gravy used to move about a bit.

Tony Hancock, English comedian (1924–68). In BBC Radio *Hancock's Half-Hour*, 'A Sunday Afternoon at Home' (22 April 1958). Script by Alan Simpson and Ray Galton.

9 Nearly every woman in England is competent to write an authoritative article on how not to cook cabbage.

Vyvyan Holland, English writer (1886–1967). *Wine and Food* (1935).

Of a hostess:

10 She did not so much cook as assassinate food.

Storm Jameson, English novelist (1891–1986). Quoted in *The Penguin Dictionary of Modern Quotations* (1980 edn).

11 The greatest animal in creation, the animal who cooks.

Douglas Jerrold, English humorist and editor (1803–57). Quoted in *The Treasury of Humorous Quotations*, eds Evan Esar & Nicolas Bentley (1951).

12 The cook was a good cook, as cooks go; and as cooks go she went.

Saki (H.H. Munro), English writer (1870–1916). *Reginald*, 'Reginald on Besetting Sins' (1904).

1 [Landor] had one day, after an imperfect dinner, thrown the cook out of the window, and, while the man was writhing with a broken limb, ejaculated, 'Good God! I forgot the violets!'

Walter Savage Landor, English poet (1775–1864). Quoted in Richard Monckton Milnes, *Monographs by Lord Houghton* (1873).

2 'Turbot, Sir,' said the waiter, placing before me two fishbones, two eyeballs, and a bit of black mackintosh.

Thomas Earle Welby, English writer (1881–1933). *The Dinner Knell*, 'Birmingham or Crewe?' (1932).

Cool

3 Keep cool: it will be all one a hundred years hence.

Ralph Waldo Emerson, American philosopher and poet (1803–82). *Representative Men*, 'Montaigne; or The Skeptic' (1850).

Coolidge, Calvin

AMERICAN REPUBLICAN PRESIDENT (1872–1933)

4 He opened his mouth and a moth flew out.

Anonymous. Quoted in Claude Fuess, *Calvin Coolidge* (1940).

On the Coolidge administration:

5 For six years profound silence was mistaken for profound wisdom.

Alben W. Barkley, American Democratic politician (1877–1956). Speech, Democratic national convention (1932). Also in *That Reminds Me* (1954).

6 I think the American public wants a solemn ass as a President. And I think I'll go along with them.

Calvin Coolidge. Quoted in Herbert V. Prochnow, Snr & Jnr, *A Treasury of Humorous Quotations* (1969).

7 Calvin Coolidge – The greatest man who ever came out of Plymouth Corner, Vermont.

Clarence Darrow, American lawyer (1857–1938). Quoted in *The Home Book of Humorous Quotations*, ed. A.K. Adams (1969).

8 Looked as if he had been weaned on a pickle.

Alice Roosevelt Longworth, American political hostess (1884–1980). She admitted hearing this 'at my dentist's office. The last patient had said it to him and I just seized on it. I didn't originate it – but didn't it describe him exactly?' (*The New York Times*, 25 February 1980). It first appeared as an 'anonymous remark' quoted in Longworth's *Crowded Hours* (1933).

9 He laughed until you could hear a pin drop.

Ring Lardner, American screenwriter (1915–). Quoted in *Wit's End*, ed. Robert E. Drennan (1973).

10 Here, indeed, was his one really notable talent. He slept more than any other President, whether by day or by night ... Nero fiddled, but Coolidge only snored ... He had no ideas, and he was not a nuisance.

H.L. Mencken, American journalist and linguist (1880–1956). In the *American Mercury* (April 1933).

When told Coolidge had died:

11 How can they tell?

Dorothy Parker, American writer (1893–1967). Quoted in Bennett Cerf, *Try and Stop Me* (1944). As 'How do they know?', it appears in Malcolm Cowley, *Writers at Work*, Series 1 (1958). In that form it is also attributed to Wilson Mizner (Alva Johnston, *The Legendary Mizners*, 1953).

Cormorants

12 The common cormorant (or shag)
Lays eggs inside a paper bag,
You follow the idea, no doubt?
It's to keep the lightning out.

But what these unobservant birds
Have never thought of, is that herds
Of wandering bears might come with buns
And steal the bags to hold the crumbs.

Christopher Isherwood, English-born American writer (1904–86). 'The Common Cormorant' (*c.* 1925).

Coughing

1 I tried to say more, but the Cough had come upon me, as it does these days. It starts as the smallest tickle in the throat and can build, though I say so myself as shouldn't, into a not unimpressive display. Something between a vomiting donkey and an explosion at a custard factory.

Stephen Fry, English novelist and actor (1957–). *The Hippopotamus*, Chap. 1 (1995).

To an expectorating concert audience when he was at a pianissimo point:

2 I can hear you, but you can't hear me.

Alfred Brendel, Austrian pianist (1931–). Quoted in *The Observer* (20 May 1991). By saying this he ensured absolute silence for the remainder of his recital.

3 When you get to the cough drop shop,
Remember when you're coughing,
It's not the cough that carries you off,
It's the coffin they carry you off in!

Leslie Sarony, English entertainer and writer (1897–1985). Song, 'The Cough-Drop Shop' (1932). The last couplet may be quoted from an earlier song.

Countryside

4 I am at two with nature.

Woody Allen, American film actor, writer and director (1937–). Quoted in *OK!* Magazine (7 January 2000).

5 You can take a boy out of the country but you can't take the country out of the boy.

Arthur ('Bugs') Baer, American humorist (1897?–1969). Quoted in *The Treasury of Humorous Quotations*, eds Evan Esar & Nicolas Bentley (1951).

6 Sylvia ... was accustomed to nothing much more sylvan than 'leafy Kensington'. She looked on the country as something excellent and wholesome in its way, which was apt to become troublesome if you encouraged it overmuch.

Saki (H.H. Munro), English writer (1870–1916). *The Chronicles of Clovis* (1911). Compare: 'Sir Leicester Dedlock is only a baronet, but there is no mightier baronet than he. His family is as old as the hills, and infinitely more respectable. He has a general opinion that the world might get on without hills, but would be done up without Dedlocks. He would on the whole admit Nature to be a good idea (a little low, perhaps, when not enclosed with a park-fence), but an idea dependent for its execution on your great county families' – Charles Dickens, *Bleak House*, Chap. 2 (1853).

7 The summer and the country have no charms for me. I look forward anxiously to the return of bad weather, coal fires, and good society in a crowded city. I have no relish for the country; it is a kind of healthy grave.

(Revd) Sydney Smith, English clergyman, essayist and wit (1771–1845). Letter to Miss G. Harcourt (1838).

8 My living in Yorkshire was so far out of the way that it was actually twelve miles from a lemon.

(Revd) Sydney Smith. Quoted in Lady Holland, *A Memoir of Sydney Smith* (1855).

9 Country life is very good; in fact, the best – for cattle.

(Revd) Sydney Smith. *Bon-mots of Sydney Smith &c.*, ed. Walter Jerrold (1893).

10 It is pure unadulterated country life. They get up early, because they have so much to do, and go to bed early because they have so little to think about.

Oscar Wilde. *The Picture of Dorian Gray*, Chap. 15 (1891).

11 Anybody can be good in the country. There are no temptations there. That is the reason why people who live out of town are so uncivilised.

Oscar Wilde. In the same book, Chap. 19.

1 I see a little time in the country makes a man turn wild and unsociable, and only fit to converse with his horses, dogs, and his herds.

William Wycherley, English playwright (1640?–1716). *The Country Wife*, Act 3 (1675).

Courage

2 No man in the world has more courage than the man who can stop after eating one peanut.

Channing Pollock, American writer and critic (1880–1946). Attributed remark.

Of Oscar Wilde:

3 He has the courage of the opinions of others.

James McNeill Whistler, American painter (1834–1903). Quoted in *The World* (London) (17 November 1886). Wilde himself subsequently used the line in his dialogue 'The Decay of Lying' (1889): 'The modern novelist presents us with dull facts under the guise of fiction ... He has not even the courage of other people's ideas, but insists on going directly to life for everything.'

Courtesy

4 The American characteristic is Uncourteousness. We are the impolite Nation ... It is only in uncourteousness, incivility, impoliteness, that we stand alone – until hell shall be heard from.

Mark Twain, American writer (1835–1910). *Mark Twain's Notebook*, ed. A.B. Paine (1935).

Replying to an actress, not noted for her good looks, who had said to him, 'Mr Wilde, you are looking at the ugliest woman in Paris':

5 In the world, madam.

Oscar Wilde, Irish playwright, poet and wit (1854–1900). Quoted on BBC Radio *Quote ... Unquote* (5 April 1978) and in Richard Ellman, *Oscar Wilde*, Chap. 13 (1987). Before this in Frank Harris, *Oscar Wilde, His Life and Confessions*, Chap. 20 (1930): 'Mdlle. Marie Anne de Bovet ... was a writer of talent and knew English uncommonly well; but in spite of masses of fair hair and vivacious eyes she was certainly very plain. As soon as she heard I was in Paris, she asked me to present Oscar Wilde to her. He had no objection, and so I made a meeting between them. When he caught sight of her, he stopped short: seeing his astonishment, she cried to him in her quick, abrupt way: "*N'est-ce pas, M. Wilde, que je suis la femme la plus laide de France?* [Come, confess, Mr Wilde, that I am the ugliest woman in France]." Bowing low, Oscar replied with smiling courtesy: "*Du monde, Madame, du monde* [In the world, madame, in the world]." No one could help laughing; the retort was irresistible. He should have said: "*Au monde, madame, au monde*," but the meaning was clear.'

When going through a swing-door together, Clare Booth Luce had used the customary phrase 'Age before beauty'. Came this response:

6 Pearls before swine.

Dorothy Parker, American writer (1893–1967). Quoted in John Keats, *You Might as Well Live* (1970). In answer to a question from Keats, Mrs Luce described this account as completely apocryphal.

Courtship

7 Have the florist send some roses to Mrs Upjohn and write 'Emily I love you' on the back of the bill.

Line from film *A Day At the Races* (US 1937). Screenwriters: Robert Pirosh, George Seaton and George Oppenheimer. Spoken by Groucho Marx (Dr Hackenbush). Compare this from the earlier film *Trouble in Paradise* (US 1932): *Gaston:* 'I want you to take five dozen roses – deep red roses – and I want you to put them in a basket and send them to Madame Colet ... Charge it to Madame Colet.' Screenwriters: Grover Jones, Samson Raphaelson. Spoken by Herbert Marshall (Gaston Monescu) referring to Kay Francis (Mariette Colet).

8 Courtship is to marriage, as a very witty prologue to a very dull play.

William Congreve, English playwright (1670–1729). *The Old Bachelor* (1693).

Coward, (Sir) Noël

ENGLISH ENTERTAINER AND WRITER (1899–1973)

9 Forty years ago he was Slightly in Peter Pan, and you might say that he has been wholly in Peter Pan ever since.

Kenneth Tynan, English critic (1927–80). Article on Coward (1953), collected in *Curtains* (1961). He went on: 'Even the youngest of us will know, in fifty years' time, exactly what we mean by "a very Noël Coward sort of person".'

Cowardice

1 Coward: one who in a perilous emergency thinks with his legs.

Ambrose Bierce, American journalist (1842–?1914). *The Cynic's Word Book* (later retitled *The Devil's Dictionary*) (1906).

When French marshals turned their backs on him at a reception:

2 I have seen their backs before.

1st Duke of Wellington (Arthur Wellesley), Irish-born soldier and British Prime Minister (1769–1852). Quoted in *The Home Book of Humorous Quotations*, ed. A.K. Adams (1969).

Cows

3 Condensed milk is wonderful. I don't see how they can get a cow to sit down on those little cans.

Fred Allen, American comedian (1894–1956). *Much Ado About Me* (1956).

4 I never saw a purple cow,
I never hope to see one;
But I can tell you anyhow,
I'd rather see than be one.

Gelett Burgess, American writer (1866–1951). 'The Purple Cow', in *The Lark* (San Francisco, May 1895).

Credit

5 There is no limit to what a man can do or where he can go, if he doesn't mind who gets the credit.

Anonymous. A sign bearing this text was displayed on the Oval Office desk of President Ronald Reagan. Shown in a *Daily Mail* photograph (14 September 1981).

Credits

Apocryphal screen credit on the 1929 film of The Taming of the Shrew:

6 With additional dialogue by William Shakespeare.

Anonymous. What, in fact, the screen credit does say is 'with additional dialogue by Sam Taylor', which is fair enough since Taylor was the director. Compare the film *My Own Private Idaho* (1992), which *does* have the credit 'With additional dialogue by William Shakespeare' – legitimately, as it is a re-telling of the Prince Hal / Falstaff story using some of the dialogue from *Henry IV*.

Cremation

7 We hold these truths to be self-evident: All men could be cremated equal.

Vern Partlow. Quoted in Laurence J. Peter, *Quotations for Our Time* (1977). Also ascribed to Goodman Ace in *The New Yorker* (1977).

Cricket

On women playing cricket:

8 It's a bit like watching men knitting.

(Sir) Len Hutton, English cricketer (1916–90). Quoted by Rachael Heyhoe-Flint on BBC Radio *Quote ... Unquote* (20 October 1998).

9 Cricket – a game which the English, not being a spiritual people, have invented in order to give themselves a conception of eternity.

Lord Mancroft, English writer (1914–87). *Bees in Some Bonnets* (1979).

A cricket enthusiast on baseball:

10 I don't think I can be expected to take seriously any game which takes less than three days to reach its conclusion.

(Sir) Tom Stoppard, English playwright (1937–). In *The Guardian* (24 December 1984).

11 Personally, I have always looked on cricket as organized loafing.

William Temple, English theologian and Archbishop

(1881–1944). Remark to parents when Headmaster of Repton School. Quoted in *The Penguin Dictionary of Modern Quotations* (1971).

Crime

1 My rackets are run on strictly American lines and they're going to stay that way.

Al Capone, American gangster (1899–1947). Quoted in Claud Cockburn, *In Time of Trouble* (1956).

2 One murder made a villain,
Millions a hero.

Beilby Porteus, English Anglican bishop and writer (1731–1808). 'Death' (1759).

3 The criminal classes are so close to us that even the policeman can see them. They are so far away from us that only the poet can understand them.

Oscar Wilde. In *Saturday Review* (17 November 1894).

Cripps, Sir Stafford

ENGLISH LABOUR POLITICIAN AND ECONOMIST (1889–1952)

4 He has a brilliant mind until he makes it up.

Margot Asquith (Countess of Oxford and Asquith) (1864–1945). *The Autobiography of Margot Asquith* (1936 edn).

5 There, but for the grace of God, goes God.

(Sir) Winston S. Churchill, British Conservative Prime Minister and writer (1874–1965). Quoted in Willans & Roetter, *The Wit of Winston Churchill* (1954), but had already been noted by Geoffrey Madan, who died in July 1947 (see his *Notebooks*, published in 1981).

Of Cripps at a dinner:

6 Who will relieve me of this Wuthering Height?

(Sir) Winston S. Churchill. Quoted in Leslie Frewin, *Immortal Jester* (1973).

Critics and criticism

7 My native habitat is the theatre. I toil not, neither do I spin. I am a critic and a commentator. I am essential to the theatre – as ants to a picnic, as the boll weevil to a cotton field.

Line from film *All About Eve* (US 1950). Screenwriter: Joseph L. Mankiewicz. Spoken by George Sanders (Addison de Witt).

8 It is a pity that critics should show so little sympathy with writers, and curious when we consider that most of them tried to be writers themselves, once.

(Sir) Max Beerbohm, English writer and caricaturist (1872–1956). In *The Yellow Book*, Vol. 2 (1894–7), answering serious abuse poured upon his essay in Vol. 1. Said to contain 'the second most effective comma I know in literature'.

9 Critics are like eunuchs in a harem: they know how it's done, they've seen it done every day, but they're unable to do it themselves.

Brendan Behan, Irish playwright (1923–64). Quoted in Laurence J. Peter, *Quotations for Our Time* (1977).

10 I never sleep through a performance. I always make sure that I am awake for the intermission.

Robert Benchley, American humorist and critic (1889–1945). Quoted by Michael Coveney on BBC Radio *Quote ... Unquote* (11 September 2000).

On Clive Barnes when drama critic of The New York Times:

11 He was given the CBE for services to the theatre – which seemed to me at the time like Goering being given the DSO for services to the RAF.

Alan Bennett, English playwright and actor (1934–). On BBC Radio *Today* (3 March 1977).

12 When I am abroad I always make a rule never to criticize or attack the Government of my country. I make up for lost time when I come home.

(Sir) Winston S. Churchill, British Conservative Prime Minister and writer (1874–1965). Speech, House of Commons (18 April 1947).

1 I was delighted to see that you thought I was as good as I thought I was.

(Sir) Noël Coward, English entertainer and writer (1899–1973). Quoted in *The Sayings of Noël Coward*, ed. Philip Hoare (1997), as having been in the New York press (1957).

2 I can take any amount of criticism, so long as it is unqualified praise.

(Sir) Noël Coward. Quoted in Laurence J. Peter, *Quotations for Our Time* (1977).

3 You know who the critics are? – the men who have failed in literature and art.

Benjamin Disraeli (1st Earl of Beaconsfield), British Conservative Prime Minister and writer (1804–81). *Lothair*, Chap. 35 (1870).

4 One of the most characteristic sounds of the English Sunday is the sound of Harold Hobson barking up the wrong tree.

Penelope Gilliatt, English writer and critic (1933–93). In *Encore* (November–December 1959). Hobson was for many years drama critic of *The Sunday Times*.

5 Asking a working writer what he thinks about critics is like asking a lamp-post how it feels about dogs.

Christopher Hampton, English playwright (1946–). In *The Sunday Times* Magazine (16 October 1977).

6 Nature when she invented, manufactured and patented her authors, contrived to make critics out of the chips that were left.

Oliver Wendell Holmes Snr, American writer and physician (1809–94). Quoted in *The Treasury of Humorous Quotations*, eds Evan Esar & Nicolas Bentley (1951).

7 All any author wants from a review is six thousand words of closely reasoned adulation.

(Sir) Antony Jay, English writer (1930–). Speech at booksellers' luncheon, Birmingham (1967). Quoted in Michael Coveney, *Cats On a Chandelier*, Chap. 12 (1999).

Book review:

8 People who like this sort of thing will find this the sort of thing they like.

Abraham Lincoln, American Republican President (1809–65). Quoted in G.W.E. Russell, *Collections and Recollections*, Chap. 31 (1898). Sometimes said to be his criticism of an unreadably sentimental book. This has been called 'the world's best book review' (by Hilary Corke in *The Listener*, 28 April 1955), though it can only loosely be traced back to Lincoln. Bartlett has steadily ignored it in recent years.

In Anthony Gross, *Lincoln's Own Stories* (1912), something like the remark is said by Lincoln to Robert Dale Owen, a spiritualist, when the latter asks Lincoln for his opinion of a long article on spiritualism.

As recounted by S.N. Behrman in *Conversations with Max* (1960), Max Beerbohm once mischievously invented a classical Greek source for the remark, and passed it off in a letter to the press under Rose Macaulay's signature. Earlier, in *Zuleika Dobson*, Chap. 11 (1911), Beerbohm puts it into the mouth of Clio who, when asked by Pallas what she thinks of *The Decline and Fall of the Roman Empire*, replies in Greek (with this translation): 'For people who like that kind of thing, that is the kind of thing they like.'

9 A critic is a legless man who teaches running.

Channing Pollock, American writer and critic (1880–1946). *The Green Book*.

In a letter (1906) to the music critic Rudolph Louis:

10 I am sitting in the smallest room of my house. I have your review before me. In a moment it will be behind me.

Max Reger, German composer (1873–1916). Quoted in N. Slonimsky, *Lexicon of Musical Invective* (1953), having been translated from the German. Ned Sherrin, in *Theatrical Anecdotes* (1991), reports the similar reply from Oscar Hammerstein (grandfather of the lyricist) to a creditor: 'I am in receipt of your letter which is now before me and in a few minutes will be behind me.' (In the *Evening Standard*, 30 January 1992, Milton Shulman ascribed it to Noël Coward ...)

There seems every chance that the real originator of the remark was John Montagu, 4th Earl of Sandwich. N.A.M. Rodger in *The Insatiable Earl* (1993) suggests that when William Eden (later Lord Auckland) defected from Sandwich in 1785 he wrote him a letter: 'Contemporaries repeated with relish Sandwich's terse reply ... "Sir, your letter is before me, and will presently be behind me"." Rodger gives his source as J.H. Jesse, *George Selwyn* (1843–4) and adds, helpfully, 'Manufactured lavatory paper was not known in the eighteenth century.'

1 As a bankrupt thief turns thief-taker, so an unsuccessful author turns critic.

Percy Bysshe Shelley, English poet (1792–1822). *Adonais*, Preface (1821).

2 Pay no attention to what the critics say. No statue has ever been put up to a critic.

Jean Sibelius, Finnish composer (1865–1957). Quoted in Bengt de Törne, *Sibelius: A Close-Up* (1937).

3 Unless the bastards have the courage to give you unqualified praise, I say ignore them.

John Steinbeck, American writer (1902–68). Quoted in J.K. Galbraith, *A Life in Our Times* (1981).

4 So, naturalists observe, a flea
Hath smaller fleas that on him prey;
And these have smaller fleas to bite 'em,
And so proceed ad infinitum.
Thus every poet, in his kind,
Is bit by him that comes behind.

Jonathan Swift, Anglo-Irish writer and clergyman (1667–1745). 'On Poetry: A Rhapsody' (1733).

To a would-be dramatist:

5 Dear Sir, I have read your play. Oh, my dear Sir. Yours faithfully ...

(Sir) Herbert Beerbohm Tree, English actor-manager (1853–1917). Quoted in Edmund Fuller, *Thesaurus of Anecdotes* (1985).

6 A critic is a man who knows the way but can't drive the car.

Kenneth Tynan, English critic (1927–80). In *The New York Times* Magazine (9 January 1966). Robin May in *The Wit of the Theatre* (1969) describes all such remarks as based on the observation that 'the critic knows how it is done but can't do it himself' and adds, 'there is an early version in Farquhar' (without saying what it is) and that the idea probably goes back to the 'ancient Greeks'.

7 *Wilde:*
I shall always regard you as the best critic of my plays.
Beerbohm Tree:
But I have never criticized your plays.
Wilde:
That's why.

Oscar Wilde, Irish playwright, poet and wit (1854–1900). Quoted in Hesketh Pearson, *Beerbohm Tree* (1956). The occasion was after the first-night success of *A Woman of No Importance* (1893).

8 Ideal dramatic criticism is unqualified appreciation.

Oscar Wilde. Quoted in Herbert V. Prochnow, Snr & Jnr, *A Treasury of Humorous Quotations* (1969).

Crowds

9 Every crowd has a silver lining.

P.T. Barnum, American showman (1810–91). Quoted in *The Treasury of Humorous Quotations*, eds Evan Esar & Nicolas Bentley (1951).

Crying

10 Crying is the refuge of plain women, but the ruin of pretty ones.

Oscar Wilde, Irish playwright, poet and wit (1854–1900). *Lady Windermere's Fan*, Act 1 (1892).

Cuckoos

11 First cuckoo I ever heard outside of a clock. Was surprised how closely it imitated the clock – and yet of course it could never have heard a clock. The hatefulest thing in the world is a cuckoo clock.

Mark Twain, American writer (1835–1910). *Mark Twain's Notebook*, ed. A.B. Paine (1935).

Cucumbers

12 It has been a common saying of physicians in England, that a cucumber should be well sliced, and dressed with pepper and vinegar, and then thrown out, as good for nothing.

(Dr) Samuel Johnson, English writer and lexicographer (1709–84). In James Boswell, *The Life of Samuel Johnson* (1791) – for 5 October 1773.

Culture

1 [Virginia Woolf] was talking of her contemporaries, how she had spoken last week with Hemingway and how Ernest had said, When I reach for my gun, I hear the word culture.

Alan Bennett, English playwright and actor (1934–). *Forty Years On*, Act 2 (1968).

2 I tell you we've got every big name taking part you've ever heard of – Callas, Picasso, Barenboim, Stradivarius …

Lew Grade (Lord Grade), Russian-born British media tycoon (1906–99). Quoted in Hunter Davies, *The Grades* (1981), but no doubt apocryphal. ATV, the TV company over which Grade presided for many years, was about to present a *Golden Hour of Entertainment* as a great new artistic spectacular.

3 Culture is like jam, the less one has, the more one spreads it.

Raymond Poincare, French politician and President (1860–1934). Quoted in Roger Vadim, *Bardot, Deneuve and Fonda* (1986). Alvin Toffler, *The Culture Consumers* (1964), has 'The wider any culture is spread, the thinner it gets.'

4 Mrs Ballinger is one of the ladies who pursue Culture in bands, as though it were dangerous to meet it alone.

Edith Wharton, American novelist (1862–1937). Quoted in *The Frank Muir Book* (1976).

5 Nobody of any real culture … ever talks nowadays about the beauty of the sunset. Sunsets are quite old fashioned. They belong to a time when Turner was the last note in art. To admire them is a distinct sign of provincialism of temperament.

Oscar Wilde, Irish playwright, poet and wit (1854–1900). 'The Decay of Lying', in *Nineteenth Century* (January 1889).

Curses

6 May you live in interesting times.

Anonymous. Variously described as an 'Old Scottish' and 'Ancient Chinese' curse. Current by the early 1980s.

7 Awake, my Muse, bring bell and book
To curse the hand that cuttings took.
May every sort of garden pest
His little plot of ground infest …
Let caterpillars, capsid bugs,
Leaf-hoppers, thrips, all sorts of slugs,
Play havoc with his garden plot,
And a late frost destroy the lot.

Laura Maconochie, Scottish versifier (1887–1972). 'The Gardener's Curse'. In *The Scotsman* (11 September 1967). When her daughter Alice, who ran the National Trust for Scotland garden at Inverewe in Wester Ross, complained about visitors to the gardens stealing plants, this was Lady Maconochie's response. It has been used by the National Trust for Scotland ever since.

Curves

8 A curved line is the loveliest distance between two points.

Mae West, American vaudeville and film actress (1893–1980). Quoted in the *Daily Mail* (1980).

9 [Daphne Dolores Moorhead had] a figure as full of curves as a scenic railway.

(Sir) P(elham) G. Wodehouse, English-born novelist and lyricist (1881–1975). *Jeeves and the Feudal Spirit*, Chap. 17 (1954). Later, in *Much Obliged, Jeeves*, Chap. 12 (1971), it is said of Florence Craye that, 'She has as many curves as a scenic railway.'

Curzon, George (1st Marquis Curzon)

ENGLISH VICEROY AND CONSERVATIVE POLITICIAN (1859–1925)

10 My name is George Nathaniel Curzon,
I am a most superior person.
My cheek is pink, my hair is sleek,
I dine at Blenheim once a week.

Anonymous. Written for *The Masque of Balliol* (*c.* 1880).

Hence, *Superior Person*, the title of Kenneth Rose's biography of Lord Curzon (1969).

Custody

1 I suppose they'll give you the custody of the Daimler?

(Sir) Noël Coward, English entertainer and writer (1899–1973). Quoted in *The Treasury of Humorous Quotations*, eds Evan Esar & Nicolas Bentley (1951).

Cynics and cynicism

2 Cynic: a blackguard whose faulty vision sees things as they are, not as they ought to be.

Ambrose Bierce, American journalist (1842–?1914). *The Cynic's Word Book* (later retitled *The Devil's Dictionary*) (1906).

3 Major Strasser has been shot. Round up the usual suspects.

Line from film *Casablanca* (US 1942). Screenwriters: Julius J. Epstein, Philip G. Epstein and Howard Koch, from an unproduced play *Everybody Comes To Rick's* by Murray Burnett and Joan Alison. Spoken by Claude Rains (Louis Renault).

4 A cynic is what an idealist calls a realist.

(Sir) Antony Jay (1930–) and Jonathan Lynn (1943–), English writers. Spoken by Sir Humphrey Appleby in the episode entitled 'The Moral Dimension' in BBC TV *Yes Minister* (1980–2). Tony Jay has confirmed that this was original.

5 A cynic is a man who looks at the world with a monocle in his mind's eye.

Carolyn Wells, American writer (187?–1942). Quoted in *The Treasury of Humorous Quotations*, eds Evan Esar & Nicolas Bentley (1951).

Lord Darlington's definition:

6 A man who knows the price of everything and the value of nothing.

Oscar Wilde, Irish playwright, poet and wit (1854–1900). *Lady Windermere's Fan*, Act 3 (1892).

7 Cynicism is merely the art of seeing things as they are instead of as they ought to be.

Oscar Wilde. *Oscariana* (1910).

D

Dancers and dancing

On Fred Astaire's first screen test:

1 Can't act, can't sing, slightly bald. Can dance a little.

Anonymous (Hollywood executive). Quoted in Leslie Halliwell, *The Filmgoer's Book of Quotes* (1973) and in David Niven, *Bring On the Empty Horses* (1975). Ned Sherrin's *Theatrical Anecdotes* (1991) has the additional information that the test was for RKO in 1933 and that the test report also stated: 'Enormous ears and bad chin-line [but] his charm is tremendous.'

2 My own personal reaction is that most ballets would be quite delightful if it were not for the dancing.

Anonymous. In the *Evening Standard*, quoted in *This England: Selections from the New Statesman column 1934–1968*, ed. Michael Bateman, Pt 1 (1969).

To Latin temptress:

3 I could dance with you till the cows come home. On second thought, I'd rather dance with the cows and you come home.

Line from film *Duck Soup* (US 1933). Screenwriters: Bert Kalmar, Harry Ruby, Arthur Sheekman, Nat Perrin. Spoken by Groucho Marx (Rufus T. Firefly).

After the opening night of Oh, Calcutta!:

4 The trouble with nude dancing is that not everything stops when the music stops.

(Sir) Robert Helpmann, Australian dancer and choreographer (1909–86). Quoted in *The Frank Muir Book* (1976). Also in the form: 'No. You see there are portions of the human anatomy which would keep swinging after the music had finished', when asked if the fashion for nudity on stage would extend to dance (Elizabeth Salter, *Helpmann*, 1978).

5 Fred Astaire, when his miraculous feet are quiet, gives a curious impression of unemployment.

Harold Lockridge, American critic. Reviewing *The Gay Divorce* in the New York *Sun* (1934).

6 Dancing is wonderful training for girls; it's the first way you learn to guess what a man is going to do before he does it.

Christopher Morley, American writer and editor (1890–1957). *Kitty Foyle*, Chap. 11 (1939).

7 A perpendicular expression of a horizontal desire.

Bernard Shaw, Irish playwright and critic (1856–1950). Quoted in the *New Statesman* (23 March 1962).

8 I am now going to the ball, to save my eyes from reading and my mind from thinking.

4th Earl of Chesterfield (Philip Dormer Stanhope), English politician and writer (1694–1773). Quoted in *The 'Quote … Unquote' Newsletter* (October 1992).

Dawn

9 How I detest the dawn. The grass always looks like it's been left out all night.

Line from film *The Dark Corner* (US 1946). Screenwriters: Jay Dratler and others. Spoken by Clifton Webb (Hardy Cathcart).

Day, Doris

AMERICAN SINGER AND FILM ACTRESS (1924–)

1 Doris Day is as wholesome as a bowl of cornflakes and at least as sexy.

Dwight MacDonald, American critic. Quoted in John Robert Colombo, *Wit and Wisdom of the Moviemakers* (1979).

Days of the month

2 Thirty days hath September, and my Uncle Fred for speeding.

Morey Amsterdam, American comedian (*fl.*1950s). Quoted in *The 'Quote … Unquote' Newsletter* (October 1997).

3 Thirty days hath Septober,
April, June, and no wonder,
All the rest have peanut butter,
Except my second cousin Henry,
Who married a chiffonier,
Which is a tall thing with drawers.

Anonymous. Quoted in the same.

4 Dirty days hath September,
April, June and November.
All the rest are dirty too
Except February –
and that's positively filthy.

Anonymous. Quoted in the same (July 1997).

5 Dirty days hath September,
April, June and November.
February's days are quite all right.
It only rains from morn to night.
All the rest have thirty-one
Without a blessed gleam of sun.
And if any of them had two and thirty
They'd be just as wet and just as dirty.

Anonymous. Quoted in the same (October 1997).

6 Thirty days hath September,
April, June and no wonder,
All the rest have porridge for breakfast,
Except my grandma
And she rides a bike.

Anonymous. Quoted in the same. A bizarre disc with the title 'I'm In Love With My Little Red Tricycle' was recorded by one Napoleon XIV in 1966 and would seem to be based on a blend of this and the previous version, starting as it does: 'Thirty days hath Septober, / April, June, and no wonder, / All the rest have peanut butter, / All except my dear grandmother. / She had a little red tricycle. / I stole it. Ha ha ha!'

7 Thirty days hath September,
All the rest I can't remember.
The calendar hangs on the wall;
Why bother me with this at all?

Anonymous. Quoted in the same (January 1998).

8 My favourite poem is the one that starts 'Thirty days hath September' because it actually tells you something.

Groucho Marx, American comedian (1895–1977). Quoted in *The Faber Book of Useful Verse*, ed. Simon Brett (1984).

Days of the week

9 To me Thursday evening has always been pale pink, with a faint green stripe growing broader towards nine o'clock. I am sure that all your readers will be thrilled to know this.

Anonymous (letter writer to *Radio Times*). Quoted in 'This England' column of the *New Statesman* in 1937.

Caption to cartoon of two hippopotami lazing in the water:

10 I keep thinking it's Tuesday.

Paul Crum, English cartoonist. Drawn anonymously for *Punch* (21 July 1937). The drawing is very small but is a favourite among cartoon buffs, who see in it a strain of the surrealism more often found in *The New Yorker* at about that time. A correspondent encourages me to believe that exactly the same picture was printed three months later with the caption: 'Angela, that's a nice name.'

Days of the year

1 Hooray, Hooray, the first of May,
Outdoor fucking begins today.

Anonymous. This 'Old Thurlestone saying' (whatever that may be – from the place in Devon?) was included in *Vice: An Anthology*, ed. Richard Davenport-Hines (1993). As 'Horray, horray, It is the first of May, / Outdoor f---ing starts today,' it appears in Reisner & Wechsler, *Encyclopedia of Graffiti* (1974) from 'Ladies' room, New York City'. But the rhyme was certainly current by the 1960s at least. In May 1964, a version with 'outdoor sex' was published in the Oxford undergraduate magazine, *Isis*.

Deafness

An MP observed Churchill as a very old man paying one of his infrequent visits to the House of Commons and remarked, 'After all, they say he's potty.' Came the muttered reply:

2 They say he can't hear either.

(Sir) Winston S. Churchill, British Conservative Prime Minister and writer (1874–1965). Quoted in William Manchester, *The Last Lion* (1983).

Death

3 It's not that I'm afraid to die. I just don't want to be there when it happens.

Woody Allen, American film actor, writer and director (1937–). *Death* (1975).

4 *Little Simpkins:*
Nearly all our best men are dead! Carlyle, Tennyson, Browning, George Eliot! – I'm not feeling very well myself!

Anonymous (cartoonist). Caption to cartoon entitled 'A Lament', *Punch*, Vol. 104 (6 May 1893). This is the better known of two expressions of this idea. In *Punch* (14 August 1886), there had been this caption to a cartoon entitled 'The Bills of Mortality': '*Kirk Elder (after a look at his Morning Paper).* "Poor McStagger deid! Et's vera sad to thenk o' the great number o' Destengweshed Men that's lately been ta'en! 'Deed – I no feel vera well – mysel!"' But then along came Mark Twain who, on a visit to the Savage Club in London (9 June 1899) made some remarks on 'Statistics' (later published in his *Speeches*, 1910), and said: 'I was sorry to have my name mentioned as one of the great authors, because they have a sad habit of dying off. Chaucer is dead, Spencer is dead, so is Milton, so is Shakespeare, and I am not feeling very well myself.' It is good to know that Twain was not averse to borrowing a good joke. Then again, Alphonse Allais, the French humorist and playwright, was asked to deliver a lecture. He began: 'I have been asked to talk to you on the subject of the theatre, but I fear that it will make you melancholy. Shakespeare is dead, Molière is dead, Racine is dead, Marivaux is dead – and I am not feeling too well myself.' Quoted in Cornelia Otis Skinner, *Elegant Wits and Grand Horizontals* (1962). So, who was the first to come up with this line? Allais died in 1905.

Meanwhile, Len Deighton remembered (1999) from the 1970s: 'Alongside the Paul Bocuse restaurant near Lyon there stood a very long brick wall. Upon it someone had carefully painted in large white letters the message: '*Dieu est mort … Marx est mort … et moi je ne me sens pas très bien* [God is dead … Marx is dead … and I don't feel very well myself …].'

5 Death is nature's way of telling you to slow down.

Anonymous. Quoted in *Newsweek* Magazine (25 April 1960). Has been specifically attributed to Severn Darden (1937–), the American film character actor. It is capable of infinite variation: from *Punch* (3 January 1962): 'Some neo-Malthusians have been heard to suggest that the bomb is Nature's way … of checking … the over-spawning of our species.' In 1978, the American cartoonist Garfield produced a bumper-sticker with the slogan: 'My car is God's way of telling you to slow down.'

6 The Bells of Hell go ting-a-ling-a-ling
For you but not for me.
O, Death where is thy sting-a-ling-a-ling,
O, grave, thy victory?

Brendan Behan, Irish playwright (1923–64). Behan made notable use of this in his play *The Hostage* (1958) but he was, in fact, merely adopting a song popular in the British Army in 1914–18. Even before that, though, it was sung – just like this – as a Sunday School chorus. It may have been in a Sankey and Moody hymnal, though it has not been traced. The basic element is from 1 Corinthians 15:55: 'O death, where is thy sting? O grave, where is thy victory?'

1 He cannot read his tombstone when he's dead.

Berton Braley, American writer (b.1882). *Do It Now.*

2 The fence around a cemetery is foolish, for those inside can't come out and those outside don't want to get in.

Arthur Brisbane, American newspaper editor (1864–1936). Quoted in *The Home Book of Humorous Quotations*, ed. A.K. Adams (1969).

3 Many people's tombstones should read, 'Died at 30. Buried at 60.'

Nicholas Murray Butler, American teacher and writer (1862–1947). Quoted in Laurence J. Peter, *Quotations for Our Time* (1977).

4 [Lord] Tyrawley and I have been dead these two years; but we don't choose to have it known.

4th Earl of Chesterfield (Philip Dormer Stanhope), English politician and writer (1694–1773). Quoted by Dr Samuel Johnson in James Boswell, *The Life of Samuel Johnson* (1791) – for 3 April 1773.

5 I've been doing nothing but write royal letters of condolence. I said to Benita [Hume] on the telephone that all I expected from my friends nowadays was that they should live through dinner.

(Sir) Noël Coward, English entertainer and writer (1899–1973). Diary entry for 28 February 1960 – usually quoted as 'All I ask of my friends these days is that they last through lunch', because in a later entry (30 July 1967), he writes: 'I said to [Marlene Dietrich], with an effort at grey comedy, "All I demand from my friends nowadays is that they live through lunch." To which she replied, puzzled, "Why lunch, sweetheart?"'

6 You live and learn ... then you die and forget it all.

(Sir) Noël Coward. Quoted in Gyles Brandreth, *Breaking the Code* (1999).

7 I have never wanted to see anybody die, but there are a few obituary notices I have read with pleasure.

Clarence Darrow, American lawyer (1857–1938). Quoted in *The Treasury of Humorous Quotations*, eds Evan Esar & Nicolas Bentley (1951).

Taking a man's pulse:

8 Either this man is dead or my watch has stopped.

Line from film *A Day At the Races* (US 1937). Screenwriters: Robert Pirosh, George Seaton and George Oppenheimer. Spoken by Groucho Marx (Dr Hackenbush).

9 *Mrs Teasdale (of her husband):*
Why, he's dead.
Firefly:
I'll bet he's just using that as an excuse.
Mrs Teasdale:
I was with him to the very end.
Firefly:
No wonder he passed away.
Mrs Teasdale:
I held him in my arms and kissed him.
Firefly:
So it was murder!

Lines from film *Duck Soup* (US 1933). Screenwriters: Bert Kalmar, Harry Ruby, Arthur Sheekman, Nat Perrin. Spoken by Groucho Marx (Rufus T. Firefly) and Margaret Dumont (Mrs Teasdale).

At the age of 92, on death:

10 Sometimes I think people see it as an indecent race between me, the Pope and Boris Yeltsin.

(Sir) John Gielgud, English actor (1904–2000). Quoted in the *Independent on Sunday* (10 November 1996).

11 As far as I'm concerned, there won't be a Beatles reunion as long as John Lennon remains dead.

George Harrison, English pop singer and musician (1943–). Quoted in *The Independent* Magazine (28 October 1995).

1 'Once you're dead, you're made for life.

Jimi Hendrix, American rock musician (1942–70). This attributed remark, dating from *c.* 1968, was certainly prescient in Hendrix's own case. His success was enhanced following an early death in September 1970. Within six weeks he had a No. 1 hit in the UK with 'Voodoo Chile'.

2 It is tragic that Howard Hughes had to die to prove that he was alive.

Walter Kane. Quoted in James Phelan, *Howard Hughes, The Hidden Years* (1976).

3 But this *long run* is a misleading guide to current affairs. *In the long run* we are all dead.

John Maynard Keynes (Lord Keynes), English economist (1883–1946). *A Tract on Monetary Reform* (1923).

Reason for her refusal to say prayers on one occasion:

4 God will be too busy unpacking King Edward.

The 'little daughter of Lord Kinnoull' who had been an 'awed witness' of the funeral of King Edward VII (1910). Quoted in Lord Riddell, *More Pages from My Diary 1908–14* (1934).

5 While there's death there is hope.

Harold Laski, English political scientist (1893–1950). So attributed (in the context of British politics) by Richard Crossman in the introduction to his *Diaries of a Cabinet Minister* (1975). However, Tam Dalyell in *Dick Crossman* (1989) has Crossman himself saying it about the death of Labour Party leader Hugh Gaitskell in 1963.

To his nephew Robin, in 1965:

6 Death is a very dull, dreary affair. And my advice to you is to have nothing whatsoever to do with it.

W. Somerset Maugham, English writer (1874–1965). Quoted in Robin Maugham, *Conversations With Willie* (1978).

Man registering complaint with pet-shop owner:

7 It's not pining, it's passed on. This parrot is no more. It's ceased to be. It's expired. It's gone to meet its maker. This is a late parrot. It's a stiff. Bereft of life it rests in peace. It would be pushing up the daisies if you hadn't nailed it to the perch. It's rung down the curtain and joined the choir invisible. It's an ex-parrot.

Lines from BBC TV *Monty Python's Flying Circus*, 'The Parrot Sketch' (7 December 1969). Script by John Cleese and Graham Chapman. Spoken by John Cleese (Praline).

8 Corpses always turned me up – even when I was doing Bereaved Households on the old Maida Vale *Intelligencer* ... I remember once I was drinking tea in one of these front rooms with a middle-aged lady who'd just lost her husband, and she asked me if I'd like to have a look at him ... Over we went to the coffin ... Well, you don't really know what to say, do you, so I said, 'He looks well, doesn't he?' and she said, 'He ought to. We only came back from Brighton last week.'

Robert Robinson, English writer and broadcaster (1927–). *Landscape With Dead Dons*, Chap. 12 (1956). However, this is an old story. In Irvin S. Cobb's *A Laugh a Day Keeps the Doctor Away* (1921), story number 254 tells of 'two sympathic friends' calling at a house of mourning in the Bronx. The bereft husband of the late Mrs Levinsky sat alongside the casket. 'Doesn't she look wonderful?' said one of them. The widower replied, 'Why shouldn't she look wonderful? Didn't she spend the whole winter in Palm Beach?'

9 'Waldo is one of those people who would be enormously improved by death,' said Clovis.

Saki (H.H. Munro), English writer (1870–1916). *Beasts and Super-Beasts*, 'The Feast of Nemesis' (1914).

10 Ain't It Grand To Be Bloomin' Well Dead?

Leslie Sarony, English entertainer and writer (1897–1985). Title of song (1932).

11 Since we have to speak well of the dead, let's knock them while they're alive.

John Sloan. Quoted in Allen Churchill, *The Improper Bohemians* (1959).

Of a rock musician:

1 He died in a bizarre gardening accident.

Line from film *This Is Spinal Tap* (US 1984). Screenwriters: Christopher Guest, Michael McKean, Harry Shearer, Rob Reiner. Spoken by Michael McKean (David St Hubbins).

On hearing of the death of a corrupt politician:

2 I refused to attend his funeral. But I wrote a very nice letter explaining that I approved of it.

Mark Twain, American writer (1835–1910). Quoted in *Everybody's Mark Twain*, ed. C.T. Harnsberger (1972).

3 Let us endeavour so to live that when we come to die even the undertaker will be sorry.

Mark Twain. *Pudd'nhead Wilson*, Chap. 6 (1894).

On hearing of Truman Capote's death in 1984:

4 Good career move.

Gore Vidal, American novelist, playwright and critic (1925–). Confirmed by him in BBC TV *Gore Vidal's Gore Vidal* (1995). According to *Time* Magazine (8 April 1985), the graffito 'Good career move' had earlier appeared following Elvis Presley's death in 1977.

Death-wish

5 The minority parties have walked into a trap … It is the first time in recorded history that turkeys have been known to vote for an early Christmas.

James Callaghan (Lord Callaghan), British Labour Prime Minister (1912–). Speech, House of Commons (28 March 1979), deriding the Liberal Party and the Scottish National Party. He described the phrase as a 'joke going about the House'.

Debts

6 Blessed are the young, for they shall inherit the national debt.

Herbert Hoover, American Republican President (1874–1964). Attributed remark.

7 In the midst of life we are in debt.

Ethel Watts Mumford, American novelist and humorist (1878?–1940). Quoted in *The Treasury of Humorous Quotations*, eds Evan Esar & Nicolas Bentley (1951).

8 I owe much; I have nothing; the rest I leave to the poor.

François Rabelais, French writer (?1494–?1553). Quoted in *The Treasury of Humorous Quotations*, eds Evan Esar & Nicolas Bentley (1951).

9 He that dies pays all debts.

William Shakespeare, English playwright and poet (1564–1616). *The Tempest*, III.ii (1612).

On his promised pension:

10 I was promis'd on a time,
To have reason for my rhyme;
From that time unto this season,
I receiv'd nor rhyme nor reason.

Edmund Spenser, English Poet Laureate (*c.* 1522–99). Quoted in Thomas Birch, 'The Life of Mr Edmund Spenser' in an edition of *The Faerie Queene* (1751). Also in Theophilus Cibber, *The Lives of the Poets of Great Britain and Ireland* … (1753). When Spenser presented some poems to Queen Elizabeth I, she ordered her Lord High Treasurer, Burleigh, to pay the poet one hundred pounds. He exclaimed, famously, 'What, all this for a song?' and Spenser continued to wait for payment. In the end, Spenser reminded the Queen of her order, in verse. He was duly paid.

11 One must have some sort of occupation nowadays. If I hadn't my debts I shouldn't have anything to think about.

Oscar Wilde, Irish playwright, poet and wit (1854–1900). *A Woman of No Importance*, Act 1 (1893).

Decency

12 Every decent man carries a pencil behind his ear to write down the price of fish.

J.B. Morton (Beachcomber), English humorous writer (1893–1979). Attributed remark.

Deception

13 O what a tangled web we weave,
When first we practise to deceive.

But when we've practised for a while
How vastly we improve our style!

Anonymous. The first two lines are, of course, from Sir Walter Scott's *Marmion*, Canto 6, St. 17 (1808). The second couplet has been attributed to J.R. Pope. Phyllis McGinley, the American poet (1905–78), is said to have added: 'Which leads me to suppose the fact is / We really ought to get more practice.' Other versions of the second couplet are: 'But when we've practised it a bit / We make a better job of it!' and 'Success in this and other spheres / Comes but to him who perseveres' and 'So try again another day / Practice makes perfect, so they say.'

Decisions

1 If you can avoid a decision, do so. If you can get somebody else to avoid a decision, don't avoid it yourself. If you cannot get one person to avoid a decision, appoint a committee.

Anonymous. Attributed to Sharu S. Ragnekar in *The Art of Avoiding Decisions* by Winston Fletcher in *Meetings, Meetings* (1983).

2 The trouble with Howard [Reinheimer] is that he won't take yes for an answer.

Oscar Hammerstein II, American lyricist (1895–1960). Quoted in George Abbott, *Mister Abbott* (1963).

Decomposition

In response to a woman who had asked, 'Do tell me: what is Baytch [Bach] doing just now? Is he still composing?':

3 Now Bach is decomposing.

(Sir) W.S. Gilbert, English writer and lyricist (1836–1911). Quoted in Hesketh Pearson, *Gilbert and Sullivan* (1947). The first appearance may have been in H. Sutherland Evans, *Personal Recollections* (1900).

Dedications

4 DEDICATED GRATEFULLY TO THE WARDEN AND FELLOWS OF ST ANTONY'S COLLEGE, OXFORD. EXCEPT ONE.

Jan Morris, Welsh writer (1926–). Dedication of *The Oxford Book of Oxford* (1978). Compare the wish attributed to W.C. Fields: 'A Merry Christmas to all my friends except two.'

Dedication of his book The Heart of a Goof *(1926):*

5 To my daughter Leonora, without whose never-failing sympathy and encouragement this book would have been finished in half the time.

(Sir) P(elham) G. Wodehouse, English-born novelist and lyricist (1881–1975). Not the first use by Wodehouse of this formula. In the first edition of *A Gentleman of Leisure* (1910) appears: 'To Herbert Westbrook, without whose never-failing sympathy and encouragement this book would have been finished in half the time.'

6 To Raymond Needham, KC, who put the tax-gatherers to flight when they had their feet on my neck and their hands on my wallet.

(Sir) P(elham) G. Wodehouse. *Right Ho, Jeeves* (1934). In fact, this dedication was reduced: 'To Raymond Needham, KC, with affection and admiration' when Needham warned against antagonizing the authorities. Needham acted for Wodehouse in a successful appeal against the Inland Revenue. Sometimes, inaccurately, Wodehouse is said to have dedicated a book to an accountant.

Deeds

7 When there is a great cry that something should be done, you can depend on it that something remarkably silly probably will be done.

Anonymous (19th-century English statesman?). Quoted in *The 'Quote ... Unquote' Newsletter* (January 1997).

8 Step One: We must do something. Step Two: This is something. Step Three: Therefore we must do it.

Anonymous (civil servant?). 'The politicians' syllogism', quoted in Jonathan Lynn & Antony Jay, *Yes Prime Minister*, Vol.2 (1987).

Definitions

Of an éclair:

1 A cake, long in shape but short in duration, with cream filling and (usually) chocolate icing.

Anonymous (lexicographer). *The Chambers Dictionary* (1993). Literally, *éclair* is French for a flash of lightning. A *coup de food*, one might say.

Of a knees-up:

2 A boisterous dance involving the raising of alternate knees.

Anonymous (lexicographer). *Collins English Dictionary* (1994 edn).

3 Opening night: the night before the play is ready to open.

George Jean Nathan, American dramatic critic (1882–1958). Quoted in *The Treasury of Humorous Quotations*, eds Evan Esar & Nicolas Bentley (1951).

Deflation

4 Collapse of stout party.

Anonymous. Supposed catchphrase of 19th-century *Punch* (used as the tag line to a story about the humbling of a pompous person). The phrase has not been found. The words 'Stout Party' do, however, appear in the caption to a cartoon in the edition of 25 August 1855.

Defrocking

On a clergyman who had been involved in a scandal:

5 [Having] ceased to be a pillar of the Church, [he was] now two columns of the *Evening Standard*.

William Inge, English clergyman and theologian (1860–1954). Quoted in Alfred Noyes, *Two Worlds for Memory* (1953). Sometimes rendered as 'a lot of pillars of society end up as columns in the *News of the World*'.

De Gaulle, Charles

FRENCH SOLDIER AND POLITICIAN (1890–1970)

6 [He is] like a female llama surprised in her bath.

(Sir) Winston S. Churchill, British Conservative Prime Minister and writer (1874–1965). Quoted in Lord Moran, *The Struggle for Survival* (1966), which also includes Churchill's denial that he ever said it.

On being compared with Robespierre:

7 I always thought I was Jeanne d'Arc and Bonaparte – how little one knows oneself.

Charles de Gaulle. Quoted in *Figaro Littéraire* (1958).

DeMille, Cecil B.

AMERICAN FILM DIRECTOR (1881–1959)

8 Cecil B. DeMille,
Rather against his will,
Was persuaded to leave Moses
Out of 'The Wars of the Roses'.

Nicolas Bentley, English cartoonist and writer (1907–78). Attributed. It appeared anonymously in *Clerihews*, ed. J.W. Carter (1938).

Democracy

9 Democracy: in which you say what you like and do what you're told.

Gerald Barry, English editor and publicist (1898–1968). Quoted in *The Treasury of Humorous Quotations*, eds Evan Esar & Nicolas Bentley (1951).

10 Many forms of Government have been tried, and will be tried on this world of sin and woe. No one pretends that democracy is perfect or all-wise. Indeed, it has been said that democracy is the worst form of Government except all those other forms that have been tried from time to time.

(Sir) Winston S. Churchill, British Conservative Prime Minister and writer (1874–1965). Speech, House of Commons (11 November 1947). Note the 'it has been said'.

1 The best argument against democracy is a five-minute conversation with the average voter.

(Sir) Winston S. Churchill. Attributed remark.

2 Democracy is the theory that the common people know what they want, and deserve to get it good and hard.

H.L. Mencken, American journalist and linguist (1880–1956). *A Little Book in C major* (1916).

3 Democracy substitutes election by the incompetent many for appointment by the corrupt few.

Bernard Shaw, Irish playwright and critic (1856–1950). *Man and Superman*, 'Maxims for Revolutionaries' (1903).

4 Democracy means simply the bludgeoning of the people by the people for the people.

Oscar Wilde, Irish playwright, poet and wit (1854–1900). 'The Soul of Man Under Socialism' (1895).

Deodorants

A most ladylike American advertising slogan for a deodorant spray called Stopette:

5 Makes your armpit your charm pit!

Anonymous, c. 1953. Quoted in Isobel Barnett, *My Life Line* (1956).

Depardieu, Gérard

FRENCH ACTOR (1948–)

6 I sometimes think I shall never view
A French film lacking Gérard Depardieu.

John Updike, American novelist, poet and critic (1932–). Attributed couplet.

Deprivation

7 *Josiah:*
[When we were kids we had to live] in a small shoe box in the middle of the road.
Joshua:
A *cardboard* box?
Josiah:
Yes.
Joshua:
You were lucky. We lived for three months in a rolled-up newspaper in a septic tank. We used to get up at six, clean the newspaper, eat a crust of stale bread, work fourteen hours at the mill, day-in, day-out, for sixpence a week, come home, and dad would thrash us to sleep with his belt.
Obadiah:
Luxury!

Lines from 'The Good Old Days Skit' in ITV series *At Last the 1948 Show* (31 October 1967). Script by John Cleese, Marty Feldman, Graham Chapman, Tim Brooke-Taylor. Performed by Marty Feldman (Joshua), Obadiah (Graham Chapman), Josiah (Tim Brooke-Taylor). Also known as 'Four Yorkshireman' and performed in *The Secret Policeman's Ball* (1979) and in *Monty Python Live at the Hollywood Bowl* (1982).

8 Deprivation is for me what daffodils were for Wordsworth.

Philip Larkin, English poet (1922–85). Interviewed in *The Observer* (December 1979).

Descriptions of people

9 I met a lot of hard-boiled eggs in my life, but you – you're twenty minutes!

Line from film *Ace in the Hole* (US 1951). Screenwriters: Billy Wilder, Lesser Samuels, Walter Newman. Spoken by Jan Sterling (Lorraine) to Kirk Douglas (Tatum).

Of Fyfe Robertson, the gaunt Scots TV interviewer of yesteryear:

10 He looks as if someone has just poured cold porridge into his Wellingtons.

Anonymous. Quoted in *The 'Quote ... Unquote' Newsletter* (April 1994).

Of Andrew Neil, Scottish journalist, when editor of The Sunday Times*:*

11 If you can't plug it in the mains or fuck it, the editor's not interested.

Anonymous. Quoted in *The Independent* (31 January 1990).

Of V.M. Molotov, Soviet politician:

1 A refrigerator when the light has gone out.

Anonymous (British diplomat). Quoted in *Time* Magazine (24 November 1986). Winston Churchill said Molotov had 'a smile like the Siberian winter'.

Of his fellow conductor Sir Adrian Boult:

2 He came to see me this morning – positively reeking of Horlicks.

(Sir) Thomas Beecham, English conductor (1879–1961). Quoted in Ned Sherrin, *Cutting Edge* (1984).

3 *Lady Rumpers:*
As I say there was a black-out. I saw his face only in the fitful light of a post-coital Craven A. He was small, but perfectly proportioned. In some respects more so.

Alan Bennett, English playwright and actor (1934–). *Habeas Corpus*, Act 2 (1973).

4 Dr Polycarp was, as you all know, an unusually sallow bimetallist. 'There,' people of wide experience would say, 'There goes the sallowest bimetallist in Cheshire.'

G.K. Chesterton, English poet, novelist and critic (1874–1936). *The Napoleon of Notting Hill*, Chap. 3 (1904).
A bimetallist was one who supported the unrestricted currency of both gold and silver at a fixed ratio to each other as coinage.

Of John Foster Dulles, US Secretary of State:

5 Dull, duller, Dulles.

(Sir) Winston S. Churchill, British Conservative Prime Minister and writer (1874–1965). So ascribed in Piers Brendon, *Winston Churchill: a Brief Life* (1984).

Of Sir Hartley Shawcross (Attorney General in the 1945 Labour Government who, wearying of the party, resigned his parliamentary seat in 1958):

6 Sir Shortly Floorcross.

(Sir) Winston S. Churchill. So ascribed in Piers Brendon, *Winston Churchill: a Brief Life* (1984).

Of actress Glenda Jackson in film Women in Love:

7 She has a face to launch a thousand dredgers.

Jack De Manio, English broadcaster (1914–88). Quoted in Diana Rigg, *No Turn Unstoned* (1982).

On President Nasser and Sir Anthony Eden:

8 The camel that broke the straw's back.

11th Duke of Devonshire (Andrew Cavendish), English politician (1920–). Quoted in *The Oxford Dictionary of Humorous Quotations*, ed. Ned Sherrin (1995).

Of Jeanette Macdonald's face:

9 It reminds me of an Aardvaark's ass.

W.C. Fields, American comedian (1879–1946). Quoted in Ned Sherrin, *Cutting Edge* (1984).

Of Thomas E. Dewey:

10 He looks like the bridegroom on the wedding cake.

Grace Hodgson Flandrau. A description that helped destroy Dewey when he stood against President Truman in 1948. Usually ascribed to Alice Roosevelt Longworth, American political hostess (1884–1980), who admitted: 'I thought it frightfully funny and quoted it to everyone. Then it began to be attributed to me.' Sometimes just 'the (little) man on the wedding cake'. Dewey did indeed have a wooden appearance, and a black moustache.

About the 17th Earl of Derby:

11 A very weak-minded fellow, I'm afraid, and, like the feather pillow, bears the marks of the last person who has sat on him!

(Sir) Douglas Haig (1st Earl Haig), British soldier (1861–1928). Letter to his wife (14 January 1918). Derby was generally considered an uninspiring choice as Secretary for War (1916–18). Lloyd George, as Prime Minister, took over Derby's responsibilities the following March. Haig's private papers were made public in an edition edited by Robert Blake in 1952.

Of Malcolm Fraser when he became Prime Minister of Australia in 1975:

12 He is the cutlery man of Australian politics. He was born with a silver spoon in his mouth,

speaks with a forked tongue, and knifes his colleagues in the back.

Bob Hawke, Australian trade unionist and politician (1929–). Quoted in *The Observer*, 'Sayings of the Week' (14 December 1975). Hawke succeeded Fraser in 1983.

On being attacked in the House of Commons by Sir Geoffrey Howe:

1 That part of his speech was rather like being savaged by a dead sheep.

Denis Healey (Lord Healey), English Labour politician (1917–). Speech, House of Commons (14 June 1978). In 1987 Alan Watkins of *The Observer* suggested that Sir Roy Welensky, of Central African Federation fame, had earlier likened an attack by Iain Macleod to being *bitten* by a sheep. We had to wait until 1989 and the publication of Healey's memoirs to be told that, 'the phrase came to me while I was actually on my feet; it was an adaptation of Churchill's remark that an attack by Attlee was "like being savaged by a pet lamb". Such banter can often enliven a dull afternoon.'

The Churchill version remains untraced, but he was noted for his Attlee jokes (and busily denied that he had ever said most of them). In 1990, the victim of Healey's phrase, Geoffrey Howe, also claimed that it wasn't original. 'It came from a play,' he said sheepishly. A profile of Healey in *The Sunday Telegraph* (3 November 1996) suggested that he had appropriated the phrase 'dead sheep' without acknowledgement from the journalist Andrew Alexander.

2 Tony Blair [then newly elected leader of the British Labour Party] is a fresh face in British politics and the sort of chap the country needs, whereas John Prescott [the deputy leader] has the face of a man who clubs baby seals to death, but is, none the less, extremely pragmatic.

Denis Healey. Quoted in *The Sunday Telegraph* (17 July 1994).

3 He was so benevolent, so merciful a man that he would have held an umbrella over a duck in a shower of rain.

Douglas Jerrold, English humorist and editor (1803–57). Quoted in *The Treasury of Humorous Quotations*, eds Evan Esar & Nicolas Bentley (1951).

Of a certain person:

4 A mouse studying to be a rat.

Chuck Jones, American cartoon animator (1912–). Quoted in *The 'Quote ... Unquote' Newsletter* (October 1996).

5 In Pierre Elliott Trudeau, Canada has at last produced a political leader worthy of assassination.

Irving Layton, Romanian-born Canadian poet (1912–). *The Whole Bloody Bird*, 'Obo II' (1969).

Self-portrait:

6 'How pleasant to know Mr Lear!'
Who has written such volumes of stuff!
Some think him ill-tempered and queer,
But a few think him pleasant enough.

Edward Lear, English poet and artist (1812–88). *Nonsense Songs*, Preface (1871).

7 Richard Steele was a rake among scholars, and a scholar among rakes.

Thomas Babington Macaulay (Lord Macaulay), English historian and poet (1800–59). Quoted in *The Treasury of Humorous Quotations*, eds Evan Esar & Nicolas Bentley (1951).

Of Sir Ian McKellen, actor:

8 When he talks, he waves his arms and leaves long dramatic pauses – while he is Thinking – and his voice sounds a little as though he is eating biscuits.

Marianne Macdonald, English journalist. In *The Observer* Magazine (8 March 1998).

9 They laugh and are glad ... [and] are terrible!

'Fiona Macleod' (William Sharp), Scottish poet and novelist (1855–1905). In the libretto of *The Immortal Hour* (1914, based on his novel), an opera with music by Rutland Boughton, English composer (1878–1960).

Of Paul Johnson, journalist:

10 [He looks like] an explosion in a pubic hair factory.

Jonathan Miller, English entertainer, writer and director (1934–). Quoted in Alan Watkins, *Brief Lives* (1982).

Of G.K. Chesterton and Hilaire Belloc:

1 Two buttocks of one bum.

T. Sturge Moore, English poet and illustrator (1870–1944). Quoted in *The Frank Muir Book* (1976).

Of TV presenter Joan Bakewell in the 1960s when she introduced the discussion programme Late Night Line-Up *on BBC2:*

2 The thinking man's crumpet.

Frank Muir, English writer and broadcaster (1920–98). Muir was unable (1997) to recall quite when and where he said this but linked it to the 'thinking --'s --' format.

On Francis Wilson, TV weatherman:

3 Listen to him, and it's like sitting on wet seaweed on Land's End at the end of February.

Jean Rook, English journalist (1931–91). Quoted in my book *A Year of Stings and Squelches* (1985).

Of President McKinley:

4 McKinley has no more backbone than a chocolate eclair.

Theodore Roosevelt, American Republican President (1858–1919). Attributed remark.

On Richard Ingrams, when editor of Private Eye*:*

5 He looks like the painting in Wedgwood Benn's attic.

William Rushton, English entertainer and cartoonist (1937–96). Quoted in my book *A Year of Stings and Squelches* (1985).

6 One of the finest women who ever walked the streets.

Line from film *She Done Him Wrong* (US 1933). Screenwriter: Mae West (adapted from her stage play *Diamond Lil*, first performed 9 April 1928). Spoken by Mae West (Lady Lou).

Of Thomas Gray, the poet:

7 He *walks* as if he had fouled his smallclothes, and *looks* as if he smelt it.

Christopher Smart, English poet (1722–71). Quoted from *Facetiae Cantabrigienses*, some kind of 19th-century Cambridge University rag, in Christopher Devlin, *Poor Kit Smart* (1961). Compare from a letter written by Sir Walter Scott (7 September 1822) on a speech delivered by the Duke of Hamilton: 'He spoke as if he were b[eshit]t / And looked as if he smelt it.'

8 Daniel Webster struck me much like a steam-engine in trousers.

(Revd) Sydney Smith, English clergyman, essayist and wit (1771–1845). Quoted in Lady Holland, *A Memoir of Sydney Smith* (1855).

9 I like him and his wife. He is so ladylike, and she is such a perfect gentleman.

(Revd) Sydney Smith. Attributed remark.

When Lord Brougham arrived for a performance of Handel's Messiah*:*

10 Here comes counsel for the other side.

(Revd) Sydney Smith. Attributed remark.

Of Sir Richard Jebb, later Professor of Greek at Cambridge:

11 What time he can spare from the adornment of his person he devotes to the neglect of his duties.

William Hepworth Thompson, English scholar (1810–86). Quoted in M.R. Bobbit, *With Dearest Love to All* (1960). Has also been ascribed to Benjamin Jowett.

12 Why do you sit there looking like an envelope without any address on it?

Mark Twain, American writer (1835–1910). Attributed remark.

13 He hasn't a single redeeming vice.

Oscar Wilde, Irish playwright, poet and wit (1854–1900). Quoted in Hesketh Pearson, *The Life of Oscar Wilde* (1946).

Of the actor, Sir Henry Irving:

14 His left leg is a poem.

Oscar Wilde. Quoted in *The Frank Muir Book* (1976).

Of Dorothy Parker:

1 She is so odd a blend of Little Nell and Lady Macbeth. It is not so much the familiar phenomenon of a hand of steel in a velvet glove as a lacy sleeve with a bottle of vitriol concealed in its folds.

Alexander Woollcott, American writer and critic (1887–1943). *While Rome Burns* (1934).

See also FACES.

Deserts

2 [The Dean of York] deserves to be preached to death by wild curates.

(Revd) Sydney Smith, English clergyman, essayist and wit (1771–1845). Quoted in Lady Holland, *A Memoir of Sydney Smith* (1855).

Desires

3 *Mrs Robinson:*
Do you find me undesirable?
Ben:
Oh no, Mrs Robinson. I think ... I think you're the most attractive of all my parents' friends. I mean that.

Lines from film *The Graduate* (US 1967). Screenwriters: Buck Henry, Calder Willingham. Spoken by Anne Bancroft (Mrs Robinson) and Dustin Hoffman (Ben Braddock).

4 There are two tragedies in life. One is to lose your heart's desire. The other is to gain it.

Bernard Shaw, Irish playwright and critic (1856–1950). *Man and Superman*, Act 4 (1903).

5 The other day we had a long discourse with [Lady Orkney] about love; and she told us a saying ... which I thought excellent, that in men, desire begets love, and in women that love begets desire.

Jonathan Swift, Anglo-Irish writer and clergyman (1667–1745). *Journal to Stella* (1768) – for 30 October 1712.

6 In this world there are only two tragedies. One is not getting what one wants, and the other is getting it.

Oscar Wilde, Irish playwright, poet and wit (1854–1900). *Lady Windermere's Fan*, Act 3 (1892).

Despair

7 Been Down So Long, It Looks Like Up to Me.

Richard Farina, American author (?1936–66). Title of book (1966; film US, 1971).

Destinations

8 Very flat, Norfolk.

(Sir) Noël Coward, English entertainer and writer (1899–1973). *Private Lives*, Act 1 (1930). Amanda is honeymooning with her second husband at the same hotel as her first, Elyot, is honeymooning with his new wife. In a wonderfully clipped conversation that nevertheless hints that they are probably still in love, Elyot remarks that he met his new wife at a house party in Norfolk. This is Amanda's famously dismissive response.

9 *Boswell:*
Should you not like to see Dublin, Sir?
Johnson:
No, Sir! Dublin is only a worse capital.
Boswell:
Is not the Giant's Causeway worth seeing?
Johnson:
Worth seeing? yes; but not worth going to see.

(Dr) Samuel Johnson, English writer and lexicographer (1709–84). James Boswell, *The Life of Samuel Johnson* (1791) – for 12 October 1779. Johnson always had an aversion to visiting Ireland. In fact, he never went there, though the strength of his views as here – and next – might lead one to suppose that he had.

10 Dublin, though a place much worse than London, is not so bad as Iceland.

(Dr) Samuel Johnson. In a note to Boswell's *Life* (not first edition). Johnson visited neither Dublin nor Iceland.

Details

1 One should absorb the colour of life, but one should never remember its details. Details are always vulgar.

Oscar Wilde, Irish playwright, poet and wit (1854–1900). *The Picture of Dorian Gray*, Chap. 8 (1891).

2 Details are the only things that interest.

Oscar Wilde. *Lord Arthur Savile's Crime*, Chap. 1 (1891).

Devil

3 An apology for the devil: it must be remembered that we have heard only one side of the case; God has written all the books.

Samuel Butler, English novelist and writer (1835–1902). *Notebooks* (1912).

Diamonds

An ex-boyfriend of much-married actress Zsa Zsa Gabor commented:

4 She has proved beyond doubt that diamonds are the hardest thing in the world – to get back.

Anonymous. Quoted in my book *A Year of Stings and Squelches* (1985).

5 Kissing your hand may make you feel very very good but a diamond and safire bracelet lasts forever.

Anita Loos, American writer (1893–1981). *Gentlemen Prefer Blondes,* Chap. 4 (1925). A caption to the frontispiece of the original edition has this slightly different version: 'Kissing your hand may make you feel very good but a diamond bracelet lasts forever.' Either way, this was the inspiration for the Jule Styne / Leo Robin song 'Diamonds Are a Girl's Best Friend' in the 1949 stage musical and 1953 film based on the book.

6 Let us not be too particular. It is better to have old second-hand diamonds than none at all.

Mark Twain, American writer (1835–1910). *Following the Equator*, Vol. 1 (1897).

Diaries

7 It's the good girls keep diaries. The bad girls never have the time.

Tallulah Bankhead, American actress (1903–68). Attributed in John Robert Colombo, *Wit and Wisdom of the Moviemakers* (1979).

8 I always say, keep a diary and some day it'll keep you.

Line from film *Every Day's a Holiday* (US 1937). Screenwriter: Mae West. Spoken by Mae West (Peaches O'Day).

9 Things of so small concern or moment, who
Would stuff his Diary with, or care to know?
As what he wore, thought, laugh'd at,
  where he walked,
When farted, where he pissed, with whom
  he talked.

Robert Heath, English poet (17th century). *Clarastella*, 'Satyr 1' (1650).

10 To write a diary every day is like returning to one's own vomit.

Enoch Powell, English Conservative then Ulster Unionist politician (1912–98). In *The Sunday Times* (6 November 1977).

11 *Gwendolen*:
I never travel without my diary. One should always have something sensational to read on the train.

Oscar Wilde, Irish playwright, poet and wit (1854–1900). *The Importance of Being Earnest*, Act 2 (1895).

12 Everyone should keep someone else's diary.

Oscar Wilde. In Ada Leverson, *Letters to the Sphinx from Oscar Wilde* (1930).

Dictators

13 I believe in benevolent dictatorships, provided I am the dictator.

(Sir) Richard Branson, English entrepreneur (1950–). A much-repeated observation. Quoted in *The Observer* (25 November 1984).

Dictionaries

1 A malevolent device for cramping the growth of a language and making it hard and inelastic.

Ambrose Bierce, American journalist (1842–?1914). *The Cynic's Word Book* (later retitled *The Devil's Dictionary*) (1906).

2 Lexicographer: A writer of dictionaries; a harmless drudge, that busies himself in tracing the original, and detailing the signification of words.

(Dr) Samuel Johnson, English writer and lexicographer (1709–84). *A Dictionary of the English Language* (1755).

Diets

3 She used to diet on any kind of food she could lay her hands on.

Arthur ('Bugs') Baer, American humorist (1897?–1969). Quoted in *The Treasury of Humorous Quotations*, eds Evan Esar & Nicolas Bentley (1951).

Having taken it into his head not to eat vegetables, Brummell was asked by a lady if he had never eaten any at all in his life:

4 Yes, madam, I once ate a pea.

Beau Brummell, English dandy (1778–1840). Quoted in Charles Dickens, *Bleak House*, Chap. 12 (1852–3).

5 Don't eat too many almonds; they add weight to the breasts.

Colette, French novelist (1873–1954). *Gigi* (1944).

6 In the matter of diet – I have been persistently strict in sticking to the things that didn't agree with me until one or the other of us got the best of it.

Mark Twain, American writer (1835–1910). *Mark Twain's Speeches*, ed. A.B. Paine (1910).

Differences

7 It's a good job we are all different – otherwise they wouldn't sell many mixed biscuits.

Anonymous. Quoted on BBC Radio *Quote ... Unquote* (28 February 2000).

8 It were not best that we should all think alike; it is difference of opinion that makes horse-races.

Mark Twain, American writer (1835–1910). *Pudd'nhead Wilson*, Chap. 19 (1894).

Dignity

9 The door behind him [Lord Emsworth] opened, and Beach the butler entered, a solemn procession of one.

(Sir) P(elham) G. Wodehouse, English-born novelist and lyricist (1881–1975). *Leave It To Smith*, Chap. 1 (1923).

Dining

10 If the soup had been as warm as the wine, and the wine as old as the fish, and the fish as young as the maid, and the maid as willing as the hostess, it would have been a very good meal.

Anonymous (Austro-Hungarian). Quoted by Clement Freud on BBC Radio *Quote ... Unquote* (15 January 1979).

11 If Jesus Christ were to come today, people would not even crucify Him. They would ask Him to dinner, and hear what He had to say, and make fun of it.

Thomas Carlyle, Scottish historian and philosopher (1795–1881). Quoted in *The Treasury of Humorous Quotations*, eds Evan Esar & Nicolas Bentley (1951).

12 It isn't so much what's on the table that matters, as what's on the chairs.

(Sir) W.S. Gilbert, English writer and lyricist (1836–1911). Quoted in Hesketh Pearson, *Gilbert and Sullivan* (1935).

13 The best number for a dinner party is two: myself and a damn good head waiter.

Nubar Gulbenkian, English industrialist and philanthropist (1896–1972). Quoted in *The Daily Telegraph* (14 January 1965).

1 A man seldom thinks with more earnestness of anything than he does of his dinner.

(Dr) Samuel Johnson, English writer and lexicographer (1709–84). Quoted in *The Treasury of Humorous Quotations*, eds Evan Esar & Nicolas Bentley (1951).

2 When you ask one friend to dine,
Give him your best wine!
When you ask two,
The second best will do!

Henry Wadsworth Longfellow, American poet (1807–82). Quoted in Brander Matthews, *Recreations of an Anthologist* (1904).

3 At a dinner party one should eat wisely but not too well, and talk well but not too wisely.

W. Somerset Maugham, English writer (1874–1965). Written in 1896 but not reproduced until *A Writer's Notebook* (1949).

4 Dinner at the Huntercombes' possessed 'only two dramatic features – the wine was a farce and the food a tragedy'.

Anthony Powell, English novelist (1905–2000). *The Acceptance World* (1955).

5 The cocktail party – a device for paying off obligations to people you don't want to invite for dinner.

Charles Merrill Smith. *Instant Status* (1972).

6 Dinners are given mostly in the middle classes by way of revenge.

William Thackeray, English novelist (1811–63). *The Book of Snobs* (1847).

7 The number must neither be less than the graces, nor more than the muses.

Fanny Trollope, English novelist and travel-writer (1780–1863). *The Blue Belles of England* (1842).

See also FOOD AND FOOD CRITICISM.

Diplomacy

8 Diplomacy. The art of saying 'Nice Doggie!' till you can find a rock.

Wynn Catlin, American writer (1930–). Quoted in Bennett Cerf, *The Laugh's On Me* (1961).

9 Talking jaw to jaw is better than going to war.

(Sir) Winston S. Churchill, British Conservative Prime Minister and writer (1874–1965). At a White House lunch (26 June 1954).

10 It is fortunate that diplomats generally have long noses, since usually they cannot see beyond them.

Paul Claudel, French diplomat and writer (1868–1955). While ambassador to Washington, but denied by him in a letter to Burton Stevenson.

11 I went first to Germany, and there I spoke with the German Foreign Minister, Herr … Herr and there. And we exchanged many frank words in our respective languages.

Peter Cook, English humorist (1937–95). Impersonating Harold Macmillan in *Beyond the Fringe*, 'T.V.P.M.' (1961).

12 Diplomats are useful only in fair weather. As soon as it rains they drown in every drop.

Charles de Gaulle, French general and President (1890–1970). Quoted by a former aide, Constantin Melnick, in *Newsweek* Magazine (19 April 1967).

13 A diplomat is a man who always remembers a woman's birthday but never remembers her age.

Robert Frost, American poet (1874–1963). Quoted in *The Treasury of Humorous Quotations*, eds Evan Esar & Nicolas Bentley (1951).

14 Modern diplomats approach every problem with an open mouth.

Arthur Goldberg, American lawyer and diplomat (1908–90). Quoted in *The New York Times* (19 April 1967), when he was US Ambassador to the United Nations.

1 Diplomacy is to do and say
The nastiest thing in the nicest way.

Isaac Goldberg, American critic (1887–1938). *The Reflex.*

2 Conferences at the top level are always courteous. Name-calling is left to the foreign ministers.

W. Averell Harriman, American diplomat (1891–1986). Quoted in news summaries (1 August 1955).

3 Diplomacy – lying in state.

Oliver Herford, American humorist (1863–1935). Quoted in *The Treasury of Humorous Quotations*, eds Evan Esar & Nicolas Bentley (1951).

4 Megaphone diplomacy leads to a dialogue of the deaf.

Geoffrey Howe (Lord Howe), English Conservative politician (1926–). Quoted in *The Observer*, 'Sayings of the Week' (29 September 1985).

5 Just British diplomacy, Doctor. Never climb a fence if you can sit on it. An old foreign office proverb.

Line from film *The Lady Vanishes* (UK 1938). Screenwriters: Alma Reville, Sidney Gilliatt, Frank Launder (from a novel). Spoken by Michael Redgrave (Gilbert).

6 Diplomats are just as essential to starting a war as soldiers are for finishing it.

Will Rogers, American humorist (1879–1935). *The Autobiography of Will Rogers* (1949).

7 A diplomat these days is nothing but a head-waiter who's allowed to sit down occasionally.

(Sir) Peter Ustinov, English actor and writer (1921–). *Romanoff and Juliet*, Act 1 (1956).

8 To make a good salad is to be a brilliant diplomatist – the problem is entirely the same in both cases. To know how much oil one must mix with one's vinegar.

Oscar Wilde, Irish playwright, poet and wit (1854–1900). *Vera, or the Nihilists*, Act 2 (1880).

9 An ambassador is an honest man sent to lie abroad for the good of his country.

(Sir) Henry Wotton, English diplomat and poet (1568–1639). Quoted in Izaak Walton, *Life of Sir Henry Wotton* (1651). Wotton was England's envoy to Venice in the reign of King James I. His punning view of the diplomat's calling very nearly cost him his job. As Walton recounted, Wotton had managed to offend a Roman Catholic controversialist called Gasper Scioppius. In 1611 Scioppius produced a book called *Ecclesiasticus*, which abused James I and related an anecdote concerning Wotton: on his way out to Italy in 1604, Wotton had stayed at Augsburg where a merchant, Christoper Fleckmore, invited him to inscribe his name in an album. Wotton wrote: *'Legatus est vir bonus peregre missus ad mentiendum Reipublicae causa'* – 'which he would have been content should have been thus Englished: An ambassador is an honest man, sent to lie abroad for the good of his country.' Scioppius, on the basis of this joke, accused James I of sending a confessed liar to represent him abroad.

According to the *Dictionary of National Biography*, 'Wotton's chances of preferment were ruined by the king's discovery of the contemptuous definition of an ambassador's function … James invited explanations of the indiscreet jest. Wotton told the king that the affair was "a merriment," but he was warned to take it seriously, and he deemed it prudent to prepare two apologies.'

James said that one of these 'sufficiently commuted for a greater offence', but the joke had done its damage, and, although Wotton was later to be given further diplomatic work and become Provost of Eton, he continued to suffer for it.

Directions

10 *Motorist:*

Can you direct me to Puddleford?

Native:

Well sir, by rights, to get there I reckon yew didn't ought to start from yere at arl.

George Belcher, English cartoonist. Caption to cartoon in *Punch* (31 March 1926).

Dirt

Of Hannen Swaffer, journalist:

1 Whenever I see his fingernails, I thank God I don't have to look at his feet.

(Dame) Athene Seyler, English actress (1889–1990). Quoted in Bryan Forbes, *Ned's Girl* (1977).

2 Truly Alfred Tennyson was the dirtiest laureate that ever lived. But there was more to a man than a washed neck or clean fingernails. As he once cleverly blurted to a fellow who had impudently criticized a dirty collar, 'I dare say yours would not be as clean as mine if you had worn it a fortnight!'

Lynne Truss, English novelist. *Tennyson's Gift* (1996).

Disagreement

3 To disagree with three-fourths of the British public on all points is one of the first elements of sanity, one of the deepest consolations in all moments of spiritual doubt.

Oscar Wilde, Irish playwright, poet and wit (1854–1900). Quoted in Herbert V. Prochnow, Snr & Jnr, *A Treasury of Humorous Quotations* (1969).

Disappointment

4 Nothing is so good as it seems beforehand.

George Eliot, English novelist (1819–80). *Silas Marner*, Chap. 18 (1861).

When asked how he felt after a defeat in the New York elections:

5 Somewhat like that boy in Kentucky, who stubbed his toe while running to see his sweetheart. The boy said he was too big to cry, and far too badly hurt to laugh.

Abraham Lincoln, American Republican President (1809–65). Quoted in *Frank Leslie's Illustrated Weekly* (22 November 1862).

6 Blessed is the man who expects nothing, for he shall never be disappointed.

Alexander Pope, English poet (1688–1744). In a joint letter to William Fortescue (23 September 1725), Pope – in his section – quotes this 'ninth beatitude' from a man of wit 'who like a man of wit was a long time in gaol,' but his identity has not been established. Pope repeated the quotation in a letter *to* John Gay, when he was commiserating with him on lack of preferment at court (16 October 1727). The saying has also been ascribed to the (later) 'Peter Pindar' (John Wolcot), English satirist and physician (1738–1819), as the first lines of his 'Ode to Pitt', 'Blessed are they that nought expect, / For they shall not be disappointed'.

Disbelief

7 My god, my god, I shall die a happy man if I can make one person disbelieve in God.

(Sir) A(lfred) J. Ayer, English philosopher (1910–89). Quoted in *The Observer*, 'Sayings of the Week' (1 July 1989).

8 Oh, life is a glorious cycle of song,
A medley of extemporanea;
And love is a thing that can never go wrong –
And I am Marie of Roumania.

Dorothy Parker, American writer (1893–1967). *Not So Deep as a Well*, 'Comment' (1937).

Disc jockeys

9 The wriggling ponces of the spoken word.

D.G. Bridson, English radio producer (1910–80). Attributed on BBC Radio *Quote ... Unquote* (10 May 1978).

Disclaimers

10 No fish were killed or injured during the making of the film.

Screen title from film *A River Runs Through It* (US 1992). Screenwriter: Richard Friedenburg. However, it is said that salmon was served at the Hollywood premiere ...

11 NO DINOSAURS WERE HARMED IN THE MAKING OF THIS MOTION PICTURE.

Screen title from film *The Flintstones* (US 1994). Screenwriters: various (after TV series).

Disgruntlement

1 He spoke with a certain what-is-it in his voice, and I could see that, if not actually disgruntled, he was far from being gruntled.

(Sir) P(elham) G. Wodehouse, English-born novelist and lyricist (1881–1975). *The Code of the Woosters*, Chap. 1 (1938).

Dishevelment

Of a close friend:

2 One cannot say that she was dressed. She was clothed. And so uncertainly that it was unsure she would remain even that.

(Dame) Ivy Compton-Burnett, English novelist (1884–1969). Quoted by Julian Mitchell on BBC Radio *Quote … Unquote* (5 January 1982).

Dismissal

3 Go, and never darken my towels again!

Line from film *Duck Soup* (US 1933). Screenwriters: Bert Kalmar, Harry Ruby, Arthur Sheekman, Nat Perrin. Spoken by Groucho Marx (Rufus T. Firefly).

Divorce

4 It was partially my fault that we got divorced … I tended to place my wife under a pedestal.

Woody Allen, American film actor, writer and director (1937–). In monologue 'I Had a Rough Marriage' (1964).

5 Divorces are made in heaven.

Oscar Wilde, Irish playwright, poet and wit (1854–1900). *The Importance of Being Earnest*, Act 1 (1895).

Dobedobedo

6 To do is to be – Rousseau.
To be is to do – Sartre.
Dobedobedo – Sinatra.

Anonymous (graffito). A version is included in Reisner & Wechsler, *Encyclopedia of Graffiti* (1974).

Doctors

7 Doctor Bell fell down the well
And broke his collar-bone.
Doctors should attend the sick
And leave the well alone.

Anonymous (18th century?). Quoted in *Verse and Worse*, ed. Arnold Silcock (1958 edn).

To Christine Keeler, the 'good time girl' in the British political Profumo scandal of 1963:

8 A few days on your feet and we'll soon have you back in bed.

Anonymous (doctor). Quoted in H. Montgomery Hyde, *A Tangled Web*, Chap. 10 (1986).

9 My dear old friend King George V told me he would never have died but for that vile doctor, Lord Dawson of Penn.

Margot Asquith (Countess of Oxford and Asquith) (1864–1945). An observation that Lady Asquith made several times in her old age, but especially to Lord David Cecil (and recorded first by Mark Bonham Carter in his introduction to *The Autobiography of Margot Asquith*, 1962 edn).

10 Physicians of the Utmost Fame
Were called at once; but when they came
They answered, as they took their fees,
'There is no cure for this disease.'

Hilaire Belloc, French-born English poet and writer (1870–1953). *Cautionary Tales*, 'Henry King' (1907).

11 Thou shalt not kill; but need'st not strive
Officiously to keep alive.

Arthur Hugh Clough, English poet (1819–61). 'The Latest Decalogue' (1862). Clough was writing an *ironical* version of the Ten Commandments – so these lines were not serious advice to doctors (in which sense they have sometimes been quoted, however).

12 I don't know much about his ability, but he's got a good bedside manner.

George Du Maurier, French-born British artist, cartoonist and novelist (1834–96). Caption to cartoon in *Punch* (15 March 1884).

1 God heals and the doctor takes the fee.

Benjamin Franklin, American politician and scientist (1706–90). *Poor Richard's Almanack* (November 1736). But the proverb, 'God heals, and the physician hath the thanks' was known by 1640. This has also been attributed to Bernard Shaw as 'Nature effects the cure, all the doctor does is pass the hat round.'

2 He's a Fool that makes his Doctor his Heir.

Benjamin Franklin. In the same publication (February 1733).

3 Doctors know what you tell them.

Don Herold, American humorist and artist (1889–1966). Quoted in *The Treasury of Humorous Quotations*, eds Evan Esar & Nicolas Bentley (1951).

4 From New Delhi to Darjeeling
I have done my share of healing
And I've never yet been beaten or outboxed.

Herbert Kretzmer, English lyricist. Song, 'Goodness Gracious Me', to music by Dave Lee. Sung in a 1960 recording by Peter Sellers and Sophia Loren as the characters (poor Indian doctor and the richest woman in the world) they were playing in the film of Shaw's *The Millionairess*.

5 Cur'd yesterday of my disease,
I died last night of my physician.

Matthew Prior, English poet and diplomat (1664–1721). 'The Remedy Worse Than the Disease' (1727).

6 The best doctors in the world are Doctor Diet, Doctor Quiet and Doctor Merryman.

Jonathan Swift, Anglo-Irish writer and clergyman (1667–1745). *Polite Conversation*, 2 (1738) – a work made up of well-established sayings and expressions.

7 It's amazing the little harm they do when one considers the opportunities they have.

Mark Twain, American writer (1835–1910). Attributed remark.

8 He had had much experience of physicians, and said 'the only way to keep your health is to eat what you don't want, drink what you don't like, and do what you'd druther not.'

Mark Twain. *Following the Equator* (1897).

9 I only care to see doctors when I am in perfect health; then they comfort one, but when one is ill they are most depressing.

Oscar Wilde, Irish playwright, poet and wit (1854–1900). In *The Letters of Oscar Wilde*, ed. Rupert Hart-Davis (1962).

Dogs and dog-owners

10 I am his Highness' dog at Kew;
Pray tell me, sir, whose dog are you?

Alexander Pope, English poet (1688–1744). 'Epigram Engraved on the Collar of a Dog which I gave to his Royal Highness' – i.e. Frederick, Prince of Wales (1738).

11 The dogs bark but the caravan passes.

Anonymous (proverb). Meaning 'critics make a noise, but it does not last'. Peter Hall, the theatre director, was given to quoting this 'Turkish proverb' during outbursts of public hostility in the mid-1970s. In *Within a Budding Grove* – the 1924 translation of Marcel Proust's *A l'Ombre des Jeunes Filles en Fleurs* (1918) – C.K. Scott Moncrieff has: 'The fine Arab proverb, "The dogs may bark; the caravan goes on!"' In the film *The Lives of a Bengal Lancer* (US 1934), 'Mohammed Khan' quotes a proverb, 'The little jackal barks, but the caravan passes.' Truman Capote entitled a book, *Dogs Bark: Public People and Private Places* (1973). As an 'Arab proverb', it is quoted by George Tabori in his book entitled *The Caravan Passes* (1951).

12 'Is there any other point to which you would wish to draw my attention?' 'To the curious incident of the dog in the night-time.' 'The dog did nothing in the night-time.' 'That was the curious incident,' remarked Sherlock Holmes.

(Sir) Arthur Conan Doyle, Scottish-born novelist (1859–1930). *The Memoirs of Sherlock Holmes*, 'Silver Blaze' (1894). A much quoted example of an absence of fact that could provide an important clue in detection. Possibly most usually alluded to now as 'the dog that did not bark in the night'.

1 I loathe people who keep dogs. They're cowards who have not got the guts to bite people themselves.

August Strindberg, Swedish playwright and novelist (1849–1912). Attributed remark.

Doing

2 Go directly, and see what she's doing, and tell her she mustn't!

Anonymous cartoonist (possibly George Du Maurier). Caption to cartoon entitled 'EXPERIENTIA DOCET' in *Punch*, Vol. 63 (16 November 1872). It shows a girl, Emily, talking to her nanny. 'Where's baby, Madge?' Madge replies, 'In the other room, I think, Emily.' And then Emily comes up with this pronouncement.

3 Everyone said it couldn't be done,
And if he tried, he'd rue it.
But he tackled the thing that couldn't
be done–
And found that he couldn't do it.

Anonymous. A version of this parody is quoted in *The Fireside Book of Humorous Poetry*, ed. William Cole (1959), but it dates back to the 1930s. Should you wonder what it was parodying – the answer is a bit of uplift called 'It Couldn't Be Done' by Edgar A. Guest, the American poet (1881–1959), which begins: 'Somebody said that it couldn't be done, but he with a chuckle replied / That "maybe it couldn't but he would be one that wouldn't say no 'till he'd tried". / So he buckled right in with a trace of a grin on his face. If he worried, he hid it. / He started to sing as he tackled the thing that couldn't be done. And he did it!'

4 The prime truth of woman, the universal mother … that if a thing is worth doing, it is worth doing badly.

G.K. Chesterton, English poet, novelist and critic (1874–1936). *What's Wrong with the World*, 'Folly and Female Education' (1910). When the Prince of Wales made his maiden speech to the House of Lords (13 June 1974), he began by ascribing this to Oscar Wilde. Frank Muir pointed out this solecism to *The Times* and added, 'If a thing is worth quoting, it is worth quoting badly.'

The father of someone I know always used to say: 'If a thing's worth doing, it's worth doing *well enough*.'

5 Let's find out what everyone is doing,
And then stop everyone from doing it.

(Sir) A(lan) P. Herbert, English writer and politician (1890–1971). 'Let's Stop Somebody from Doing Something' (1930).

6 Positively the best thing a man can have to do is nothing, and next to that, perhaps, good works.

Charles Lamb, English essayist (1775–1834). Quoted in *The Treasury of Humorous Quotations*, eds Evan Esar & Nicolas Bentley (1951).

7 Do not do unto others as you would that they should do unto you. Their tastes may not be the same.

Bernard Shaw, Irish playwright and critic (1856–1950). *Man and Superman*, 'Maxims for Revolutionaries' (1903).

8 All the things I really like to do are either illegal, immoral or fattening.

Alexander Woollcott, American writer and critic (1887–1943). *The Knock at the Stage Door* (1933). In 1934, W.C. Fields uttered the line, 'According to you, everything I like to do is either illegal, immoral or fattening' in the film *Six of a Kind* (US). Hence, presumably, the song, 'It's Illegal, It's Immoral Or It Makes You Fat' by Griffin, Hecht and Bruce, and popularized in the UK by the Beverley Sisters (1950s).

Domestic life

9 They that wash on Monday
Have all the week to dry;
They that wash on Tuesday
Are not so much awry;
They that wash on Wednesday
Are not so much to blame;
They that wash on Thursday
Wash for shame;
They that wash on Friday
Wash in need;
And they that wash on Saturday,
Oh! they're sluts indeed.

Anonymous. Quoted in *The Oxford Dictionary of Quotations* (1953 edn). Known since 1865. *Scottish Nursery Ryhmes*, ed. Norah and William Montgomerie (1947), has a concluding: 'They that wash on Friday / Hae gey muckle need. / They that wash on Saturday / Are dirty daws indeed.'

1 Sex and socks are not compatible.

Angela Carter, English writer (1940–92). Quoted in *The Observer*, 'Sayings of the Year' (27 December 1987).

Donkeys

2 A donkey is a horse translated into Dutch.

George Christoph Lichtenberg, German scientist and drama critic (1742–99). *Aphorisms*.

Donne, John

ENGLISH POET AND PRIEST (1572–1631)

3 As a youth, John Donne
Had a lot of fun.
After he hung up his balls
He became Dean of St Paul's.

Ivan Berger. Attributed verse.

Doors

4 When one door closes another door closes.

Anonymous. A cynical variant (which I first heard in 1969) of the proverb 'God never shuts one door but He opens another' (known by 1586). The variant also comes – perhaps more usually – in the form 'one door closes, another door shuts'.

Double-entendres

5 There is nothing I like better than to lie on my bed for an hour with my favourite Trollope.

Anonymous (Bishop of Bath and Wells). Quoted in *Chips: The Diaries of Sir Henry Channon*, ed. Robert Rhodes James (1967) – entry for 4 April 1943. Channon records that he visited Wells Cathedral and then lunched at the Palace with the Bishop of Bath and Wells. Inevitably, there was much talk of Barchester, and the Bishop said this, to everybody's consternation.

To Howard Dietz on his musical Beat the Devil:

6 I understand your play is full of single entendre.

George S. Kaufman, American playwright (1889–1961). Quoted in Ned Sherrin, *Cutting Edge* (1984).

7 It was good to be ashore. I hadn't felt my legs on land for a long while – or anybody else's for that matter. I undressed and lay on my bed looking up my Baedeker.

Lines from BBC Radio *Round the Horne* (14 May 1967). Script by Barry Took and Marty Feldman. Spoken by Kenneth Horne.

Speaking at Carlton Club dinner to mark Lord Whitelaw's retirement:

8 Every Prime Minister needs a Willie.

Margaret Thatcher (Baroness Thatcher), British Conservative Prime Minister (1925–). Quoted by Michael Cockerell in *The Guardian* (8 April 1989). Possibly appreciating the double entendre, she is said to have added, without effect, 'That is not to go beyond this room.'

Doubt

9 If you are ever in doubt as to whether or not you should kiss a pretty girl, always give her the benefit of the doubt.

Thomas Carlyle, Scottish historian and philosopher (1795–1881). Quoted in *The Treasury of Humorous Quotations*, eds Evan Esar & Nicolas Bentley (1951).

Dreams

10 He dreamed he was eating Shredded Wheat and woke up to find the mattress half gone.

Fred Allen, American comedian (1894–1956). Quoted in *The Treasury of Humorous Quotations*, eds Evan Esar & Nicolas Bentley (1951).

11 Last night I dreamt I ate a ten-pound marshmallow. When I woke up the pillow was gone.

Tommy Cooper, English comedian (1921–84). Quoted in John Fisher, *Funny Way To Be a Hero* (1973).

12 I dreamt that I was making a speech in the House. I woke up, and by Jove I was!

10th Duke of Devonshire, English politician (1895–1950). Quoted in Winston S. Churchill, *Thoughts and Adventures* (1932).

Dress

1 The miniskirt is a functional thing. It enables young ladies to run faster – and because of it they may have to.

Anonymous. In *Time* Magazine (1960s).

Edward VII had an obsessive interest in correct attire. On one occasion when a courtier unwisely appeared in a loud check suit, the King said:

2 Goin' rattin', 'arris?

Edward VII, British King (1841–1910). Quoted on BBC Radio *Quote ... Unquote* (25 June 1986). Another version is that the offending Harris appeared at Ascot in a brown bowler hat.

When Chauncey Depew asked what was holding up her daringly low-cut gown:

3 Your age and my discretion.

Mary Garden, Scottish-born singer (1877–1967). Quoted in *Time* Magazine (13 January 1967).

4 Boy George is all England needs – another queen who can't dress.

Joan Rivers, American entertainer (1937–). Quoted in *Scorn*, ed. Matthew Parris (1995 edn).

5 'You got to be awful rich to dress as bad as you do,' he said.

John Steinbeck, American novelist (1902–68). *Travels With Charley In Search of America* (1962).

Drinks and drinking

6 If all be true that I do think,
There are five reasons we should drink:
Good wine – a friend – or being dry –
Or lest we should be by and by –
Or any other reason why.

Henry Aldrich, English academic (1647–1710) – after the French of Jacques Sirmond (1559–1651). Quoted in *The Faber Book of Epigrams and Epitaphs*, ed. Geoffrey Grigson (1977). Aldrich was Dean of Christ Church, Oxford. Sirmond was a French Jesuit and scholar.

7 I feel no pain, dear mother, now,
But oh, I am so dry!
O take me to a brewery
And leave me there to die.

Anonymous. The *Penguin Dictionary of Quotations* (1960) gives this as an anonymous 'shanty', but really it is just a parody of an old weepie, 'The Collier's Dying Child' – sometimes known as 'Little Jim' – by the English poet Edward Farmer (*c.*1809–76), of which the eighth verse is: 'I have no pain, dear mother, now / But oh! I am so dry: / Just moisten poor Jim's lips once more; / And, mother, don't you cry!'

8 'I love a Martini,' said Mabel,
'I only have two at the most.
After three, I am under the table,
After four, I am under my host.'

Anonymous. Quoted by John Julius Norwich on BBC Radio *Quote ... Unquote* (30 October 2000). Dorothy Parker is supposed to have said, 'One more drink and I'd be under the host' – quoted in John Keats, *You Might as Well Live* (1970).

9 'Indeed, senora,' said Sancho, 'I never yet drank out of wickedness; from thirst I have very likely, for I have nothing of the hypocrite in me; I drink when I'm inclined, or, if I'm not inclined, when they offer it to me, so as not to look either strait-laced or ill-bred; for when a friend drinks one's health what heart can be so hard as not to return it?'

Miguel de Cervantes, Spanish novelist (1547–1616). *Don Quixote*, Pt 2, Chap. 33 (1615).

10 I have taken more out of alcohol than alcohol has taken out of me.

(Sir) Winston S. Churchill, British Conservative Prime Minister and writer (1874–1965). Quoted in Willans & Roetter, *The Wit of Winston Churchill* (1954). Also later in Quentin Reynolds, *By Quentin Reynolds* (1963).

In reply to his wife's remark, I hate the taste of beer':

11 So do many people – to begin with. It is, however, a prejudice that many have been able to overcome.

(Sir) Winston S. Churchill. Quoted in *The Wit of Sir Winston* (1965).

1 When I was younger, I made it a rule never to take a strong drink before lunch. It is now my rule never to do so before breakfast.

(Sir) Winston S. Churchill. Quoted in the same collection as above.

2 You can no more keep a martini in the refrigerator than you can keep a kiss there. The proper union of gin and vermouth … is one of the happiest marriages on earth and one of the shortest lived.

Bernard De Voto, American historian and writer (1897–1955). In *Harper's Magazine* (December 1949).

3 'Mrs Harris,' I says, 'Leave the bottle on the chimley-piece, and don't ask me to take none, but let me put my lips to it when I am so dispoged.'

Charles Dickens, English novelist (1812–70). *Martin Chuzzlewit*, Chap. 19 (1844). Mrs Gamp speaking.

4 Sherry gives rise to no thoughts.

R. Druitt. Quoted in *Geoffrey Madan's Notebooks* (1981).

5 'I've brought you a glass of wine, Mr Professor. Please drink it!' 'Vat! Pefore tinner? Ach, vy?' 'Because Mummy says you drink like a fish, and I want to see you – !'

George du Maurier, French-born British artist, cartoonist and novelist (1834–96). Caption to cartoon in *Punch* (1 November 1890) with the title 'Enfant Terrible'.

6 A man shouldn't fool with booze until he's fifty; then he's a damn fool if he doesn't.

William Faulkner, American novelist (1897–1962). Quoted in Webb & Green, *William Faulkner of Oxford* (1965).

7 I was in love with a beautiful blonde once, dear. She drove me to drink. That's the one thing I'm indebted to her for.

W.C. Fields, American comedian (1879–1946). In film *Never Give a Sucker an Even Break* (US 1941). Screenwriters: John T. Neville, Prescot Chaplin (from story by Otis Criblecoblis, i.e. Fields). Spoken by Fields (The Great Man).

When asked why he did not drink water:

8 Fish fuck in it.

W.C. Fields. Quoted in Leslie Halliwell, *The Filmgoer's Book of Quotes* (1973).

9 Some weasel took the cork out of my lunch.

W.C. Fields. In film, *You Can't Cheat an Honest Man* (US 1939). Screenwriters: various, from story by Charles Bogle (W.C. Fields).

10 I exercise strong self-control. I never drink anything stronger than gin before breakfast.

W.C. Fields. Quoted in Robert Lewis Taylor, *W.C. Fields* (1950).

11 I always keep a supply of stimulant handy in case I see a snake – which I also keep handy.

W.C. Fields. Quoted in Corey Ford, *The Time of Laughter* (1967).

12 A soft drink turneth away company.

Oliver Herford, American humorist (1863–1935). Quoted in Herbert V. Prochnow, Snr & Jnr, *A Treasury of Humorous Quotations* (1969).

13 Malt does more than Milton can
To justify God's ways to man.

A.E. Housman, English poet (1859–36). *A Shropshire Lad*, 56 (1896).

14 I like liquor – its taste and its effects – and that is just the reason why I never drink it.

T.J. ('Stonewall') Jackson, American general (1824–63). Quoted in *The Life and Letters of Robert Edward Lee, Soldier and Man*, ed. William Jones (1906).

15 Cocktails have all the disagreeability without the utility of a disinfectant.

(Sir) Shane Leslie, Irish writer (1885–1971). Quoted in *The Observer* (1939).

16 I've made it a rule never to drink by daylight and never to refuse a drink after dark.

H.L. Mencken, American journalist and linguist (1880–1956). Quoted in the *New York Post* (18 September 1945).

1 A prohibitionist is the sort of man one wouldn't care to drink with – even if he drank.

H.L. Mencken. Attributed remark in 1920.

2 Candy
Is dandy
But liquor
Is quicker.

Ogden Nash, American poet (1902–71). *Hard Lines*, 'Reflection on Ice-Breaking' (1931).

3 I only drink to make other people seem more interesting.

George Jean Nathan, American drama critic (1882–1958). Quoted in news summaries (8 April 1958) and inscribed beneath his portrait in Charley O's bar, New York City, in 1958. Also attributed to Don Marquis as 'I drink only to make my friends seem interesting' in Edward Anthony, *O Rare Don Marquis* (1962).

4 Three highballs, and I think I'm St Francis of Assisi.

Dorothy Parker, American writer (1893–1967). 'Just a Little One' (1929).

5 There are two reasons for drinking: one is, when you are thirsty, to cure it; the other, when you are not thirsty, to prevent it.

Thomas Love Peacock, English poet and novelist (1785–1866). *Melincourt* (1817).

6 I don't have a drink problem except when I can't get one.

Tom Waits, American singer (1949–). Attributed remark in 1979.

7 I have made an important discovery … that alcohol, taken in sufficient quantities, produces all the effects of intoxication.

Oscar Wilde, Irish playwright, poet and wit (1854–1900). Attributed remark.

Drugs

On being asked to autograph a fan's school chemistry book:

8 Sure thing, man. I used to be a laboratory myself once.

Keith Richard, English rock musician and songwriter (1943–). Quoted in *The Independent on Sunday* (7 August 1994).

9 Cocaine is God's way of saying you're making too much money.

Robin Williams, American comic and actor (1951–). Quoted in *Screen International* (15 December 1990).

Drunks

10 Show me the way to go way
I'm bed and I want to go to tired.
I had a little hour about a drink ago
And it's head right to my gone.

Anonymous. Quoted as 'having been sung during the Second World War' on BBC Radio *Quote … Unquote* (17 November 1998).

11 Starkle, starkle, little twink,
Who the hell you are, you think?
I'm not under the alcofluence of incohol,
Though some thinkle peep I am.
I fool so feelish. I don't know who is me
For the drunker I sit here, the longer I get.

Anonymous. A drunken parody of 'Twinkle, twinkle, little star'. Said to have been published in the small magazine *Argosy* (*c.* 1943). A musical version was recorded by the English comedian Charlie Drake in 1959.

12 An alcoholic is someone who drinks too much – and you don't like anyway.

Anonymous. Quoted in *The Home Book of Humorous Quotations*, ed. A.K. Adams (1969).

13 I saw a notice which said 'Drink Canada Dry' and I've just started.

Brendan Behan, Irish playwright (1923–64). Quoted in my book *The 'Quote … Unquote' Book of Love, Death and the Universe* (1980), but probably a line ascribed to any famous drinker. The following version was used in his act by the American comedian Pat Henning (*fl.* 1950s): 'He was a drinkin' man, my fadder. One day he's standin' onna banks of the river, wonderin' what the hell folks can do with all that water, when suddenly he sees a great sign on the other side DRINK CANADA DRY. [Pause] So he went up there.'

When asked how often he drank:

1 Only twice a day – when I'm thirsty and when I'm not.

Brendan Behan. Quoted in *The Wit of Brendan Behan* (1968).

When John B. Keane's son Billy implored him not to have another drink:

2 Whatever you say, Bill, whatever you say. But I'll just have one more to wash down the last one.

Brendan Behan. Quoted in Gus Smith & Des Hickey, *The Real Keane* (1992).

In response to being told that all the martinis he was drinking were slow poison:

3 I'm in no hurry.

Robert Benchley, American humorist (1889–1945). Attributed remark.

4 Most British statesmen have either drunk too much or womanised too much. I never fell into the second category.

George Brown (Lord George-Brown), English Labour politician (1914–85). Quoted in *The Observer* (11 November 1974).

5 One evening in October, when I was one-
third sober,
An' taking home a 'load' with manly pride;
My poor feet began to stutter, so I lay
down in the gutter,
And a pig came up an' lay down by my side;
Then we sang 'It's all fair weather when
good fellows get together,'
Till a lady passing by was heard to say:
'You can tell a man who "boozes" by the
company he chooses'
And the pig got up and slowly walked away.

Benjamin Hapgood Burt, American songwriter (1880–1950). Song, 'The Pig Got Up and Slowly Walked Away' (1896), to music by F.V. Bowers. It is yet to be confirmed whether Burt originated these lines or whether they were based on something by another hand. Various versions of the lyrics are in circulation. *The Frank Muir Book* (1976) suggests that it was first attributed to Burt by the actor DeWolf Hopper in his book *Once a Clown, Always a Clown*, but that it has also been attributed to Aimor A. Dickson. Frank Muir seems to think the chances are, it began life in Ireland …

6 What's the use of getting sober, when you're gonna get drunk again?

Louis Jordan, American singer, musician and songwriter (1908–75). Attributed remark on a record made in 1942.

7 You're not drunk if you can lie on the floor without holding on.

Dean Martin, American entertainer (1917–95). Quoted in Paul Dickson, *The Official Rules* (1978). However, this is a venerable saying. 'No man is drunk so long as he can lie on the floor without holding on' is attributed to 'Author unidentified' in *H.L. Mencken's Dictionary of Quotations* (1942).

8 Not drunk is he who from the floor
Can rise alone and still drink more;
But drunk is he who prostrate lies,
Without the power to drink or rise.

Thomas Love Peacock, English novelist and poet (1785–1866). *The Misfortunes of Elfin* (1829).

9 Anybody that can't get drunk by midnight ain't trying.

Toots Shor. Quoted in Joey Adams, *Cindy and I*, Chap. 11 (1957).

10 'Can I liquor my stand?' Why, yes, like hell!
I care not how many a tossed I've pot,
I shall stralk quite weight and not yutter an ell,
My feech will not spalter the least little jot:

If you knownly had own! – well, I gave
him a dot,
And I said to him, 'Sergeant, I'll come like
a lamb –
The floor it seems like a storm in a yacht,
But I'm not so think as you drunk I am.'

(Sir) J(ohn) C. Squire, English poet, essayist and critic (1884–1958). 'Ballade of Soporific Absorption', in Maurice Baring, *One Hundred and One Ballades* (1931).

1 An alcoholic is someone you don't like who drinks as much as you do.

Dylan Thomas, Welsh poet (1914–53). Quoted in Constantine Fitzgibbon, *Life of Dylan Thomas* (1965).

2 I always say that if you've seen one Gentleman of the Press having delirium tremens, you've seen them all.

(Sir) P(elham) G. Wodehouse, English-born novelist and lyricist (1881–1975). *Bachelors Anonymous* (1973).

Dullness

Of Thomas Gray:

3 He was dull in a new way, and that made many people think him great.

(Dr) Samuel Johnson, English writer and lexicographer (1709–84). Quoted in James Boswell, *The Life of Samuel Johnson* (1791) – for 28 March 1775.

Of a law lord:

4 He is not only dull himself, but the cause of dullness in others.

(Dr) Samuel Johnson. Quoted in the same book as above – for 1783. In fact, Johnson is himself quoting Samuel Foote.

Duty

With a deep sigh, entering the bedchamber where Anne of Cleves awaits him:

5 The things I've done for England!

Line from film *The Private Life of Henry VIII* (UK 1933). Screenwriters: Lajos Biro, Arthur Wimperis. Spoken by Charles Laughton (Henry VIII). Popularly misquoted as 'the things I *do* for England'.

6 The first duty in life is to be as artificial as possible. What the second duty is no one has as yet discovered.

Oscar Wilde, Irish playwright, poet and wit (1854–1900). 'Phrases and Philosophies for the Use of the Young', in *The Chameleon* (December 1894).

7 Duty is what one expects from others, it is not what one does oneself.

Oscar Wilde. *A Woman of No Importance*, Act 2 (1893). Lord Illingworth speaking.

8 Duty ... merely means doing what other people want because they want it.

Oscar Wilde. 'The Soul of Man Under Socialism' (1895).

9 My duty to myself is to amuse myself terrifically.

Oscar Wilde. Quoted in André Gide, *Oscar Wilde: In Memoriam* (1910, 1949).

Dying words

10 I am dying with the help of too many physicians.

Alexander the Great, King of Macedonia (356–323 BC). Quoted in *The Treasury of Humorous Quotations*, Evan Esar & Nicolas Bentley (1951), and earlier, in the form, 'I die by the help of too many physicians' in *H.L. Mencken's Dictionary of Quotations* (1942). No other evidence has been found to support this attribution. The idea, however, surfaces elsewhere in the classical world. The dying Emperor Hadrian (AD 76–138) apparently came out with 'the popular saying "many physicians have slain a king"' (according to Chap. 69 of the Roman history by the Greek historian Dion Cassius). Pliny the Elder quoted an epitaph in AD 77 which goes *turba se medicorum periisse* or, in another version, *turba medicorum perii* (translated as, 'the brawling of the doctors killed me'). There is also said to be a more recent Czech proverb, 'Many doctors, death accomplished.' In addition, Molière, in the opening line of Act 2 of *L'Amour Médecin*, comes close to the sense: '*Que voulez-vous donc faire, Monsieur, de quatre médecins? N'est-ce pas assez d'un pour tuer une personne?* [What do you want with four doctors? Isn't one enough to kill someone?]' One might also compare the fable of Aesop's variously entitled 'The Sick Man and the Doctor' or 'Favourable Omens' etc. in which a sick man goes to the doctor and describes a symptom, to which the doctor replies, 'Ah, that's a good sign.' This happens again and again with different symptoms but the same reply from the doctor. Finally, a friend asks the sick man how he is doing, and the sick man replies, 'My friend, I am dying of good signs.'

Expiring in her one hundredth year during the course of a good meal:

1 Quick! Serve the dessert! I think I am dying.

Paulette Brillat-Savarin. She was the sister of Jean-Anthelme Brillat-Savarin, the celebrated French gastronome who died in 1826. Quoted on BBC Radio *Quote ... Unquote* (6 February 1979).

2 A certain amount of research on Last Despatches from the edge of the tomb has been made, but I feel there has always been a tendency on the part of the imminent mourners to tart the script up a bit.

Cassandra (Sir William Connor), English journalist (1909–67). Quoted in A. Andrews, *Quotations for Speakers and Writers* (1969).

3 Twiddly widdly toodle-oo,
I can no longer stay with you.
My time is short, I'll not prevail,
I'm off to seek the Holy Grail,
Twiddly widdly toodle-oo.

Clarence Day, American humorist (1874–1935). Reportedly written on his own deathbed.

During his final illness when it was suggested that he might like to receive a visit from Queen Victoria:

4 No, it is better not ... she would only ask me to take a message to Albert.

Benjamin Disraeli (1st Earl of Beaconsfield), British Conservative Prime Minister and writer (1804–81). Quoted by Robert Blake in his life, *Disraeli* (1966).

5 If Mr Selwyn calls again, shew him up; if I am alive I shall be delighted to see him; and if I am dead, he would like to see me.

Henry Fox Holland (1st Baron Holland), English Whig politician (1773–1840). Deathbed words, concerning George Selwyn, who, apparently, enjoyed executions and corpses. Quoted in J.H. Jesse, *George Selwyn and his Contemporaries* (1844).

6 Keep Paddy behind the big mixer.

(Sir) Alfred McAlpine, British civil engineer (1881–1944). Attributed last words, presumably encouraging the use of Irish labour in British building works. Could it rather have been said by Robert McAlpine, another member of the family? In 1999, John Lee commented: 'The version heard around Co. Kerry in the early 1960s was that McAlpine's last words of advice to his family were, "Keep the big mixer going and don't sack Paddy." I do not remember hearing a first name for the man but since he died prior to 1960, Sir Alf might fit the bill.'

Suggested dying words of a notable gourmand:

7 My exit is the result of too many entrées.

Richard Monckton Milnes (1st Baron Houghton), English politician and writer (1809–85). Quoted in Barnaby Conrad, *Famous Last Words* (1961).

8 It has all been very interesting.

Lady Mary Wortley Montagu, English writer (1689–1762). Lady Mary's wonderful 'dying words' (as given, for example, in Barnaby Conrad, *Famous Last Words*, 1961) have, unfortunately, not been authenticated. Robert Halsband in his *Life of Lady Mary Wortley Montagu* (1956) remarks that 'they are nowhere unequivocally recorded' and notes that the source – Iris Barry's *Portrait of Lady Mary Montagu* (1928) – is 'clearly fictitious'.

Last words:

9 Die, my dear doctor? That's the last thing I shall do.

Lord Palmerston, British Prime Minister (1784–1865). Quoted in E. Latham, *Famous Sayings and their Authors* (1961).

10 I think I could eat one of Bellamy's veal pies.

William Pitt (Pitt the Younger), British Prime Minister (1759–1806). Quoted in *The Oxford Dictionary of Quotations* (1941). Oral tradition. Pitt's formal last words' Oh, my country! how I leave my country!' refer to the breaking up of the British-led coalition in the wake of the defeat of Austro-Russian forces by Napoleon at the Battle of Austerlitz in 1805. Often given as ' ... how I love my country!'

Dying words

Last words before being shot by a sniper at the Battle of Spotsylvania in the American Civil War:

1 They couldn't hit an elephant at this dist–.

John Sedgwick, American general (1813–64). Quoted in J. Green, *Famous Last Words* (1979). Sedgwick was with the Union Army.

2 What *is* the answer? … In that case, what is the question?

Gertrude Stein, American poet (1874–1946). Quoted in D. Sutherland, *G.S., a Biography of her Work* (1951).

3 If this is dying, then I don't think much of it.

Lytton Strachey, English biographer (1880–1932). Quoted in Michael Holroyd, *Lytton Strachey*, Vol. 2 (1968).

As he called for champagne when he was approaching death in 1900:

4 'Ah, well then,' said Oscar, 'I suppose that I shall have to die beyond my means.'

Oscar Wilde, Irish playwright, poet and wit (1854–1900). Quoted in R.H. Sherard, *Life of Oscar Wilde* (1906). Alternatively, 'I am dying, as I have lived, beyond my means' – quoted in Barnaby Conrad, *Famous Last Words* (1961). Richard Ellman, in *Oscar Wilde* (1987), has: 'I am dying beyond my means, I will never outlive the century' as said to Wilde's sister-in-law. Either way, they were not his 'dying words'. He lived for another month or so.

About the furnishings in his room:

5 This wallpaper'll be the death of me – one of us'll have to go.

Oscar Wilde. Quoted in Sherard (same book.). *Not* said *in extremis*. Another version is that Wilde said to Claire de Pratz: 'My wallpaper and I are fighting a duel to the death. One or the other of us has to go' – reported in Guillot de Saix, 'Souvenirs inédits', also in Frank Harris, *Oscar Wilde, His Life and Confessions* (1930).

6 No one on his deathbed ever said, 'I wish I had spent more time on my business.'

Arnold Zack. Quoted in Paul Tsongas, *Heading Home* (1984).

Ears

1 One should never listen. To listen is a sign of indifference to one's hearer.

Oscar Wilde, Irish playwright, poet and wit (1854–1900). In *Saturday Review* (17 November 1894).

Eccentricity

2 'You are old, father William,' the young
man said,
'And your hair has become very white;
And yet you incessantly stand on your head –
Do you think, at your age, it is right?'

Lewis Carroll, English writer (1832–98). *Alice's Adventures in Wonderland*, Chap. 5 (1865). Alice's recitation is a parody of a much more sober piece – 'The Old Man's Comforts and How He Gained Them' (1799) by Robert Southey: 'You are old, father William,' the young man cried, / 'The few locks which are left you are grey; / You are hale, father William, a hearty old man; / Now tell me the reason, I pray.'

One day Morton was walking down a crowded Fleet Street with Rupert Hart-Davis, the publisher. He suddenly went up to a pillar box and shouted into the slot:

3 You can come out now!

J.B. Morton (Beachcomber), English humorous writer (1893–1979). Quoted in *The Lyttelton Hart-Davis Letters* – for 5 February 1956 – where it is said to have happened '20 years ago'.

Economics and economists

4 Due to the present financial situation, the light at the end of the tunnel will be turned off at the week-ends.

Anonymous (graffito) from Dublin. Reported by Darren Hickey, Leixlip, Co. Kildare, in 1987.

5 I am a great friend of Israel. Any country that can stand Milton Friedman as an adviser has nothing to fear from a few million Arabs.

John Kenneth Galbraith, Canadian-born American economist (1908–). Quoted in my book *A Year of Stings and Squelches* (1985).

To Franco Zeffirelli who explained that the high cost of the TV film Jesus of Nazareth *(1977) was partly because there had to be twelve apostles:*

6 Twelve! So who needs *twelve*? Couldn't we make do with *six*?

Lew Grade (Lord Grade), Russian-born English media tycoon (1906–98). Quoted in *Radio Times* (October 1983).

On producing the famously expensive and unsuccessful film Raise the Titanic *(1980):*

7 It would have been cheaper to lower the Atlantic.

Lew Grade (Lord Grade). Attributed remark. Alas, on TV-am's *Frost on Sunday* (23 November 1987), Grade denied having said it. All he had actually managed was, 'I didn't raise the Titanic high enough'.

To J.K. Galbraith:

1 Did y'ever think, Ken, that making a speech on economics is a lot like pissing down your leg? It seems hot to you, but it never does to anyone else.

Lyndon B. Johnson, American Democratic President (1908–73). Quoted in J.K. Galbraith, *A Life in Our Times* (1981).

2 An economist is a man who couldn't tell the difference between chicken salad and chicken shit.

Lyndon B. Johnson. Attributed remark. In Ned Sherrin, *Cutting Edge* (1984), this is given as a comment on a speech by Richard Nixon: 'Boys, I may not know much, but I know chicken shit from chicken salad!'

3 If all economists were laid end to end, they would not reach a conclusion.

Bernard Shaw, Irish playwright and critic (1856–1950). Quoted in Laurence J. Peter, *Quotations for Our Time* (1977).

Eden, Anthony (1st Earl of Avon)

BRITISH CONSERVATIVE PRIME MINISTER (1897–1977)

When Eden had been described as the offspring of a mad baronet and a beautiful woman:

4 That's Anthony for you – half mad baronet, half beautiful woman.

R.A. Butler (Lord Butler), English Conservative politician (1902–82). Untraced quotation in David Carlton, *Anthony Eden* (1981).

Edinburgh

5 McFee ... whose chief delusion is that Edinburgh is the Athens of the North ... McFee's dead ... He took offence at my description of Edinburgh as the Reykjavik of the South.

(Sir) Tom Stoppard, English playwright (1937–). *Jumpers* (1972).

Editors

6 Editor: a person employed by a newspaper whose business it is to separate the wheat from the chaff and to see that the chaff is printed.

Elbert Hubbard, American writer and editor (1856–1915). *The Roycroft Dictionary* (1914). As 'An editor is one who separates the wheat from the chaff and prints the chaff,', this was ascribed to Adlai Stevenson, American Democratic politician (190065), in Bill Adler, *The Stevenson Wit* (1966).

7 The conscience of an editor is purely decorative.

Oscar Wilde, Irish playwright, poet and wit (1854–1900). Quoted in Lloyd Lewis & Henry Justin Smith, *Oscar Wilde Discovers America* (1936).

Education

8 Gentlemen: I have not had your advantages. What poor education I have received has been gained in the University of Life.

Horatio Bottomley, English journalist, financier and politician (1860–1933). Speech at the Oxford Union (2 December 1920), quoted in Beverley Nichols, *25* (1926).

9 'That's the reason they're called lessons,' the Gryphon remarked: 'because they lessen from day to day.'

Lewis Carroll, English writer (1832–98). *Alice's Adventures in Wonderland*, Chap. 9 (1865).

10 'Reeling and Writhing, of course, to begin with,' the Mock Turtle replied; 'and then the different branches of Arithmetic – Ambition, Distraction, Uglification, and Derision.'

Lewis Carroll. In the same book, Chap. 10.

11 The average PhD thesis is nothing but a transference of bones from one graveyard to another.

J. Frank Dobie, American writer (1888–1964). *A Texan in England*, Chap. 1 (1946).

1 How do you explain school to a higher intelligence?

Line from film *E.T. The Extra-Terrestrial* (US 1982). Screenwriter: Melissa Matthison. Spoken by Henry Thomas (Elliott).

On receiving an honorary degree from Yale University:

2 It might be said now that I have the best of worlds: a Harvard education and a Yale degree.

John F. Kennedy, American Democratic President (1917–63). Speech (June 1962).

3 Educated: in the holidays from Eton.

Sir Osbert Sitwell, English writer (1892–1969). Entry in *Who's Who* (1929).

4 Education is what survives when what has been learned has been forgotten.

B.F. Skinner, American psychologist (1904–90). In *New Scientist* (21 May 1964).

5 The Battle of Yorktown was lost on the playing fields of Eton.

H. Allen Smith, American writer (1906–). Quoted in *The Frank Muir Book* (1976). Compare what George Orwell (an Old Etonian himself) wrote: 'Probably the Battle of Waterloo *was* won on the playing fields of Eton, but the opening battles of all subsequent wars have been lost there' (*The Lion and the Unicorn*, 1941).

6 Nothing that you will learn in the course of your studies will be of the slightest possible use to you in after life – save only this – that if you work hard and intelligently you should be able to detect when a man is talking rot, and that, in my view, is the main, if not the sole, purpose of education.

J.A. Smith, Professor of Moral Philosophy at Oxford (1863–1939). Quoted in John Julius Norwich, *A Christmas Cracker* (1980). Opening a lecture course (1914).

7 What does education often do? It makes a straight-cut ditch of a free, meandering brook.

Henry David Thoreau, American writer (1817–62). Journal entry – for October 1850.

8 Soap and education are not as sudden as a massacre, but they are more deadly in the long run.

Mark Twain, American writer (1835–1910). *A Curious Dream*, 'Facts Concerning the Recent Resignation' (1872).

9 I never let my schooling interfere with my education.

Mark Twain. Quoted in *The Sayings of Mark Twain*, ed. James Munson (1992).

10 Education is an admirable thing, but it is well to remember from time to time that nothing that is worth knowing can be taught.

Oscar Wilde, Irish playwright, poet and wit (1854–1900). 'The Critic As Artist' (1890).

11 *Lady Bracknell:*
Ignorance is like a delicate exotic fruit; touch it and the bloom is gone. The whole theory of modern education is radically unsound. Fortunately, in England, at any rate, education produces no effect whatsoever. If it did, it would prove a serious danger to the upper classes, and probably lead to acts of violence in Grosvenor Square.

Oscar Wilde. *The Importance of Being Earnest*, Act 1 (1895).

Edward the Confessor

KING OF ENGLAND (*c.*1003–66)

12 Edward the Confessor
Slept under the dresser.
When that began to pall,
He slept in the hall.

E.C. Bentley, English novelist, journalist and poet (1875–1956). *Biography for Beginners* (1905).

Egotism

13 The most humane of the group was Alfred Adler, a stout cherub with a pursed mouth and a gay sparkle in his eyes. When he heard

that an egocentric had fallen in love, he said: 'Against whom?'

Alfred Adler, Austrian psychiatrist (1870–1937). Quoted in Jim Bishop, *Some of My Very Best*, 'Exponent of the Soul' (1960).

On studying the Ptolemaic system:

1 Had I been present at the Creation, I would have given some useful hints for the better ordering of the universe.

Alfonso X, the Wise, King of Castile (1221–84). Quoted in Thomas Carlyle, *Life of Frederick the Great* (1858–65). In Bishop Berkeley's *Three Dialogues Between Hylas and Philonus* (1713), Philonus says: 'Why, I imagine that if I had been present at the Creation, I should have seen things produced into being; that is, become perceptible, in the order described by the sacred historian.'

2 That favourite subject, Myself.

James Boswell, Scottish lawyer, biographer and diarist (1740–95). Letter to William Temple (26 July 1763), quoted in Boswell's *The Life of Samuel Johnson* (1791). The biographer was, indeed, rather too interested in himself but, without that obsession, his voluminous diaries would not be the extraordinary documents that they are.

3 *Oscar Wilde:*
When you and I are together, we never talk about anything except ourselves.
Whistler:
No, no, Oscar, you forget – when you and I are together, we never talk about anything except me.

James McNeill Whistler. American painter (1834–1903). *The Gentle Art of Making Enemies* (1890).

Eisenhower, Dwight D.

AMERICAN GENERAL AND REPUBLICAN PRESIDENT (1890–1969).

4 I doubt very much if a man whose main literary interests were in works by Mr Zane Grey, admirable as they may be, is particularly well equipped to be chief executive of this country, particularly where Indian affairs are concerned.

Dean Acheson, American Democratic politician (1893–1971). Attributed remark (1953).

His speaking style applied to the Gettysburg address:

5 I haven't checked these figures, but 87 years ago, I think it was, a number of individuals organized a governmental set-up here in this country, I believe it covered certain eastern areas, with this idea they were following up based on a sort of national-independence arrangement and the program that every individual is just as good as every other individual ... that government of all individuals, by all individuals and for the individuals shall not pass out of the world picture.

Oliver Jensen, American writer (1914–). Quoted in Willard R. Espy, *An Almanac of Words at Play* (1975).

Elections

6 If voting changed anything they would make it illegal.

Anonymous. Has been dubiously ascribed to Tony Benn, English Labour politician (1925–). Fred Metcalf in *The Penguin Dictionary of Modern Humorous Quotations* (1987) merely places the slogan as on a 'badge, London, 1983'. In Rennie Ellis's *Australian Graffiti Revisited* (1979), there is a photograph of a wall slogan in Carlton, Victoria: 'IF VOTING COULD CHANGE THINGS, IT WOULD BE ILLEGAL.' This may predate the original publication of the book in 1975. In 1987, the Labour MP Ken Livingstone published a book with the title *If Voting Changed Anything, They'd Abolish It.*

7 Don't vote. The Government will get in.

Anonymous (graffito). Included in my book *Graffiti Lives, OK* (1979). From Oxford.

8 Don't vote. You'll only encourage them.

Anonymous (graffito). Quoted in my book *Graffiti 4* (1982). From Oxford.

9 The trouble with free elections is, you never know who is going to win.

Leonid Brezhnev, Soviet politician (1906–82). Attributed remark. It is, however, just the kind of thing Joseph Stalin might have said at the Potsdam Conference in 1945 when Winston Churchill's fate in the British General Election hung in the balance. V.M. Molotov has also been suggested.

1 'Who are you going to vote for, Uncle Willie?' asked Fowler. 'Hell, I never vote *for* anybody,' cried Fields, incensed. 'I always vote *against*.'

W.C. Fields, American comedian (1879–1946). Quoted in Robert Lewis Taylor, *W.C. Fields* (1950).

2 So that's the choice before the electorate. On the one side, Lord Home; on the other, Harold Wilson. Dull Alec versus Smart Alec.

(Sir) David Frost, English broadcaster (1939–). On BBC TV *That Was the Week That Was* (19 October 1963). Lord Home had just become British Prime Minister and Leader of the Conservative Party. In his memoirs, Frost suggests this was 'a quick ad-lib'; there were six hundred phone calls of complaint.

3 I just received the following wire from my generous Daddy – 'Dear Jack. Don't buy a single vote more than is necessary. I'll be damned if I'm going to pay for a landslide.'

John F. Kennedy, American Democratic President (1917–63). Speech, Washington DC (1958). Quoted in Bill Adler, *The Wit of President Kennedy* (1964).

4 There is no city in the United States in which I get a warmer welcome and fewer votes than Columbus, Ohio.

John F. Kennedy. Quoted in Herbert V. Prochnow, Snr & Jnr, *A Treasury of Humorous Quotations* (1969).

5 Bad officials are elected by good citizens who do not vote.

George Jean Nathan, American dramatic critic (1882–1958). Quoted in *The Home Book of Humorous Quotations*, ed. A.K. Adams (1969).

On the British General Election fight between Harold Wilson and Edward Heath, 1970:

6 A choice between a man with a pipe and a man with a boat.

Enoch Powell, English Conservative then Ulster Unionist politician (1912–98). Quoted in *The Independent* (9 February 1998).

7 'Vote early and vote often' is the Politishun's golden rule.

Henry Wheeler Shaw, American humorist (1818–85). *Josh Billings' Wit and Humour* (1874). Earlier, William Porcher Miles had said in a speech to the House of Representatives (31 March 1858): '"Vote early and vote often", the advice openly displayed on the election banners in one of our northern cities.' William Safire, *Safire's Political Dictionary* (1978), ignores both these sources but mentions that historian James Morgan found 'in his 1926 book of biographies' that the original jokester was John Van Buren (d. 1866), a New York lawyer and son of President Martin Van Buren.

8 You won the elections, but I won the count.

Anastasio Somoza, Nicaraguan dictator (1925–80). Quoted in *The Guardian* (17 June 1977). Ironically, this remark had been anticipated by Tom Stoppard in his play *Jumpers* (1972): 'It's not the voting that's democracy, it's the counting.'

9 If we would learn what the human race really *is* at bottom, we need only observe it at election times.

Mark Twain, American writer (1835–1910). *Mark Twain's Autobiography*, ed. A.B. Paine (1924).

Elephants

10 Useful friends – with handles at both ends.

(Sir) Noël Coward, English entertainer and writer (1899–1973). Attributed in Dick Richards, *The Wit of Noël Coward* (1968).

11 *Sheriff:*
Where are you going with that elephant?
Jimmy Durante:
What elephant?

Lines from film *Jumbo* (also known as *Billy Rose's Jumbo*) (US 1962). Screenwriter: Sidney Sheldon (based on the 1935 Rodgers-Hart-Hecht-MacArthur stage show), but this joke is specifically credited to Charles Lederer.

Elevators

1 Lift under repair. Use other lift.
– This Otis regrets it is unable to lift today.

Anonymous (graffito). Included in my book *Graffiti 3* (1981).

Embarrassment

On arriving at a Tomorrow Club meeting in full evening dress and finding himself the only person so dressed:

2 Now, I don't want anybody to feel embarrassed.

(Sir) Noël Coward, English entertainer and writer (1899–1973). Quoted in Cole Lesley, *The Life of Noël Coward* (1976).

Employment

3 I should like to think that the gentleman who created *King Kong* would have been more gainfully employed in making a set of concrete steps at the Ashton Road end of Bracebridge Street to help old people to get to the bus stops, without making half mile detours.

Anonymous (letter writer to the *Birmingham Evening Mail* in May 1972). Contributed by Sheila Fielding of Menston, West Yorkshire, to BBC Radio *Quote ... Unquote* (15 June 1977).

4 In a hierarchy, every employee tends to rise to his level of incompetence.

Laurence J. Peter, Canadian writer (1919–90). *The Peter Principle – Why Things Always Go Wrong* (with R. Hull) (1969). Intoning his principle on TV (1982) he added, '... and stays there'.

Encounters

5 A Petty Sneaking Knave I knew –
O! Mr Cr---, how do ye do?

William Blake, English poet and artist, 1757–1827. This was addressed to Robert Cromek, an engraver and devious publisher who did Blake and other artists out of money to which they were entitled.

6 As I was going up the stair
I met a man who wasn't there.
He wasn't there again today.
I wish, I wish he'd stay away!

Hughes Mearns, American writer (1875–1965). *Bartlett's Familiar Quotations* (1951 edn) puts this in 'Antigonish' from *The Psycho-Ed* (1922). This attribution is presumably accurate. Mearns also appears to have written several parodies of the verse. *Verse and Worse*, ed. Arnold Silcock (1958 edn), credits him with: 'As I was letting down my hair / I met a guy who didn't care; / He didn't care again today – / I *love* 'em when they get that way!' (1939) – and – 'As I was sitting in my chair / I *knew* the bottom wasn't there, / Nor legs nor back, but *I just sat*, / Ignoring little things like that.'

7 Oh wad some power the giftie gie us to see some people before they see us.

Ethel Watts Mumford, American novelist and humorist (1878?–1940). Quoted in *The Treasury of Humorous Quotations*, eds Evan Esar & Nicolas Bentley (1951).

Encouragement

8 In this country [England] it is thought well to kill an admiral from time to time to encourage the others.

Voltaire, French writer and philosopher (1694–1778). *Candide*, Chap. 23 (1759). This was a reference to the case of Admiral Byng who, in 1756, was sent to relieve Minorca, which was blockaded by a French fleet. He failed and, when found guilty of neglect of duty, he was condemned to death and shot on board the *Monarque* at Portsmouth.

Endings

9 In a *viva voce* examination at Oxford, Wilde was required to translate from a Greek version of the New Testament. When the examiners were satisfied, they told him he could stop, but Wilde went on, explaining, 'I want to see how it ends.'

Oscar Wilde, Irish playwright, poet and wit (1854–1900). Recounted by Joyce Hawkins for *The Oxford Book of Literary Anecdotes* (1975).

Enemies

On being told that another Labourite was 'his own worst enemy', Bevin replied:

1 Not while I'm alive, he ain't.

Ernest Bevin, English Labour politician (1881–1951). Reputedly levelled at Aneurin Bevan, Herbert Morrison, Emanuel Shinwell and others, and quoted by Michael Foot in *Aneurin Bevan* (Vol. 2, 1973). Foot footnoted: 'Perhaps once [Bevin] had made it he recited it about all of them. Impossible to determine who was the original victim.' Douglas Jay in *Change and Fortune* (1980) adds that it was, 'Made, I have little doubt, though there is no conclusive proof, about Bevan [being the victim] ... I could never discover direct evidence for this oft-told story.'

2 Beware of meat twice boil'd, and an old foe reconciled.

Benjamin Franklin, American politician and scientist (1706–90). *Poor Richard's Almanack* (April 1733) – a work in which Franklin often revised already existing sayings.

3 Nobody ever fergits where he buried a hatchet.

Frank McKinney ('Kin') Hubbard, American humorist (1868–1930). *Abe Martin's Broadcast* (1930).

4 H.L. Mencken's war aims, according to the handful of observers who deigned to notice his conflict, were the overthrow of American Democracy, the Christian religion, and the YMCA. He was also credited with trying to wipe out poets and luncheon orators.

H.L. Mencken, American journalist and linguist (1880–1956). Quoted in Ben Hecht, *Letters from Bohemia* (1964).

5 My prayer to God is a very short one: 'O Lord, make my enemies ridiculous.' God has granted it.

Voltaire, French writer and philosopher (1694–1778). Attributed remark.

6 I'm lonesome. They are all dying. I have hardly a warm personal enemy left.

James McNeill Whistler. American painter (1834–1903). Quoted in D.C. Seitz, *Whistler Stories* (1913).

7 I choose my friends for their good looks, my acquaintances for their good characters, and my enemies for their good intellects. A man cannot be too careful in the choice of his enemies. I have not one who is a fool. They are all men of some intellectual power, and consequently they all appreciate me.

Oscar Wilde, Irish playwright, poet and wit (1854–1900). *The Picture of Dorian Gray*, Chap. 1 (1891).

8 Be careful to choose your enemies well. Friends don't much matter. But the choice of enemies is very important.

Oscar Wilde. Quoted in Vincent O'Sullivan, *Aspects of Oscar Wilde* (1936).

9 Next to having a staunch friend is the pleasure of having a brilliant enemy.

Oscar Wilde. Quoted in Lloyd Lewis & Henry Justin Smith, *Oscar Wilde Discovers America* (1936).

Engagements

10 An engagement should come on a young girl as a surprise, pleasant or unpleasant, as the case may be.

Oscar Wilde, Irish playwright, poet and wit (1854–1900). *The Importance of Being Earnest*, Act 1 (1895).

11 I am not in favour of long engagements. They give people the opportunity of finding out each other's characters before marriage, which I think is never advisable.

Oscar Wilde. In the same play, Act 3.

12 An engagement is hardly a serious one that has not been broken off at least once.

Oscar Wilde. Quoted in Herbert V. Prochnow, Snr & Jnr, *A Treasury of Humorous Quotations* (1969).

Engineers

13 Yesterday I couldn't spell engineer – now I are one.

Anonymous (graffito). Included in my book *Graffiti 2* (1980). From Loughborough University.

England and the English

1 I know why the sun never sets on the British Empire: God wouldn't trust an Englishman in the dark.

Anonymous. In Nancy McPhee, *The Book of Insults* (1978), this is ascribed to 'Duncan Spaeth' (is this John Duncan Spaeth, the US educator?). An Irish Republican placard held up during Prince Charles's visit to New York in June 1981 had the slogan: 'The sun never sets on the British Empire because God doesn't trust the Brits in the dark.'

2 Don't trust any Englishman who speaks French with a correct accent.

Anonymous (French proverb).

3 Englishmen hate two things – racial discrimination and Irishmen.

Anonymous (Irishman).

4 Most Englishmen can never get over the embarrassing fact that they were born in bed with a woman.

Anonymous (Scotsman).

5 They tell me that the English are a people who travel all over the world to laugh at other people.

Anonymous (Spaniard). Quoted in Gerald Brenan, *The Face of Spain* (1950).

6 The English may not like music – but they absolutely love the noise it makes.

(Sir) Thomas Beecham, English conductor (1879–1961). Quoted in L. Ayre, *The Wit of Music* (1966).

7 When I warned [the French] that Britain would fight on alone ... their General [Weygand] told their Prime Minister ... in three weeks England will have her neck wrung like a chicken – some chicken, some neck.

(Sir) Winston S. Churchill, British Conservative Prime Minister and writer (1874–1965). Speech, Canadian Parliament (30 December 1941).

8 I remember remarking bitterly at the time [1933] that if I wrote a book about England I should call it 'What about Wednesday Week?' which is what English people say when they are making what they believe to be an urgent appointment.

Claud Cockburn, English journalist (1904–81). *In Time of Trouble* (1956).

9 In Bangkok at twelve o'clock
They foam at the mouth and run,
But mad dogs and Englishmen
Go out in the mid-day sun.

(Sir) Noël Coward, English entertainer and writer (1899–1973). Song, 'Mad Dogs and Englishmen' from *Words and Music* (1932). In *The Life of Noël Coward* (1976), Cole Lesley commented on the 'Mad Dogs' phrase: 'Many fans had been sending slight traces of its origins from obscure books of travel, the earliest in *Rough Leaves from a Journal* by Lt.-Col. Lovell Badcock, published in 1835: "It happened to be during the heat of the day, when dogs and English alone are seen to move." The first mention of mad dogs we ever came across was an 1874 *Guide to Malta* by the Reverend G.N. Goodwin, Chaplain to the Forces there: "Only newly arrived Englishmen and mad dogs expose themselves to it."'

In *The Nöel Coward Song Book* (1953), the composer wrote: 'I have sung it myself *ad nauseam*. On one occasion it achieved international significance. This was a dinner party given by Mr Winston Churchill on board HMS *Prince of Wales* in honour of President Roosevelt on the evening following the signing of the Atlantic Charter ... The two world leaders became involved in a heated argument as to whether "In Bangkok at twelve o'clock they foam at the mouth and run" came at the end of the first refrain or at the end of the second. President Roosevelt held firmly to the latter view and refused to budge even under the impact of Churchillian rhetoric. In this he was right and when, a little while later, I asked Mr Churchill about the incident he admitted defeat like a man.'

10 Toward people with whom they disagree, the English gentry, or at any rate that small cross-section of them I have seen, are tranquilly good-natured. It is not *comme il faut* to establish the supremacy of an idea by smashing in the faces of all the people who try to

contradict it. The English never smash it in the face. They merely refrain from asking it to dinner.

Margaret Halsey, American writer (1910–). *With Malice Toward Some* (1938).

1 Englishwomen's shoes look as if they had been made by someone who had often heard shoes described, but had never seen any.

Margaret Halsey. In the same book as above.

2 If an Englishman gets run down by a truck, he apologises to the truck.

Jackie Mason, American comedian (1931–). Quoted in *The Observer*, 'Sayings of the Week' (23 September 1990).

3 Continental people have sex lives; the English have hot-water bottles.

George Mikes, Hungarian-born writer in Britain (1912–87). *How To Be An Alien* (1946). Later, in *How To Be Decadent* (1977), Mikes commented: 'Things *have* progressed. Not on the continent, where people still have sex lives; but they have progressed here because the English now have electric blankets. It's a pity that electricity so often fails in this country.'

4 An Englishman, even if he is alone, forms an orderly queue of one.

George Mikes. In the same book as above.

5 The cold of the polar regions was nothing to the chill of an English bedroom.

Fridtjof Nansen, Norwegian explorer (1861–1930). Quoted in *The Laughing Diplomat* (1939) by Daniele Varè. Nansen made several voyages in the Arctic regions. He was also the first Norwegian ambassador to London (1906–8), which is when he presumably acquired his knowledge of the bedrooms.

6 Let us pause to consider the English,
Who when they pause to consider
  themselves they get all
reticently thrilled and tinglish,
Because every Englishman is convinced of
  one thing, viz.:
That to be an Englishman is to belong to
  the most exclusive club there is.

Ogden Nash, American poet (1902–71). *I'm a Stranger Here Myself*, 'England Expects' (1938).

7 An Englishman thinks he is moral when he is only uncomfortable.

Bernard Shaw, Irish playwright and critic (1856–1950). *Man and Superman*, Act 3 (1903). The Devil speaking.

8 The English are mentioned in the Bible: Blessed are the meek, for they shall inherit the earth.

Mark Twain, American writer (1835–1910). *Following the Equator*, Vol. 1 (1897).

9 Those things which the English public never forgives – youth, power, and enthusiasm.

Oscar Wilde, Irish playwright, poet and wit (1854–1900). Lecture in New York, 'The English Renaissance of Art' (9 January 1882).

10 I did a picture in England one winter and it was so cold I almost got married.

Shelley Winters, American actress (1922–). Quoted in *The New York Times* (29 April 1956), but possibly not mentioning the England bit. In *The Sunday Times* (2 May 1971) she said she'd been so cold on a winter sports holiday she almost got married.

English language

11 English is the great vacuum cleaner of languages: it sucks in anything it can get.

David Crystal, English lexicographer (1941–). Quoted in 'They Said It In 1995', *The Daily Telegraph* (30 December 1995).

Enough

Said by Mr Bennet to his daughter Mary who has been singing:

12 You have delighted us long enough.

Jane Austen, English novelist (1775–1817). *Pride and Prejudice*, Chap. 18 (1813).

Envy

1 The dullard's envy of brilliant men is always assuaged by the suspicion that they will come to a bad end.

(Sir) Max Beerbohm, English writer and caricaturist (1872–1956). *Zuleika Dobson*, Chap. 4 (1911).

Epigrams

2 The day of the jewelled epigram is past and, whether one likes it or not, one is moving into the stern puritanical era of the four-letter word.

Noël Annan (Lord Annan), English academic and writer (1916–2000). Quoted in *The Observer* (20 February 1966) as having being spoke in the House of Lords. Compare Curzon on Disraeli: 'Men were on the look out for the jewelled phrase, the exquisite epigram, the stinging sneer' – quoted in Kenneth Rose, *Superior Person* (1969).

3 An epigram is only a wisecrack that's played Carnegie Hall.

Oscar Levant, American pianist and actor (1906–72). Quoted in *The Treasury of Humorous Quotations*, eds Evan Esar & Nicolas Bentley (1951).

Epitaphs

4 Stop, passenger, as you pass by,
As you are now so once was I.
As I am now so you will be,
So be prepared to follow me.
– To follow you I'd be content
If I only knew which way you went.

Anonymous. The last couplet is a graffitoed addition, quoted in my book *Graffiti 3* (1981). 'To follow you I'm not content. / How do I know which way you went?' is given as 'The Wife's Epitaph' in *More Comic and Curious Verse*, ed. J.M. Cohen (1956).

On the memorial to Sir Christopher Wren, architect, in St Paul's Cathedral:

5 LECTOR, SI MONUMENTUM REQUIRIS, CIRCUMSPICE... [*Reader, if you seek his monument, look around* ...]

Anonymous, though reputedly composed by his son. Horace Smith (1779–1849) commented dryly that it would 'be equally applicable to a physician buried in a churchyard'.

Epitaph on a hypochondriac – from the southern USA:

6 I told you I was sick.

Anonymous. Quoted on BBC Radio *Quote ... Unquote* (22 December 1981). In January 1994, it was reported that the dying wish of Keith Woodward of Shrivenham, Wiltshire, had been to have a tombstone bearing the joke 'I told them I was ill'. However, parish councillors ordered the message to be removed.

On a mule, in the USA:

7 Here lies Bill. He done his damnedest.

Anonymous. Quoted by Naomi Lewis on BBC Radio *Quote ... Unquote* (1 December 1981). Compare what President Harry S. Truman said in Winslow, Arizona, on 15 June 1948: 'You know, the greatest epitaph in the country is here in Arizona. It's in Tombstone and says, "Here lies Jack Williams. He done his damnedest." I think that is the greatest epitaph a man could have. Whenever a man does the best he can, then that is all he can do; and that is what your President has been trying to do for the last three years for this country.' In 1964, Truman more precisely located the epitaph in Boot Hill Cemetery, Tombstone, and said that it went on, 'What more could a person do?' He added, of himself, 'Well, that's all I could do. I did my damnedest and that's all there is to it.'

8 Here lies
Captain Ernest Bloomfield
Accidentally shot by his Orderly
March 2nd 1789
'Well done, thou good and faithful servant'.

Anonymous. Quoted in W.H. Beable, *Epitaphs: Graveyard Humour & Eulogy* (1925), which has not only this, but also a version involving 'Major James Brush ... 1831 (Woolwich Churchyard)'. Beable also finds the similar, 'Erected to the Memory of / John Phillips / Accidentally Shot / As a mark of affection by his brother'. Earlier, David Mackae, *A Pennyworth of Queer Epitaphs* (?1910), had found the same epitaph in India. *Pass the Port Again* (1980) ascribed it confidently to the grave of David Warnock in Simla. The *Faber Book of Anecdotes* has it that James Whitcomb Riley (1849–1916), the American poet, said of a cook who had worked for a family many years, and who fell asleep over her stove and was burned to death, 'Well done, good and faithful servant'.

On a dentist:

1 Stranger! Approach this spot with gravity!
John Brown is filling his last cavity.

Anonymous. Quoted in *A Dictionary of Famous Quotations*, ed. Robin Hyman (1967). Peter Haining, *Graveyard Wit* (1973), has a similar rhyme more precisely from 'St George's Church, Edinburgh'.

2 Here lies John Bunn
Who was killed by a gun.
His name wasn't Bunn, but his real name
was Wood,
But Wood wouldn't rhyme with gun,
So I thought Bunn should.

Anonymous. W. Fairley, *Epitaphiana: or the Curiosities of Churchyard Literature* (1875) and W. H. Beable, *Epitaphs: Graveyard Humour & Eulogy* (1925) both have this, the latter noting 'a distinctly American flavour'. William Tegg, *Epitaphs, Witty, Grotesque, Elegant & c.* (1876), has the similar: 'Underneath this ancient pew / Lie the remains of Jonathan Blue; / His name was Black, but that wouldn't do.'

3 Here lies the body of Joan Carthew,
Born at St Columb, buried at St Kew.
Children she had five,
Three are dead, and two alive.
Those that are dead chusing rather
To die with their Mother
Than live with their Father.

Anonymous. Quoted in Anonymous, *A Collection of Epitaphs and Monumental Inscriptions* (1806). 'Unfortunately cannot now be found, but was inscribed on an 18th Century headstone' – according to the guidebook (1982) of the church at St Ewe, near St Austell, Cornwall. Joan Bakewell and John Drummond, *A Fine and Private Place* (1977), give the version as above from St Agnes, which is on the north coast of Cornwall, near Redruth. However, St Agnes *is* nearer to St Columb, if that is relevant.

4 Dorothy Cecil Unmarried
As Yet.

Anonymous. Quoted in an undated newspaper cutting (possibly from the early 1900s): '"C.W." writes: "While lately strolling through an old Surrey church containing altar-tombs, escutcheons and memorials of the House of Exeter, [this] epitaph on a large marble slab, suspended high in the mortuary chapel, arrested my attention. It is printed in uncials, and I reproduce the arrangement in facsimile".'

5 Here lies the bones of Copperstone
Charlotte
Born a virgin, died a harlot.
For sixteen years she kep' her virginity
A damn'd long time in this vicinity.

Anonymous. Quoted in Raymond Lamont Brown, *A New Book of Epitaphs* (1973), which has it 'from the US'. Compare: 'Here lie the bones of Elizabeth Charlotte, / That was born a virgin and died a harlot. / She was aye a virgin till seventeen – / An extraordinary thing for Aberdeen' – quoted in Donald and Catherine Carswell, *The Scots Week-End* (1936).

6 Deep in this grave lies lazy Dai
Waiting the last great trump on high.
If he's as fond of his grave as he's fond
of his bed
He'll be the last man up when that roll
call's said.

Anonymous. 'From Nevern – translated from the Welsh'. Quoted by Wynford Vaughan-Thomas on BBC Radio *Quote … Unquote* (26 January 1982).

7 Here lies the body of *Martha Dias*,
Who was always uneasy, and not over pious.
She liv'd to the age of threescore and ten,
And gave that to the worms she refus'd
to the men.

Anonymous. Quoted in Anonymous, *A Collection of Epitaphs and Monumental Inscriptions* (1806), from 'Shrewsbury church-yard'.

8 John Edwards who perished in a fire 1904.
None could hold a candle to him.

Anonymous. An epitaph from the burial ground near the present Anglican Cathedral in Liverpool. Quoted by Beryl Bainbridge on BBC Radio *Quote … Unquote* (29 June 1988). She said that another in the same place, on a certain 'G. Wild', bore the words, 'Not worth remembering'.

Epitaphs

1 Jonathan Grober
Died dead sober.
Lord thy wonders never cease.

Anonymous. Quoted on BBC Radio *Quote ... Unquote* (22 December 1981).

2 Here lie I by the churchyard door.
Here lie I because I'm poor.
The farther in, the more you pay,
But here lie I as warm as they.

Anonymous. Revd John Booth, *Metrical Epitaphs, Ancient and Modern* (1868) has 'Here I lie at the chancel door...'; William Tegg, *Epitaphs, Witty, Grotesque, Elegant & c.* (1876) has it in Dawlish churchyard and at Kingsbridge Church, Devon; W.H.Beable, *Epitaphs: Graveyard Humour & Eulogy* (1925), has it as being 'outside the Priest's Door, Kingsbridge Church, Devon ... in memory of Robert Phillip, commonly called Bone (due to he being the chief parish gravedigger) died 1795'.

3 Here lies the body of Mary Gwynne,
Who was so very pure within,
She cracked the shell of her earthly skin,
And hatched herself a cherubim.

Anonymous. Said to be in Cambridge – W. Fairley, *Epitaphiana: or the Curiosities of Churchyard Literature* (1875); in St Alban's, Hertfordshire – J. Potter Briscoe, *Gleanings from God's Acre Being a Collection of Epitaphs* (1901).

4 Here lies John Higley whose father and mother were drowned in the passage from America. Had they both lived, they would have been buried here.

Anonymous. Quoted in W. Fairley, *Epitaphiana: or the Curiosities of Churchyard Literature* (1875). In 'Belturbet Churchyard, Ireland'.

5 In joyous memory of
George Jones
who was president of
the Newport Rifle Club
for twenty years.
'Always missed'.

Anonymous. 'From America, I think' – A. Bune, Cambridge (1982).

6 Here lies the body of Mary,
wife of John Jones of this parish.

Here lies the body of Martha,
wife of John Jones of this parish.

Here lies the body of Jane,
wife of John Jones of this parish.

John Jones. At rest.

Anonymous. Adjacent epitaphs which used to be quoted by Lt Commander D. Gill Jones in his talk 'A quiet hour among the dead' (mid-20th century).

7 Here lies the body of Mary Ann Lowder,
She burst while drinking a seidlitz powder.
Called from the world to her heavenly rest,
She should have waited till it effervesced.

Anonymous. Quoted in W.H. Beable, *Epitaphs: Graveyard Humour & Eulogy* (1925) – 'in Burlington Churchyard'. John Diprose, *Diprose's Book of Epitaphs: Humorous, Eccentric, Ancient & Remarkable* (1879) had earlier put it in 'Burlington, Mass.'

8 Erected to the memory of
John MacFarlane
Drowned in the Water of Leith
By a few affectionate friends.

Anonymous. Quoted in W.H. Beable, *Epitaphs: Graveyard Humour & Eulogy* (1925).

9 In memory of
MAGGIE
Who in her time kicked
Two colonels,
Four majors,
Ten captains,
Twenty-four lieutenants,
Forty-two sergeants,
Four hundred and thirty-two other ranks
AND
One Mills Bomb.

Anonymous. 'On the last resting place of an Army mule somewhere in France' – J.H.A. Dick, Currie, Midlothian (1981).

1 Born a dog. Died a gentleman.

Anonymous. Quoted by Naomi Lewis on BBC Radio *Quote … Unquote* (1 December 1981). It seems to have been a Victorian epitaph from an unidentified pets' cemetery.

2 Here lies the body of Mary Anne
Safe in the arms of Abraham.
All very well for Mary Anne
But how about poor Abraham?

Anonymous. 'In a North Devon churchyard' – D. Whitmore, Liphook, Hants. (1982); 'Mary Ann has gone to rest, / Safe at last on Abraham's breast, / Which may be nuts for Mary Ann, / But is certainly rough on Abraham' – quoted in *A Dictionary of Famous Quotations*, ed. Robin Hyman (1967).

3 Here lies the body of
LADY O'LOONEY
Great niece of BURKE
Commonly called the Sublime
She was Bland, Passionate
and deeply Religious, also
she painted in water colours
and sent several pictures
to the Exhibition
She was first Cousin to
LADY JONES
and of such is the
Kingdom of Heaven.

Anonymous. This most delightful of epitaphs can no longer be found. *Punch* (29 January 1870) referred to it as 'a famous Irish epitaph'. W. Fairley, *Epitaphiana: or the Curiosities of Churchyard Literature* (1875), placed it in 'Pewsey churchyard'; William Tegg, *Epitaphs, Witty, Grotesque, Elegant & c.* (1876), in 'Pewsey, Bedfordshire' (which does not exist); Aubrey Stewart, *English Epigrams and Epitaphs* (1897), in 'Pewsey, Wiltshire'; J. Potter Briscoe, *Gleanings from God's Acre Being a Collection of Epitaphs* (1901), in Dorset; David Mackae, *A Pennyworth of Queer Epitaphs* (?1910), placed it in Devon; Peter Haining, *Graveyard Wit* (1973), in Bridgewater Cemetery, Somerset. Compare from Philip Reder, *Epitaphs* (1969), in Bandon, Ireland: 'Sacred to the memory of Mrs Maria Boyle / Who was a good wife, a devoted Mother / And a kind and charitable neighbour. / She painted in water colours, / And was the first cousin to the Earl of Cork, / And of such is the Kingdom of Heaven.' At which point one wonders whether what G.W.E. Russell, *Collections and Recollections* (1898), calls 'the best-known of all epitaphs' ever existed anywhere at all.

4 Here lies, in horizontal position,
the outside case of
GEORGE ROUTLEIGH, Watchmaker;
Whose abilities in that line
Were an honour to his profession.
Integrity was the Mainspring, and prudence
the Regulator
Of all the actions of his life.
Humane, generous and liberal,
his Hand never stopped
till he had relieved Distress.
So nicely regulated were all his motions,
that he never went wrong,
except when set a-going
by people
who did not know his Key;
Even then he was easily
set right again.
He had the art of disposing his time so well,
that his hours glided away
in one continual round
of pleasure and delight,
until an unlucky minute put a period
to his existence.
He departed this life,
Nov. 14, 1802,
aged 57:
wound up,
in hopes of being taken in hand
by his Maker;
and of being thoroughly cleaned, repaired,
and set a-going
in the world to come.

Anonymous. Quoted in full in Geoffrey N. Wright, *Discovering Epitaphs* (1972). In church at Lydford, Devon. *Benham's Book of Quotations* (1948) has only an extract and puts the name as 'George Roughfield'.

5 In memory of Jane Emily Smith
Died 10 Apr. 1804, aged 74
'Believing, we rejoice to see the curse
removed'.

Anonymous. 'In South Ealing cemetery', according to a correspondent, but untraced.

1 Her Time Was Short.

Anonymous. Quoted in Michael Holroyd, *Bernard Shaw Vol.II: The Pursuit of Power* (1989). On the tombstone of Mary Ann South in Ayot St Lawrence churchyard, Hertfordshire. She had lived in the village for seventy years, from 1825 to 1895. Bernard Shaw, when asked why he had chosen to live in the same village, would explain that if the biblical span of three score years and ten was considered short there, it had to be a good place to live. He himself managed to live to the age of 94.

2 IN LOVING MEMORY
OF
FRANK STANIER
OF
STAFFORDSHIRE
WHO LEFT US IN PEACE
FEB. 2ND. 1910

Anonymous. In the English cemetery on the island of San Michele, Venice. Quoted (correctly) by a correspondent, Margaret R. Jackson of Chipping Camden (1982), though it had already been transcribed (differently) in James Morris, *Venice* (1960/1974).

3 Here lies a poor woman who always was tired,
For she lived in a place where help wasn't hired,
Her last words on earth were, 'Dear friends, I am going,
Where washing ain't done nor cooking nor sewing,
And everything there is exact to my wishes,
For there they don't eat, there's no washing of dishes,
I'll be where loud anthems will always be ringing
(But having no voice, I'll be out of the singing).
Don't mourn for me now, don't grieve for me never,
For I'm going to do nothing for ever and ever.'

Anonymous. Quoted in E. Jameson, *1000 Curiosities of Britain* (1937). Sometimes referred to as 'The Maid-of-all-Works' Epitaph' or 'The Tired Woman's Epitaph', this has two possible sources. As 'an epitaph for Catherine Alsopp, a Sheffield washerwoman, who hanged herself, 7 August 1905', it was composed by herself and included in Jameson. But a letter in the *Spectator* (2 December 1922) from a correspondent at the British Museum states that the inscription was once to be found in Bushey churchyard. A copy of the text was made before 1860, but the actual stone had been destroyed by 1916. Aubrey Stewart, *English Epigrams and Epitaphs* (1897), has it as 'quoted by James Payn in the *Cornhill Magazine*'. It was also discussed in *Notes and Queries* for March 1889 and *Longman's Magazine* for January 1884. W. Gurney Benham, *Cassell's Book of Quotations* (1907), states that it had been quoted 'before 1850'.

4 Wherever you be
Let your wind go free.
For it was keeping it in
That was the death of me.

Anonymous. 'Traditional, from Ireland', quoted on BBC Radio *Quote ... Unquote* (2 March 1982).

5 Beneath this Marble is Buried
Tho. Welsted
Who was Struck Down by the Throwing of a Stone.
He was First in this School
And we Hope is not Last in Heaven
Whither he went
Instead of to Oxford.
January 13, 1676
Aged 18.

Anonymous. Quoted in *The Oxford Book of Oxford*, ed. Jan Morris (1978). Translation of a Latin inscription to be found in the Old Cloisters at Winchester College.

A widow's epitaph for her husband:

6 Rest in peace – until we meet again.

Anonymous. Quoted in Jessica Mitford, *The American Way of Death* (1963).

1 Lord she is thin.

Anonymous. The story has it that this epitaph appears at the bottom of a Tasmanian tombstone. The 'e' is on the back, the stonemason not having left himself enough room to carve it on the front. Also told of a Presbyterian churchyard in Charles L. Wallis, *Stories On Stone: A Book of American Epitaphs* (1954).

2 Man is a noble animal, splendid in ashes, and pompous in the grave.

(Sir) Thomas Browne, English author and physician (1605–82). *Hydriotaphia* (*Urn-Burial*), Chap. 5 (1658).

3 Epitaph: a belated advertisement for a line that has been permanently discontinued.

Irvin S. Cobb, American humorist and journalist (1876–1944). Quoted in *The Treasury of Humorous Quotations*, eds Evan Esar & Nicolas Bentley (1951).

4 Reading the epitaphs, our only salvation lies in resurrecting the dead and burying the living.

Paul Eldridge, American writer and poet (b. 1888). Quoted in *The Treasury of Humorous Quotations*, eds Evan Esar & Nicolas Bentley (1951).

5 In lapidary inscriptions a man is not upon oath.

(Dr) Samuel Johnson, English writer and lexicographer (1709–84). Quoted in James Boswell, *The Life of Samuel Johnson* (1791) – for 1775.

Observing the fulsome epitaphs in a churchyard in the 1780s:

6 Mary, where are all the naughty people buried?

Charles Lamb, English writer (1775–1834). As a boy, to his sister. Quoted in Leonard Russell, *English Wits* (1940). Compare: William Wordsworth, in the second of his essays on epitaphs (possibly written about 1812), recalling the story (old even in his day, one imagines) of the person who, tired of reading so many fulsome epitaphs on 'faithful wives, tender husbands, dutiful children and good men of all classes', exclaimed, 'Where are all the *bad* people buried?' Perhaps he was referring to Lamb? Whoever first made the comment, Wordsworth argues that there is a lot to be said for having, 'in an unkind world, one enclosure where the voice of Detraction is not heard … and there is no jarring tone in the peaceful concert of amity and gratitude'.

7 The rarest quality in an epitaph is truth.

Henry David Thoreau, American writer (1817–62). Quoted in *The Treasury of Humorous Quotations*, eds Evan Esar & Nicolas Bentley (1951).

Epitaphs, literary and suggested

8 Here lies an honest lawyer, –
That is Strange.

Anonymous. On the 'eminent barrister, Sir John Strange' – quoted in W. Fairley, *Epitaphiana: or the Curiosities of Churchyard Literature* (1875); 'on Mr Strange, a lawyer' – William Tegg, *Epitaphs, Witty, Grotesque, Elegant & c.* (1876). The only notable lawyer of this name mentioned in the *Dictionary of National Biography* is Sir John Strange (1696–1754), who was Master of the Rolls. Compare what John Aubrey earlier recorded: 'Ben JO(H)NSON, riding through Surrey, found the Women weeping and wailing, lamenting the Death of a Lawyer, who lived there: He enquired why so great Grief for the Loss of a Lawyer? Oh, said they, we have the greatest Loss imaginable; he kept us all in Peace and Quietness, and was a most charitable good Man: Whereupon Ben made this Distich: "God works Wonders now and then, / Behold a Miracle, deny't who can, / Here lies a *Lawyer* and an *honest* man." 'Tis Pity that good Man's Name should not be remember'd.'

Epitaph on an unknown man:

9 Under this sod lies another one.

Anonymous. Quoted on BBC Radio *Quote … Unquote* (8 June 1977).

10 Below the high Cathedral stairs,
Lie the remains of Agnes Pears.
Her name was Wiggs; it was not Pears.
But Pears was put to rhyme with stairs.

Anonymous. Quoted in Edward Lear's diary (entry for 20 April 1887). With 'Susan Pares' replacing 'Agnes Pears', the rhyme was first published without date in *Queery Leary Nonsense* (1911), edited from manuscripts by Lady Constance Strachey.

11 This is the grave of Mike O'Day
Who died maintaining his right of way.

His right was clear, his will was strong.
But he's just as dead as if he'd been wrong.

Anonymous. Quoted in *Bartlett's Familiar Quotations* (1968 edn). Another version: 'Here lies the body of Edmund Gray / died maintaining his right of way. / He was right – dead right – as he drove along. / But he's just as dead as if he'd been wrong' – quoted by Sir Huw Wheldon on BBC Radio *Quote ... Unquote* (1 December 1981). There is also one to 'Timothy Jay', as in 'jay-walking'.

1 Miss Emily Stamp, postmistress.
Returned opened.

Anonymous. 'On a comic post card [of a gravestone] at Blackpool' – quoted by Bryan Glover on BBC Radio *Quote ... Unquote* (9 February 1982). Jaap Engelsman commented (1999): 'The late Dutch author S. Carmiggelt once described having heard a somewhat similar joke. Freely translated from Dutch: 'After the death of a pious nun the stone on her grave was going to be inscribed: "Here rests sister Magdalen Mary, born a virgin, and as a virgin carried off to eternal bliss". There was money for just a tiny stone, but the mason promised to do his best. He chiselled: "Here rests Magdalen Mary, unused returned to sender".' This was published in a book in 1965, having previously appeared as a daily column in an Amsterdam newspaper, probably in 1964 or 1965. Carmiggelt heard the joke in Rome, at a Vatican Council (1962–5) press conference, when, during a summary in Chinese, a French Jesuit priest sitting in front of C. told it to his neighbour.

2 Down the lanes of memory
The lights are never dim
Until the stars forget to shine
We shall remember her.

Anonymous. Quoted by Alan Bennett from 'a Lancashire newspaper' on BBC Radio *Quote ... Unquote* (26 January 1982). He had earlier included the lines in 'The English Way of Death' in *Beyond the Fringe* (Broadway version, 1964).

3 The angel's trumpet sounded,
St Peter called out 'Come',
The pearly gates swung open,
And in walked Mum.

Anonymous. 'This must have appeared at least 30 years ago ... I remember a correspondence about it in the Live Letters column of the *Daily Mirror*, where some readers condemned its tastelessness, and others praised its simple sentiment' – letter from Margaret Holt, Manchester (1981). In *Ego 7* (for 6 March 1944), James Agate stakes an earlier claim: 'The members [of the Column Club] were delighted with something I bagged out of the obituary notices in an august paper a few days ago: "The silver trumpets sounded loud, / The angels shouted 'Come!' / Opened wide the Golden Gate, / And in walked Mum!"'

Epitaph on Frederick Louis, Prince of Wales (1707–51), eldest son of George II and father of George III:

4 Here lies Fred,
Who was alive and is dead:
Had it been his father,
I had much rather;
Had it been his brother,
Still better than another;
Had it been his sister
No one would have missed her;
Had it been the whole generation,
Still better for the nation:
But since 'tis only Fred,
Who was alive and is dead, –
There's no more to be said.

Anonymous. Quoted by Horace Walpole in an appendix to his *Memoirs of George II* (1847). Compare from *Frobisher's New Select Collection of Epitaphs ...* (?1790), 'On a tombstone in Cornwall: Here lies honest Ned, / Because he is dead. / Had it been his father ... ' *A Collection of Epitaphs ...* (1806) has from 'a headstone in the churchyard of Storrington in the County of Sussex: Here lies the body of Edward Hide; / We laid him here because he died. / We had rather it had been his father. / If it had been his sister, / We should not have miss'd her. / But since 'tis honest Ned / No more shall be said ... ' Peter Haining, *Graveyard Wit* (1973), has a version beginning 'Here lies HONEST NED ... ' from 'Kirkby Stephen parish church, Westmorland'.

5 Here lies the grave of Keelin,
And on it his wife is kneeling;
If he were alive, she would be lying,
And he would be kneeling.

Anonymous (graffito). Quoted in Oliver St John Gogarty, *As I Was Going Down Sackville Street* (1937).

Suggested epitaph for one Thomas Longbottom who died young:

1 *Ars longa, vita brevis.*

Anonymous. Contributed to BBC Radio *Quote … Unquote* (17 May 1978). In the same edition, Richard Stilgoe suggested rather that *Punch* in its early days had reproduced the death announcement of a man called 'Longbottom' and put over it the headline 'Vita brevis'. Hence, also, 'Ars Longa, Vita Sackville-West', which was quoted in the same edition of *Quote … Unquote*.

2 Here lies one Foote, whose death may
thousands save,
For death has now one foot within the
grave.

Anonymous. Quoted in Anonymous, *A Collection of Epitaphs and Monumental Inscriptions* (1806). A punning epitaph on Samuel Foote (1720–77), actor and dramatist, famous for his mimicry and for making Samuel Johnson laugh against his will. He was, however, buried in the cloister of Westminster Abbey, by torchlight and in an unmarked grave.

3 Here lies the body of Charlotte Greer,
Whose mouth would stretch from ear to ear.
Be careful as you tread this sod
For if she gapes, you're gone, by God!

Anonymous. 'My father maintained that in the Vale of Aylesbury about 1900 he encountered this epitaph … I'm afraid it was apocryphal' – E.J. Burdon, Preston, Lancs. (1982).

4 When I am dead, I hope it may be said:
'His sins were scarlet, but his books were
read'.

Hilaire Belloc, French-born English poet and writer (1870–1953). *Sonnets and Verse*, 'On his Books' (1923).

Suggested epitaph for an actress:

5 She sleeps alone at last.

Robert Benchley, American humorist (1889–1945). Quoted in Edmund Fuller, *2500 Anecdotes for All Occasions* (1943).

Of Sir Henry Campbell-Bannerman (1836–1908), British Liberal Prime Minister from 1905 to 1908:

6 He is remembered chiefly as the man about whom all is forgotten.

Nicolas Bentley, English cartoonist and writer (1907–78). *An Edwardian Album* (1974).

At the funeral of Humphrey Sumner, the Oxford historian and Warden of All Souls, in 1951:

7 Sumner is a-going out
Loud sing boo-hoo.

(Sir) Maurice Bowra, English academic (1898–1971). Quoted by Alan Bennett on BBC Radio *Quote…Unquote* (26 January 1982). This alluded to the 13th-century rhyme, 'Sumer is icumen in, / Lhude sing cuccu!'

8 Posterity will ne'er survey
A nobler grave than this.
Here lie the bones of Castlereagh.
Stop, Traveller –

Lord Byron, English poet (1788–1824). 'Epitaph' (1821). Byron wrote this epitaph on Viscount Castlereagh (1769–1822) apparently the year *before* the Foreign Secretary's death by suicide. Castlereagh is actually buried in Westminster Abbey and attracted the poet's enmity either because Byron supported Napoleon or on account of Castlereagh's presumed role in the Peterloo massacre of 1819.

9 Been there, done that.

(Sir) Michael Caine, English actor (1933–). 'Caine was once asked if he had a motto: "Yeah – Been There, Done That. It'll certainly be on my tombstone. It'll just say, "Been There, Done That"' – quoted in Elaine Gallagher and others, *Candidly Caine* (1990).

10 Believing that his hate for queers
Proclaimed his love for God,
He now (of all queer things, my dears)
Lies under his first sod.

Paul Dehn, English writer (1912–76). He won a *New Statesman* competition in 1962 with this epitaph on John Gordon (1890–1974), editor-in-chief of the *Sunday Express*, and a columnist famous for his outspoken views.

1 Here lies my wife: here let her lie.
Now she's at rest, and so am I.

John Dryden, English poet and playwright (1631–1700). Quoted in *The Treasury of Humorous Quotations*, eds Evan Esar & Nicolas Bentley (1951).

On Sir John Vanbrugh (1664–1726), the dramatist and architect:

2 Under this stone, Reader, survey
Dead Sir John Vanbrugh's house of clay.
Lie heavy on him, Earth! for he
Laid many heavy loads on thee!

(Dr) Abel Evans (1679–1737), though it has also been ascribed to the architect Nicholas Hawksmoor. Thinking of Blenheim Palace, Castle Howard, and so on. This version is the one in Revd John Booth, *Metrical Epitaphs, Ancient and Modern* (1868). Anonymous, *A Collection of Epitaphs and Monumental Inscriptions* (1806), has: 'Lie *light* upon him earth! tho' he / Laid many a heavy load on thee.' (Compare, on Pelham, a former Treasury minister: 'Lie heavy on him, land, for he / Laid many a heavy tax on thee'.)

3 On the whole I'd rather be in Philadelphia.

W.C. Fields, American comedian (1879–1946). What the comedian actually submitted as a suggested epitaph to *Vanity Fair* Magazine in 1925 was: 'Here lies W.C. Fields. I would rather be living in Philadelphia.'

4 At last I get top billing.

Wallace Ford, English film actor (1897–1966). Quoted by Terence Frisby on BBC Radio *Quote … Unquote* (16 February 1979). Ford went to Hollywood in the early 1930s. After a number of 'semi-leads', he was condemned to a succession of supporting roles in Hollywood films and decided that his gravestone epitaph should read, 'At last – I get top billing.' This inscription was duly put on his grave. Then along came a graffiti artist and chalked above it, 'Clark Gable and Myrna Loy supported by … '

5 Here Skugg
Lies snug
As a bug
In a rug.

Benjamin Franklin, American politician and scientist (1706–90). Letter to Miss Georgiana Shipley (26 September 1772) on the death of her pet squirrel. However, lest it be thought that, by its inclusion in dictionaries of quotations, Franklin originated the phrase 'snug as a bug in a rug', note that there are earlier uses. In an anonymous work *Stratford Jubilee* (commemorating David Garrick's Shakespeare Festival in 1769) we find: 'If she [a rich widow] has the mopus's [money] / I'll have her, as snug as a bug in a rug.' Probably, however, it was an established expression even by that date, if only because in 1706 Edward Ward in *The Wooden World Dissected* had the similar 'He sits as snug as a Bee in a Box', and in Thomas Heywood's play *A Woman Killed with Kindness* (1603) there is 'Let us sleep as snug as pigs in pease-straw.' A little after Franklin's use: in the July 1816 edition of the *New Monthly Magazine*, among the curious epitaphs printed from Waddington in Yorkshire (now in Lancashire) was one, 'In memory of WILLIAM RICHARD PHELPS, late Boatswain of H.M.S. *Invincible*. He accompanied Lord Anson in his cruise round the world, and died April 21, 1789'. It reads: 'When I was like you, / For years not a few, / On the ocean I toil'd, / On the line I have broil'd / In Greenland I've shiver'd, / Now from hardship deliver'd, / Capsiz'd by old death, / I surrender'd my breath, / And now I lie snug / As a bug in a rug.'

6 The body
of Benjamin Franklin, printer,
(Like the cover of an old book,
Its contents worn out,
And stript of its lettering and gilding)
Lies here, food for worms!
Yet the work itself shall not be lost,
For it will, as he believed, appear once more
In a new
And more beautiful edition,
Corrected and amended
By its Author!

Benjamin Franklin, who began his career as a printer. Written *c.*1728. William Andrews, *Curious Epitaphs* (1899), compares it to other similarly punning printers' epitaphs. W. Gurney Benham, *Cassell's Book of Quotations* (1907), quotes the Revd Joseph Capen (19th century), 'Lines on Mr John Foster': 'Yet at the resurrection we shall see / A fair edition, and of matchless worth, / Free from erratas, new in heaven set forth.' Benham also suggests that the idea was borrowed from the Revd Benjamin Woodbridge, chaplain to Charles II, who wrote these 'Lines of John Cotton' (1652): 'O what a monument of glorious worth, / When in a new edition he comes forth, / Without erratas, may we think he'll be / In leaves and covers of eternity!' In fact, Franklin lies with his wife under a simple inscription in Christ Church, Philadelphia: 'Benjamin and Deborah Franklin 1790'.

Epitaph for himself:

1 Here lies Fuller's Earth.

Thomas Fuller, English preacher and historian (1608–61). Quoted in T. Webb, *A New Select Collection of Epitaphs* (1775). Fuller was buried in the church of which he had been rector, at Cranford, west London, but the grave no longer survives. His actual epitaph was a sober Latin text.

2 Life is a jest, and all things show it;
I thought so once; and now I know it.

John Gay, English poet and playwright (1685–1732). The couplet forms part of the inscription on the pedestal of Gay's monument in Westminster Abbey. The lines were written by Gay himself as 'My Epitaph' (1720).

3 Pardon me for not getting up.

Ernest Hemingway, American novelist (1899–1961). One of the playful epitaphs that celebrities were invited to suggest for themselves, usually by American magazines in the 1920s/30s. He is buried at Ketchum, Idaho, where he shot himself.

4 Over my dead body.

George S. Kaufman, American playwright (1889–1961). Quoted in *The Book of Hollywood Quotes*, ed. Gary Herman (1979).

Mock epitaph on G.K. Chesterton:

5 Poor G.K.C., his day is past –
Now God will know the truth at last.

E.V. Lucas, English writer (1868–1938). Quoted in Dudley Barker, *G.K. Chesterton* (1973).

6 Here lies Groucho Marx
and Lies and Lies and Lies.
PS He never kissed an ugly girl.

Groucho Marx, American comedian (1895–1977). *The Secret Word is Groucho* (1976).

7 If after I depart this vale you ever remember me and have thought to please my ghost, forgive some sinner and wink your eye at some homely girl.

H.L. Mencken, American journalist and linguist (1880–1956). Mencken suggested this epitaph for himself in the *Smart Set* (December 1921). After his death, it was inscribed on a plaque in the lobby of the offices of the Baltimore *Sun* newspapers (with which he had been associated most of his working life).

8 This is on me.

Dorothy Parker, American writer (1893–1967). Quoted in Alexander Woollcott, *While Rome Burns* (1934). Other epitaphs she suggested for herself, *c.* 1925, were 'Excuse my dust' and 'If you can read this you are standing too close.'

9 Here lye two poor Lovers, who had the mishap
Tho very chaste people, to die of a Clap.

Alexander Pope, English poet (1688–1744). This was one of several epitaphs that Pope showed to Lady Mary Wortley Montagu in a letter (dated 1 September 1718), referring to the deaths by lightning of John Hewet and Sarah Drew in July 1718. A more respectable verse by Pope on the 'Stanton Harcourt Lovers' is to be found on a tablet on the exterior south wall of St Michael's Church, Stanton Harcourt, Oxfordshire.

10 Nature, and Nature's Laws lay hid in Night:
GOD said, *Let Newton be!* and all was Light.

Alexander Pope. 'Epitaph: Intended for Sir Isaac Newton' (1730), in Westminster Abbey. Sir John Squire later suggested this response (in his *Poems*, 1926): 'It did not last: the Devil howling 'Ho! / Let Einstein be!' restored the status quo.'

11 Here lies one whose name was writ in hot water.

Robert Ross, English writer (1869–1918). This, his own suggestion for an epitaph, is quoted in Osbert Sitwell, *Noble Essences* (1950). Ross, who had a stormy life, was a friend of Oscar Wilde and is buried with him in Paris.

On Sir John, later Viscount, Simon (1873–1954), lawyer and Liberal politician:

12 This stone with not unpardonable pride,
Proves by its record what the world denied:

Simon could do a natural thing – he died.

John Sparrow, English scholar (1906–92). *Grave Epigrams and Other Verses* (1981) – where 'Simon' is replaced with '*Nemo*'. 'Lord Simon has died ... John Sparrow wrote this epitaph many years ago ... But then John Simon helped John Sparrow to become Warden of All Souls, and the latter came to regret his epigram' – *Harold Nicolson's Diaries and Letters 1945–1962* (entry for 11 January 1954).

Epitaph for himself:

1 This is where the real fun starts.

Ben Travers, English playwright (1886–1980). Quoted in *The Listener* (31 December 1981).

Epitaph for himself:

2 He never used a sentence if a paragraph would do.

(Sir) Huw Wheldon, Welsh broadcaster and TV executive (1916–86). Quoted in the *Daily Mail* (9 June 1976). The actual headstone of his grave in St Peris churchyard, Nant Peris, Snowdonia, calls him 'Soldier, Broadcaster, Administrator'.

Epitaph for his cat Bathsheba:

3 To whom none ever said scat,
No worthier cat
Ever sat on a mat
Or caught a rat:
Requies – cat.

John Greenleaf Whittier, American poet (1807–92). Quoted in Janice Anderson, *The Cat-a-Logue* (1987).

Equality

4 His lordship may compel us to be equal upstairs, but there will never be equality in the servants' hall.

(Sir) J(ames) M. Barrie, Scottish playwright (1860–1937). *The Admirable Crichton*, Act 1, Sc. 1 (1902). Crichton speaking.

5 ALL ANIMALS ARE EQUAL
BUT SOME ANIMALS ARE MORE
EQUAL THAN OTHERS.

George Orwell, English novelist and journalist (1903–50). *Animal Farm*, Chap. 10 (1945), which was a commentary on the totalitarian excesses of Communism. It had been anticipated: Hesketh Pearson recalled in his biography of the actor/manager Sir Herbert Beerbohm Tree (1956) that Tree wished to insert one of his own epigrams in a play called *Nero* by Stephen Phillips (1906). It was: 'All men are equal – except myself.' In Noël Coward's *This Year of Grace* (1928) there is the exchange: Pellet: 'Men are all alike.' Wendle: 'Only some more than others'. Compare also: 'Men were all alike – men of Bill Bannister's kind especially so' – P.G. Wodehouse, *Doctor Sally*, Chap. 9 (1932).

The saying alludes, of course, to Thomas Jefferson's 'All men are created equal and independent', from the 'rough draft' of the American Declaration of Independence (1776). It has the makings of a formula phrase in that it is more likely to be used to refer to humans than to animals. Only the second half of the phrase need actually be spoken, the first half being understood: 'You-Know-Who [Mrs Thatcher] is against the idea [televising parliament]. There aren't card votes at Westminster, but some votes are more equal than others.' (*The Guardian*, 15 February 1989).

Eroticism

6 Erotic is when you do something sensitive and imaginative with a feather. Kinky is when you use the whole chicken.

Elmore Leonard, American novelist (1925–). Attributed to Leonard by William Rushton in 1987, but otherwise untraced. However, in a BBC TV *Moving Pictures* profile of Roman Polanski (reviewed in *The Guardian*, 25 November 1991), Peter Coyote ascribed the remark to Polanski in the form: 'Eroticism is using a feather, while pornography is using the whole chicken.' Another version uses 'perverted' instead of 'kinky'.

Errata

7 Erratum. In my article on the Price of Milk, 'Horses' should have read 'Cows' throughout.

J.B. Morton (Beachcomber), English humorous writer (1893–1979). *The Best of Beachcomber* (1963).

Eskimos

8 Eskimos are God's frozen people.

Anonymous (graffito). Included in my book *Graffiti 3* (1981).

Etiquette

1 Dunking is bad taste but tastes good.

Franklin P. Adams, American journalist, poet and humorist (1881–1960). Quoted in *The Treasury of Humorous Quotations*, eds Evan Esar & Nicolas Bentley (1951).

The Red Queen to Alice:

2 It isn't etiquette to cut any one you've been introduced to. Remove the joint!

Lewis Carroll, *Through the Looking-Glass and What Alice Found There*, Chap. 9 (1872).

Having left the table to be sick, at a formal dinner in the home of the producer Arthur Hornblow Jnr:

3 It's all right, Arthur. The white wine came up with the fish.

Herman J. Mankiewicz, American screenwriter (1897–1953). Quoted in Max Wilk, *The Wit and Wisdom of Hollywood* (1972). Also attributed to Howard Dietz.

4 Etiquette is knowing how to yawn with your mouth closed.

Herbert V. Prochnow, American writer (b. 1897). Quoted in Herbert V. Prochnow, Snr & Jnr, *A Treasury of Humorous Quotations* (1969).

See also MANNERS.

Euphemisms

5 *Honey*:
I wonder if you could show me where the …
I want to … put some powder on my nose.
George:
Martha, won't you show her where we keep the … euphemism?'

Edward Albee, American playwright (1928–). *Who's Afraid of Virginia Woolf?*, Act 1 (1962).

6 The answer is in the plural and they bounce.

(Sir) Edwin Lutyens, English architect (1869–1944). Said to have been the euphemistic response given by Lutyens to a Royal Commission (quoted without source in *The Penguin Dictionary of Modern Quotations*, 1971). However, according to Robert Jackson, *The Chief* (1959), when Gordon (later Lord) Hewart was in the House of Commons, he was answering questions on behalf of David Lloyd George. For some time, one afternoon, he had given answers in the customary brief parliamentary manner – 'The answer is in the affirmative' or 'The answer is in the negative'. After one such non-committal reply, several members arose to bait Hewart with a series of rapid supplementary questions. He waited until they had all finished and then replied: 'The answer is in the plural!'

Europe

7 Baldwin thought Europe was a bore, and Chamberlain thought it was only a greater Birmingham.

(Sir) Winston S. Churchill, British Conservative Prime Minister and writer (1874–1965). Attributed remark in 1953.

8 The only cultural heritage that the 321 peoples of Europe share is that of America. That is why the organisers of Euro-Disneyland are on safe ground.

Kenneth Hudson, English museums expert (1916–99). Quoted in *The Independent*, 'Quote Unquote' (30 June 1990).

Everest

When asked why he wanted to climb Mount Everest:

9 Because it's there.

George Leigh Mallory, English mountaineer (1886–1924). Mallory disappeared in 1924 on his last attempt to scale Mount Everest. The previous year, during a lecture tour of the US, he had frequently been asked why he wanted to achieve this goal. On one such occasion he replied: 'Because it's there.'

In 1911, at Cambridge, A.C. Benson had urged Mallory to read Carlyle's life of John Sterling – a book that achieved high quality simply 'by being *there*'. Perhaps that is how the construction entered Mallory's mind. On the other hand, Tom Holzel and Audrey Salkeld in *The Mystery of Mallory and Irvine* (1986) suggest that 'the four most famous words in mountaineering' may have been invented for the climber by a reporter named Benson in *The New York Times* (18 March 1923). A report in *The Observer* (2 November 1986) noted that Howard Somervell, one of Mallory's climbing colleagues in the 1924 expedition, declared forty years later that the 'much-quoted remark' had always given him a 'shiver down the spine – it doesn't smell of George Mallory one bit'. Mallory's niece, Mrs B.M. Newton Dunn, claimed in a letter to *The Daily Telegraph* (11 November 1986) that the mountaineer had once given the reply to his sister (Mrs Newton Dunn's mother) 'because a silly question deserves a silly answer'.

The saying has become a catchphrase in situations where the speaker wishes to dismiss an impossible question about motives and also to express his acceptance of a challenge that is in some way daunting or maybe foolish. In September 1962 President Kennedy said: 'We choose to go to the moon in this decade, and do the other things, not because they are easy but because they are hard; because that goal will serve to organize and measure the best of our energies and skills ... Many years ago the great British explorer George Mallory, who was to die on Mount Everest, was asked why did he want to climb it, and he said, "Because it is there." Well, space is there, and ... the moon and the planets are there, and new hopes for knowledge and peace are there.'

There have been many variations (and misattributions). Sir Edmund Hillary repeated it regarding his own attempt on Everest in 1953. It was quoted in John Hunt, *The Ascent of Everest* (1953) which may have contributed to the remark's modern popularity.

Evidence

At the conclusion of the trial of the 'Luncheon Voucher' Madam, Cynthia Payne:

1 M'lud, we find the defendant not guilty – but we would love to hear all the evidence again.

Anonymous (jury foreman). Quoted in *Sunday Today*, 'Quotes of the Week' (15 February 1987). In fact, this was not actually said in court (as a member of the jury pointed out to the author) but may have appeared as the caption to a cartoon.

2 Some circumstantial evidence is very strong, as when you find a trout in the milk.

Henry David Thoreau, American writer (1817–62). Diary note (11 November 1850).

Evolution

On being informed of Charles Darwin's theory of evolution:

3 Descended from the apes! My dear, we hope it is not true. But if it is, let us pray that it may not become generally known.

Anonymous (wife of a canon of Worcester Cathedral). Quoted in the first article/lecture 'Man's Kinship with Nature' in Theodosius Dobzhansky, *The Biological Basis of Human Freedom* (1956). Where he got the story from, he does not say. Yves Pleven of Ville d'Avray near Paris wrote to assure me that in the form, *'Ainsi l'homme descendrait du singe, pourvu que cela ne s'ébruite pas ...* [roughly: Maybe man is descended from the apes, but no need to spread it about ...]' it came from an 'XVIIIth century salon held by one of the following hostesses: Julie de Lespinasse, Madame du Deffand or Madame de Tencin'. He adds: 'The quotation is well-known in France.' This rather surprised me in that I should have thought the concept of men being descended from apes was not known before Darwin. However, Jaap Engelsman reminded me that Voltaire once remarked: *'Cela est fort beau, mais j'ai du mal à croire que je descends d'une morue* [roughly: that's all very fine, but I hate to think that I am descended from a cod]' – apparently referring to some earlier theory of evolution put forward by Maillet and Maupertuis. Indeed, the idea of man being descended from the apes does predate Darwin's theory. Of Lord Monboddo, the Scottish judge and author (1714–90), the *Dictionary of National Biography* states: 'Among other curious and interesting opinions ... he maintained that the orang-utang was a class of the human species and that its want of speech was purely accidental.' Douglas Woodruff in *More Talking at Random* (1944) mentioned *Vestiges of the Natural History of Creation*, published anonymously in 1844, 15 years before *The Origin of Species*: 'When Disraeli parodied drawing-room talk of the forties – "We have been fishes and shall be crows" – it was with the effects of the *Vestiges* that he was dealing. Darwin walked into a well-prepared house.'

4 The question is this: Is man an ape or an angel? Now I am on the side of the angels.

Benjamin Disraeli (1st Earl of Beaconsfield), English politician and writer (1804–81). Speech on evolution to the Oxford Diocesan Society (25 November 1864).

Examinations

5 I would like to have been examined in history, poetry and writing essays. The examiners, on the other hand, were partial to Latin and mathematics. And their will prevailed

... I should have liked to be asked to say what I knew. They always tried to ask what I did not know.

(Sir) Winston S. Churchill, British Conservative Prime Minister and writer (1874–1965). *My Early Life*, Chap. 2 (1930).

1 Examinations are formidable even to the best prepared, for the greatest fool may ask more than the wisest man can answer.

Charles Caleb Colton, English clergyman and writer (*c.* 1780–1832). *Lacon* (1820).

2 In an examination those who do not wish to know ask questions of those who cannot tell.

(Sir) Walter Raleigh, English scholar (1861–1922). *Laughter from a Cloud*, 'Some Thoughts on Examinations' (1923).

3 Expostulate (chiefly) on
(a) The Curfew
(b) Gray's Energy in the Country Churchyard.

W.C. Sellar and R.J. Yeatman, English humorists (1898–1951) and (1897–1968). *1066 and All That*, Chap. 21 – 'Test Paper II, Up to the End of Henry III' (1930).

4 Do not on any account attempt to write on both sides of the paper at once.

W.C. Sellar and R.J. Yeatman. In the same book, Chap. 62 – 'Test Paper V, Up to the End of History.'

5 Examinations are of no value whatsoever. If a man is a gentleman, he knows quite enough, and if he is not a gentleman, whatever he knows is bad for him.

Oscar Wilde, Irish playwright, poet and wit (1854–1900). *A Woman of No Importance*, Act 3 (1893).

6 In examinations the foolish ask questions that the wise cannot answer.

Oscar Wilde, Irish playwright, poet and wit (1854–1900). 'Phrases and Philosophies for the Use of the Young', in *The Chameleon* (December 1894). Compare Colton above.

Example

7 Few things are harder to put up with than the annoyance of a good example.

Mark Twain, American writer (1835–1910). *Pudd'nhead Wilson*, Chap. 19 (1894).

Excess

8 Too much of a good thing can be wonderful.

Mae West, American vaudeville and film actress (1893–1980). Quoted in the *Daily Mail* (1980).

9 Moderation is a fatal thing, Lady Hunstanton. Nothing succeeds like excess.

Oscar Wilde, Irish playwright, poet and wit (1854–1900). *A Woman of No Importance*, Act 3 (1893).

Exclamation marks

Editing a radio script by Sheilah Graham:

10 Cut out all the exclamation points. An exclamation point is like laughing at your own joke.

F. Scott Fitzgerald, American novelist (1896–1940). Quoted in Sheilah Graham and Gerald Frank, *Beloved Infidel* (1959).

Exclamations

11 We was robbed!

Joe Jacobs, American boxing manager (1896–1940). Quoted in Peter Heller, *In This Corner* (1975). Believing that his client, Max Schmeling, had been cheated of a heavyweight title by Jack Sharkey (21 June 1932), Jacobs shouted this protest into a microphone.

12 I should have stood in bed!

Joe Jacobs. Quoted in John Lardner, *Strong Cigars and Lovely Women* (1951). Jacobs left his sick-bed to attend the baseball World Series in October 1935. He bet on the losers. Leo Rosten in *Hooray for Yiddish* (1983) puts his own gloss on the expression: 'The most celebrated instance of this usage was when Mike [*sic*] Jacobs, the fight promoter, observing the small line at his ticket window, moaned, "I should of stood in bed!" *Stood* is a calque for the Yiddish *geshtanen*, which can mean both "stood" and "remained". Mr Jacobs' use of "of" simply followed the speech pattern of his childhood.'

1 Hallelujah, I'm a Bum.

Harry Kirby McClintock, American songwriter (1882–1967). Title of song (1928), based on the traditional hymn 'Revive Us Again'. This formed the basis of the film *Hallelujah, I'm a Bum* (US 1933), for which a new song with the title was written by Lorenz Hart (music by Richard Rodgers). In fact, it only included the line 'Hallelujah, I'm a bum again!' Even so, a separate version had to be made for the sensitive British censor who also insisted on the film being re-titled *Hallelujah, I'm a Tramp* for British audiences.

2 Heavens, eleven o'clock and not a whore in the house dressed!

Anonymous. Variations on this exclamation were recalled by listeners to BBC Radio *Quote … Unquote* in 1992, though whether it was an actual quotation could not be established. They included: 'Heavens, eleven o'clock and not a whore in the house dressed, not a po emptied, and the streets full of Spanish sailors … '; 'Heavens! four o'clock and not a whore washed and the street full of sailors'; 'Heavens! Ten o'clock! Not a bed made, not a po emptied, not a whore in the house dressed, and the Spanish soldiers in the courtyard!'; 'Ten o'clock already no pos emptied, no beds made and a street full of matelots'; 'Eight o'clock, and not a whore in the house washed and a troopship in the bay'; 'Eleven o'clock, not a whore washed, not a bed made, and the *Japanese fleet* in town!' In the 1980s, the comedian Les Dawson in drag is reliably reported to have uttered the 'no pos emptied' part of the expression. Rupert Hart-Davis in *The Lyttelton Hart-Davis Letters*, Vol.3 (1981), has a letter dated 9 June 1958: 'In the words of the harassed theatrical landlady, "Half-past four, and not a po emptied".' Whether all or part of the expression is a quotation from a play, or not, one does keep on being drawn back to a possible theatrical origin. The earliest printed reference found to date is in the *Spectator* (24 April 1959). Patrick Campbell recorded that 'Ten-thirty, and not a strumpet in the house painted!' was a favourite saying (apparently in the late 1930s) of Robert Smyllie, editor of *The Irish Times*.

Excuses

3 I'd like to kiss you, but I just washed my hair. Bye!

Line from film *Cabin in the Cotton* (US 1932). Screenwriter: Paul Green (from novel by Harry Harrison Knoll). Spoken by Bette Davis (Madge).

When asked about an unmarried mother's baby:

4 If you please, ma'am, it was a very little one.

Frederick Marryat, English novelist (1792–1848). *Mr Midshipman Easy*, Chap. 3 (1836). Although often given as the source of this limp excuse, it is not. For example, in a letter of 9 March 1811 to William Godwin, William Wordsworth wrote: 'You remember the story of the poor Girl who being reproached with having brought forth an illegitimate Child said it was true, but added that it was a very little one: insinuating thereby that her offence was small in proportion. But the plea does not hold good.' What a characteristic it is of the humourless to explain the joke, though this does not apply, of course, to Mark Twain who (later) merely put, 'The girl who was rebuked for having borne an illegitimate child excused herself by saying, "But it is such a little one"' – in *Europe and Elsewhere*, ed. James Brander (1923). This pales besides the version of the story that Frank Muir found for *The Oxford Book of Humorous Prose* in *Gratiae Ludentes* – of which the date is 1638.

When a man asked to be excused to go to the men's room:

5 He really needs to telephone, but he's too embarrassed to say so.

Dorothy Parker, American writer (1893–1967). Quoted in John Keats, *You Might as Well Live* (1970). Cole Lesley, in his *Life of Noël Coward* (1976), tells it like this, and describes it as a Coward favourite: 'She [Parker] produced a personable young man, of which she seemed to have a supply, to fill in a last-minute cancellation at a literary dinner-party. Faced with such distinguished guests, through nerves he knocked back too many martinis and was drunk by the time he got to a table, from which he soon got up, loudly announced, "I wanna piss," and staggered from the room. "He's very shy," said Mrs Parker. "Actually he only wants to telephone".'

On hearing that Harold Ross, editor of The New Yorker, *had called while she was on her honeymoon, demanding late copy:*

6 Tell him I've been too fucking busy – or vice versa.

Dorothy Parker. Quoted in the same book as above.

Asked by Harold Ross, editor of The New Yorker, *why she hadn't been in to the office during the week to write her piece:*

1 Someone was using the pencil.

Dorothy Parker. Quoted in *The Sayings of Dorothy Parker*, ed. S.T. Brownlow (1992).

On why snow had disrupted rail services, even though a big chill had been correctly forecast:

2 It was the wrong kind of snow.

Terry Worrall, British Rail's director of operations. Quoted in *The Independent* (16 February 1991). This remark became part of British folklore as the archetypal limp excuse. In an interview with the BBC Radio *Today* programme on 11 February (presumably after he had made the original remark), Worrall said, 'We have had a particular problem with this type of snow ... it has ... been very dry and powdery and it has actually penetrated all the protection that we have on our traction motors, beneath our multiple units and on some of our locomotives.'

Exercise

When asked how he kept fit:

3 Exercise is the most *awful* illusion. The secret is a lot of aspirin and *marrons glacés*.

(Sir) Noël Coward, English entertainer and writer (1899–1973). In *The Observer* (1969). Compare how he explained his longevity: 'To constant smoking and *marrons glacés*' – quoted in *Noël Coward: A Life in Quotes*, ed. Barry Day (1999).

On Mickey Rooney:

4 His favourite exercise is climbing tall people.

Phyllis Diller, American comic performer (1917–). Attributed remark.

5 Exercise is bunk. If you are healthy, you don't need it. If you are sick, you shouldn't take it.

Henry Ford, American industrialist (1863–1947). Quoted in *The Penguin Dictionary of Modern Quotations*, eds J.M. & M.J. Cohen (1971).

6 Whenever I feel like exercise, I lie down until the feeling passes.

Robert M. Hutchins, American educator (1899–1977). Untraced, but apparently said by the former University of Chicago President rather than all the other candidates (Wilde, Twain, W.C. Fields, and so on). Ascribed by J.P. McEvoy in *Young Man Looking Backwards* (1938). However, Hutchins's biographer, Harry S. Ashmore, ascribes it to *McEvoy* and says that it was merely one of many sayings Hutchins collected to use when appropriate. In the film *Mr Smith Goes to Washington* (US 1939), Thomas Mitchell speaks the line: 'Every time I think of exercise, I have to lie down till the feeling leaves me.' In his introduction to the *Speeches* volume of the Oxford Mark Twain (1996), the actor Hal Holbrook, noted for his performances 'as' Mark Twain, mentions an attributed remark: 'When the urge to exercise comes over me I lie down until it passes away.' He does not say where he got this from, however.

7 The only exercise I get is when I take the studs out of one shirt and put them in another.

Ring Lardner, American humorist (1885–1933). Quoted in *The Treasury of Humorous Quotations*, eds Evan Esar & Nicolas Bentley (1951).

8 I take my only exercise acting as pallbearer at the funerals of my friends who exercise regularly.

Mark Twain, American writer (1835–1910). Quoted in *The Sayings of Mark Twain*, ed. James Munson (1992). Also attributed to Chauncey Depew.

9 I am pushing sixty. That is enough exercise for me.

Mark Twain. Quoted in the same book as above.

10 I have never taken any exercise, except for sleeping and resting, and I never intend to take any. Exercise is loathsome.

Mark Twain. Speech at his seventieth birthday dinner, New York City (5 December 1905).

11 No gentleman ever takes exercise.

Oscar Wilde, Irish playwright, poet and wit (1854–1900). *The Importance of Being Earnest*, Act 2 (1895).

Exits

1 He flung himself from the room, flung himself upon his horse and rode madly off in all directions.

Stephen Leacock, English-born Canadian writer and economist (1869–1944). *Nonsense Novels*, 'Gertrude the Governess' (1911).

Expenditure

When the future King Edward VII said to his mistress, 'I've spent enough on you to buy a battleship', she replied:

2 And you've spent enough in me to float one.

Lily Langtry, English actress (1852–1929). Quoted in Irving Wallace and others, *Intimate Sex Lives of Famous People* (1981).

3 I'm living so far beyond my income that we may almost be said to be living apart.

Saki (H.H. Munro), English writer (1870–1916). Quoted in *The Treasury of Humorous Quotations*, eds Evan Esar & Nicolas Bentley (1951).

Experience

4 You should make a point of trying every experience once, excepting incest and folk-dancing.

Anonymous ('sympathetic Scotsman'). Quoted in Sir Arnold Bax, *Farewell, My Youth* (1943).

5 Experience is the comb that Nature gives us when we are bald.

Anonymous (Belgian proverb). Quoted in Herbert V. Prochnow, Snr & Jnr, *A Treasury of Humorous Quotations* (1969).

6 Experience is a revelation in the light of which we renounce our errors of youth for those of age.

Ambrose Bierce, American journalist (1842–?1914). Quoted in *The Treasury of Humorous Quotations*, eds Evan Esar & Nicolas Bentley (1951).

7 The only thing experience teaches us is that experience teaches us nothing.

André Maurois, French biographer and writer (1885–1967). Quoted in the same collection as above.

8 We should be careful to get out of an experience only the wisdom that is in it – and stop there; lest we be like the cat that sits down on a hot stove-lid. She will never sit down on a hot stove-lid again – and that is well; but also she will never sit down on a cold one any more.

Mark Twain, American writer (1835–1910). *Following the Equator*, Vol. 1 (1897).

9 Experience was of no ethical value. It was merely the name men gave to their mistakes.

Oscar Wilde, Irish playwright, poet and wit (1854–1900). *The Picture of Dorian Gray*, Chap. 4 (1891). Compare, also by Wilde: 'Experience is the name every one gives to their mistakes' – *Lady Windermere's Fan*, Act 3 (1892), which is also to be found in *Vera: Or The Nihilists*, Act 2 (1880).

10 What a pity in life that we only get our lessons when they are of no use to us!

Oscar Wilde. In *Lady Windermere's Fan*, Act 4.

11 He is old enough to know worse.

Oscar Wilde. Quoted in Hesketh Pearson, *The Life of Oscar Wilde* (1946).

Experts

12 An expert is one who knows more and more about less and less.

Nicholas Murray Butler, American teacher and writer (1862–1947). Remark in a commencement address at Columbia University (of which he was President 1901–45). Quoted in *The Treasury of Humorous Quotations*, eds Evan Esar & Nicolas Bentley (1951). Sometimes completed with, ' … until finally he knows everything about nothing'. Compare: 'Every day you seem to know less and less about more and more' – P.G. Wodehouse, *Summer Lightning*, Chap. 8 (1929). To Dr William J. Mayo has been attributed: 'Specialist – A man who knows more and more about less and less.'

Explanations

1 Are you lost daddy I arsked tenderly. 'Shut up,' he explained.

Ring Lardner, American humorist (1885–1933). *The Young Immigrunts* (1920).

2 Never Explain – your friends do not need it and your enemies will not believe you anyway.

Elbert Hubbard, American writer and editor (1856–1915). *The Motto Book* (1907).

When his wife caught him kissing a chorus girl, he explained, creatively:

3 But, you see, I wasn't kissing her. I was whispering in her mouth.

Chico Marx, American comedian (1886–1961). Quoted in Groucho Marx & Richard Anobile, *The Marx Brothers Scrapbook* (1974).

An actor was appearing in a long-running melodrama during which he had to stab another in the last act with a stiletto-type letter opener. One day, the props man forgot to put the knife on the table and there was no other murder implement to hand. Instead of throttling his victim, the actor apparently kicked him up the backside. The man fell down dead. The actor turned to the audience and said:

4 Fortunately, the toe of my boot was poisoned!

Osgood Perkins, American character actor (1892–1937). Quoted by Stanley Donen to Richard Burton who recorded it in his diary for 16 October 1968 (included in Melvyn Bragg, *Rich: The Life of Richard Burton*, 1988).

5 'But what would you say your plays were *about*, Mr Pinter?'
'The weasel under the cocktail cabinet.'

Harold Pinter, English playwright (1930–). 'Exchange at a new writers' brains trust', quoted in John Russell Taylor, *Anger and After* (1962).

Extremes

6 'Extremes meet,' as the whiting said with its tail in its mouth.

Thomas Hood, English poet and humorist (1799–1845). *Comic Annual*, 'The Doves and the Crows' (1839).

Eyesight

7 My eyes are dim
I cannot see
I have not brought my specs with me.

Anonymous. Song, 'In the Quartermaster's Stores', known by at least the 1930s. A version 'with words and music adapted by Elton Box, Desmond Cox and Bert Reed' was copyrighted in 1940.

8 Sir Thomas Robinson was always complaining that he kept seeing double and asked what he should do about it. Samuel Johnson said: Count your money.

(Dr) Samuel Johnson, English writer and lexicographer (1709–84). Quoted in my book *A Year of Stings and Squelches* (1985).

F

Faces

1 He thought what a pity it was that all his faces were designed to express rage or loathing. Now that something had happened that really deserved a face, he'd none to celebrate it with. As a kind of token he made his Sex Life in Ancient Rome face.

(Sir) Kingsley Amis, English novelist, poet and critic (1922–95). *Lucky Jim*, Chap. 25 (1954).

Of Sir Ralph Richardson, the actor:

2 I don't know his name but he's got a face like half a teapot.

George VI, British King (1895–1952). Quoted in *The Guinness Dictionary of Theatrical Quotations*, ed. Michèle Brown (1993).

3 Her face was her chaperone.

Rupert Hughes, American novelist and playwright (1872–1956). Quoted in *The Treasury of Humorous Quotations*, eds Evan Esar & Nicolas Bentley (1951).

4 *Of Lester Piggott, the English jockey:*

He has a face like a well-kept grave.

Jack Leach, English sportswriter. Attributed remark (by 1990). This clearly echoes W.C. Fields's description of an elderly woman dressed to kill in the film *The Old-Fashioned Way* (US 1934): '[She's] all dressed up like a well-kept grave.'

When a drunk lurched up to Groucho and said, 'You old son-of-a-gun, you probably don't remember me':

5 I never forget a face, but in your case I'll be glad to make an exception.

Groucho Marx, American comedian (1895–1977). Quoted in Leo Rosten, *People I Have Loved, Known or Admired*, 'Groucho' (1970).

6 At 50, everyone has the face he deserves.

George Orwell, English novelist and journalist (1903–50). In *The Collected Essays*, Vol. 4 (1968) – notebook entry for 17 April 1949 – when he was 46 and had only one year to live.

7 A dowdy dull girl, with one of those characteristic British faces that, once seen, are never remembered.

Oscar Wilde, Irish playwright, poet and wit (1854–1900). *The Picture of Dorian Gray*, Chap. 15 (1891).

8 She certainly has a wonderful faculty of remembering people's names, and forgetting their faces.

Oscar Wilde. *A Woman of No Importance*, Act 1 (1893).

See also DESCRIPTIONS OF PEOPLE.

Facetiousness

9 You call me in your speech 'my facetious friend', and I hasten to denominate you 'my solemn friend'; but you and I must not run into common-place errors; you must not think me necessarily foolish because I am

facetious, nor will I consider you necessarily wise because you are grave.

(Revd) Sydney Smith, English clergyman, essayist and wit (1771–1845). Letter to Bishop Bloomfield (1840).

Facts

1 Never check an interesting fact.

Howard Hughes, American film producer and industrialist (1905–76). Quoted in Peter Hay, *Harrap's Book of Business Anecdotes* (1988). Hughes, when in Hollywood, was producing a mighty historical film. A lowly assistant pointed out that there were several historical errors in the script for one scene, and volunteered to go and check them out in the library. Hughes told him to forget it, with this remark.

2 Comment is free but facts are on expenses.

(Sir) Tom Stoppard, English playwright (1937–). *Night and Day* (1978).

Failures

3 Failure has gone to his head.

Wilson Mizner, American playwright (1876–1933). Quoted in Alva Johnston, *The Legendary Mizners* (1953).

4 There are interesting failures. There are prestige failures, and there are financial failures, but this is the sort of failure that gives failures a bad name.

Line from film *Please Don't Eat the Daisies* (US 1960). Screenwriter: Isobel Lennart (from Jean Kerr novel). Spoken by David Niven (Lawrence Mackay). An earlyish outing for the 'gives – a bad name' critical format. *See also* THEATRICAL CRITICISM 428:6 and 430:7.

5 I haven't had a hit film since Joan Collins was a virgin.

Burt Reynolds, American film actor (1936–). Quoted in *The Observer*, 'Sayings of the Week' (27 March 1988).

6 I have done my best to die before this book is published.

Robert Runcie (Lord Runcie), English Archbishop of Canterbury (1921–2000). Letter to Humphrey Carpenter quoted in the biographer's *Robert Runcie, The Reluctant Archbishop* (1996). Runcie had cooperated with Carpenter (indeed, had invited him to write the biography), believing that the book would not be published until after his death.

7 Anybody seen in a bus after the age of thirty has been a failure in life.

Loelia Westminster, English duchess (1902–93). Quoted in *The Daily Telegraph* (*c.* 1980).

Fairness

8 One should always play fairly ... when one has the winning cards.

Oscar Wilde, Irish playwright, poet and wit (1854–1900). *An Ideal Husband*, Act 1 (1895).

Faith

9 He was of the faith chiefly in the sense that the church he currently did not attend was Catholic.

(Sir) Kingsley Amis, English novelist, poet and critic (1922–95). *One Fat Englishman*, Chap. 8 (1963).

10 There are those who scoff at the schoolboy, calling him frivolous and shallow. Yet it was the schoolboy who said, 'Faith is believing what you know ain't so.'

Mark Twain, American writer (1835–1910). *Following the Equator* (1897).

Faithfulness

11 Your idea of fidelity is not having more than one man in the bed at the same time ... You're a whore, baby, that's all, just a whore, and I don't take whores in taxis.

Line from film *Darling* (UK, 1965). Screenwriter: Frederic Raphael. Spoken by Dirk Bogarde (Robert Gold) to Julie Christie (Diana Scott).

12 Those who are faithful know only the trivial side of love: it is the faithless who know love's tragedies.

Oscar Wilde, Irish playwright, poet and wit (1854–1900). *The Picture of Dorian Gray*, Chap. 1 (1891).

1 Faithfulness is to the emotional life what consistency is to the life of the intellect, simply a confession of failure.

Oscar Wilde. In the same book, Chap. 4.

2 Young men want to be faithful and are not; old men want to be faithless and are not.

Oscar Wilde. In the same book, Chap. 37.

Falsehood

Squashing a critic (Aneurin Bevan) in the House of Commons by replying thus to one of his questions:

3 I should think it hardly possible to state the opposite of the truth with more precision.

(Sir) Winston S. Churchill, British Conservative Prime Minister and writer (1874–1965). Quoted in *The Sayings of Winston Churchill*, ed. J.A. Sutcliffe (1992).

Fame

4 You're famous when they can spell your name in Karachi.

Anonymous (American showbiz observation). Quoted in Steve Aronson, *Hype* (1983). In David Brown, *Star Billing* (1985), 'You're not a star until they can spell your name in Karachi' is ascribed to Humphrey Bogart.

5 A test of whether you have achieved true fame is when a deranged person believes himself to be you.

Anonymous. Quoted by Denis Norden on BBC Radio *Quote … Unquote* (11 October 1999). *H. L. Mencken's Dictionary of Quotations* (1942) has: 'The final test of fame is to have a crazy person imagine he is you' – Author unidentified.

6 Fame is failure disguised as money.

Brendan Behan, Irish playwright (1923–64). Quoted in *The Irish Digest* (1963).

7 In the march up to the heights of fame there comes a spot close to the summit in which man reads 'nothing but detective stories'.

Heywood Broun, American journalist (1888–1939). *G.K.C.* (1922).

8 In short, whoever you may be,
To this conclusion you'll agree,
When everyone is somebodee,
Then no one's anybody.

(Sir) W.S. Gilbert, English writer and lyricist (1836–1911). *The Gondoliers*, Act 2 (1889).

Of Charles Dickens:

9 He writes too often and too fast … If he persists much longer in this course, it requires no gift of prophecy to foretell his fate – he has risen like a rocket, and he will come down like a stick.

Abraham Hayward, English essayist (1801–84). Hayward was reviewing *Pickwick Papers* for *The Quarterly Review* (October 1838). Not entirely original: Tom Paine had said of Edmund Burke, 'As he rose like the rocket, he fell like the stick' – *Letter to the Addressers on the late Proclamation* (1792).

When asked what he proposed to do when he had taken his university degree:

10 Somehow or other I'll be famous, and if not famous, I'll be notorious.

Oscar Wilde, Irish playwright, poet and wit (1854–1900). Quoted in *The Oxford Book of Oxford* (1978).

Familiarity

11 Dear 338171 (May I call you 338?)

(Sir) Noël Coward, English entertainer and writer (1899–1973). Writing to T.E. Lawrence in the RAF, when Lawrence was hiding under the name 'Brown'. Included in *Letters to T.E. Lawrence*, ed. D. Garnett (1938). The letter was dated 25 August 1930 and sent from the Adelphi Hotel, Liverpool, where Coward stayed on the tour of his play *Private Lives*. Lawrence replied on 6 September: 'It is very good to laugh: and I laughed so much, and made so many people laugh over your "May I call you 338" that I became too busy and happy to acknowledge your letter.' A kindly pedant has pointed out to me that the really individual part of one's number in the services is at the end, so Coward should have put: 'May I call you 171?'

1 The first Rotarian was the first man to call John the Baptist Jack.

H.L. Mencken, American journalist and linguist (1880–1956). Quoted in *The Treasury of Humorous Quotations*, eds Evan Esar & Nicolas Bentley (1951).

2 Familiarity breeds contempt – and children.

Mark Twain, American writer (1835–1910). *Notebooks* (published 1935).

3 Familiarity breeds consent.

Oscar Wilde, Irish playwright, poet and wit (1854–1900). Quoted in E.H. Mikhail, *Oscar Wilde: Interviews and Recollections* (1979).

Families

4 There's a wonderful family called Stein,
There's Gert and there's Epp and there's Ein;
Gert's poems are bunk,
Epp's statues are junk,
And no one can understand Ein.

Anonymous. Quoted in *The Home Book of Humorous Quotations*, ed. A.K. Adams (1969 edn). A different version is quoted in Robert Graves & Alan Hodge, *The Long Weekend*, Chap. 12 (1940): 'I don't like the family Stein! / There is Gert, there is Ep, there is Ein. / Gert's writings are punk, / Ep's statues are junk, / Nor can anyone understand Ein.' The limerick was current in the 1920s.

5 Where does the family start? It starts with a young man falling in love with a girl – no superior alternative has yet been found.

(Sir) Winston S. Churchill, British Conservative Prime Minister and writer (1874–1965). Speech, House of Commons (6 November 1950).

6 To the family – that dear octopus from whose tentacles we never quite escape nor, in our inmost hearts, ever quite wish to.

Dodie Smith, English novelist and playwright (1896–1990). *Dear Octopus* (1938). Nicholas gives this toast at a family dinner marking his grandparents' Golden Wedding.

7 A family is a terrible encumbrance, especially when one is not married.

Oscar Wilde, Irish playwright, poet and wit (1854–1900). *Vera: Or The Nihilists*, Act 3 (1880). Prince Paul speaking.

Lady Bracknell:

8 To be born, or at any rate bred, in a hand-bag, whether it had handles or not, seems to me to display a contempt for the ordinary decencies of family life that reminds one of the worst excesses of the French Revolution.

Oscar Wilde. *The Importance of Being Earnest*, Act 1 (1895).

Fanatic

9 A fanatic is one who can't change his mind and won't change his subject.

(Sir) Winston S. Churchill, British Conservative Prime Minister and writer (1874–1965). Quoted in *Reader's Digest* (December 1954).

Farce

When someone said to Gwenn, on his deathbed, 'It must be hard, very hard, Ed?', he replied:

10 It is. But not as hard as farce.

Edmund Gwenn, Welsh-born character actor (1875–1959). Quoted in *Time* Magazine (30 January 1984). One version has it that the visitor was Jack Lemmon.

11 Sergeant, arrest several of these vicars!

Philip King, English playwright (1904–79). Tom Stoppard once claimed this as the funniest line anywhere in English farce. Alas, King's *See How They Run* (first performed in 1944) does not have quite this line in it. For reasons it would be exhausting to go into, the stage gets filled with various people who are, or are dressed up as, vicars, and the order is given: 'Sergeant, arrest most of these people.'

Farewells

12 *Burns*:
Say goodnight, Gracie.
Allen:
Goodnight, Gracie.

George Burns, American comedian (1896–1996). Exchange with his wife, Gracie Allen – the customary ending of their TV series, *The George Burns and Gracie Allen Show* (1950–8).

Subsequently, in NBC TV *Rowan and Martin's Laugh-In* (1967–73), Dan Rowan would say, 'Say goodnight, Dick' and Dick Martin would reply, 'Goodnight, Dick.'

Farming

1 I believe the first receipt [i.e. recipe] to farm well is to be rich.

(Revd) Sydney Smith, English clergyman, essayist and wit (1771–1845). Letter to John Wishaw (13 April 1818).

2 He was a very inferior farmer when he first began, and he is now fast rising from affluence to poverty.

Mark Twain, American writer (1835–1910). *Choice Bits from Mark Twain*, 'Rev. Henry Ward Beecher's Farm' (1885).

Farts

3 Every man likes the smell of his own farts.

Anonymous (Icelandic proverb). Quoted in W.H. Auden and Louis MacNeice, *Letters from Iceland* (1937). *Compare* HANDWRITING 200:10.

The Earl of Oxford, Edward de Vere, 'making of his low obeisance to Queen Elizabeth, happened to let a fart, at which he was so abashed and ashamed that he went to travel, seven years.' On his return, the Queen welcomed him by saying:

4 My lord, we have forgot the fart.

Elizabeth I, English Queen (1533–1603). Quoted in John Aubrey, *Brief Lives* (*c.* 1693). There is, coincidentally, a parallel story in the *Arabian Nights' Entertainment*: 'How Abu Hasan Brake Wind' tells of the poor chap who had too much to eat and drink at his wedding-banquet and 'let fly a fart, great and terrible' in front of the guests and before he was able to make it to the bridal chamber. In his embarrassment he instantly exiled himself for ten years. On his return, he overheard a girl asking her mother about her birth date. The mother replied: 'Thou was born, O my daughter, on the very night when Abu Hasan farted.' At this he said to himself, 'Verily thy fart hath become a date, which shall last for ever and ever' and went off into exile until he died.

Fascination

5 Mrs Skinner told Jones that Mrs N. was a very fascinating woman, and that Mr W. was very fond of fascinating with her.

Samuel Butler, English author (1835–1902). *Notebooks* (1912) – for *c.* 1890.

6 There is no fascination so irresistible to a boy as the smile of a married woman.

Benjamin Disraeli (1st Earl of Beaconsfield), English politician and writer (1804–81). *Vivian Grey*, Bk 1, Chap. 7 (1826–7).

Fashion

7 Her hat is a creation that will never go out of style; it will just look ridiculous year after year.

Fred Allen, American comedian (1894–1956). Quoted in *The Treasury of Humorous Quotations*, eds Evan Esar & Nicolas Bentley (1951).

Defining style:

8 A candy-striped jeep, Jane Austen, Cassius Clay, *The Times* before it changed, Danny La Rue, Charleston in South Carolina, 'Monsieur de Givenchy', a zebra (but not a zebra crossing), evading boredom, Gertrude Lawrence, the Paris Opera House, white, a seagull, a Brixham trawler, Margot Fonteyn, any Cole Porter song, English pageantry, Marlene's voice ... and ... Lingfield has a tiny bit.

(Sir) Noël Coward, English entertainer and writer (1899–1973). Copy for Gillette razor blade advertisement, shortly before he died. Quoted in Kenneth Tynan article in *The Observer* (1 April 1973).

On army uniforms:

9 Excuse me, sir. Is green the only colour these come in?

Line from film *Private Benjamin* (US 1980). Screenwriters: Nancy Meyers and others. Spoken by Goldie Hawn (Judy Benjamin).

1 Writing fashion articles, like wet-nursing, can only be done properly by women.

Mark Twain, American writer (1835–1910). *The Washoe Giant in San Francisco*, 'The Lick House Ball' (1938).

2 Fashion is what one wears oneself. What is unfashionable is what other people wear.

Oscar Wilde, Irish playwright, poet and wit (1854–1900). *An Ideal Husband*, Act 3 (1895).

3 Style largely depends on the way the chin is worn. They are worn very high, just at present.

Oscar Wilde, Irish playwright, poet and wit (1854–1900). *The Importance of Being Earnest*, Act 3 (1895).

4 Women's styles may change but their designs remain the same.

Oscar Wilde. Quoted in *The Home Book of Humorous Quotations*, ed. A.K. Adams (1969).

5 After all, what is a fashion? From the artistic point of view, it is usually a form of ugliness so intolerable that we have to alter it every six months.

Oscar Wilde. Attributed remark.

See also STYLE.

Fast-talking

6 Hubert Humphrey talks so fast that listening to him is like trying to read *Playboy* magazine with your wife turning the pages.

Barry Goldwater, American Republican politician (1909–98). Quoted in Ned Sherrin, *Cutting Edge* (1984).

Fate

7 I'm not absolutely certain of my facts, but I rather fancy it's Shakespeare – or, if not, it's some equally brainy bird – who says that it's always just when a fellow is feeling particularly braced with things in general that Fate sneaks up behind him with the bit of lead piping. And what I'm driving at is that the man is perfectly right.

(Sir) P(elham) G. Wodehouse, English-born novelist and lyricist (1881–1975). *Carry on, Jeeves!*, 'Jeeves and the Unbidden Guest' (1925).

8 Unseen in the background, Fate was quietly slipping the lead into the boxing-glove.

(Sir) P(elham) G. Wodehouse. *Very Good, Jeeves*, 'Jeeves and the Old School Chum' (1930).

Fathers

9 When I was a boy of fourteen, my father was so ignorant I could hardly stand to have the old man around. But when I got to be twenty-one, I was astonished at how much he had learned in seven years.

Mark Twain, American writer (1835–1910). Quoted in *Reader's Digest* (September 1939). But if Twain ever said this, there was more than a hint of poetic licence about it. His own father died when Twain was eleven.

10 Fathers should be neither seen nor heard. That is the only proper basis for family life.

Oscar Wilde, Irish playwright, poet and wit (1854–1900). *An Ideal Husband*, Act 4 (1895). Lord Goring speaking.

Fatness

Fat woman looking at skeleton:

11 Lor! Miss – are we really as thin as that inside?

Anonymous. Caption to cartoon in *Punch* (28 August 1907).

12 Outside every fat man there was an even fatter man trying to close in.

(Sir) Kingsley Amis, English novelist, poet and critic (1922–95). *One Fat Englishman* (1963).

During the First World War, a patriotic hostess pointedly asked the more than portly G.K. Chesterton, 'Why are you not out at the Front?' He replied to her, gently:

13 Madam, if you go round to the side, you will find that I am.

G.K. Chesterton, English poet, novelist and critic (1874–1936). Quoted in A.N. Wilson, *Hilaire Belloc* (1984).

1 Imprisoned in every fat man a thin one is wildly signalling to be let out.

Cyril Connolly, English writer and critic (1903–74). *The Unquiet Grave* (1944).

2 I see no objection to stoutness – in moderation.

(Sir) W.S. Gilbert, English writer and lyricist (1836–1911). *Iolanthe*, Act 1 (1882).

3 I cannot but bless the memory of Julius Caesar, for the great esteem he expressed for fat men, and his aversion to lean ones.

David Hume, Scottish historian and philosopher (1711–76). Quoted in *The Treasury of Humorous Quotations*, eds Evan Esar & Nicolas Bentley (1951).

4 Inside every fat Englishman is a thin Hindu trying to get out.

Timothy Leary, American hippie guru (1920–96).

5 I'm fat, but I'm thin inside. Has it ever struck you that there's a thin man inside every fat man, just as they say there's a statue inside every block of stone?

George Orwell, English novelist and journalist (1903–50). *Coming Up for Air* (1939).

Driver to stout countrywoman trying to board an omnibus:

6 Try zideways, Mrs Jones, try zideways!
To which Mrs Jones replies:
Lar' bless 'ee, John, I ain't got no zideways.'

L. Raven-Hill, English cartoonist. Caption to cartoon in *Punch* (17 October 1900). Earlier in *Punch* (27 June 1885) there had been the caption to a cartoon of a Pew-opener saying to a fat woman with a bustle: 'Try it *sideways*, Miss!' Recalled when opera diva Jessye Norman (who has a big voice and body to match) complained about an otherwise admiring article in *Classic CD* Magazine. It had jokingly told of the occasion when, trapped in swing doors on the way to a concert, she was advised to turn sideways and release herself. In ringing tones, Norman declared: 'Honey, I ain't got no sideways.'

Norman attempted to sue for libel on the grounds that the words conformed to a 'degrading, racist stereotype of a person of African-American heritage'. Striking out her claim, in a ruling at the Court of Appeal in London (November 1998), Lord Justice Gibson said he wished 'that Miss Norman had told the hoary old joke contained in the anecdote' as it would have 'shown she had a sense of humour as well as her other talents.'

Muriel Smith spotted another appearance of this old chestnut in Maisie Ward's *Gilbert Keith Chesterton* (1944) in an account of Chesterton's visit to the United States in 1930–31, when he gave a course of lectures at Notre Dame. The chauffeur there, Johnny Mangan, said: 'I brought him under the main building and he got stuck in the door of the car. Father O'Donnell tried to help. Mr Chesterton said it reminded him of an old Irishwoman: "Why don't you get out sideways?" "I have no sideways".'

7 Elizabeth Taylor is wearing Orson Welles designer jeans.

Joan Rivers, American entertainer (1937–). Quoted in Ned Sherrin, *Cutting Edge* (1984).

8 Elizabeth Taylor's so fat, she puts mayonnaise on an aspirin.

Joan Rivers. Quoted in my book *A Year of Stings and Squelches* (1985).

9 *Alfred Hitchcock*:
One look at you, Mr Shaw, and I know there's famine in the land.
Bernard Shaw:
One look at you, Mr Hitchcock, and I know who caused it.

Bernard Shaw, Irish playwright and critic (1856–1950). Quoted in Blanche Patch, *Thirty Years With GBS* (1951).

10 If the fence is strong enough I'll sit on it.

(Sir) Cyril Smith, English Liberal politician (1928–). Quoted in *The Observer* (15 September 1974). Member of Parliament for Rochdale (1972–92), 'Big Cyril' weighed something like twenty-five stones.

To a young Scot who was about to marry an Irish widow twice his age and twice his size:

11 Going to marry her! Impossible! You mean a part of her; he could not marry her all him-

self ... There is enough of her to furnish wives for a whole parish ... You might people a colony with her; or give an assembly with her; or perhaps take your morning's walk round her, always provided there were frequent resting-places, and you were in rude health.

(Revd) Sydney Smith, English clergyman, essayist and wit (1771–1845). Quoted in Hesketh Pearson, *The Smith of Smiths*, Chap. 11 (1934).

1 She fitted into my biggest arm-chair as if it had been built round her by someone who knew they were wearing arm-chairs tight about the hips that season.

(Sir) P(elham) G. Wodehouse, English-born novelist and lyricist (1881–1975). *My Man Jeeves*, 'Jeeves and the Unbidden Guest' (1919).

2 The Right Hon was a tubby little chap who looked as if he had been poured into his clothes and had forgotten to say 'When!'

(Sir) P(elham) G. Wodehouse. *Very Good, Jeeves*, 'Jeeves and the Impending Doom' (1930).

3 A fat man should not play the concertina.

Mao Zedong, Chinese revolutionary and Communist leader (1893–1976). Quoted on BBC Radio *Quote ... Unquote* (10 May 1978). Perhaps attributed to Mao simply as a change from Confucius?

Faults

4 *Si nous n'avions point de défauts, nous ne prendrions pas tant de plaisir à en remarquer dans les autres* [If we had no faults, we should not take so much pleasure in remarking them in others].

François, Duc de La Rochefoucauld, French writer (1613–80). *Maximes*, No. 31 (1678).

5 Don't tell your friends their social faults; they will cure the fault and never forgive you.

Logan Pearsall Smith, American writer (1865–1946). *All Trivia* (1933).

6 When you have done a fault, be always pert and insolent, and behave yourself as if you were the injured person; this will immediately put your master or lady off their mettle.

Jonathan Swift, Anglo-Irish writer and clergyman (1667–1745). *Directions to Servants* (1745).

7 Always acknowledge a fault frankly. This will throw those in authority off their guard and give you opportunity to commit more.

Mark Twain, American writer (1835–1910). *More Maxims of Mark Twain*, ed. Merle Johnson (1927).

8 It is easy to find fault, if one has that disposition. There was once a man who, not being able to find any other fault with his coal, complained that there were too many prehistoric toads in it.

Mark Twain. *Pudd'nhead Wilson*, Chap. 9 (1894).

Fear

9 I get goose pimples. Even my goose pimples get goose pimples.

Line from film *The Cat and the Canary* (US 1939). Screenwriters: Walter de Leon, Lynn Starling. Spoken by Bob Hope (Wally Campbell).

Fecundity

The children of a famous diplomat, Lord Lytton, organized a charade. The scene displayed a Crusader knight returning from the wars to his ancestral castle. At the castle-gate he was welcomed by his beautiful and rejoicing wife, to whom, after tender salutations, he recounted his triumphs on the tented fields and the number of paynim whom he had slain. Replied his wife, pointing with conscious pride to a long row of dolls of various sizes:

10 And I, too, my lord, have not been idle.

Anonymous. Quoted in G.W.E. Russell, *Collections and Recollections* (1898).

Feelings

Retiring from the US Supreme Court in 1992, Marshall was asked at a press conference the cliché question, 'How do you feel?' He replied:

1 With my hands.

Thurgood Marshall, American judge (1908–93). Quoted in the *Texas Lawyer* (6 January 1992).

2 The advantage of the emotions is that they lead us astray.

Oscar Wilde, Irish playwright, poet and wit (1854–1900). *The Picture of Dorian Gray*, Chap. 3 (1891).

3 The secret of life is never to have an emotion that is unbecoming.

Oscar Wilde. *A Woman of No Importance*, Act 3 (1893).

Feminism

4 I was the first woman to burn my bra – it took the fire department four days to put it out.

Dolly Parton, American singer (1946–). Quoted in Barbara Rowes, *The Book of Quotes* (1979).

5 Ginger Rogers did everything that Fred Astaire did. She just did it backward and in high heels.

Ann Richards, American Democratic politician (1933–). *Straight from the Heart* (1989). This familiar feminist line has also been attributed to Linda Ellerbee and Faith Whittlesey.

6 We are becoming the men we wanted to marry.

Gloria Steinem, American feminist writer (1934–). In *Ms* Magazine (July/August 1982).

7 I myself have never been able to find out precisely what feminism is: I only know that people call me a feminist whenever I express sentiments that differentiate me from a doormat or a prostitute.

(Dame) Rebecca West, Irish-born writer (1892–1983). 'Mr Chesterton in Hysterics: A Study in Prejudice', in *The Clarion* (14 November 1913).

Fence-sitting

On Sir John Simon:

8 Simon has sat on the fence so long that the iron has entered into his soul.

David Lloyd George (1st Earl Lloyd George of Dwyfor), British Liberal Prime Minister (1863–1945). Quoted in A.J.P. Taylor, *English History 1914–1945* (1965). Simon had been Attorney General and Home Secretary in Asquith's Liberal government but had resigned by the time Lloyd George became PM in 1916. He formed a division of the Liberal Party in the 1920s which Lloyd George scorned.

Fiction

9 'Very strange!' he said to himself, vacantly. 'It's like a scene in a novel – it's like nothing in real life.'

Wilkie Collins, English novelist (1824–89). *No Name* (1862–3).

10 I'm really very sorry for you all, but it's an unjust world, and virtue is triumphant only in theatrical performances.

(Sir) W.S. Gilbert, English writer and lyricist (1836–1911). *The Mikado*, Act 2 (1885).

11 If this were played upon a stage now, I could condemn it as an improbable fiction.

William Shakespeare, English playwright and poet (1564–1616). *Twelfth Night*, III.iv.128 (1600). Fabian speaking.

12 The author of this novel and all the characters mentioned in it are completely fictitious. There is no such city as Manchester.

Howard Spring, Welsh novelist (1889–1965). *Shabby Tiger*, Epigraph (1934).

13 *Miss Prism*:

The good ended happily, and the bad unhappily. That is what fiction means.

Oscar Wilde, Irish playwright, poet and wit (1854–1900). *The Importance of Being Earnest*, Act 2 (1895).

Film criticism

Reviewing the film Random Harvest *(US 1942):*

1 I would like to recommend this film to those who can stay interested in Ronald Colman's amnesia for two hours and who could with pleasure eat a bowl of Yardley's shaving soap for breakfast.

James Agee, American critic and screenwriter (1909–55). Quoted in Leslie Halliwell, *The Filmgoer's Book of Quotes* (1973).

On the 1959 remake of Ben-Hur*:*

2 Loved Ben, hated Hur.

Anonymous (critic). Quoted in the same collection as above.

On the 1972 film of Shakespeare's Antony and Cleopatra, *starring and directed by Charlton Heston:*

3 The Biggest Asp Disaster in the World.

Anonymous tabloid newspaper journalist. Quoted by Richard Boston on BBC Radio *Quote ... Unquote* (4 January 1976).

On the film I Am a Camera *(US 1955):*

4 Me no Leica.

Anonymous (critic). Quoted in Leslie Halliwell, *The Filmgoer's Book of Quotes* (1973). Ascribed to C.A. Lejeune in *The Penguin Dictionary of Modern Quotations* (1980 edn). Also attributed to George Jean Nathan, Walter Kerr and Kenneth Tynan. But in a review of the film by the critic of the *Sunday Dispatch* (16 October 1955) appears: 'No Leica, snarled a New York critic.'

To Tennessee Williams at premiere of film based on his play Orpheus Descending *(US 1957):*

5 Darling, they've absolutely ruined your perfectly dreadful play!

Tallulah Bankhead, American actress (1903–68). Quoted in Peter Hay, *Broadway Anecdotes* (1989).

Of Peter O'Toole in the film Lawrence of Arabia *(UK 1962):*

6 If it had been any prettier, it would have been *Florence of Arabia*.

(Sir) Noël Coward, English entertainer and writer (1899–1973). Quoted in *The Sayings of Noël Coward*, ed. Philip Hoare (1997).

On the film Love Story *(US 1970):*

7 Happiness is a warm bed pan.

Christopher Hudson. Quoted in my book *A Year of Stings and Squelches* (1985).

On the film My Son My Son *(US 1940):*

8 My Son My Son, my sainted aunt!

C(aroline) A. Lejeune, English film critic (1897–1973). Attributed criticism.

On the film No Leave No Love *(US 1946):*

9 No comment.

C.A. Lejeune. Attributed criticism.

On the film I Was Framed *(US 1942):*

10 Yes, but was you hung?

C.A. Lejeune. In the *News Chronicle*. Quoted in *The Observer* (21 December 1997).

On the film Anything Goes *(US 1956):*

11 Obviously.

C.A. Lejeune. Quoted in *The Observer* (4 January 1998).

On the film Her Primitive Man *(US 1944):*

12 *Cave*.

C.A. Lejeune. Quoted in *The Observer* (11 January 1998).

On the film Gilda *(US 1946) and its slogan, 'There never was a woman like Gilda!':*

13 There never was.

C.A. Lejeune. Quoted in *The Observer* (18 January 1998).

On Charlton Heston's performance as a doctor:

14 It makes me want to call out, Is there an apple in the house?

C.A. Lejeune. Quoted in my book *The 'Quote ... Unquote' Book of Love, Death and the Universe* (1980).

During a viewing of the lengthy film Exodus *(US 1960):*

1 Let my people go!

Mort Sahl, American satirist (1926–). As told on his record album 'The New Frontier' (1961). Another version is that Sahl, invited by the director, Otto Preminger, to a preview, stood up after three hours and said, 'Otto – let my people go!'

Films

2 *Per essere considerato un classico un film deve riuscire a far sbadigliare almeno tre generazoni di spetattori* [To be considered a classic, a film must succeed in making at least three generations of moviegoers yawn].

Marco Ferreri, Italian film director (1928–). Attributed remark.

3 Every film should have a beginning, a middle and an end – but not necessarily in that order.

Jean-Luc Godard, French film director (1930–). Quoted in Len Deighton, *Close Up* (1972). Has also been ascribed to the French film director Georges Franju (1912–87) – as in *Time* Magazine (14 September 1981).

4 French films follow a basic formula: Husband sleeps with Jeanne because Bernadette cuckolded him by sleeping with Christophe, and in the end they all go off to a restaurant.

Sophie Marceau, French actress (1967–). Quoted in *The Observer*, 'Sayings of the Week' (26 March 1995).

5 *Joe:*

You're Norma Desmond – used to be in silent pictures – used to be big.

Norma:

I *am* big. It's the pictures that got small.

Line from film *Sunset Boulevard* (US 1950). Screenwriters: Charles Brackett, Billy Wilder, D.M. Marshman Jnr. Spoken by Gloria Swanson (Norma Desmond) and William Holden (Joe Gillis).

Finance and Financiers

6 A financier is a pawnbroker with imagination.

(Sir) Arthur Wing Pinero, English playwright (1855–1934). Quoted in *The Treasury of Humorous Quotations*, eds Evan Esar & Nicolas Bentley (1951).

7 Finance is the art of passing currency from hand to hand until it finally disappears.

Robert Sarnoff, American TV executive (1918–). Quoted in *The Executive's Quotation Book*, ed. James Charlton (1983).

Fishing

8 I never lost a little fish. Yes, I am free to say,
It always was the biggest fish I caught that
got away.

Eugene Field, American journalist and humorist (1850–95). Quoted in *The Treasury of Humorous Quotations*, eds Evan Esar & Nicolas Bentley (1951).

9 There are more fish taken out of a stream than ever were in it.

Oliver Herford, American humorist (1863–1935). Quoted in the same collection as above.

10 Fly fishing may be a very pleasant amusement; but angling or float fishing I can only compare to a stick and a string, with a worm at one end and a fool at the other.

(Dr) Samuel Johnson, English writer and lexicographer (1709–84). Quoted in Hawker, *Instructions to Young Sportsmen* (1859).

11 It is to be observed that 'angling' is the name given to fishing by people who can't fish.

Stephen Leacock, Canadian economist and humorist (1869–1944). 'When Fellers Go Fishing'.

Flattery

A schoolboy applicant for a naval college is being interviewed. An examining admiral asks him, 'Now mention three great admirals.' The candidate replies:

12 Drake, Nelson and – I beg your pardon, Sir, I didn't quite catch your name.

Anonymous (cartoonist). Caption to cartoon in *Punch* (24 June 1914).

1 Everyone likes flattery; and when you come to Royalty you should lay it on with a trowel.

Benjamin Disraeli (1st Earl of Beaconsfield), English politician and writer (1804–81). Remark to Matthew Arnold, quoted in G.W.E. Russell, *Collections and Recollections*, Chap.23 (1898). The most notable example of Disraeli's own use of the trowel must be his saying 'We authors, Ma'am' to Queen Victoria when she published her Highland journals and on several other occasions (asserted by Monypenny and Buckle, *Life of Disraeli*, 1910–20, though G.W.E. Russell had already had it in his book).

To a young lady:

2 Won't you come into the garden? I would like my roses to see you.

Richard Brinsley Sheridan, English dramatist and politician (1751–1816). Quoted in Rose Heniker Heaton, *The Perfect Hostess* (1931).

3 I suppose flattery hurts no one – that is, if he doesn't inhale.

Adlai Stevenson, American Democratic politician (1900–65). On *Meet the Press*, TV broadcast (29 March 1952).

4 'Tis an old maxim in the schools,
That Vanity's the food of fools;
Yet now and then your men of wit
Will condescend to taste a bit.

Jonathan Swift, Anglo-Irish writer and clergyman (1667–1745). *Cadenus and Vanessa* (written 1713). George Crabbe, in quoting this, used the words 'flattery' in place of 'vanity'.

Flirting

5 Flirt: a woman who thinks it's every man for herself.

Anonymous. Quoted in *The Penguin Dictionary of Modern Humorous Quotations*, ed. Fred Metcalf (1987).

Man flirting with a woman:

6 Tell me about yourself – your struggles, your dreams, your telephone number.

Peter Arno, American cartoonist (1904–68). Quoted in A. Andrews, *Quotations for Speakers and Writers* (1969).

7 Nothing sharpens the wits like promiscuous flirtation.

George Moore, Irish novelist (1852–1933). Quoted in *The Treasury of Humorous Quotations*, eds Evan Esar & Nicolas Bentley (1951).

To Bernard Shaw after an empty flirtation (1887):

8 You had no right to write the Preface if you were not going to write the book.

E(dith) Nesbit, English writer (1858–1924). Quoted in Michael Holroyd, *Bernard Shaw*, Vol. 1 (1988).

9 *Algernon*:
The amount of women in London who flirt with their husbands is perfectly scandalous. It looks so bad. It is simply washing one's clean linen in public.

Oscar Wilde, Irish playwright, poet and wit (1854–1900). *The Importance of Being Earnest*, Act 1 (1895).

See also CHATTING UP.

Flynn, Errol

AUSTRALIAN-BORN AMERICAN ACTOR (1909–59)

10 The great thing about Errol was – you always knew precisely where you stood with him because he *always* let you down. He let himself down too, from time to time, but that was his prerogative.

David Niven, English actor (1909–83). *Bring On the Empty Horses*, 'Errol' (1975).

Food and food criticism

11 Eating cottage cheese is like kissing your sister.

Anonymous. Overheard remark quoted by Isabelle Lucas on BBC Radio *Quote ... Unquote* (19 January 1982).

12 *Wife of Two Years' Standing:*
Oh yes! I'm sure he's not so fond of me as at first. He's away so much, neglects me dreadfully, and he's so cross when he comes home. What shall I do?

Widow:
Feed the brute!

Anonymous. Cartoon caption in *Punch* (31 October 1885).

On a piece of pie:

1 Age cannot wither it, nor custard stale its infinite variety.

Anonymous. Quoted in my book *Quote ... Unquote* (1978).

2 And what they could not eat that night,
The queen next morning fried.

Anonymous (nursery rhyme). 'When good King Arthur ruled this land, / He was a goodly king.' *The Oxford Dictionary of Nursery Rhymes* (1951) finds a version *c.* 1799. Referring to a bag pudding, well-stuffed with plums.

3 There is no such thing as a little garlic.

Arthur ('Bugs') Baer, American humorist (1897?–1969). Quoted in *The Frank Muir Book* (1976).

4 A gourmet who thinks of calories is like a tart who looks at her watch.

James Beard, American food writer (1903–). Inscribed beneath his portrait in Charley O's bar, New York City.

5 'Oh my friends be warned by me,
That breakfast, dinner, lunch and tea
Are all the human frame requires ... '
With that, the wretched child expires.

Hilaire Belloc, French-born English poet and writer (1870–1953). *Cautionary Tales*, 'Henry King' (whose 'chief defect ... was chewing little bits of string') (1907).

6 There are in England sixty different religions and only one gravy [or sauce], melted butter.

(Marquis) Francesco Caraccioli, Neapolitan diplomat (1752–99). Quoted in *The Home Book of Humorous Quotations*, ed. A.K. Adams (1969).

7 The turkey has practically no taste except a dry fibrous flavour reminiscent of a mixture of warmed-up plaster of Paris and horsehair. The texture is like wet sawdust and the whole vast feathered swindle has the piquancy of a boiled mattress.

Cassandra (Sir William Connor), English journalist (1909–67). In the *Daily Mirror* (24 December 1953).

When waiter expressed concern that he had found too much shot in his woodcock:

8 No ... No, it died a natural death. Trouble is, there's too much wood and not enough cock.

(Sir) Noël Coward, English entertainer and writer (1899–1973). Quoted in Richard Briers, *Coward and Company* (1987).

Of champagne arriving with the pudding after a series of poorly heated courses at a public dinner:

9 Thank God for something warm at last.

Benjamin Disraeli (1st Earl of Beaconsfield), English politician and writer (1804–81). Quoted in *The Sayings of Disraeli*, ed. Robert Blake (1992).

As an elderly man, asked why he did not take supper:

10 For my part, now, I consider supper as a turnpike through which one must pass, in order to get to bed.

Oliver Edwards, English lawyer (1711–91). Quoted in James Boswell, *The Life of Samuel Johnson* (1791) – for 17 April 1778.

11 Eat to live, and not live to eat.

Benjamin Franklin, American politician and scientist (1706–90). *Poor Richard's Almanack* (May 1733) – a work in which Franklin often revised already existing sayings.

12 To barbecue is a way of life rather than a desirable method of cooking.

(Sir) Clement Freud, English humorist and politician (1924–). *Freud on Food* (1978).

13 If eels only looked a little less like eels more people would want to eat them.

(Sir) Clement Freud. In the same book as above.

14 It Must Be Jelly ('Cause Jam Don't Shake Like That).

Sunny Skylar, American songwriter. Title of song, with music by George Williams and J. Chalmers (Chummy)

McGregor (1942). It was introduced and first recorded in that year by Glen Miller (and sung by The Modernaires). Later associated with 'Fats' Waller.

1 The piece of cod passeth all understanding.

Sir Edwin Lutyens, English architect (1869–1944). Quoted in Robert Lutyens, *Sir Edwin Lutyens* (1942).

2 Parsley
Is gharsely.

Ogden Nash, American poet (1902–71). *Good Intentions*, 'Further Reflections on Parsley' (1942).

3 The mountain sheep are sweeter,
But the valley sheep are fatter,
We therefore deemed it meeter
To carry off the latter.

Thomas Love Peacock, English poet and novelist (1785–1866). *The Misfortunes of Elphin*, 'The War-Song of Dinas Vawr' (1829).

4 After all the trouble you go to, you get about as much actual 'food' out of eating artichoke as you would licking thirty or forty postage stamps. Have the shrimp cocktail instead.

Miss Piggy, *Miss Piggy's Guide to Life (as told to Henry Beard)* (1981).

5 The goose is a silly bird – too much for one to eat, and not enough for two.

Charles H. Poole. *Archaic Words*.

6 I heard a lady who sat next me, in a low, sweet voice, say, 'No gravy, Sir.' I had never seen her before, but I turned suddenly round and said, 'Madam, I have been looking for a person who disliked gravy all my life; let us swear eternal friendship.'

(Revd) Sydney Smith, English clergyman, essayist and wit (1771–1845). Quoted in Lady Holland, *A Memoir of Sydney Smith* (1855).

7 He was a bold man that first eat an oyster.

Jonathan Swift, Anglo-Irish writer and clergyman (1667–1745). *Polite Conversation*, Dialogue 2 (1738). There is an earlier version in Thomas Fuller's *History of the Worthies of England* (1662): 'He was a very valiant man who first ventured on eating of oysters.'

8 It was only when we arrived [at the inn of Dalwhinnie] that one of the maids recognized me … We had a very good-sized bedroom. Albert had a dressing-room of equal size … But unfortunately there was hardly anything to eat, and there was only tea, and two miserable starved Highland chickens, without any potatoes! No pudding, and no fun! … It was not a nice supper.

Victoria, British Queen (1819–1901). Journal entry (8 October 1861). Victoria published *Leaves from a Journal of our Life in the Highlands* (1868) and *More Leaves* (1883).

To a waiter:

9 When I ask for a watercress sandwich, I do not mean a loaf with a field in the middle of it.

Oscar Wilde, Irish playwright, poet and wit (1854–1900). Recounted in a letter from Max Beerbohm to Reggie Turner (15 April 1893).

10 After a good dinner, one can forgive anybody, even one's own relations.

Oscar Wilde. *A Woman of No Importance*, Act 2 (1893).

See also DINING.

Fools

11 It is better to be silent and be thought a fool than to speak out and remove all doubt.

Anonymous (proverb). *Compare* SILENCE 398:3.

12 The traditional fool and his money are lucky ever to have got together in the first place.

Anonymous. Quoted in *The Home Book of Humorous Quotations*, ed. A.K. Adams (1969).

13 Fools' names, like fools' faces,
Are often seen in public places.

Anonymous (graffito). Recorded as a comment from 1928 in Allen Walker Read, *Lexical Evidence From Folk Epigraphy in Western North America* (1935).

1 I have always heard it said, that to do a kindness to clowns, is like throwing water into the sea.

Miguel de Cervantes, Spanish novelist (1547–1616). *Don Quixote*, Pt 1, Chap. 23 (1605).

2 When he said we were trying to make a fool of him, I could only murmur that the Creator had beat us to it.

Ilka Chase, American actress and author (1900–78). Quoted in *The Treasury of Humorous Quotations*, eds Evan Esar & Nicolas Bentley (1951).

3 If you once forfeit the confidence of your fellow citizens, you can never regain their respect and esteem. You may fool all the people some of the time; you can even fool some of the people all the time; but you can't fool all of the people all the time.

Abraham Lincoln, American Republican President (1809–65). Quoted in Alexander K. McLure, *Lincoln's Yarns and Stories* (1904). There is so much Lincolniana – and so much that can't be verified – but this has the authentic ring. Lincoln reportedly made the remark during a senatorial campaign speech in Illinois (May 1856 – other dates are mentioned), but it was not quoted at the time and it does not appear in his published works. The saying has also been ascribed to P.T. Barnum – this, however, presumably out of confusion with 'There's a sucker born every minute.'

To a tiresome escort who exclaimed, 'I can't bear fools':

4 That's queer. Your mother could.

Dorothy Parker, American writer (1893–1967). Quoted in Ned Sherrin, *Cutting Edge* (1984). Compare: 'If I had a son who was a fool I'd make him [a cook or a diplomatist]' – 'I see your father did not hold the same opinion' – exchange from Oscar Wilde, *Vera, or the Nihilist*. Act 2 (1880).

5 Ah, well, I am a great and sublime fool. But then I am God's fool, and all His work must be contemplated with respect.

Mark Twain, American writer (1835–1910). Quoted in A.B. Paine, *Mark Twain: A Biography* (1912).

Foot-in-mouth remarks

Of the athlete Alberto Juantorena, competing in the 400 metres heats at the 1976 Montreal Olympics:

6 Juantorena opens wide his legs and shows his class.

Ron Pickering, English broadcaster (1930–91). Attributed remark, long ascribed to David Coleman. Since the late 1970s, *Private Eye* Magazine has had a column with the title 'Colemanballs' devoted chiefly to the inanities of TV and radio sports commentators. The name was derived from David Coleman (1926–), BBC TV's principal sports commentator at the time. Coleman was generally supposed to have committed any number of solecisms, tautologies and what-have-you in the cause of keeping his tongue wagging. Hearers who report his sayings have often been inaccurate. It is believed, however, that he did say, among other things, 'This man could be a black horse', 'There is only one winner in this race' and – of the footballer Asa Hartford who had a hole-in-the-heart operation – 'He is a whole-hearted player'.

7 I say that if Lincoln were living today, he would turn over in his grave.

Gerald R. Ford, American Republican President (1913–). Said when House Minority Leader at a Lincoln Day Republican rally (quoted in *Time Magazine*, 17 February 1967). Suggested as one of Ford's idiocies in *c.* 1975, but a traditional joke. In Roger Woddis's poem 'Final Curtain' (written about and probably near the time of Watergate, 1973–4) he has: 'George Washington's dead, / Like the pledge that I gave, / But if he were alive / He would turn in his grave.'

8 'Dentopedology' is the science of opening your mouth and putting your foot in it. I've been practising it for years.

Philip, Greek-born British Prince and consort of Queen Elizabeth II (1921–). Quoted in Herbert V. Prochnow, Snr & Jnr, *A Treasury of Humorous Quotations* (1969). As 'dontopedology', this view is said to have been expressed in a speech to the (British) General Dental Council and quoted in *Time* Magazine (21 November 1960).

1 Every time he opens his mouth at the Town Hall, he puts his foot in it, so they call him 'the foot and mouth disease'. Ha. Ha.

J.B. Priestley, English novelist and playwright (1894–1984). *When We Are Married* (1938).

Football

Of footballer Kevin Keegan:

2 He is not fit to lace George Best's drinks.

John Roberts, English football journalist. Attributed remark (by 1990).

In a football match:

3 The first ninety minutes are the most important.

Bobby Robson, English football manager (1933–). Quoted as title of TV documentary (1983). He was manager of the England football team at the time.

4 Some people think football is a matter of life and death. I don't like that attitude. I can assure them it is much more serious than that.

Bill Shankly, Scottish football manager (1914–81). Quoted in *The Guardian*, 'Sports Quotes of the Year' (24 December 1973).

Forbidding Cornell's first intercollegiate football game with the University of Michigan at Cleveland, Ohio, in 1873:

5 I will not permit thirty men to travel four hundred miles to agitate a bag of wind.

Andrew D. White, American academic (1832–1918). Quoted in Stuart Berg Flexner, *Listening to America* (1982). White was the first President of Cornell University (1867–85).

Ford, Gerald R.

AMERICAN REPUBLICAN PRESIDENT (1913–)

6 He played too much football without a helmet.

Anonymous. Quoted in my book *Quote ... Unquote* (1978). Other criticisms: 'He'd fuck up a two-car funeral'; 'He couldn't find the seat of his pants with both hands.'

7 He looks like the guy in a science fiction movie who is the first to see the Creature.

David Frye, American impressionist and comedian (1934–). Attributed in 1975. Quoted in the same book as above.

8 A year ago Gerald Ford was unknown throughout America, now he's unknown throughout the world.

Anonymous. Quoted in *The Guardian* (August 1974) and then in *The Penguin Dictionary of Modern Quotations* (1980). When he replaced Spiro Agnew as US Vice-President.

9 That Gerald Ford. He can't fart and chew gum at the same time.

Lyndon B. Johnson, American Democratic President (1908–73). Quoted in Richard Reeves, *A Ford Not a Lincoln* (1975) and J.K. Galbraith, *A Life in Our Times* (1981).

10 Ford is bunk, says history.

Miles Kington, English humorist (1941–). Ascribed by Alan Brien on BBC Radio *Quote ... Unquote* (13 October 1984).

Foreign affairs

11 I'd never heard of this place Guatemala until I was in my seventy-ninth year.

(Sir) Winston S. Churchill, British Conservative Prime Minister and writer (1874–1965). During his visit to the US (June 1954), recorded by Lord Moran in *The Struggle for Survival* (1966). Earlier, Moran recorded Churchill saying on 28 April 1953: 'I have lived seventy-eight years without hearing of bloody places like Cambodia.'

Foreign policy

On his foreign policy when Labour Foreign Secretary:

12 My policy is to be able to take a ticket at Victoria Station and go anywhere I damn well please.

Ernest Bevin, English Labour politician (1881–1951). Quoted in *The Spectator* (20 April 1951).

Foreigners

1 Everybody has the right to pronounce foreign names as he chooses.

(Sir) Winston S. Churchill, British Conservative Prime Minister and writer (1874–1965). Quoted in *The Observer* (5 August 1951).

2 'Frogs,' he would say, 'are slightly better than Huns or Wops, but abroad is unutterably bloody and foreigners are fiends.'

Nancy Mitford, English novelist (1904–73). *The Pursuit of Love*, Chap. 15 (1945). Compare from Chap. 10: 'I loathe abroad, nothing would induce me to live there ... and, as for foreigners, they are all the same, and they all make me sick.' Mitford wrote both these passages in the character of 'Uncle Matthew'. This no great opinion of foreigners is put down to his four years in France and Italy between 1914 and 1918. It certainly does not reflect her own view – she lived in France for many years until her death.

Foreplay

3 He twisted my nipples as though tuning a radio.

Lisa Alther, American writer (1944–). *Kinflicks* (1976).

Foresight

4 When a man buys a motor car, he doesn't always know what he is letting himself in for.

Jaroslav Hašek, Czechoslovakian writer (1883–1923). *The Good Soldier Švejk* (*c*.1923). Švejk's charwoman tells him of the assassination of Franz Ferdinand – the event that triggered the First World War – as the Archduke drove through Sarajevo in a motor car. Švejk deduces the above from this occurrence. Hašek's humour is oblique at the best of times (some would say imperceptible) and another translator renders this passage much more meekly, thus: 'Yes, of course, a gentleman like him can afford it, but he never imagines that a drive like that might finish up badly.'

Forgetfulness

5 One always forgets the most important things. It's the things that one can't remember that stay with you.

Alan Bennett, English playwright and actor (1934–). *Forty Years On*, Act 1 (1969).

6 Only three men in Europe had ever understood [the Schleswig-Holstein question], and of these the Prince Consort is dead, a Danish statesman is in an asylum, and I myself have forgotten it.

Lord Palmerston, British Prime Minister (1784–1865). Quoted in R.W. Seton-Watson, *Britain in Europe 1789–1914* (1937).

Of Richard Porson, English scholar (1759–1808):

7 There were moments when his memory failed him; and he would forget to eat dinner, though he never forgot a quotation.

(Dame) Edith Sitwell, English poet (1887–1964). *English Eccentrics* (1933). Just prior to this remark she has described how Porson, Regius Professor of Greek at Cambridge, set about a young man in a hackney coach who had produced inaccurate quotations to impress the ladies.

8 There are three things I always forget. Names, faces, and – the third I can't remember.

Italo Svevo, Italian novelist (1861–1928). Quoted in *The Penguin Dictionary of Modern Quotations*, eds J.M. & M.J. Cohen (1971).

Forster, E. M.

ENGLISH NOVELIST (1879–1970)

9 E.M. Forster never gets any further than warming the teapot. He's a rare fine hand at that. Feel this teapot. Is it not beautifully warm? Yes, but there ain't going to be no tea.

Katherine Mansfield, New Zealand-born writer (1888–1923). *Journal* (1927) – entry for May 1917.

Forty

One actress about another:

10 Pushing forty? She's clinging on to it for dear life!

Anonymous. Quoted by Julian Mitchell on BBC Radio *Quote ... Unquote* (5 January 1982).

Fragility

1 He was in the sort of overwrought state when a fly treading a little too heavily on the carpet is enough to make a man think he's one of the extras in *All Quiet On the Western Front*.

(Sir) P(elham) G. Wodehouse, English-born novelist and lyricist (1881–1975). *Young Men in Spats,* 'The Luck of the Stiffhams' (1936).

2 He says his memory is blurred. All he can recall is waking next morning on the floor of his bedroom and shooting up to the ceiling when a sparrow on the window-sill chirped unexpectedly.

(Sir) P(elham) G. Wodehouse. *A Few Quick Ones,* 'The Right Approach' (1936).

3 'Have you an aspirin about you?'
'Certainly, m'lord. I have just been taking one myself.'
He produced a small tin box, and held it out.
'Thank you, Jeeves. Don't slam the lid.'

(Sir) P(elham) G. Wodehouse. *Ring for Jeeves*, Chap. 18 (1953).

Having had too little to smoke:

4 Yes, he felt, analysing his emotions, he was distinctly nervous. The noise of the cat stamping about in the passage outside caused him exquisite discomfort.

(Sir) P(elham) G. Wodehouse. *Mr Mulliner Speaking,* 'The Man Who Gave Up Smoking' (1929).

France and the French

5 Fifty million Frenchmen can't be wrong.

Anonymous. A good deal of confusion surrounds this phrase. As a slightly grudging expression it appears to have originated with American servicemen during the First World War, justifying support for their French allies. The precise number of millions was variable. Eric Partridge, *A Dictionary of Catch Phrases* (1985 edn), suggests that it was the last line of a First World War song 'extolling the supreme virtue of copulation, though in veiled terms'. Partridge may, however, have been referring to a song with the title (by Rose, Raskin & Fisher), which was not recorded by Sophie Tucker until 15 April 1927. Cole Porter's musical *Fifty Million Frenchmen* opened in New York on 27 November 1929. An unrelated US film with this three-word title was released in 1931.

Where the confusion has crept in is that Texas Guinan, an American nightclub hostess (1884–1933), was refused entry into France with her girls in 1931 and said: 'It goes to show that fifty million Frenchmen *can* be wrong.' She returned to America and renamed her show *Too Hot for Paris*. Perversely, the *Oxford Dictionary of Quotations* (1979, 1992) has her saying 'Fifty million Frenchmen *can't* be wrong' in the *New York World-Telegram* on 21 March 1931, and seems to be arguing that she originated the phrase as she had been using it 'six or seven years earlier'. Sometimes it is quoted as '*forty* million Frenchmen ... '

Bernard Shaw also held out against the phrase. He insisted: 'Fifty million Frenchmen can't be right.'

6 France was long a despotism tempered by epigrams.

Thomas Carlyle, Scottish historian and philosopher (1795–1881). *History of the French Revolution*, Vol. 3, Bk 7, Chap. 7 (1837).

7 France is the only place where you can make love in the afternoon without people hammering on your door.

(Dame) Barbara Cartland, English romantic novelist (1902–2000). Quoted in *The Observer*, 'Sayings of the Week' (28 October 1984).

8 France is an absolute monarchy, tempered by songs.

Nicolas-Sébastien Chamfort, French writer (1741–94). *Characters and Anecdotes* (1795).

9 If it were not for the government, we should have nothing left to laugh at in France.

Nicolas-Sébastien Chamfort. Attributed remark.

On the French actress Simone Signoret playing Lady Macbeth in English for the first time:

10 *Aimez-vous Glamis?*

(Sir) Noël Coward, English entertainer and writer (1899–

1973). Quoted in *Noël Coward: A Life in Quotes*, ed. Barry Day (1999), as having appeared in *The Washington Post* in 1969.

1 *Comment voulez-vous gouverner un pays qui a deux cent quarante-six variétés de fromage?* [How can you govern a country which produces 246 different kinds of cheese?].

Charles de Gaulle, French soldier and President (1890–1970). There are many versions of de Gaulle's aphorisms but this is probably an accurate summing up of his view of the French people, although the number of cheeses varies. 246 is Ernest Mignon's version in *Les Mots du Général* (1962). The *Oxford Dictionary of Quotations* (1979) has 265 – the occasion given for this version is the 1951 election when de Gaulle's political party, though the largest, still did not have an overall majority.

Compare the older view of De la Reyniere (d. 1838): '*On connoit en France 685 manières differentes d'accommoder les oeufs* [in France, there are 685 different ways of using eggs]'.

2 The cross of the Legion of Honor has been conferred upon me. However, few escape that distinction.

Mark Twain, American writer (1835–1910). *A Tramp Abroad*, Chap. 8 (1880).

3 France is a country where the money falls apart in your hands and you can't tear the toilet paper.

Billy Wilder, American film director and writer (1906–). Quoted in Leslie Halliwell, *The Filmgoer's Book of Quotes* (1973).

Freedom

4 Man is born free but everywhere is in cellular underwear.

Jonathan Miller, English entertainer, writer and director (1934–). *Beyond the Fringe*, 'The Heat-Death of the Universe' (1961).

Freudian slips

5 Two women stopped in front of a drugstore, and one said to her companion, 'If you will wait a few *moments* I'll soon be back.' But she said *movements* instead. She was on her way to buy some castor-oil for her child.

Sigmund Freud, Austrian psychiatrist (1856–1939). *The Psychopathology of Everyday Life* (1904).

Friends and friendship

6 God protect me from my friends.

Anonymous. Used as the title of a book (1956) by Gavin Maxwell about Salvatore Giuliano, the Sicilian bandit. From the proverbial expression: 'I can look after my enemies, but God protect me from my friends.'

7 With friends like that, who needs enemies? With a Hungarian for a friend, who needs an enemy?

Anonymous. Quoted in Eric Partridge, *A Dictionary of Catch Phrases* (1977). Referring to the Germans, the first remark has been ascribed to Joey Adams, *Cindy and I*, Chap. 30 (1957).

8 A friend married is a friend lost.

Anonymous (proverb). Quoted in Henrik Ibsen, *Love's Comedy*, Act 2 (1862).

9 Give me the avowed, the erect, the manly foe,
Bold I can meet – perhaps may turn his blow!
But of all plagues, Good Heaven, thy wrath can send,
Save, save, Oh, save me from the candid friend!

George Canning, British Prime Minister (1770–1827). 'New Morality' (1821).

10 There is no spectacle more agreeable than to observe an old friend fall from a roof-top.

Confucius, Chinese philosopher (551–479 BC). Sometimes it is a 'neighbour' as in: 'Even a virtuous and high-minded man may experience a little pleasure when he sees his neighbour falling from a roof.' The earliest citation to hand dates only from 1970, and one suspects that, like so many other Confucian sayings, it has nothing whatever to do with the Chinese philosopher who, nevertheless, undoubtedly did exist and did say a number of wise things (some through his followers). Even when not prefaced by 'Confucius, he say ...' there is a tendency –

particularly in the US – to ascribe any wry saying to him. In John G. Murray, *A Gentleman Publisher's Commonplace Book* (1996), the above precise form is ascribed to 'Kai Lung' – by which he presumably means Ernest Bramah's fictional Chinese philosopher.

Similar thoughts have occurred to others: 'Philosophy may teach us to bear with equanimity the misfortunes of our neighbours' – *see* NEIGHBOURS 302:7; 'I am convinced that we have a degree of delight, and that no small one, in the real misfortunes and pains of others' – Edmund Burke, *On the Sublime and Beautiful* (1756); and, especially, see La Rochefoucauld below.

1 A friend that ain't in need is a friend indeed.

Frank McKinney ('Kin') Hubbard, American humorist and caricaturist (1868–1930). Quoted in *The Treasury of Humorous Quotations*, eds Evan Esar & Nicolas Bentley (1951).

2 Making and preserving friends. Select some sound hearts. Be careful not to bruise them with unfeeling words. Take of milk of human kindness one heartful. Add to this plenty of tact. Warm the mixture with plenty of sympathy. Do not let it get *too* hot at first, lest it only ferment mischief. Knead with plenty of oil of unselfishness to make all smooth. Beware of jars (lovely wording). The mixture should be kept in a warm corner of the heart. Years only serve to improve the flavour of friends thus preserved.

Barry Humphries, Australian entertainer (1934–). 'A Recipe for Happiness' (1959) included in *A Nice Night's Entertainment* (1981). Humphries has admitted that this recipe was taken in its entirety from a women's magazine.

3 The feeling of friendship is like that of being comfortably filled with roast beef; love, like being enlivened with champagne.

James Boswell, Scottish lawyer, biographer and diarist (1740–95). *The Life of Samuel Johnson* (1791) – for 16 April 1775.

4 *Dans l'adversité de nos meilleurs amis, nous trouvons toujours quelque chose qui ne nous deplaît pas* [In the misfortune of our best friends, we find something that is not displeasing to us].

François, Duc de La Rochefoucauld, French moralist (1613–80). *Réflexions ou Maximes Morales*, No. 99 (1665).

5 The best friend of a boy is his mother, of a man his horse; only it's not clear when the transition takes place.

Joseph L. Mankiewicz, American screenwriter, producer and director (1909–93). Quoted in J.M. & M.J. Cohen, *The Penguin Dictionary of Modern Quotations* (1971).

On the 'Night of the Long Knives', when Prime Minister Harold Macmillan sacked half his Cabinet (13 July 1962):

6 Greater love hath no man than this, that he lay down his friends for his life.

Jeremy Thorpe, English liberal politician (1929–). Quoted in D.E. Butler & A. King, *The General Election of 1964* (1965).

7 That is just the way of the world; an enemy can partly ruin a man, but it takes a good-natured injudicious friend to complete the thing and make it perfect.

Mark Twain, American writer (1835–1910). *Pudd'nhead Wilson* (1894).

8 The proper office of a friend is to side with you when you are in the wrong. Nearly everybody will side with you when you are in the right.

Mark Twain. *Mark Twain's Notebook*, ed. A.B. Paine (1935).

9 Whenever a friend succeeds, a little something in me dies.

Gore Vidal, American novelist, playwright and critic (1925–). Interviewed on TV by David Frost and quoted in *The Sunday Times* Magazine (16 September 1973).

10 If you want a friend, get a dog.

Line from film *Wall Street* (US 1987). Screenwriters: Stanley Weiser and Oliver Stone. Spoken by Michael Douglas (Gordon Gekko).

11 Friendship is far more tragic than love. It lasts longer.

Oscar Wilde, Irish playwright, poet and wit (1854–1900). In *Saturday Review* (17 November 1894).

1 Anybody can sympathize with the sufferings of a friend, but it requires a very fine nature … to sympathize with a friend's success.

Oscar Wilde.'The Soul of Man Under Socialism' (1895).

Frogs

2 What a wonderful bird the frog are!
When he walk, he fly almost;
When he sing, he cry almost.
He ain't got no tail hardly, either.
He sit on what he ain't got almost.

Anonymous. A leading article in *The Times* (20 May 1948) ascribed these lines to the pen of an African schoolgirl, causing one reader to write in and say he had always believed they had come from the mouth of a French Canadian. He also said he had an idea that he had first seen them in the *Manchester Guardian* 'about twenty years ago'. The version that appears in Arnold Silcock's *Verse and Worse* (1952) is also ascribed to 'Anon (French Canadian)' and is fractionally different.

Frost, (Sir) David

ENGLISH BROADCASTER (1939–)

3 *On rescuing David Frost from drowning:*

I had to pull him out, otherwise nobody would have believed I didn't push him in.

Peter Cook, English humorist (1937–95). Quoted in my book *A Year of Stings and Squelches* (1985).

When asked by a nun if her future husband was religious:

4 Oh, yes, he thinks he's God Almighty.

Lady Carina Frost (1952–). Quoted in *The Sunday Times* (28 July 1985).

5 He rose without trace.

Kitty Muggeridge, English writer (1903–94). Remark made *c.* 1965, quoted in my book *Quote … Unquote* (1978). Curiously delighting in it, Frost provides the context in the first volume of his autobiography (1993): Malcolm Muggeridge (Kitty's husband) had predicted that after *That Was the Week That Was*, Frost would sink without trace. She said, 'Instead, he has risen without trace'.

Fun

6 There is some fun going forward.

Oliver Goldsmith, Irish-born playwright and writer (1730–74). *She Stoops to Conquer*, Act 1, Sc. 1 (1773). Tony Lumpkin speaking. Hence, *There Is Some Fun Going Forward*, the somewhat unexpected title of a compilation album (material recorded 1969–72) from Dandelion Records, the label co-established by John Peel, the English disc jockey.

Funerals

7 The last one [funeral] I went to had people in the front pew that I wouldn't have to my funeral over my dead body.

Anonymous. Quoted in Cleveland Amory, *Who Killed Society* (1960).

8 'If you don't go to other men's funerals,' he told Father stiffly, 'they won't go to yours.'

Clarence Day, American humorist (1874–1935). *Life with Father* (1935).

On Louis B. Mayer's funeral:

9 The reason so many people showed up at his funeral was because they wanted to make sure he was dead.

Sam Goldwyn, Polish-born American film producer (1882–1974). Quoted in Bosley Crowther, *Hollywood Rajah* (1960). Probably apocryphal, if only because the funeral was in fact sparsely attended.

On the large number of mourners at film producer Harry Cohn's funeral (in 1958):

10 Same old story: you give 'em what they want and they'll fill the theatre.

George Jessel, American entertainer (1898–1981). Quoted in Lillian Hellman, *Scoundrel Time* (1976). Earlier quoted, as said on TV by Red Skelton (1910–97), in Philip French, *The Movie Moguls* (1969), and, in the form, 'Well, it only proves what they say – give the public something they want to see, and they'll come out for it', in Bob Thomas, *King Cohn* (1967). An unattributed version appears in Oscar Levant, *The Unimportance of Being Oscar* (1968).

1 There is nothing like a morning funeral for sharpening the appetite for lunch.

Arthur Marshall, English writer and entertainer (1910–89). *Life's Rich Pageant* (1984). It was quoted at his own (pre-lunch) memorial service in 1989.

When asked if he would attend his ex-wife Marilyn Monroe's funeral (1962):

2 Why should I go? She won't be there.

Arthur Miller, American playwright (1915–). Attributed remark.

Attending a funeral towards the end of his life:

3 There's not much point going home really, is there?

Robb Wilton, English comedian (1881–1957). Quoted on BBC Radio *Quote ... Unquote* (1991). Ned Sherrin, in *Theatrical Anecdotes* (1991), has Lorenz Hart saying something similar about his Uncle Willie, at his (Hart's) mother's funeral in 1943. As it happens, Hart himself died first.

Funny

4 'I liked that song, myself,' he said, 'even if it isn't classical. It's funny, anyhow.'

Genevieve Gertrude raised her hand. 'Do you mean funny peculiar, or funny ha-ha?' she inquired politely ... ''Cause,' explained his mentor gravely, 'our teacher don't allow us to say funny when we mean peculiar. It's bad English, you know.'

Meriel Brady, American novelist. *Genevieve Gertrude*, Chap. 7 (1928). Mae West in her autobiography, *Goodness Had Nothing To Do With It*, Chap. 9 (1959), writing of the period before her play *Pleasure Man* opened in New York (17 September 1928), quotes a male friend as saying: 'Men can get funny over a woman. Funny peculiar that is.' Note what year it was.

5 What do you mean, funny? Funny peculiar, or funny ha-ha?

Ian Hay, Scottish novelist and playwright (1876–1952). Play, *Housemaster*, Act 3 (1936).

Futures

Of Marilyn Monroe:

6 There's a broad with her future behind her.

Constance Bennett, American film actress (1904–65). Quoted in John Robert Colombo, *Wit and Wisdom of the Moviemakers* (1979).

7 He was a man with a great future behind him.

Angela Carter, English novelist (1940–92). *Wise Children*, Chap. 3 (1991).

Of Bill Clinton, when the youngest defeated state governor in US history:

8 At 34, he fit the ironic description of the quintessential Rhodes Scholar: someone with a great future behind him.

David Maraniss, American journalist and author (1949–). *First in His Class* (1995).

9 He did not seem to mind having a future behind him.

C.P. Snow (Lord Snow), English novelist and scientist (1905–80). *The Affair*, Chap. 2 (1960). An early appearance of this line.

10 I like men who have a future, and women who have a past.

Oscar Wilde, Irish playwright, poet and wit (1854–1900). *The Picture of Dorian Gray*, Chap. 15 (1891).

G

Gable, Clark

AMERICAN FILM ACTOR (1901–60)

Verdict on Clark Gable's first screen test:

1 Ears too big.

Anonymous (studio executive). Quoted in Charles Higham and Joel Greenberg, *Celluloid Muse* (1969).

2 That man's ears make him look like a taxi-cab with both doors open.

Howard Hughes, American industrialist and film producer (1905–76). Quoted in the same book as above. Supposedly said after Gable auditioned for *The Front Page* (1931).

3 Clark Gable has the best ears of our lives.

Milton Berle, American comedian (1908–). Quoted in Leslie Halliwell, *The Filmgoer's Book of Quotes* (1973).

Gabor, Zsa Zsa

AMERICAN FILM ACTRESS (1919–)

4 She not only worships the Golden Calf, she barbecues it for lunch.

Oscar Levant, American pianist and actor (1906–72). Quoted in *The Penguin Dictionary of Modern Quotations*, eds J.M. & M.J. Cohen (1980 edn).

Gambling

5 Horse sense is a good judgement which keeps horses from betting on people.

W.C. Fields, American comedian (1879–1946). Quoted by Sam Ervin on record album *Senator Sam at Home* (1974).

When a gambler asks Cuthbert J. Twillie, 'Is this a game of chance?':

6 Not the way I play it.

Line from film *My Little Chickadee* (US 1939). Screen-writers: Mae West, W.C. Fields. Spoken by W.C. Fields (Cuthbert J. Twillie).

7 The race is not always to the swift nor the battle to the strong, but that's the way to bet.

Damon Runyon, American writer (1884–1946). Quoted in *The Treasury of Humorous Quotations*, eds Evan Esar & Nicolas Bentley (1951).

Games-playing

8 It is a silly game where nobody wins.

Thomas Fuller, English writer and physician (1654–1734). *Gnomologia* (1732).

When a poor bridge partner asked how he should have played a hand:

9 Under an assumed name.

George S. Kaufman, American playwright (1889–1961). Quoted in Scott Meredith, *George S. Kaufman and the Algonquin Round Table* (1974).

10 I am afraid I play no outdoor games at all, except dominoes. I have sometimes played dominoes outside French cafés.

Oscar Wilde, Irish playwright, poet and wit (1854–1900). Quoted in Gelett Burgess, 'A Talk With Mr Oscar Wilde', in *The Sketch* (January 1895).

Gardening

1 No matter how small your garden, always leave a few acres down to wild woodland.

Anonymous. Variously ascribed (in 2000) to 'one of the Rothschilds', 'a landowner in his club' and to 'a Royal Horticultural Society lecturer' – the latter in the form, 'Every garden, no matter how small, should set aside two or three acres for woodland'.

2 A garden is a loathsome thing, God wot!
… That geezer should be shot
What wrote that lot
Of Palgrave's Golden Tommy-rot …
I'd rather sun myself on Uncle's yacht.

Gerard Benson. Included in *Imitations of Immortality*, ed. E.O. Parrott (1986).

3 A garden is a lovesome thing? What rot!

J.A. Lindon. 'My Garden with a stern look at T.E. Brown'. In *Yet More Comic and Curious Verse*, ed. J.M. Cohen (1959).

4 Our England is a garden, and such gardens are not made
By singing: – 'Oh, how beautiful!' and sitting in the shade.

Rudyard Kipling, English poet and novelist (1865–1936). 'The Glory of the Garden' (1911).

5 Oh, Adam was a gardener, and God who made him sees
That half a proper gardener's work is done upon the knees.

Rudyard Kipling. In the same poem.

6 I have nothing against gardening. I just prefer not to be there when it happens.

Tracey Macleod, English broadcaster and journalist. On BBC Radio *Quote … Unquote* (25 September 2000). Paraphrasing Woody Allen (DEATH 107:3).

On finding that a grand Italian house had a garden that was a shambles:

7 This garden rather looks as if it was laid out by Incapability Bruno.

Leonard Miall, English broadcasting executive, historian and obituarist (1914–). Quoted by Sir Huw Wheldon on BBC Radio *Quote … Unquote* (10 August 1985).

Generalization

8 For parlor use, the vague generality is a life-saver.

George Ade, American humorist and playwright (1866–1944). Quoted in *The Treasury of Humorous Quotations*, eds Evan Esar & Nicolas Bentley (1951).

9 He who generalizes generally lies.

Anonymous. Quoted in *The 'Quote … Unquote' Newsletter* (January 1997). Note: Mary Pierrepoint (who became Lady Mary Wortley Montagu, 1689–1762) wrote 'General notions are generally wrong' in a letter (28 March 1710) to her future husband Edward Wortley Montagu.

10 A generalizer is a man who learns less and less about more and more until he knows nothing about everything.

Anonymous. Quoted in the same publication.

11 All generalizations are dangerous, even this one.

Alexandre Dumas *fils*, French writer (1824–95). Quoted in *The Treasury of Humorous Quotations*, ed. Evan Esar & Nicholas Bentley (1951).

12 No generalization is wholly true, not even this one.

Oliver Wendell Holmes Jnr, American judge (1841–1935). Attributed remark in *The Home Book of Humorous Quotations*, ed. A.K. Adams (1969). Also ascribed to Benjamin Disraeli.

Genetics

13 If a queen bee were crossed with a Fresian bull, would not the land flow with milk and honey?

Oliver St John Gogarty, Irish writer (1878–1957). Quoted on BBC Radio *Quote … Unquote* (8 September 1984).

1 Varicose veins are the result of an improper selection of grandparents.

(Sir) William Osler, Canadian-born physician (1849–1919). *Aphorisms from his Bedside Teachings*, Chap. 5 (1961).

Genius

Contrasting Mozart and Salieri in Pushkin's play Mozart and Salieri:

2 We see the contrast between the genius which does what it must and the talent which does what it can.

Maurice Baring, English writer (1874–1945). *An Outline of Russian Literature*, Chap. 3 (1914). Compare: 'Genius does what it must, and Talent does what it can' – Owen Meredith (1st Earl of Lytton), English poet (1831–91). 'Last Words of a Sensitive Second-Rate Poet' (1868).

3 Genius ... has been described as a supreme capacity for taking trouble ... It might be more fitly described as a supreme capacity for getting its possessors into trouble of all kinds and keeping them therein so long as the genius remains.

Samuel Butler, English novelist and writer (1835–1902). *Notebooks* (1912).

Discussing H. G. Wells:

4 If a man is going to behave like a bastard, he'd better be a genius.

Jill Craigie, English writer and film-maker (1914–2000). On BBC2 TV *Bookmark* (24 August 1996), in conversation with her husband, Michael Foot.

5 Genius is one per cent inspiration and ninety-nine per cent perspiration.

Thomas Alva Edison, American inventor (1847–1931). Quoted in *Life/Harper's Monthly Magazine* (September 1932), having originally been said by him *c.*1903. Earlier, the French naturalist, the Comte de Buffon (1707–88), was quoted in 1803 as having said, 'Genius is only a greater aptitude for patience.'

6 Genius is the talent of a man who is dead.

Edmond de Goncourt, French writer and artist (1822–96). Attributed remark.

7 Some people's genius lies in giving infinite pains.

Addison Mizner, American architect (1872–1933). Quoted in *The Treasury of Humorous Quotations*, eds Evan Esar & Nicolas Bentley (1951). Compare: 'Genius is an infinite capacity for giving pains' – Don Herold, American humorist and artist (1889–1966). Quoted in the same book.

8 Genius, cried the commuter,
As he ran for the 8:13,
Consists of an infinite capacity
For catching trains.

Christopher Morley, American writer and editor (1890–1957). 'An Ejaculation'.

9 When a true genius appears in the world, you may know him by this sign, that the dunces are all in confederacy against him.

Jonathan Swift, Anglo-Irish writer and clergyman (1667–1745). *Thoughts on Various Subjects* (1706).

10 To the question: 'Do you think genius is hereditary?' he replied: 'I can't tell you; heaven has granted me no offspring.'

James McNeill Whistler. American painter (1834–1903). Quoted in Hesketh Pearson, *Lives of the Wits* (1962).

At the New York Custom House, on arriving in the United States (1882) and asked by the customs officer if he had anything to declare:

11 I have nothing to declare except my genius.

Oscar Wilde, Irish playwright, poet and wit (1854–1900). Quoted in Frank Harris, *Oscar Wilde* (1918).

12 The public is wonderfully tolerant. It forgives everything except genius.

Oscar Wilde. 'The Critic As Artist' (1890).

1 Genius is born, not paid.

Oscar Wilde, Irish playwright, poet and wit (1854–1900). Quoted in *The Treasury of Humorous Quotations*, eds Evan Esar & Nicolas Bentley (1951).

Gentility

2 Phone for the fish knives, Norman,
As Cook is a little unnerved.

(Sir) John Betjeman, English poet (1906–84). 'How to Get on in Society' (1954). The poem concerns the 'Non-U' language and behaviour of the would-be 'genteel' classes, as opposed to the 'U' language and behaviour of the upper classes. In the latter milieu, special knives for eating fish are frowned upon, the full word 'telephone' is preferred, and so on.

Gentlemen

3 A gentleman is any man who wouldn't hit a woman with his hat on.

Fred Allen, American comedian (1894–1956). Quoted in Laurence J. Peter, *Quotations for Our Time* (1977).

Definition of an English gentleman:

4 Useful at a hunt ball. Invaluable in a shipwreck.

Anonymous. Quoted on BBC Radio *Quote ... Unquote* (18 June 1986).

5 A gentleman should be able to play the flute, but not too expertly.

Aristotle, Greek philosopher (384–322 BC). Attributed remark – possibly an encapsulation of the point he makes in his *Politics* (Bk 8), where he says that children of free men should learn and practise music only until they are able to feel delight in it and should not become professional musicians because this would make them vulgar.

6 I do hope I shall enjoy myself with you ... I am parshial to ladies if they are nice I suppose it is my nature. I am not quite a gentleman but you would hardly notice it.

Daisy Ashford, English child author (1881–1972). *The Young Visiters*, Chap. 1 (1919).

7 No gentleman writes about his private life.

Hilaire Belloc, French-born English poet and writer (1870–1953). Quoted in Hugh Kingsmill and Hesketh Pearson, *Talking About Dick Whittington* (1947).

8 Gentlemen do not take soup at luncheon.

George Curzon (1st Marquess Curzon), English Conservative politician (1859–1925). Quoted in E.L. Woodward, *Short Journey* (1912). However, in *The Oxford Book of Oxford*, the remark is said to have been made in 1921 when Curzon was Chancellor of the University of Oxford. Queen Mary was to be awarded an honorary degree and Curzon was asked to approve of the luncheon to which she was to be invited at Balliol. 'He returned it to the bursar with a single comment written in the corner.' Curzon also said: 'Gentlemen never wear brown in London.'

9 Gentlemen prefer blondes, but take what they can get.

Don Herold, American humorist and artist (1889–1966). Quoted in *The Treasury of Humorous Quotations*, eds Evan Esar & Nicolas Bentley (1951).

To a certain person:

10 Had your father spent more of your mother's immoral earnings on your education you would not even then have been a gentleman.

(Sir) Seymour Hicks, English actor-manager (1871–1949). *Vintage Years* (1943).

11 A gentleman is one who never strikes a woman without provocation.

H.L. Mencken, American journalist and linguist (1880–1956). Quoted in *The Treasury of Humorous Quotations*, eds Evan Esar & Nicolas Bentley (1951).

When his statement that he weighed 199 pounds was questioned:

12 No gentleman ever weighs more than two hundred pounds.

Thomas B. Reed, American Speaker of the House of Representatives (1839–1902). Quoted in *The Home Book of Humorous Quotations*, ed. A.K. Adams (1969).

1 The only infallible rule we know is, that the man who is always talking about being a gentleman never is one.

R.S. Surtees, English novelist and journalist (1803–64). *Ask Mamma*, Chap. 1 (1858).

2 *Dumby*:
Awful manners young Hopper has!
Cecil Graham:
Ah! Hopper is one of Nature's gentlemen, the worst type of gentleman I know.

Oscar Wilde, Irish playwright, poet and wit (1854–1900). *Lady Windermere's Fan*, Act 2 (1892).

3 No gentleman ever has any money.

Oscar Wilde. *The Importance of Being Earnest*, Act 2 (1895). In a scene cut when the play was reduced from four to three acts. Quoted in H. Montgomery Hyde, *Oscar Wilde* (1976).

On being shown into a hotel room in Paris with a fine view over the River Seine and the Louvre:

4 Oh, that is altogether immaterial, except to the hotelier, who of course charges it in the bill. A gentlemen never looks out of the window.

Oscar Wilde. Said to Robert H. Sherard and quoted by him in *Oscar Wilde: Story of an Unhappy Friendship* (1902).

5 A gentleman is one who never hurts anyone's feelings unintentionally.

Oscar Wilde. Quoted in *The Treasury of Humorous Quotations*, eds Evan Esar & Nicolas Bentley (1951). Has also been ascribed to Oliver Herford.

6 It is the first duty of a gentleman to dream.

Oscar Wilde. Quoted in Richard Le Gallienne, *The Romantic 90s* (1926).

Of the writer Michael Arlen:

7 For all his reputation [he] is not a bounder. He is every other inch a gentleman.

Alexander Woollcott, American writer and critic (1887–1943). Quoted in R.E. Drennan, *Wit's End* (1973). The same remark has also been attributed to Rebecca West (by Ted Morgan in *Somerset Maugham*, 1980) on the same person.

Geography

8 Geography is everywhere.

G.V. Desani, Indian-born novelist (1909–). In the days when humorous graffiti were all the rage, I was sent a photograph of a curious daub on a brick wall in the middle of a field in Bedworth, Warwickshire. It proclaimed: 'GEOGRAPHY IS EVERYWHERE – G.V. DESANI.' The identity of the given author of this profound thought puzzled me, but latterly I have learned that Desani actually exists. His novel *All About H. Hatterr* was published to acclaim in 1948. Until his retirement he was a visiting professor at the University of Austin, Texas. The last line of *Hatterr* is the (seemingly very Indian), 'Carry on, boys, and continue like hell!'

George III

BRITISH KING (1738–1820)

9 George the Third
Ought never to have occurred.
One can only wonder
At so grotesque a blunder.

E. Clerihew Bentley, English novelist, journalist and poet (1875–1956). *Biography for Beginners* (1905).

The Georges

10 George the First was always reckoned
Vile, but viler George the Second;
And what mortal ever heard
Any good of George the Third?
When from earth the Fourth descended
God be praised, the Georges ended!

Walter Savage Landor, English poet (1775–1864). Epigram in *The Atlas* (28 April 1855).

German language

11 Life is too short to learn German.

Richard Porson, English Professor of Greek at Cambridge (1759–1808). Quoted in Thomas Love Peacock, *Gryll Grange* (1861).

12 The great majority of Germans, realizing the impossibility of talking their language with any degree of success, abandon it altogether, and communicate with one another

on brass bands. German sounds better on a band, but not much.

Frank Richardson, English novelist. *Love, and All About It* (1907).

1 I heard a Californian student in Heidelberg, say, in one of his calmest moods, that he would rather decline two drinks than one German adjective.

Mark Twain, American writer (1835–1910). *A Tramp Abroad*, Appendix D (1880).

2 My philological studies have satisfied me that a gifted person ought to learn English (barring spelling and pronouncing) in thirty hours, French in thirty days, and German in thirty years.

Mark Twain. In the same book as above.

3 Whatever music sounds like, I am glad to say that it does not sound in the smallest degree like German.

Oscar Wilde, Irish playwright, poet and wit (1854–1900). 'The Critic As Artist' (1890).

Germans and Germany

4 The only way to treat a Prussian is to step on his toes until he apologizes.

Anonymous (Austrian proverb).

5 The proud German Army by its sudden collapse, sudden crumbling and breaking up, has once again proved the truth of the saying 'The Hun is always either at your throat or at your feet.'

(Sir) Winston S. Churchill, British Conservative Prime Minister and writer (1874–1965). Speech to the US Congress (19 May 1943). Quoted by Marlon Brando in *Playboy* (January 1979): 'Chaplin reminded me of what Churchill said about the Germans: either at your feet or at your throat.' According to John Robert Colombo's *Wit and Wisdom of the Moviemakers* (1979), Ava Gardner said about a well-known American film critic: 'Rex Reed is either at your feet or at your throat.'

6 Springtime for Hitler and Germany,
Deutschland is happy and gay.
We're marching to a faster pace,
Look out, here comes the Master Race!

Lines from song in musical *Springtime for Hitler* from film *The Producers* (US 1967). Screenwriter: Mel Brooks. Dubbed by Brooks himself.

7 Don't be stupid, be a smarty
Come and join the Nazi party.

From the same song.

Gifts

His idea of the gift he would give his worst enemy for Christmas:

8 Dinner with Princess Michael of Kent.

Viscount Linley, English designer (1961–). Quoted in the *Daily Mail* (16 April 1985). Allegedly spoken in November 1983.

9 'Tis more blessed to give than to receive; for example, wedding presents.

H.L. Mencken, American journalist and linguist (1880–1956). Quoted in *The Treasury of Humorous Quotations*, eds Evan Esar & Nicolas Bentley (1951).

On her ex-husband, pop singer Rod Stewart:

10 What do you give the man who's had everyone?

Alana Stewart. Quoted in *Sunday Today*, 'Quotes of the Week' (4 January 1987).

Gilbert and Sullivan

11 One can always count on Gilbert and Sullivan for a rousing finale, full of words and music, signifying nothing.

Tom Lehrer, American songwriter and entertainer (1928–). On record album *An Evening Wasted with Tom Lehrer* (1953).

Gin

12 The wages of gin is breath.

Oliver Herford, American humorist (1863–1935), and Addison Mizner, American architect (1872–1933). *The Cynic's Calendar* (1902).

Girls

1 Good girls go to heaven, bad girls go everywhere.

Helen Gurley Brown, American journalist (1922–). Her promotional line for *Cosmopolitan* Magazine when she relaunched it in 1965.

2 I am fond of children (except boys).

Lewis Carroll (Revd C.L. Dodgson), English writer (1832–98). Letter to Kathleen Eschwege (1879), quoted in Stuart Dodgson Collingwood, *The Life and Letters of Lewis Carroll* (1898).

Gladstone, W.E.

BRITISH LIBERAL PRIME MINISTER (1809–98)

3 For the purposes of recreation he has selected the felling of trees, and we may usefully remark that his amusements, like his politics, are essentially destructive ... The forest laments that Mr Gladstone may perspire.

Lord Randolph Churchill, English politician (1849–94). Speech on financial reform, Blackpool (24 January 1884). Gladstone's 'arboreal assaults' (in Roy Jenkins's phrase) became one of his central occupations, almost akin – though publicly better known – to his picking up of fallen women.

4 An old man in a hurry.

Lord Randolph Churchill. In an address to the electors of South Paddington (19 June 1886): 'This monstrous mixture of imbecility, extravagance and political hysterias, better known as "the bill for the future government of Ireland" [the Home Rule Bill] – this farrago of superlative nonsense – is to be put into motion –for this reason and no other: to gratify the ambitions of an old man in a hurry.'

5 Mr Gladstone read Homer for fun, which I thought served him right.

(Sir) Winston S. Churchill, British Conservative Prime Minister and writer (1874–1965). *My Early Life*, Chap. 2 (1930).

6 He has not a single redeeming defect.

Benjamin Disraeli (1st Earl of Beaconsfield), English politician and writer (1804–81). Quoted in A.K. Adams, *The Home Book of Humorous Quotations* (1969).

7 Oh, William dear, if you weren't such a great man you would be a terrible bore.

Catherine Gladstone, his wife (1812–1900). Quoted in Georgina Battiscombe, *Mrs Gladstone* (1956). Roy Jenkins in *Gladstone* (1995) describes this as 'a rarely illuminating expression of exasperated affection'.

8 He speaks to Me as if I was a public meeting.

Victoria, British Queen (1819–1901). Quoted in G.W.E. Russell, *Collections and Recollections* (1898) – '... is a complaint which is said to have proceeded from illustrious lips.' It has been objected that, if she did indeed say any such thing, Victoria would have said '... as if I *were* a public meeting'. But what we have here is only a report (albeit published while she was still alive). As her published letters and journals show, she wrote in a very emphatic manner and often referred to herself in the third person, but she did not usually capitalize 'Me' as here. It is not clear, either, how unthinkable it really is for her to have committed the solecism.

By a curious coincidence, that same year, Bismarck in his memoirs *Gedanken und Erinnerungen* looked back on an unsatisfactory conversation he had had in private in 1850 with Heinrich von Gagern, former President of the first National Assembly in Frankfurt. When someone asked Bismarck what Gagern said, he replied: '*Er hat mir eine Rede gehalten, als ob ich eine Volksversammlung wäre* [He made a speech to me as if I were a public meeting].'

Glasses (= spectacles)

9 A girl who is bespectacled,
She may not get her nectacled.

Ogden Nash, American poet (1902–71). 'Lines written to console those Ladies distressed by the Lines "Men seldom make Passes, etc."'

10 Men seldom make passes
At girls who wear glasses.

Dorothy Parker, American writer (1893–1967). *Enough Rope*, 'News Item' (1927).

Glyn, Elinor

ENGLISH ROMANTIC NOVELIST (1864–1943)

1 Would you like to sin
With Elinor Glyn
On a tiger-skin?
Or would you prefer
To err with her
On some other fur?

Anonymous. Quoted in A. Glyn, *Elinor Glyn* (1955). Written *c.* 1907.

God

2 God don't make mistakes. That's how he got to be God.

Line from US TV series *All in the Family* (1971–80). Script by various. Spoken by Carroll O'Connor (Archie Bunker).

3 Not only is there no God, but try getting a plumber on weekends.

Woody Allen, American film actor, writer and director (1937–). *Getting Even*, 'My Philosophy' (1975).

4 God is not dead but alive and working on a much less ambitious project.

Anonymous (graffito). Quoted in *The Guardian* (26 November 1975).

5 When God made man she was only testing.

Anonymous (graffito), North Kensington, London. Contributed to BBC Radio *Quote... Unquote* (26 April 1978).

6 Never mind, God isn't an Albanian ...

Anonymous (Greek saying). Contributed to BBC Radio *Quote ... Unquote* (7 November 1989).

7 *14th Earl of Gurney*:
I know I am God because when I pray to him I find I'm talking to myself.

Peter Barnes, English playwright (1931–). *The Ruling Class* (1968).

8 God, whatever else He is, and of course He is everything else, – is not a fool.

Alan Bennett, English playwright and actor (1934–). *Forty Years On*, Act 2 (1969).

9 To the lexicographer, God is simply the word that comes next to go-cart.

Samuel Butler, English writer (1835–1902). Quoted in *The Treasury of Humorous Quotations*, eds Evan Esar & Nicolas Bentley (1951).

While reading the Bible from cover to cover in response to a bet:

10 Isn't God a shit!

Randolph Churchill, English journalist and politician (1911–68). Quoted in Evelyn Waugh, *The Diaries of Evelyn Waugh* (1976) – entry for 11 November 1944.

On his 75th birthday:

11 I am ready to meet my Maker. Whether my Maker is ready for the ordeal of meeting me is another matter.

(Sir) Winston S. Churchill, British Conservative Prime Minister and writer (1874–1965). Speech (30 November 1949).

12 Forgive, O Lord, my little jokes on Thee
And I'll forgive Thy great big one on me.

Robert Frost, American poet (1874–1963). 'Cluster of Faith' (1962).

On why he omitted all passages glorifying God when he read aloud to his household from the Prayer Book:

13 God is a gentleman and no gentleman cares to be praised to his face.

Augustus Hare, English clergyman and writer (1792–1834). Somerset Maugham once quoted this as by Hare. Possibly a confusion with his nephew, also called Augustus Hare, who was a biographer and writer of guide books (1834–1903).

14 An honest God is the noblest work of man.

Robert Green Ingersoll, American lawyer and writer (1833–99). *The Gods and Other Lectures*, Chap. 1 (1876). Has also been ascribed to Samuel Butler (*Further Extracts from the Notebooks*, 1934).

1 God said: 'Let us make man in our image'; and Man said, 'Let us make God in our image'.

Douglas Jerrold, English humorist and editor (1803–57). Quoted in *The Treasury of Humorous Quotations*, eds Evan Esar & Nicolas Bentley (1951).

2 There once was a man who said, 'God
Must think it exceedingly odd
If he finds that this tree
Continues to be
When there's no one about in the Quad.'

Ronald Knox, English priest and writer (1888–1957). Quoted in Langford Reed, *The Complete Limerick Book* (1924). To which Anonymous wrote the following reply: 'Dear Sir, / Your astonishment's odd: / / I am always about in the Quad. / And that's why the tree / Will continue to be, / Since observed by / Yours faithfully, / God.'

3 The ordinary Britisher imagines that God is an Englishman.

Bernard Shaw, Irish playwright and critic (1856–1950). Quoted in Herbert V. Prochnow, Snr & Jnr, *A Treasury of Humorous Quotations* (1969). Hence, perhaps, *God is an Englishman*, the title of a novel by R.F. Delderfield (published in 1970). But, however expressed, the arrogant assumption is almost traditional. Harold Nicolson recorded in his diary for 3 June 1942 that three years previously, R.S. Hudson, the Minister of Agriculture, was being told by the Yugoslav minister in London of the dangers facing Britain. 'Yes,' replied Hudson, 'you are probably correct and these things may well happen. But you forget that God is English.'

In his introduction to *The British Character* (1951) by 'Pont', E.M. Delafield writes: 'Most Englishmen, if forced into analysing their own creeds – which Heaven forbid – are convinced that God is an Englishman – probably educated at Eton.'

James Morris in *Farewell the Trumpets* (1978) has a Dublin balladeer at the time of the 1916 Easter Rising singing: 'God is not an Englishman and truth will tell in time.' The closing line of the Gilbert and Sullivan opera *HMS Pinafore* (1878) is 'That he is an Englishman!', but it is sung to such grandiose music that it tends to sound like, '*He* is an Englishman!'

And then God is sometimes included in other groups. As R.A. Austen-Leigh's *Eton Guide* (1964) points out, on the south wall of Lower Chapel an inscription begins, 'You who in the chapel worship God, an Etonian like yourselves ...' When H.M. Butler, Master of Trinity College, Cambridge, said, 'It was well to remember that, at this moment, both the Sovereign and the Prime Minister are Trinity men', Augustine Birrell replied: 'The Master should have added that he can go further, for it is obvious that the affairs of the world are built upon the momentous fact that God is also a Trinity man' (quoted by Harold Laski in a letter to Oliver Wendell Holmes, 4 December 1926).

4 *Si Dieu n'existait pas, il faudrait l'inventer* [If God did not exist, it would be necessary to invent him].

Voltaire, French philosopher and writer (1694–1778). *Epîtres*, No. 96 (1770). Hence, the formula, 'If -- did not exist it would have to be invented'. Other examples include: 'If Austria did not exist it would have to be invented' (Frantisek Palacky, *c.* 1845); 'If he [Auberon Waugh, a literary critic] did not exist, it would be un-necessary to invent him' (Desmond Elliott, literary agent, *c.* 1977); 'What becomes clear is that Olivier developed his own vivid, earthy classical style as a reaction to Gielgud's more ethereal one ... So if Gielgud did not exist would Olivier have found it necessary to invent himself?' (review in *The Observer*, 1988); 'If Tony Benn did not exist, the old Right of the Labour Party would have had to invent him' (*The Observer*, 15 October 1989).

5 I sometimes think that God in creating man somewhat overestimated his ability.

Oscar Wilde, Irish playwright, poet and wit (1854–1900). Quoted in Herbert V. Prochnow, Snr & Jnr, *A Treasury of Humorous Quotations* (1969).

Godfathers

On being invited to be a godparent by Kenneth Tynan (1967):

6 Always a godfather, never a God.

Gore Vidal, American novelist, playwright and critic (1925–). Quoted in Kathleen Tynan, *The Life of Kenneth Tynan* (1987). Has also been ascribed to Alexander Woollcott.

Goldwynisms

THE MOSTLY APOCRYPHAL SAYINGS OF SAMUEL GOLDWYN, POLISH-BORN AMERICAN FILM PRODUCER (1882–1974)

1 Let's have some new clichés.

Quoted in *The Observer* (24 October 1948).

2 An oral [*or* verbal] contract isn't worth the paper it's written on.

Quoted in Alva Johnston, *The Great Goldwyn* (1937). Whilst this is one of the best known Goldwynisms, it is far from original to him. The Irish *Bulls Ancient and Modern* (1912) by J.C. Percy contains this: '"Verbal agreements," said the Irish attorney, "are not worth the paper they are written on".'

3 That's the way with these directors, they're always biting the hand that lays the golden egg.

Quoted in the same book as above.

4 In two words – impossible!

Quoted in the same book as above – along with the information that the joke appeared in a humour magazine late in 1925, and was subsequently imposed upon Goldwyn. *H.L. Mencken's Dictionary of Quotations* (1942) has: 'I can answer in two words – im possible' and ascribes it to 'an American movie magnate, 1930'. Curiously, however, the following is to be found in *Punch* (10 June 1931) – caption to cartoon by George Belcher: 'Harassed Film-Producer. "This business can be summed up in two words: IM-POSSIBLE".'

5 A secretary came to Goldwyn saying, 'Our files are so crowded that I suggest destroying all correspondence more than six years old.' 'By all means,' said Goldwyn, 'but be sure to make copies.'

Quoted in *The Home Book of Humorous Quotations*, ed. A.K. Adams (1969).

When told by the head of his script department that they could not film Lillian Hellman's play The Children's Hour *because it dealt with lesbians:*

6 OK, so we make them Albanians.

Quoted by Philip French in *The Observer* (10 May 1992). Sounds pretty unlikely. This anecdote made an early appearance in Edmund Fuller, *2500 Anecdotes for All Occasions* (1943) with the contentious script being, rather, Radclyffe Hall's *The Well of Loneliness*, and the reply: 'All right – where they got lesbians, we'll use Austrians.'

7 We're overpaying him, but he's worth it.

Quoted in *The Home Book of Humorous Quotations*, ed. A.K. Adams (1969).

8 What we want is a story that starts with an earthquake and works its way up to a climax ...

Quoted in Leslie Halliwell, *The Filmgoer's Book of Quotes* (1973). Note, however, that in John Robert Colombo, *Wit and Wisdom of the Moviemakers* (1979), this is ascribed to Cecil B. DeMille.

9 Tell me, how did you love the picture?

From the same Halliwell book as above.

10 Let's bring it up to date with some snappy nineteenth century dialogue.

From the same Halliwell book as above.

11 I had a great idea this morning but I didn't like it.

From the same Halliwell book as above.

12 Next time I want to send an idiot on some errand, I'll go myself.

Attributed remark. Note, however, that in John Robert Colombo, *Wit and Wisdom of the Moviemakers* (1979), 'The next time I send a fool for something, I go myself', is ascribed rather to Michael Curtiz.

13 If you can't give me your word of honour, will you give me your promise?

Quoted in my book *Quote ... Unquote* (1978).

14 I would be sticking my head in a moose.

Quoted in the same book as above.

1 First you have a good story, then a good treatment, and next a first-rate director. After that you hire a competent cast and even then you have only the mucus of a good picture.

Quoted in John Robert Colombo, *Wit and Wisdom of the Moviemakers* (1979). In P.G. Wodehouse's Mr Mulliner story 'The Castaways' (1933), set in Hollywood, Mr Schnellenhamer, the film mogul, says of a script he has bought, 'It has the mucus of a good story. See what you can do with it.'

2 Why should people go out and pay to see bad movies when they can stay at home and see bad television for nothing?

Quoted in *The Observer* (9 September 1956). As 'Who wants to go out and see a bad movie when they can stay at home and see a bad one free on television' – quoted in Philip French, *The Movie Moguls* (1969).

3 We have all passed a lot of water since then.

Quoted in Ezra Goodman, *The Fifty Year Decline of Hollywood* (1961).

4 Anyone who goes to a psychiatrist needs to have his head examined.

Quoted in Norman Zierold, *Moguls* (1969).

When Busby Berkeley, who had made his first musical for Goldwyn, was discovered moonlighting for Warner Brothers, Goldwyn said to Warner:

5 How can we sit together and deal with this industry if you're going to do things like this to me? If this is the way you do it, gentlemen, include me out!

Attributed remark. Goldwyn himself appeared to acknowledge ownership of this when speaking at Balliol College, Oxford (1 March 1945): 'For years I have been known for saying "Include me out" but today I am giving it up for ever.' On the other hand, Boller & George, in *They Never Said It* (1989), report Goldwyn as having denied saying it, claiming rather to have said to members of the Motion Picture Producers and Distributors of America: 'Gentlemen, I'm withdrawing from the association.'

Waving from an ocean-going liner to friends on the quayside:

6 Bon Voyage!

Quoted in Lillian Hellman, *Pentimento* (1974).

7 I took it all with a dose of salts.

Quoted in the same book as above.

Proposing toast at banquet to Field Marshal Montgomery:

8 A long life to Marshall Field Montgomery Ward.

Quoted in the same book as above. Also quoted in David Niven, *Bring On the Empty Horses* (1975).

When James Thurber was arguing with Goldwyn over the amount of violence that had crept in to a film treatment of his story The Secret Life of Walter Mitty, *eventually released in 1947, Goldwyn said:*

9 I'm sorry you felt it was too bloody and thirsty.

Quoted in Arthur Marx, *Goldwyn: A Biography of the Man Behind the Myth* (1976). Thurber, with commendable presence of mind, replied, 'Not only did I think so, I was horror and struck.'

10 Goldwynisms! Don't talk to me about Goldwynisms. Talk to Jesse Lasky!

Attributed remark. Lasky (1880–1958) was a pioneer American film producer.

11 Going to call him William? What kind of a name is that? Every Tom, Dick and Harry's called William. Why don't you call him Bill?

Quoted by Benny Green on BBC Radio *Quote ... Unquote* (22 June 1977).

12 I read part of the book all the way through.

Quoted in Philip French, *The Movie Moguls* (1969).

13 The trouble with this business is the dearth of bad pictures.

Quoted in the same book as above.

1 It rolls off my back like a duck.

Quoted in the same book as above – invented for him by George Oppenheimer.

2 I'll give you a definite maybe.

Quoted in Evan Esar, *The Humor of Humor* (1952).

3 It's more than magnificent – it's mediocre.

Quoted in the same book as above.

During filming of The Last Supper:

4 'Why only *twelve* [apostles]?' 'That's the original number.' 'Well, go out and get thousands!'

Quoted in the same book as above.

To a man who said, 'What beautiful hands your wife has':

5 Yes, I'm going to have a bust made of them.

Quoted in the same book as above.

6 You ought to take the bull between the teeth.

Quoted in the same book as above.

7 Chaplin is no businessman – all he knows is that he can't take anything less.

Quoted in Charles Chaplin, *My Autobiography*, Chap. 19 (1964).

8 This makes me so sore, it gets my dandruff up.

Quoted in Herbert V. Prochnow, Snr & Jnr, *A Treasury of Humorous Quotations* (1969).

9 That's my *Toujours* Lautrec.

Quoted in Lillian Ross, *Picture*, 'Throw the Little Old Lady Down the Stairs' (1952).

10 I want you to be sure and see my *Hans Christian Andersen*. It's full of charmth and warmth.

Quoted in my book *Foot in Mouth* (1982). The second sentence is quoted as said about an actual person in John Robert Colombo, *Wit and Wisdom of the Moviemakers* (1979).

11 Too caustic? To hell with the cost, we'll make the picture anyway.

Quoted in the same book (*Foot in Mouth*) as above.

12 It's spreading like wildflowers!

Quoted in the same book as above.

13 The A-bomb – that's dynamite!

Quoted in the same book as above.

14 I don't remember where I got this new Picasso. In Paris, I think. Somewhere over there on the Left Wing.

Quoted in the same book as above.

15 You just don't realise what life is all about until you have found yourself lying on the brink of a great abscess.

Quoted in the same book as above.

16 This is written in blank werse.

Quoted in the same book as above.

17 We can get all the Indians we need at the reservoir.

Quoted in John Robert Colombo, *Wit and Wisdom of the Moviemakers* (1979).

18 If Roosevelt were alive today, he'd turn over in his grave.

Quoted in the *The Penguin Dictionary of Modern Quotations*, eds J.M. & M.J. Cohen (1971). *Compare* FOOT-IN-MOUTH REMARKS 175:7.

In answer to Samuel Goldwyn's inquiry, 'Do you really say all those things which the papers report that you say?':

19 Do *you*?

Dorothy Parker, American writer (1893–1967). Quoted in *The Sayings of Dorothy Parker*, ed. S.T. Brownlow (1992).

Golf

1 [Golf is] cow-pasture pool.

O.K. Bovard, American executive. When he was managing editor of the *St Louis Post-Dispatch*. Quoted in *The Home Book of Humorous Quotations*, ed. A.K. Adams (1969).

2 If I had my way no man guilty of golf would be eligible to any office of trust or profit under the United States.

H.L. Mencken, American journalist and linguist (1880–1956). *Heathen Days* (1943).

3 Golf is a good walk spoiled.

Mark Twain, American writer (1835–1910). Quoted by Laurence J. Peter in *Quotations for Our Time* (1977). The German author Kurt Tucholsky (1890–1935) wrote: '*Golf, sagte einmal jemand, ist ein verdorbener Spaziergang* [Golf, someone once said, is a walk spoiled]'.

4 I've been studying the game of golf pretty considerably. I guess I understand now how it's played. It's this way. You take a small ball into a big field and you try to hit it – the ball not the field. At the first attempt you hit the field and not the ball. After that you probably hit the air or else the boy who is carrying your bag of utensils. When you've gone on long enough you possibly succeed in obtaining your original object. If the boy's alive you send him off to look for the ball. If he finds it the same day, you've won the game.

Mark Twain. In *The Mark Twain Jest Book*, ed. Cyril Clemens (1957).

Good news

5 Good news rarely comes in a brown envelope.

(Sir) Henry D'Avigdor Goldsmid, English politician and bullion broker (1909–76). Quoted by John Betjeman in a letter to Tom Driberg (21 July 1976).

Goodness

6 The word 'good' has many meanings. For example, if a man were to shoot his grandmother at a range of five hundred yards, I should call him a good shot, but not *necessarily* a good man.

G.K. Chesterton, English poet, novelist and critic (1874–1936). Quoted in Hesketh Pearson, *Lives of the Wits* (1962).

7 When I'm good, I'm very, very good. But when I'm bad, I'm better.

Line from film *I'm No Angel* (US 1933). Screenwriters: Mae West, Harlan Thompson. Spoken by Mae West (Tira).

Replying to exclamation, 'Goodness, what beautiful diamonds!':

8 Goodness had nothing to do with it, dearie.

Line from film *Night After Night* (US 1932). Screenwriter: Vincent Laurence (from novel by Louis Bromfield) 'with additional dialogue' by Mae West. Spoken by Mae West (Mandie Triplett). Hence the title of West's autobiography *Goodness Had Nothing To Do With It* (1959).

9 To be good is noble; but to show others how to be good is nobler and no trouble.

Mark Twain, American writer (1835–1910). *Following the Equator*, Epigraph (1897).

10 No good deed goes unpunished.

Oscar Wilde, Irish playwright, poet and wit (1854–1900). Attributed remark. Joe Orton recorded in his diary for 13 June 1967: 'Very good line George [Greeves] came out with at dinner: "No good deed ever goes unpunished".' James Agate in *Ego 3* (for 25 January 1938) states: '[Isidore Leo] Pavia was in great form today: "Every good deed brings its own punishment".' Note that neither of these sources mentions Wilde.

11 It is absurd to divide people into good and bad. People are either charming or tedious.

Oscar Wilde. *Lady Windermere's Fan*, Act 1 (1892).

Government

On the nature of Russian government:

12 Despotism tempered by assassination, that is our Magna Carta.

Anonymous (Russian noble) to Count Münster on the assassination of Emperor Paul I in 1800. Quoted in

Quotations for Speakers and Writers, ed. A. Andrews (1969). So also replied Lord Reith, the BBC's first Director General, when asked by Malcolm Muggeridge in the TV programme *Lord Reith Looks Back* (1970) what he considered the best form of government. The *Oxford Dictionary of Quotations* (1992) prefers a direct quote from Count Münster's *Political Sketches of the State of Europe, 1814–1867* (1868): 'An intelligent Russian once remarked to us, "Every country has its own constitution; ours is absolutism moderated by assassination".' *Bartlett's Familiar Quotations* (1980) attributes 'Absolutism tempered by assassination' direct to the earlier Ernst Friedrich Herbert von Münster (1766–1839).

The dates are rather important. How else is one to know whether Thomas Carlyle in his *History of the French Revolution* (1837) was alluding to the saying, when he wrote: 'France was long a despotism tempered by epigrams'? In a speech to the International Socialist Congress (Paris, 17 July 1889), the Austrian Victor Adler followed up with: 'The Austrian government ... is a system of despotism tempered by casualness.'

Notes and Queries, Vol. 202 (1957) has earlier sources, including Mme de Staël.

1 Too bad that all the people who know how to run the country are busy driving taxicabs and cutting hair.

George Burns, American comedian (1896–1996). Remark attributed to him, by 1977. Also quoted in *Life* Magazine (December 1979).

2 Of course government in general, any government anywhere, is a thing of exquisite comicality to a discerning mind.

Joseph Conrad, Polish-born novelist (1857–1924). *Nostromo*, Pt 2, Chap. 3 (1904).

3 I don't make jokes; I just watch the government and report the facts.

Will Rogers, American humorist (1879–1935). Quoted in 'A Rogers Thesaurus' in *The Saturday Review* (25 August 1962).

Graces

4 For rabbits young and rabbits old,
For rabbits hot and rabbits cold,
For rabbits tender, rabbits tough,
We thank Thee, Lord: we've had enough.

Anonymous. Quoted in *The Frank Muir Book* (1976).

Graffiti

5 I love grils.
You mean girls, stupid!
What about us grils?

Anonymous (graffito). Included in my book *Graffiti Lives, OK* (1979).

6 If God had not meant us to write on walls, he would never have given us the example.

Anonymous. Quoted in my book *Graffiti 2* (1980).

7 Graffiti should be obscene and not heard.

Anonymous. Quoted in the same book as above.

8 When a society has to resort to the lavatory for its humour, the writing is on the wall.

Alan Bennett, English playwright and actor (1934–). *Forty Years On*, Act 2 (1969).

9 Popular education was bringing the graffito lower on the walls.

Oliver St John Gogarty, Irish writer (1878–1957). *As I Was Going Down Sackville Street* (1937).

Grammar

10 *Old Gentleman (who has a sensitive ear for Grammar):*
My dears, there's your Mother calling you.
Wild Boy of the West:
'O, her ain't callin' o' we; us don't belong to she.

Anonymous (cartoonist). Caption to cartoon in *Punch* (30 October 1858).

Gratitude

In speech accepting Oscar:

11 I just want to thank everyone I met in my entire life.

Kim Basinger, American actress (1953–). Quoted in *The Observer*, 'Sayings of the Week' (29 March 1998).

To a nun nursing him on his deathbed:

1 Thank you, Sister. May you be the mother of a bishop!

Brendan Behan, Irish playwright (1923–64). Quoted in *The Sayings of Brendan Behan*, ed. Aubrey Dillon-Malone (1997).

Of Marilyn Monroe:

2 Copulation was, I'm sure, Marilyn's uncomplicated way of saying thank you.

Nunnally Johnson, American screenwriter, director and producer (1897–1977). Quoted in Maria Leach, *The Ultimate Insult* (1996).

3 The gratitude of place-expectants is a lively sense of future favours.

Sir Robert Walpole (1st Earl of Orford), British Whig Prime Minister (1676–1745). Quoted in William Hazlitt, *Lectures on the English Comic Writers*, 'On Wit and Humour' (1819). By the 20th century, the *Dictionary of American Proverbs* had, as simply proverbial, 'Gratitude is a lively expression of favours yet to come.' Prior to Walpole, La Rochefoucauld had said, 'The gratitude of most men is merely a secret desire to receive greater benefits [*La reconnaissance de la plupart des hommes n'est qu'une secrète envie de recevoir de plus grands bienfaits*]' – *Maxims*, No. 298 (1678).

4 A formidable woman he did not admire encountered Oscar Wilde one evening at a party. 'Ah, Mr Wilde,' she said, beaming at him, 'I passed your house this afternoon.' 'Thank you so much,' he replied.

Oscar Wilde, Irish playwright, poet and wit (1854–1900). Contributed to BBC Radio *Quote ... Unquote* (1 January 1979).

5 Wilde was receiving bouquets, both spoken and floral, after the first night of one of his plays, when a would-be critic slipped in with a rotten cabbage. Wilde took it, smiled, and said: 'Thank you, my dear fellow. Every time I smell it I shall think of you.'

Oscar Wilde. Attributed remark. As Frank Harris described in *Oscar Wilde* (1938), Lord Queensberry did, of course, appear at the first production of *The Importance of Being Earnest* carrying a large bouquet of turnips and carrots, but was refused admission. Could these stories be linked?

Greatness

6 All my shows are great. Some of them are bad. But they are all great.

Lew Grade (Lord Grade), Russian-born English media tycoon (1906–98). Quoted in *The Observer* (14 September 1975).

Greetings

7 I met Curzon in Downing Street, from whom I got the sort of greeting a corpse would give to an undertaker.

Stanley Baldwin (1st Earl Baldwin of Bewdley), British Conservative Prime Minister (1867–1947). Quoted in A. & V. Palmer, *Quotations from History* (1976). On becoming Prime Minister – a job Curzon had always wanted – in 1933.

8 Hello, I must be going.

Line from song 'Hooray for Captain Spaulding' in film *Animal Crackers* (US 1930). Song written by Harry Ruby and Bert Kalmar. Sung by Groucho Marx (Capt. Spaulding). Hence, 'Hello I Must be Going!', title of a record album (1982) by Phil Collins.

Growing up

To Nina Hamnett:

9 We have become, Nina, the sort of people our parents warned us about.

Augustus John, Welsh artist (1878–1961). This was quoted about the time Michael Holroyd's two-volume biography of John appeared (1974–5), but it is not in that book. It was quoted in the form 'We are the sort of people, Nina, our fathers warned us against', on BBC Radio *Quote ... Unquote* (11 May 1977). Holroyd confirmed that it *was* addressed to Nina Hamnett (1890–1956), the painter and something of a figure in London Bohemia, but says that he encountered it only *after* he had written his biography. He first used it in 1981 in his entry on John in *Makers of Modern Culture*. In the 1996 revision of the biography, Holroyd gives it as 'We are the sort of people our fathers warned us against.'

When my version appeared in the second *Quote ... Unquote* book, Bernard Davis wrote in 1981 from Turkish Cyprus, saying: 'An acquaintance of mine, York-Lodge, a close friend of Claud Cockburn and Evelyn Waugh, was continually saying, "We are the sort of people our parents warned us against," and claiming it as his own. This was about 1924.'

It was probably a common expression dating from between the wars, if not before. In Brendan Behan's *Borstal Boy* (1958), there is: 'We're all good kids. We're all the kids our mothers warned us against.' The saying was reported as graffiti from New York City in the early 1970s ('We are the people our parents warned us about') and a placard carried at a demonstration by homosexuals in New York in 1970 asserted, 'We're the people our parents warned us against'. In 1968, Nicholas Von Hoffman brought out a book on hippies with the title *We Are the People Our Parents Warned Us Against*.

Grumbling

1 There are two powers at which men should never grumble – the weather and their wives.

Benjamin Disraeli (1st Earl of Beaconsfield), English politician and writer (1804–81). Quoted in Wilfrid Meynell, *The Man Disraeli* (1927 edn).

Guests

2 *George*:
I'll tell you what game we'll play. We're done with Humiliate the Host ... and we don't want to play Hump the Hostess, yet ... We'll play a round of Get the Guests.

Edward Albee, American playwright (1928–). *Who's Afraid of Virginia Woolf?*, Act 2 (1962).

On visiting royalty who overstayed their welcome:

3 Don't these people have palaces to go to?

Anonymous (old duke). Quoted by Patrick Garland on BBC Radio *Quote ... Unquote* (11 September 1979).

In her hostess's elaborate visitor's book:

4 'Quoth the raven ... '

Mrs Patrick Campbell, English actress (1865–1940). Quoted in Bennett Cerf, *Shake Well Before Using* (1948). Also ascribed to John Barrymore.

5 I'm a particularly loathsome guest and I eat like a vulture. Unfortunately, the resemblance doesn't end there.

Groucho Marx, American comedian (1895–1977). *The Groucho Letters* (1967) – for 15 August 1956.

When he felt his Rothschild relatives had kept him up long enough:

6 To your tents, O Israel!

Archibald Philip Primrose (5th Earl of Rosebery), British Liberal Prime Minister (1847–1929). Attributed remark.

In reply to hostess's inquiry whether he was enjoying himself at party:

7 Certainly, there is nothing else here to enjoy.

Bernard Shaw, Irish playwright and critic (1856–1950). Quoted in *The Sayings of Bernard Shaw*, ed. Joseph Spence (1993).

8 Yes, dear Frank [Harris], we believe you: you have dined in every house in London, *once*.

Oscar Wilde, Irish playwright, poet and wit (1854–1900). Quoted in William Rothenstein, *Men and Memories* (1931).

See also VISITS AND VISITORS.

Habit

1 Habit with him was all the test of truth,
It must be right: I've done it from my youth.

George Crabbe, English poet (1754–1832). Quoted in Laurence J. Peter, *Quotations for Our Time* (1977).

Hair and hairdressers

2 What's the point of getting your hair cut? It only grows again.

Alphonse Allais, French humorist (1854–1905). Attributed remark.

3 Grey hair is a sign of age, not of wisdom.

Anonymous (Greek proverb). Quoted in *The Home Book of Humorous Quotations*, ed. A.K. Adams (1969).

When asked by a barber how he would like his hair cut:

4 In silence.

Archelaus, Macedonian King (reigned 413–399 BC). Quoted by W. & A. Durant in *The Story of Civilization* (1935–64). Possibly said, rather, by a successor, Philip II. Plutarch, however, in his *Moralia*, attributes it to Archelaus. Curiously, this is the caption to a Bernard Partridge cartoon entitled 'A DAMPER' in *Punch* (27 February 1897): '*Chatty Barber:* "'Ow would you like to be shaved, sir?" *Grumpy Customer:* "In perfect silence, please."'

5 Young man, if she asks you if you like her hair that way, beware; the woman has already committed matrimony in her heart.

Don Marquis, American journalist and humorist (1878–1937). Quoted in the same collection as above.

Of Ronald Reagan in 1974:

6 He doesn't dye his hair. He's just prematurely orange.

Gerald Ford, American Republican President (1913–). Quoted in Ned Sherrin, *Cutting Edge* (1984). Note: in Harry Thompson, *Peter Cook* (1997), Jonathan Miller's wife Rachel is quoted as having said of Cook's dyeing his hair a virulent orange-brown in 1975: 'Peter's gone prematurely orange.'

7 When red-haired people are above a certain social grade their hair is auburn.

Mark Twain, American writer (1835–1910). Quoted in *The Home Book of Humorous Quotations*, ed. A.K. Adams (1969).

8 'And go and get your hair cut,' screamed Beatrice. 'You look like a chrysanthemum.'

(Sir) P(elham) G. Wodehouse, English-born novelist and lyricist (1881–1975). *Hot Water*, Chap. 2 (1932).

Halitosis

Of Professor Tancred Borenius:

9 Oh! that halitosis. It's so thick – a greyhound couldn't jump it.

(Sir) Cecil Beaton, English designer and photographer (1904–80). Quoted in Hugo Vickers, *Cecil Beaton* (1985).

Hamlet

In answer to the question much puzzled over by Shakespearean scholars, 'Did Hamlet actually sleep with Ophelia?', an old actor-manager is said to have replied:

1 In our company – *always*!

Anonymous remark. Quoted in Sir Cedric Hardwicke, *A Victorian in Orbit* (1961). Peter Hay in *Broadway Anecdotes* (1989) identifies the actor specifically as John Barrymore.

2 A ghost and a prince meet
And everyone ends in mincemeat.

Howard Dietz, American writer and film executive (1896–1983). Song, 'That's Entertainment', from the film *The Band Wagon* (US 1953).

To Sir Henry Beerbohm Tree about his Hamlet:

3 Funny without being vulgar.

(Sir) W.S. Gilbert, English writer and lyricist (1836–1911). Quoted in David Bispham, *Recollections* (1920). He claimed to have heard Gilbert say something like this to Tree on the stage of the Haymarket Theatre, London, after the first performance: 'My dear fellow, I never saw anything so funny in my life, and yet it was not in the least vulgar.' Presumably related to this is a music-hall song 'Funny Without Being Vulgar', words by Harry Brett, music by Charles Ingle (1891). Performed by Albert Chevalier, it begins: 'I am told that you can't get a good comic song / Which is funny without being vulgar … '

4 Hamlet is the tragedy of tackling a family problem too soon after college.

Tom Masson, American humorist (1866–1934). Quoted in *The Treasury of Humorous Quotations*, eds Evan Esar & Nicolas Bentley (1951).

5 To sum up: your father, whom you love, dies, you are his heir, you come back to find that hardly was the corpse cold before his younger brother popped on to his throne and into his sheets, thereby offending both legal and natural practice. Now why exactly are you behaving in this extraordinary manner?

(Sir) Tom Stoppard, British playwright (1937–). *Rosencrantz and Guildenstern Are Dead,* Act 1 (1966).

Hampstead

6 In fact when somebody from Hampstead is drowning, all their previous furniture passes in front of them.

Alexei Sayle, English comedian (1952–). In BBC TV, *Comic Roots*, quoted in *The Listener* (1 September 1983).

Handicaps

In answer to the question, 'What's your golf handicap?':

7 I'm a coloured, one-eyed Jew – do I need anything else?

Sammy Davis Jnr, American entertainer (1925–90). *Yes I Can* (1966).

Handshakes

When a young man accosted him in Zurich and asked, 'May I kiss the hand that wrote Ulysses?*':*

8 No, it did a lot of other things, too.

James Joyce, Irish novelist (1882–1941). Quoted in Richard Ellman, *James Joyce* (1959).

Handwriting

Of a child's handwriting:

9 With the dawn of legibility comes the horrendous revelation that he cannot spell.

Anonymous. Geoffrey J. Toye, a schoolmaster, vaguely remembered having read this in a report and contributed it to BBC Radio *Quote … Unquote* (1 August 1987). On the same programme, Arthur Marshall had earlier quoted a school report (possibly as coming from *The Daily Telegraph*), 'Now that her handwriting has improved we can tell how very little she knows … ' (14 August 1980). Unconfirmed is a suggestion that it originated with Ian Hay, Scottish novelist and playwright (1876–1952). But it is not from his book *The Lighter Side of School Life* (1914), nor from his play or book *Housemaster* (both 1936).

10 Most people enjoy the sight of their own handwriting as they enjoy the smell of their own farts.

W.H. Auden, Anglo-American poet (1907–73). *The Dyer's Hand*, 'Writing' (1962). *Compare* FARTS 165:3.

1 I never saw Monty James's writing but doubt whether he can have been more illegible than Lady Colefax: the only hope of deciphering *her* invitations, someone said, was to pin them up against the wall and *run* past them!

Rupert Hart-Davis, English publisher (1907–). Letter to George Lyttelton (13 November 1955).

2 My handwriting looks as if a swarm of ants, escaping from an ink bottle, had walked over a sheet of paper without wiping their legs.

(Revd) Sydney Smith, English clergyman, essayist and wit (1771–1845). Attributed remark.

Hanging

3 Yes, we must indeed all hang together, or, most assuredly, we shall all hang separately.

Benjamin Franklin, American politician and scientist (1706–90). Quoted in *A Book of Anecdotes*, ed. Daniel George (1958.) Remark to John Hancock at the signing of the Declaration of Independence (4 July 1776), though possibly not original. Hancock had said in his address to the Continental Congress, just previous to this: 'It is too late to pull different ways; the members of the Continental Congress must hang together.'

4 Hanging was the worst use a man could be put to.

(Sir) Henry Wotton, English diplomat and poet (1568–1639). *The Disparity Between Buckingham and Essex* (1651).

Happiness

5 Happiness? A good cigar, a good meal, and a good woman – or a bad woman. It depends on how much happiness you can handle.

George Burns, American comedian (1896–1996). Attributed remark.

Lunching with friends at the time of her husband's retirement, Madame de Gaulle was asked what she was looking forward to in the years ahead. 'A penis', she replied without hesitation. The embarrassed silence that followed was broken by the former President:

6 My dear, I don't think the English pronounce the word like that. It is ''appiness'.

Charles de Gaulle, French general and President (1890–1970). Quoted in Robert Morley, *Book of Bricks* (1978) – but probably applied to de Gaulle and 'Tante Yvonne' simply because they were a famous French couple. The same pronunciation is delivered as a joke in the film version of Terence Frisby's *There's A Girl in My Soup* (1970) – by a French hotel manager welcoming a honeymoon couple. In *The Diaries of Kenneth Williams* (1993), the entry for 10 April 1966 has it as told by Michael Codron and involving Lady Dorothy Macmillan who asks Mme de Gaulle if there is any desire she has for the future and the reply is, 'Yes – a penis.'

7 No, Sir, there is nothing which has yet been contrived by man by which so much happiness is produced as by a good tavern or inn.

(Dr) Samuel Johnson, English writer and lexicographer (1709–84). Quoted in James Boswell, *The Life of Samuel Johnson* (1791) – for 21 March 1776.

8 [He] is as happy as a martyr when the fire won't burn.

Mark Twain, American writer (1835–1910). Quoted in Mark Webster, *Mark Twain, Business Man* (1946).

9 Leavin' me as happy as a dog with two tails.

Mark Twain. Quoted in *The Adventures of Thomas Jefferson Snodgrass* (1928).

10 Happiness is no laughing matter.

Richard Whately, English philosopher, theologian and archbishop (1787–1863). *Apothegms* (1854).

11 A man can be happy with any woman as long as he does not love her.

Oscar Wilde, Irish playwright, poet and wit (1854–1900). *The Picture of Dorian Gray*, Chap. 15 (1891).

12 Some cause happiness wherever they go; others whenever they go.

Oscar Wilde, Irish playwright, poet and wit (1854–1900). Quoted in Herbert V. Prochnow, Snr & Jnr, *A Treasury of Humorous Quotations* (1969).

Harpsichords

1 [A harpsichord] sounds like two skeletons copulating on a corrugated tin roof.

(Sir) Thomas Beecham, English conductor (1879–1961). Quoted in Harold Atkins and Archie Newman, *Beecham Stories* (1978). Sometimes quoted as 'resembles a bird-cage played with toasting-forks'.

Haste

2 Here's your hat, what's your hurry?

Bartley C. Costello. Title and refrain of song (1904).

3 Here lies, extinguished in his prime,
a victim of modernity;
but yesterday he hadn't time –
and now he has eternity.

Piet Hein, Danish poet, designer and inventor (1905–96). *Grooks* (1969).

On the impossibility of quick economic change:

4 You can't set a hen in one morning and have chicken salad for lunch.

George Humphrey, American Secretary of the Treasury (1890–1970). Quoted in *Time* Magazine (26 January 1953).

Hatred

5 Now Hatred is by far the longest pleasure;
Men love in haste, but they detest at leisure.

Lord Byron, English poet (1788–1824). *Don Juan*, Canto 13, St. 6 (1819–24). Hence, the title of Anne Mather's novel *The Longest Pleasure* (1986).

6 I am free of all prejudice. I hate everyone equally.

W.C. Fields, American comedian (1879–1946). Quoted by Jerome Beatty Jnr in *The Saturday Review* (28 January 1967).

Headlines

On the Wall Street crash (30 October 1929):

7 WALL ST. LAYS AN EGG.

Anonymous. In *Variety*, American show business newspaper. When the stock market plummeted again in October 1987, *Variety* had the headline: 'WALL STREET LAYS AN EGG: THE SEQUEL.'

Meaning that cinema-goers in rural areas were not attracted to films with bucolic themes:

8 STICKS NIX HICKS PIX.

From the same newspaper (17 July 1935). Credited to Sime Silverman.

9 EIGHTH ARMY PUSH BOTTLES UP GERMANS.

Anonymous. Possibly apocryphal headline, said to have appeared in a British newspaper – presumably during the Second World War. Quoted by Robert Lacey on BBC Radio *Quote ... Unquote* (5 February 1979). He said it came from the *News Chronicle* in 1942.

On the marriage of playwright Arthur Miller to Marilyn Monroe (1956):

10 EGGHEAD WEDS HOURGLASS.

Anonymous. In *Variety*. Quoted in Leslie Halliwell, *The Filmgoer's Book of Quotes* (1973).

11 TEENAGE DOG-LOVING DOCTOR-PRIEST IN SEX-CHANGE MERCY DASH TO PALACE.

Anonymous. Untraced and apocryphal all-embracing headline, mentioned in *The Lyttelton Hart-Davis Letters*, Vol. 4 (1959).

12 BOOK LACK IN ONGAR.

Anonymous. In *Private Eye* – on a report of strikes at lending libraries in Essex. Quoted on BBC Radio *Quote ... Unquote* (20 July 1977).

13 THE EGO HAS LANDED.

Anonymous. In *The Observer* Magazine (24 June 1990) – on a profile of the tycoon and crook, Robert Maxwell. The feature made much of Maxwell's helicopter habit.

14 SUPER CALEY GO BALLISTIC, CELTIC ARE ATROCIOUS.

Anonymous. *The Sun* (February 2000). Over a football report of the shock defeat of Celtic by the tiny Scottish club Caledonian-Thistle. It has been suggested that something like this headline had appeared elsewhere before. Here referring, of course, to the song title 'Supercalifragilisticexpialidocious' from the film *Mary Poppins* (1964). The song containing the word was the subject of a copyright infringement suit brought in 1965 against the makers of the film by Life Music Co. and the writers of two earlier songs: 'Supercalafajalistickespiala-dojus' had been the title of an (unpublished) song in 1949; 'Supercalafajalistickespeealadojus; or, The super song' followed in 1951. The ruling went against the plaintiffs in view of earlier oral uses of the word sworn to in affidavits, and of dissimilarity between the songs.

1 SMALL EARTHQUAKE IN CHILE. NOT MANY DEAD.

Claud Cockburn, English journalist (1904–81). *In Time of Trouble* (1956) (incorporated in *I Claud ...*, 1967). Cockburn claimed to have won a competition for dullness among sub-editors on *The Times* with this headline in the late 1920s: 'It had to be a genuine headline, that is to say one which was actually in the next morning's newspaper. I won it only once.' At Cockburn's death it was said, however, that an exhaustive search had failed to find this particular headline. In 2000, Mark English made the intriguing discovery that in 1929 (when Cockburn started work on *The Times* in London, before becoming its correspondent in New York and Washington), there occurred two similar entries in the paper's 'Telegrams in Brief' column. 'An earthquake was felt yesterday between Illapel, to the north, and Talca, to the south, in Chile. No damage was done' (6 August 1929); 'An earthquake shock was felt in Melilla [which is in Chile] on Wednesday, but no one was injured' (16 August 1929). Could Cockburn have embroidered the story in the telling and asserted that the 'Telegrams in Brief' were in fact headlines?

Healey, Denis (Lord Healey)

ENGLISH LABOUR POLITICIAN (1917–)

2 I plan to be the Gromyko of the Labour Party for the next thirty years.

Denis Healey. Quoted in *The Observer*, 'Sayings of the Week' (5 February 1984).

Health and illness

3 I reckon being ill as one of the greatest pleasures of life, provided one is not too ill and is not obliged to work until one is better.

Samuel Butler, English novelist and writer (1835–1902). *The Way of All Flesh*, Chap. 80 (1903).

4 One of the minor pleasures in life is to be slightly ill.

(Sir) Harold Nicolson, English writer and politician (1886–1968). Quoted in *The Observer*, 'Sayings of the Week' (22 January 1950). Compare this from C.S. Lewis, *Surprised by Joy*, Chap. 12 (1955): 'Perhaps I ought to have mentioned before that I had had a weak chest ever since childhood, and had very early learned to make a minor illness one of the pleasures in life, even in peace-time.' The point about the last phrase is that it comes in the context of the First World War, when the convalescent home was particularly attractive as an alternative to the trenches.

Faulkland:

5 [No one would wish to be ill] yet surely a little trifling indisposition ... Now confess – isn't there something unkind in this violent, robust, unfeeling health?

Richard Brinsley Sheridan, English dramatist and politician (1751–1816). *The Rivals*, Act 2 Sc. 1 (1775).

6 One evil in old age is that as your time is come you think every little illness is the beginning of the end. When a man expects to be arrested every knock at the door is an alarm.

(Revd) Sydney Smith, English clergyman, essayist and wit (1771–1845). Letter (1836), quoted in *The Sayings of Sydney Smith*, ed. Alan Bell (1993).

7 Sydney Smith feeling so ill and confused that he could not remember whether there were nine Articles and thirty-nine Muses, or the contrary.

(Revd) Sydney Smith. Quoted by Richard Monckton Milnes, in the same book as above.

8 Early to rise and early to bed makes a male healthy and wealthy and dead.

James Thurber, American cartoonist and writer (1894–1961). In *The New Yorker*, 'The Shrike and the Chipmunks' (1939).

Heartbreak

1 When people say, 'You're breaking my heart,' they do in fact usually mean that you're breaking their genitals.

Jeffrey Bernard, English journalist (1932–97). In *The Spectator* (31 May 1986). However, this saying had appeared earlier, quoted in *The Observer*, 'Sayings of the Week' (19 May 1985), suggesting he used it more than once.

Heaven

2 Heaven protects children, sailors, and drunken men.

Anonymous. Compare 'God protects fools, drunks and the United States of America', sometimes attributed to Bismarck (29:1). W. Eric Gustafson commented (1995): 'My history teacher, the great Henry Wilkinson Bragdon, used to ascribe to Bismarck the saying that "There is a special providence that protects idiots, drunkards, children, and the United States of America".' There is a French proverb that states: 'God helps three sorts of people, fools, children and drunkards'. As 'children, sailors and drunken men', this was known in English by 1861 (Thomas Hughes, *Tom Brown at Oxford*). On 9 January 1995, *US News and World Report* quoted Daniel P. Moynihan as saying of the avoidance of casualties in the Haitian intervention: 'The Lord looks after drunks and Americans.'

3 At any rate there will be no wedding presents in heaven.

Samuel Butler, English author (1835–1902). Quoted in *The Treasury of Humorous Quotations*, eds Evan Esar & Nicolas Bentley (1951).

4 —'s idea of heaven is eating *pâté de foie gras* to the sound of trumpets.

(Revd) Sydney Smith, English clergyman, essayist and wit (1771–1845). Quoted in *Recollections of the Table-Talk of Samuel Rogers* (1887). Smith did not mean that this was his own view of heaven. It seems probable that he was referring to his friend Henry Luttrell.

5 Heaven: the Coney Island of the Christian imagination.

Elbert Hubbard, American writer and editor (1856–1915). *The Notebook* (1927).

On the existence of heaven and hell:

6 I don't want to express an opinion. You see, I have friends in both places.

Mark Twain, American writer (1835–1910). Quoted in Archibald Henderson, *Mark Twain* (1911).

7 Whenever cannibals are on the brink of starvation, Heaven in its infinite mercy sends them a nice plump missionary.

Oscar Wilde, Irish playwright, poet and wit (1854–1900). Quoted in *The Treasury of Humorous Quotations*, eds Evan Esar & Nicolas Bentley (1951).

Heckling

When Harold Wilson asked rhetorically, 'Why do I emphasize the importance of the Royal Navy?':

8 Because you're in Chatham.

Anonymous (heckler). During the British General Election (1964). Quoted in A. Andrews, *Quotations for Speakers and Writers* (1969).

Heels

9 High heels were invented by a woman who had been kissed on the forehead.

Christopher Morley, American writer and editor (1890–1957). Quoted in *The Treasury of Humorous Quotations*, eds Evan Esar & Nicolas Bentley (1951).

Hell

10 There have been many definitions of hell, but for the English the best definition is that it is a place where the Germans are the police, the Swedish are the comedians, and the Italians are the defence force, Frenchmen dig the roads, the Belgians are the pop singers, the Spanish run the railways, the Turks cook the food, the Irish are the waiters, the Greeks run the government and the common language is Dutch.

(Sir) David Frost & (Sir) Antony Jay, English writers and broadcasters (1939–) and (1930–). *To England with Love* (1967). Compare this anonymous version: 'Heaven is an English policeman, a French cook, a German engineer, an

Italian lover and everything organized by the Swiss. Hell is an English cook, a French engineer, a German policeman, a Swiss lover and everything organized by the Italians.' And: 'It is said that Hell is where the food is British and the police are French. And Heaven is the other way about' – attributed to Lord Bethell, British Conservative peer, in 1990.

1 *L'Enfer, c'est les Autres* [Hell is other people].

Jean-Paul Sartre, French philosopher and writer (1905–80). *Huis Clos* (1944). Subsequently, T.S. Eliot, *The Cocktail Party* (1950), had: 'What is hell? / Hell is oneself.' A character in Henry Reed, *A Very Great Man Indeed* (1953), quotes Sartre as 'one of our modern neo-pessimists' saying 'Hell consists of other people' and adds: 'We know what Shewin's comment on that would have been … "Yes, but so does heaven".'

2 Heaven for climate; hell for society.

Mark Twain, American writer (1835–1910). *Mark Twain's Speeches*, ed. A.B. Paine (1910). J.M. Barrie wrote, 'If it's heaven for climate, it's hell for company' in *The Little Minister* (1891).

Hemingway, Ernest

AMERICAN NOVELIST (1899–1961)

3 Always willing to lend a helping hand to the one above him.

F. Scott Fitzgerald, American novelist (1896–1940). Quoted in my book *A Year of Stings and Squelches* (1985).

Henry VIII

ENGLISH KING (1491–1547)

4 Have you ever noticed … that all hot-water bottles look like Henry the Eighth?

(Sir) Max Beerbohm, English writer and caricaturist (1872–1956). Quoted in S.N. Behrman, *Conversations with Max* (1960).

Heroes and heroines

5 No man is a hero to his undertaker.

Finley Peter Dunne, American humorist (1867–1936). *Mr Dooley Remembers* (1963 edn).

6 Hail, the conquering hero comes,
Surrounded by a bunch of bums.

George E. Phair. Quoted by Gene Fowler in *Skyline: a reporter's reminiscences of the 1920s* (1961).

7 Heroine: girl who is perfectly charming to live with in a book.

Mark Twain, American writer (1835–1910). In *More Maxims of Mark Twain*, ed. Merle Johnson (1927).

8 Formerly we used to canonise our heroes. The modern method is to vulgarise them. Cheap editions of great books may be delightful, but cheap editions of great men are absolutely detestable.

Oscar Wilde, Irish playwright, poet and wit (1854–1900). 'The Critic As Artist' (1890).

9 The crude commercialism of America, its materializing spirit, its indifference to the poetical side of things, its lack of imagination and of high unattainable ideals, are entirely due to that country having adopted for its national hero one who, according to his own confession, was incapable of telling a lie; and it is not too much to say that the story of George Washington has done more harm, and in a shorter space of time, than any other moral tale in the whole of literature.

Oscar Wilde, Irish playwright, poet and wit (1854–1900). Quoted in Herbert V. Prochnow, Snr & Jnr, *A Treasury of Humorous Quotations* (1969).

Highbrow

10 What is a highbrow? He is a man who has found something more interesting than women.

Edgar Wallace, English writer (1875–1932). In *The New York Times* (24 January 1932), having been interviewed in Hollywood (December 1931). *Compare* INTELLECTUALS 225:6.

Hindsight

1 Hindsight is always twenty-twenty.

Billy Wilder, American film director and screenwriter (1906–). Quoted in John Robert Colombo, *Wit and Wisdom of the Moviemakers* (1979).

Hippies

2 A hippie is someone who looks like Tarzan, walks like Jane, and smells like Cheeta.

Ronald Reagan, American film actor and President (1911–). Attributed remark.

Hippopotamus

3 I shoot the Hippopotamus
with bullets made of platinum,
Because if I use leaden ones
his hide is sure to flatten 'em.

Hilaire Belloc, French-born English poet and writer (1870–1953). *The Bad Child's Book of Beasts*, 'The Hippopotamus' (1896).

4 He thought he saw a Banker's Clerk
Descending from a bus:
He looked again, and found it was
A Hippopotamus:
'If this should stay to dine,' he said,
'There won't be much for us!'

Lewis Carroll, English writer (1832–98). *Sylvie and Bruno*, Chap. 7 (1889).

5 The broad-backed hippopotamus
Rests on his belly in the mud;
Although he seems so firm to us
He is merely flesh and blood.

T.S. Eliot, American-born English poet, playwright and critic (1888–1965). 'The Hippopotamus' (1920).

6 Mud, mud, glorious mud,
Nothing quite like it for cooling the blood.

Michael Flanders, English writer and entertainer (1922–75). 'The Hippopotamus Song' (1953), with music by Donald Swann. It has been pointed out that this bears a more than passing resemblance to James Thurber's apparently later 'The Lover and His Lass' in *Further Fables of Our Time* (1956). In both, the hippos are courting; in the Flanders, the female is referred to as 'his inamorata' and in the Thurber, the male is 'her inamoratus'.

History and historians

7 History is something that never happened, written by someone who wasn't there.

Anonymous. Quoted in *The Home Book of Humorous Quotations*, ed. A.K. Adams (1969).

8 Until lions have their own historians, history will always glorify the hunter.

Anonymous 'Zimbabwean proverb'.

During the Second World War, Winston Churchill had to announce to the House of Commons that the British had, rather illicitly, taken bases in the Azores. He apparently thought he could gloss it over with a splendid speech, so he rose and said, 'I must ask the House now to come with me back over four hundred years of our eventful history ...' Bevan interrupted:

9 Good God, he's looked into his in-tray at last!

Aneurin Bevan, Welsh Labour politician (1897–1960). Quoted by Wynford Vaughan-Thomas on BBC Radio *Quote ... Unquote* (12 June 1980).

10 History is simply a piece of paper covered with print; the main thing is still to make history, not to write it.

Otto von Bismarck, Prusso-German statesman (1815–98). *Prussian Chamber*.

11 God cannot alter the past; that is why he is obliged to connive at the existence of historians.

Samuel Butler, English author (1835–1902). Quoted in *The Treasury of Humorous Quotations*, eds Evan Esar & Nicolas Bentley (1951). This may be a paraphrase of the passage in *Erewhon Revisited* (1901): 'It has been said that though God cannot alter the past, historians can; it is perhaps because they can be useful to Him in this respect that He tolerates their existence.'

1 History books which contain no lies are extremely dull.

Anatole France, French writer (1844–1924). Quoted in *The Treasury of Humorous Quotations*, eds Evan Esar & Nicolas Bentley (1951).

2 It was Quintilian or Max Beerbohm who said, 'History repeats itself: historians repeat each other.'

Philip Guedalla, English biographer and historian (1889–1944). *Supers and Supermen*, 'Some Historians' (1920). Also ascribed to Arthur Balfour. Actually it was Oscar Wilde who said it – as 'History never repeats itself ... ' – at least according to Richard Ellman, *Oscar Wilde* (1987).

3 Very few things happen at the right time, and the rest do not happen at all; the conscientious historian will correct these defects.

Herodotus, Greek historian (484?–425 BC). Quoted in *The Treasury of Humorous Quotations*, eds Evan Esar & Nicolas Bentley (1951).

As 'Edna Everage', on seeing a Morris Traveller in Stratford-upon-Avon:

4 Why, even the cars are half-timbered here!

Barry Humphries, Australian entertainer (1934–). On BBC TV *Line-Up* (1970s).

5 History is too serious to be left to historians.

Iain Macleod, English Conservative politician (1913–70). Quoted in *The Observer*, 'Sayings of the Week' (16 July 1961).

6 Historian: An unsuccessful novelist.

H.L. Mencken, American journalist and linguist (1880–1956). *A Mencken Chrestomathy* (1949).

7 Statesmen think that they make history; but history makes itself and drags the statesmen along.

Will Rogers, American humorist (1879–1935). Quoted in Alastair Cooke, *One Man's America* (1952).

8 Alas! Hegel was right when he said that we learn from history that men never learn anything from history.

Bernard Shaw, Irish playwright and critic (1856–1950). *Heartbreak House*, Preface (1919).

9 More difficult to do a thing than to talk about it? Not at all. That is a gross popular error. It is very much more difficult to talk about a thing than to do it. In the sphere of actual life that is of course obvious. Anybody can make history. Only a great man can write it.

Oscar Wilde, Irish playwright, poet and wit (1854–1900). 'The Critic As Artist' (1890).

10 The one duty we owe to history is to rewrite it.

Oscar Wilde, in the same work as above.

11 To give an accurate description of what has never occurred is not merely the proper occupation of the historian, but the inalienable privilege of any man of parts and culture.

Oscar Wilde, in the same work as above.

Hitler, Adolf

GERMAN NAZI LEADER (1889–1945)

12 Hitler
Has only got one ball!
Goering
Has two, but very small!
Himmler
Has something similar,
But poor old Goebbels
Has no balls at all!

Anonymous song (sung to the tune of 'Colonel Bogey'), in existence by 1940. As with 'Not tonight Josephine', the basis for this assertion about the sexuality of a political figure is obscure. The rumour had been widespread in Central Europe in the 1930s, and Martin Page in *Kiss Me Goodnight, Sergeant Major* (1973) wrote of a Czech refugee who had referred in 1938 to the fact that Hitler had been wounded in the First World War, since when *'ihm fehlt einer'* [he lacks one]. Perhaps it was no more than a generalized slight against the Nazi leader's virility, which conveniently fitted the tune and also permitted a 'Goebbels / no balls' rhyme. There had earlier been a 19th-century American ballad about a trade-union leader that began: 'Arthur Hall / Has only got one ball.'

Famous for never having a bad word to say about anybody, he said of Hitler:

1 Well, he was the best in his field.

Bobby Hackett, jazz musician (1915–76). Quoted in *Jazz Anecdotes*, ed. Bill Crow (1991).

2 Hitler, there was a painter! He could paint an entire apartment in one afternoon. Two coats!

Line from film *The Producers* (US 1967). Screenwriter: Mel Brooks. Spoken by Kenneth Mars (Frank Liebklnd).

3 Let me tell you this, and you are hearing this straight from the horse, Hitler was better looking than Churchill, he was a better dresser than Churchill, he had more hair, he told funnier jokes and he could dance the pants off of Churchill.

Line from the same film. Spoken by Kenneth Mars (Frank Liebkind).

4 I wouldn't believe Hitler was dead, even if he told me so himself.

Hjalmar Schacht, German banker (1877–1970). Attributed remark on 8 May 1945. Quoted on BBC Radio *Quote ... Unquote* (15 June 1977). Schacht was Hitler's Central Bank Governor.

5 And looking very relaxed – Adolf Hitler on vibes.

Vivian Stanshall, English entertainer and eccentric (1942–95). Written and spoken by Stanshall in a number called 'The Intro and the Outro' (1967), performed by the Bonzo Dog Band.

Holes

6 Well, if you knows of a better 'ole, go to it.

Bruce Bairnsfather, British cartoonist (1888–1959). Caption to cartoon published in *Fragments from France* (1915), depicting the gloomy soldier 'Old Bill' sitting on a shell crater in the mud of the Western Front during the First World War. The cartoon series was enormously popular. A musical (London, 1917; New York, 1918) and two films (UK, 1918; US, 1926), based on the strip, all had the title *The Better 'Ole*.

On US politicians having got themselves into a hole over the arms race:

7 When you are in a hole, stop digging.

Denis Healey (Lord Healey), English politician (1917–). Remark, September 1983. Earlier, however, on 7 January 1983, the *Financial Times* had quoted Kenneth Mayland, an economist with the First Pennsylvania Bank, as saying: 'The first rule of holes; when you're in one, stop digging.'

Hollywood

8 Hollywood is a place where people from Iowa mistake themselves for movie stars.

Fred Allen, American comedian (1894–1956). Quoted in Maurice Zolotow, *No People Like Show People* (1951). Said in about 1941.

9 Hollywood is no place for a professional comedian; the amateur competition is too great.

Fred Allen. Quoted in *The Treasury of Humorous Quotations*, eds Evan Esar & Nicolas Bentley (1951 edn).

10 An associate producer is the only guy in Hollywood who will associate with a producer.

Fred Allen. Quoted in the same book as above.

11 You can take all the sincerity in Hollywood, put it in a flea's navel, and still have room left over for three caraway seeds and an agent's heart.

Fred Allen. Quoted in Silver & Haiblum, *Faster Than a Speeding Bullet* (1980). Quoted earlier in John Robert Colombo, *Wit and Wisdom of the Moviemakers* (1979) as, '... place it in the navel of a fruit fly and still have room enough for three caraway seeds and a producer's heart.'

Collecting an Oscar:

12 If New York is the Big Apple, tonight Hollywood is the Big Nipple.

Bernardo Bertolucci, Italian film director (1940–). Speech at the Academy Awards ceremony, Los Angeles (1988). Quoted in *The Observer*, 'Sayings of the Week' (17 April 1988). In an attempt at clarification, the film director explained: 'It is a big suck for me.'

1 Hollywood – an emotional Detroit.

Lillian Gish, American actress (1899–1993). Attributed remark, quoted in *Hollywood Wits*, ed. K. Madsen Roth (1995).

2 Strip the phoney tinsel off Hollywood and you'll find the real tinsel underneath.

Oscar Levant, American pianist and actor (1906–72). Quoted in Leslie Halliwell, *The Filmgoer's Book of Quotes* (1973). In the early 1940s.

3 Hollywood is a sewer with service from the Ritz Carlton.

Wilson Mizner, American playwright (1876–1933). Quoted in Leslie Halliwell, *The Filmgoer's Book of Quotes* (1973).

4 A trip through a sewer in a glass-bottomed boat.

Wilson Mizner. Quoted in Alva Johnston, *The Legendary Mizners* (1953).

5 In Hollywood, if you don't have happiness you send out for it.

Rex Reed, American journalist and critic (1938–). Quoted in John Robert Colombo, *Wit and Wisdom of the Moviemakers* (1979).

6 Hollywood – a place where the inmates are in charge of the asylum.

Laurence Stallings, American writer (1894–1968). Quoted in Laurence J. Peter, *Quotations for Our Time* (1977).

When asked after a visit to Hollywood what it was like out there:

7 There is no 'There' – there.

Gertrude Stein, American poet (1874–1946). Quoted in David Niven, *Bring on the Empty Horses* (1975).

8 You can seduce a man's wife there, attack his daughter and wipe your hands on his canary, but if you don't like his movie, you're dead.

Joseph von Sternberg, Austrian-born film director (1894–1969). Quoted in the book *Quote ... Unquote* (1978).

Home

9 Home is where the television is.

Anonymous (graffito). From Covent Garden, London. In my book *Graffiti 4* (1982).

10 'Home, Sweet Home' must surely have been written by a bachelor.

Samuel Butler, English novelist and writer (1835–1902). *Notebooks* (1912).

Parodying official jargon which had become all the rage under the then Labour government and which had redesignated 'homes' as 'accommodation units':

11 Accommodation Unit Sweet Accommodation Unit.

(Sir) Winston S. Churchill, British Conservative Prime Minister and writer (1874–1965). In speech at Cardiff in 1950. Quoted in Leslie Frewin, *Immortal Jester* (1973). Compare the graffito found in Notting Hill and quoted in my book *Graffiti Lives OK* (1979): 'Dwelling unit sweet dwelling unit.'

12 Be it ever so humbug, there's no place like home.

(Sir) Noël Coward, English entertainer and writer (1899–1973). Quoted in *The Treasury of Humorous Quotations*, eds Evan Esar & Nicolas Bentley (1951).

13 Home is where you go to when you've nowhere to go.

Bette Davis, American film actress (1908–89). Quoted by Katharine Whitehorn in *The Observer* (20 September 1987).

14 Many a man who thinks to found a home discovers that he has merely opened a tavern for his friends.

Norman Douglas, Scottish novelist and essayist (1868–1952). *South Wind* (1917).

15 Home is the place where, when you have to go there, they have to take you in.

Robert Frost, American poet (1874–1963). Quoted in *The Treasury of Humorous Quotations*, eds Evan Esar & Nicolas Bentley (1951).

Homosexuality

1 A far from whole-hearted devotion to the pursuit of girls had sometimes struck him as a kind of selection-board requirement for writers and artists. (Musicians showed up in a different light whenever they were sober enough.)

(Sir) Kingsley Amis, English novelist, poet and critic (1922–95). *I Like It Here*, Chap. 7 (1958).

Written by another hand under the graffito, 'My mother made me a homosexual':

2 If I got her the wool, would she make me one?

Anonymous. Quoted in Norton Mockridge, *The Scrawl of the Wild* (1968).

On being asked if he was homosexual:

3 Well, if I had to choose between Michaelangelo's David and Whistler's mother …

Brendan Behan, Irish playwright (1923–64). Quoted in Joan Littlewood, *Joan's Book* (1994).

About his affection for a rather plain young lady:

4 Buggers can't be choosers.

(Sir) Maurice Bowra, English academic (1898–1971). Quoted in Jan Morris, *The Oxford Book of Oxford* (1978). The story comes from Francis King and is taken from Hugh Lloyd-Jones, *Maurice Bowra: A Celebration* (1974).

5 If God had meant to have homosexuals, he would have created Adam and Bruce.

Anita Bryant, American anti-gay campaigner. Quoted in Barbara Rowes, *The Book of Quotes* (1979). Earlier this had appeared in *The New York Times* (5 June 1977) as: 'If homosexuality were the normal way, God would have made Adam and Bruce.'

6 *Winston Churchill*:
I once went to bed with a man to see what it was like.
Somerset Maugham:
Who was the man?
Winston Churchill:
Ivor Novello.
Somerset Maugham:
And what was it like?
Winston Churchill:
Musical.

(Sir) Winston S. Churchill, British Conservative Prime Minister and writer (1874–1965). Quoted in Ted Morgan, *Somerset Maugham* (1980). The source for this story was Alan Searle, one of Maugham's acolytes. Churchill's daughter, Mary Soames, questioned it when it was included in my *Dictionary of Twentieth Century Quotations* (1987), and it is surely of dubious veracity.

When Sheridan Morley was keen to discuss Coward's sexuality in his biography and pointed out that theatre critic T.C. Worsley had recently 'come out':

7 There is one essential difference between me and Cuthbert Worsley. The British public at large would not care if Cuthbert Worsley had slept with mice.

(Sir) Noël Coward, English entertainer and writer (1899–1973). Quoted in *The Times* (1994).

8 I became one of the stately homos of England.

Quentin Crisp, English homosexual celebrity (1908–99). *The Naked Civil Servant* (1968).

9 I have heard some say … [homosexual] practices are allowed in France and in other NATO countries. We are not French, and we are not other nationals. We are British, thank God!

Bernard Montgomery (1st Viscount Montgomery of Alamein), English field marshal (1887–1976). Commenting on a bill to relax the laws against homosexuals (House of Lords, 24 May 1965). Fundamentally opposed to what he termed a 'Buggers' Charter', Montgomery, at the committee stage of the parliamentary bill, suggested raising the age of consent from the age of 21 to 80. He added, disarmingly, that he would himself be reaching his fourscore years at his next birthday. Recounted in Mervyn Stockwood, *Chanctonbury Ring* (1982).

Telegram said to have been sent to Tom Driberg MP on the occasion of his marriage (to a woman) (1951):

1 I pray that the church is not struck by lightning.

Evelyn Waugh, English novelist (1903–66). Attributed remark. According to Alan Watkins, *Brief Lives* (1982), Waugh in fact wrote – rather than telegraphed – to the effect: 'I will think of you intently on the day and pray that the church is not struck by lightning.' The letter is not, alas, included in Waugh's published correspondence. Watkins adds: 'This sentence in this same connection is, oddly enough, attributed to Aneurin Bevan and Winston Churchill also.' Driberg was a notorious and active homosexual.

Honesty

2 No man, the late Charles May Oelrichs used to say, ever made more than a million dol lars honestly.

Charles May Oelrichs. Quoted in Cleveland Amory, *The Last Resorts* (1952).

Of physicians:

3 First they get *on*, then they get *honour*, then they get *honest*.

(Sir) Humphry Rolleston, English consultant physician (1862–1944). Quoted in David Ogilvy, *Confessions of an Advertising Man* (1963).

4 Honesty is the best policy, but it is not the cheapest.

Mark Twain, American writer (1835–1910). In *The Mark Twain-Howells Letters*, eds Smith & Gibson (1960).

Honey

5 When Rabbit said, 'Honey or condensed milk with your bread?' [Pooh] was so excited he said, 'Both,' and then, so as not to seem greedy, he added, 'But don't bother about the bread, please.'

A.A. Milne, English writer (1882–1956). *Winnie-The-Pooh*, Chap. 2 (1926).

Honeymoons

6 The success of the marriage comes after the failure of the honeymoon.

G.K. Chesterton, English poet, novelist and critic (1874–1936). Quoted in *The Treasury of Humorous Quotations*, eds Evan Esar & Nicolas Bentley (1951).

Returning with his second wife from Venice:

7 We have been on a working honeymoon.

(Sir) David Frost, English broadcaster (1939–). Remark to reporters (March 1983). Frost, an inveterate business person, had got married and taken his honeymoon at the height of a cataclysm that was afflicting TV-am, the breakfast TV station, of which he was a prominent part.

Honour

8 Remember, you're fighting for this woman's honour ... which is probably more than she ever did.

Line from film *Duck Soup* (US 1933). Screenwriters: Bert Kalmar, Harry Ruby, Arthur Sheekman, Nat Perrin. Spoken by Groucho Marx (Rufus T. Firefly).

9 The louder he talked of his honour, the faster we counted our spoons.

Ralph Waldo Emerson, American poet and essayist (1803–82). *The Conduct of Life*, 'Worship' (1860). This had been anticipated by Samuel Johnson, as reported in Boswell's *Life* (1791 – for 14 July 1763): 'But if he [Macpherson] does really think that there is no distinction between virtue and vice, why, Sir, when he leaves our houses, let us count our spoons.'

Honours

10 This indiscriminate flinging about of knighthoods is making me very nervous; it's quite possible they may give one to my butler next.

(Sir) W.S. Gilbert, English writer and lyricist (1836–1911). Quoted in Hesketh Pearson, *Lives of the Wits* (1962). Gilbert received his knighthood in 1907, and proceeded to describe it as 'a tin-pot, two-penny-halfpenny sort of distinction', 'a mere triviality' and 'an unmeaning scrap of tinsel'. He also referred to his knighthood as 'a commuted Old Age Pension.'

Hope

1 When I am sad and weary
When I think all hope has gone
When I walk along High Holborn
I think of you with nothing on.

Adrian Mitchell, English poet and playwright (1932–). 'Celia Celia' (1968).

Hopelessness

2 If we see light at the end of the tunnel,
It's the light of the oncoming train.

Robert Lowell, American poet (1917–77). 'Since 1939' (1977). Probably not original. Paul Dickson cited 'Rowe's Rule: the odds are five to six that the light at the end of the tunnel is the headlight of an oncoming train' in *Washingtonian* (November 1978). On BBC Radio *Quote … Unquote* (1980), John Lahr said it had been a favourite remark of his father – the actor Bert Lahr (d. 1967).

Refusing any last-ditch attempts to rescue President Ford's re-election campaign in 1976:

3 I'm not going to do anything to rearrange the furniture on the deck of the *Titanic*.

Rogers Morton, American government official (1914–79). Quoted in *The Times* (13 May 1976). He was Ford's campaign manager.

4 Since I gave up hope, I feel so much better.

John Osborne, English playwright (1929–94). Quoted in *The Independent* (26 April 1994). This was a badge displayed in his bathroom – 'it always made him smile'. Virgil may have anticipated this with '*Una salus victis nullam sperare salutem* [Losers have one salvation – to give up all hope of salvation]' (*Aeneid*, Bk 2, Verse 354).

Horses

On her first encounter with a horse (as a child):

5 One was presented with a small, hairy individual and, out of general curiosity, one climbed on.

Anne, British Princess Royal (1950–). Quoted in *Princess Anne and Mark Phillips Talking Horses with Genevieve Murphy* (1976).

6 There is nothing better for the inside of a man than the outside of a horse.

Anonymous. When *Time* Magazine quoted President Reagan as saying this (28 December 1987), it received many letters from readers saying such things as: 'This quotation bears a striking resemblance to a remark made by the California educator and prep school founder Sherman Thacher: "There's something about the outside of a horse that's good for the inside of a boy"'; and, 'Rear Admiral Grayson, President Woodrow Wilson's personal physician put it … "The outside of a horse is good for the inside of a man"'; and, 'Lord Palmerston said it.' The latter ascription is given in *The Home Book of Humorous Quotations*, ed. A.K. Adams (1969). *Time* sensibly replied (19 January 1988): 'Everyone is right. The origin of the saying is unknown. It is one of the President's favorite expressions.'

7 I know two things about the horse
And one of them is rather coarse.

Anonymous. However, in *The Weekend Book* (1928), it is attributed to Naomi Royde-Smith (*c.* 1875–1964).

8 Dangerous at both ends and uncomfortable in the middle.

Ian Fleming, English novelist and journalist (1908–64). Quoted in *The Sunday Times* (9 October 1966).

9 Take most people, they're crazy about cars … I'd rather have a goddamn horse. A horse is at least *human*, for Christ's sake.

J.D. Salinger, American novelist (1919–). *The Catcher in the Rye*, Chap. 17 (1951).

Hosts and hostesses

10 I maintain that though you would often in the fifteenth century have heard the snobbish Roman say, 'I am dining with the Borgias to-night,' no Roman ever was able to say, 'I dined last night with the Borgias.'

(Sir) Max Beerbohm, English writer and caricaturist (1872–1956). *Hosts and Guests* (1920).

11 To mankind in general, Macbeth and Lady Macbeth stand out as the supreme type of

all that host and hostess should not be.

(Sir) Max Beerbohm. In the same book as above.

1 Mankind is divisible into two great classes: hosts and guests.

Max Beerbohm. In the same book as above. Also quoted as: 'People are either born hosts or born guests.'

2 I am a man more dined against than dining.

(Sir) Maurice Bowra, English academic (1898–1971). Quoted in John Betjeman, *Summoned by Bells* (1960).

When asked to add Lady Macbeth to her repertoire:

3 I could never impersonate a woman with such peculiar notions of hospitality!

(Dame) Edith Evans, English actress (1888–1976). Quoted in Richard Huggett, *The Curse of Macbeth* (1981).

To a visitor, Denton Welch:

4 Come again when you can't stay so long.

Walter Sickert, German-born English painter (1860–1942). Quoted by Welch in 'Sickert at St Peter's' in *Horizon*, Vol. 6, No. 32 (1942). In *Taken Care of* (1965), Edith Sitwell comments on the article but gives the tag as 'Come again – when you have a little less time.' Either way, this farewell was not originated by Sickert. Indeed, Welch ends his article by saying, 'And at these words a strange pang went through me, for it was what my father had always said as he closed the book, when I had finished my bread and butter and milk, and it was time for bed.'

Hot dogs

5 The noblest of all dogs is the hot-dog; it feeds the hand that bites it.

Laurence J. Peter, Canadian writer (1919–90). *Quotations for Our Time* (1977). Although compiling a book of quotations, Peter inserted several observations of his own.

Hot pants

6 Those hot pants of hers were so damned tight, I could hardly breathe.

Benny Hill, English television comedian (1924–92). Quoted in *The Penguin Dictionary of Modern Humorous Quotations*, ed. Fred Metcalf (1987).

House of Commons

7 Being an MP is a good job, the sort of job all working-class parents want for their children – clean, indoors and no heavy lifting. What could be nicer?

Diane Abbott, British Labour politician (1953–). In an interview with Hunter Davies in *The Independent* (18 January 1994). Much the same claim had earlier been made by Senator Robert Dole about the US vice-presidency (ABC TV broadcast, 24 July 1988): 'It is inside work with no heavy lifting.'

8 Both acting and the House of Commons are about people – but the House is remarkably under-rehearsed and very poorly lit; and the acoustics are appalling.

Glenda Jackson, English actress and politician (1936–). Interviewed in *The Independent* (26 January 2000) – but a view also expressed by her previously.

9 Only people who look dull ever get into the House of Commons, and only people who are dull ever succeed there.

Oscar Wilde, Irish playwright, poet and wit (1854–1900). *An Ideal Husband*, Act 4 (1895).

See also PARLIAMENT.

House of Lords

10 The House of Lords is like a glass of champagne which has stood for five days.

Clement Attlee (1st Earl Attlee), British Labour Prime Minister (1883–1967). Quoted in *The Fine Art of Political Wit*, ed. Leon A. Harris (1966).

11 A severe though not unfriendly critic of our institutions said that 'the *cure* for admiring the House of Lords was to go and look at it'.

Walter Bagehot, English constitutional historian (1826–77). *The English Constitution*, 'The House of Lords' (1867).

On renouncing his own peerage:

12 The British House of Lords is the British Outer Mongolia for retired politicians.

Tony Benn, English Labour politician (1925–). Quoted in

The Observer (4 February 1962). Also ascribed to V.M. Molotov. Compare, from Malcolm Muggeridge, *Tread Softly for You Tread On My Jokes* (1966): 'Stalin when he killed off his egg-heads like Bukharin, was only establishing a sound and stable government. In this country the victims would have been given the OM and sent to the House of Lords, but the end result would have been the same.'

1 My Lord Tomnoddy is thirty-four;
The Earl can last but a few years more.
My Lord in the Peers will take his place:
Her Majesty's councils his words will grace.
Office he'll hold and patronage sway;
Fortunes and lives he will vote away;
And what are his qualifications? – ONE!
He's the Earl of Fitzdotterel's eldest son.

Robert Barnabas Brough, English writer (1828–60). 'My Lord Tomnoddy' (1855).

On learning that the elder Pitt had accepted an earldom:

2 Pitt has had a bad fall upstairs to that Hospital for Incurables, the House of Lords.

4th Earl of Chesterfield (Philip Dormer Stanhope), English politician and writer (1694–1773).

On becoming a peer:

3 I am dead, dead but in the Elysian Fields.

Benjamin Disraeli (1st Earl of Beaconsfield), English politician and writer (1804–81). Quoted in Moneypenny & Buckle, *Life of Disraeli* (1910–20).

4 The House of Lords is a model of how to care for the elderly.

Frank Field, English Labour politician (1942–). Quoted in *The Observer* (24 May 1981).

5 This is the leal [*sic*] and trusty mastiff which is to watch over our interests, but which runs away at the first snarl of the trade unions? A mastiff? It is the right hon. Gentleman's Poodle. It fetches and carries for him. It barks for him. It bites anybody that he sets it on to.

David Lloyd George (1st Earl Lloyd George of Dwyfor), British Liberal Prime Minister (1863–1945). Speech in the House of Commons (26 June 1907) on the controversy over the power of the upper House. He questioned the House of Lords' role as a 'watchdog' of the constitution and suggested that A.J. Balfour, the Conservative leader, was using the party's majority in the upper chamber to block legislation by the Liberal government (in which Lloyd George was President of the Board of Trade). Hence, the phrase 'Mr Balfour's poodle'.

6 The House of Peers, throughout the war,
Did nothing in particular,
And did it very well.

(Sir) W.S. Gilbert, English writer and lyricist (1836–1911). *Iolanthe*, Act 2 (1882).

7 The House of Lords must be the only institution in the world that is kept efficient by the persistent absenteeism of its members.

1st Viscount Samuel, English Liberal politician and philosopher (1870–1963). Quoted in *American News Review* (5 February 1948).

8 The House of Lords is a perfect eventide home.

Mary Stocks (Baroness Stocks), English academic (1891–1975). *My Commonplace Book* (1970).

9 The House of Lords, an illusion to which I have never been able to subscribe – responsibility without power, the prerogative of the eunuch throughout the ages.

(Sir) Tom Stoppard, English playwright (1937–). *Lord Malquist and Mr Moon* (1966).

10 We in the House of Lords are never in touch with public opinion. That makes us a civilised body.

Oscar Wilde, Irish playwright, poet and wit (1854–1900). *A Woman of No Importance*, Act 1 (1893).

See also PARLIAMENT.

Housework

1 There was no need to do any housework at all. After the first four years the dirt doesn't get any worse.

Quentin Crisp, English homosexual celebrity (1908–99). *The Naked Civil Servant* (1968).

Hughes, Ted

ENGLISH POET LAUREATE (1930–98)

2 We had the old crow over at Hull recently, looking like a Christmas present from Easter Island.

Philip Larkin, English poet (1922–85). Letter of 15 June 1975, included in *Required Writing* (1983).

Human race

3 The human race, to which so many of my readers belong, has been playing at children's games from the beginning, and will probably do it till the end, which is a nuisance for the few people who grow up.

G.K. Chesterton, English poet, novelist and critic (1874–1936). *The Napoleon of Notting Hill*, Chap. 1 (1904).

4 I wish I loved the Human Race;
I wish I loved its silly face;
I wish I liked the way it walks;
I wish I liked the way it talks;
And when I'm introduced to one
I wish I thought, *What Jolly Fun!*

(Sir) Walter Raleigh, English scholar (1861–1922). *Laughter from a Cloud*, 'The Wishes of an Elderly Man: Wished at a Garden Party, June, 1914' (1923).

Humiliation

On the climate of Washington DC when McCarthyism was at its height:

5 It's not so much the heat, it's the humiliation.

Anonymous. Quoted by Leonard Miall in *The 'Quote ... Unquote' Newsletter* (October 1992).

Humility

6 In 1969 I published a small book on Humility. It was a pioneering work which has not, to my knowledge, been superseded.

7th Earl of Longford (Francis Pakenham), English writer and politician (1905–). In *The Tablet* (22 January 1994).

Humming

7 *He:*
Of course, you know the 'Heir of Redclyffe'?
She:
I'm not sure. Would you mind just humming it?

Anonymous. Cartoon caption in the series 'Conversational Inanities' from *Punch* (16 April 1887). The reference is to a novel by C.M. Yonge. Earlier in *Punch* (26 October 1872) there had been the similar cartoon in which a 'Kirk Elder' asks, 'My friend, do you know the chief end of man?' A Scots piper replies, 'Na, I dinae mind the chune! Can you whistle it?' All this may be the origin of the modern joke exchange: 'Do you know --?' / 'No, but if you hum it, I'll pick out the tune / fake it.' A comic exchange, current in the US and the UK by the 1960s. From BBC radio show *Round the Horne* (29 May 1966): 'Do you know Limehouse?' / 'No, but if you hum a few bars, I'll soon pick it up.'

Humour

8 Every good joke has a philosophical idea somewhere inside it.

G.K. Chesterton, English poet, novelist and critic (1874–1936). Attributed remark. Possibly a rendering of the view put forward in his essay 'Cockneys and Their Jokes': 'When once you have got hold of a vulgar joke, you may be certain that you have got hold of a subtle and spiritual idea.'

9 I think there's a terrific merit in having no sense of humour, no sense of irony, practically no sense of anything at all. If you're born with these so-called defects you have a very good chance of getting to the top. That's what's enabled her [Mrs Thatcher] to turn Britain into a cross between Singapore and Telford.

Peter Cook, English humorist (1937–95). In *The Guardian* (23 July 1988).

Of Charlie Chaplin:

1 Chaplin's genius was in comedy. He had no sense of humour.

Lita Grey, American actress (1908). His ex-wife. Quoted in Richard Lamparski, *Whatever Became of --?* (1983).

Distinguishing between amateur and professional senses of humour:

2 For the amateur the funniest thing in the world is the sight of a man dressed up as an old woman rolling down a steep hill in a wheel-chair and crashing into a wall at the bottom of it. But to make a pro laugh, it would have to be a real old woman.

Groucho Marx, American comedian (1895–1977). Quoted in Kenneth Tynan in 'The Crazy Gang', *Persona Grata* (1953). In John Robert Colombo, *Wit and Wisdom of the Moviemakers* (1979), this has become: 'An amateur thinks it's funny if you dress a man up as an old lady, put him in a wheelchair, and give the wheelchair a push that sends it spinning down a slope toward a stone wall. For a pro it's got to be a real old lady.'

3 Performers who began their career playing some kind of part in Windmill productions included ... Bruce Forsyth, Jimmy Edwards ... Peter Sellers, Arthur English, and many others too humorous to mention.

Frank Muir, English writer and broadcaster (1920–98). *A Kentish Lad*, Chap. 7 (1997). My recollection is that Muir was using the 'too humorous to mention' line by 1971.

4 Mark Twain and I are in very much the same position. We have to put things in such a way as to make people, who would otherwise hang us, believe that we are joking.

Bernard Shaw, Irish playwright and critic (1856–1950). *Table Talk* (1924).

5 Humor ... is emotional chaos remembered in tranquillity.

James Thurber, American cartoonist and writer (1894–1961). Quoted in the *New York Post* (29 February 1960).

6 Everything human is pathetic. The secret source of humor itself is not joy but sorrow. There is no humor in heaven.

Mark Twain, American writer (1835–1910). *Following the Equator* (1897).

Hunting

7 When a man wants to murder a tiger he calls it sport; when a tiger wants to murder him, he calls it ferocity.

Bernard Shaw, Irish playwright and critic (1856–1950). Quoted in *The Treasury of Humorous Quotations*, eds Evan Esar & Nicolas Bentley (1951).

8 'Unting is all that's worth living for – all time is lost wot is not spent in 'unting – it is like the hair we breathe – if we have it not we die – it's the sport of kings, the image of war without its guilt, and only five-and-twenty per cent of its danger.

R.S. Surtees, English novelist and journalist (1805–64). *Handley Cross*, Chap. 7 (1843).

9 The English country gentleman galloping after a fox – the unspeakable in full pursuit of the uneatable.

Oscar Wilde, Irish playwright, poet and wit (1854–1900). *A Woman of No Importance*, Act 1 (1893).

Husbands

10 Husbands are like fires. They go out when unattended.

Zsa Zsa Gabor, Hungarian-born film actress (1919–). Quoted in *Newsweek* Magazine (28 March 1960).

In answer to the question 'How many husbands have you had?':

11 You mean apart from my own?

Zsa Zsa Gabor. Quoted in Kenneth Edwards, *I Wish I'd Said That!* (1976).

On her second husband:

12 I only saw him twice and we have two children.

Sheilah Graham, British-born Hollywood gossip columnist (1904–88). Quoted in *The Observer*, 'Sayings of the Week' (25 March 1984).

1 Do married men make the best husbands?

James Gibbons Huneker, American writer (1860–1921). Quoted in *The Treasury of Humorous Quotations*, eds Evan Esar & Nicolas Bentley (1951).

2 American women expect to find in their husbands a perfection that English women only hope to find in their butlers.

W. Somerset Maugham, English writer (1874–1965). Quoted in the same collection as above.

3 A husband is what is left of the lover after the nerve has been extracted.

Helen Rowland, American humorous columnist and writer (1875–1950). Quoted in the same collection as above.

4 I am, dear Prue, a little in drink, but at all times yr faithful husband.

(Sir) Richard Steele, Irish-born essayist (1672–1729). Letter to his wife (27 September 1708).

5 The husbands of very beautiful women belong to the criminal classes.

Oscar Wilde, Irish playwright, poet and wit (1854–1900). *The Picture of Dorian Gray*, Chap. 15 (1891).

6 Chumps always make the best husbands. When you marry, Sally, grab a chump. Tap his forehead first, and if it rings solid, don't hesitate. All the unhappy marriages come from the husbands having brains. What good are brains to a man? They only unsettle him.

(Sir) P(elham) G. Wodehouse, English-born novelist and lyricist (1881–1975). *The Adventures of Sally*, Chap. 10 (1920).

Hymns

7 Our Lady sings Magnificat
With tune surpassing sweet;
And all the Virgins bear their parts,
Sitting about her feet.

Anonymous. Verse 23 (of 26), No. 638 in *The English Hymnal*.

Hypochondria

8 If you're a hypochondriac, first class, you awaken each morning with the firm resolve not to worry; everything is going to turn out all wrong.

Goodman Ace, American writer (1899–1982). *The Fine Art of Hypochondria* (1966).

9 Hypochondria is the one disease I haven't got.

David Renwick and Andrew Marshall, English writers (1951–) and (1954–). In BBC Radio *The Burkiss Way* (14 February 1978).

Hypocrisy

10 Making the world safe for hypocrisy.

Thomas Wolfe, American novelist (1900–38). *Look Homeward, Angel*, Pt 3 (1929).

11 I hope you have not been leading a double life, pretending to be wicked, and being really good all the time. That would be hypocrisy.

Oscar Wilde, Irish playwright, poet and wit (1854–1900). *The Importance of Being Earnest*, Act 2 (1895).

Hypotheses

On being asked what would have happened if Khruschev rather than Kennedy had been assassinated in 1963:

12 With history one can never be certain, but I think I can safely say that Aristotle Onassis would not have married Mrs Khruschev.

Gore Vidal, American novelist, playwright and critic (1925–). Quoted in *The Sunday Times* (4 June 1989).

I

Ibsen, Henrik

NORWEGIAN PLAYWRIGHT (1828–1906)

1 In every play a stranger comes into the room, opens a window to let in fresh air and everyone dies of pneumonia.

W. Somerset Maugham, English novelist and short-story writer (1874–1965). Attributed remark. Quoted by Robin Bailey on BBC Radio *Quote ... Unquote* (27 July 1985).

Ideals

2 An idealist is one who, on noticing that a rose smells better than a cabbage, concludes that it will also make a better soup.

H.L. Mencken, American journalist and linguist (1880–1956). *A Mencken Chrestomathy* (1949).

Ideas

3 That fellow seems to me to possess but one idea, and that is a wrong one.

(Dr) Samuel Johnson, English writer and lexicographer (1709–84). Quoted in James Boswell, *The Life of Samuel Johnson* (1791) – for 1770.

4 The three stages of a new idea. 1. The idea is nonsense. 2. Somebody else thought of it before you did. 3. We believed it all the time.

Ray Lyttelton. Quoted in Fred Hoyle, *Home Is Where the Wind Blows* (1994).

In answer to boy's question, 'Where do you get your incredible ideas from?':

5 There's this warehouse called Ideas Are Us.

Terry Pratchett, English novelist (1948–). Quoted in *The Observer* (8 November 1992).

6 All I know is, if someone says, 'Hey, what a great idea for a musical', it usually isn't.

(Sir) Tim Rice, English lyricist (1944–). Quoted in *The Independent* (19 August 1989).

In answer to the journalists' clichéd question 'Where do you get your ideas from?':

7 If I knew, I'd go there.

(Sir) Tom Stoppard, English playwright (1937–). Attributed remark. In *Joyce Grenfell Requests the Pleasure* (1976), Joyce Grenfell wrote that she gave the same reply to the question, 'Where do you get the ideas for your monologues?'

8 When you convert someone to an idea ... you lose your faith in it.

Oscar Wilde, Irish playwright, poet and wit (1854–1900). Quoted in Herbert V. Prochnow, Snr & Jnr, *A Treasury of Humorous Quotations* (1969).

Identification

9 Mr George Robey is the Darling of the music-halls, m'lud.

F.E. Smith (1st Earl of Birkenhead), English Conservative politician and lawyer (1872–1930). To Mr Justice Darling who had asked, as judges do, who George Robey the comedian was. Quoted in A.E. Wilson, *The Prime Minister of Mirth* (1956).

10 A nobleman (as he was riding) met with a yeoman of the country, to whom he said,

'My friend, I should know thee. I do remember I have often seen thee.' 'My good lord,' said the countryman, 'I am one of your honour's poor tenants, and my name is T. I.' 'I remember thee better now' (saith my lord) 'There were two brothers but one is dead. I pray thee, which of you doth remain alive?'

John Taylor, English poet and writer (?1578–1653). *Wit and Mirth* (1630).

Identifying marks

Until quite recently a small spot was reserved by the River Cherwell in Oxford for dons to swim in the nude. Some young wags decided to go up the river in a punt in order to be able to see their tutors so disporting themselves. They braved the rapids and came into the quiet patch of the river where these rather corpulent dons were sitting naked on the sward. As the old gentlemen saw their pupils going past, they all – except Bowra – covered their loins with their hands. Bowra put his hands over his eyes – and explained to his colleagues:

1 In Oxford I'm known by my face …

(Sir) Maurice Bowra, English academic (1898–1971). Quoted by A N Wilson on BBC Radio *Quote … Unquote* (20 November 1990). In his published diary for 4 February 1992, Anthony Powell notes how he had written to *The Daily Telegraph* about this story, adding: 'It was a chestnut when Maurice was born, as usual journalists missing the point, especially as they were all Balliol dons. As it was, just as the punt was disappearing, a lady was heard to say: "I think that must have been Mr Paravicini. He is the only *red-haired* don in Balliol".'

Identity

When he was President, George Bush paid a visit to an old people's home. After chatting to patients for a little while, he asked one of them, 'And do you know who I am?' Came the reply from one old biddie:

2 No, but if you ask in reception I'm sure they will be able to tell you.

Anonymous. Quoted by Derek Parker in *The Author* (Summer 1993). Also told variously about other celebrities.

Idleness

3 Cultivated idleness seems to me to be the proper occupation for man.

Oscar Wilde, Irish playwright, poet and wit (1854–1900). In *The Letters of Oscar Wilde*, ed. Rupert Hart-Davis (1962).

4 *Lady Bracknell:*
Do you smoke?
Jack Worthing:
Well, yes, I must admit I smoke.
Lady Bracknell:
I am glad to hear it. A man should always have an occupation of some kind. There are far too many idle men in London as it is.

Oscar Wilde. *The Importance of Being Earnest*, Act 1 (1895).

If God …

5 If God had intended us to fly, He would have sent us tickets.

Mel Brooks, American writer and actor (1926–). Quoted by Frederic Raphael in 1994. Frank Muir, *A Kentish Lad* (1997), mentions that the line, 'If God had meant us to fly he would have given us the money' was spoken in a TV series called *Thingummybob* (*c.* 1969).

These two 'If Gods …' on flying are part of a long tradition of such remarks. Compare from Lord Berners, *First Childhood* (1934): 'My [model flying machine] elicited a reproof from the Headmaster, who happened to see it [c.1893]. "Men," he said, "were never meant to fly; otherwise God would have given them wings." The argument was convincing, if not strikingly, having been used previously, if I am not mistaken, by Mr Chadband.' Indeed, in Charles Dickens, *Bleak House* (1852–3) we have: [Chadband] 'Why can't we not fly, my friends?' [Mr Snagsby] 'No wings.'

6 If God had intended us to fly, he'd never have given us the railways.

Michael Flanders, English writer and entertainer (1922–75). *At the Drop of Another Hat*, 'By Air' (1963).

7 If God had not meant everyone to be in bed by ten-thirty, He would never have provided the ten o'clock newscast.

Garrison Keillor, American writer (1942–). *Lake Wobegon Days* (1985).

1 If the Lord had meant us to pay income taxes, He'd have made us smart enough to prepare the return.

Kirk Kirkpatrick. Attributed remark.

2 I've always figured that if God wanted us to go to church a lot, he'd have given us bigger behinds to sit on and smaller heads to think with.

P.J. O'Rourke, American humorist (1947–), 'Holidays in Hell' (1988).

3 *Ruby:*
Me mother says if God had intended men to smoke He'd have put chimneys in their heads.
Ormonroyd:
Tell your mother from me that if God had intended men to wear clothes He'd have put collar studs at back of their necks.

J.B. Priestley, English novelist and playwright (1894–1984). *When We Are Married* (1938).

4 If God had meant us to travel tourist class, He would have made us narrower.

Martha Zimmerman, American air hostess. Quoted in *The Wall Street Journal* (1977).

Ignorance

5 Gross ignorance –144 times worse than ordinary ignorance.

Bennett Cerf, American humorist (1898–1971). *The Laugh's On Me* (1961).

6 Even his ignorance is encyclopedic.

Stanislaw J. Lec, Polish poet and aphorist (1909–66). *Unkempt Thoughts* (1962).

7 Presently Mr Bixby turned on me and said: 'What is the name of the first point above New Orleans?' I was gratified to be able to answer promptly and I did. I said I didn't know.

Mark Twain, American writer (1835–1910). *Life on the Mississippi* (1883).

Immaturity

8 Basically my wife was immature. I'd be at home in the bath and she'd come in and sink my boats.

Woody Allen, American film actor, writer and director (1937–). Quoted in *Nudge Nudge Wink Wink* (1986).

Immortality

9 I don't want to achieve immortality through my work. I want to achieve it through not dying.

Woody Allen, American actor, screenwriter and director (1935–). Quoted in Eric Lax, *Woody Allen and His Comedy* (1975).

To Parker Pillsbury who 'would fain talk with Thoreau in this last winter concerning the next world':

10 One world at a time.

Henry David Thoreau, American writer (1817–62). Quoted in *The Home Book of Humorous Quotations*, ed. A.K. Adams (1969).

Impossible

11 The difficult is what takes a little time; the impossible is what takes a little longer.

Fridtjof Nansen, Norwegian explorer (1861–1930). Quoted in *The Listener* (14 December 1939). *Bartlett's Familiar Quotations* (1980) places this slogan specifically with the US Army Service Forces, but the idea has been traced back to Charles Alexandre de Calonne (1734–1802), who said: *'Madame, si c'est possible, c'est fait; impossible? cela se fera* [if it is possible, it is already done; if it is impossible, it will be done]' – quoted in J. Michelet, *Histoire de la Révolution Française* (1847). Compare: 'The Difficult is that which can be done immediately; the Impossible that which takes a little longer' – George Santayana, Spanish-born American poet and philosopher (1863–1952), quoted in *The Treasury of Humorous Quotations*, eds Evan Esar & Nicolas Bentley (1951). Henry Kissinger once joked: 'The illegal we do immediately, the unconstitutional takes a little longer' – quoted in William Shawcross, *Sideshow*, (1979).

Impropriety

1 Impropriety is the soul of wit.

W. Somerset Maugham, English writer (1874–1965). *The Moon and Sixpence*, Chap. 4 (1919).

2 An improper mind is a perpetual feast.

Logan Pearsall Smith, American writer (1865–1946). *Afterthoughts* (1931). As 'a filthy mind is a continual feast' this has also been ascribed to Edward Heron-Allen and Vyvyan Holland, acquaintance of and son of Oscar Wilde, respectively. In John G. Murray's *A Gentleman Publisher's Commonplace Book* (1996), there is a version '*from* [note rather than *by*] Osbert Lancaster' with 'perpetual feast'. There is little reason to doubt that Smith was the originator, however.

Impulses

3 *Ne suivez jamais votre premier mouvement car il est bon* [Mistrust first impulses, they are always good].

Charles-Maurice de Talleyrand, French politician (1754–1838). Quoted in *Biographie Universelle*.

Incest

4 Incest – a game the whole family can play.

Anonymous. Included in my book *Graffiti 3* (1981). But on 14 November 1959, Rupert Hart-Davis was already writing: 'I'm also told that the latest popular game is called Incest – all the family can join in!' (*The Lyttelton Hart-Davis Letters*, 1982).

Incompatibility

5 I believe a little incompatibility
is the spice of life, particularly
if he has income and she is pattable.

Ogden Nash, American poet (1902–71). *Versus*, 'I Do, I Will, I Have' (1949).

Indecision

6 *Philip (bewildered)*:
I'm sorry. (*Pause*.) I suppose I am indecisive. (*Pause*.) My trouble is, I'm a man of no convictions. (*Longish pause*.) At least, I think I am.

Christopher Hampton, English playwright (1946–). *The Philanthropist* (1970).

7 I used to be indecisive, but now I'm not so sure.

Boscoe Pertwee (18th century). M.M. Harvey of Andover sent this quotation to BBC Radio *Quote ... Unquote* in 1977, but it has proved impossible to trace a source or, indeed, the existence of its author. A little later it was said to be a graffito and was quoted as such by Brian Johnston on *Quote ... Unquote* (21 August 1979).

Indexers and indexes

8 *Index entry for one of James Boswell's mistresses, slightly edited:*

LEWIS, Mrs (Louisa), actress. JB anticipates delight with, 96. JB lends two guineas to, 97. Consummation with JB interrupted, 117. Spends night with JB at Hayward's, 137–40. JB enraged at perfidy of, 158. JB asks his two guineas back, 174.

Anonymous. *James Boswell's London Journal*, ed. Frederick A. Pottle (1950).

Index entry for one of Samuel Pepys's mistresses, slightly abbreviated:

9 BAGWELL, Mrs, wife of William: her good looks, 4/222; P plans to seduce, 4/222, 266; visits, 4/233–4; finds her virtuous, 4/234; and modest, 5/163; asks P for place for husband, 5/65–6, 163; P kisses, 5/287; she grows affectionate, 5/301–2; he caresses, 5/313; she visits him, 5/316, 339; her resistance collapses in alehouse, 5/322; amorous encounters with: at her house, 5/350–1; 6/40, 162, 189, 201, 253, 294; 7/166 ... asks for promotion for husband, 6/39–40; P strains a finger, 6/40; has sore face, 7/191; servant dies of plague, 7/166.

Anonymous. *The Diary of Samuel Pepys*, ed. Latham & Matthews, Vol. 11 (1983).

10 So essential did I consider an index to be to every book, that I proposed to bring a bill into parliament, to deprive an author who publishes a book without an index of the privilege of copyright, and, moreover, to subject him for his offense to a pecuniary penalty.

John Campbell (1st Baron Campbell), Scottish judge (1779–1861). *Lives of the Chief Justices of England*, Preface to Vol. 3 (1845–7).

1 Should not the Society of Indexers be known as Indexers, Society of, The?

Keith Waterhouse, English journalist, novelist and playwright (1929–). *Bookends* (1990).

Indiscretion

To Mrs Grote:

2 Go where you will, do what you please. I have the most perfect confidence in your indiscretion.

(Revd) Sydney Smith, English clergyman, essayist and wit (1771–1845). Letter (1843), quoted in *The Sayings of Sydney Smith*, ed. Alan Bell (1993).

3 Indiscretion is the better part of valour. The sure way of knowing nothing about life is to try and make oneself useful.

Oscar Wilde, Irish playwright, poet and wit (1854–1900). 'The Critic As Artist' (1890).

Indispensability

4 Some time when you're feeling important
Some time when your ego's in bloom
Some time when you feel you are
The best qualified man in the room,
Some time when you feel that your going
Would leave an unfillable hole,
Just follow this simple instruction
And see how it humbles the soul.
Take a bucket and fill it with water
Place you hands in it up to your wrists
Take them out and the hole that remains
Is a measure of how you'll be missed.
You may splash all you like as they enter
You may stir up the water galore
But take them out and in just a moment
It will look just the same as before.
The moral of this is quite simple
Just do the best that you can.
Be proud of yourself but remember
There is no indispensable man.

Anonymous. Quoted in various versions by 1989.

5 The graveyards are full of people the world could not do without.

Elbert Hubbard, American writer and editor (1856–1915). Quoted in *The Treasury of Humorous Quotations*, eds Evan Esar & Nicolas Bentley (1951). Compare: 'Graveyards are full of indispensable men' – attributed to Charles de Gaulle in *The Penguin Dictionary of Modern Quotations* (1980 edn), but a proverbial view in any language.

Individuality

6 Away he went, to live in a tent;
Over in France with his regiment.
Were you there, and tell me, did you notice?
They were all out of step but Jim.

Irving Berlin, American composer and lyricist (1888–1989). Song, 'They Were All Out of Step But Jim' (1918).

7 If you choose to represent the various parts in life by holes upon a table, of different shapes, – some circular, some triangular, some square, some oblong, – and the persons acting these parts by bits of wood of similar shapes, we shall generally find that the triangular person has got into the square hole, and a square person has squeezed himself into the round hole.

Sydney Smith, English clergyman, essayist and wit (1771–1845). *Sketches of Moral Philosophy*, Lecture 9 (1804). An early formulation of the 'square peg in a round hole' idea, meaning 'someone badly suited to his job or position'. The more familiar phrase was known by 1836. *Punch* once ascribed the following to the philosopher Bishop George Berkeley (1685–1753), but it has not been found in his works: 'The world is like a board with holes in it, and the square men have got into the round holes, and the round into the square.' James Agate in *Ego 5* (1942) wrote: 'Will somebody please tell me the address of the Ministry for Round Pegs in Square Holes?' Compare Twain below.

8 I have ever hated all nations, professions and communities, and all my love is towards individuals ... I hate and detest that animal

called man; although I heartily love John, Peter, Thomas and so forth. This is the system upon which I have governed myself many years.

Jonathan Swift, Anglo-Irish writer and clergyman (1667–1745). Letter to Alexander Pope (29 September 1725).

1 A round man cannot be expected to fit a square hole right away. He must have time to modify his shape.

Mark Twain, American writer (1835–1910). *More Tramps Abroad*, Chap. 71 (1897).

Infamy

Julius Caesar fending off the knives in an assassination attempt:

2 Infamy, infamy – they've all got it in for me!

Line from film *Carry on Cleo* (UK 1964). Screenwriter: Talbot Rothwell. Spoken by Kenneth Williams (Julius Caesar). *However*, Frank Muir wrote to *The Guardian* (22 July 1995), asserting that this line was the product of his and Denis Norden's joint pen. It was spoken by Dick Bentley as Caesar in a sketch for the BBC radio show *Take It From Here* (1948–59). Moreover, Muir added, Talbot Rothwell had very properly asked their permission to use the line. So it was a bit much always hearing Rothwell praised for writing it. The letter concluded, 'Please may we have our line back.'

Inflation

3 Having a little inflation is like being a little pregnant.

Leon Henderson, American economist (1895–1986). Quoted by John Kenneth Galbraith in *A Life in Our Times* (1981). Henderson was appointed by President Roosevelt to the National Defense Advisory Commission in 1940.

Information

4 Sure, the next train has gone ten minutes ago.

Anonymous (cartoonist). Caption to cartoon in *Punch*, Vol. 60 (20 May 1871). Actually this is an early Irish joke: the caption reads in full – '*Gent.* I say, Porter, when does the next train start? *Irish Porter:* The next train! Sure, the nixt train has gone tin minutes ago.' The joke reappeared in the Will Hay film *Oh Mr Porter!* (UK 1937). Screenwriters: Marriott Edgar and others. Spoken by Moore Marriott (Jeremiah Harbottle) to Will Hay (William Porter). As a ticket seller, he slings up his shutter, shouts 'Next train gone!' and slams it down again.

5 *Vincent:*
I'm gonna take a piss.
Mia:
That's a little bit more information than I needed, Vince, but go right ahead.

Line from film *Pulp Fiction* (US 1994). Screenwriter: Quentin Tarantino. Spoken by John Travolta (Vincent Vega) and Uma Thurman (Mia Wallace).

Inhumanity

At Lord's, a South African googly bowler named 'Tufty' Mann was tying a Middlesex tail-end batsman named George Mann into such knots that the crowd was reduced to laughter. When it occurred for the fourth time in a single over, the BBC radio commentator, apparently without a moment's thought, reported:

6 So what we are watching here is a clear case of Mann's inhumanity to Mann.

John Arlott, English journalist and radio cricket commentator (1914–91). Quoted in the *Daily Mail* (3 September 1980).

Innocence

Of the actress Maureen O'Hara:

7 She looked as though butter wouldn't melt in her mouth. Or anywhere else.

Elsa Lanchester, English film actress (1902–86). Quoted in news summaries (30 January 1950).

8 Oh, *that's* what hay looks like, is it? I never knew that.

Mary, British Queen of King George V (1867–1953). The Duchess of Beaufort told James Pope-Hennessy about Queen Mary's evacuation to Badminton House during the Second World War: 'When she came here, she didn't even know what hay was – when I pointed to a hayfield and said look at our hay, she replied [as quoted above], studying it … She was totally urban, but got used to the country.' Pope-Hennessy reported this in his official biography *Queen Mary* (1959) and also in a memoir of the interview with the Duchess, that was included in *A Lonely Business, A Self-Portrait of James Pope-Hennessy* (1981).

Insanity

1 Insanity runs in my family. It practically gallops.

Line from film *Arsenic and Old Lace* (US 1944). Screenwriters: Julius J. & Philip G. Epstein and others (from Joseph Kesselring play). Spoken by Cary Grant (Mortimer Brewster).

2 Insanity is hereditary: you can get it from your children.

Sam Levenson, American writer (1911–). Quoted in *The Home Book of Humorous Quotations*, ed. A.K. Adams (1969).

Insomnia

Private Peter Able:

3 Try thinking of love, or something.
Amor vincit insomnia.

Christopher Fry, English playwright (1907–). *A Sleep of Prisoners* (1951).

Insularity

4 Channel storms. Continent isolated.

Anonymous. This English newspaper headline remains untraced (if, indeed, it ever existed). In Maurice Bowra's *Memories 1898–1939* (1966) he recalled Ernst Kantorowicz, a refugee from Germany in the 1930s: 'He liked the insularity of England and was much pleased by the newspaper headline, "Channel storms. Continent isolated", just as he liked the imagery in, "Shepherd's Bush combed for dead girl's body".'

As an indicator of English isolationism, the phrase does indeed seem to have surfaced in the 1930s. John Gunther in his *Inside Europe* (1938 edn) had: 'Two or three winters ago a heavy storm completely blocked traffic across the Channel. "CONTINENT ISOLATED", the newspapers couldn't help saying.' The cartoonist Russell Brockbank drew a newspaper placard stating 'FOG IN CHANNEL – CONTINENT ISOLATED' (as shown in his book *Round the Bend with Brockbank*, published by Temple Press, 1948). By the 1960s and 1970s, and by the time of Britain's attempts to join the European Community, the headline was more often invoked as: 'FOG IN CHANNEL. EUROPE ISOLATED.'

Insults

5 Do not insult the mother alligator until after you have crossed the river.

Anonymous (Haitian proverb). Quoted in Herbert V. Prochnow, Snr & Jnr, *A Treasury of Humorous Quotations* (1969). Compare the reputed Chinese proverb: 'One does not insult the River God while crossing the river.'

6 *Flo:*
I've never been so insulted in my life.
Hackenbush:
Well, it's early yet.

Line from film *A Day at the Races* (US 1937). Screenwriters: Robert Pirosh, George Seaton, George Oppenheimer. Spoken by Groucho Marx (Dr Hackenbush) and Esther Muir (Flo).

See also ABUSE.

Insurance

7 Certainly there is no nobler field for human effort than the insurance line of business – especially accident insurance. Ever since I have been a director in an accident-insurance company I have felt that I am a better man. Life has seemed more precious ... I do not care for politics – even agriculture does not excite me. But to me now there is a charm about a railway collision that is unspeakable.

Mark Twain, American writer (1835–1910). *Mark Twain's Speeches*, ed. A.B. Paine (1923).

Integrity

8 Integrity is a lofty attitude assumed by someone who is unemployed.

Oscar Levant, American pianist and actor (1906–72). *Memoirs of an Amnesiac* (1965).

Intellect

Of his son, later Edward VII:

9 His intellect is no more use than a pistol packed in the bottom of a trunk if one were attacked in the robber-infested Apennines.

Prince Albert, German-born British Prince (1819–61). Attributed remark.

On Huey Long:

1 The trouble with Senator Long is that he is suffering from halitosis of the intellect. That's presuming Emperor Long has an intellect.

Harold L. Ickes, American politician (1874–1952). Quoted in Arthur M. Schlesinger, *The Politics of Upheaval* (1960). *Compare* BORES 61:12.

Intellectuals

2 Intellectual – one educated beyond the bounds of common sense.

Anonymous. Quoted in Peter & Josie Holtom, *Quote and Unquote* (1970). Or should this be '... educated beyond their intelligence'? Compare the epigram ascribed to Brander Matthews, American writer (1852–1929): 'A high-brow is a person educated beyond his intelligence.'

3 I've never been an intellectual, but I have this look.

Woody Allen, American actor, screenwriter and director (1935–). Quoted in *The Observer*, 'Sayings of the Week' (22 March 1992).

4 To the man-in-the-street, who, I'm sorry to say
Is a keen observer of life,
The word Intellectual suggests straight away
A man who's untrue to his wife.

W.H. Auden, Anglo-American poet (1907–73). *New Year Letter* (1941), also published as 'Note on Intellectuals' (1947).

5 The movie [*Independence Day*] ... has a role I could have played – a character identified in the cast list as 'Intellectual on roof'.

Philip French, English film critic (1933–). In *The Observer* (11 August 1996).

6 An intellectual is someone who has found something more interesting to think about than sex.

Aldous Huxley, English novelist and writer (1894–1963). Quoted in Robert Irwin, *Exquisite Corpse* (1996).

7 Making political hay of the fact that Adlai [Stevenson] had a special appeal to the intellectuals, Eisenhower came up with one of his rare witticisms when he told a rally: 'An intellectual is a man who takes more words than necessary to tell more than he knows.'

Dwight D. Eisenhower, American general and Republican 34th President (1890–1969). Quoted in Paul Steiner, *The Stevenson Wit and Wisdom* (1965).

8 An 'egghead' is a person who stands firmly on both feet in mid-air on both sides of an issue.

Homer Ferguson, American senator. Quoted in news summaries (28 May 1954).

9 Eggheads of the world, arise – I was even going to add that you have nothing to lose but your yolks.

Adlai Stevenson, American Democratic politician (1900–65). Speech at Oakland, California (1 February 1956).

Intelligence

10 The only thing the good Lord has distributed fairly is Intelligence. Everyone is quite sure that they have more of it than anyone else.

Anonymous. However, it is possible that the origin of this thought is in the opening words of René Descartes, *Le Discours de la méthode* (1637): 'Common sense is the most widely distributed commodity in the world, for everyone thinks himself so well endowed with it that those who are hardest to please in every other respect generally have no desire to possess more of it than they have.' Much the same idea is expressed, more long-windedly of course, in Thomas Hobbes, *Leviathan*, Pt 1, Chap. 13 (1651): 'For such is the nature of man, that howsoever they may acknowledge many others to be more witty, or more eloquent, or more learned; Yet they will hardly believe there be many so wise as themselves; ... But this proveth rather that men are in that point equall than unequall. For there is not ordinarily a greater sign of the equall distribution of any thing, than that every man is contented with his share.' There is also more than a hint of La Rochefoucauld's Maxim no. 89 (1678): *'Tout le monde se plaint de sa mémoire, et personne ne se plaint de son jugement* [Everyone complains of his memory, and no one complains of his judgement].'

Intelligibility

1 Nowadays to be intelligible is to be found out.

Oscar Wilde, Irish playwright, poet and wit (1854–1900). *Lady Windermere's Fan*, Act 1 (1892).

Interruptions

2 As I was saying when I was interrupted, it is a powerful hard thing to please all the people all the time.

Cassandra (Sir William Connor), English journalist (1909–67). In September 1946, Cassandra resumed his column in the *Daily Mirror* after the Second World War with quite a common form of words. In June of that same year, announcer Leslie Mitchell is also reported to have begun BBC TV's resumed transmissions with: 'As I was saying before I was so rudely interrupted.' The phrase sounds as if it might have originated in music-hall routines of the 'I don't wish to know that, kindly leave the stage' type. Compare: Eamonn De Valera, the Irish politician, is said to have started a public speech at Ennis in 1924, 'As I was saying before I was interrupted ... ' – referring to the fact that he had been arrested at the same venue a year before. A.A. Milne, *Winnie-the-Pooh* (1926): '"AS – I – WAS – SAYING," said Eeyore loudly and sternly, "as I was saying when I was interrupted by various Loud Sounds, I feel that – ".'

Long before any of these: Fary Luis de León, the Spanish poet and religious writer, is believed to have resumed a lecture at Salamanca University in 1577 with, '*Dicebamus hesterno die* ... [We were saying yesterday].' He had been in prison for five years.

Preparing for his sacred afternoon nap:

3 If *God* rings, tell Him I'm not in.

(Sir) Noël Coward, English entertainer and writer (1899– 1973). Quoted in Cole Lesley, *the Life of Coward* (1976).

4 There's nothing so annoying as to have two people go right on talking when you're interrupting.

Mark Twain, American writer (1835–1910). Quoted in *The Sayings of Mark Twain*, ed. James Munson (1992).

Intervention

Objecting to government meddling:

5 Don't just do something, stand there.

George Shultz, American Republican politician (1920–). As Labor Secretary, in a speech (1970). Quoted in William Safire, *Safire's Political Dictionary* (1978). The expression appears earlier, however, said by the White Rabbit in the Walt Disney version of *Alice In Wonderland* (US 1951), while Adlai Stevenson said of his opponents (in 1956): 'I have finally figured out what the Republican orators mean by what they call "moderate progressivism". All they mean is: "Don't do something. Stand there".'

Intolerance

6 If Woody Allen were a Muslim, he'd be dead by now.

Salman Rushdie, Indian-born author (1947–). Quoted in *The Observer*, 'Sayings of the Week' (18 February 1989).

Intuition

7 Intuition: the strange instinct that tells a woman she is right, whether she is or not.

Oscar Wilde, Irish playwright, poet and wit (1854–1900). Quoted in Herbert V. Prochnow, Snr & Jnr, *A Treasury of Humorous Quotations* (1969).

Invitations

8 As somebody always said, if you can't say anything nice about anybody, come sit by me.

Line from film *Steel Magnolias* (US 1989). Screenwriter: Robert Harling. Spoken by Olympia Dukakis (Clairee Belcher). The 'somebody' was, in fact, Alice Roosevelt Longworth, American political hostess (1884–1980), and daughter of President Theodore Roosevelt. 'If you haven't got anything nice to say about anyone, come and sit by me' was embroidered on a cushion at Longworth's Washington, DC, home. She had a reputation for barbed wit, but many of her lines were not entirely original.

9 I am engaged to dine with Mrs Sartoris the singing woman. Not that I have any pleasure in the voice of singing men or singing women – but as Adam said when they found

him in breeches, 'The woman asked me and I did eat.'

(Revd) Sydney Smith, English clergyman, essayist and wit (1771–1845). Letter (1843), quoted in *The Sayings of Sydney Smith*, ed. Alan Bell (1993).

1 I must decline your invitation owing to a subsequent engagement.

Oscar Wilde, Irish playwright, poet and wit (1854–1900). Quoted in Hesketh Pearson, *The Life of Oscar Wilde* (1946).

Irish Question

On how to resolve the Irish Question:

2 You've got to exchange the populations of Holland and Ireland. Then the Dutch will turn Ireland into a beautiful garden and the Irish will forget to mend the dikes and will all be drowned.

Otto von Bismarck, Prusso-German statesman (1815–98). Quoted by Lord Healey on BBC Radio *Quote ... Unquote* (23 May 1995).

3 [Gladstone] spent his declining years trying to guess the answer to the Irish Question; unfortunately, whenever he was getting warm, the Irish secretly changed the question.

W.C. Sellar & R.J. Yeatman, English humorists (1898–1951) and (1897–1968). *1066 and All That*, Chap. 57 (1930).

4 So great and so long has been the misgovernment of Ireland, that we verily believe the empire would be much stronger if every thing was open sea between England and the Atlantic, and if skates and cod-fish swam over the fair land of Ulster.

(Revd) Sydney Smith, English clergyman, essayist and wit (1771–1845). In *The Edinburgh Review* (1820).

5 The only way to deal with such a man as O'Connell is to hang him up and erect a statue to him under the gallows.

(Revd) Sydney Smith. Quoted in Hesketh Pearson, *The Smith of Smiths* (1934). Daniel O'Connell was the Irish nationalist, known as 'The Liberator'.

Irishness and the Irish

6 Anyone who isn't confused here doesn't really understand what's going on.

Anonymous (Belfast citizen) (1970). Quoted in my book *Quote ... Unquote* (1978). However, Walter Bryan, *The Improbable Irish* (1969), has: 'As Ed Murrow once said about Vietnam, anyone who isn't confused doesn't really understand the situation.'

On the situation in Ulster, 1970s:

7 Ah, well, they say it's not as bad as they say it is.

Anonymous (Irish woman). Quoted in book *Quote ... Unquote* (1978).

8 The Irish don't know what they want and won't be happy till they get it.

Anonymous (graffito). Quoted in my book *Graffiti 5* (1986).

9 There are three things I don't like about New York: the water, the buses and the professional Irishmen. A professional Irishman is one who is terribly anxious to pass as a middle-class Englishman.

Brendan Behan, Irish playwright (1923–64). Quoted in the *Daily News* (1961) and included in *The Sayings of Brendan Behan*, ed. Aubrey Dillon-Malone (1997).

10 I believe they manage things better across the other side [in America]. Sure God help the Irish, if it was raining soup, they'd be out with forks.

Brendan Behan. *Brendan Behan's Island* (1962).

11 I said, 'It is most extraordinary weather for this time of year.' He replied, 'Ah, it isn't this time of year at all.'

Oliver St John Gogarty, Irish writer (1878–1957). *It Isn't This Time of Year at All* (1954).

12 The Irish are a fair people; – they never speak well of one another.

(Dr) Samuel Johnson, English writer and lexicographer (1709–84). Quoted in James Boswell, *The Life of*

Samuel Johnson (1791) – for 1775. Remark to Dr Barnard, Bishop of Killaloe.

1 Ireland is a country in which the probable never happens and the impossible always does.

John Pentland Mahaffy, Irish scholar (1839–1919). Quoted in *The Treasury of Humorous Quotations*, eds Evan Esar & Nicolas Bentley (1951).

2 The Irish do not want anyone to wish them well; they want everyone to wish their enemies ill.

(Sir) Harold Nicolson, English politician and writer (1886–1968). Quoted in the same collection as above.

3 Put an Irishman on the spit, and you can always get another Irishman to turn him.

Bernard Shaw, Irish playwright and critic (1856–1950). Quoted in the same collection as above.

Irony

4 The only people really keeping the spirit of irony alive in Australia are taxi-drivers and homosexuals.

Barry Humphries, Australian entertainer (1934–). In *Australian Women's Weekly* (February 1983).

5 Ten years later, in the mid-sixties, the theatrical slang of the previous decade percolated into the middle-class vernacular, and even housewives were saying, 'Are you sending me up?' Just as America had, in Bernard Shaw's perception, moved from barbarism to decadence without an intervening period of civilization, Australian humour had somehow skipped the ironic and gone from folksy to camp.

Barry Humphries. *More Please*, 'Sinny' (1992). Actually, Georges Clemenceau is usually credited with the 'barbarism' remark. *See* AMERICA 29:2.

6 Oh, oh, irony! Oh, no, no. We don't get that here. See, uh, people ski topless here while smoking dope, so irony's not really a high priority. We haven't had any irony here since about '83, when I was the only practitioner of it, and I stopped because I was tired of being stared at.

Line from film *Roxanne* (US 1987). Screenwriter: Steve Martin (after Edmond Rostand play *Cyrano de Bergerac*). Spoken by Steve Martin (Charlie C.D. Bales).

7 I have been assured by a very knowing American of my acquaintance in London, that a young healthy child well nursed is at a year old a most delicious, nourishing, and wholesome food, whether stewed, roasted, baked, or boiled, and I make no doubt that it will equally serve in a fricassee, or a ragout.

Jonathan Swift, Anglo-Irish writer and clergyman (1667–1745). *A Modest Proposal for Preventing the Children of Ireland from being a Burden to their parents or country* (1729).

Italy and the Italians

8 In Italy, the whole country is a theatre and the worst actors are on the stage.

Bernard Shaw, Irish playwright and critic (1856–1950). Quoted in *The Home Book of Humorous Quotations*, ed. A.K. Adams (1969).

9 Lump the whole thing! Say that the Creator made Italy from designs by Michael Angelo!

Mark Twain, American writer (1835–1910). *The Innocents Abroad* (1869).

J

James, Henry

AMERICAN NOVELIST (1843–1916)

1 The nicest old lady I ever met.

William Faulkner, American novelist (1897–1962). Quoted in Edward Stone, *The Battle and the Books* (1964).

2 The work of Henry James has always seemed divisible by a simple dynastic arrangement into three reigns: James I, James II, and the Old Pretender.

Philip Guedalla, English writer (1889–1944). *Collected Essays*, 'Men of Letters: Mr Henry James' (1920). Guedalla also used this device in his introduction to *The Queen and Mr Gladstone* (1933). There were really three Queen Victorias, he wrote: 'The youngest of the three was Queen Victoria I ... distinguished by a romping sort of innocence ... She was succeeded shortly after marriage by Victoria II ... [bearing] the unmistakable impress of her married life ... [Then] the Queen became Queen-Empress ... her third and final manner.'

3 Henry James writes fiction as if it were a painful duty.

Oscar Wilde, Irish playwright, poet and wit (1854–1900). Quoted in *The Treasury of Humorous Quotations*, eds Evan Esar & Nicolas Bentley (1951).

Jazz

When asked what jazz was:

4 If you still have to ask ... shame on you.

Louis Armstrong, American jazzman (1901–71). Quoted in Max Jones and others, *Salute to Satchmo* (1970). Often rendered as, 'Man, if you gotta ask you'll never know.' Fats Waller, when asked the same question, replied: 'Madam, if you don't know by now, don't mess with it!'

Jefferson, Thomas

AMERICAN POLYMATH AND PRESIDENT (1743–1826)

5 I think it's the most extraordinary collection of talent, of human knowledge, that has ever been gathered together at the White House – with the possible exception of when Thomas Jefferson dined alone.

John F. Kennedy, American Democratic President (1917–63). Speech at dinner for Nobel prizewinners (29 April 1962).

Jesus Christ

FOUNDER OF CHRISTIANITY (*c.* 6 BC–*c.* 30 AD)

6 Jesus! with all thy faults I love thee still.

Samuel Butler, English author (1835–1902). *Further Extracts from Notebooks* (1934).

Jews and Jewishness

Leaping out of a second-floor window:

7 I'm Super-jew!

Lenny Bruce, American satirist (1923–66). Quoted in *The Observer* (21 August 1966). He sustained only a broken leg.

1 How odd
Of God
To choose
The Jews.

W.N. Ewer, English journalist and poet (1885–1976). Quoted in *The Week-End Book* (1924).

2 But not so odd
As those who choose
A Jewish God
Yet spurn the Jews.

Rejoinder to the above by Cecil Browne (untraced) – apparently published in 1924.

3 Not odd
Of God.
Goyim
Annoy 'im.

Rejoinder to Ewer's rhyme (see above) by Anonymous. Quoted in *Christian Wisdom* (1997).

4 Who said he did?
Moses. But he's a yid.

Rejoinder to Ewer's rhyme (see above) by Anonymous. Current by the 1960s.

5 When they circumcised Herbert Samuel they threw away the wrong bit.

David Lloyd George (1st Earl Lloyd George of Dwyfor), British Liberal Prime Minister (1863–1945). Quoted by John Grigg in *The Listener* (7 September 1978). Samuel was a prominent Jewish Liberal politician in the early part of the 20th century.

Reply to small child who asked, 'What does two and two make?':

6 Are you buying or selling?

Lew Grade (Lord Grade), Russian-born English media tycoon (1906–98). Quoted in *The Observer* during 1962. Apocryphal, according to Grade, but an essential piece of Gradiana.

When told by the membership secretary of a beach club that he couldn't become a member because he was Jewish:

7 My son's only half Jewish. Would it be all right if he went in the water up to his knees?

Groucho Marx, American comedian (1895–1977). Quoted in Arthur Marx, *Son of Groucho* (1973). Also told by Dick Cavett in 'An Evening With Groucho Marx' at Carnegie Hall, New York (1972).

8 I'm not really a Jew; just Jew-ish, not the whole hog, you know.

Jonathan Miller, English entertainer, writer and director (1934–). *Beyond the Fringe*, 'Real Class' (1961).

9 Q. Are you Jewish?
A. No, a tree fell on me.

Spike Milligan, Irish entertainer and writer (1918–). This exchange comes from one of Milligan's *Q* comedy series on BBC TV in the early 1980s, but the business originated in his earlier scripts for BBC radio's *The Goon Show*. In 'The Moriarty Murder Mystery' (2 December 1957) is this: Eccles: 'He died in bed.' Bluebottle: 'What happened?' Eccles: 'A tree fell on him.'

10 If God had intended Jewish women to exercise, he'd have put diamonds on the floor.

Joan Rivers, American entertainer (1937–). Quoted in *The 'Quote . . . Unquote' Newsletter* (April 1995).

11 Otto Kahn, the banker [1867–1934], was a convert to Christianity. One day he was walking up Fifth Avenue in New York with a banker [Marshall P. Wilder] who had a hunchback. Kahn pointed to the Temple Emmanuel Synagogue and remarked, 'I used to be a Jew.' 'Yeah,' said Wilder, 'and I used to be a hunchback.'

Marshall P. Wilder, American banker. Quoted by Larry Adler on BBC Radio *Quote . . . Unquote* (22 June 1977). Also told by Groucho Marx in 'An Evening With Groucho Marx' at Carnegie Hall, New York (1972).

Jogging

1 The only reason I would take up jogging is so that I could hear heavy breathing again.

Erma Bombeck, American humorous columnist (1927–96). Quoted in Robert Byrne, *The 637 Best Things Anybody Ever Said* (1982).

John, Augustus

WELSH ARTIST (1878–1961)

2 I understand he was a sober and pleasant young man until he fell on his head in Wales, whereupon he became the slap-dash goat of his later years.

George Melly, English writer, singer and critic (1926–). On BBC Radio *Quote ... Unquote* (11 May 1977). Compare Virginia Shankland's earlier remark concerning the occasion when John, out swimming one day, as a young man, dived into shallow water and cut his head on a rock: 'He hit his head whilst diving and emerged from the water a genius!' As noted by Michael Holroyd in Vol. 1 of his biography of John (1974), Shankland's comment appeared on the back of a Brooke Bond Tea Card, one of a series of 'Fifty Famous People'.

Johnson, Samuel

ENGLISH WRITER AND LEXICOGRAPHER (1709–84)

3 When I called upon Dr. Johnson next morning, I found him highly satisfied with his colloquial prowess the preceding evening. 'Well, (said he) we had a good talk.' BOSWELL. 'Yes, Sir; you tossed and gored several persons.'

James Boswell, Scottish lawyer, biographer and diarist (1740–95). *The Life of Samuel Johnson* (1791) – relating to the summer of 1768.

4 There is no arguing with Johnson; for when his pistol misses fire, he knocks you down with the butt end of it.

Oliver Goldsmith, Irish-born playwright and writer (1730–74). Quoted in James Boswell, *The Life of Samuel Johnson* (1791) – for 26 October 1769.

Jokes

5 When is a door not a door? When it's ajar.

Anonymous. *Punch* in its 'comic chronology' (17 December 1872, i.e. its *Almanack for 1873*) has 'AD 1001 invention of the riddle "When is a door not a door?"'

6 'By the way, Mrs Jocelyn, I hear you've taken a rippin' little place on the river this year.' 'Yes. I hope, when you're passing, that you'll – er – drop in!'

Anonymous. Caption to cartoon in *Punch* (15 August 1900).

7 The Lord said unto Moses come forth, and 'e come fifth an' lorst the cup.

Anonymous. Quoted in Herbert Jenkins, *The Adventures of Bindle* (1917). Bindle, who 'likes his little joke', is at a very joyless wedding, and tells Mr Sopley, the Minister, that he 'ad a little argument with a cove the other day, as to where this 'ere was to be found. I said it's from the Bible, 'e says it's from *The Pink 'Un*.' This last was the nickname for *The Sporting Times*. The implication is that it was an old joke even then.

8 The marvellous thing about a joke with a double meaning is that it can only mean one thing.

Ronnie Barker, English comedian and actor (1929–). *Sauce*, 'Daddie's Sauce' (1977).

9 Anyone like myself who thinks making jokes is a serious matter must regret the eclipse of the Book of Common Prayer because it has diminished the common stock of shared reference on which jokes – and of course it's not only jokes – depend.

Alan Bennett, English playwright and actor (1934–). *Writing Home* (1994).

10 If Adam came on earth again the only thing he would recognize would be the old jokes.

Lord (Thomas Robert) Dewar, Scottish distiller (1864–1930). Quoted in *The Treasury of Humorous Quotations*, eds Evan Esar & Nicolas Bentley (1951).

1 A different taste in jokes is a great strain on the affections.

George Eliot, English novelist (1819–80). *Daniel Deronda*, Chap. 15 (1876).

Defining a joke:

2 An idea going in one direction meets an idea going in the opposite direction.

Mack Sennett, Canadian-born comedy film maker (1880–1960). Quoted in *The 'Quote ... Unquote' Newsletter* (July 1994).

3 A joke goes a great way in the country. I have known one last pretty well for seven years.

(Revd) Sydney Smith, English clergyman, essayist and wit (1771–1845). Quoted in Lady Holland, *A Memoir of Sydney Smith* (1855).

4 It is only the dull who like practical jokes.

Oscar Wilde, Irish playwright, poet and wit (1854–1900). Quoted in Herbert V. Prochnow, Snr & Jnr, *A Treasury of Humorous Quotations* (1969).

Jolson, Al

AMERICAN ENTERTAINER (1888–1950)

Of his voice:

5 Like playing a trombone underwater.

Anonymous. Quoted by Humphrey Lyttelton on BBC Radio *Quote ... Unquote* (13 July 1988).

Journalism

6 Journalism could be described as turning one's enemies into money.

Craig Brown, English journalist (1957–). In *The Daily Telegraph* (28 September 1990).

7 Journalism largely consists in saying 'Lord Jones Dead' to people who never knew Lord Jones was alive.

G.K. Chesterton, English poet, novelist and critic (1874–1936). *The Wisdom of Father Brown*, 'The Purple Wig' (1914).

8 If you don't know what's going on in Portugal, you must have been reading the papers.

Paul Foot, English journalist (1937–). Attributed in 1975. This was at the time when Portugal was undergoing political upheaval following a revolution against a dictatorship.

9 Journalism is to politician as dog is to lamppost.

H.L. Mencken, American journalist and linguist (1880–1956). Attributed in *The Oxford Dictionary of Literary Quotations*, ed. Peter Kemp (1997).

10 That awful power, the public opinion of a nation, is created in America by a horde of ignorant, self-complacent simpletons who failed at ditching and shoemaking and fetched up in journalism on their way to the poorhouse.

Mark Twain, American writer (1835–1910). In *Mark Twain's Speeches*, ed. A.B. Paine (1923).

11 'What is the difference between literature and journalism?'
'Oh! journalism is unreadable, and literature is not read. That is all.'

Oscar Wilde, Irish playwright, poet and wit (1854–1900). 'The Critic As Artist' (1890).

12 There is much to be said in favour of modern journalism. By giving us the opinions of the uneducated, it keeps us in touch with the ignorance of the community.

Oscar Wilde. In the same work as above.

13 Modern journalism justifies its own existence by the great Darwinian principle of the survival of the vulgarest.

Oscar Wilde. 'The Critic As Artist' (1890).

14 They [newspapers] give us the bald, sordid, disgusting facts of life. They chronicle, with degrading avidity, the sins of the second-rate, and with the conscientiousness of the illit-

erate give us accurate and prosaic details of the doings of people of absolutely no interest whatsoever.

Oscar Wilde. In the same work as above.

1 Rock journalism is people who can't write interviewing people who can't talk for people who can't read.

Frank Zappa, American rock musician (1940–93). Quoted in L. Botts, *Loose Talk* (1980). Originally in *Rolling Stone* Magazine (1970).

See also JOURNALISTS; NEWS AND NEWSPAPERS; PRESS.

Journalists

Definition of a journalist:

2 Someone who stays sober right up to lunchtime.

Anonymous. Quoted by Godfrey Smith on BBC Radio *Quote ... Unquote* (27 July 1985).

3 Journalists say a thing that they know isn't true, in the hope that if they keep on saying it long enough it *will* be true.

Arnold Bennett, English novelist (1867–1931). *The Title*, Act 1 (1918).

4 No news is good news; no journalists is even better.

Nicolas Bentley, English cartoonist and writer (1907–78). Quoted in *The Treasury of Humorous Quotations*, eds Evan Esar & Nicolas Bentley (1951).

5 A journalist is one who has missed his calling.

Otto von Bismarck, Prusso-German statesman (1815–98). Not said in precisely this form. According to *H.L. Mencken's Dictionary of Quotations* (1942): 'On Nov. 10, 1862, in a statement printed on the island of Rügen, he spoke of the opposition press as being "in large part in the hands of Jews and malcontents who have missed their calling".'

6 All journalists are spies – I know, I have been one.

Sese Seko Mobuto, Zaïrean President (1930–). Quoted in *The Sunday Times* (28 May 1978).

7 I'll tell you briefly what I think of newspapermen. The hand of God, reaching down into the mire, couldn't elevate one of them to the depths of degradation.

Line from film *Nothing Sacred* (US 1937). Screenwriter: Ben Hecht. Spoken by Charles Winninger (Dr Enoch Downer) to Fredric March (Wally Cook).

Of a foreign correspondent:

8 He's someone who flies around from hotel to hotel and thinks the most interesting thing about any story is the fact that he has arrived to cover it.

(Sir) Tom Stoppard, English playwright (1937–). *Night and Day*, Act 1 (1978).

9 The only qualities essential for real success in journalism are rat-like cunning, a plausible manner, and a little literary ability.

Nicholas Tomalin, English journalist (1931–73). In *The Sunday Times* Magazine (26 October 1969). Tomalin was writing on careers in journalism and his view, though a touch self-serving, has continued to be quoted admiringly by other journalists. The passage continues: 'Other qualities are helpful but not essential. These include a knack with telephones, trains and petty officials, a good digestion and a steady head ... The capacity to steal other people's ideas and phrases – that one about rat-like cunning was invented by my colleague Murray Sayle – is also invaluable.' Tomalin himself was killed while covering the Arab-Israeli war in 1973.

10 I am not an editor of a newspaper and shall always try to do right and be good so that God will not make me one.

Mark Twain, American writer (1835–1910). Attributed remark.

11 Bad manners make a journalist.

Oscar Wilde, Irish playwright, poet and wit (1854–1900). Quoted in Lloyd Lewis & Henry Justin Smith, *Oscar Wilde Discovers America* (1936).

1 You cannot hope
to bribe or twist,
thank God! the
British journalist.

But, seeing what
the man will do
unbribed, there's
no occasion to.

Humbert Wolfe, English poet and critic (1885–1940). *The Uncelestial City*,'Over the Fire' (1930).

Of the sports journalist Clifford Makins (1924–90):

2 A legend in his own lunchtime.

Christopher Wordsworth, English journalist and critic (1914–98). In book review (by 1976). However, according to Ned Sherrin, *Theatrical Anecdotes* (1991),'David Climie, the witty revue and comedy writer ... claims to have invented the phrase "A legend in his own lunchtime" and to have lavished it on the mercurial BBC comedy innovator, Dennis Main Wilson.'

See also JOURNALISM; NEWS AND NEWSPAPERS; PRESS.

Judges

To a convicted criminal who had exclaimed, 'As God is my judge – I am innocent':

3 He isn't; I am, and you're not!

Norman Birkett (Lord Birkett), English barrister and judge (1883–1962). Quoted in Matthew Parris, *Scorn* (1994).

4 And what's more, being a miner, as soon as you're too old and tired and ill and sick and stupid to do the job properly, you have to go. Well, the very opposite applies with the judges.

Peter Cook, English humorist (1937–95). *Beyond the Fringe*,'Sitting on the Bench' (1961).

To a hopeless drunken tramp, shaking with DTs, who appeared in court before him, having told him that he must at all costs eschew alcohol entirely forthwith:

5 Mind now, not even a tiny glass of sherry before luncheon!

John Maude, English judge (1901–86). Quoted in *The Times* (4 May 1998).

6 Judge – A law student who marks his own examination papers.

H.L. Mencken, American journalist and linguist (1880–1956).'Sententiae' (1912–48).

7 *F.E. Smith*:
He was drunk as a judge.
Judge:
The expression as I have always understood it is 'sober as a judge'. Perhaps you mean 'as drunk as a lord'?
F. E. Smith:
Yes, my lord.

F.E. Smith (1st Earl of Birkenhead), English politician and lawyer (1872–1930). Smith was placed in this famous exchange by Bryan Magee in BBC Radio *Quote ... Unquote* (26 April 1994).

July the fourth

8 *July 4*. Statistics show that we lose more fools on this day than in all the other days of the year put together. This proves, by the number left in stock, that one Fourth of July per year is now inadequate, the country has grown so.

Mark Twain, American writer (1835–1910). *Puddn'head Wilson* (1894).

Juries

9 A jury consists of twelve persons chosen to decide who has the better lawyer.

Robert Frost, American poet (1874–1963). Quoted in *The Treasury of Humorous Quotations*, eds Evan Esar & Nicolas Bentley (1951).

Jury foreman:

10 We find the defendants incredibly guilty.

Line from film *The Producers* (US 1967). Screenwriter: Mel Brooks. Spoken by Bill Macy (Jury Foreman).

1 We have a criminal system which is superior to any in the world; and its efficiency is only marred by the difficulty of finding twelve men every day who don't know anything and can't read.

Mark Twain, American writer (1835–1910). *Sketches New and Old* (1875).

Justice

On being defeated in a libel action, when editor of Private Eye*:*

2 If this is justice, I'm a banana.

Ian Hislop, English journalist (1960–). Quoted in *The Observer*, 'Sayings of the Week' (28 May 1989). *Private Eye*, edited by Hislop, had been sued by Sonia Sutcliffe, wife of the 'Yorkshire Ripper'.

3 In England, Justice is open to all, like the Ritz hotel.

(Sir) James Mathew, Irish judge (1830–1908). Quoted in R.E. Megarry in *Miscellany-at-Law* (1955).

4 Justice must not only be seen to be done but has to be seen to be believed.

J.B. Morton (Beachcomber), English humorous writer (1893–1979). Quoted by Peter Cook on BBC Radio *Quote ... Unquote* (5 June 1980).

Kennedy, John F.

AMERICAN DEMOCRATIC PRESIDENT (1917–63)

1 President Kennedy is a great one for the girls, and during the election his opponents said that if he got to the White House they only hoped he would do for fornication what Eisenhower did for golf.

Anonymous. Quoted by Rupert Hart-Davis in *The Lyttelton Hart-Davis Letters* (1984) – letter of 25 February 1961.

Ketchup

2 Shake and shake
The catsup bottle.
None will come,
And then a lot'll.

Richard Armour, American writer (1906–89). *Going to Extremes* (1949). There is a feeling that this should have been written by Ogden Nash, but apparently not'll. 'Catsup' is an American variant of 'ketchup'.

Kilts

3 Join a Highland regiment, my boy. The kilt is an unrivalled garment for fornication and diarrhoea.

John Masters, Indian-born English novelist (1914–83). *Bugles and a Tiger* (1956).

Kindness

4 One can always be kind to people about whom one cares nothing.

Oscar Wilde, Irish playwright, poet and wit (1854–1900). *The Picture of Dorian Gray*, Chap. 8 (1891).

Kings

5 The whole world is in revolt. Soon there will be only five kings left – the King of England, the King of Spades, the King of Clubs, the King of Hearts and the King of Diamonds.

Farouk I, Egyptian King (1920–65). Remark to Lord Boyd-Orr (1948). Quoted in *Life* Magazine (10 April 1950).

Remark on declining a formal coronation (1740):

6 *Une couronne n'est qu'un chapeau qui laisse passer la pluie* [A crown is no more than a hat that lets in the rain].

Frederick the Great, Prussian King (1712–86). Quoted in Alan and Veronica Palmer, *Quotations in History* (1976).

7 My people and I have come to an agreement which satisfies us both. They are to say what they please, and I am to do what I please.

Frederick the Great. Attributed definition of 'benevolent despotism' in *The Oxford Dictionary of Quotations* (1953).

Jesting epitaph on Charles II:

8 Here lies a great and mighty king
Whose promise none relies on;
He never said a foolish thing,
Nor ever did a wise one.

John Wilmot, 2nd Earl of Rochester, English poet (1647–80). Quoted in *Thomas Traherne: Remarks and Collections* (1885–1921). Other versions include, 'Here lies our sovereign Lord the King ... ' and 'Here lies our mutton-eating king' (where 'mutton' = prostitute). Charles II's reply is said to have been: 'This is very true: for my words are my own, and my actions are my ministers' (also in *Traherne* ...).

Kipling, Rudyard

ENGLISH POET AND NOVELIST (1865–1936)

1 Do you like Kipling?
I don't know, you naughty boy, I've never kippled.

Donald McGill, English comic postcard artist (1875–1962). Caption to one of McGill's postcards – undated, but possibly from the 1930s.

2 Will there ever come a season
Which shall rid us from the curse
Of a prose which knows no reason
And an unmelodious verse ...
When there stands a muzzled stripling,
Mute, beside a muzzled bore:
When the Rudyards cease from kipling
And the Haggards ride no more.

J.K. Stephen, English journalist and light versifier (1859–92). 'To R.K.' (1891).

3 He is a stranger to me but he is a most remarkable man – and I am the other one. Between us, we cover all knowledge; he knows all that can be known and I know all the rest.

Mark Twain, American writer (1835–1910). *Autobiography*, Chap. 59 (1924).

4 From the point of view of literature Mr Kipling is a genius who drops his aspirates.

Oscar Wilde, Irish playwright, poet and wit (1854–1900). 'The Critic As Artist' (1890).

Kissing

5 I don't know how to kiss, or I would kiss you. Where do the noses go?

Line from film *For Whom the Bell Tolls* (US 1943). Screenwriter: Dudley Nicholls (from Ernest Hemingway novel). Spoken by Ingrid Bergman (Maria).

6 Being kissed by a man who *didn't* wax his moustache was – like eating an egg without salt.

Rudyard Kipling, English poet and novelist (1865–1936). *The Story of the Gadsbys*, 'Poor Dear Mamma' (1890). Probably based on a Spanish proverbial saying, 'A kiss without a moustache is like an egg without salt.'

7 Kissing don't last: cookery do!

George Meredith, English novelist and poet (1828–1909). *The Ordeal of Richard Feverel* (1859).

On kissing Margaret Thatcher (when they were both candidates for the Conservative leadership, 1975):

8 I have over a period of time, when I have met her – as indeed one does – I have kissed her often before. We have not done it on a pavement outside a hotel in Eastbourne before. But we have done it in various rooms in one way and another at various functions – it is perfectly genuine and normal – and normal and right – so to do.

William Whitelaw (1st Viscount Whitelaw), English Conservative politician (1918–99). Reported in *The Observer* (9 February 1975).

Knees

Of a Shubert musical show 'with a preponderance of leg' (c. 1912):

9 The female knee is a joint, and not an entertainment.

Percy Hammond, American theatre critic (1873–1936). Review in *Chicago Tribune*, quoted in Mark Sullivan, *Our Times, III, Pre-War America*, Chap. 10 (1930). *See also* THEATRICAL CRITICISM 430:3.

Knickers

Of Jilly Cooper as romantic novelist:

10 Barbara Cartland without the iron knickers.

Anonymous. Quoted in my book *A Year of Stings and Squelches* (1985).

11 Why can't a woman with a wooden leg give change for a pound note?
Because she's only got half a nicker!

Anonymous. Revived by Spike Milligan in his script for

BBC Radio *The Last Goon Show Of All* (5 October 1972) – though it had been used in the original *Goon Show* in the 1950s – e.g. the episodes entitled 'The £50 Cure' (23 February 1959) and 'A Christmas Carol' (24 December 1959).

Knowledge

1 It ain't the thing you don't know that gets you into trouble; it's the things you know for sure what ain't so.

Anonymous. Sometimes ascribed to Will Rogers. A 1940 joke book stated that it was a 'Negro saying'.

2 First come I; my name is Jowett.
There's no knowledge but I know it.
I am the Master of this College:
What I don't know isn't knowledge.

H.C. Beeching, English clergyman and writer (1859–1919). In 'The Masque of Balliol' (1870s). Benjamin Jowett was Master of Balliol College, Oxford, from 1870.

3 Every library should try to be complete on something, if it were only the history of pin-heads.

Oliver Wendell Holmes Snr, American writer and physician (1809–94). Quoted in *The Treasury of Humorous Quotations*, eds Evan Esar & Nicolas Bentley (1951).

4 Dear Mr Coolidge: Well all I know is just what I read in the papers.

Will Rogers, American humorist (1879–1935). *The Letters of a Self-Made Diplomat to His President* (1927).

5 It is a very sad thing that nowadays there is so little useless information.

Oscar Wilde, Irish playwright, poet and wit (1854–1900). In *Saturday Review* (17 November 1894).

L

Labour Party

1 A divorced woman on the throne of the house of Windsor would be a pretty big feather in the cap of that bunch of rootless intellectuals, alien Jews and international pederasts who call themselves the Labour Party.

Alan Bennett, English playwright and actor (1934–). *Forty Years On*, Act 2 (1969). In Bulldog Drummond parody.

2 I do not often attack the Labour Party. They do it so well themselves.

(Sir) Edward Heath, British Conservative Prime Minister (1916–). Quoted in my book *A Year of Stings and Squelches* (1985).

Language and languages

3 *Maid Marian:*
Why, you speak treason.
Robin Hood:
Fluently.

Lines from film *The Adventures of Robin Hood* (US 1938). Screenwriters: Seton I. Miller, Norman Reilly Raine. Spoken by Olivia de Havilland (Maid Marian) and Erroll Flynn (Robin Hood).

4 English as she is spoke.

Anonymous phrase-book author, probably Pedro Carolino (*fl.* 1860s). This way of referring to the language as it might be spoken by foreigners or the illiterate comes from an actual 'guide of the conversation in Portuguese and English' published in the 19th century. In *Baldness Be My Friend* (1977) Richard Boston explored the facts. Originally, there was a French-Portuguese phrase book, *O Novo Guia da Conversacão em frances e portuguez* by José da Fonseca, published in Paris in 1836. The text was in parallel columns. Then in 1865 a third column, carrying English translations, was added by one Pedro Carolino. His excellence as a translator can be shown by quoting from a section he cleverly but unwittingly called 'Idiotisms and Proverbs'. It included:

5 In the country of blinds, the one-eyed men are kings.
To do a wink to some body.
The stone as roll not, heap up not foam.
After the paunch comes the dance.
To craunch the marmoset.
To come back to their muttons.
He sin in trouble water.

Source as above. By 1883, the awfulness of this non-joke was known in London. Publishers Field and Tuer brought out a selection under the title *English as She is Spoke* (a phrase taken from the chapter on 'Familiar Dialogues'). The same year, Mark Twain introduced an edition of the complete work in the US.

6 The postillion has been struck by lightning.

Anonymous saying, said to be a useful expression from an old phrase book. Hence, *A Postillion Struck by Lightning*, title of the first volume of Dirk Bogarde's autobiography (1977). Describing a holiday in early childhood (the 1920s presumably), he mentions an old phrase book (seemingly dated 1898), which contained lines like: 'This muslin is too thin, have you something thicker?'; 'My leg, arm, foot, elbow, nose, finger is broken'; and 'The postillion has been struck by lightning'. Which phrase book is this? Not *English as She is Spoke* (as above), in which the 'postillion' line does not occur.

In the third volume of Bogarde's autobiography, *An Orderly Man* (1983), describing the writing of the first, he says: 'My sister-in-law, Cilla, on a wet camping holiday somewhere in northern France ... once sent me a postcard on which she said ... she had been forced to learn a little more French than the phrase "Help! My postillion has been struck by lightning!" I took the old phrase for the title of my book.'

A similarly untraced Russian/English phrase book is said to have included: 'Don't bother to unsaddle the horses, lightning has struck the innkeeper.' In Karl Baedeker's *The Traveller's Manual of Conversation in Four Languages* (1836 edn) is: 'Postilion, stop; we wish to get down; a spoke of one of the wheels is broken.' In an 1886 edition I have found: 'Are the postilions insolent?; the lightning has struck; the coachman is drunk.' From these examples it is quite clear that the preposterous phrase could quite likely have appeared in Baedeker or somewhere similar.

A writer in *The Times* (30 July 1983) noted: '"Look, the front postillion has been struck by lightning" ... supposed to feature in a Scandinavian phrase book: but it may well be apocryphal.' *Punch* (22 April 1970) contains a headline with the earliest allusion found so far: 'My postilion has been struck by the vice-consul.'

Now I see that *More Comic and Curious Verse*, ed. J.M. Cohen (1956) contains a poem entitled 'Ballad of Domestic Calamity' by M.H. Longson, apparently extracted from *Punch*. The last line is 'For our postillion has been struck by lightning', and an introductory note explains: '"Our postillion has been struck by lightning" is one of the "useful Common Phrases" appearing in a Dutch manual on the speaking of English.' One is reminded that Dirk Bogarde was of Dutch ancestry.

1 I speak Spanish to God, Italian to women, French to men – and German to my horse.

Charles V, Holy Roman Emperor (1500–58). Attributed remark. Alluded to in Lord Chesterfield, *Letters to His Son* (1832 edn)

Presenting the Thomas Cranmer Schools Prize, organized by the Prayer Book Society, in 1989, Prince Charles delivered an attack on the 'dismal wasteland of banality, cliché and casual obscenity' of everyday language. 'Is it entirely an accident,' he wondered, 'that the defacing of Cranmer's Prayer Book has coincided with a calamitous decline in literacy and the quality of English?' He went on to deliver a rendering of Hamlet's 'To be or not to be' speech in modern English:

2 Well, frankly, the problem as I see it
At this moment in time is whether I
Should just lie down under all this hassle
And let them walk all over me.
Or, whether I should just say: 'OK,
I get the message', and do myself in.
I mean, let's face it, I'm in a no-win situation,
And quite honestly, I'm so stuffed up to
 here with the
Whole stupid mess that, I can tell you,
 I've just
Got a good mind to take the quick way out.
That's the bottom line. The only problem is:
What happens if I find that when I've
 bumped
Myself off, there's some kind of a, you
 know,
All that mystical stuff about when you die,
You might find you're still – know what I
 mean?

Charles, British Prince of Wales (1948–). Quoted in *The Independent* (20 December 1989). Full marks to the speechwriter. Compare Quiller-Couch below.

Marginal comment on document:

3 This is the sort of English up with which I will not put.

(Sir) Winston S. Churchill, British Conservative Prime Minister and writer (1874–1965). Quoted in Sir Ernest Gowers, 'Troubles with Prepositions', *Plain Words* (1948).

4 Be on your guard! I am going to speak in French – a formidable undertaking and one which will put great demands upon your friendship for Great Britain.

(Sir) Winston S. Churchill. Speech, in Paris, after the Liberation of France (1944).

5 Tim was so learned that he could name a Horse in nine languages, but bought a cow to ride on.

Benjamin Franklin, American politician and scientist (1706–90). *Poor Richard's Almanack* (November 1750) – a work in which Franklin often revised already existing sayings.

1 The Romans would never have had time to conquer the world if they had been obliged to learn Latin first of all.

Heinrich Heine, German poet and writer (1797–1856). *Idéen, Das Buch Le Grand* (1835).

To a young man who had bemoaned that he had lost all his Greek:

2 I believe it happened at the same time, Sir, that I lost all my large estates in Scotland.

(Dr) Samuel Johnson, English writer and lexicographer (1709–84). Attributed remark. Frank Muir, *A Kentish Lad* (1997) has it rather as 'lost all my large *estate* in *Yorkshire*' and seems to suggest it was reported in a letter by a friend and not by Boswell.

3 If English was good enough for Jesus Christ, it is good enough for me.

Ralph Melnyk, Saskatchewan farmer. Quoted in John Robert Colombo, *Colombo's All Time Great Canadian Quotations* (1994). In 1963, Canada's Royal Commission on Bilingualism and Biculturalism criss-crossed the country to ask ordinary citizens their feelings about the possibility of French becoming the official language. This is what Mr Melnyk told the Commission.

4 You English … think we know damn nothing *but I tell you we know damn all.*

Nicholas Monsarrat, English novelist (1910–79). *The Cruel Sea* (1951). Compare this: in the second volume of David Niven's autobiography to which he gave the title *Bring On the Empty Horses* (1975), he talked of Michael Curtiz, the Hungarian-born American film director (1888–1962). During the filming of *The Charge of the Light Brigade* (1936), Curtiz ordered the release of a hundred riderless steeds by shouting: 'Bring on the empty horses!' David Niven and Errol Flynn fell about with laughter at this. Curtiz rounded on them and said, 'You and your stinking language! You think I know f–– nothing. Well, let me tell you, I know f–– all!'

5 When Abraham Lincoln was murdered
The one thing that interested Matthew
  Arnold
Was that the assassin shouted in Latin
As he leapt on the stage.
This convinced Matthew
That there was still hope for America.

Christopher Morley, American novelist and editor (1890–1957). 'Points of View'.

6 *Mike*
There's no word in the Irish language for what you were doing.
Wilson:
In Lapland they have no word for snow.

Joe Orton, English playwright (1933–67). *The Ruffian on the Stair* (rev. edn 1967). What they were doing was, naturally, of a homosexual and possibly incestuous nature. The observation about Lapland amounts to artistic licence: rather the reverse is believed to be the case. Far from having no word for snow, the Laps have any number to describe all the different types. Indeed, it is sometimes said that 'Eskimos have two hundred different words for snow.'

William Hartston of *The Independent* investigated this canard in an article on 15 January 1998: 'I have just received a copy of a paper entitled "The great Eskimo vocabulary hoax" by Geoffrey Pullum (*Natural Language and Linguistic Theory*, Vol. 7, 1989). This is the paper that nails, once and for all, the myth that Eskimos have hundreds of different words for snow … The original source of the myth about "these lexically profligate hyperborean nomads", as Pullum describes them, is Franz Boas's introduction to *The Handbook of North American Indians* (1911) … It is one of the most entertaining shaggy academic tales I have read for a long time.' Compare this from a famous fashion person (quoted in *Diana Vreeland*, ed. George Plimpton & Charles Hemphill, 1984): 'The Eskimos, I'm told, have seventeen different words for shades of white. This is even more than there are in "my" imagination.'

Hamlet's soliloquy jargonized:

7 To be, or the contrary? Whether the former or the latter be preferable would seem to admit of some difference of opinion; the answer in the present case being of an

affirmative or of a negative character according as to whether one elects on the one hand to mentally suffer the disfavour of fortune, albeit in an extreme degree, or on the other to boldly envisage adverse conditions in the prospect of eventually bringing them to a conclusion.

(Sir) Arthur Quiller-Couch, English critic and academic (1863–1944). *On the Art of Writing*, Lecture 5 (1916). Compare Prince Charles above.

1 It is a misfortune for Anglo-American friendship that the two countries are supposed to have a common language.

Bertrand Russell (3rd Earl Russell), English mathematician and philosopher (1872–1970). In the *Saturday Evening Post* (3 June 1944).

2 England and America are two countries separated by the same language.

Bernard Shaw, Irish playwright and critic (1856–1950). Quoted in *Reader's Digest* (November 1942) and *The Treasury of Humorous Quotations*, eds Evan Esar & Nicolas Bentley (1951).

3 [European writers and scholars in America are] up against the barrier of a common language.

Dylan Thomas, Welsh poet (1914–53). Radio talk published in *The Listener* (April 1954).

4 We have really everything in common with America nowadays except, of course, language.

Oscar Wilde, Irish playwright, poet and wit (1854–1900). *The Canterville Ghost* (1887).

Last person

5 Would the last person to leave the country please switch off the lights.

Anonymous. Quoted in my book *Graffiti 2* (1980). On 9 April 1992, this line suffered a revival when, on the day of the British General Election, *The Sun* newspaper's front page headline was: 'IF KINNOCK WINS TODAY WILL THE LAST PERSON IN BRITAIN PLEASE TURN OUT THE LIGHTS.' In Maxime Rodinson, *Israel and the Arabs* (1969), it is reported that in c. 1966, when due to the political situation many people decided to leave Israel, a notice was put up at Lydda Airport near Tel Aviv: 'Will the last to leave kindly turn out the light.'

Lateness (1)

6 I have noticed that people who are late are often so much jollier than the people who have to wait for them.

E.V. Lucas, English essayist and writer (1868–1938). *365 Days and One More* (1926).

Lateness (2)

7 He that riseth late must trot all day, and shall scarce overtake his business at night.

Benjamin Franklin, American politician and scientist (1706–90). Included in *Poor Richard's Almanack* (1742).

8 Whoever thinks of going to bed before twelve o'clock is a scoundrel.

(Dr) Samuel Johnson, English writer and lexicographer (1709–84). Quoted in *The Treasury of Humorous Quotations*, eds Evan Esar & Nicolas Bentley (1951).

Laughs and laughter

9 In the language of screen comedians four of the main grades of laugh are the titter, the yowl, the belly laugh and the boffo. The titter is just a titter. The yowl is a runaway titter. Anyone who has ever had the pleasure knows all about a belly laugh. The boffo is the laugh that kills.

James Agee, American film critic and screenwriter (1909–55). In *Life* Magazine (5 September 1949).

10 Laughter is the hiccup of a fool.

Anonymous (English proverb). In John Ray, *English Proverbs* (1670).

11 A merry heart doeth good like a medicine.

The Bible. Proverbs 17:22.

1 As the crackling of thorns under a pot, so is the laughter of a fool.

The Bible. Ecclesiastes 7:6.

2 You know what my philosophy of life is? That it's important to have some laughs, no question about it, but you got to suffer a little, too, because otherwise you miss the whole point of life.

Lines from film *Broadway Danny Rose* (US 1984). Screenwriter: Woody Allen. Spoken by Woody Allen (Danny Rose).

3 I remember a Methodist preacher who on perceiving a profane grin on the faces of part of his congregation – exclaimed 'no *hopes* for *them* as *laughs*'.

Lord Byron, English poet (1788–1824). Letter to Augusta Leigh (19 December 1816). In a note to *Hints from Horace*, Byron gave the name of the preacher as John Stickles.

4 The day most wholly lost is the one on which one does not laugh.

Nicholas-Sébastien Chamfort, French writer (1741–94). *Maximes et pensées* (1785).

5 Laughter does not seem to be a sin, but it leads to sin.

John Chrysostom, Syrian saint and churchman (*c.* 347–407). *Homilies*, 15 (*c.* 388).

Advice to a young speaker:

6 Never make people laugh. If you would succeed in life, you must be solemn, solemn as an ass. All the great monuments are built over solemn asses.

Thomas Corwin, American politician (1794–1865). Quoted in *The Home Book of Humorous Quotations*, ed. A.K. Adams (1969).

7 I can teach you with a quip if I've a mind,
I can trick you into learning with a laugh;
Oh, winnow all my folly, folly, folly and
you'll find
A grain or two of truth among the chaff.

(Sir) W.S. Gilbert, English writer and lyricist (1836–1911). *The Yeomen of the Guard*, Act 1 (1888). Jack Point sings 'I've Jibe and Joke'.

8 *Quamquam ridentem dicere verum / Quid vetat?* [Why should one not speak the truth, laughing?].

Horace, Roman poet (65–8 BC). *Satires*, I.i.24. Used as a justification of satire. Other translations: 'Why should truth not be impress'd / Beneath the cover of a jest'; 'Nevertheless, what prevents us from telling the truth cheerfully?'

9 Born with the gift of laughter and a sense that the world was mad.

Rafael Sabatini, Italian-born novelist (1875–1950). *Scaramouche*, Chap. 1 (1921). Opening line.

10 I come no more to make you laugh.

William Shakespeare, English playwright and poet (1564–1616). *King Henry VIII* (1613). First words of the Prologue.

11 [Mankind] in its poverty, has unquestionably one really effective weapon – laughter. Power, money, persuasion, supplication, persecution – these can lift at a colossal humbug – push it a little, weaken it a little, century by century; but only laughter can blow it to rags and atoms at a blast. Against the assault of laughter nothing can stand.

Mark Twain, American writer (1835–1910). *The Mysterious Stranger, Etc.*, ed. A.B. Paine (1922).

12 Laughter without a tinge of philosophy is but a sneeze of humour. Genuine humour is replete with wisdom.

Mark Twain. Quoted in Opie Read, *Mark Twain and I* (1940).

13 Humour must be one of the chief attributes of God. Plants and animals that are distinctly humorous in form and characteristics are God's jokes.

Mark Twain. Quoted in A.B. Paine, *Mark Twain: A Biography* (1912).

1 Laugh and the world laughs with you
Weep and you weep alone.

Ella Wheeler Wilcox, American poet (1855–1919). 'Solitude', in the *New York Sun* (25 February 1883) – and, as the *Concise Oxford Dictionary of Proverbs* points out, an alteration of the sentiment expressed by Horace in his *Ars Poetica*: 'Men's faces laugh on those who laugh, and correspondingly weep on those who weep.'

2 Laughter is not at all a bad beginning for a friendship, and is far the best ending for one.

Oscar Wilde, Irish playwright, poet and wit (1854–1900). *The Picture of Dorian Gray*, Chap. 1 (1891).

3 Humanity takes itself too seriously. It is the world's original sin. If the cavemen had known how to laugh, History would have been different.

Oscar Wilde. In the same book, Chap. 3.

4 One must have a heart of stone to read the death of Little Nell without laughing.

Oscar Wilde. Quoted in Ada Leverson, *Letters to the Sphinx from Oscar Wilde and Reminiscences of the Author* (1930).

5 Honoria ... is one of those robust, dynamic girls with the muscles of a welter-weight and a laugh like a squadron of cavalry charging on a tin bridge.

(Sir) P(elham) G. Wodehouse, English-born novelist and lyricist (1881–1975). *Carry On, Jeeves*, 'The Rummy Affair of Old Biffy' (1925).

6 I once got engaged to his daughter Honoria, a ghastly dynamic exhibit who read Nietzsche and had a laugh like waves breaking on a stern and rock-bound coast.

(Sir) P(elham) G. Wodehouse. 'Jeeves and and the Yule-Tide Spirit' (1927).

Lavatories

On being approached by the Secretary of the Athenaeum whose lavatory he was in the habit of using on his way to the office:

7 Good God, do you mean to say this place is a club?

F.E. Smith (1st Earl of Birkenhead), English politician and lawyer (1872–1930). Quoted in John Campbell, *F.E. Smith, First Earl of Birkenhead* (1983). Campbell claims to have established that it must have been, rather, the National Liberal Club.

8 Men are never so serious, thoughtful, and intent, as when they are at stool.

Jonathan Swift, Anglo-Irish writer and clergyman (1667–1745). *Gulliver's Travels* (1726).

Law

When a Yorkshire miner put in a very late claim for compensation, the judge told his counsel: 'Your client is no doubt aware of vigilantibus, et non dormientibus, jura subveniunt?' *The counsel replied:*

9 Why, in Barnsley, m'lud, they speak of little else.

Anonymous. In *Pass the Port Again* (1980), there is a version quoted involving Serjeant Sullivan – 'the last serjeant of the Irish Bar to practise in the English courts' (Alexander Martin Sullivan, 1871–1959). Here, the legal tag is '*Assignatus utitur jure auctoris*' and the place where they speak of little else is Ballynattery. The legal maxims in each case are genuine. The first means, 'The laws assist the watchful, not the sleepers' and the second, 'An assignee is clothed with the right of his principal.'

10 'In my youth,' said his father, 'I took to the law,
And argued each case with my wife;
And the muscular strength, which it gave to my jaw,
Has lasted the rest of my life.'

Lewis Carroll, English writer (1832–98). *Alice's Adventures in Wonderland*, Chap. 5 (1865).

1 If the law supposes that … the law is a ass – a idiot.

Charles Dickens, English novelist (1812–70). *Oliver Twist*, Chap. 51 (1837). Mr Bumble is dismayed that the law holds him responsible for his wife's actions.

2 The Law is the true embodiment
Of everything that's excellent.
It has no kind of fault or flaw,
And I, my Lord, embody the Law.

(Sir) W.S. Gilbert, English writer and lyricist (1836–1911). *Iolanthe*, Act 1 (1882).

3 Johnson observed that 'he did not care to speak ill of any man behind his back, but he believed the gentleman was an *attorney*'.

(Dr) Samuel Johnson, English writer and lexicographer (1709–84). Quoted in James Boswell, *The Life of Samuel Johnson* (1791) – for 1770.

4 There is a general prejudice to the effect that lawyers are more honourable than politicians but less honourable than prostitutes. This is an exaggeration.

Alexander King, American writer (1900–65). *Rich Man, Poor Man, Freud and Fruit*, Chap. 3 (1965).

5 The penalty for laughing in the courtroom is six months in jail: if it were not for this penalty, the jury would never hear the evidence.

H.L. Mencken, American journalist and linguist (1880–1956). Quoted in Andrew & Jonathan Roth, *Devil's Advocates* (1989).

When a magistrate asked if he was trying to show contempt for the court:

6 No, I'm trying to conceal it.

Wilson Mizner, American playwright (1876–1933). Quoted in Alva Johnston, *The Legendary Mizners* (1953).

7 No brilliance is needed in the law. Nothing but common sense, and relatively clean finger nails.

(Sir) John Mortimer, English author, playwright and lawyer (1923–). *A Voyage Round My Father* (1970).

On the Kennedy administration's reliance on lawyers from his Chicago practice:

8 I regret that I have but one law firm to give to my country.

Adlai Stevenson, American Democratic politician (1900–65). Quoted in *The Home Book of Humorous Quotations*, ed. A.K. Adams (1969).

9 To succeed in the other trades, capacity must be shown; in the law, concealment of it will do.

Mark Twain, American writer (1835–1910). *Following the Equator*, Vol. 2 (1897).

Law-making

10 If you like laws and sausages, you should never watch either one being made.

Otto von Bismarck, Prusso-German statesman (1815–98). Unverified. A slightly different version, 'Laws are like sausages; you should never watch them being made', has been credited to the French revolutionary statesman Honoré Gabriel de Riqueti, Comte de Mirabeau (1749–91). Comparison has been made with a Dutch proverb (by 1861): 'Who marries a widow or chews a sausage, doesn't know what has been put into them.'

11 One would risk being disgusted if one saw politics, justice, and one's dinner in the making.

Nicolas-Sébastien Chamfort, French writer (1741–94). Quoted in *The Treasury of Humorous Quotations*, eds Evan Esar & Nicolas Bentley (1951).

Lawrence of Arabia (T.E. Lawrence)

ENGLISH SOLDIER AND WRITER (1888–1935)

12 He's always backing into the limelight.

Lord Berners, English writer and composer (1883–1950). Quoted in the *Oxford Dictionary of Quotations* (1979), citing 'oral tradition'. Winston Churchill said the same thing, according to his Private Secretary 1952–65, Anthony Montague Brown (speech to the International

Churchill Societies, 25 September 1986): 'He had the art of backing uneasily into the limelight. He was a very remarkable character and very careful of that fact.'

Laws, informal

1 When your cat has fallen asleep on your lap and looks utterly content and adorable you will suddenly have to go to the bathroom.

Anonymous ('Rule of Feline Frustration'). Quoted in Arthur Bloch, *Murphy's Law and Other Reasons Why Things Go Wrong* (1977).

2 The amount of flak received on any subject is inversely proportional to the subject's true value.

Anonymous ('Potter's Law'). In the same book as above.

3 When all else fails, read the instructions.

Anonymous ('Cahn's Axiom'). Quoted by Paul Dickson in *Playboy* (April 1978).

4 If anything can go wrong, it will.

Anonymous ('Murphy's Law'). Quoted in *Scientific American* (April 1956), but said to date from the late 1940s. *The Macquarie Dictionary* (1981) suggests that it was named after a character who always made mistakes in a series of educational cartoons published by the US Navy. *The Concise Oxford Dictionary of Proverbs* (1982) hints that it was invented by George Nichols, a project manager for Northrop, the Californian aviation firm, in 1949. He developed the idea from a remark by a colleague, Captain Edward A. Murphy Jnr of the Wright Field-Aircraft Laboratory: 'If there is a wrong way to do something, then someone will do it.'

The most notable demonstration of Murphy's Law is that a piece of bread when dropped on the floor will always fall with its buttered side facing down (otherwise known as the Law of Universal Cussedness). This, however, pre-dates the promulgation of the Law. *Punch* (2 February 1856) had this observation: 'Such is Life. A Little School-girl makes the following pathetic inquiry: "Did you ever know a piece of bread and butter fall on the ground but it was sure to fall on the buttered side?"' In 1867, A.D. Eichardson wrote in *Beyond Mississippi*: 'His bread never fell on the buttered side.' In 1884 James Payn composed the lines:

I never had a piece of toast
Particularly long and wide,
But fell upon the sanded floor
And always on the buttered side.

The corollary of this aspect of the Law is that bread always falls buttered side down *except when demonstrating the Law …*

Some have argued that the point of Captain Murphy's original observation was constructive rather than defeatist – it was a prescription for avoiding mistakes in the design of a valve for an aircraft's hydraulic system. If the valve could be fitted in more than one way, then sooner or later someone would fit it the wrong way. The idea was to design it so that the valve could be fitted only the right way.

5 Whenever you're in the bathtub and the telephone rings, it invariably is the wrong number.

Anonymous. Quoted in *The Home Book of Humorous Quotations*, ed. A.K. Adams (1969).

6 Did you ever notice how much faster wood burns when you personally cut and chop it yourself?

Anonymous. Quoted on CBS TV *Apple's Way* (12 January 1975).

7 Seven-eighths of everything can't be seen.

Anonymous ('Iceberg Theorem'). Quoted in the *Daily Mail* (10 March 1979).

8 The easiest way to find something lost around the house is to buy a replacement.

Anonymous ('Rosenbaum's Law'). Quoted in the same article as above. Compare: 'As soon as you replace a lost object, you will find it' – David Brinkley, American broadcaster (1920–). Quoted by Ann Landers, in the *Poughkeepsie Journal* (26 March 1978).

9 When all else fails – and the instructions are missing – kick it.

Anonymous (in the Department of Anaesthetics at Harrow Hospital). Contributed to BBC Radio *Quote … Unquote* and quoted in my book *Say No More* (1987).

10 Acceptable invitations only arrive when you can't accept them.

Anonymous. Contributed as above.

1 If you buy a record for the A side, in time you will find that you are only able to tolerate the B side.

Anonymous. Contributed as above.

2 When your car or central heating is due for servicing – and nothing is positively wrong with it – the servicing will result in the machine *having* to be serviced again within the month.

Anonymous. Contributed as above.

3 The possibility of a young man meeting a desirable and receptive young female increases by pyramidal progression when he is already in the company of (1) a date (2) his wife (3) a better-looking and richer male friend.

Ronald Beifield. Quoted by Allan L. Otten, in *The Wall Street Journal* (2 February 1975).

4 A falling body always rolls to the most inaccessible place.

Theodore M. Bernstein, American writer (1904–). *The Careful Writer* (1967).

5 The longer one saves something before throwing it away, the sooner it will be needed after it is thrown away.

James J. Caulfield. Quoted in Harold Faber, *The Book of Laws* (1979). Promulgated in March 1968.

6 When the weight of the paperwork equals the weight of the plane, the plane will fly.

Donald Douglas, American aircraft designer and manufacturer (1892–1981). Quoted by Alan L. Otten in *The Wall Street Journal* (26 February 1976).

7 Whatever happens in government could have happened differently, and it usually would have been better if it had.

Charles Frankel, American writer (1917–). *High on Foggy Bottom* (1970).

8 When ripping an article from a newspaper, the tear is always into and never away from the required article.

Alan Fraser of Stockport. Contributed to BBC Radio *Quote ... Unquote* and quoted in book *Say No More* (1987).

9 The more underdeveloped the country, the more overdeveloped the women.

John Kenneth Galbraith, Canadian-born American economist (1908–). Quoted in *Time* Magazine (17 October 1969).

10 Anyone who says he isn't going to resign four times, definitely will.

John Kenneth Galbraith. Quoted in *Time* Magazine (7 November 1973).

11 Gnomes always draw curtains where there are views.

Ada Louise Huxtable, American architectural critic (*c.* 1921–). In *The New York Times* (16 November 1975).

12 A shortcut is the longest distance between two points.

Charles Issawi. In *Columbia Forum* (Summer, 1970).

13 If it works well, they'll stop making it.

Jane Otten, and Russell Baker, American humorist (1925–). Quoted by Alan L. Otten in *The Wall Street Journal* (26 February 1976). As 'If it's good, they'll stop making it', this has also been attributed to Herbert Block (Herblock), the American political cartoonist (1909–).

14 It is impossible to make anything foolproof because fools are so ingenious.

H.W. Robinson of Co. Down. Quoted in the *Daily Mail* (29 November 1980).

15 The place you are trying to get to is always on the extreme edge of the page on the street-map.

Violet Rutter of London W6. Contributed to BBC Radio *Quote ... Unquote* and quoted in my book *Say No More* (1987).

1 No matter how you have searched, there will always be one teaspoon left at the bottom of the washing-up water.

Irene Thomas, English broadcaster (1920–2001). *The Bandsman's Daughter* (1979).

2 At bank, post office or supermarket, there is one universal law which you ignore at your own peril: the shortest line moves the slowest.

Bill Vaughan. Quoted in *Reader's Digest* (July 1977).

Lawyers

3 Lawyers should never marry other lawyers. This is called inbreeding, from which comes idiot children and more lawyers.

Line from film *Adam's Rib* (US 1949). Screenwriters: Ruth Gordon, Garson Kanin. Spoken by David Wayne (Kip Laurie).

4 A man who is his own lawyer has a fool for a client.

Anonymous (proverb). First recorded in Philadelphia (1809).

5 A man may as well open an oyster without a knife as a lawyer's mouth without a fee.

Barten Holyday, English divine and translator (1593–1661). Quoted in *The Treasury of Humorous Quotations*, eds Evan Esar & Nicolas Bentley (1951).

6 A lawyer with his briefcase can steal more than a thousand men with guns.

Mario Puzo, American novelist (1920–99). *The Godfather*, Bk 1, Chap. 1 (1969). A saying of Don Corleone's. Compare: 'Pen and ink are now my surest means of vengeance; and more land is won by the lawyer with the ram-skin [parchment], than by the Andrea Ferrara [sword] with his sheepshead handle' – Sir Walter Scott, *The Fortunes of Nigel*, Chap. 32 (1822).

7 As scarce as lawyers in heaven.

Mark Twain, American writer (1835–1910). *The Celebrated Jumping Frog of Calaveras County*, 'Information for the Millions' (1867).

Lays, good

8 And there was that wholesale libel on a Yale prom. If all the girls attending it were laid end to end, Mrs Parker said, she wouldn't be at all surprised.

Dorothy Parker, American writer (1893–1967). Quoted in Alexander Woollcott, *While Rome Burns* (1934).

On her requirements for an apartment:

9 [Enough space] to lay a hat – and a few friends.

Dorothy Parker. Quoted in John Keats, *You Might as Well Live* (1970).

Leadership

10 I must follow them for I am their leader.

Alexandre Auguste Ledru-Rollin, French politician (1807–74). Quoted in E. de Mirecourt, *Histoire contemporaire* (1857). Ledru-Rollin became Minister of the Interior in the provisional government during the 1848 Paris revolution. He was looking from his window one day as a mob passed by and he said: '*Eh, je suis leur chef, il fallait bien les suivre* [Ah well, I'm their leader, I really ought to follow them].' It is said that 'he gave offence by his arbitrary conduct' (of which this would seem to be a prime example) and had to resign.

11 The question, 'Who ought to be boss?' is like asking, 'Who ought to be the tenor in the quartet?' Obviously, the man who can sing tenor.

Henry Ford, American industrialist (1863–1947). Quoted in *Forbes Magazine* (undated).

12 Leadership, like swimming, cannot be learned by reading about it.

Henry Mintzberg, American business expert (1939–). At McGill University School of Management.

Leaks

How Noah plugged a leak in the Ark using various parts of the anatomy, including a bloodhound's:

13 And that is how Noah got 'em all safe
ashore,

But ever since then, strange to tell,
Them as helped save the Ark has all
carried a mark,
Aye, and all their descendants as well.

That's why dog has a cold nose, and ladies
cold elbows
– You'll also find if you enquire
That that's why a man takes his coat-tails
in hand
And stands with his back to the fire.

Marriott Edgar, English writer (1880–1951). 'The 'Ole in the Ark' (1937). Famously recited by Stanley Holloway.

Legends

1 Legend – a lie that has attained the dignity of age.

Harry Oliver. *The Desert Rat Scrap Book*.

Legs

2 There are two reasons why I'm in show business, and I'm standing on both of them.

Betty Grable, American actress (1916–73). Quoted in Barbara Rowes, *The Book of Quotes* (1979).

Leisure

3 Leisure tends to corrupt, and absolute leisure corrupts absolutely.

Edgar A. Shoaff. Quoted in Laurence J. Peter, *Quotations for Our Time* (1977).

Lending

4 I don't trust a bank that would lend money to such a poor risk.

Robert Benchley, American humorist (1889–1945). Quoted in *The Bloomsbury Dictionary of Quotations* (1987). *Compare* CLUBS 85:2.

5 Never lend books, for no one ever returns them; the only books I have in my library are books that other people have lent me.

Anatole France, French novelist and critic (1844–1924). Quoted in *The Treasury of Humorous Quotations*, eds Evan Esar & Nicolas Bentley (1951).

6 Please return this book; I find that though many of my friends are poor arithmeticians, they are nearly all good bookkeepers.

Sir Walter Scott, Scottish novelist (1771–1832). Quoted in the same collection as above.

Length

Of an article (said by Frank Muir to be 'full of declamation and invective') submitted by Lord Brougham to Smith's Edinburgh Review*:*

7 Brougham's review is not in good taste; he should have put on an air of serious concern, not raillery and ridicule; things are too serious for that. It is long yet vigorous, like the penis of a jackass.

(Revd) Sydney Smith, English clergyman, essayist and wit (1771–1845). Letter (1809), quoted in *The Oxford Book of Humorous Prose* (1990).

Lesbianism

8 Many years ago I chased a woman for almost two years, only to discover her tastes were exactly like mine: we were both crazy about girls.

Groucho Marx, American comedian (1895–1977). In *The Groucho Letters* (1967) – letter of 28 March 1955.

9 No woman would do that.

Victoria, British Queen (1819–1901). Commenting on the fact that the Criminal Law Amendment Act of 1885 (which outlawed indecent relations between same sex adults in public and in private) made no mention of women. Another version: originally the wording had been 'any male or female person', but when the text was shown to the Queen, no one had the nerve to answer her query of 'Why women were included in the Act as surely it was impossible for them' (source: Ted Morgan, *Somerset Maugham*, 1980). Dermod Quirke commented (1999): 'There are many versions of this old chestnut – I like the lesbian one, which has Victoria saying, "I'll be damned if I'll let them spoil the fun for us girls." But they're all nonsense: there is absolutely no evidence that Victoria made any comment on the Act of 1885 ... [besides] women were never included in any draft of sect. 11 ... and they were certainly not included in the definitive text submitted to

Victoria for her assent. Labouchère's draft read "if any male person ... ", and it was adopted by parliament in precisely that form.

'Richard Ellman's version [in his *Oscar Wilde*, 1987] is more subtle. He recognizes that the Act referred only to men, and so has Victoria asking why women were not included. Nice try, but it still doesn't really hold water.'

Lesser of two evils

On the first wife (with whom he was having a feud) of the composer Frank Loesser:

1 Lynn is the evil of two Loessers.

Harry Kurnitz, American screenwriter (c. 1907–68). Quoted in *The Observer* (31 March 1968).

Letters

2 I would have answered your letter sooner, but you didn't send one.

Goodman Ace, American writer (1899–1982). Letter (1950) to Groucho Marx, quoted in *The Groucho Letters* (1967).

3 Never burn an uninteresting letter is the first rule of British aristocracy.

Frank Moore Colby, American editor and writer (1865–1925). Quoted in *The Treasury of Humorous Quotations*, eds Evan Esar & Nicolas Bentley (1951).

Replying to letter headed, 'From the desk of ... ':

4 Dear Desk.

(Sir) Noël Coward, English entertainer and writer (1899–1973). Attributed.

5 An odd thought strikes me: we shall receive no letters in the grave.

(Dr) Samuel Johnson, English writer and lexicographer (1709–84). Quoted in James Boswell, *The Life of Samuel Johnson* (1791) – a remark from the last few weeks of his life in December 1784.

6 Paddy wrote a letter to his Irish Molly O',
Saying 'Should you not receive it, write
and let me know.'

Jack Judge and Harry J. Williams, British songwriters (1878–1938) and (1858–1924). 'Tipperary' (1912).

Of Charles Lamb:

7 His sayings are generally like women's letters; all the pith is in the postscript.

William Hazlitt, English essayist (1778–1830). *Boswell Redivivus* (1827). Compare: 'A woman seldom writes her mind but in her postscript' – (Sir) Richard Steele, Irish essayist and playwright (1672–1729), quoted in *The Treasury of Humorous Quotations*, eds Evan Esar & Nicolas Bentley (1951).

8 My dear McClellan:
If you don't want to use the army, I should like to borrow it for a while.
Yours respectfully,
A. Lincoln.

Abraham Lincoln, American Republican President (1809–65). Quoted in Carl Sandburg, *Abraham Lincoln, The War Years* (1939). During the American Civil War, Lincoln became concerned that General George Brinton McClellan was failing in his duties as Commander in Chief of the Army of the Potomac and duly sent him this message.

9 Do right and fear no man; don't write and fear no woman.

Luke McLuke (J.S. Hastings), American columnist. 'Epigram' from the Cincinnati *Enquirer* (c. 1918). Quoted in *The Home Book of Proverbs, & c.*, ed. Burton Stevenson (1948). Elbert Hubbard is credited with 'Wrong no man and write no woman' in *The Treasury of Humorous Quotations*, eds Evan Esar & Nicolas Bentley (1951).

10 Letter-writing: that most delightful way of wasting time.

John Morley (Lord Morley), English biographer and politician (1838–1923). *Critical Miscellanies*, 'The Life of George Eliot' (1886).

11 Sydney Smith, or Napoleon or Marcus Aurelius (somebody about that time) said that after ten days any letter would answer itself. You see what he meant.

A.A. Milne, English writer (1882–1956). Attributed remark. In fact, it was Arthur Binstead, the English journalist (1861–1914) in *Pitcher's Proverbs* (1909), who said, 'The great secret in life ... [is] not to open letters for a fortnight. At the expiration of that period you will find that nearly all of them have answered themselves.'

1 Correspondences are like small-clothes before the invention of suspenders; it is impossible to keep them up.

(Revd) Sydney Smith, English clergyman, essayist and wit (1771–1845). Letter to Catherine Crowe (31 January 1841).

2 Beware of writing to me. I always answer ... My father spent the last 20 years of his life writing letters. If someone thanked him for a wedding present, he thanked them for thanking him and there was no end to the exchange but death.

Evelyn Waugh, English novelist (1903–66). Letter to Lady Mosley (30 March 1966). In *Life* Magazine (8 April 1946), he made the same point: 'His courtesy was somewhat extravagant. He would write and thank people who wrote to thank him for wedding presents and when he encountered anyone as punctilious as himself the correspondence ended only with death.'

Levity

3 Nothing like a little judicious levity.

Robert Louis Stevenson, Scottish writer (1850–94) and Lloyd Osbourne, American writer (1868–1947). *The Wrong Box*, Chap. 7 (1889).

Libels

When Confidential *magazine ran a muck-raking article, going over every area of his life, Groucho dashed off one of his famous letters to the editor:*

4 Dear Sir, If you persist in publishing libellous articles about me, I will have to cancel my subscription.

Groucho Marx, American comedian (1895–1977). Quoted in Arthur Marx, *Son of Groucho* (1973). In *The Groucho Letters*, Introduction (1967), there is this version: 'If you continue to publish slanderous pieces about me, I shall feel compelled to cancel my subscription.'

Liberals

5 A liberal is a conservative who has been arrested.

Anonymous. Quoted (twice) in Tom Wolfe, *The Bonfire of the Vanities* (1987).

6 There aren't any liberals left in New York. They've all been mugged.

James Q. Wilson. Quoted in *Policy Review* (Fall 1993).

Lies

During the Profumo affair (1963):

7 What have you done? cried Christine,
You've wrecked the whole party machine.
To lie in the nude may be rude,
But to lie in the House is obscene.

Anonymous. Secretary of State for War John Profumo carried on with Christine Keeler who was also allegedly sharing her favours with the Soviet military attaché. Profumo at first denied this in the House of Commons but then had to own up and resign.

Of Harold Wilson:

8 How can you tell when he's lying? When his lips are moving.

Anonymous. Quoted in my book *A Year of Stings and Squelches* (1985).

Of a friend:

9 She tells enough white lies to ice a wedding cake.

Margot Asquith (Countess of Oxford and Asquith) (1864–1945). Quoted by Baroness Asquith in BBC TV *As I Remember* (30 April 1967).

10 I have been thinking that I would make a proposition to my Republican friends ... That if they will stop telling lies about the Democrats, we will stop telling the truth about them.

Adlai Stevenson, American Democratic politician (1900–65). Remark during election campaign (10 September 1952). However, it was originated by Chauncey Depew about the *Democrats* earlier in the century. Depew was a Republican Senator in 1899–1911.

1 A lie is an abomination unto the Lord and a very present help in time of trouble.

Adlai Stevenson. Attributed saying – an amalgamation of Proverbs 12:22 and Psalms 46:1. However, the remark is not original to him. *Symons's Meteorological Magazine* (May 1916) recalled: 'That urchin when asked for the Scriptural definition of a lie is reported to have answered glibly, "A lie which is an abomination unto the Lord is a very present help in time of trouble".' The following month, a (British) reader stated that the 'true version of what he said' was: 'A lie is an abomination to the Lord, but a very present help in trouble' – and surmised that it was said by an American 'Sunday school boy'.

2 He was not a direct liar but he would subtly convey untruths.

Mark Twain, American writer (1835–1910). *Mark Twain's Notebook*, ed. A.B. Paine (1935).

3 The only form of lying that is absolutely beyond reproach is lying for its own sake.

Oscar Wilde, Irish playwright, poet and wit (1854–1900). 'The Decay of Lying', in *Nineteenth Century* (January 1889).

Life

4 If I had to live my life all over again, I would change one thing: I wouldn't read *Moby Dick*.

Woody Allen, American film actor, writer and director (1937–). Quoted in *The Daily Telegraph* (24 February 1994). Allen is also reported to have said, similarly: 'If I had my life to live over again, I would do everything the exact same way, with the possible exception of seeing the movie remake of *Lost Horizon*' – remark attributed in *The Guinness Book of Movie Facts & Feats* (ed. Patrick Robertson) (1993 edn).

5 Life is just a bowl of toenails.

Anonymous (graffito). On the wall of an Oxford college. Contributed to BBC Radio *Quote...Unquote* (31 May 1978).

6 This is not a dress rehearsal, this is real life.

Anonymous (graffito). Collected at the Eight-O Club, Dallas, Texas. Quoted in my book *Graffiti 3* (1981).

7 No good worry worry anything. By'm by, we all asame – Nothing!

Anonymous (Australian aborigine). Quoted in *The 'Quote ... Unquote' Newsletter* (April 1994).

8 Someone has said that the ideal life is to live in an English country home, engage a Chinese cook, marry a Japanese wife, and take a French mistress.

Anonymous. Quoted in Lin Yutang, *With Love and Irony* (1940).

9 Life ... is like a cup of tea; the more heartily we drink, the sooner we reach the dregs.

(Sir) J(ames) M. Barrie, Scottish playwright (1860–1937). *The Admirable Crichton*, Act 1, Sc. 1 (1902).

In parody of an Anglican church sermon:

10 Life, you know, is rather like opening a tin of sardines. We're all of us looking for the key.

Alan Bennett, English playwright and actor (1934–). *Beyond the Fringe*, 'Take a Pew' (1961).

11 If Life Is a Bowl of Cherries, What Am I Doing in the Pits?

Erma Bombeck, American humorous columnist (1927–96). Title of book (1979).

12 Life is like playing a violin solo in public and learning the instrument as one goes on.

Edward Bulwer-Lytton (1st Baron Lytton), English novelist and politician (1803–73). Quoted in *The Treasury of Humorous Quotations*, eds Evan Esar & Nicolas Bentley (1951). Later quoted by Samuel Butler, English author (1835–1902) during a speech at the Somerville Club (27 February 1895).

13 When one subtracts from life infancy (which is vegetation), – sleep, eating, and swilling – buttoning and unbuttoning – how much remains of downright existence? The summer of a dormouse.

Lord Byron, English poet (1788–1824). Journal (7 December 1813). 'If I ever write an autobiography,

Byron has found me the title' – Kenneth Tynan, letter of 17 November 1972. Hence, *The Summer of a Dormouse*, title of a novel (1967) by Monica Stirling and of memoirs (2000) by John Mortimer. *The Oxford Dictionary of Quotations* (1992) finds the phrase 'all this buttoning and unbuttoning' from an anonymous '18th-century suicide note'.

1 For there is good news yet to hear and
fine things to be seen,
Before we go to Paradise by way of
Kensal Green.

G.K. Chesterton, English poet, novelist and critic (1874–1936). 'The Rolling English Road' (1914).

2 If life has a second edition, how I would correct the proofs.

John Clare, English poet (1793–1864). Attributed remark in a letter to a friend.

3 Life is like a B-picture script. It is that corny. If I had my life story offered to me to film, I'd turn it down.

Kirk Douglas, American actor (1916–). Quoted in *Look* Magazine (4 October 1955).

4 My momma always said, life was like a box of chocolates ... you never know what you're gonna get.

Line from film *Forrest Gump* (US 1994). Screenwriter: Eric Ross. Spoken by Tom Hanks (Forrest Gump).

5 Is there a life before death? That's chalked
up
In Ballymurphy. Competence with pain,
Coherent miseries, a bite and sup,
We hug our little destiny again.

Seamus Heaney, Irish poet (1939–). *North*, 'Whatever You Say Say Nothing' (1975). Earlier, 'Is there life before death?' was the epigraph to Chap. 9 of Stephen Vizinczey's novel *In Praise of Older Women* (1966). There, it is credited to 'Anon. Hungarian'.

6 In the midst of life we are in Brooklyn.

Oliver Herford, American humorist (1863–1935). Quoted in *The Treasury of Humorous Quotations*, eds Evan Esar & Nicolas Bentley (1951).

7 Life is just one damned thing after another.

Elbert Hubbard, American writer and editor (1856–1915). In *The Philistine* (December 1909). Also attributed to Frank Ward O'Malley (1875–1932).

Quoting, with approval, a remark in his student Rain's story:

8 'Life doesn't imitate art. It imitates bad television.'

Line from film *Husbands and Wives* (US 1992). Screenwriter: Woody Allen. Spoken by Woody Allen (Gabe Roth).

9 Don't worry – it's quite suitable for the children. This is a story about passion, bloodshed, desire and death. Everything in fact that makes life worth living.

Line from stage musical *Irma La Douce* (1958). Book and lyrics by More, Heneker and Norman based on originals by Alexandre Breffort. Opening line.

10 Life is like a sewer. What you get out of it depends on what you put in.

Tom Lehrer, US songwriter and entertainer (1928–). On record album, *An Evening Wasted with Tom Lehrer* (1953).

11 Life would be tolerable if it were not for its amusements.

(Sir) George Cornewall Lewis, English Liberal politician and editor (1806–63). In *The Times* (18 September 1872). Quoted by Lord Grey of Fallodon in the *Dictionary of National Biography*.

12 Laugh it off, laugh it off; it's all part of life's rich pageant.

Arthur Marshall, English writer and entertainer (1910–89). In recorded monologue 'The Games Mistress' (1937). Compare: *Elke (a maid, to Clouseau who has fallen into a fountain):* 'You should get out of these clothes immediately. You'll catch your death of pneumonia, you will.' *Clouseau:* 'Yes, I probably will. It's all part of life's rich pageant, you know' – lines from film *A Shot in the Dark* (US

1964). Screenwriters: Blake Edwards, William Peter Blatty. Spoken by Elke Sommer (Maria Gambrelli) and Peter Sellers (Inspector Clouseau).

1 Life's a tough proposition, and the first hundred years are the hardest.

Wilson Mizner, American playwright (1876–1933). Quoted in *A Treasury of Laughter*, ed. Louis Untermeyer (1946).

2 Life is not being told a man has just waxed the floor.

Ogden Nash, American poet (1902–71). Attributed remark.

3 Take me or leave me. Or as most people do: both.

Dorothy Parker, American writer (1893–1967). Quoted in book *Nudge Nudge, Wink Wink* (1986).

When someone said, 'They're ducking for apples' at a Hallowe'en party:

4 There, but for a typographical error, is the story of my life.

Dorothy Parker. Quoted in John Keats, *You Might as Well Live* (1970).

5 People say that life is the thing, but I prefer reading.

Logan Pearsall Smith, American writer (1865–1946). *Afterthoughts*, 'Myself' (1931).

6 Oh, isn't life a terrible thing, thank God?

Dylan Thomas, Welsh poet (1914–53). Radio play, *Under Milk Wood* (1954), opening words.

7 The events of life are mainly small events – they only seem large when we are close to them. By and by they settle down and we see that one doesn't show above another. They are all about one general low altitude, and inconsequential.

Mark Twain, American writer (1835–1910). *Mark Twain's Autobiography*, ed. A.B. Paine (1924).

8 What a pity that in life we only get our lessons when they are of no use to us.

Oscar Wilde, Irish playwright, poet and wit (1854–1900). *Lady Windermere's Fan*, Act 4 (1892).

Lifts *See* ELEVATORS

Liking

9 Will Rogers never met Marvin Hamlisch.

Anonymous (car sticker in New York). Quoted in *The Independent*, (15 May 1987). Will Rogers, the folksy American comedian, had been famous for saying, 'When I die, my epitaph is going to read, "I never met a man I didn't like."'

Limericks

10 There was a young lady of Tottenham,
Who'd no manners or else she'd forgotten 'em.
At tea at the vicar's
She tore off her knickers,
Because, she explained, she felt 'ot in 'em.

Anonymous. G. Legman's magisterial survey *The Limerick* (two vols, 1964, 1969) finds a source for this in 1903.

11 There was a young girl of Madras
Who had the most beautiful ass.
But not as you'd think
Firm, round and pink,
But grey, with long ears, and eats grass.

Anonymous. Legman finds a source for this in 1940.

12 There was a young lady of Exeter
So pretty that men craned their nexetter.
One was even so brave
As to take out and wave
The distinguishing mark of his sexetter.

Anonymous. Legman finds this '1927–1941'.

13 There once was a young man called Stencil
Whose prick was as sharp as a pencil.
He punctured an actress,
Two sheets and a mattress,
And dented the bedroom utensil.

Anonymous (current in the early 1980s). Does not appear in Legman.

1 A tired old fairy from Rome
Took a leprechaun back to his home.
As he entered the elf
He said to himself
I'd be much better off in a gnome.

Anonymous. Ditto.

2 Nymphomaniacal Alice
Used a dynamite stick for a phallus.
They found her vagina
In North Carolina
And her ass-hole in Buckingham Palace.

Anonymous. Legman dates this '1942–1951'.

3 On the chest of a barmaid in Sale
Were tattooed the prices of ale,
And on her behind,
For the sake of the blind,
Was the same information in Braille.

Anonymous. Legman has a version of this about a 'harlot from Yale', dated 1941.

4 There was a young man from Calcutta
Who had the most terrible stutta.
He said, 'Pass the h-ham
And the j-j-j-jam,
And the b-b-b-b-b-b-butta.'

Anonymous. Source forgotten, not in Legman.

5 There was a young man in Florence
To whom all art was abhorrence.
So he got slightly tipsy
Went to the Uffizi
And peed on the paintings in torrents.

Anonymous. Quoted in my book *Graffiti 2* (1980). Legman finds two limericks from 1941–2 that both make use of the Florence/abhorrence/torrents rhyme, but on different themes.

6 There was a young gaucho named Bruno
Who said, 'Screwing is one thing I do know.
A woman is fine,
And a sheep is divine,
But a llama is Numero Uno.

Anonymous. Legman has this from 1942.

7 There was an old man of Dunoon
Who always ate soup with a fork,
For he said, 'As I eat
Neither fish, fowl nor flesh,
I should finish my dinner too quick.'

Anonymous non-rhyming limerick. Included in *Comic and Curious Verse*, ed. J.M. Cohen (1952).

8 There was a young man of Tralee
Who was stung on the neck by a wasp
When asked if it hurt
He replied, 'Not a bit.
It can do it again if it likes.'

Anonymous non-rhyming anti-limerick. Compare these other versions: 'There was a young man of St Bees / Who was stung on his wrist by his watch. / When asked if it hurt, / He said, 'I knew ticks could bite, / It's lucky it wasn't Big Ben.' And: 'There was a young man of St Bees / Who was stung on the arm by a wasp; / When they said, 'Does it hurt?' / He replied, 'No, it doesn't: / 'It's a good job it wasn't a hornet.'

9 There was a young curate of Salisbury
Who was terribly halisbury-scalisbury:
He ran about Hampshire
Without any pampshire
Till his bishop compelled him to walisbury.

Anonymous. Quoted in *The Faber Book of Comic Verse*, ed. Michael Roberts (1974 edn). For anyone who does not understand this, the key rests in the alternative name Sarum for Salisbury and the abbreviation Hants. for Hampshire.

10 There was a young gourmet of Crediton
Who took pâté de foie gras and spread it on
A chocolate biscuit
He murmured 'I'll risk it.'
His tomb bears the date that he said it on.

Anonymous. Known by 1981. Not found in Legman.

1 There was a young lady named Bright,
Whose speed was far faster than light;
She set out one day
In a relative way,
And returned on the previous night.

A.H. Reginald Buller, Canadian botanist (1874–1944). Anonymously in *Punch* (19 December 1923). Buller's authorship was recorded in W.S. Baring-Gould, *The Lure of the Limerick* (1968).

2 I wish that my room had a floor.
I don't so much care for a door
But this crawling around
Without touching the ground
Is beginning to be quite a bore.

Gelett Burgess, American writer and illustrator (1866–1951). Attributed.

Limits

3 Everything has its limit – iron ore cannot be educated into gold.

Mark Twain, American writer (1835–1910). *What Is Man? and Other Essays* (1917).

Lingerie

4 Brevity is the soul of lingerie – as the Petticoat said to the Chemise.

Dorothy Parker, American writer (1893–1967). Quoted in Alexander Woollcott, *While Rome Burns* (1934). Said to have been written as a caption for *Vogue* in 1916.

Lips

5 With Mick Jagger's lips, he could French kiss a moose.

Joan Rivers, American entertainer (1937–). Quoted in my book *A Year of Stings and Squelches* (1985).

Lisps

6 Lisp: to call a spade a thpade.

Oliver Herford, American humorist (1863–1935). Quoted in *The Treasury of Humorous Quotations*, eds Evan Esar & Nicolas Bentley (1951).

Literary criticism

On Sir Arthur Conan Doyle's The Return of Sherlock Holmes *(1905):*

7 I think, sir, when Holmes fell over that cliff he may not have killed himself, but he was never quite the same man afterwards.

Anonymous (Cornish boatman) – whom Conan Doyle liked to quote himself. Howard Haycraft, *Murder for Pleasure: the Life and Times of the Detective Story* (1942) comments: '*The Return of Sherlock Holmes* was purchasable on both sides of the Atlantic in 1905. The reading public was properly grateful and would not for any known worlds have had matters otherwise. And yet – the reception of the new tales was not entirely unmixed. Doyle enjoyed relating a homely incident that expressed the state of the popular mind neatly ... '

Of the novelist R.S. Surtees:

8 Dickens with horse dung.

Anonymous.

Of James Laver's memoirs Museum Piece *(1963):*

9 Like someone coming for tea and staying a month.

Anonymous (critic in *The Times*). Quoted in Roy Strong, *The Roy Strong Diaries 1967–1987* (1997).

Of Abraham Cowley:

10 He more had pleased us, had he pleased us less.

Joseph Addison, English essayist and politician (1672–1719). *An Account of the Greatest English Poets* (1694).

Reviewing a TV adaptation of M.M. Kaye's The Far Pavilions*:*

11 One of those big, fat paperbacks, intended to while away a monsoon or two, which, if thrown with a good overarm action, will bring a water buffalo to its knees.

Nancy Banks-Smith, English journalist and critic (1929–). In *The Guardian* (4 January 1984).

An early book-reviewer writes:

1 And it shall be, when thou hast made an end of reading this book, that thou shalt bind a stone to it, and cast it into the midst of Euphrates.

The Bible. Jeremiah 51:63.

2 The covers of this book are too far apart.

Ambrose Bierce, American journalist (1842–?1914). One-sentence review quoted in C.H. Grattan, *Bitter Bierce* (1929).

On hearing that Watership Down *was a novel about rabbits written by a civil servant:*

3 I would rather read a novel about civil servants written by a rabbit.

Craig Brown, English journalist (1957–). Attributed in *The Oxford Dictionary of Literary Quotations*, ed. Peter Kemp (1997).

Of Monckton Milnes's Life of Keats*:*

4 A fricassee of dead dog.

Thomas Carlyle, Scottish historian and philosopher (1795–1881). Quoted in *The Frank Muir Book* (1976).

On a book by John O'Hara:

5 Hard to lay down and easy not to pick up.

Malcolm Cowley, American critic (1898–1989). Quoted in Ned Sherrin, *Cutting Edge* (1984).

On Scott's 'The Field of Waterloo', a patriotic poem written to raise money for soldiers' widows (1815):

6 The corpse of many a hero slain
Pressed Waterloo's ensanguined plain;
But none by salvo or by shot
Fell half so flat as Walter Scott!

Thomas Erskine (1st Baron Erskine), Scottish lawyer (1750–1823). Quoted in *The Home Book of Humorous Quotations*, ed. A.K. Adams (1969).

7 Edward Gibbon presented a copy of the first volume of his *Decline and Fall of the Roman Empire* to the Duke of Gloucester. When the second volume came out, Gibbon did likewise. The Duke appeared to be pleased by the presentation, but commented: 'Another damned, thick, square book! Always scribble, scribble, scribble! Eh! Mr Gibbon?'

William Henry, 1st Duke of Gloucester (1743–1805) – a brother of King George III. Quoted in Henry Beste, *Personal and Literary Memorials* (1829). Has also been ascribed to King George III and to a Duke of Cumberland.

Of an early work by Congreve:

8 It is praised by the biographers … I would rather praise it than read it.

(Dr) Samuel Johnson, English writer and lexicographer (1709–84). *The Lives of the English Poets*, 'Congreve' (1779–81).

9 The want of human interest is always felt. *Paradise Lost* is one of the books which the reader admires and lays down, and forgets to take up again. Its perusal is a duty rather than a pleasure. None ever wished it longer than it is.

(Dr) Samuel Johnson. In the same work, 'Milton'.

'Maudie Littlehampton' on the book Lady Chatterley's Lover *during its trial on obscenity charges:*

10 It's an odd thing, but now one knows it's profoundly moral and packed with deep spiritual significance a lot of the old charm seems to have gone.

(Sir) Osbert Lancaster, English cartoonist (1908–86). Caption to cartoon in the *Daily Express* (1961).

11 From the moment I picked up your book until I laid it down I was convulsed with laughter. Someday I intend reading it.

Groucho Marx, American comedian (1895–1977). Quoted in Hector Arce, *Groucho* (1979). Concerning *Dawn Ginsbergh's Revenge* (1928) by S.J. Perelman.

12 There is a great vogue for what is called the Woogie-Poogie-Boo kind of children's book, and I am doing my best to get one ready. I

don't know what it will be called, but I rather fancy 'Songs Through My Hat' or perhaps 'When We Were Very Silly'.

J.B. Morton (Beachcomber), English humorous writer (1893–1979). From 'When We Were Very Silly' (*c.* 1931), a comment on the works of A.A. Milne.

Reviewing Cyril Connolly's The Rock Pool:

1 Even to want to write about so-called artists who spend on sodomy what they have gained by sponging betrays a kind of spiritual inadequacy.

George Orwell, English novelist and journalist (1903–50). In the *New English Weekly* (23 July 1936).

2 This is not a novel to be tossed aside lightly. It should be thrown with great force.

Dorothy Parker, American writer (1893–1967). Quoted in R.E. Drennan, *Wit's End* (1973). In Matthew Parris, *Scorn* (1994), this is said to refer to Benito Mussolini's novel *Claudia Particella, L'Amante del Cardinale: Grande Romanzo dei Tempi del Cardinal Emanuel Madruzzo*. When this was published in the US as *The Cardinal's Mistress*, Parker reviewed it devastatingly (15 September 1928), but did not actually include this put-down.

As 'Constant reader', reviewing A.A. Milne:

3 And it is that word 'hummy', my darlings, that marks the first place in 'The House at Pooh Corner' at which Tonstant Weader fwowed up.

Dorothy Parker. In *The New Yorker* (20 October 1928).

4 To say Agatha [Christie]'s characters are cardboard cut-outs is an insult to cardboard.

Ruth Rendell (Baroness Rendell), English crime novelist (1930–). Quoted in *The Independent* 'Quote Unquote' (3 April 1993). This has become a common critical format. For example, Peter Preston in *The Guardian* (2 May 1998), writing of the novelist Jeffrey Archer: 'Who else would cheerily permutate characters of such vestigiality that calling them cardboard is an to insult the British packaging industry?'

On a two-line poem:

5 Very nice, though there are dull stretches.

Antoine de Rivarol, French satirist and pamphleteer (1753–1801). Attributed remark.

6 I never read a book before reviewing it; it prejudices a man so.

(Revd) Sydney Smith, English clergyman, essayist and wit (1771–1845). Quoted in Hesketh Pearson, *The Smith of Smiths* (1934).

7 [The Mormon Bible] is chloroform in print. If Joseph Smith composed this book, the act was a miracle – keeping awake while he did it was, at any rate.

Mark Twain, American writer (1835–1910). *Roughing It* (1872).

8 It is a thoroughly well-intentioned book, and eminently suitable for invalids.

Oscar Wilde, Irish playwright, poet and wit (1854–1900). Quoted in *The Fireworks of Oscar Wilde*, ed. Owen Dudley Edwards (1989).

9 *Astray: A Tale of a Country Town* is a very serious volume. It has taken four people to write it, and even to read it requires assistance.

Oscar Wilde. Quoted in the same book as above.

10 *Andiatoroctè* is the title of a volume of poems by the Rev. Clarence Walworth, of Albany N.Y. It is a word borrowed from the Indians, and should, we think, be returned to them as soon as possible.

Oscar Wilde. Quoted in *A Critic in Pall Mall*, ed. E.V. Lucas (1919).

On George Meredith:

11 Meredith! Who can define him? His style is chaos, illumined by flashes of lightning. As a writer, he has mastered everything, except language: as a novelist he can do everything except tell a story. As an artist he is everything, except articulate.

Oscar Wilde. 'The Decay of Lying', in *Nineteenth Century* (January 1889).

On George Moore:

1 He wrote excellent English until he discovered grammar.

Oscar Wilde. Quoted in *The Home Book of Humorous Quotations*, ed. A.K. Adams (1969).

Reviewing D.H. Lawrence's novel Lady Chatterley's Lover *when it was reissued by the Grove Press in the United States in 1959. Rather oddly, this was in the pages of* Field and Stream, *a journal aimed at followers of outdoor pursuits:*

2 This pictorial account of the day-by-day life of an English gamekeeper is full of considerable interest to outdoor-minded readers, as it contains many passages on pheasant-raising, the apprehending of poachers, ways to control vermin, and other chores and duties of the professional gamekeeper. Unfortunately, one is obliged to wade through many pages of extraneous material in order to discover and savour those sidelights on the management of a Midland shooting estate, and in this reviewer's opinion, the book cannot take the place of J.R. Miller's *Practical Gamekeeper*.

Ed Zern, American writer (1910–). In *Field and Stream*, 'Exit Laughing' column (November 1959). Quoted anonymously in the seventh volume of Rupert Furneaux's *Famous Criminal Cases* (1962) in its account of The Penguin Books/*Lady Chatterley* trial.

Literary lapses

3 Flash'd from his bed the electric tidings came,
'He is no better, he is much the same.'

Anonymous. The lines are often ascribed, however, to Alfred Austin, English Poet Laureate (1835–1913), as in A. & V. Palmer, *Quotations in History* (1976), and sometimes remembered as 'Across/along the electric wire the message came ... ' The couplet is quoted as an example of bathos and of a Poet Laureate writing to order at his worst. As such, it needs some qualification, if not an actual apology to the poet's shade. D.B. Wyndham Lewis and Charles Lee in their noted selection of bad verse, *The Stuffed Owl* (1930), interestingly included a similar couplet, but ascribed it to a 'university poet unknown', and quite right, too. F.H. Gribble had included the slightly different version, 'Along the electric wire ...' in his *Romance of the Cambridge Colleges* (1913).

What is not in dispute is that the lines were written to mark the Prince of Wales's illness in 1871. Unfortunately, to spoil a good story, it has to be pointed out that Austin never wrote them (though he *did* match them in awfulness on other occasions) and he did not become Poet Laureate until 1896, following in the illustrious footsteps of Tennyson. As J. Lewis May observed in *The Dublin Review* (July 1937), in an article about Austin as 'a neglected poet', the couplet was written 'when the then Prince of Wales (he who afterwards became King Edward VII) had recovered from the attack of typhoid fever which had caused the gravest anxiety throughout the country, [and] the subject set for the Newdigate Prize Poem at Oxford was "The Prince of Wales's illness"; whereupon some wag, with consequences of which he never dreamed, produced the following couplet, as a specimen of the sort of thing that might be sent in by competitors for the coveted guerdon ... The name of the inventor of those immortal lines has not been handed down.'

4 Men of the Middle Ages, tomorrow sees the beginning of the Hundred Years' War.

Anonymous (screenwriter). Quoted by Chris Langham on BBC Radio *Quote ... Unquote* (5 June 1998), though in fact he reported the line of dialogue as lip-read from an actor in a silent epic. Probably apocryphal – indeed, it may be no more than a development of a joke ending for a play, as told by Max Beerbohm to his actor brother Herbert Beerbohm Tree and recorded in Hesketh Pearson, *Lives of the Wits* (1962): 'Herbert ... howled with laughter when Max suggested an effective line to bring the curtain down on a play, "Where are you going?" asks the sorrowful heroine. "I am going to the Thirty Years' War," answers the distraught hero.'

5 And from this chasm, with ceaseless turmoil seething,
As if this earth in fast thick pants were breathing,
A mighty fountain momently was forced.

Samuel Taylor Coleridge, English poet and critic (1772–1834). *Kubla Kahn* (1816). The 'fast thick pants' have occasioned much schoolboy laughter over the years. C.S.

Lewis evidently posed the question as to whether the pants were 'woollen or fur' (according to Ann Thwaite in *My Oxford*, 1977).

1 She felt them coming, but no power
Had she the words to smother;
And with a kind of shriek she cried,
'Oh Christ! you're like your mother.'

Samuel Taylor Coleridge. *Sybilline Leaves*, 'The Three Graves', Pt 4 (1817).

2 When she sang, he sat like one entranced. She touched his organ, and from that bright epoch, even it, the old companion of his happiest hours, incapable as he had thought of elevation, began a new and deified existence.

Charles Dickens, English novelist (1812–70). *Martin Chuzzlewit*, Chap. 24 (1843–4). A passage one feels Dickens might have felt the need to improve, if he were writing today. It is included in Edward Gathorne-Hardy, *An Adult's Garden of Bloomers* (1966).

3 I had cherished a profound conviction that her bringing me up by hand gave her no right to bring me up by jerks.

Charles Dickens. *Great Expectations*, Chap. 8 (1860–1). (Jerks = strokes with whip, lash.)

4 They had proceeded thus gropingly two or three miles further when on a sudden Clare became conscious of some vast erection in his front.

Thomas Hardy, English novelist and poet (1840–1928). *Tess of the D'Urbervilles*, Chap. 58 (1891). It was Stonehenge.

5 The chicken is a noble beast,
But the cow it is forlorner.
Standing in the pouring rain,
With a leg at every corner.

William McGonagall, Scottish poet (*c.* 1830–1902). Attributed.

6 When cares attack and life seems black,
How sweet it is to pot a yak …
A brief suspense, and then at last
The waiting o'er, the vigil past:
A careful aim. A spurt of flame.
It's done. You've pulled the trigger,
And one more gnu, so fair and frail,
Has handed in its dinner-pail:
(The females all are rather small,
The males are somewhat bigger.)

(Sir) P(elham) G. Wodehouse, English-born novelist and lyricist (1881–1975). 'Good Gnus' is an intentional literary lapse. The poem is written as though by 'Charlotte Mulliner' in the story 'Unpleasantness at Bludleigh Court' (1929). She is very put out when her poem is turned down by the *Animal Lovers' Gazette*.

7 And to the left, three yards beyond,
You see a little muddy pond,
Though but of compass small, and bare
To thirsty suns and parching air.
I've measured it from side to side;
'Tis three feet long, and two feet wide.

William Wordsworth, English poet (1770–1850). 'The Thorn' (original version – but not in the poem as it was published in 1798).

Literature

8 There was a time when I thought my only connection with the literary world would be that I had once delivered meat to T.S. Eliot's mother-in-law.

Alan Bennett, English playwright and actor (1934–). Quoted in *The Observer* (26 April 1992). Bennett's father was indeed a butcher and T.S. Eliot's second wife, Valerie Fletcher, came from the same town in Yorkshire. Bennett recounted this once more in the Introduction to his *Writing Home* (1994).

9 Literature is mostly about having sex and not much about having children. Life is the other way round.

David Lodge, English academic and novelist (1935–). *The British Museum is Falling Down* (1965).

10 Literature always anticipates life. It does not copy it, but moulds it to its purpose. The

nineteenth century, as we know it, is largely an invention of Balzac.

Oscar Wilde, Irish playwright, poet and wit (1854–1900). 'The Decay of Lying', in *Nineteenth Century* (January 1889).

Living (1)

1 The living are just the dead on holiday.

Maurice Maeterlinck, Belgian poet and playwright (1862–1949). Quoted in *The Treasury of Humorous Quotations*, eds Evan Esar & Nicolas Bentley (1951).

Living (2)

2 Earned a precarious living by taking in one another's washing.

Mark Twain, American writer (1835–1910). Attributed remark. In *The Commonweal* (6 August 1887) an article entitled 'Bourgeois Versus Socialist' signed by William Morris ends: 'A bourgeois paradise will supervene, in which everyone will be free to exploit – but there will be no one to exploit ... On the whole, one must suppose that the type of it would be that town (surely in America and in the neighbourhood of Mark Twain) that I have heard of, whose inhabitants lived by taking in each other's washing.' Compare what Robert Graves says in the Preface to his *Collected Poems 1938–1945*: 'The moral of the Scilly Islanders who earned a precarious livelihood by taking in one another's washing is that they never upset their carefully balanced island economy by trying to horn into the laundry trade of the mainland; and that nowhere in the Western Hemisphere was washing so well done.'

Lloyd George, David (1st Earl Lloyd George of Dywfor)

BRITISH PRIME MINISTER (1863–1945)

3 Lloyd George knew my father,
My father knew Lloyd George.

Anonymous, sung to the tune of 'Onward Christian Soldiers'. Known before Lloyd George's death in 1945. In Welsh legal and Liberal circles the credit for the coinage has been given to Tommy Rhys Roberts QC (1910–75), whose father did indeed know Lloyd George.

4 He couldn't see a belt without hitting below it.

Margot Asquith (Countess of Oxford and Asquith) (1864–1945). Quoted in Mark Bonham Carter's Introduction to *The Autobiography of Margot Asquith* (1962 edn).

5 He did not care which direction the car was travelling, so long as he was in the driver's seat.

1st Baron Beaverbrook (Maxwell Aitken), Canadian-born English politician and newspaper proprietor (1879–1964). *The Decline and Fall of Lloyd George* (1963).

6 Mr Lloyd George spoke for a hundred and seventeen minutes, in which period he was detected only once in the use of an argument.

Arnold Bennett, English novelist (1867–1931). *Things That Have Interested Me*, 'After the March Offensive' (1921–25).

7 *Ah, si je pouvais pisser comme il parle!* [If I could piss the way he speaks!]

George Clemenceau, French Prime Minister (1841–1929). Quoted in A. Andrews, *Quotations for Speakers and Writers* (1969).

8 When he's alone in a room, there's nobody there.

John Maynard Keynes, English economist (1883–1946). Quoted by Baroness Asquith in BBC TV *As I Remember* (30 April 1967). However, James Agate in *Ego 5* (for 30 September 1941): 'Sat next to Lady Oxford, who was in great form ... "Lloyd George? There is no Lloyd George. There is a marvellous brain; but if you were to shut him in a room and look through the keyhole there would be nobody there".'

Lobotomies

9 I'd rather have a full bottle in front of me than a full frontal lobotomy.

Anonymous (graffito). From Leicester University. Contributed to BBC Radio *Quote ... Unquote* (19 February 1979) by Bob Baker.

Longevity

Asked, on her eightieth birthday (13 January 1964), the secret of longevity:

1 Keep breathing.

Sophie Tucker, Russian-born American entertainer (1884–1966). Quoted in *The Home Book of Humorous Quotations*, ed. A.K. Adams (1969).

Looks (1)

Of a certain actress not noted for her looks:

2 If she played Lady Godiva, the horse would have stolen the show.

Anonymous. Quoted in *The Penguin Dictionary of Modern Quotations*, eds J.M. & M.J. Cohen (1971).

When a proud mother said her baby looked like him:

3 Madam, all babies look like me.

(Sir) Winston S. Churchill, British Conservative Prime Minister and writer (1874–1965). Quoted in *Book of the Month Club News* (April 1954).

On Ian Mikardo MP:

4 He's not as nice as he looks.

(Sir) Winston S. Churchill. Quoted by Richard Boston on BBC Radio *Quote ... Unquote* (4 January 1976). Said to have been spoken to Christopher Soames, Churchill's PPS. According to Matthew Parris, *Scorn* (1994): 'Sir Edward Heath told us that this remark was made after a debate in the House of Commons in which Mr Mikardo "pressed the Prime Minister about anti-Semitic practices at the Mid-Ocean Club, Bermuda, somewhat to the irritation of the Prime Minister".' Perhaps it should be explained that Mr Mikardo was no oil painting, as the saying has it.

Looks (2)

5 He gave her a look that you could have poured on a waffle.

Ring Lardner, American humorist and writer (1885–1933). Quoted in *The Treasury of Humorous Quotations*, eds Evan Esar & Nicolas Bentley (1951).

Referring to President Taft:

6 He looked at me as if I was a side dish he hadn't ordered.

Ring Lardner. Quoted in the same book as above.

Lord Privy Seal

7 It has been said that this minister is neither a Lord, nor a privy, nor a seal.

Sydney D. Bailey, English writer (1916–). *British Parliamentary Democracy* (3rd edn, 1971). However, this was not an original observation and had already been made on BBC TV's *The Frost Report* (1966–7). It was possibly inspired by Voltaire's joke that the Holy Roman Empire was neither holy, nor Roman, nor an empire (*Essai sur l'histoire générale et sur les moeurs et l'esprit des nations*, 1756). By the late 1960s there was also an observation current that the YMCA was joined by those who were neither young, male nor Christian.

Lords

8 It is always said that an Englishman loves a lord. It would be more exact to say that he is in love with lordliness.

Anonymous. Quoted in *The Spectator* (3 July 1908).

See also HOUSE OF LORDS.

Los Angeles

9 I don't want to live in a city where the only cultural advantage is that you can make a right turn on a red light.

Line from film *Annie Hall* (US 1977). Screenwriters: Woody Allen, Marshall Brickman. Spoken by Woody Allen (Alvy).

10 They don't throw their garbage away. They make it into television shows.

Line from same film. Spoken by Woody Allen (Alvy).

11 A big hard-boiled city with no more personality than a paper cup.

Raymond Chandler, American novelist (1888–1959). *The Little Sister* (1949).

1 The difference between Los Angeles and yogurt is that yogurt has real culture.

Tom Taussik, American humorist. *Legless in Gaza*.

See also HOLLYWOOD.

Losers

2 Show me a good loser and I'll show you a loser.

Anonymous. Variously attributed, e.g. to Knute Rockne, as in Jerry Brondfield, *Rockne* (1976).

Loss

3 Losing one glove is sorrow enough
But nothing compared with the pain
Of losing one glove
Discarding the other
Then finding the first one again.

Piet Hein, Danish poet, designer and inventor (1905–96). Translation of one of his aphoristic 'Grooks', though as Hein lived from 1969 to 1976 in Britain, it may have been written in English originally.

Love

4 *'Lisa:*
Wot's it feel like bein' in love. Kytie?
Katie:
Ow, it's prime, 'Liza. It's like 'avin 'ot treacle runnin' daown yer back!

Anonymous (cartoonist). Cartoon caption in *Punch* (25 January 1899).

Promotional slogan for the film The Abominable Dr Phibes *(UK, 1971):*

5 Love means never having to say you're ugly.

Anonymous. Quoted in John Robert Colombo, *The Wit and Wisdom of the Movie Makers* (1979).

6 Love – the delightful interval between meeting a beautiful girl and discovering that she looks like a haddock.

John Barrymore, American actor (1882–1942). Quoted in *The Treasury of Humorous Quotations*, eds Evan Esar & Nicolas Bentley (1951).

7 I do not love thee, Dr Fell.
The reason why I cannot tell;
But this I know, and know full well,
I do not love thee, Dr Fell.

Thomas Brown, English satirist (1663–1704). On the Dean of Christ Church, Oxford, when Brown was an undergraduate at the college. Based on an epigram of Martial's, which translates as: 'I do not love you, Sabidius, and I cannot say why: this only I can say, I do not love you.'

8 'Tis better to have loved and lost than never to have lost at all.

Samuel Butler, English author (1835–1902). *The Way of All Flesh*, Chap. 77 (1903).

9 Love and a cottage! Eh, Fanny! Ah, give me indifference and a coach and six!

George Colman (the Elder), English playwright (1732–94). *The Clandestine Marriage*, Act 1 (1766).

10 See how love and murder will out.

William Congreve, English playwright (1670–1729). *The Double Dealer*, Act 4, Sc. 2 (1694). The proverb 'murder will out' (i.e. will be found out, will reveal itself) goes back at least to 1325, and 'truth will out' to 1439. Later, Hannah Cowley in *The Belle's Stratagem*, Act 1, Sc. 4 (1782) has: 'Vanity, like murder, will out.'

11 Running after women never hurt anybody – it's catching 'em that does the damage.

Jack Davies, English screenwriter and critic (1913–94). Quoted in *The Treasury of Humorous Quotations*, eds Evan Esar & Nicolas Bentley (1951).

12 When love congeals
It soon reveals
The faint aroma of performing seals,
The double-crossing of a pair of heels.

Lorenz Hart, American lyricist (1895–1943). Song, 'I Wish I Were in Love Again' from *Babes in Arms* (1937).

13 Love is like the measles; we all have to go through it.

Jerome K. Jerome, English writer (1859–1927). *Idle Thoughts of an Idle Fellow* (1886).

1 Love's like the measles – all the worse when it comes late in life.

Douglas Jerrold, English writer (1803–57). *The Wit and Opinions of Douglas Jerrold*, 'Love' (1859).

2 I loved Kirk so much, I would have skied down Mount Everest in the nude with a carnation up my nose.

Joyce McKinney, American beauty queen (1950–). A former Miss Wyoming, McKinney was charged in an English court with kidnapping Kirk Anderson, a Mormon missionary, who was her ex-lover. She allegedly abducted Mr Anderson to a remote country cottage where he was chained to a bed and forced to make love to her. In Epsom Magistrates' Court (6 December 1977) McKinney told a stunned jury of her feelings on the matter.

To woman appearing on quiz show whose justification for bearing 22 children was, 'I love my husband':

3 I like my cigar, too, but I take it out once in a while.

Groucho Marx, American comedian (1895–1977). Quoted in Dorothy Herrman, *With Malice Toward All* (1982). History suggests that this was cut from the broadcast – which was *probably* on his radio and TV quiz show *You Bet Your Life?* This ran from 1947 to 1961 (and also ran in London, disastrously, for a season as plain *Groucho*). A story is also told of another quiz show host – perhaps Jackie Gleason? – who, confronted with a similarly prolific mother, asked her why she had so many children. She replied, 'I guess there must be something in the air back home in Montana', to which he replied, 'Your legs, by the sound of it.'

4 It is better to have loved a short man, than never to have loved a tall.

Miles Kington, English humorist (1941–). A 'cod' Albanian proverb, in *The Independent* (27 December 1991).

5 It is difficult to love mankind unless one has a reasonable private income and when one has a reasonable private income one has better things to do than loving mankind.

Hugh Kingsmill, English writer (1889–1949). Quoted in Richard Ingrams, *God's Apology* (1977).

6 Love is not the dying moan of a distant violin – it is the triumphant twang of a bedspring.

S.J. Perelman, American writer (1904–79). Quoted in Fred Metcalf, *The Penguin Dictionary of Modern Humorous Quotations* (1987).

7 I picked a lemon in the garden of love
Where I thought only roses bloom.

M.E. Rourke, American songwriter (1867–1933). Said in reference to an unloved wife. From the song 'A Lemon in the Garden of Love', with music by Richard Carle, dating from 1906 when it was sung in the New York production of *The Spring Chicken*. This comic number of romantic misjudgement was reprised in the 1940 film *Ma! He's Making Eyes at Me*, which starred Constance Moore and Tom Brown. There may also have been a parody entitled 'I Picked a Pansy in the Garden of Love', which Sophie Tucker sang in London around 1925.

8 If love is the answer could you rephrase the question?

Lily Tomlin, American actress (1939–). Quoted in Barbara Rowes, *The Book of Quotes* (1979).

9 Men always want to be a woman's first love. We women have a more subtle instinct about things. What we like is to be a man's last romance.

Oscar Wilde, Irish playwright, poet and wit (1854–1900). *A Woman of No Importance*, Act 2 (1893).

10 Woman begins by resisting a man's advances and ends by blocking his retreat.

Oscar Wilde. Quoted in *The Treasury of Humorous Quotations*, eds Evan Esar & Nicolas Bentley (1951).

Love-making

11 Mrs Laye … told a good thing of a very old man on his dying bed giving advice to a youngster: 'I've had a long life, and it's been a merry one. Take my advice. Make love to every pretty woman you meet. And remember, if you get 5 per cent on your outlay it's a good return.'

Arnold Bennett, English novelist (1867–1931). Diary entry for 24 May 1904, published in *The Journals* (1971). *The Treasury of Humorous Quotations*, eds Evan Esar & Nicolas Bentley (1951), has this as though said by Bennett himself, in the form: 'Make love to every woman you meet; if you get five per cent on your outlay, it's a good investment.'

1 The only way to behave to a woman is to make love to her, if she is pretty, and to someone else, if she is plain.

Oscar Wilde, Irish playwright, poet and wit (1854–1900). *The Importance of Being Earnest*, Act 1 (1895).

Loyalty

Of a politician:

2 T.T. Claypoole has all the characteristics of a dog except loyalty.

Line from film *The Best Man* (US 1964). Screenwriter: Gore Vidal (from his play). Spoken by Henry Fonda (William Russell). Said to be after a remark by Alamo hero Sam Houston. Also, about a colleague, by Senator Thomas P. Gore – quoted in George E. Allen, *Presidents Who Have Known Me* (1950).

3 When you are down and out, something always turns up – and it is usually the noses of your friends.

Orson Welles, American film director, writer and actor (1915–85). Quoted in *The New York Times* (1 April 1962).

Luck

4 Throw a lucky man into the sea and he will come up with a fish in his mouth.

Anonymous (Arab proverb).

5 Just my luck! If I had been born a hatter, little boys would have come into the world without heads.

Edward Bulwer-Lytton (1st Baron Lytton), English novelist, playwright and politician (1803–73). *Money*, Act 2 (1840).

Lyrics

6 I could eat alphabet soup and *shit* better lyrics.

Johnny Mercer, American lyricist (1909–76). Attributed remark. On seeing a British musical (1975), possibly *Jeeves* – lyrics by Alan Ayckbourn (after Tim Rice had withdrawn from the production), music by Andrew Lloyd Webber.

Macaulay, Thomas Babington (Lord Macaulay)

ENGLISH HISTORIAN, POET AND POLITICIAN (1800–59)

1 Macaulay is well for a while, but one wouldn't *live* under Niagara.

Thomas Carlyle, Scottish historian and philosopher (1795–1881). Quoted in Richard Monckton Milnes, *Notebook* (1838).

2 He was a most disagreeable companion to my fancy ... His conversation was a procession of one.

Florence Nightingale, English nurse (1820–1910). In letter, quoted in Cecil Woodham-Smith, *Florence Nightingale* (1950).

3 [Macaulay's] enemies might perhaps have said before (though I never did so) that he talked rather too much; but now he has occasional flashes of silence, that make his conversation perfectly delightful.

(Revd) Sydney Smith, English clergyman, essayist and wit (1771–1845). Quoted in Lady Holland, *A Memoir of Sydney Smith* (1855). Harriet Martineau recalled Smith's remark as, 'Macaulay improves. I have observed in him, of late, flashes of silence.'

4 There is no limit to Macaulay's knowledge, on small subjects as well as great – he is like a book in breeches.

(Revd) Sydney Smith. Quoted in the same book as above.

5 Literature is [Macaulay's] vocation. Nothing would do him more good than a course of the Waters of Lethe; if he could forget half of what he reads he would be less suffocating than he is.

(Revd) Sydney Smith. In letter (1841).

6 He not only overflowed with learning, but stood in the slop.

(Revd) Sydney Smith. Quoted by Peter Quennell in the *New Statesman* (25 August 1934).

MacDonald, Ramsay

BRITISH LABOUR PRIME MINISTER (1866–1937)

7 He died as he lived – at sea.

Anonymous. Quoted in Atyeo & Green, *Don't Quote Me* (1981). He died during a cruise. However, Hesketh Pearson, *Lives of the Wits* (1962), has this: 'Whistler had an unforgiving nature, and on hearing some years later that [William Stott, a disciple] had expired during an ocean voyage he merely remarked: "So he died at sea, where he always was".'

8 [At Barnum's Circus] the exhibit on the programme I most desired to see was the one described as the Boneless Wonder. My parents judged that the spectacle would be too revolting and demoralizing for my youthful eyes, and I have waited fifty years to see the boneless wonder sitting on the Treasury bench.

(Sir) Winston S. Churchill, British Conservative Prime

Minister and writer (1874–1965). Speech, House of Commons (28 January 1931).

1 He has, more than any other man, the gift of compressing the largest amount of words into the smallest amount of thought.

(Sir) Winston S. Churchill. Speech, House of Commons (23 March 1933).

Madness

2 A visitor inquired as to what was the problem with a certain patient in a mental institution. 'Ah,' came the reply, 'he thinks he is a poached egg and spends his days seeking a suitable piece of toast upon which to sit.'

Anonymous (cartoonist). Caption to cartoon in *Punch*, Vol. 122 (1902). Compare the music-hall song 'Slowly But Surely', words and music by James Godden (1911), which contains the verse:
Strolling one day in a garden fair
At an asylum (I visited there),
I rested awhile underneath a tree
When a man quite excited made straight for me,
Slowly but surely towards me he came,
'Hast thou some toast?' he began to exclaim,
'I must find some toast,' said he with a frown,
'For I'm a poached egg and I want to sit down.'

Replying to the Duke of Newcastle who had said that General Wolfe was a madman:

3 Mad is he? Then I hope he will *bite* some of my other generals.

George II, British King (1683–1760). Quoted in Henry Beckles Wilson, *The Life and Letters of James Wolfe* (1909).

4 *Hamlet:*
Ay, marry. Why was he sent into England?
Gravedigger:
Why, because a was mad. A shall recover his wits there. Or if a do not, 'tis no great matter there.

William Shakespeare, English playwright and poet (1564–1616). *Hamlet*, V.i.145 (1600–1).

5 Those comfortably padded lunatic asylums which are known, euphemistically, as the stately homes of England.

Virginia Woolf, English novelist and critic (1882–1941). *The Common Reader*, 'Lady Dorothy Nevill' (1925).

Maiden speeches

To A.P. Herbert (1935):

6 Call that a maiden speech? It was a brazen hussy of a speech. Never did such a painted lady of a speech parade itself before a modest parliament.

(Sir) Winston S. Churchill, British Conservative Prime Minister and writer (1874–1965). Quoted in A.P. Herbert, *Independent Member* (1950).

Mail

7 Hate mail is the only kind of letter that never gets lost by the Post Office.

Philip Kerr, English novelist (1956–). *Dead Meat* (1993).

Make-up

8 Most women are not so young as they are painted.

(Sir) Max Beerbohm, English writer and caricaturist (1872–1956). In *The Yellow Book* (1894).

9 She had a beautiful complexion when she first came, but it faded out by degrees in an unaccountable way. However, it is not lost for good. I found the most of it on my shoulder afterwards.

Mark Twain, American writer (1835–1910). *Sketches New and Old* (1899).

Malapropisms

10 My son, the world is your lobster.

Leon Griffiths, English TV playwright (1928–92). In TV series *Minder*, quoted in *The Guardian* (16 June 1992). Compare: 'Of her son, taking his finals before embarking on an international job, a cousin of mine said: "Of course, if he does well in them, the world is his lobster"' – contributed to BBC Radio *Quote... Unquote* (21 August 1980) by A.M.D. Carrier, London SW7.

1 He's so poor – he hasn't got a rag to stand on.

Linley Sambourne, English cartoonist and illustrator, principally for *Punch* (1844–1910). Quoted in literature on display at the 'Linley Sambourne House' in Kensington, which is preserved by the Victorian Society and open to visitors.

2 There was such a silence afterwards that you could have picked up a pin in it.

Linley Sambourne. From the same.

3 You're digging nails in your coffin with every stroke of your tongue.

Linley Sambourne. From the same.

4 I don't care for Lady Macbeth in the street-walking scene.

Linley Sambourne. Quoted in R.G.G. Price, *A History of Punch* (1957).

5 Illiterate him, I say, quite from your memory.

Richard Brinsley Sheridan, English dramatist and politician (1751–1816). *The Rivals*, Act 1, Sc. 2 (1775). Mrs Malaprop speaking – after whom 'malapropisms' are called. 'Her select words [are] so ingeniously *misapplied*, without being *mispronounced*' (Act 2, Sc. 2). She was not the first character to have such an entertaining affliction: Shakespeare's Dogberry and Mistress Quickly are similarly troubled. After the French phrase *mal à propos* ('awkward, inopportune').

6 A progeny of learning.

Richard Brinsley Sheridan. From the same play and act.

7 He is the very pineapple of politeness!

Richard Brinsley Sheridan. From the same play, Act 3, Sc. 3. In this instance, she is attempting to say 'the very pinnacle of politeness'.

8 If I reprehend any thing in this world, it is the use of my oracular tongue, and a nice derangement of epitaphs!

Richard Brinsley Sheridan. From the same play and scene. Hence, *A Nice Derangement of Epitaphs*, title of a novel (1988) by Ellis Peters, about a medieval monk detective, Father Cadfael.

9 She's as headstrong as an allegory on the banks of the Nile.

Richard Brinsley Sheridan. From the same play and scene.

10 It is no further from the north coast of Spitsbergen to the North Pole than it is from Land's End to John of Gaunt.

(Revd) William Spooner, English clergyman and academic (1844–1930). A malapropism spoken to Julian Huxley and recalled by him in *SEAC* (Calcutta) (27 February 1944). Also quoted in William Hayter, *Spooner* (1977).

11 Poor soul – very sad; her late husband, you know, a very sad death – eaten by missionaries – poor soul!

(Revd) William Spooner. A further malapropism, demonstrating that Spooner's talent did not just lie with Spoonerisms.

Malignancy

When Randolph Churchill went into hospital to have a lung removed and the trouble was found to be non-malignant:

12 A typical triumph of modern science to find the only part of Randolph that was not malignant and remove it.

Evelyn Waugh, English novelist (1903–66). *The Diaries of Evelyn Waugh* (entry for March 1964).

Man

13 If they can put a man on the moon, why don't they put them all there?

Anonymous (graffito). Contributed by Ann Osborne to BBC Radio *Quote … Unquote* (March 1998). From London.

14 Man is the only animal that eats when he is not hungry, drinks when he is not thirsty, and makes love at all seasons.

Anonymous.

15 Man is the only animal that can remain on friendly terms with the victims he intends to eat until he eats them.

Samuel Butler, English novelist and writer (1835–1902). Quoted in *Samuel Butler's Notebooks,* eds Keynes & Hill (1951).

1 *Cada uno es como Dios le hizo, y aun peor muchas veces* [Every man is as God made him, and often even worse].

Miguel de Cervantes, Spanish novelist (1547–1616). *Don Quixote,* Pt 2, Chap. 4. (1615). Sancho Panza's comment.

2 *Gil:*
Are you a man or a mouse?
Hackenbush:
You put a piece of cheese down there and you'll find out.

Lines from film *A Day at the Races* (US 1937). Screenwriters: Robert Pirosh, George Seaton, George Oppenheimer. Spoken by Allan Jones (Gil) and Groucho Marx (Dr Hackenbush). This challenge to a man has been proverbial since 1541.

3 There was a young man who said, 'Damn!
At last I've found out who I am:
A creature that moves
In determinate grooves,
In fact not a bus but a tram.'

Maurice Evan Hare, English writer (1886–67). 'Limerick' (1905).

4 Man is the only animal that laughs and weeps; for he is the only animal that is struck with the difference between what things are, and what they ought to be.

William Hazlitt, English essayist (1778–1830). Attributed remark.

5 Man is the only animal that blushes. Or needs to.

Mark Twain, American writer (1835–1910). *Following the Equator* (1897).

6 Man was made at the end of a week's work when God was tired.

Mark Twain. Quoted in A.B. Paine, *Mark Twain: A Biography* (1912).

Manchester (England)

7 The shortest way out of Manchester is notoriously a bottle of Gordon's gin.

William Bolitho, English writer (1890–1930). *Twelve Against the Gods,* 'Caliogstro and Seraphina' (1930). However, *The Times* (21 June 1921) was writing: 'Certainly if drink, in the proverbial saying, has proved on occasion "the shortest way out of Manchester ... "' – evidence of some earlier source.

On living in Manchester, to the husband in a divorce case:

8 A totally incomprehensible choice for any free human being to make.

(Sir) Melford Stevenson, English judge (1902–87). Quoted in *The Daily Telegraph* (11 April 1979).

9 I looked out of the train window and all I could see was rain and fog. 'I know I'm going to love Manchester,' I told Jim, 'if I can only see it.'

Mae West, American vaudeville and film actress (1893–1980). *Goodness Had Nothing To Do With It,* Chap. 19 (1959).

Manners

On going into a bathroom and finding his hostess in the bath:

10 I beg your pardon, *sir!*

Anonymous – traditionally given as the correct thing to say in this situation. Compare John Michaelhouse (a pen name of the Revd Joseph McCulloch), *Charming Manners* (1932): in the story, a group of Oxford undergraduates happen upon half-a-dozen naked nymphs dancing in the sunlight on the banks of the River Cherwell. 'We all collapsed in the punt at once, there being no chance of saying, "Sorry, gentlemen" in the approved style.'

In François Truffaut's film *Baisers Volés* (1968), the character played by Delphine Seyrig says that she was taught the difference between tact and politeness – if a man surprises a naked lady in the bathroom, politeness is to say 'Sorry', tact is to say, 'Sorry, *sir.*'

The boot is on the other foot, so to speak, in a glancing comment in E.M. Forster's *A Room with a View* (1908): 'Mr Beebe [the clergyman] was not able to tell the ladies of his adventure at Modena, where the chambermaid burst in upon him in his bath, exclaiming cheerfully, "*Fa niente, sono vecchia*" [It doesn't matter, I'm an old woman].'

1 A gentleman always gives up his seat to a lady in a public convenience.

Anonymous (platoon sergeant). Quoted in Gerald Kersh, *They Die With Their Boots Clean* (1941) – a record of his experiences in the Guards. Some young soldiers were being given a homily by their platoon sergeant on the subject of 'public duties' – that is, how they should behave when they were out of the barracks and moving about among civilians. He volunteered what would otherwise seem to be a music-hall joke.

2 I eat my peas with honey,
I've done it all my life.
It makes the peas taste funny
But it keeps 'em on the knife!

Anonymous. Known by the early 1950s and included in *Verse and Worse*, ed. Arnold Silcock (1958 edn).

One of Berners's acquaintances had the impertinent habit of saying to him, 'I've been sticking up for you.' He repeated this once too often and Berners replied:

3 Yes, and I have been sticking up for you. Someone said you aren't fit to live with pigs and I said you were.

Lord (Gerald) Berners, English writer, composer, painter and eccentric (1883–1950). Quoted in Edith Sitwell, *Taken Care Of* (1965). Compare the caption to a cartoon by A. Wallis Mills in *Punch* (28 June 1905): '*Lady A.* "HERE COMES THAT DREADFUL MAN WHO SAT NEXT TO ME AT DINNER. HE HASN'T THE MANNERS OF A PIG!" *Mrs B.* "HOW FUNNY! I THOUGHT HE *HAD!*"'

4 I don't mind if you don't like my manners. I don't like them myself. They're pretty bad. I grieve over them long winter evenings.

Line from film *The Big Sleep* (US 1946). Screenwriters: William Faulkner and others (from Raymond Chandler novel). Spoken by Humphrey Bogart (Philip Marlowe).

5 I don't recall your name, but your manners are familiar.

Oliver Herford, American humorist (1863–1935). Quoted in *The Treasury of Humorous Quotations*, eds Evan Esar & Nicolas Bentley (1951).

See also ETIQUETTE.

Manuscripts

6 Manuscript: something submitted in haste and returned at leisure.

Oliver Herford, American humorist (1863–1935). Quoted in *The Treasury of Humorous Quotations*, eds Evan Esar & Nicolas Bentley (1951).

Marginal comments

In the margin of a medieval manuscript:

7• *Nunc scripsi totum, pro Christo da mihi potum* [I have now written everything, for the sake of Christ give me a drink].

Anonymous. Quoted in the *Blue Guide Belgium and Luxembourg*, Preface (8th edition, 1993). It has been claimed that the comment may have appeared in the margins of the Domesday Book or in the Little Domesday (a set of working notes). In the University of Durham Library there is a medieval manuscript (Ms Cosin V.III.11 Recipes, etc.), dating from about 1435–56, which contains this: 'To make Frumente. Tak clene whete & braye yt wel ... For to claryfyen hony ... tak of e whye with a sklyse. Nunc scripsi totum pro cristo da mihi potum.' Some would suggest that this was a fairly common signing-off phrase to mark the end of the day's work.

In a routine letter to the Foreign Office, the British Minister in Athens reported that the monks in some of the monasteries in northern Greece had allegedly violated their monastic vows. Unfortunately, due to a typing error, 'cows' appeared in the letter instead of 'vows'. On receiving this report, the Foreign Secretary pencilled a note in the margin:

8 Appears to be a case for a Papal Bull.

Arthur Balfour (1st Earl Balfour), British Conservative Prime Minister (1848–1930). Quoted on BBC Radio *Quote ... Unquote* (5 June 1979). In Lewis Broad, *Sir Anthony Eden* (1955), the marginal comment is said to have been written by Lord Curzon.

Marriage

To Lord Snowdon on the break-up of his marriage to Princess Margaret:

9 Your experience will be a lesson to all of us

men to be careful not to marry ladies in very high positions.

Idi Amin, Ugandan soldier and President (1925–). Quoted in Barbara Rowes, *The Book of Quotes* (1979).

1 WORTHY OF ATTENTION. ADVICE TO PERSONS ABOUT TO MARRY, – Don't.

Anonymous. *Punch*, Vol. 8 (1845). What is probably the most famous of all *Punch* jokes appeared on the January page of the 1845 *Almanack*. R.G.G. Price, in his history of the magazine, wonders whether it is perhaps 'the most famous joke ever made' and remarks that 'it needs an effort to realise how neat, ingenious and profound it must have seemed at the time'. It was based on an advertisement put out by a house furnisher of the day and was probably contributed by Henry Mayhew, better known for his serious surveys of *London Labour and the London Poor*, though others also claimed to have thought of it. At about this period *Punch* also ran other jokes obviously based on the same advert – 'To persons about to marry ….', 'Persons about to marry should … ' etc.

2 All marriages are happy. It's the living together afterward that causes all the trouble.

Anonymous. Quoted in *Farmer's Almanac* (1966).

3 All men are born free, but some get married.

Anonymous. Quoted in Herbert V. Prochnow, Snr & Jnr, *A Treasury of Humorous Quotations* (1969).

Law student (in viva voce *examination) when asked what was necessary to render a marriage valid in Scotland:*

4 For a marriage to be valid in Scotland it is absolutely necessary that it should be consummated in the presence of two policemen.

Anonymous. Quoted in *Samuel Butler's Notebooks* (towards the end of the period 1874–1902).

5 Marriage is a wonderful institution – but who wants to live in an institution?

Anonymous (graffito). Included in my book *Graffiti 2* (1980).

Conversation heard at a Hollywood wedding reception:

6 'What are you giving the bride and groom?' Reply: 'Oh, about three months.'

Anonymous. Quoted by Rula Lenska on BBC Radio *Quote … Unquote* (16 February 1982).

7 He was reputed one of the wise men that made answer to the question when a man should marry? 'A young man not yet, an elder man not at all.'

Francis Bacon (1st Baron Verulam and Viscount St Albans), English philosopher and politician (1561–1626). *Essays*, 'Of Marriage and Single Life' (1625).

In answer to question, Is it true that married people live longer?:

8 No, it just seems longer.

Line from film *The Bank Dick* (US 1940). Screenwriter: Mahatma Kane Jeeves (W.C. Fields). Spoken by W.C. Fields (Egbert Sousè) (*sic*).

Of marriage:

9 I'm not going to make the same mistake once.

Warren Beatty, American actor and director (1937–). Quoted in Bob Chieger, *Was It Good For You Too?* (1983). In fact, this is a line from *North West Mounted Police* (US 1940), in which Texas Ranger Gary Cooper says to Madeleine Carroll, 'I've always held that a bachelor is a feller who never made the same mistake once.' Ed Wynn is also credited with, 'Bachelor – A man who never makes the same mistake once' – quoted in *The Home Book of Humorous Quotations*, ed. A.K. Adams (1969). Beatty eventually relented.

10 Marriage: the state of condition of a community consisting of a master, a mistress, and two slaves, making, in all, two.

Ambrose Bierce, American journalist (1842–?1914). *The Cynic's Word Book* (later retitled *The Devil's Dictionary*) (1906).

11 'Are you married, Mr Willoughby?' asked the wife of the Vice-Chancellor … 'I don't

suppose he believes in it,' said the Vice-Chancellor in disgruntled tones. 'Well, why buy the cow,' asked Willoughby reasonably, 'when you can steal milk through the fence?'

(Sir) Malcolm Bradbury, English academic and novelist (1932–2000). *Eating People Is Wrong*, Chap. 8 (1959). Using an established phrase.

1 It was very good of God to let Carlyle and Mrs Carlyle marry one another and so make only two people miserable instead of four, besides being very amusing.

Samuel Butler, English author (1835–1902). Letter to Miss E.M.A. Savage (21 November 1884). As part of their long correspondence, Miss Savage had written to Butler on 18 November: 'Are you not glad that Mr and Mrs Carlyle were married to one another, and not to other people? They certainly were justly formed to meet by nature.' In my very first quotation book I mistakenly attributed to Tennyson this view on the marriage of Thomas and Jane Carlyle. When it was suggested that the marriage had been a mistake – because with anyone but each other they might have been perfectly happy – I said that Tennyson had opined: 'I totally disagree with you. By any other arrangement *four* people would have been unhappy instead of *two*.' The remark should have been credited to Butler. My inaccurate version was taken up by *The Faber Book of Anecdotes* (1985). However, I now know why I made the misattribution. In *The Autobiography of Margot Asquith* (1936) she recounts a meeting with Tennyson at which they discussed the Carlyles. She said, 'With anyone but each other, they might have been perfectly happy.' He said: 'I totally disagree with you. By any other arrangement four people would have been unhappy instead of two.' This exchange occurred in 1885 (if Margot Asquith was not inventing the whole episode), which is very close to the year of Butler's letter. In the end, perhaps one might allow that both men independently had the same bright view.

2 Greater luck hath no man than this, that he lay down his wife at the right moment.

Samuel Butler. *Notebooks* (1912) – for *c.* 1890.

3 Marriage is distinctly and repeatedly excluded from heaven. Is this because it is thought likely to mar the general felicity?

Samuel Butler. In the same work as above.

4 Still I can't contradict, what so oft has
been said,
'Though women are angels, yet wedlock's
the devil.'

Lord Byron, English poet (1788–1824). 'To Eliza' (1806).

5 All tragedies are finish'd by death,
All comedies are ended by a marriage.

Lord Byron. *Don Juan*, Canto 3, St. 9 (1819–24).

6 I shall marry in haste and repeat at leisure.

James Branch Cabell, American novelist (1879–1958). *Jurgen*, Chap. 38 (1919).

7 The deep, deep peace of the double-bed after the hurly-burly of the chaise longue.

Mrs Patrick Campbell, English actress (1865–1940). Quoted in Alexander Woollcott, *While Rome Burns*, 'The First Mrs Tanqueray' (1934).

8 A man and woman marry because both of them don't know what to do with themselves.

Anton Chekhov, Russian playwright (1860–1904). Quoted in *The Treasury of Humorous Quotations*, eds Evan Esar & Nicolas Bentley (1951).

9 Marriage is a feast where the grace is sometimes better than the dinner.

Charles Caleb Colton, English clergyman and writer (1780–1832). Quoted in *The Treasury of Humorous Quotations*, eds Evan Esar & Nicolas Bentley (1951).

10 Marriage is a wonderful invention; but, then again, so is a bicycle repair kit.

Billy Connolly, Scottish comedian (1942–). Quoted in Duncan Campbell, *Billy Connolly, the Authorised Version* (1976).

11 She married in haste and repented at Brixton.

(Sir) Noël Coward, English entertainer and writer (1899–1973). Quoted in *Noël Coward: A Life in Quotes*, ed. Barry Day (1999), as a 'line of unused dialogue (*c.* 1918)'.

1 I've sometimes thought of marrying – and then I've thought again.

(Sir) Noël Coward, English entertainer and writer (1899–1973). Quoted by Ward Morehouse in 'Dear Noel on Love and Marriage' in *Theatre Arts* Magazine (November 1956).

2 Marriage isn't a word … it's a sentence!

Line/screen title from silent film *The Crowd* (US 1928). Screenwriter/director: King Vidor.

3 Wedlock, indeed, hath oft compared been
To public feasts where meet a public rout,
Where they that are without would fain go in
And they that are within would fain go out.

(Sir) John Davies, English poet (1569–1626). 'A Contention Betwixt a Wife, a Widow, and a Maid for Precedence' (1608). Compare Montaigne below.

4 Never go to bed mad. Stay up and fight.

Phyllis Diller, American comic performer (1917–). *Phyllis Diller's Housekeeping Hints*.

5 I have always thought that every woman should marry, and no man.

Benjamin Disraeli (1st Earl of Beaconsfield), British Conservative Prime Minister and writer (1804–81). *Lothair*, Chap. 30 (1830).

6 One fool at least in every married couple.

Henry Fielding, English novelist and judge (1707–54). *Amelia*, Bk 9, Chap. 4 (1751).

7 Keep your eyes wide open before marriage, half shut afterwards.

Benjamin Franklin, American politician and scientist (1706–90). *Poor Richard's Almanack* (June 1738) – a work in which Franklin often revised already existing sayings.

8 It's a funny thing that when a man hasn't got anything on earth to worry about, he goes off and gets married.

Robert Frost, American poet (1874–1963). Quoted in *The Treasury of Humorous Quotations*, eds Evan Esar & Nicolas Bentley (1951).

9 A man in love is incomplete until he has married. Then he's finished.

Zsa Zsa Gabor, Hungarian-born film actress (1919–). Quoted in *Newsweek* Magazine (28 March 1960).

10 How To Be Happy Though Married.

(Revd) E.J. Hardy, Irish army chaplain and writer (1849–1920). Title of book (1885).

11 They say a parson first invented gunpowder, but one cannot believe it till one is married.

Douglas Jerrold, English humorist and editor (1803–57). Quoted in *The Treasury of Humorous Quotations*, eds Evan Esar & Nicolas Bentley (1951).

12 Marriage is a mistake every man should make.

George Jessel, American entertainer (1898–1981). Quoted in Fred Allen, *Treadmill to Oblivion* (1956).

13 Marriage has many pains, but celibacy has no pleasures.

(Dr) Samuel Johnson, English writer and lexicographer (1709–84). *Rasselas* (1759).

When told that a gentleman who had been very unhappy in marriage had married again immediately after his wife died:

14 It was the triumph of hope over experience.

(Dr) Samuel Johnson. Quoted by Johnson's friend, the Revd Dr Maxwell, and inserted by James Boswell in *The Life of Samuel Johnson* (1791) in the year 1770. Johnson had a very positive view of marriage (though it is sometimes forgotten that he was himself married for a while), hence, his remark, 'Even ill assorted marriages were preferable to cheerless celibacy.'

15 Believing the phrase 'happy marriage' to be a contradiction in terms (like 'young poet').

Philip Larkin, English librarian and poet (1922–85). Letter to Andrew Motion (28 March 1983).

16 Many a man in love with a dimple makes the mistake of marrying the whole girl.

Stephen Leacock, Canadian economist and humorist

(1869–1944). Quoted in *The Treasury of Humorous Quotations*, eds Evan Esar & Nicolas Bentley (1951).

1 The trouble with marriage is that, while every woman is at heart a mother, every man is at heart a bachelor.

E.V. Lucas, English essayist and writer (1868–1938). Quoted in *The Treasury of Humorous Quotations*, eds Evan Esar & Nicolas Bentley (1951).

2 After all, a man marries to have a home, but also because he doesn't want to be bothered with sex and all that sort of thing.

W. Somerset Maugham, English writer (1874–1965). *The Circle*, Act 2 (1921).

3 The only really happy people are married women and single men.

H.L. Mencken, American journalist and linguist (1880–1956). Quoted in Laurence J. Peter, *Quotations for Our Time* (1977).

4 *Il en advient ce qui se voit aux cages, les oyseaux qui en sont dehors, desperent d'y entrer; et d'un pareil soing en sortir, ceux qui sont au dedans* [It [marriage] happens as with cages: the birds outside despair to get in, and those inside despair of getting out.

Michel de Montaigne, French essayist (1533–92). *Essais*, Bk 2, Cap. 12 (1580).

5 A good marriage would be between a blind wife and a deaf husband.

Michel de Montaigne. Attributed remark. Compare: 'Wedded persons may thus pass over their lives quietly ... if the husband becomes deaf and the wife blind' – Richard Taverner, English religious reformer (1505?–77), quoted in *The Treasury of Humorous Quotations*, eds Evan Esar & Nicolas Bentley (1951).

6 To keep your marriage brimming
With love in the loving cup,
Whenever you're wrong, admit it,
Whenever you're right, shut up.

Ogden Nash, American poet (1902–71). 'A Word to Husbands' (1957).

On marriage (in his case to the actress Joanne Woodward):

7 Why fool around with hamburger when you have steak at home?

Paul Newman, American film actor (1925–). Quoted in *Radio Times* (24 June 1971). In *The Observer* (11 March 1984), he was quoted as adding: 'That doesn't mean it's always tender.'

8 Marriage is a book of which the first chapter is written in poetry and the remaining chapters in prose.

Beverley Nichols, English journalist and writer (1898–1983). Quoted in *The Treasury of Humorous Quotations*, eds Evan Esar & Nicolas Bentley (1951).

9 Marriage is a meal where the soup is better than the dessert.

Austin O'Malley, American oculist and humorist (1858–1932). Quoted in the same collection as above.

10 My Lord told me that among his father's many old sayings that he had writ in a book of his, this is one: that he that doth get a wench with child and marries her afterward it is as if a man should shit in his hat and then clap it upon his head.

Samuel Pepys, English civil servant and diarist (1633–1703). *Diary* (7 October 1660). 'My lord' was Pepys's patron (also his first cousin once removed), the politician, naval commander and diplomat, Edward Mountagu, created 1st Earl of Sandwich in 1660. His father had been a royalist, whereas Mountagu espoused the parliamentarian cause. The book in question remains untraced.

11 Strange to say what delight we married people have to see these poor fools decoyed into our condition.

Samuel Pepys. In the same (25 December 1665). On Christmas Day, Pepys saw 'a wedding in the church, which I have not seen many a day', and was particularly struck by how merry the young couple were with each other.

12 It does not much signify whom one marries, as one is sure to find next morning that it is someone else.

Samuel Rogers, English poet (1763–1855). In *Recollection of the Table-talk of Samuel Rogers* (1856).

1 Marriage is popular because it combines the maximum of temptation with the maximum of opportunity.

Bernard Shaw, Irish playwright and critic (1856–1950). *Man and Superman*, 'Maxims for Revolutionists' (1903).

2 It's a woman's business to get married as soon as possible, and a man's to keep unmarried as long as he can.

Bernard Shaw. *Man and Superman*, Act 2 (1903).

3 What God hath joined together no man shall ever put asunder: God will take care of that.

Bernard Shaw. *Getting Married* (1908).

4 What business have you, miss, with preference and aversion? … You ought to know, that as both always wear off, 'tis safest in matrimony to begin with a little aversion.

Richard Brinsley Sheridan, English playwright and politician (1751–1816). *The Rivals*, Act 1, Sc. 2 (1775). Mrs Malaprop to Lydia.

5 [Marriage] resembles a pair of shears, so joined that they cannot be separated; often moving in opposite directions, yet always punishing any one who comes between them.

(Revd) Sydney Smith, English clergyman, essayist and wit (1771–1845). Quoted in Lady Holland, *A Memoir of Sydney Smith* (1855).

6 Marriage: a ceremony in which rings are put on the finger of the lady and through the nose of the gentleman.

Herbert Spencer, English philosopher (1820–1903). Quoted in *The Treasury of Humorous Quotations*, eds Evan Esar & Nicolas Bentley (1951).

7 Even if we take matrimony at its lowest, even if we regard it as a sort of friendship recognised by the police.

Robert Louis Stevenson, Scottish writer (1850–94). *Travels With a Donkey*, Title essay (1879).

8 Marriage is one long conversation, chequered by disputes.

Robert Louis Stevenson. Quoted in *The Treasury of Humorous Quotations*, eds Evan Esar & Nicolas Bentley (1951).

9 What they do in heaven we are ignorant of; what they do *not* we are told expressly, that they neither marry, nor are given in marriage.

Jonathan Swift, Anglo-Irish writer and clergyman (1667–1745). *Thoughts on Various Subjects* (1706).

10 A woman with fair opportunities and without a positive hump, may marry whom she likes.

William Makepeace Thackeray, English novelist (1811–63). *Vanity Fair*, Chap. 4 (1847–8).

11 Will you take this woman Matti Richards … to be your awful wedded wife?

Dylan Thomas, Welsh poet (1914–53). Radio play, *Under Milk Wood* (1954).

When asked if she had ever considered divorce during her long marriage to Sir Lewis Casson:

12 Divorce? Never. But murder often!

(Dame) Sybil Thorndike, English actress (1882–1976). Attributed remark. The Scottish Liberal politician David Steel apparently said of his ally Dr David Owen on one occasion: 'I am reminded of Dame Sybil Thorndike's comment on her long marriage. She considered divorce never, murder frequently. With Dr Owen it is murder, occasionally.' Also attributed to Elizabeth Longford, historian wife of the 7th Earl of Longford, in John G. Murray, *A Gentleman Publisher's Commonplace Book* (1996).

13 Love seems the swiftest but it is the slowest of all growths. No man or woman really knows what perfect love is until they have been married for a quarter of a century.

Mark Twain, American writer (1835–1910). *Notebooks* (published 1935).

1 Marriage is a great institution, but I'm not ready for an institution yet.

Mae West, American vaudeville and film actress (1893–1980). Quoted in Laurence J. Peter, *Quotations for Our Time* (1977). In the film *Look Who's Laughing* (1941), Lucille Ball says to Charlie McCarthy: 'Marriage is like an institution.' He replies: 'So is Alcatraz, but I wouldn't want to live in it.'

2 The one charm of marriage is that it makes a life of deception absolutely necessary for both parties.

Oscar Wilde, Irish playwright, poet and wit (1854–1900). *The Picture of Dorian Gray*, Chap. 1 (1891).

3 Men marry because they are tired; women because they are curious; both are disappointed.

Oscar Wilde. In the same book, Chap. 4. And later in *A Woman of No Importance*, Act 3 (1893).

4 How marriage ruins a man! It's as demoralizing as cigarettes, and far more expensive.

Oscar Wilde. *Lady Windermere's Fan*, Act 3 (1892).

5 There's nothing in the world like the devotion of a married woman. It's a thing no married man knows anything about.

Oscar Wilde. In the same act of the same play.

6 One should always be in love. That is the reason one should never marry,

Oscar Wilde. In the same play, Act 3.

7 In married life, three is company and two is none.

Oscar Wilde. *The Importance of Being Earnest*, Act 1 (1895).

8 *Miss Prism:*
No married man is ever attractive except to his wife.
Chasuble:
And often, I've been told, not even to her.

Oscar Wilde. In the same play, Act 2.

9 The London season is entirely matrimonial; people are either hunting for husbands or hiding from them.

Oscar Wilde. Quoted in *The Home Book of Humorous Quotations*, ed. A.K. Adams (1969).

10 Marriage is hardly a thing one can do now and then – except in America.

Oscar Wilde. Quoted in Herbert V. Prochnow, Snr & Jnr, *A Treasury of Humorous Quotations* (1969).

11 I married him for better or worse, but not for lunch.

Duchess of Windsor (formerly Mrs Wallis Simpson), American-born wife of the Duke of Windsor (1896–1986). Quoted in J. Bryan III & Charles J.V. Murphy, *The Windsor Story* (1979). '[The Duke of Windsor] usually lunched alone on a salad while the duchess went out ("I married the Duke for better or worse but not for lunch").'

Marx, Chico

AMERICAN FILM COMEDIAN (1886–1961)

12 There are three things that my brother Chico is always on: a phone, a horse or a broad.

Groucho Marx, American comedian (1895–1977). Quoted in John Robert Colombo, *Wit and Wisdom of the Moviemakers* (1979).

Marxism

13 *Je suis Marxiste – tendance Groucho* [I am a Marxist – of the Groucho tendency].

Anonymous (graffito). Included in my book *Graffiti Lives, OK* (1979). From Paris (May 1968).

14 Karl Marx – is he one of the Marx Brothers?

Line from film *Auntie Mame* (US 1958). Screenwriters: Betty Comden, Adolph Green (from Patrick Dennis novel and Jerome Lawrence play). Spoken by Jan Handzlik (Patrick Dennis as child) to Rosalind Russell (Auntie Mame Dennis).

Masturbation

15 One thing about masturbation: you don't have to look your best.

Anonymous (graffito). Included in book *Graffiti 2* (1980). Also reportedly spoken in film *The Boys in the Band* (US 1970).

1 Hey! Don't knock masturbation. It's sex with someone I love.

Line from film *Annie Hall* (US 1977). Screenwriters: Woody Allen, Marshall Brickman. Spoken by Woody Allen (Alvy).

2 The good thing about masturbation is that you don't have to dress up for it.

Truman Capote, American writer (1924–84). Quoted in Bob Chieger, *Was It Good For You Too?* (1983).

3 You know what I like about masturbation? You don't have to talk afterwards.

Milos Forman, Czech film director (1932–). Quoted in the same collection as above.

4 Masturbation is the thinking man's television.

Christopher Hampton, English playwright (1946–). *The Philanthropist* (1970).

5 A woman occasionally is quite a serviceable substitute for masturbation. It takes an abundance of imagination to be sure.

Karl Kraus, Austrian satirist (1874–1936). Quoted in Bob Chieger, *Was It Good For You Too?* (1983). Possibly from *Aphorisms* (1909).

6 *Countess Alexandrovna:*
You are the greatest lover I have ever known.
Boris:
Well, I practise a lot when I'm on my own.

Lines from film *Love and Death* (US 1975). Screenwriter: Woody Allen. Spoken by Woody Allen (Boris) and Olga Georges-Picot (Countess Alexandrovna).

On why she named her canary 'Onan':

7 Because he spills his seed on the ground.

Dorothy Parker, American writer (1893–1967). Quoted in John Keats, *You Might as Well Live* (1970).

Matzoh balls

On being served matzoh balls for supper at Arthur Miller's parents' house:

8 Isn't there another part of the matzoh you can eat?

Marilyn Monroe, American film actress (1926–62). Oral tradition, no doubt apocryphal. Gore Vidal merely cited 'the dumb starlet [who] would ask, What do they do with the rest of the matzoh?' in *The New York Review of Books* (17/31 May 1973).

Maxims

9 Today I have been having an experience – and it results in this maxim: To man all things are possible but one – he cannot have a hole in the seat of his breeches and keep his fingers out of it.

Mark Twain, American writer (1835–1910). In *The Mark Twain–Howells Letters*, eds Smith & Gibson (1960).

Mayors

10 After you've met one hundred and fifty Lord Mayors, they all begin to look the same.

George V, British King (1865–1936). Quoted in my book *A Dictionary of Twentieth Century Quotations* (1987).

Meanness

In reply to robber demanding 'Your money or your life!':

11 I'm thinking it over.

Jack Benny, American comedian (1894–1974). Quoted in Silver & Haiblum, *Faster Than a Speeding Bullet* (1980). His basic joke, from the 1930s onwards.

In reply to advertising slogan 'If —— Offered You A Cigarette, It Would Be A De Reszke':

12 If Godfrey Winn offered you a cigarette … it would be a bloody miracle!

(Sir) Noël Coward, English entertainer and writer (1899–1973). Quoted by Jonathan Cecil on BBC Radio *Quote … Unquote* (11 June 1996). In the 1940s, there was a brand of cigarette called De Reszke that was promoted in advertisements featuring various movie stars and with slogans like 'If Clark Gable Offered You a Cigarette ... '. Accordingly, Coward is said to have remarked this of the somewhat tight-fisted journalist Godfrey Winn.

On Bing Crosby:

1 If he can't take it with him, he's not going.

Bob Hope, English-born American comedian (1903–). Attributed remark.

Medals

To a soldier who had exclaimed 'No more bloody wars for me' as she presented medals during the First World War:

2 No more bloody wars, no more bloody medals.

Mary, British Queen of King George V (1867–1953). Quoted by Robert Lacey on BBC Radio *Quote ... Unquote* (19 February 1979).

Media

3 The media. It sounds like a convention of spiritualists.

(Sir) Tom Stoppard, English playwright (1937–). *Night and Day* (1978).

Medicine

4 A miracle drug is any drug that will do what the label says it will do.

Eric Hodgins, American writer and editor (1899–1971). *Episode: Report On the Accident Inside My Head* (1981).

5 I don't know much about medicine, but I know what I like.

S.J. Perelman, American humorist (1904–79). Quoted in Herbert V. Prochnow, Snr & Jnr, *A Treasury of Humorous Quotations* (1969).

6 The art of medicine consists of amusing the patient while nature cures the disease.

Voltaire, French writer and philosopher (1694–1778). Quoted in *The Treasury of Humorous Quotations*, eds Evan Esar & Nicolas Bentley (1951).

See also DOCTORS.

Mediocrity

Of the British music-hall comic Dan Leno:

7 Often, even in his heyday, his acting and his waggishness did not carry him very far. Only mediocrity can be trusted to be always at its best. Genius must always have lapses proportionate to its triumphs.

(Sir) Max Beerbohm, English writer and caricaturist (1872–1956). In the *Saturday Review* (5 November 1904).

8 Mediocrity knows nothing higher than itself, but talent instantly recognizes genius.

(Sir) Arthur Conan Doyle, Scottish-born novelist (1859–1930). *The Valley of Fear*, Chap. 1 (1915).

9 Some men are born mediocre, some men achieve mediocrity, and some men have mediocrity thrust upon them. With Major Major it was all three.

Joseph Heller, American novelist (1923–). *Catch-22*, Chap. 9 (1961).

10 I sometimes make pictures which are not up to my standard, but then it can only be said of mediocrity that all his work is up to his standard.

Ernst Lubitsch, German film director (1892–1947). Quoted in Leslie Halliwell, *The Filmgoer's Book of Quotes* (1973).

11 Only a very mediocre writer is always at his best, and Dorothy Parker is not a mediocre writer.

W. Somerset Maugham, English writer (1874–1965). In introduction to *The Portable Dorothy Parker* (1944).

12 Modesty is the fig-leaf of mediocrity.

Charles Osborne, Australian-born writer and arts administrator (1927–). *Giving It Away: Memoirs of an Uncivil Servant* (1986). Compare: 'The man who is ostentatious of his modesty is twin to the statue that wears a fig-leaf' – Mark Twain, *Following the Equator*, Pt 2, Chap. 14 (1897).

13 Indifference is the revenge the world takes on mediocrities.

Oscar Wilde, Irish playwright, poet and wit (1854–1900). *Vera: Or The Nihilists*, Act 2 (1880).

Meekness

1 The meek shall inherit the earth, but not the mineral rights.

Anonymous. Quoted in my book *Graffiti 3* (1981). Had also been attributed to J. Paul Getty, the American oil tycoon (1892–1976) by that date.

2 It's going to be fun to watch and see how long the meek can keep the earth after they inherit it.

Frank McKinney ('Kin') Hubbard, American humorist and caricaturist (1868–1930). Quoted in *The Treasury of Humorous Quotations*, eds Evan Esar & Nicolas Bentley (1951).

3 We have the highest authority for believing that the meek shall inherit the earth; though I have never found any particular corroboration of this aphorism in the records of Somerset House.

F.E. Smith (1st Earl of Birkenhead), English politician and lawyer (1872–1930). *Contemporary Personalities* 'Marquess Curzon' (1924). Somerset House was once the depository for British wills and testaments.

Meetings

4 If you have enough meetings over a long enough period of time, the meetings become more important than the problem the meetings were intended to solve.

(Dr) E.R. Hendrickson, President of Environmental Engineering Inc. of Gainseville, Florida. In 1971. Quoted in Thomas L. Martin Jnr, *Malice in Blunderland* (1973) – 'Hendrickson's Law'.

Melons

5 It is a good fruit: you eat, you drink, you wash your face.

Enrico Caruso, Italian singer (1873–1921). Quoted in Herbert V. Prochnow, Snr & Jnr, *A Treasury of Humorous Quotations* (1969).

Memoirs

6 If I were to say all the unpleasant things that occur to me about posthumous memoirs, I should have nothing left for my posthumous memoirs.

Samuel Butler, English author (1835–1902). Quoted in *The Treasury of Humorous Quotations*, eds Evan Esar & Nicolas Bentley (1951).

7 I dislike modern memoirs. They are generally written by people who have either entirely lost their memories, or have never done anything worth remembering; which, however, is, no doubt, the true explanation of their popularity, as the English public always feels perfectly at its ease when a mediocrity is talking to it.

Oscar Wilde, Irish playwright, poet and wit (1854–1900). 'The Critic As Artist' (1890).

Memorandums

8 A memorandum is written not to inform the reader but to protect the writer.

Dean Acheson, American Democratic politician (1893–1971). Quoted in *The Wall Street Journal* (8 September 1977).

To the economist Leon Henderson:

9 Are you labouring under the impression that I read these memoranda of yours? I can't even lift them.

Franklin D. Roosevelt, American Democratic President (1882–1945). Quoted in J.K. Galbraith, *Ambassador's Journal* (1969).

Memorial services

10 Memorial services are the cocktail parties of the geriatric set.

(Sir) Ralph Richardson, English actor (1902–83). Sometimes misattributed to Harold Macmillan, as in Alastair Horne, *Macmillan 1957-1986* (1989). In Ruth Dudley Edwards, *Harold Macmillan: a life in pictures* (1983), Macmillan (who is purported to have written the picture captions) states: 'I rather agree with Ralph Richardson [the actor] that Memorial Services are the "cocktail parties of the geriatric set".'

Memory

1 'It's a poor sort of memory that only works backwards', the Queen remarked.

Lewis Carroll, English writer (1832–98). *Through the Looking-Glass and What Alice Found There*, Chap. 5 (1872).

2 It is a natural enough malaise, this idealized remembering, but should not be encouraged too much. There is no future in the past.

(Sir) Noël Coward, English entertainer and writer (1899–1973). *Diaries* – for 10 December 1954.

3 My own wife, as some people know, had a lot of children – eight if I remember rightly.

7th Earl of Longford (Francis Pakenham), English writer and politician (1905–). Quoted in *The Observer*, 'Sayings of the Week' (5 May 1985).

Celebrating his 75th birthday:

4 When I look back, the fondest memory I have is not really of the Goons. It is of a girl called Julia with enormous breasts.

Spike Milligan, Irish entertainer and writer (1918–). Quoted in *The Independent* 'Quote Unquote' (24 April 1993).

5 Women and elephants never forget an injury.

Saki (H.H. Munro), English writer (1870–1916). *Reginald*, 'Reginald on Besetting Sins' (1904). The basic expression 'an elephant never forgets' is what one might say of one's self when complimented on remembering a piece of information forgotten by others. As such, it is based on the view that elephants are supposed to remember trainers, keepers and so on, especially those who have been unkind to them. A song with the title 'The Elephant Never Forgets' was featured in the play *The Golden Toy* by Carl Zuckmayer (London, 1934) and recorded by Lupino Lane. *Stevenson's Book of Proverbs, Maxims and Familiar Phrases* (1949) has that the modern saying really derives from a Greek proverb: 'The camel [*sic*] never forgets an injury' – which is exactly how Saki uses it.

6 Among the more elderly inhabitants of the South I found a melancholy tendency to date every event of importance on the late War. 'How beautiful the moon is tonight,' I once remarked to a gentleman standing near me. 'Yes,' was his reply, 'but you should have seen it before the War.'

Oscar Wilde, Irish playwright, poet and wit (1854–1900). *Impressions of America* (pub. 1906).

7 No woman should have a memory. Memory in a woman is the beginning of dowdiness.

Oscar Wilde. *A Woman of No Importance*, Act 3 (1893).

8 It is only by paying one's bills that one can hope to live in the memory of the commercial classes.

Oscar Wilde. 'Phrases and Philosophies for the Use of the Young', in *The Chameleon* (December 1894).

9 *Miss Prism:*
Memory, my dear Cecily, is the diary that we all carry about with us.
Cecily:
[Yes, but it] usually chronicles things that have never happened, and couldn't possibly have happened.

Oscar Wilde. *The Importance of Being Earnest*, Act 2 (1895).

Men

10 Women's faults are many
Men have only two:
Everything they say
And everything they do.

Anonymous. Reproduced on T-shirts, badges, and so on in the 1970s. Compare, however, from *H.L. Mencken's Dictionary of Quotations* (1942), this well-documented rhyme from the 18th century – and note the change of gender: 'We men have many faults: / Poor women have but two – / There's nothing good they say, / There's nothing good they do.'

11 I married beneath me. All women do.

Nancy Astor (Viscountess Astor), American-born English politician (1879–1964). Speech, Oldham (1951). Quoted in the *Dictionary of National Biography 1961–70* (1981). She was the first British woman MP to take her seat in the House of Commons and, in fact, was wealthy in her own right.

1 The more I see of men, the less I like them. If I could but say so of women too, all would be well.

Lord Byron, English poet (1788–1824). *Journal* (1814).

2 I tell you there isn't a thing under the sun that needs to be done at all, but what a man can do better than a woman, unless it's bearing children; and they do that in a poor makeshift way; it had better ha' been left to the men.

George Eliot, English novelist (1819–80). *Adam Bede*, Chap. 21 (1859).

On being told by a 'modern' woman of the 1890s that there was almost no difference between men and women at that time:

3 *Vive la différence!*

Anatole France, French writer (1844–1924). Attributed remark.

4 The trouble with Ian [Fleming] is that he gets off with women because he can't get on with them.

Rosamund Lehmann, English novelist (1901–90). Quoted in John Pearson, *The Life of Ian Fleming* (1966). Apparently, Lehmann was borrowing a line from Elizabeth Bowen.

5 Men are those creatures with two legs and eight hands.

Jayne Mansfield, American film actress (1932–67). Quoted in John Robert Colombo, *Wit and Wisdom of the Movie-makers* (1979).

6 Men have a much better time of it than women; for one thing, they marry later; for another thing, they die earlier.

H.L. Mencken, American journalist and linguist (1880–1956). *A Mencken Chrestomathy*, Chap. 30 (1949).

7 The more I see of men, the more I like dogs.

Madame Roland, French revolutionary (1756–93). Attributed in the *Oxford Dictionary of Quotations* (1979). However, after Roland's time, Alphonse de Lamartine, French poet and politician (1790–1869), is reported to have said: 'The more I see of the representatives of the people, the more I admire my dogs'; and A. Toussenel wrote in *L'Esprit des bêtes* (1847): 'The more one gets to know of men, the more one values dogs [*Plus on apprend à connaître l'homme, plus on apprend à estimer le chien*].'

8 It's not the men in my life, but the life in my men.

Mae West, American film actress (1893–1980). As Tira in the film *I'm No Angel* (US 1933), for which she wrote the script.

9 Give a man a free hand and he'll try to put it all over you.

Mae West. As Annie in the film *Klondike Annie* (US 1936), for which she wrote the script.

10 A hard man is good to find.

Mae West. Quoted in my book *Nudge Nudge, Wink Wink* (1986).

Meretricious

When Richard Adams chose to describe Vidal's novel about Abraham Lincoln as 'meretricious':

11 Really? Well, meretricious and a happy New Year!

Gore Vidal, American novelist, playwright and critic (1925–). On the BBC Radio show *Start the Week*. Quoted in Alan Bennett, *Writing Home* (1995) – entry for 25 September 1984. Bennett comments: 'That's the way to do it.' But, unusually for Vidal, it now appears Vidal was quoting another's line (a 'meretricious and a happy New Year'), ascribed to Franklin Pierce Adams in Scott Meredith, *George S. Kaufman and the Algonquin Round Table* (1977). It was also delivered by Chico Marx on the NBC Radio series *Flywheel, Shyster and Flywheel* (13 March 1933).

Merman, Ethel

AMERICAN ENTERTAINER (1908–84)

On her voice:

12 A chorus of taxi horns.

Anonymous. Quoted in *Time* Magazine (27 February 1984).

1 A brass band going by.

Cole Porter, American songwriter (1891–1964). Quoted in *The Guardian* (16 February 1984).

Messages

After Japanese claims that most of the American Third Fleet had been sunk or was retiring:

2 Our ships have been salvaged and are retiring at high speed toward the Japanese fleet.

Anonymous (radio message). From a US Navy ship (October 1944). Quoted in *The Home Book of Humorous Quotations*, ed. A.K. Adams (1969).

On being asked about the messages in his plays:

3 I'm a playwright, not a bloody postman.

Brendan Behan, Irish playwright (1923–64). Quoted in *The Sayings of Brendan Behan*, ed. Aubrey Dillon-Malone (1997). Remark addressed to Colin MacInnes of the *The Daily Telegraph.*

On films with a 'message':

4 Messages are for Western Union.

Samuel Goldwyn, Polish-born American film producer (1882–1974). Quoted in Alva Johnston, *The Great Goldwyn* (1937). Arthux Marx, *Goldwyn* (1976) has Goldwyn saying: 'Pictures are for entertainment, messages should be delivered by Western Union.' In the 1978 edition of *The Filmgoer's Book of Quotes*, Leslie Halliwell also attributes to Jack Warner: 'We'll make the pictures: let Western Union deliver the messages.' The line has been used frequently in film dialogue.

5 Sighted sub, sank same.

Donald Mason, American Navy pilot (1913–). Radio message (28 January 1942), from this US Navy flyer after he had dropped a depth charge on a surfaced Japanese submarine in the South Pacific. 'This concise message was one of the first pieces of good news to come after Pearl Harbor and was given wide publicity as showing the good spirit of our armed forces' – comments Stuart Flexner in *I Hear America Talking* (1976).

Metaphors

6 The cure for mixed metaphors, I have always found, is for the patient to be obliged to draw a picture of the result.

Bernard Levin, English journalist and critic (1928–). *In These Times* (1986).

7 Mr Speaker, I smell a rat; I see him forming in the air and darkening the sky; but I'll nip him in the bud.

(Sir) Boyle Roche, Irish politician (1743–1807). Attributed remark in the Irish Parliament. In F. Wills, *The Irish Nation* (1871–5) – it is conceded that the chamberlain to the vice-regal court (in Dublin), as Roche later became, had a 'graceful address and ready wit', but, additionally, 'it was usual for members of the cabinet to write speeches for him, which he committed to memory, and, while mastering the substance, generally contrived to travesty the language and ornament with peculiar graces of his own'. Could this be the reason for Roche's peculiar sayings? The *Dictionary of National Biography* adds that 'he gained his lasting reputation as an inveterate perpetrator of "bulls" [i.e., ludicrous, self-contradictory propositions, often associated with the Irish]'.

8 How could the sergeant-at-arms stop him in the rear, while he was catching him at the front? Could he like a bird be in two places at once?

(Sir) Boyle Roche. Quoted in *A Book of Irish Quotations* (1984). Supposedly said in the Irish Parliament. *Brewer's Dictionary of Phrase and Fable* (1989) suggests that he was quoting from 'Jevon's play *The Devil of a Wife*' (untraced) and that what he said was, 'Mr Speaker, it is impossible I could have been in two places at once, unless I were a bird' – adding that the phrase was probably of even earlier origin.

9 Ice formed on the butler's upper slopes.

(Sir) P(elham) G. Wodehouse, English-born novelist and lyricist (1881–1975). *Pigs Have Wings* (1952).

Metaphysics

10 A Short Cut to Metaphysics. What is Matter? – Never mind. What is Mind? – No matter.

Anonymous (writer). In *Punch* (14 July 1855). Sometimes ascribed to T.H. Key.

1 On a metaphysician: A blind man in a dark room, looking for a black hat which isn't there.

Lord Bowen, English judge (1835–94). Quoted in J.A.K. Foote KC, *Pie-Powder &c.* (1911). Discussed in *Notes & Queries*, Vol.182 (14 March 1942), where it is stated that Bowen would not have approved of any 'black *cat*' version.

2 I take the liberty to send you two brace of grouse – curious, because killed by a Scotch metaphysician. In other and better language, they are mere ideas, shot by other ideas, out of a pure intellectual notion called a gun.

(Revd) Sydney Smith, English clergyman, essayist and wit (1771–1845). Letter (1808), quoted in *The Sayings of Sydney Smith*, ed. Alan Bell (1993).

See also PHILOSOPHERS AND PHILOSOPHY.

Methods

Supposedly Chinese proverb:

3 Do not remove a fly from your friend's forehead with a hatchet.

Anonymous. Quoted in *H. Allen Smith's Almanac* (1965).

Mexico

4 Poor Mexico! So far from God, so close to the United States.

Porfirio Diaz, Mexican President (1830–1915). Attributed in *Bartlett's Familiar Quotations* (1980).

Middle age

5 Middle age occurs when you are too young to take up golf and too old to rush up to the net.

Franklin P. Adams, American journalist, poet and humorist (1881–1960). Quoted in *The Treasury of Humorous Quotations*, eds Evan Esar & Nicolas Bentley (1951).

6 You know you are getting old when the policemen start looking younger.

Arnold Bennett, English novelist (1867–1931). Quoted in Arnold Bax, *Farewell My Youth* (1943). What Bax actually said of Bennett was: '[He] once remarked that his earliest recognition of his own middle age came at a certain appalling moment when he realized for the first time that the policeman at the corner was a mere youth.' This realization also came to Sir Seymour Hicks (1871–1949), the actor, in connection with *old* age, as stated in his *Between Ourselves* (1930): 'You will recognize, my boy, the first sign of age: it is when you go out into the streets of London and realize for the first time how young the policemen look.'

7 The really frightening thing about middle age is the knowledge that you'll grow out of it.

Doris Day, American singer and actress (1924–). Quoted in A.E. Hotchner, *Doris Day* (1978).

8 Boys will be boys, and so will a lot of middle-aged men.

Frank McKinney ('Kin') Hubbard, American humorist and caricaturist (1868–1930). Quoted in *The Treasury of Humorous Quotations*, eds Evan Esar & Nicolas Bentley (1951).

9 I wouldn't mind being called middle-aged if only I knew a few more 100-year-old people.

Dean Martin, American entertainer (1917–95). Quoted in *OK!* Magazine (7 January 2000).

10 Middle age is when, wherever you go on holiday, you pack a sweater.

Denis Norden, English humorist (1922–). On Thames TV, *Looks Familiar* (1976).

Military leadership

On a general who had let him down on the battlefield:

11 He has managed to snatch defeat from the jaws of victory.

Abraham Lincoln, American Republican President (1809–65). Unverified, though General Ambrose Burnside is generally thought to be the one criticized. 'Only Burnside could have managed such a coup, wringing one last spectacular defeat from the jaws of victory' is the version given in Stephen Pile, *The Book of Heroic Failures* (1979). Sean O'Connor noted (1999): 'Burnside never missed an opportunity to give up strategic positions and was never known to win an engagement. I *think* Lincoln's comment came after the Battle of Fredericksburg when the Civil

War was as good as won. It was completely unnecessary for Burnside to fight the engagement but, needless to say, he lost and I always thought that Lincoln had said that he had taken "one last glorious opportunity to snatch defeat from the very jaws of victory"." Others would argue that Burnside was so inept that he was never close enough to victory to be able to snatch defeat from it.

1 Russia has two generals in whom she can confide – Generals Janvier and Février.

Nicholas I, Russian Tsar (1796–1855). Caption to cartoon at his death in *Punch* (10 March 1855), ascribing this well-known observation to him.

Mill, John Stuart

ENGLISH PHILOSOPHER AND ECONOMIST (1806–73)

2 John Stuart Mill
By a mighty effort of will,
Overcame his natural bonhomie
And wrote 'Principles of Political Economy'.

E. Clerihew Bentley, English novelist, journalist and poet (1875–1956). *Biography for Beginners* (1905).

3 [He is] prominent because of the flatness of the surrounding countryside.

Karl Marx, German political theorist (1818–83). *Das Kapital*, Vol. 1, Chap. 16 (1867). After having demolished one of Mill's arguments, Marx actually wrote of Mill in the following terms: 'On a level plain, simple mounds look like hills; and the insipid flatness of our present bourgeoisie is to be measured by the altitude of its "great intellects".'

Mimicry

4 *Commenting on the performance of a mimic/impressionist at a music hall:*

Perfectly splendid. And I do think it so kind of him to tell us who he is imitating. It avoids discussion, doesn't it.

Oscar Wilde, Irish playwright, poet and wit (1854–1900). Quoted in E.H. Mikhail, *Oscar Wilde: Interviews and Recollections* (1979).

Mind

To a solicitor:

5 You will turn it over in what you are pleased to call your mind.

Richard Bethell (Baron Westbury), English judge (1800–73). Quoted in Nash, *Life of Westbury*. 'Noted for his sarcastic wit, he was an unpopular judge', notes *Chambers Biographical Dictionary* (1990).

6 Minds are like parachutes: they only function when they are open.

Lord (Thomas Robert) Dewar, Scottish distiller (1864–1930). Quoted in *The Treasury of Humorous Quotations*, eds Evan Esar & Nicolas Bentley (1951). In the film *Charlie Chan's Murder Cruise* (US 1940), Chan tells one of his children, 'Mind like parachute – only function when open.' *The Oxford Dictionary of Quotations* (1992) attributes it, rather, to Sir James Dewar, Scottish physicist (1842–1923). Sometimes quoted as 'Minds are like umbrellas ... '

Diary entry for 14 February 1995:

7 A Valentine card in a tiny illiterate hand; surely I can't have sent a card to myself. Now that Dr Alzheimer looks as if he may be extending a welcome to me I can no longer be sure of these things.

(Sir) Alec Guinness, English actor (1914–2000). *My Name Escapes Me* (1996).

8 A woman's mind is cleaner than a man's; she changes it more often.

Oliver Herford, American humorist (1863–1935). Quoted in *The Treasury of Humorous Quotations*, eds Evan Esar & Nicolas Bentley (1951).

9 As to those who can find it in them to employ the doubtlessly useful word 'brunch', do they, I wonder, ever up-grade it to 'bruncheon'? This is the kind of question I ponder on while waiting for the kettle to boil. The active mind is never at rest.

Arthur Marshall, English writer and entertainer (1910–89). *Life's Rich Pageant* (1984).

On trying to engage in debate with Nancy Astor in the House of Commons:

1 It was like playing squash with a dish of scrambled eggs.

(Sir) Harold Nicolson, English writer and politician (1886–1968). Letter to his sons (18 March 1943). Nancy Astor was famous for not being able to stick to the point.

2 I shall be like that tree, I shall die at the top.

Jonathan Swift, Anglo-Irish writer and clergyman (1667–1745). Quoted in *The Sayings of Jonathan Swift*, ed. Joseph Spence (1994).

Mini-skirts

3 We Bishops, in our proper dress, originated the mini-skirt. But we allowed Mary Quant to steal the thunder and make three million quid out of it last year.

(Dr) Victor J. Pike, English bishop (1907–). When Bishop Suffragan of Sherborne. Quoted in 1967 and re-quoted in *The Observer*, 'Sayings of the Decade' (1970).

Minorities

After a General Election that resulted in no party having a clear majority:

4 Looking around the House, one realises that we are all minorities now.

Jeremy Thorpe, English Liberal politician (1929–). Speech, House of Commons (6 March 1974), alluding to Edward VII's alleged remark 'We are all socialists nowadays.'

Miracles

5 A Miracle: an event described by those to whom it was told by men who did not see it.

Elbert Hubbard, American writer and editor (1856–1915). Quoted in *The Treasury of Humorous Quotations*, eds Evan Esar & Nicolas Bentley (1951).

6 It would have approached nearer to the idea of miracle if Jonah had swallowed the whale.

Thomas Paine, English-born American revolutionary and political theorist (1737–1809). Quoted in *The Treasury of Humorous Quotations*, eds Evan Esar & Nicolas Bentley (1951).

On Niagara Falls:

7 The wonder would be if the water did not fall.

Oscar Wilde, Irish playwright, poet and wit (1854–1900). Quoted in Hesketh Pearson, *Lives of the Wits* (1962).

8 There is absolutely nothing wrong with Oscar Levant that a miracle cannot fix.

Alexander Woollcott, American writer and critic (1887–1943). Quoted in M.C. Harriman, *The Vicious Circle* (1951).

Misapprehensions

9 *Railway Porter:*
Weybridge! Weybridge! Any one for V'rgin'a Water!
Thirsty passenger (waking up at the sound of the last word):
Gin 'an water! 'Ere y'are, Porter! Bring 'sh four penn'th!!

Anonymous (cartoonist). Caption to cartoon in *Punch* (25 December 1869). This idea resurfaced in *Punch* (31 October 1900): Hostess: 'Come and hear a whistling solo by my husband.' Smith (whose hearing is a trifle indistinct): 'A whiskey and soda with your husband? Well, thanks. I don't mind if I do have just one!' In the end this contributed to the catchphrase 'I don't mind if I do' uttered by Colonel Chinstrap at the slightest hint of a drink in the BBC Radio show *ITMA* (1939–49).

A Sympathetic Soul. Bluejacket (in charge of Party of Sightseers):

10 Here Nelson fell.
Old lady:
An' I don't wonder at, poor dear. Nasty slippery place! I nearly fell there myself.

Anonymous (cartoonist). Caption to cartoon in *Punch* (3 May 1899).

Dialogue between a Medical Officer and a recruit:

11 *M.O.*: How are your bowels working?
R.: Haven't been issued with any, sir.
M.O.: I mean, are you constipated?
R.: No, sir, I volunteered.
M.O.: Heaven's man, don't you know the

King's English?
R.: No sir, is he?

Anonymous. Quoted in Edward Marsh, *Ambrosia and Small Beer*, Chap. 4 (1964).

1 Now, on the St Louis team we have Who's on first, What's on second, I Don't Know is on third.

Bud Abbott, American comedian (1895–1974). From a classic routine based on misunderstanding and performed by Abbott and his partner Lou Costello (1906–59). Included in the film *Naughty Nineties* (US 1945). Accordingly, Richard J. Anobile's celebration of their act was entitled *Who's On First?* (1973).

Misfortunes

2 Misfortunes and twins never come singly.

'Josh Billings' (Henry Wheeler Shaw), American humorist (1818–85). Quoted in *The Home Book of Humorous Quotations*, ed. A.K. Adams (1969).

Asked to define the difference between a calamity and a misfortune:

3 If, for instance, Mr Gladstone were to fall into the river, that would be a misfortune. But if anyone were to pull him out, that would be a calamity.

Benjamin Disraeli (1st Earl of Beaconsfield), British Conservative Prime Minister and writer (1804–81). Quoted in Hesketh Pearson, *Lives of the Wits* (1962). Almost certainly apocryphal. A similar story is told concerning Napoleon III and Plon-Plon, once designated as his heir, concerning the difference between an accident and a misfortune (related in Felix Markham, *The Bonapartes*, 1975).

4 Ay, people are generally calm at the misfortunes of others.

Oliver Goldsmith, Irish-born playwright and writer (1730–74). *She Stoops to Conquer*, Act 3 (1773).

5 We all have enough strength to bear the misfortunes of others.

François, Duc de La Rochefoucauld, French writer (1613–80). Quoted in *The Treasury of Humorous Quotations*, eds Evan Esar & Nicolas Bentley (1951).

6 I never knew a man in my life who could not bear another's misfortune perfectly like a Christian.

Jonathan Swift, Anglo-Irish writer and clergyman (1667–1745). Quoted in the same collection as above.

Mishearings

7 When God gave out heads,
I thought He said Beds,
and I asked for a soft one.

When God gave out looks,
I thought He said books,
and I didn't want any.

When God gave out noses,
I thought He said roses
and I asked for a red one.

When God gave out ears,
I thought He said beers,
and I asked for two big ones.

When God gave out chins,
I thought He said gins,
and I asked for a double.

When God gave out brains,
I thought He said trains
and I said I'd take the next one.

When God gave out legs,
I thought He said kegs,
So I ordered two fat ones.

Since then I'm trying to listen better.

Anonymous. This is a composite of versions that have been in circulation since the 1940s.

8 *Hammer:*
I say here is a little peninsula, and here's a viaduct leading over to the mainland.
Chico:
All right. Why a duck?

Line from film *The Cocoanuts* (US 1929). Screenwriters: George S. Kaufman, Morrie Ryskind. Spoken by Groucho Marx (Hammer) and Chico Marx (Chico).

See also MONDEGREENS.

Misperceptions

When a drunken reveller decides to look out and see what sort of a night it is and stumbles into a larder by mistake, he reports that it is:

1 Hellish dark, and smells of cheese!

R.S. Surtees, *Handley Cross*, Chap. 50 (1843 edn).

Misprints

2 Printers indeed should be very careful how they omit a Figure or a Letter; For by such Means sometimes a terrible Alteration is made in the Sense. I have heard, that once, in a new edition of the *Common Prayer*, the following Sentence, *We shall all be changed in a Moment, in the Twinkling of an Eye*; by the omission of a single Letter, became, *We shall all be hanged in a Moment*, &c. to the no small Surprize of the first Congregation it was read to.

Benjamin Franklin, American politician and scientist (1706–90). *Poor Richard's Almanack* (Preface 1750). Franklin began his career as a printer.

3 What do you think of this for a misprint: 'Idle vistas and melancholy nooks' – '*idle sisters and melancholy monks*'!!

Henry James, American novelist (1843–1916). Letter (13 June 1874).

4 I am told that printer's readers no longer exist because clergymen are no longer unfrocked for sodomy.

Evelyn Waugh, English novelist (1903–66). Letter to Tom Driberg (11 June 1960).

Mistakes

5 Archduke Franz Ferdinand found alive. First World War a mistake.

Anonymous (graffito). Contributed to BBC Radio *Quote ... Unquote* (29 January 1979) by John Butcher, who said he saw it in the British Museum. Compare what Alan Clark, the English politician, wrote in his published *Diaries* (entry for 28 June 1983): 'I often think of that prize-winning spoof headline in the *New York Daily News* in 1920: "Archduke found alive, World War a Mistake".'

6 I have made mistakes, but I have never made the mistake of claiming that I never made one.

James Gordon Bennett II, American newspaper proprietor (1841–1918). Quoted in *The Treasury of Humorous Quotations*, eds Evan Esar & Nicolas Bentley (1951).

7 Now let me correct you on a couple of things, okay? Aristotle was not Belgian. The central message of Buddhism is not every man for himself ... And the London Underground is not a political movement. Those are all mistakes, Otto. I looked them up.

Line from film *A Fish Called Wanda* (UK 1988). Screenwriters: John Cleese, Charles Crichton. Spoken by Jamie Lee Curtis (Wanda Gerschwitz) to Kevin Kline (Otto).

8 The man who makes no mistakes does not usually make anything.

Edward John Phelps, American lawyer and diplomat (1822–1900). Speech, Mansion House, London (24 January 1899). It has also been ascribed to Bishop W.C. Magee in an 1868 sermon.

9 Nowadays most people die of a sort of creeping common sense, and discover, when it is too late, that the only thing one never regrets are one's mistakes.

Oscar Wilde, Irish playwright, poet and wit (1854–1900). *The Picture of Dorian Gray*, Chap. 3 (1891).

10 Murder is always a mistake. One should never do anything that one cannot talk about after dinner.

Oscar Wilde. In the same book, Chap. 19

Mistresses

11 A miss for pleasure, and a wife for breed.

John Gay, English poet and playwright (1685–1732). 'The Toilette' (1716).

In reply to the wish of his dying wife, Caroline, that he marry again:

1 No, I shall have mistresses [*Non, j'aurai des maîtresses*].

George II, British King (1683–1760). She then commented, 'Good Lord, that doesn't prevent it [*Ah! mon Dieu! cela n'empêche pas*].' Quoted in John Hervey, *Memoirs of the Reign of George II*, vol. 2 (1848).

2 When you marry your mistress, you create a job vacancy.

(Sir) James Goldsmith, English businessman (1933–97). Attributed in about 1978, in which year he married his third wife, Lady Annabel Birley. Within six months of this marriage he did indeed acquire another mistress and had two children by her. He admitted that the remark was not original.

3 Next to the pleasure of taking a new mistress is that of being rid of an old one.

William Wycherley, English playwright and poet (*c.* 1640–1716). *The Country Wife*, Act 1 (1675).

4 A mistress should be like a little country retreat near the town, not to dwell in constantly, but only for a night and away.

William Wycherley. From the same play and act.

Moderation

5 You should take everything in moderation ... including moderation.

Anonymous. Compare, however, from Samuel Butler, *The Way of All Flesh*, Chap. 50 (1903): '[Ernest] brought out his pipes and tobacco again. There should be moderation, he felt, in all things, even in virtue; so for that night he smoked immoderately.'

6 We know what happens to people who stay in the middle of the road. They get run over.

Aneurin Bevan, Welsh Labour politician (1897–1960). Quoted in *The Observer* (9 December 1953). According to Kenneth Harris, *Thatcher* (1988), Margaret Thatcher later said to James Prior: 'Standing in the middle of the road is very dangerous, you get knocked down by traffic from both sides.' And a TV play called *A Very British Coup* (1988) had a fictional Prime Minister saying, 'I once tried the middle of the road ... but I was knocked down by traffic in both directions.'

7 A middle-of-the-roader is one who's apt to have trouble on the one hand and on the other.

Franklin P. Jones. In *The Saturday Evening Post*.

8 An Iranian moderate is one who has run out of ammunition.

Henry Kissinger, American Republican politician (1923–). Quoted in *Today* (23 July 1987).

Modesty

9 The English instinctively admire any man who has no talent and is modest about it.

James Agate, English drama critic (1877–1947). *Ego 9* (1948).

Of her husband, H.H. Asquith:

10 His modesty amounts to deformity.

Margot Asquith (later Countess of Oxford and Asquith) (1864–1945). Quoted by her stepdaughter Baroness Asquith in BBC TV programme *As I Remember* (30 April 1967).

11 Modesty is the only sure bait when you angle for praise.

4th Earl of Chesterfield (Philip Dormer Stanhope), English politician and writer (1694–1773). *Letters to His Son* (1774) – for 7 May 1750.

Of Melvyn Bragg, TV presenter and novelist:

12 Modest? He's as modest as Larry Adler.

Jonathan Miller, English entertainer, writer and director (1934–). Quoted on BBC Radio *Quote ... Unquote* (13 July 1977).

13 I have often wished I had time to cultivate modesty ... But I am too busy thinking about myself.

(Dame) Edith Sitwell, English poet (1887–1964). Quoted in *The Observer* (30 April 1950).

1 I was born modest, but it didn't last.

Mark Twain, American writer (1835–1910). In *Mark Twain's Speeches*, ed. A. B. Paine (1910).

Mona Lisa

2 [She has] the smile of a woman who has just dined off her husband.

Lawrence Durrell, English novelist (1912–90). *Justine*, Pt 2 (1957). The passage reads in full: 'Nearby hangs a small print of the Mona Lisa whose enigmatic smile has always reminded Scobie of his mother. (For my part the famous smile has always seemed to me to be the smile of a woman who has just dined off her husband).'

Mondegreens

3 Ye Highlands and ye Lawlands
O where hae ye been?
They hae slain the Earl of Murray
And laid him on the green.

Anonymous. From the old Scottish ballad, 'The Bonny Earl of Murray'. 'And Lady Mondegreen' gives us the word 'Mondegreen' for a misquotation or mishearing of verse. It was coined by Sylvia Wright in a 1954 *Harper's Magazine* article.

4 Gladly, my cross-eyed bear.

Anonymous. Known since the 1950s or 1960s at least, and clearly the tale must have been told by the time that John Hopkins so entitled an episode of his TV drama *Talking To a Stranger* (1966). The joke rather depends on there having been a line 'gladly my [*or* the] cross I'd bear' in some hymn or other. But which hymn? The hymn popularly known as 'The Old Rugged Cross' written by the Revd George Bennard in 1913 contains the lines, 'To the old rugged cross I will ever be true, / Its shame and reproach gladly bear ... ' Ed McBain's thriller entitled *Gladly the Cross-Eyed Bear* (1996) attributes the quotation, however, to a hymn called 'Keep Thou My Way' by the blind American hymnodist Fanny Crosby (1820–1915), who is credited with writing more than 9,000 of the things ... The line alluded to occurs in the third stanza, thus:

Keep Thou my all, O Lord,
Hide my life in Thine;
O let Thy sacred light,
O'er my pathway shine;
Kept by Thy tender care,
Gladly the cross I'll bear,
Hear Thou and grant my prayer,
Hide my life in Thine.

5 Can a mother's tender care cease towards the child she-bear?

Anonymous. Alluding to the hymn 'Lovest thou me?' beginning 'Hark! my soul! it is the Lord', based on lines in one of William Cowper's *Olney Hymns* (1779): 'Can a woman's tender care / Cease towards the child she bare? / Yes, she may forgetful be, / Yet will I remember thee.'

6 A four-year-old Roman Catholic child used to pray: 'Hail, Mary, full of grace ... blessed art thou swimming ... '

Anonymous. Contributed to BBC Radio *Quote... Unquote* (4 June 1986) by Margaret Drake of Nelson, Lancashire. Compare how Malachy McCourt explains the title of his book *A Monk Swimming* (1998): *'Hail Mary, full of grace, The Lord is with Thee. Blessed art thou amongst women* – or, as I misheard it as a child, and still to this day on occasion, *Blessed art thou, a monk swimming ... '*

7 I will make you vicious old men.

Anonymous (schoolboy). Rendering 'I will make you fishers of men'. Contributed to BBC Radio *Quote... Unquote* (10 May 1994) by Shirley Firth of Budleigh Salterton, Devon.

8 The little Lord Jesus lay down his wee ted.

Anonymous (five-year-old). In the run-up to the nativity play. Contributed to BBC Radio *Quote... Unquote* (1 May 2000) by Frances McMillan of Midlothian.

9 The girl with colitis goes by.

Anonymous. Quoted in *Babes and Sucklings* (1983). Said to have been reported first by William Safire of *The New York Times* and known by 1981. Alluding to the line 'The girl with kaleidoscope eyes' from 'Lucy in the Sky with Diamonds' on The Beatles' *Sgt. Pepper* album (1967).

10 I Lost My Heart To a Draught Excluder.

Anonymous. Quoted as from Heather Knowles on BBC Radio *Quote ... Unquote* (9 October 2000). Referring to the Sarah Brightman record 'I Lost My Heart To a Starship Trooper' (1978).

Member of crowd (mishearing Christ's Sermon on the Mount):

1 I think it was 'Blessed are the cheese-makers'.

Line from film *Monty Python's Life of Brian* (UK 1979). Written and performed by the Monty Python team.

Money

2 What this country needs is a good five-cent nickel.

Franklin P. Adams, American journalist, poet and humorist (1881–1960). *The Sun Dial* (1932).

3 It has always been said that money talks, but I rather think that it is beginning to talk too loudly.

James Agate, English dramatic critic (1877–1947). Quoted in *The Treasury of Humorous Quotations*, eds Evan Esar & Nicolas Bentley (1951).

4 Money can't buy you happiness but you can be miserable in comfort.

Anonymous. Something to this effect appears in exchanges between Topaze (the schoolmaster who gets rich by falling in with shady businessmen) and Tamise in Marcel Pagnol's *Topaze* (1930) – *'L'argent ne fait pas le bonheur …* ' Perhaps the precise saying occurred in one of the two English-language film versions.

5 A tip is a small sum of money you give to somebody because you're afraid he won't like not being paid for something you haven't asked him to do.

Anonymous. In *The Baile* (Glasgow) (*c.* 1913).

6 There are no pockets in shrouds.

Anonymous (proverb). R.C. Trench, *On Lessons in Proverbs* (1854), refers to an Italian proverb: 'With an image Dantesque in its vigour, that "a man shall carry nothing away with him when he dieth", take this Italian, *Our last robe that is our winding sheet,* is made *without pockets.*' 'There'll be no pockets in your shroud' has been ascribed to James T. Hill.

7 Never marry for money, but marry where money is.

Anonymous (proverb). Little recorded, but see Tennyson's dialect poem 'Northern Farmer, New Style' (1869): 'But I knaw'd a Quaäker feller as often 'as towd ma this: / 'Doänt thou marry for munny, but goä wheer munny is!'

8 The money that men make lives after them.

Samuel Butler, English author (1835–1902). Quoted in *The Treasury of Humorous Quotations*, eds Evan Esar & Nicolas Bentley (1951).

9 If you would know the value of Money, go and borrow some.

Benjamin Franklin, American politician and scientist (1706–90). *Poor Richard's Almanack* (April 1754) – a work in which Franklin often revised already existing sayings.

10 The sordid topic of coin.

Joyce Grenfell, English entertainer (1910–80). A delightful term for the matter of payment due or cash. Not from any sketch but mentioned by her in discussing a woman who inspired the creation of one of her characters. In *Joyce Grenfell Requests the Pleasure* (1976), she writes about the wife of an Oxbridge vice chancellor who featured in three monologues called 'Eng. Lit.'. The character was based partly on Grenfell's own expression while cleaning her teeth, partly on the playwright Clemence Dane (Winifred Ashton) and partly on the idiosyncratic speech patterns of Hester Alington, wife of the Dean of Durham, and a distant relative of Grenfell's husband. 'On a postcard addressed to a shoe-shop in Sloane Street she had written: "Gently fussed about non-appearance of dim pair of shoes sent to you for heeling" … And when Viola [Tunnard, Grenfell's accompanist] and I went to Durham to perform in aid of one of her charities she introduced the paying of our expenses: "My dears, we have not yet touched on the sordid topic of coin … "'

11 You Can't Take It With You.

Moss Hart and George S. Kaufman, American playwrights (1904–61) and (1889–1961). Title of play (1937).

12 The safest way to double your money is to fold it over once and put it in your pocket.

Frank McKinney ('Kin') Hubbard, American humorist and caricaturist (1868–1930). Quoted in *The Treasury of Humorous Quotations*, eds Evan Esar & Nicolas Bentley (1951).

1 Money can't buy friends, but you can get a better class of enemy.

Spike Milligan, Irish entertainer and writer (1918–). *Puckoon*, Chap. 6 (1963).

2 Money talks, they say. All it ever said to me was 'goodbye'.

Line from film *None But the Lonely Heart* (US 1944). Screenwriter: Clifford Odets (from Richard Llewellyn novel). Spoken by Cary Grant (Ernie Mott).

3 I shall benefit [from my brother's estate] to the amount of about £30,000 or more, which will come just in time to gild the nails of my coffin.

(Revd) Sydney Smith, English clergyman, essayist and wit (1771–1845). Letter (1843), quoted in *The Sayings of Sydney Smith*, ed. Alan Bell (1993).

Asked in old age why he persisted in robbing banks:

4 Because that's where the money is.

Willie Sutton, American criminal (1901–80). 'The most publicized bank robber since Jesse James' did, however, tell CBS TV's *Sixty Minutes* (8 August 1976) that, in fact, a reporter made it up and attributed it to him. His book *I, Willie Sutton* (1953) apparently does contain the observation: 'It is a rather pleasant experience to be alone in a bank at night.'

5 The lack of money is the root of all evil.

Mark Twain, American writer (1835–1910). In *More Maxims of Mark Twain*, ed. Merle Johnson (1927).

6 When I was young I used to think that money was the most important thing in life; now that I am old, I know that it is.

Oscar Wilde, Irish playwright, poet and wit (1854–1900). Quoted in *The Treasury of Humorous Quotations*, eds Evan Esar & Nicolas Bentley (1951).

Montgomery, Bernard (1st Viscount Montgomery of Alamein)

ENGLISH FIELD MARSHAL (1887–1976)

7 In defeat unbeatable; in victory unbearable.

(Sir) Winston S. Churchill, British Conservative Prime Minister and writer (1874–1965). Quoted in Edward Marsh, *Ambrosia and Small Beer* (1964).

Morals and moralizing

8 *Erst kommt das Fressen, dann kommt die Moral* [Food comes first, then morals].

Bertolt Brecht, German playwright (1898–1956). *The Threepenny Opera*, Act 2, Sc. 3 (1928). Variously translated: 'Eats first, morals after'; W.H. Auden wrote a poem entitled 'Grub First, Then Ethics (Brecht)' (1958).

On George Orwell whose copious essays and journalism were later to fill three sizeable volumes:

9 He would not blow his nose without moralizing on conditions in the handkerchief industry.

Cyril Connolly, English writer and critic (1903–74). *The Evening Colonnade* (1973).

10 Morality consists of suspecting other people of not being legally married.

Bernard Shaw, Irish playwright and critic (1856–1950). *The Doctor's Dilemma*, Act 3 (1906).

11 *Pickering*:
Have you no morals, man?
Doolittle:
Can't afford them, Governor.

Bernard Shaw. *Pygmalion*, Act 2 (1913).

12 Morality is simply the attitude we adopt towards people whom we personally dislike.

Oscar Wilde, Irish playwright, poet and wit (1854–1900). *An Ideal Husband*, Act 2 (1895).

Morons

13 See the happy moron,
He doesn't give a damn,

I wish I were a moron,
My god! perhaps I am!

Anonymous. In *The Eugenics Review* (July 1929). In Herbert V. Prochnow, Snr & Jnr, *A Treasury of Humorous Quotations* (1969), Henry Pratt Fairchild is credited with this version: 'I don't know what a moron is, / And I don't give a damn. / I'm thankful that I am not one – / My God, perhaps I am.' This is said to have appeared in *Harper's* Magazine (May 1932).

Moses

1 *Q.*:
Where was Moses when the light went out?
A.:
In the dark.

Anonymous. Quoted in I. & P. Opie, *The Lore and Language of Schoolchildren* (1959), as an 'almost proverbial' riddle having been found in *The Riddler's Oracle* (*c.* 1821). It is retold in Mark Twain, *The Adventures of Huckleberry Finn*, Chap. 17 (1884). Out of this may have grown the rhyme:

2 Where was Moses when the light went out?
Down in the cellar eating sauerkraut.

John J. Stamford, American songwriter (*c.* 1840–99). Song 'Where Was Moses When the Light Went Out?' (1878).

Mothers

3 Who took me from my bed so hot
And placed me shivering on the pot,
Nor asked me whether I would or not?
My Mother!

Anonymous. Parody of Ann and Jane Taylor's 'My Mother' in *Original Poems for Infant Minds* (1804). Known by 1978.

4 See the mothers in the park,
Ugly creatures chiefly.
Someone must have loved them, once,
But in the dark, and briefly.

Anonymous. Quoted in *The 'Quote ... Unquote' Newsletter* (October 1997) and earlier in *A World of Love*, ed. Godfrey Smith (1982). However, it has been reported from the early 1960s.

5 All women dress like their mothers, that is their tragedy. No man ever does. That is his.

Alan Bennett, English playwright and actor (1934–). *Forty Years On*, Act 1 (1969). Compare Wilde below.

6 Sometimes when I look at my children I say to myself, 'Lillian, you should have stayed a virgin.'

Lillian Carter, American mother of President Jimmy Carter (1898–1983). Quoted in *Woman* Magazine (9 April 1977), also recorded in the form, 'Wherever there's trouble – that's where Billy is! Sometimes ... I say to myself, "Lillian, you should have stayed a virgin"' – in Bob Chieger, *Was It Good For You Too?* (1983).

7 *Algernon*:
All women become like their mothers. That is their tragedy. No man does. That's his.

Oscar Wilde, Irish playwright, poet and wit (1854–1900). *The Importance of Being Earnest*, Act 1 (1895). The same words occur earlier (between two characters) in *A Woman of No Importance*, Act 2 (1893).

Mothers-in-law

8 There are only three basic jokes, but since the mother-in-law joke is not a joke but a very serious question, there are only two.

George Ade, American humorist and playwright (1866–1944). Quoted in *The Treasury of Humorous Quotations*, eds Evan Esar & Nicolas Bentley (1951).

Of his ex-wife Elaine:

9 She is the kind of girl who will not go anywhere without her mother. And her mother will go anywhere.

John Barrymore, American actor (1882–1942). Quoted in the same collection as above.

10 My mother-in-law broke up my marriage. One day my wife came home early and found us in bed together.

Lenny Bruce, American satirist (1923–66). Quoted in *The Penguin Dictionary of Modern Humorous Quotations*, ed. Fred Metcalf (1987).

1 Peter remained on friendly terms with Christ notwithstanding Christ's having healed his mother-in-law.

Samuel Butler, English writer (1835–1902). Quoted in *The Treasury of Humorous Quotations*, eds Evan Esar & Nicolas Bentley (1951).

2 My mother-in-law has come round to our house at Christmas seven years running. This year we're having a change. We're going to let her in.

Les Dawson, English comedian (1934–93). On BBC TV *Pebble Mill* (27 December 1979).

On the Grand Canyon:

3 What a marvellous place to drop one's mother-in-law.

Ferdinand Foch, French soldier (1851–1929). Quoted in Edmund Fuller, *2500 Anecdotes for All Occasions* (1943).

4 The awe and dread with which the untutored savage contemplates his mother-in-law are amongst the most familiar facts of anthropology.

(Sir) James George Frazer, Scottish anthropologist and folklorist (1854–1941). *The Golden Bough*, 2nd edn (1900).

5 But there, everything has its drawbacks, as the man said when his mother-in-law died, and they came down upon him for the funeral expenses.

Jerome K. Jerome, English writer (1859–1927). *Three Men In a Boat*, Chap. 3 (1889).

6 *Desperanda tibi salva concordia socru* [Give up all hope of peace so long as your mother-in-law is alive].

Juvenal, Roman poet and satirist (*c.* AD 40–125. *Satires*, 6.

7 I just came from a pleasure trip: I took my mother-in-law to the airport.

Henny Youngman, British-born American comedian (1906–98). Quoted in *The Times* (26 February 1998).

Motivation

When an actor, no doubt under the influence of The Method, was agonizing over his 'motivation' and asked his director, 'Just why do I cross the stage? Why, why?', Abbott told him:

8 To pick up your pay check.

George Abbott, American playwright, producer and director (1887–1995). Quoted by Mark Steyn on BBC Radio *Quote ... Unquote* (1990). *The Faber Book of Anecdotes* (1985) ascribes the remark to Noël Coward. *Compare* ADVICE 22:9.

Telegraphed version of the outcome of a conversation with the film producer Sam Goldwyn:

9 The trouble, Mr Goldwyn, is that you are only interested in art and I am only interested in money.

Bernard Shaw, Irish playwright and critic (1856–1950). Quoted in Alva Johnson, *The Great Goldwyn* (1937). It has been said that this witticism was, in fact, the creation of Howard Dietz but that Shaw approved it.

On the death of the Turkish ambassador to France:

10 What does he mean by that?

Charles Maurice de Talleyrand, French statesman (1754–1838). Alluded to in Ben Pimlott, *Harold Wilson*, Chap. 29 (1992). However, another version is that it was said in the form 'Died, has he? Now I wonder what he meant by that?', *about* Talleyrand and *by* King Louis Philippe.

Author's notice:

11 Persons attempting to find a motive in this narrative will be prosecuted; persons attempting to find a moral in it will be banished; persons attempting to find a plot in it will be shot.

Mark Twain, American writer (1835–1910). *The Adventures of Huckleberry Finn* (1884).

12 When a man does a thoroughly stupid thing, it is always from the noblest motives.

Oscar Wilde, Irish playwright, poet and wit (1854–1900). Quoted in *The Treasury of Humorous Quotations*, eds Evan Esar & Nicolas Bentley (1951).

Motoring and motorists

To Daisy, when she blames her car for an accident:

1 Mama, cars don't behave. They are behaved upon.

Line from film *Driving Miss Daisy* (US 1989). Screenwriter: Alfred Uhry (from his play). Spoken by Dan Aykroyd (Boolie Werthan) to Jessica Tandy (Daisy Werthan).

Toad on the joys of motoring:

2 The poetry of motion! The *real* way to travel! The *only* way to travel! Here today – in next week tomorrow! Villages skipped, towns and cities jumped – always somebody else's horizon! O bliss! O poop-poop! O my! O my!

Kenneth Grahame, Scottish-born writer (1859–1932). *The Wind in the Willows*, Chap. 2 (1908).

3 God would not have invented the automobile if he had intended me to walk.

J(ack) E. Morpurgo, English academic (1918–2000). *The Road to Athens* (1963).

4 There are a number of mechanical devices which increase sexual arousal, particularly in women. Chief among these is the Mercedes 380SL convertible.

P.J. O'Rourke, American humorist (1947–). *Modern Manners* (1983).

5 It is the overtakers who keep the undertakers busy.

William Pitts (1900–80). Quoted in *The Observer*, 'Sayings of the Week' (22 December 1963).

Mottoes

6 Hope for the best, expect the worst and take what comes.

Anonymous. Quoted by Arthur Marshall on BBC Radio *Quote … Unquote* (1 August 1987), who said that he was told it by a no-nonsense President of a Women's Institute. Apparently, it originated with Queen Alexandra, who used to write it in people's birthday books.

7 Our motto: Life is too short to stuff a mushroom.

Shirley Conran, English novelist and journalist (1932–). *Superwoman*, Epigraph (1975).

8 A lady once asked me for a motto for her dog Spot. I proposed, 'Out, damned Spot!' but strange to say, she did not think it sentimental enough.

(Revd) Sydney Smith, English clergyman, essayist and wit (1771–1845). Quoted in Lady Holland, *A Memoir of Sydney Smith*, Chap. 11 (1855).

9 Everybody's private motto: It's better to be popular than right.

Mark Twain, American writer (1835–1910). *More Maxims of Mark Twain*, ed. Merle Johnson (1927).

Mourning

10 Mrs Fitz-Adam reappeared in Cranford ('as bold as a lion,' Miss Pole said), a well-to-do widow, dressed in black rustling silk, so soon after her husband's death that poor Miss Jenkyns was justified in the remark she made, that 'bombazine would have shown a deeper sense of her loss'.

Elizabeth Gaskell, English novelist and biographer (1810–65). *Cranford*, Chap. 7 (1851–3).

Mozart, Wolfgang Amadeus

AUSTRIAN COMPOSER (1756–91)

His opinion of Mozart; walking out of a Glyndebourne performance:

11 Like piddling on flannel.

(Sir) Noël Coward, English entertainer and writer (1899–1973). Quoted in Cole Lesley, *The Life of Noël Coward* (1976). Mozart would have appreciated this comment, as he once said, 'I write [music] as a sow piddles' – quoted by Laurence J. Peter in *Quotations for Our Time* (1977) – source untraced, but using imagery of which Mozart was typically fond. Compare John Aubrey's memoir of Dr Kettle who, 'was wont to say that "Seneca writes, as a boare doth pisse", *scilicet*, by jirkes' (*Brief Lives*, from *c.* 1690).

Muddling through

On the American Civil War:

1 My opinion is that the Northern States will manage somehow to muddle through.

John Bright, English Radical politician (1811–89). Quoted in Justin McCarthy, *Reminiscences* (1899). Ironically, in the light of this earliest citation of the phrase, muddling through came to be known as what the British had a great talent for. *H.L. Mencken's Dictionary of Quotations* (1942) has, 'The English always manage to muddle through' – 'author unidentified; first heard *c.* 1885'. Ira Gershwin celebrated the trait in the song 'Stiff Upper Lip' from *A Damsel in Distress* (1937). He remembered the phrase 'keep muddling through' from much use at the time of the First World War.

Mugwumps

2 A mugwump is a sort of bird that sits on a fence with his mug on one side and his wump on the other.

Anonymous. In the *Blue Earth Post* (Minnesota), early 1930s. In a political context, the saying may have been introduced by Albert J. Engel in a House of Representatives speech (23 April 1936), though it has also been credited to Harold W. Dodds.

Murder and murderers

3 Lizzie Borden took an axe
And gave her mother forty whacks;
When she saw what she had done
She gave her father forty-one.

Anonymous. Lizzie Borden, the American axe-woman, was acquitted of murdering her father and stepmother at Fall River, Mass., in 1892.

4 Television has brought murder back into the home – where it belongs.

(Sir) Alfred Hitchcock, English film director (1899–1980). Quoted in *The Observer*, 'Sayings of the Week' (19 December 1965).

5 Murderer: one who is presumed to be innocent until he is proved insane.

Oscar Wilde, Irish playwright, poet and wit (1854–1900). Quoted in Herbert V. Prochnow, Snr & Jnr, *A Treasury of Humorous Quotations* (1969).

Museums

Towards the end of his life, the English music-hall comedian Wee Georgie Wood (1895–1979) hailed a taxi and said to the driver, 'Take me to the British Museum.' The driver looked alarmed at this and said:

6 You're taking a bloody chance, aren't you?

Anonymous. Quoted by Peter Jones on BBC Radio *Quote ... Unquote* (5 January 1982). Joe Ging, who was curator of the National Museum Hall in Sunderland wrote (8 May 1984) that Wood performed his museum's opening ceremony in July 1975. During his speech, Wood said, 'I was picked up at the Post House Hotel, Washington, by a taxi-driver from Sunderland. "Where are you going to, Mr Wood?" asked the taxi-driver. "I'm going to open a museum," I replied, proudly. To which he replied, "You're taking a bloody chance, aren't you?"' Joe Ging concedes that this was too good a story for Wood only to have used on one occasion.

Music

7 Of all modern phenomena, the most monstrous and ominous, the most manifestly rotting with disease, the most grimly prophetic of destruction, the most clearly and unmistakably inspired by evil spirits, the most instantly and awfully overshadowed by the wrath of heaven, the most near to madness and moral chaos, the most vivid with devilry and despair, is the practice of having to listen to loud music while eating a meal in a restaurant.

G.K. Chesterton, English poet, novelist and critic (1874–1936). 'On the Prison of Jazz' in 'Our Notebook', *Illustrated London News* (22 April 1933).

8 I hate music – especially when it is played.

Jimmy Durante, American comedian (1893–1980). Quoted in *An Encyclopedia of Quotations About Music*, ed. Nat Shapiro (1978).

When, as President and tone-deaf, he had to attend a concert:

1 I know only two tunes. One of them is 'Yankee Doodle' and the other isn't.

Ulysses S. Grant, American soldier and President (1822–85). Quoted in Louis Untermeyer, *A Treasury of Laughter* (1946).

2 Live music is an anachronism, and now is the winter of our discothèque.

Benny Green, English writer and broadcaster (1927–98). Recalled by him on BBC Radio *Quote ... Unquote* (1 June 1977).

3 The public doesn't want new music; the main thing it demands of a composer is that he be dead.

Arthur Honegger, Swiss composer (1892–1955). Quoted in *The Frank Muir Book* (1976).

4 Classical music is the kind that we keep hoping will turn into a tune.

Frank McKinney ('Kin') Hubbard, American humorist and caricaturist (1868–1930). Quoted in the same book as above.

5 Talking about music is like dancing about architecture.

Steve Martin, American comic actor and writer (1945–). Quoted in J.M. & M.J. Cohen, *The Penguin Dictionary of Twentieth-Century Quotations* (1993) as from *The Independent*. Has also been attributed to the jazz musician Thelonius Monk.

6 *Datemi una nota della lavandaia e la metterò in musica* [Give me a laundry-list and I will set it to music].

Gioachino Rossini, Italian composer (1792–1868). Quoted in *The Treasury of Humorous Quotations*, eds Evan Esar & Nicolas Bentley (1951).

When told his violin concerto needed a soloist with six fingers:

7 Very well, I can wait.

Arnold Schoenberg, German composer (1874–1951). Quoted in *The Penguin Dictionary of Modern Quotations*, eds J.M. & M.J. Cohen (1971) and Nat Shapiro, *An Encyclopedia of Quotations About Music* (1978). In Joseph Machlis, *Introduction to Contemporary Music* (1963), Schoenberg is quoted as having said of his violin concerto: 'I am delighted to add another unplayable work to the repertoire. I want the Concerto to be difficult and I want the little finger to become longer. I can wait.'

8 [Music is] the only cheap and unpunished rapture upon earth.

(Revd) Sydney Smith, English clergyman, essayist and wit (1771–1845). Quoted in *The Frank Muir Book* (1976).

Music-making

9 The music teacher came twice a week to bridge the awful gap between Dorothy and Chopin.

George Ade, American humorist and playwright (1866–1944). Quoted in *The Treasury of Humorous Quotations*, eds Evan Esar & Nicolas Bentley (1951).

To a female cellist:

10 Madam, you have between your legs an instrument capable of giving pleasure to thousands – and all you can do is scratch it.

(Sir) Thomas Beecham, English conductor (1879–1961). Quoted in Ned Sherrin, *Cutting Edge* (1984). Also attributed to Arturo Toscanini.

11 There are two golden rules for an orchestra: start together and finish together. The public doesn't give a damn what goes on in between.

(Sir) Thomas Beecham. Quoted in Harold Atkins & Archie Newman, *Beecham Stories* (1978). On the LP *Sir Thomas Beecham in Rehearsal* (WRC SH 147), he actually says: 'I have always laid it down as a golden rule that there are only two things requisite so far as the public is concerned for a good performance. That is, for the orchestra to begin together and end together. In between it doesn't matter much.'

12 Dr Johnson was observed by a musical friend of his to be extremely inattentive at a concert, whilst a celebrated solo player was run-

ning up the divisions and subdivisions of notes upon his violin. His friend, to induce him to take a greater notice of what was going on, told him how extremely difficult it was. 'Difficult do you call it, Sir?' replied the Doctor; 'I wish it were impossible.'

(Dr) Samuel Johnson, English writer and lexicographer (1709–84). Quoted in William Seward, *Supplement to the Anecdotes of Distinguished Persons* (1797).

1 After playing Chopin, I feel as if I had been weeping over sins that I had never committed.

Oscar Wilde, Irish playwright, poet and wit (1854–1900). 'The Critic As Artist' (1890).

Musical criticism

2 If white bread could sing, it would sound like Olivia Newton-John.

Anonymous. Quoted in *The Sunday Telegraph* Magazine (September 1980).

Of Madonna:

3 [Sings] like Mickey Mouse on helium … Like a sheep in pain.

Anonymous. Quoted in *Time* Magazine (1985).

4 I love Wagner, but the music I prefer is that of a cat hung up by its tail outside a window and trying to stick to the panes of glass with its claws.

Charles Baudelaire, French poet (1821–67). Quoted in *An Encyclopedia of Quotations About Music*, ed. Nat Shapiro (1978).

On Herbert von Karajan:

5 [He's a kind] of musical Malcolm Sargent.

(Sir) Thomas Beecham, English conductor (1879–1961). Quoted in Harold Atkins & Archie Newman, *Beecham Stories* (1978).

On Elgar's A Flat Symphony:

6 He [Elgar] is furious with me for drastically cutting his A flat symphony – it's a very long work, the musical equivalent of the towers of St Pancras station – neo-Gothic, you know.

(Sir) Thomas Beecham. Quoted in Neville Cardus, *Sir Thomas Beecham* (1961).

On being asked if he had ever heard any Stockhausen:

7 No, but I once stepped in some.

(Sir) Thomas Beecham. Quoted on BBC Radio *Quote … Unquote* (16 February 1979).

8 'I don't,' she added, 'know anything about music, really. But I know what I like.'

(Sir) Max Beerbohm, English writer and caricaturist (1872–1956). *Zuleika Dobson*, Chap. 16 (1911). In Chap. 9, Beerbohm had already commented of his heroine at a college concert: 'She was one of the people who say, "I don't know anything about music really, but I know what I like".' In the same year (1911), Gelett Burgess identified this philistine's slogan (also applied to art and literature) as a platitude in *Are You a Bromide?*

Having listened to a performance of an opera by a somewhat lesser composer:

9 I like your opera – I think I will set it to music.

Ludwig van Beethoven, German composer (1770–1827). Contributed to BBC Radio *Quote … Unquote* (6 July 1977). Also attributed to Richard Wagner.

To a fellow musician:

10 Oh, well, you play Bach *your* way. I'll play him *his*.

Wanda Landowska, Polish-born harpsichordist (1877–1959). Quoted in Harold C. Schonberg, *The Great Pianists* (1963).

On the song, 'The Red Flag':

11 The funeral march of a fried eel.

Bernard Shaw, Irish playwright and critic (1856–1950). Quoted in Winston S. Churchill, *Great Contemporaries* (1937).

Of Dame Ethel Smythe:

1 She would be like Richard Wagner, if only she looked a bit more feminine.

(Sir) Osbert Sitwell, English writer (1892–1969). Quoted in Elizabeth Lutyens, *A Goldfish Bowl* (1972).

To members of his orchestra:

2 After I die I shall return to earth as the doorkeeper of a bordello, and I won't let one of you in.

Arturo Toscanini, Italian conductor (1867–1957). Quoted in *The Home Book of Humorous Quotations*, ed. A.K. Adams (1969).

3 If one hears bad music, it is one's duty to drown it in conversation.

Oscar Wilde, Irish playwright, poet and wit (1854–1900). *The Picture of Dorian Gray*, Chap. 4 (1891).

Of Richard Clayderman, a popular pianist:

4 He is to piano playing as David Soul is to acting; he makes Jacques Loussier sound like Bach; he reminds us how cheap potent music can be.

Richard Williams, English music critic. Writing in *The Times*. Quoted in Ned Sherrin, *Cutting Edge* (1984).

5 [Andrew] Lloyd Webber's music is everywhere, but so is AIDS.

Malcolm Williamson, Australian-born Master of the Queen's Musick (1931–). Quoted in *The Daily Telegraph* (27 January 1992).

Musicians

6 Please don't shoot the pianist; he is doing his best.

Anonymous. Quoted in Oscar Wilde, *Impressions of America*, 'Leadville' (1906). Wilde reports having seen this notice in a bar or dancing saloon in the Rocky Mountains.

To a player in his orchestra:

7 We can't expect you to be with us all the time, but perhaps you would be good enough to keep in touch now and again.

(Sir) Thomas Beecham, English conductor (1879–1961). Quoted in Ned Sherrin, *Cutting Edge* (1984).

8 The chief objection to playing wind instruments is that it prolongs the life of the player.

Bernard Shaw, Irish playwright and critic (1856–1950). Quoted in *The Treasury of Humorous Quotations*, eds Evan Esar & Nicolas Bentley (1951).

9 Every member of the orchestra carries a conductor's baton in his knapsack.

(Sir) Tom Stoppard, English playwright (1937–). *Every Good Boy Deserves Favour* (1978).

10 It's organ organ all the time with him … Up every night until midnight playing the organ … I'm a martyr to music.

Dylan Thomas, Welsh poet (1914–53). Radio play, *Under Milk Wood* (1954).

N

Nakedness

1 I have seen three emperors in their nakedness, and the sight was not inspiring.

Otto von Bismarck, Prusso-German statesman (1815–98). Quoted in *The Treasury of Humorous Quotations*, eds Evan Esar & Nicolas Bentley (1951), but otherwise unverified.

When asked if she had really posed for a 1947 calendar with nothing on:

2 I had the radio on.

Marilyn Monroe, American film actress (1926–62). Quoted in *Time* Magazine (11 August 1952).

On being asked what she wore in bed:

3 Chanel No. 5.

Marilyn Monroe. Quoted in Pete Martin, *Marilyn Monroe* (1956).

On David Storey's play The Changing Room, *which included a male nude scene:*

4 I didn't pay three pounds fifty just to see half a dozen acorns and a chipolata.

(Sir) Noël Coward, English entertainer and writer (1899–1973). Quoted in Ned Sherrin, *Cutting Edge* (1984). *See also* SIZE 400:8.

Name-calling

When Eva Perón complained to him that she had been called a 'whore' on a visit to northern Italy:

5 Quite so. But I have not been on a ship for fifteen years and they still call me 'Admiral'.

Anonymous (Italian admiral). Quoted in 'The Power Behind the Glory', *Penthouse* Magazine (UK, August 1977).

Said first to have appeared in an anecdotal notebook kept by Adlai Stevenson, where the exchange takes place with a general in Barcelona.

Names

6 I agree with you that the name of Spiro Agnew is not a household name. I certainly hope that it will become one within the next couple of months.

Spiro T. Agnew, American Republican Vice President (1918–96). In interview with Mike Wallace of ABC TV, on becoming US vice-presidential candidate (8–9 August 1968).

7 *Striker:*
Surely you can't be serious!
Dr Rumack:
I am serious. And don't call me Shirley.

Lines from film *Airplane* (US 1980). Screenwriters: Jim Abrahams, David Zucker, Jerry Zucker. Spoken by Robert Hays (Ted Striker) and Leslie Nielsen (Dr Rumack).

8 I often think life must be quite different to a man called Smith; it can have neither poetry nor distinction.

'Annandale'. Quoted in W. Somerset Maugham, *A Writer's Notebook* (1949) – from his journal for 1894.

9 He (who has tried to catch his companion's name, and wishes to find it out indirectly): 'BY THE WAY, HOW DO YOU SPELL YOUR NAME?' She: 'J-O-N-E-S'.

Anonymous (cartoonist). Caption to cartoon in *Punch*, Vol. 122 (8 January 1902).

On being told that a woodwind player's name was 'Ball':

1 Ball? Ah, *Ball*. Very singular.

(Sir) Thomas Beecham, English conductor (1879–1961). Quoted in Neville Cardus, *Sir Thomas Beecham* (1961).

Of Sir Alfred Bossom MP:

2 Bossom? What an extraordinary name. Neither one thing nor the other!

(Sir) Winston S. Churchill, British Conservative Prime Minister and writer (1874–1965). Quoted in Willans & Roetter, *The Wit of Winston Churchill* (1954).

At Christmas 1944, Churchill paid a visit to Athens. This resulted in the appointment of Archbishop Damaskinos as Regent of Greece and General Plastiras as Prime Minister. Of the latter, Churchill commented:

3 Well, I hope he doesn't have feet of clay, too.

(Sir) Winston S. Churchill. Quoted in Leon Harris, *The Fine Art of Political Wit* (1966). In *Geoffrey Madan's Notebooks* (1981 – but Madan in 1947), Churchill's remark is quoted as: 'A bewhiskered ecclesiastic, and a certain General Plastiras. I hope his feet are not of clay.'

Of Samuel Francis Smith:

4 Fate tried to conceal him by naming him Smith.

Oliver Wendell Holmes Snr, American writer and physician (1809–94). 'The Boys' (1859).

5 I'm ashamed to be your father. You're a disgrace to our family name of Wagstaff, if such a thing is possible.

Line from film *Horse Feathers* (US 1932). Screenwriters: Bert Kalmar and others. Spoken by Groucho Marx (Prof. Wagstaff) to Zeppo Marx (Frank Wagstaff).

6 *Kornblow:*
Call me Montgomery.
Beatrice:
Is that your name?
Kornblow:
No, I'm just breaking it in for a friend.

Lines from film *A Night in Casablanca* (US 1946). Screenwriters: Joseph Fields, Roland Kibbee. Spoken by Groucho Marx (Ronald Kornblow) and Lisette Verea (Beatrice).

7 I've got Bright's Disease. And he's got mine.

S.J. Perelman, American humorist (1904–79). Caption to cartoon in *Judge* (16 November 1929).

On having an inflatable life-jacket named after her:

8 I've been in *Who's Who*, and I know what's what, but it'll be the first time I ever made the dictionary.

Mae West, American vaudeville and film actress (1893–1980). Letter to the 'Boys of the RAF' in 1941. Quoted by her in *Goodness Had Nothing To Do With It*, Chap. 17 (1959).

9 This agglomeration which was called and which still calls itself the Holy Roman Empire is neither holy, nor Roman, nor an empire.

Voltaire, French writer and philosopher (1694–1778). *Essai sur les Moeurs* (1756).

10 A journalist who had attacked Oscar Wilde in print on a number of occasions came up to him in the street one day and attempted to strike up a conversation. Wilde stared at him for a moment or two and then said: 'You will pardon me: I remember your name but I can't recall your face.'

Oscar Wilde, Irish playwright, poet and wit (1854–1900). Recounted by Max Beerbohm in one of the published *Letters to Reggie Turner* (1964). Compare, however: 'I remember your name perfectly; but I just can't think of your face' – ascribed to Revd William Spooner, English clergyman and academic (1844–1930) in *The Penguin Dictionary of Quotations*, eds J.M. & M.J. Cohen (1960). Both of these may be no more than re-attributions of the caption to a Phil May cartoon in *Punch* (9 August 1899): 'I know your name so well, but I can't remember your face.'

To somebody he ought to have known:

11 I can't remember your name. But don't tell me.

Alexander Woollcott, American writer and critic (1887–1943). Quoted by Lynne Truss on BBC Radio *Quote … Unquote* 13 September 1999).

Nannies

1 And always keep a hold of Nurse
For fear of finding something worse.

Hilaire Belloc, French-born English poet and writer (1870–1953). *Cautionary Tales*, 'Jim' (1907).

Napoleon I

FRENCH EMPEROR (1769–1821)

2 I don't care a twopenny damn [or I care not one twopenny damn …] what becomes of the ashes of Napoleon Bonaparte.

1st Duke of Wellington (Arthur Wellesley), Irish-born soldier and British Prime Minister (1769–1852). Attributed, but unverified – as e.g. in Farmer and Henley, *Slang and its Analogues* (1890–1904). In *Notes and Queries* (1879), the source is given as a *Life*, ii.257 (1878 edn), presumably that by Brialmont and Gleig. Lord Macaulay in a letter of 6 March 1849 wrote: 'How they settle the matter I care not, as the duke says, one twopenny damn.' James Morris in Pax Britannica (1968) comments: 'a dam was a small Indian coin, as Wellington knew when he popularized the phrase "a twopenny dam".' *Brewer's Dictionary of Phrase & Fable* (1989) says: 'The derivation … from the coin, a dam, is without foundation.' *The Oxford English Dictionary* (2nd edn) has: 'The conjecture that … the word is the Hindi *dam, dawm*, an ancient copper coin … is ingenious, but has no basis in fact.'

Nations

3 The great nations have always acted like gangsters and the small nations like prostitutes.

Stanley Kubrick, American film director (1928–99). In *The Guardian* (5 June 1963).

Nature

4 Nature, Mr Allnutt, is what we are put in this world to rise above.

Line from film *The African Queen* (UK 1951). Screenwriter: James Agee (from C.S. Forester novel). Spoken by Katharine Hepburn (Rose Sayer) to Humphrey Bogart (Charlie Allnutt).

5 Nature has good intentions, of course, but as Aristotle once said, she cannot carry them out.

Oscar Wilde, Irish playwright, poet and wit (1854–1900). 'The Decay of Lying', in *Nineteenth Century* (January 1889).

Navy

6 We joined the Navy to see the world,
And what did we see? We saw the sea.

Irving Berlin, American composer and lyricist (1888–1989). Song 'We Saw the Sea' from *Follow the Fleet* (1936).

When a naval officer objected that a wartime operation the Prime Minister was supporting ran against the traditions of the Royal Navy:

7 Don't talk to me about naval tradition. It's nothing but rum, sodomy, and the lash.

(Sir) Winston S. Churchill, British Conservative Prime Minister and writer (1874–1965). Quoted in Sir Peter Gretton, *Former Naval Person* (1968). In Harold Nicolson's diary (17 August 1950), this appears as: 'Naval tradition? Monstrous. Nothing but rum, sodomy, prayers and the lash.' Hence, *Rum Bum and Concertina*, the title of a volume of George Melly's autobiography (1977), which he prefers to derive from 'an old naval saying': 'Ashore it's wine, women and song, aboard it's rum, bum and concertina.' However, according to Churchill's Private Secretary 1952–65, Anthony Montague Brown (speech to the International Churchill Societies, 25 September 1986), 'He [Churchill] liked it very much, but he had never heard it before … ' Brown gave the phrase as 'Rum, lice, sodomy and the lash – those are the traditions of the British Navy.'

8 When I was a lad I served a term
As office boy to an Attorney's firm.
I cleaned the windows and I swept the floor,
And I polished up the handle of the big
front door.
I polished up the handle so carefullee
That now I am the Ruler of the Queen's
Navee!

(Sir) W.S. Gilbert, English writer and lyricist (1836–1911). *H.M.S. Pinafore*, Act 1 (1878).

On the state of England:

1 Everything's at sea – except the Fleet.

Horace Walpole (4th Earl of Orford), English writer (1717–97). Quoted by Malcolm Muggeridge on BBC Radio *Quote ... Unquote* (21 June 1978).

Necking

2 Whoever named it necking was a poor judge of anatomy.

Groucho Marx, American comedian (1895–1977). In 1970. Quoted in Laurence J. Peter, *Quotations for Our Time* (1977).

Negotiation

3 Negotiating with [Eamon] de Valera [Irish politician] ... is like trying to pick up mercury with a fork.

David Lloyd George (1st Earl Lloyd George of Dwyfor), British Liberal Prime Minister (1863–1945). Quoted in M.J. MacManus, *Eamon de Valera* (1944). To which de Valera is said to have replied: 'Why doesn't he use a spoon?'

Neighbours

Mr Bennet speaking:

4 For what do we live, but to make sport for our neighbours, and laugh at them in our turn?

Jane Austen, English novelist (1775–1817). *Pride and Prejudice*, Chap. 57 (1813).

5 For my part I keep the commandments, I love my neighbour as myself, and to avoid coveting my neighbour's wife I desire to be coveted by her; which you know is quite another thing.

William Congreve, English playwright (1670–1729). Letter to Mrs Edward Porter (27 September 1700).

6 It is an offence to have a wireless on too loud these still summer evenings. It can annoy your neighbour. An even better way is to throw a dead cat on the lawn ...

Ronald Fletcher, English broadcaster (1910–96). Quoted in Bernard Braden, *The Kindness of Strangers* (1990). From Braden radio shows of the 1950s. Scripts by various.

7 Philosophy may teach us to bear with equanimity the misfortunes of our neighbours.

Oscar Wilde, Irish playwright, poet and wit (1854–1900). Lecture 'The English Renaissance of Art' in New York (9 January 1882).

Neurotics

8 Neurotics build castles in the air. Psychotics live in them. Psychiatrists charge the rent.

Anonymous (graffito). From Birmingham University, included in my book *Graffiti* 2 (1980). In Laurence J. Peter, *Quotations for Our Time* (1977), this observation is ascribed to Jerome Lawrence (1916–). Sometimes 'Psychotics smash the windows' is inserted.

9 A neurotic is a man who builds a castle in the air. A psychotic is the man who lives in it. And a psychiatrist is the man who collects the rent.

Alfred Edward (Lord) Webb-Johnson, English surgeon (1880–1958). Quoted in *Look* Magazine (4 October 1955).

Neutrality

10 As the poet Dante once said, 'The hottest places in hell are reserved for those who, in a time of great moral crisis, maintain their neutrality.'

John F. Kennedy, American Democratic President (1917–63). Quoted in *The Quotable Mr Kennedy*, ed. Gerald C. Gardner (1962).

Never-never

11 Live now, pay later.

Anonymous (graffito). In Los Angeles (1970), quoted in Reisner & Wechsler, *The Encyclopedia of Graffiti* (1974). Earlier, however, it had been the title of a screenplay (1962) based on the novel *All On the Never Never* by Jack Lindsay.

New York City

12 When I first went to New York, I was warned to look out for the pitfalls, and I did. But it was Sunday, and they were all closed.

Robert Benchley, American humorist (1889–1945). Quoted by Earl Wilson in *New York Post* (no date).

1 The city of Dreadful Height.

James Bone, Scottish journalist (b. 1872). In *Manchester Guardian* (undated). Quoted in *The Home Book of Humorous Quotations*, ed. A.K. Adams (1969).

2 When I had looked at the lights of Broadway by night, I said to my American friends: what a glorious garden of wonders this would be to anyone who was lucky enough to be unable to read.

G.K. Chesterton, English poet, novelist and critic (1874–1936). *What I Saw in America* (1922).

3 Nearly all th' most foolish people in th' country an' manny iv th' wisest goes to Noo York. Th'wise people ar-re there because th' foolish wint first. That's th' way th'wise men make a livin'.

Finley Peter Dunne, American writer (1867–1936). *Mr Dooley's Opinions* (1902).

4 If they had as much adultery going on in New York as they said in the divorce courts, they … would never have a chance to make the beds at the Plaza.

Zsa Zsa Gabor, Hungarian-born film actress (1919–). Quoted in Barbara Rowes, *The Book of Quotes* (1979).

5 Baghdad-on-the-Subway.

O. Henry, American writer (1862–1910). *A Madison Square Arabian Night* (*c.* 1913) and in other stories.

6 If ever there was an aviary overstocked with jays it is that Yaptown-on-the-Hudson, called New York.

O. Henry. *Gentle Grafter*, 'A Tempered Wind' (1908).

7 Most of the people living in New York have come here from the farm to try to make enough money to go back to the farm.

Don Marquis, American writer (1878–1937). Quoted in Herbert V. Prochnow, Snr & Jnr, *A Treasury of Humorous Quotations* (1969).

8 When it's three o'clock in New York, it's still 1938 in London.

Bette Midler, American entertainer (1945–). Quoted in *The Times* (21 September 1978). However, in Vanessa Letts, *New York* (1991), 'When it's 9.30 in New York, it's 1937 in Los Angeles' is ascribed to Groucho Marx.

9 The Bronx?
No thonx.

Ogden Nash, American poet (1902–71). In *The New Yorker* (1931).

10 New York is not the centre of the goddamn universe. I grant you it's an exciting, vibrant, stimulating, fabulous city, but it is not Mecca. It just smells like it.

Neil Simon, American playwright (1927–). *California Suite* (1976).

11 Coney Island, where the surf is one-third water and two-thirds people.

John Steinbeck, American writer (1902–68). Quoted in Herbert V. Prochnow, Snr & Jnr, *A Treasury of Humorous Quotations* (1969).

12 New York is like a disco, but without the music.

Elaine Stritch, American actress (1926–). Quoted in *The Observer*, 'Sayings of the Week' (17 February 1980).

13 New York is a small place when it comes to the part of it that wakes up just as the rest is going to bed.

(Sir) P(elham) G. Wodehouse, English-born novelist and lyricist (1881–1975). *My Man Jeeves*, 'The Aunt and the Sluggard' (1919).

14 There's no more crime in New York – there's nothing left to steal.

Henny Youngman, British-born American comedian (1906–98). Quoted in Barbara Rowes, *The Book of Quotes* (1979).

New Zealand

15 I went to New Zealand but it was closed.

Anonymous. A line that gets rediscovered every so often. The Beatles found it in the 1960s; slightly before then, Anna Russell, the musical comedienne, said it on one of her records. It has also been attributed to Clement Freud. William Franklyn, son of the Antipodean actor Leo Franklyn, says that his father was saying it in the 1920s. Perhaps W.C. Fields began it all by saying 'Last week, I went to Philadelphia, but it was closed' about the same time (if indeed he did). This last attribution comes from Richard J. Anobile, *Godfrey Daniels* (1975).

News and newspapers

1 He had been kicked in the head by a mule when young, and believed everything he read in the Sunday papers.

George Ade, American humorist and playwright (1866–1944). Quoted in *The Treasury of Humorous Quotations*, eds Evan Esar & Nicolas Bentley (1951).

2 I read the newspaper avidly. It is my one form of continuous fiction.

Aneurin Bevan, Welsh Labour politician (1897–1960). Quoted in *The Times* (29 March 1960).

3 When a dog bites a man, that is not news, because it happens so often. But if a man bites a dog, that is news.

John B. Bogart, American journalist (1845–1921). As a definition of news, this has been variously ascribed. Chiefly, in this form, to Bogart, city editor of the New York *Sun*, 1873–90. To Charles A. Dana, the editor of the same paper from 1868 to 1897, it has been ascribed in the form: 'If a dog bites a man, it's a story; if a man bites a dog, it's a good story.'

4 The man who reads nothing at all is better educated than the man who reads nothing but newspapers.

Thomas R. Jefferson, American President and polymath (1743–1826). Quoted in *The Treasury of Humorous Quotations*, eds Evan Esar & Nicolas Bentley (1951).

5 News expands to fill the time and space allocated to its coverage.

William Safire, American journalist (1929–). In *The New York Times* (6 September 1973).

Of the Daily Mail:

6 By office boys for office boys.

3rd Marquess of Salisbury (Robert Cecil), British Conservative Prime Minister (1830–1903). Quoted in H. Hamilton Fyfe, *Northcliffe, an Intimate Biography* (1930).

7 The *newspapers*! Sir, they are the most villainous – licentious – abominable – infernal – Not that I ever read them – No – I make it a rule never to look into a newspaper.

Richard Brinsley Sheridan, English playwright and politician (1751–1816). *The Critic*, Act 1 Sc. 1 (1779).

8 Editorial is what keeps the ads apart.

Roy Thomson (Lord Thomson), Canadian-born newspaper proprietor (1894–1976). Attributed remark.

9 He was as shy as a newspaper is when referring to its own merits.

Mark Twain, American writer (1835–1910). *Following the Equator* (1897).

10 You try to tell *me* anything about the newspaper business! Sir! I have been through it from Alpha to Omega, and I tell you the less a man knows the bigger the noise he makes and the higher the salary he commands.

Mark Twain. *Sketches New and Old* (1899).

11 I became a newspaperman. I hated to do it, but I couldn't find honest employment.

Mark Twain. Quoted in *The Sayings of Mark Twain*, ed. James Munson (1992).

12 News is what a chap who doesn't care much about anything wants to read. And it's only news until he's read it. After that it's dead.

Evelyn Waugh, English novelist (1903–66). *Scoop*, Bk 1, Chap. 5 (1938).

See also JOURNALISM, JOURNALISTS, PRESS.

Niagara

13 Every American bride is taken there, and the sight of the stupendous waterfall must be one of the earliest, if not the keenest, disappointments in American married life.

Oscar Wilde, Irish playwright, poet and wit (1854–1900). *Impressions of America* (1906). Sometimes rendered as 'Niagara is only the second biggest disappointment of the standard honeymoon' and '[Niagara] is the first disappointment in the married life of many Americans who spend their honeymoon there.' Wilde visited Niagara in February 1882.

Nightmares

1 Have you noticed ... there is never any third act in a nightmare? They bring you to a climax of terror and then leave you there. They are the work of poor dramatists.

(Sir) Max Beerbohm, English writer and caricaturist (1872–1956). Quoted in S.N. Behrman, *Conversations with Max* (1960).

Nincompoops

2 *Someone described the late wealthy actor Raymond Massey as a nincompoop. When asked why, he said:*

Because he's a poop with an income.

Anonymous. Quoted in The *'Quote ... Unquote' Newsletter* (January 1997).

Nixon, Richard M.

AMERICAN REPUBLICAN PRESIDENT (1913–94)

3 [President Nixon] told us he was going to take crime out of the streets. He did. He took it into the damn White House.

(Revd) Ralph Abernathy, American civil rights leader and minister (1926–90). Attributed remark.

4 Would you buy a used car from this man?

Anonymous. Although attributed by some to Mort Sahl and by others to Lenny Bruce, and though the cartoonist Herblock denied that he was responsible (*The Guardian*, 24 December 1975), this is just a joke *about* Nixon and one is no more going to find an origin for it than for most such. As to *when* it arose, this is Hugh Brogan, writing in *New Society* (4 November 1982): 'Nixon is a double-barrelled, treble-shotted twister, as my old history master would have remarked; and the fact has been a matter of universal knowledge since at least 1952, when, if I remember aright the joke, "Would you buy a second-hand car from this man?" began to circulate.' It was a very effective slur and, by 1968, when the politician was running (successfully) for President, a poster of a shifty-looking Nixon with the line as caption was in circulation.

The phrase is now used of anybody one has doubts about. In a Mahood cartoon of Prime Minister Edward Heath (*Punch*, 7 January 1970): 'Would you buy a used boat from this man?' *The Encyclopedia of Graffiti*, eds R. Reisner & L. Wechsler (1974) even finds: 'Governor Romney – would you buy a *new* car from this man?' *See also* TRUST 438:8.

5 He could tell two separate lies out of different corners of his mouth at the same time.

Anonymous. Quoted by Robin Oakley on BBC Radio *Quote ... Unquote* (9 September 2000).

6 President Nixon's motto was, if two wrongs don't make a right, try three.

Norman Cousins, American writer (1915–). Quoted by Christie Davies in *The Daily Telegraph* (17 July 1979).

7 Nixon just isn't half the man Hitler was.

Richard Dudman, American Journalist. In *St Louis Post Dispatch* (undated).

8 [Nixon has] the integrity of a hyena and the style of a poison toad.

Hunter S. Thompson, American writer and journalist (1939–). Attributed remark.

Nobel Prize

9 [Nobel Prize] money is a lifebelt thrown to a swimmer who has already reached the shore in safety.

Bernard Shaw, Irish playwright and critic (1856–1950). Quoted in Hesketh Pearson, *Lives of the Wits* (1962). Shaw was awarded the Nobel Prize for Literature in 1925 but refused it. Here he is merely paraphrasing Samuel Johnson's pointed remark to Lord Chesterfield: *see* PATRON 328:6.

Noise

10 The rooster makes more racket than the hen that lays the egg.

Joel Chandler Harris, American writer (1848–1908). Quoted in *The Treasury of Humorous Quotations*, eds Evan

Esar & Nicolas Bentley (1951). This would seem to be a version of a proverbial saying 'The cock crows but the hen goes', recorded by 1659. At a private dinner party in 1987, Margaret Thatcher quoted, 'The cocks may crow but it's the hen that lays the egg' – reported in *The Sunday Times* (9 April 1989).

1 Of all noises I think music the least disagreeable.

(Dr) Samuel Johnson, English writer and lexicographer (1709–84). Quoted in *The Morning Chronicle* (1816).

2 Noise proves nothing. Often a hen who has merely laid an egg cackles as if she had laid an asteroid.

Mark Twain, American writer (1835–1910). *Following the Equator*, Vol. 1 (1897).

3 Thunder is good, thunder is impressive; but it is the lightning that does the work.

Mark Twain. *Mark Twain's Letters*, ed. A.B. Paine (1917).

4 When some men discharge an obligation you can hear the report for miles around.

Mark Twain. Quoted in *The Sayings of Mark Twain*, ed. James Munson (1992).

5 The type-writing machine, when played with expression, is not more annoying than the piano when played by a sister or near relation.

Oscar Wilde, Irish playwright, poet and wit (1854–1900). In *The Letters of Oscar Wilde*, ed. Rupert Hart-Davis (1962) – letter to Robert Ross from Reading Prison (1 April 1897).

6 The drowsy stillness of the summer afternoon was shattered by what sounded to his strained senses like G.K. Chesterton falling on a sheet of tin.

(Sir) P(elham) G. Wodehouse, English-born novelist and lyricist (1881–1975). *Mr Mulliner Speaking* (1929).

Nonsense

7 Parding Mrs Harding,
Is our kitting in your garding,
Eating of a mutting-bone?
No, he's gone to Londing.
How many miles to Londing?
Eleving? I thought it was only seving.
Heavings! *What* a long way from home!

Anonymous (popular song). Known by the 1870s. Quoted in Vyvyan Holland, *Son of Oscar Wilde* (1954). This has also been quoted beginning, 'Beg your parding, Mrs Harding ... '

8 I had a duck-billed platypus when I was up at Trinity
With whom I soon discovered a remarkable affinity.
He used to live in lodgings with myself and Arthur Purvis,
And we all went up together for the Diplomatic Service.

Patrick Barrington (11th Viscount Barrington), English poet (1908–90). Probably written in the 1930s and contributed to *Punch*. Included in *Verse and Worse*, ed. Arnold Silcock (1958 edn).

9 I dreamt I dwelt in marble halls,
And each damp thing that creeps and crawls
Went wobble-wobble on the walls.

Lewis Carroll, English writer (1832–98). *Lays of Mystery, Imagination, and Humour* (1855).

10 They told me you had been to her,
And mentioned me to him:
She gave me a good character,
But said I could not swim.

Lewis Carroll. *Alice's Adventures in Wonderland*, Chap. 12 (1865).

11 'Twas brillig, and the slithy toves
Did gyre and gimble in the wabe;
All mimsy were the borogoves,
And the mome raths outgrabe.

Lewis Carroll. *Through the Looking-Glass and What Alice Found There*, Chap. 1 (1872). This opening stanza of the poem 'Jabberwocky' first appeared in a periodical that Carroll wrote and published for his brothers and sisters in 1855. There it is headed 'Stanza of Anglo-Saxon Poetry' and the following translations given of the difficult words: brillig = the close of the afternoon; slithy = smooth and active; tove = a species of badger; gyre = scratch like a dog; gimble = screw out holes in anything; wabe = side of a hill; mimsy = unhappy; borogove = extinct kind of parrot; mome = grave; rath = species of land turtle; outrabe = squeaked.

1 The Jabberwock, with eyes of flame,
Came whiffling through the tulgey wood,
And burbled as it came.

Lewis Carroll. In the same poem. Carroll subsequently explained the name Jabberwock as meaning 'the result of much excited discussion'; whiffling is not a Carrollian invention but means something like blowing; tulgey (his invention) = thick, dense, dark; burbling, though an established word, was derived, according to Carroll, from an amalgam of 'bleat', 'murmur' and 'warble'.

2 'And hast thou slain the Jabberwock?
Come to my arms, my beamish boy!
O frabjous day! Callooh! Callay!'
He chortled in his joy.

Lewis Carroll. In the same poem. Beamish (an old word) = shining brightly; frabjous (Carroll's invention) = fair and joyous; chortled (Carroll's invention, surprisingly perhaps) = chuckled and snorted.

3 Tweedledum and Tweedledee
Agreed to have a battle;
For Tweedledum said Tweedledee
Had spoiled his nice new rattle.

Lewis Carroll. In the same book, Chap. 4.

4 The sun was shining on the sea,
Shining with all his might:
He did his very best to make
The billows smooth and bright –
And this was odd, because it was
The middle of the night.

Lewis Carroll. In the same book and chapter.

5 But four young Oysters hurried up,
All eager for the treat:
Their coats were brushed, their faces washed,
Their shoes were clean and neat –
And this was odd, because, you know,
They hadn't any feet.

Lewis Carroll. In the same poem.

6 'O Oysters,' said the Carpenter,
'You've had a pleasant run!
Shall we be trotting home again?'
But answer came there none –
And this was scarcely odd, because
They'd eaten every one.

Lewis Carroll. In the same poem.

7 He thought he saw an Elephant,
That practised on a fife:
He looked again, and found it was
A letter from his wife.
'At length I realize,' he said,
'The bitterness of Life!'

Lewis Carroll. *Sylvie and Bruno*, Chap 5. (1889).

8 When it's night-time in Italy it's Wednesday over here.

James Kendis and Lew Brown, American songwriters (1883–1946) and (1893–1958). Title of nonsense song, recorded by Billy Jones with orchestra in New York (1922).

9 On the coast of Coromandel
Where the early pumpkins blow,
In the middle of the woods,
Lived the Yonghy-Bonghy-Bó.
Two old chairs, and half a candle; –
One old jug without a handle, –
These were all his worldly goods.

Edward Lear, English poet and artist (1812–88). 'The Courtship of the Yonghy-Bonghy-Bó' (1871). This poem was itself parodied in 1943 by Sir Osbert Sitwell who wrote: 'On the coast of Coromandel / Dance they to the tunes of Handel'.

10 Show me a rose and I'll show you a girl named Sam.

Groucho Marx, American comedian (1895–1977). Line from song, 'Show Me a Rose'. In fact, written by Harry Ruby and Bert Kalmar, though popularized by Groucho. Not included in any of his films.

About F.D. Roosevelt's New Deal during campaign speeches in 1936:

1 No matter how thin you slice it, it's still baloney.

Alfred E. Smith, American politician (1873–1944). Roosevelt had supported Smith in 1928 but they fell out when Roosevelt himself ran for the presidency. However, Brendan Gill in *Here at the New Yorker* (1975), ascribes the remark to Rube Goldberg. Clare Booth Luce, in a speech to the House of Representatives (9 February 1943) said: 'Much of what Mr [H.G.] Wallace calls his global thinking is, no matter how you slice it, still globaloney.'

2 One man's caviar is another man's major general, as the old saw has it.

(Sir) P(elham) G. Wodehouse, English-born novelist and lyricist (1881–1975): *Jeeves in the Offing* (1949).

Normality

3 Young normal tigers do not eat people. If eaten by a tiger you may rest assured that he was abnormal.

Will Cuppy, American humorist (1884–1949). *How To Tell Your Friends From the Apes*, 'The Tiger' (1934).

4 We are normal and we dig Bert Weedon.

Line from song, 'We Are Normal', written and performed by the Bonzo Dog Band (1968). Bert Weedon was a notable guitar soloist in those days.

Norwegians

5 The Norwegian language has been described as German spoken underwater.

Anonymous. Quoted by Christopher Hampton in programme note to his translation of Ibsen's *An Enemy of the People*, Royal National Theatre, London (1997).

6 It is difficult to describe Norwegian charisma precisely but it is somewhere between a Presbyterian minister and a tree.

Johnny Carson, American comedian (1925–). Attributed remark dating from 1984 when Walter Mondale, the American politician of Norwegian stock, challenged President Reagan unsuccessfully.

7 I don't like Norwegians at all. The sun never sets, the bar never opens, and the whole country smells of kippers.

Evelyn Waugh, English novelist (1903–66). Letter to Lady Diana Cooper (13 July 1934).

Noses

8 Red roses blow but thrice a year,
In June, July and May.
But those who have red noses
Can blow them every day.

Gerald Berners (Lord Berners), English composer and writer (1883–1950). Poem 'Some People Praise Red Roses' (which he also set to music), from the 1930s. Included in *Mark Amory*, Lord Berners (1998).

9 If Cleopatra's nose had been shorter the whole face of the earth would have changed.

Blaise Pascal, French philosopher and mathematician (1623–62). *Pensées*, Bk 2, No. 62 (1670). That is to say, if the Queen of Egypt had not attracted both Julius Caesar and Mark Antony, and become embroiled with the affairs of the Roman empire, history might have taken a different course.

Suggesting better insults about his nose:

10 Obvious: Excuse me, is that your nose, or did a bus park on your face? Meteorological: Everybody take cover! She's going to blow! Fashionable: You know, you could de-emphasize your nose if you wore something larger, like Wyoming. Personal: Well, here we are, just the three of us … Laugh and the world laughs with you. Sneeze and it's 'Goodbye Seattle' … Dirty: Your name wouldn't be Dick, would it?

Lines from film *Roxanne* (US 1987). Screenwriter: Steve Martin (after Edmond Rostand play *Cyrano de Bergerac*). Spoken by Steve Martin (Charlie C.D. Bales).

11 It is a nose once seen never to be forgotten, and which requires the utmost strength of Christian charity to forgive.

Percy Bysshe Shelley, English poet (1792–1822). Quoted

in *The Treasury of Humorous Quotations*, eds Evan Esar & Nicolas Bentley (1951).

Nostalgia

1 Nostalgia isn't what it used to be.

Anonymous (graffito). In New York City. Used as the title of the autobiography (1978) of Simone Signoret, the French film actress (1921–85). As 'Nostalgia ain't what it used to be', the remark has been attributed to the American novelist Peter de Vries.

Notes

When Miller was an undergraduate at Cambridge, he called on a friend whom he found in flagrante. *So he left a note saying:*

2 Called to see you but you were in.

Karl Miller, Scottish editor and academic (1931–). Quoted in *Cosmopolitan* (UK) (*c.* 1979).

Notices and signs

Warning notice near Milan cathedral:

3 The Sisters, so called, of Mercy solicit tender alms. They harbour all kinds of diseases and have no respect for religion.

Anonymous. Said to have been observed by Mark Twain, but untraced. A version appeared in *Pass the Port Again* (1981 edn) In John G. Murray, *A Gentleman Publisher's Commonplace Book* (1996), this version is said to have appeared outside an Italian hospital run by nuns: 'These little sisters solicit gentle alms, they do not respect religion and harbour all manner of disease.'

Sign from a pub:

4 LADIES UNACCOMPANIED ARE RESPECTFULLY REQUESTED TO USE TABLES FOR THEIR REFRESHMENTS AND NOT TO STAND AT THE BAR AND OBLIGE.

Anonymous. Quoted in James Agate, *Ego 3* (1938).

5 NO SPITTING – ON THURSDAYS.

Anonymous. Sign in Hollywood studio, quoted on BBC Radio *Quote … Unquote* (11 July 1987).

6 Please smoke. Thank you for not jogging.

Anonymous. Sign in New York taxi, quoted on BBC Radio *Quote … Unquote* (11 July 1987).

7 ANYONE THROWING STONES AT THIS NOTICE WILL BE PROSECUTED.

Gerald Berners (Lord Berners), English writer and composer (1883–1950). Quoted in *The Independent on Sunday* (25 July 1993). At least he is said to have had this sign put up at his home, Faringdon House, in Oxfordshire. Compare David Frost's narration from BBC TV's *The Frost Report* (*c.* 1966): 'For many of us, authority is summed up by the sign that one of the team found on the Yorkshire Moors which said simply, "It is forbidden to throw stones at this notice".' However, even earlier, *Punch* (22 March 1939) contained a drawing of a notice which stated: 'IT IS FORBIDDEN TO THROW STONES AT THIS NOTICE BOARD.'

8 When loading the vessel, always make sure that the center of flotation is above the center of gravity. If, however, the center of gravity is higher, do not worry, as the vessel will automatically turn over, so that the center of flotation is once more above the center of gravity. However, this has the tendency to spoil everyone's day, and is best avoided.

Anonymous (sign on American container vessel). Quoted on BBC Radio *Quote … Unquote* (18 September 2000). A chartered mechanical engineer (British) suggests that 'center of buoyancy' would be the more likely term.

9 It is no good putting up notices saying 'Beware of the bull' because very rude things are sometimes written on them. I have found one of the most effective notices is 'Beware of the Agapanthus'.

Lord Massereene and Ferrard, English politician (1914–93). Speech, House of Lords, on the Wildlife and Countryside Bill (16 December 1980).

10 When she saw the sign 'Members only' she thought of him.

Spike Milligan, Irish entertainer and writer (1918–). *Puckoon*, Chap. 3 (1963).

Notoriety

1 There is only one thing in the world worse than being talked about, and that is not being talked about.

Oscar Wilde, Irish playwright, poet and wit (1854–1900). *The Picture of Dorian Gray*, Chap. 1 (1891).

Novels

2 The trouble began with [E.M.] Forster. After him it was considered ungentlemanly to write more than five or six [novels].

Anthony Burgess, English novelist and critic (1917–93). In *The Guardian* (24 February 1989).

On the 'classic formula' for a novel:

3 A beginning, a muddle, and an end.

Philip Larkin, English poet (1922–85). When presenting the results of the Booker Prize for Fiction in 1977. Quoted in *New Fiction* (January 1978).

4 One should not be too severe on English novels; they are the only relaxation of the intellectually unemployed.

Oscar Wilde, Irish playwright, poet and wit (1854–1900). Quoted in *The Fireworks of Oscar Wilde*, ed. Owen Dudley Edwards (1989).

5 The ancient historians gave us delightful fiction in the form of fact; the modern novelist presents us with dull facts under the guise of fiction.

Oscar Wilde, Irish playwright, poet and wit (1854–1900). 'The Decay of Lying', in *Nineteenth Century* (January 1889).

6 In every first novel the hero is the author as Christ or Faust.

Oscar Wilde. Attributed remark.

Novelty

7 There are three things which the public will always clamour for, sooner or later: namely, novelty, novelty, novelty.

Thomas Hood, English poet (1799–1845). *Announcement of Comic Annual for 1836*. This is the earliest example found of the triple repetition format. By 1999, the (real) estate agent's mantra was much quoted: 'The three most important things when determining the selling price of a property: location, location, location.' In 1996, the Labour Party leader Tony Blair declared that his political priorities were: 'Education, education, education.' From Tim Rice's autobiography *Oh, What a Circus*, Chap. 11 (1999): 'There is a famous quote in theatrical circles which has been attributed to nearly every musical writer and producer over the years: the three most important things to get right when embarking on a musical are "book, book and book," the book being the storyline.'

Nuns

On reading Monica Baldwin's book I Leap Over the Wall *(1949) about her return to the world after 28 years in a convent:*

8 Very interesting, I must say. It has strengthened my decision not to become a nun.

(Sir) Noël Coward, English entertainer and writer (1899–1973). *The Noël Coward Diaries* (1982) – entry for 1 December 1949.

Nursery rhymes

9 Little Miss Muffet
Sat on her tuffet,
So nobody could get at it.
There came a big spider,
Who sat down beside her –
But he couldn't get at it either.

Anonymous. In 1966.

10 The Grand Old Duchess of York,
She *had* ten thousand men.
She'd march them up to the top of the hill,
Then say, 'Go on, do it again!'

Anonymous. In 1966.

11 Humpty Dumpty sat on a wall
Humpty Dumpty had a great fall
All the king's horses and all the king's men
Had scrambled eggs for the next four weeks.

Anonymous (graffito). Included in my book *Graffiti 4* (1982).

O

Oafs

1 Great oafs from little ikons grow.

Anonymous. Fake Russian-style proverb concerning Nikita Khruschev. Contributed to BBC Radio *Quote ... Unquote* (1 June 1977) by Benny Green. Richard Boston ascribed to S.J. Perelman the similar 'Great oafs from little infants grow.'

Oats

2 A grain, which in England is generally given to horses, but in Scotland supports the people.

(Dr) Samuel Johnson, English writer and lexicographer (1709–84). *A Dictionary of the English Language* (1755).

Obituaries

3 He loved shooting, hunting, horses, and above all dogs. The smell of a wet dog was delicious to him, and his devoted wife never let him know that, to her, it was abominable.

Anonymous (obituarist). In *The Times* (7 August 1963), of Sir Hereward Wake, English soldier (1876–1963).

4 De mortuis nil nisi bunkum.

Anonymous. Based on the maxim *'de mortuis nil nisi bonum* [speak nothing but good of the dead – or not at all]', this remark is attributed to Harold Laski, the political scientist (in Kingsley Martin, *Harold Laski*, 1953), though in fact he was merely reviving a joke that had appeared in *Punch* (25 March 1865): 'RULE IN FUNERAL ORATIONS. De mortuis nil nisi bunkum.' Presumably it is saying that one may – or, rather, one usually does – only speak half-truths of the recently dead.

5 I always wait for *The Times* each morning. I look at the obituary column, and if I'm not in it, I go to work.

A.E. Matthews, English actor (1869–1960). Quoted in Leslie Halliwell, *The Filmgoer's Book of Quotes* (1973). Matthews's own obituary appeared on 26 July 1960. Several people have used the line subsequently. In *The Observer* (16 August 1987), William Douglas-Home, the playwright, was quoted as saying: 'Every morning I read the obits in *The Times*. If I'm not there, I carry on.'

After he reappeared having been reported dead during the Cyprus coup of 1974:

6 You should have known that it was not easy for me to die – but tell me, were my obituaries good?

Archbishop Makarios, Cypriot priest and President (1913–77). Quoted in *The Observer* (29 December 1974).

During the Boxer Rebellion (1900) in northern China, it was erroneously reported that those besieged in the Legation Quarter of Peking, including Dr Morrison, correspondent of The Times, *had been massacred. Morrison cabled the paper:*

7 Have just read obituary in *The Times*. Kindly adjust pay to suit.

George Ernest Morrison, English journalist (1862–1920). From this version one can only assume that the obituary was a glowing one. Quoted in Claud Cockburn, *In Time of Trouble* (1956).

Obscenity

Of George Melly, critic and jazz singer:

1 Mr Melly had to be obscene to be believed.

Quentin Crisp, English homosexual celebrity (1908–99). Remark recalled by Melly on BBC Radio *Quote … Unquote* (27 May 1997). This set a number of distant bells ringing in my memory and I eventually remembered having seen this couplet quoted in *Yet More Comic and Curious Verse*, ed. J.M. Cohen (1959):

Poor Mr Graham Greene is greatly grieved.
He has to be obscene to be believed.

Obscenity was hardly one of Greene's most characteristic qualities, and the whole thing was clearly built around the Greene/obscene rhyme. The similar seen/obscene pun also occurs in my *Graffiti 2* (1980): 'Graffiti should be obscene and not heard'; and, from New York, in Reisner & Wechsler's *Encyclopedia of Graffiti* (1974): 'Women should be obscene and not heard.'

2 Obscenity can be found in every book except the telephone directory.

Bernard Shaw, Irish playwright and critic (1856–1950). Quoted in *The Treasury of Humorous Quotations*, eds Evan Esar & Nicolas Bentley (1951).

Obscurity

3 Obscurity and a competence – that is the life that is best worth living.

Mark Twain, American writer (1835–1910). *Mark Twain's Notebook*, ed. A.B. Paine (1935).

Obviousness

4 Well, he would, wouldn't he?

Mandy Rice-Davies, English 'model and show girl' (1944–). At Magistrates' Court hearing, London (28 June 1963). An innocuous enough phrase but one still used allusively because of the way it was spoken by Rice-Davies during the Profumo affair in 1963 (Secretary of State for War John Profumo carried on with Rice-Davies's friend Christine Keeler, who was allegedly sharing her favours with the Soviet military attaché). Rice-Davies was called as a witness when Stephen Ward, the pimp involved, was charged under the Sexual Offences Act. During the preliminary hearing she was questioned about the men she had had sex with. When told by Ward's defence counsel that Lord Astor – one of the names on the list – had categorically denied any involvement with her, she chirpily made this reply. The court burst into laughter and the expression passed into the language.

Miss Rice-Davies's elevation to the quotation books has occasioned a good deal of humorous prevarication when it comes to giving her a job description. In *A Dictionary of Twentieth Century Quotations* (1987) I led the way with the neutral 'British woman'. The *Bloomsbury Dictionary of Quotations* (1987) boldly went for 'British call-girl'. The Oxford Dictionary of Quotations quaintly had 'English courtesan' in 1992. I switched to 'British "model and show girl"' for *Brewer's Quotations* (1994). *Collins Dictionary of Quotations* (1995) interestingly opted for 'Welsh model, nightclub performer and owner' and *The Penguin Thesaurus of Quotations* (1998) simply for 'Welsh show-girl'. Somehow I still don't think that any of us has quite got it right.

Offensiveness

5 *Judge:*
You are extremely offensive, young man.
F.E. Smith:
As a matter of fact, we both are, and the only difference between us is that I am trying to be, and you can't help it.

F.E. Smith (1st Earl of Birkenhead), English Conservative politician and lawyer (1872–1930). Quoted in 2nd Earl of Birkenhead, *The Earl of Birkenhead* (1933).

Old age

6 'Old age is coming on me rapidly,' as the urchin said when he was stealing apples from an old man's garden, and saw the owner coming.

Anonymous (Wellerism). In *Ballou's Dollar Magazine*, Vol. 1 (US 1855).

7 God grant me the senility to forget the people I never liked anyway, the good fortune to run into the ones I do, and the eyesight to tell the difference.

Anonymous. Quoted by Terry Wogan on BBC Radio *Quote … Unquote* (3 April 2000).

8 I got used to my arthritis
To my dentures I'm resigned,

I can manage my bifocals,
But Lord I miss my mind.

Anonymous. Some verses entitled 'I Can't Remember' were found among the papers of Henry Adams (1907–2000) of Milverton, Somerset, and were ostensibly original although they included these four lines that have been the subject of searches since 1998. I am inclined to think that Mr Adams must have built these already existing lines into his own poem – unless of course he acquired the whole thing from somewhere else. In Noel Annan, *The Dons* (1999), these verses are ascribed to John Sparrow with the title 'Growing Old':

I'm accustomed to my deafness,
To my dentures, I'm resigned,
I can cope with my bifocals,
But – oh dear! – I miss my mind.

Annan comments that this was frequently quoted and misquoted but seldom ascribed correctly. Sparrow, Warden of All Souls, Oxford, was no mean poet and towards the end of his life, when I met him, he was, alas, well into his 'missed mind' period, but I am not convinced that he originated this. I wonder who did? Compare 314:4 below.

1 I will never be an old man. To me, old age is always fifteen years older than I am.

Bernard Baruch, American financier (1870–1965). Quoted in *The Observer* (21 August 1955).

2 You only have to survive in England and all is forgiven you … if you can eat a boiled egg at ninety in England they think you deserve a Nobel Prize.

Alan Bennett, English playwright and actor (1934–). On ITV's *South Bank Show* (1984). In his TV film *An Englishman Abroad* (1989), this reappeared as: 'In England, you see, age wipes the slate clean … If you live to be ninety in England and can still eat a boiled egg they think you deserve the Nobel Prize.'

3 Speak, you who are older, for it is fitting that you should,
but with accurate knowledge, and
do not interrupt the music.

The Bible. Ecclesiasticus, 32:3 (Apocrypha).

On his hundredth birthday:

4 If I'd known I was gonna live this long, I'd have taken better care of myself.

Eubie Blake, American jazz musician (1883–1983). Quoted in *The Observer* (13 February 1983). Unfortunately, five days after marking his centennial, Blake died. Even so, his felicitous remark was not original. In *Radio Times* (17 February 1979), Benny Green quoted Adolph Zukor, founder of Paramount Pictures, as having said on the approach to his 100th birthday: 'If I'd known how old I was going to be I'd have taken better care of myself.'

5 Old age is the outpatients' department of Purgatory.

Hugh Cecil (Lord Quickswood), English Conservative politician (1869–1956). Quoted by John Betjeman in a letter to Tom Driberg (21 July 1976).

6 Old age isn't so bad when you consider the alternative.

Maurice Chevalier, French entertainer (1888–1972). Quoted in *The New York Times* (9 October 1960) on his 72nd birthday. Or 'Growing old isn't so bad when you consider the alternative' – quoted in Laurence J. Peter, *Quotations for Our Time* (1977).

Towards the end of his life, Churchill was sitting in the House of Commons smoking room with his fly-buttons undone. When this was pointed out to him, he said:

7 Dead birds don't fall out of nests.

(Sir) Winston S. Churchill, British Conservative Prime Minister and writer (1874–1965). Quoted in *The Lyttelton Hart-Davis Letters*, Vol. 2 (1979) (from a letter dated 5 January 1957, where the reply is given as: 'No matter. The dead bird does not leave the nest.')

On seeing a pretty girl in the Champs-Élysées on his 80th birthday:

8 Oh, to be seventy again!

Georges Clemenceau, French Prime Minister (1841–1929). Quoted in James Agate, *Ego 3* (1938). The same remark is ascribed to Oliver Wendell Holmes Jnr (1841–1935), the American jurist, on reaching his 87th year (by Fadiman & van Doren in *The American Treasury*, 1955). Bernard de Fontenelle (1657–1757), the French writer and philosopher, is said in great old age to have attempted with difficulty to pick up a young lady's fan, murmuring,'Ah, if I were only eighty again!' (Pedrazzini & Gris, *Autant en apportent les mots*, 1969).

1 The older I grow, the more I distrust the familiar doctrine that age brings wisdom.

H.L. Mencken, American journalist and linguist (1880–1956). Quoted in *The Treasury of Humorous Quotations*, eds Evan Esar & Nicolas Bentley (1951).

2 King David and King Solomon
Had merry, merry lives,
With many, many lady friends,
And many, many wives.
But when old age came over them
With many, many qualms,
King Solomon wrote Proverbs
And King David wrote the Psalms.

James Ball Naylor, American physician and writer (1860–1945). 'King David and King Solomon' (1935). This later somehow became part of an anonymous song called 'The Darkie Sunday School', which was popular in informal sing-songs from the 1940s onwards. A version printed in *Rugby Songs* (1967) has this chorus: 'Young folk, old folk / Everybody come / To the darkie Sunday School / And we'll have lots of fun. / Bring your sticks of chewing gum / And sit upon the floor / And we'll tell you Bible stories / That you've never heard before … '

3 Growing old is like being increasingly penalized for a crime you haven't committed.

Anthony Powell, English novelist (1905–2000). *Temporary Kings*, Chap. 1 (1973).

4 To age and imbecility resigned,
I watch the struggles of my failing mind:
Lumbering along the all-too-well-worn grooves
The poor old thing moves slowly – but it moves!

John Sparrow, English scholar (1906–92). *Grave Epigrams and Other Verses*, 'Eppur si muove' (1981).

Resolutions when old:

5 Not to be fond of children, or let them come near me hardly … Not to talk much, nor of myself. Not to boast of my former beauty, or strength, or favour with ladies, &c.

Jonathan Swift, Anglo-Irish writer and clergyman (1667–1745). *When I Come to be Old* (1699).

6 Every man desires to live long but no man would be old.

Jonathan Swift. *Thoughts on Various Subjects* (1706).

On Max Beerbohm:

7 The gods bestowed on Max the gift of perpetual old age.

Oscar Wilde, Irish playwright, poet and wit (1854–1900). Quoted in Vincent O'Sullivan, *Aspects of Wilde* (1936). If this was said in the 1890s, Beerbohm would then have been in his twenties.

8 The old should neither be seen nor heard.

Oscar Wilde. Quoted in E.H. Mikhail, *Oscar Wilde: Interviews and Recollections* (1979).

9 Those whom the Gods hate die old.

Oscar Wilde. Quoted in R.H. Sherard, *Oscar Wilde: The Story of an Unhappy Friendship* (1917).

Old maids

10 Being an old maid is like death by drowning, a really delightful sensation after you cease to struggle.

Edna Ferber, American writer (1887–1968). Quoted in R.E. Drennan, *Wit's End* (1973).

Older women

11 Older women are best because they always think they may be doing it for the last time.

Ian Fleming, English novelist and journalist (1908–64). Quoted in John Pearson, *The Life of Ian Fleming* (1966). Compare Benjamin Franklin's *Reasons for Preferring an Elderly Mistress* (1745): '8th and lastly. They are so grateful!' Compare: 'I like older men. They are so grateful' – line from film *Two-Faced Woman* (US 1941). Screenwriters:

S.N. Behrman and others. Spoken by Greta Garbo (Katherine Borg) to Melvyn Douglas (Larry Blake).

1 When I am an old woman I shall wear purple
With a red hat which doesn't go, and doesn't suit me,
And I shall spend my pension on brandy and summer gloves
And satin sandals, and say we've no money for butter.

Jenny Joseph, English poet (1932–). 'Warning' in *New Poems* (PEN anthology, 1965).

One-upmanship

Defining 'One-Upmanship':

2 How to be one up – how to make the other man feel that something has gone wrong, however slightly.

Stephen Potter, English humorist (1900–69). *Lifemanship* (1950).

Opera

Quoting a supposed maxim concerning Italian opera:

3 That nothing is capable of being well set to music that is not nonsense.

Joseph Addison, English essayist and politician (1672–1719). In *The Spectator*, No. 18 (21 March 1711).

4 The opera ain't [or isn't] over till the fat lady sings.

Anonymous (modern proverb). Relatively few modern proverbs have caught on in a big way but, of those that have, this one has produced sharp division over its origin. It is also used with surprising vagueness and lack of perception. If it is a warning 'not to count your chickens before they are hatched', it is too often simply employed to express a generalized view that 'it isn't over till it's over'.

So how did the saying come about? A report in the *Washington Post* (13 June 1978) had this version: 'One day three years ago [i.e. 1975], Ralph Carpenter, who was then Texas Tech's sports information director, declared to the press box contingent in Austin, "The rodeo ain't over till the bull riders ride." Stirred to that deep insight, San Antonio sports editor Dan Cook countered with, "The opera ain't over till the fat lady sings".' However, proof that this 'opera' version is merely a derivative of some earlier American expression appears to be provided by *A Dictionary of American Proverbs* (1992), which lists both 'The game's not over until the last man strikes out' and 'Church is not out 'til they sing'. *Bartlett's Familiar Quotations* (1992) finds in *Southern Words and Sayings* (1976), by F.R. and C.R. Smith, the expression 'Church ain't out till the fat lady sings'.

5 No good opera plot can be sensible, for people do not sing when they are feeling sensible.

W.H. Auden, Anglo-American poet (1907–73). Quoted in *Time* Magazine (29 December 1961).

6 As for operas, they are essentially too absurd and extravagant to mention; I look upon them as a magic scene contrived to please the eyes and the ears at the expense of the understanding.

4th Earl of Chesterfield (Philip Dormer Stanhope), English politician and writer (1694–1773). *Letters to His Son* (1774) – for 23 January 1752.

7 People are wrong when they say that the opera isn't what it used to be. It is what it used to be – that's what's wrong with it.

(Sir) Noël Coward, English entertainer and writer (1899–1973). *Design for Living* (1933).

8 Opera is when a guy gets stabbed in the back and instead of bleeding he sings.

Ed Gardner, American broadcaster (1901–63). In the 1940s radio show *Duffy's Tavern*, quoted in *The Frank Muir Book* (1976). Has also been ascribed to Robert Benchley.

9 Opera in English is, in the main, just about as sensible as baseball in Italian.

H.L. Mencken, American journalist and linguist (1880–1956). Quoted in *The Treasury of Humorous Quotations*, eds Evan Esar & Nicolas Bentley (1951).

10 How wonderful opera would be if there were no singers.

Gioacchino Rossini, Italian composer (1792–1868). Quoted in the same collection as above.

1 Sleep is an excellent way of listening to an opera.

James Stephens, Irish poet and novelist (1882–1950). Quoted in the same collection as above.

2 An unalterable and unquestioned law of the musical world required that the German text of French operas sung by Swedish artists should be translated into Italian for the clearer understanding of English-speaking audiences.

Edith Wharton, American novelist (1862–1937). *The Age of Innocence*, Bk 1, Chap. 1 (1920).

Opinion

3 One man's Mede is another man's Persian.

George S. Kaufman, American playwright (1889–1961). Quoted in *The Home Book of Humorous Quotations*, ed. A.K. Adams (1969).

4 Unless they share our opinions, we seldom find people sensible.

François, Duc de La Rochefoucauld, French writer (1613–80). *Maximes*, No. 347 (1665).

5 It is only about things that do not interest one that one can give a really unbiassed opinion, which is no doubt the reason why an unbiassed opinion is always absolutely valueless.

Oscar Wilde, Irish playwright, poet and wit (1854–1900). 'The Critic As Artist' (1890).

6 Public opinion exists only where there are no ideas.

Oscar Wilde. In *Saturday Review* (17 November 1894).

Opposition

To Nancy Astor:

7 When you come into the Debating Chamber, Nancy, I feel as if you had come into my bathroom and I had only a sponge to cover myself with.

(Sir) Winston S. Churchill, British Conservative Prime Minister and writer (1874–1965). Quoted by John Beavers in the *Sunday Referee* (19 February 1939).

On why he kept J. Edgar Hoover at the FBI:

8 I'd much rather have that fellow inside my tent pissing out, than outside my tent pissing in.

Lyndon B. Johnson, American Democratic President (1908–73). Quoted in David Halberstam, *The Best and the Brightest* (1972). The same sentiment is attributed to Laurence Olivier about employing Kenneth Tynan, a critic, at the National Theatre, in John Dexter, *The Honourable Beast* (1993).

On why he was supporting the brutal, corrupt, but pro-American, Nicaraguan dictator, Tacho Somoza:

9 He may be a son of a bitch, but he's our son of a bitch.

Franklin D. Roosevelt, American Democratic President (1882–1945). In about 1938. No source. Miriam Ringo, *Nobody Said It Better!* (1980) puts this line in the mouth of Kenneth Simpson, speaking about Fiorello La Guardia, Mayor of New York, in 1937. Stimson was telling fellow Republicans why they had to endorse La Guardia for a second term.

Optimism

10 The optimist proclaims that we live in the best of all possible worlds; and the pessimist fears this is true.

James Branch Cabell, American novelist (1879–1958). *The Silver Stallion*, Pt 4, Chap. 26 (1926).

11 An optimist is a girl who mistakes a bulge for a curve.

Ring Lardner, American humorist (1885–1933). Quoted in *The Treasury of Humorous Quotations*, eds Evan Esar & Nicolas Bentley (1951).

12 Cheer up! The worst is yet to come.

Mark Twain, American writer (1835–1910). In a letter to his wife (1893/4) included in *The Love Letters of Mark Twain*. Also to be found in *Those Extraordinary Twins* (1894). The most usual attribution, though, is to the American writer

Philander Johnson (1866–1939) in *Everybody's Magazine* (May 1920). The similar expression, 'Cheer up ... you'll soon be dead!' appears in several British entertainments in the period 1909–18.

1 Optimist: Person who travels on nothing from nowhere to happiness.

Mark Twain. *More Maxims of Mark Twain*, ed. Merle Johnson (1927).

2 I'm an optimist, but I'm an optimist who takes his raincoat.

Harold Wilson (Lord Wilson of Rievaulx), British Labour Prime Minister (1916–95). Quoted in *The Observer* (18 January 1976).

Orders

3 Cancel the kitchen scraps for lepers and orphans. No more merciful beheadings. And call off Christmas.

Line from film *Robin Hood: Prince of Thieves* (US 1991). Screenwriters: Pen Densham, John Watson. Spoken by Alan Rickman (Sheriff of Nottingham).

Organization

4 This island is made mainly of coal and surrounded by fish. Only an organizing genius could produce a shortage of coal and fish at the same time.

Aneurin Bevan, Welsh Labour politician (1897–1960). Speech at Blackpool (24 May 1945).

Orgasms

5 In the case of some women, orgasms take quite a bit of time. Before signing on with such a partner, make sure you are willing to lay aside, say, the month of June, with sandwiches having to be brought in.

Bruce Jay Friedman, American writer (1930–). 'Sex and the Lonely Guy' in *Esquire* (1977).

Girl at party:

6 I finally had an orgasm ... and my doctor told me it was the *wrong* kind.

Line from film *Manhattan* (US 1979). Screenwriters: Woody Allen, Marshall Brickman.

After orgasm with French lover:

7 Now I know what I've been faking all these years.

Line from film *Private Benjamin* (US 1980). Screenwriters: Nancy Meyers and others. Spoken by Goldie Hawn (Judy Benjamin).

8 Since most men can't keep it up long enough to fulfil woman's God-given – and soon to be Constitutioned – right to orgasm, the vibrator can take over while the man takes a leak.

Gore Vidal, American novelist, playwright and critic (1925–). In *Rolling Stone* (1980) – quoted in Bob Chieger, *Was It Good For You Too?* (1983).

Orgies

9 You get a better class of person at orgies, because people have to keep in trim more. There is an awful lot of going round holding in your stomach, you know. Everybody is very polite to each other. The conversation isn't very good but you can't have everything.

Gore Vidal, American novelist, playwright and critic (1925–). Interviewed on London Weekend Television, *Russell Harty Plus* (1972).

Originality

10 Nothing should ever be done for the first time.

Francis Cornford, English academic (1874–1943). *Microcosmographia Academica* (1908). The precise context is: 'Every public action, which is not customary, either is wrong, or, if it is right, is a dangerous precedent. It follows that nothing should ever be done for the first time.' Compare: 'The conservative in financial circles I have often described as a man who thinks nothing new ought ever to be adopted for the first time' – Frank A. Vanderlip, *From Farm Boy to Financier* (1935).

1 *Pereant qui ante nos nostra dixerunt* [Damn those who have made our remarks before us]!

Aelius Donatus, Roman grammarian (AD 4th century). Quoted in this form in *The Treasury of Humorous Quotations*, eds Evan Esar & Nicolas Bentley (1951). Quoted originally by St Jerome, *Commentary on Ecclesiastes*: 'The same idea is said by the comic poet [Terence, in the Prologue to *Eunuchus*]: "Nothing is said which has not been said before." Whence my teacher Donatus when he was speaking of that verse, said, "Confound those who have said our remarks before us".'

2 As usual, the Liberals offer a mixture of sound and original ideas. Unfortunately none of the sound ideas is original and none of the original ideas is sound.

Harold Macmillan (1st Earl of Stockton), British Conservative Prime Minister (1894–1986). Speech to London Conservatives (7 March 1961). Compare what is ascribed to Dr Samuel Johnson: 'Your manuscript is both good and original; but the part that is good is not original, and the part that is original is not good' – quoted in *The Treasury of Humorous Quotations*, eds Evan Esar & Nicolas Bentley (1951); it has also been loosely ascribed to Johnson's 'Letters 1777'. If confirmed, this might be the first English example of a critical formula. But possibly the Johnson citations are misleading. He definitely quoted 'I found that generally what was new was false' as a passage that Oliver Goldsmith struck out from *The Vicar of Wakefield* (as Boswell records for 26 March 1779), but there is no confirmation yet of his using the other, formulaic saying.

Next in time comes Richard Brinsley Sheridan (1751–1816), commenting on a minister's speech in the House of Commons: 'It contained a great deal both of what was new and what was true, but unfortunately what was new was not true and what was true was not new.' Quoted in Hesketh Pearson, *Lives of the Wits* (1962).

Notes & Queries (7th series, 4 and 6, 1887) looked into the question and suggested that in the 1830s a saying was abroad: 'Some things the lady's said are new, / And some things she has said are true; / But what are true, alas! they are not new, / And what are new, alas! they are not true.' It also suggested that Daniel Webster criticized the platform of the American Free Soil Party in 1848 with the words: 'What is valuable is not new, and what is new is not valuable.'

Precisely this form is also ascribed to Lord Brougham in an 'Essay: The Work of Thomas Young' in *The Edinburgh Review* (*c.* 1839). The historian Lord Macaulay (1800–59) apparently said: 'There were gentlemen and there were seamen in the navy of Charles II. But the seamen were not gentlemen, and the gentlemen were not seamen.' Charles Darwin said of something in 1858: 'All that was new was false, and what was true was old.' Somewhat later, Arthur Balfour made a similarly structured remark, 'In that oration there were some things that were true, and some things that were trite: but what was true was trite, and what was not trite was not true' – quoted in Winston S. Churchill, *Great Contemporaries*, 'Arthur James Balfour' (1937).

In any case, *The Oxford Dictionary of English Proverbs* (1975) has an entry for 'What is new is not true and what is true is not new', suggesting that the formula is proverbial anyway. Its earliest citation is from the German author J.H. Voss (1751–1826) in the Vossischer Musenalmanach (1792): *'Auf mehrere Bücher. / Nach Lessing. / Dein redseliges Buch lehrt mancherlei Neues und Wahres, / Wäre das Wahre nur neu, wäre das Neue nur wahr!* [On several books. / After Lessing. / Your garrulous book teaches many things new and true, / If only the true were new, if only the new were true!]'

3 All that can be said is, that two people happened to hit on the same thought – and Shakespeare made use of it first, that's all.

Richard Brinsley Sheridan, English playwright and politician (1751–1816). *The Critic*, Act 3, Sc. 1 (1779).

4 Most people are other people. Their thoughts are someone else's opinions, their life a mimicry, their passions a quotation.

Oscar Wilde, Irish playwright, poet and wit (1854–1900). *De Profundis* (1905).

Orthodoxy

5 Orthodoxy is my doxy; heterodoxy is another man's doxy.

William Warburton, English theologian and bishop (1698–1779). To Lord Sandwich. Quoted in Joseph Priestley, *Memoirs*, Vol. 1 (1807).

Osteopathy

1 To ask a doctor's opinion about osteopathy is equivalent to going to Satan for information about Christianity.

Mark Twain, American writer (1835–1910). *Mark Twain's Notebook*, ed. A.B. Paine (1935).

Outspokenness

When told that she was 'very outspoken':

2 Outspoken by whom?

Dorothy Parker, American writer (1893–1967). Quoted in Ralph L. Marquard, *Jokes and Anecdotes for All Occasions* (1977).

Overheard remarks

3 Walking one day in Oxford, I saw two elderly dons coming towards me engrossed apparently in some weighty discourse. As they passed me, I overheard just two words: 'And ninthly ... '

Anonymous. Quoted by S.H. Jarvis of Bristol in my book *Eavesdroppings* (1981). The pedantic ninth point is, however, a venerable institution. In Ronald Knox's *Juxta Salices* (1910), he includes a group of poems written while he was still at Eton. 'As no less than three of them wear the aspect of a positively last appearance [i.e. a promise not to write more], they have been called in the words of so many eminent preachers "ninthlies and lastlies".' Even before this, *The Oxford English Dictionary* (2nd edition) has Thomas B. Aldrich writing in *Prudence Palfrey* (1874) of 'The poor old parson's interminable ninthlies and finallies.'

Much the same, though marginally different: in 1745, Benjamin Franklin concluded his *Reasons for Preferring an Elderly Mistress* with: 'Eighth and lastly. They are so grateful!!' And the *OED2* takes such pedantry even further back, more loosely, finding a 'fifthly and lastly' dated 1681.

Ultimately, the origin for all this sort of thing must be the kind of legal nonsense talk parodied by Shakespeare's Dogberry in *Much Ado About Nothing* (1598): 'Marry, sir, they have committed false report; moreover, they have spoken untruths; secondarily, they are slanders; sixthly and lastly, they have belied a lady; thirdly, they have verified unjust things; and to conclude, they are lying knaves.'

Whatever the origin, this is a story that will not go away. On BBC Radio *Quote ... Unquote* (24 April 1998), the Oxford philosopher Anthony Quinton told a version involving Dean Hastings Rashdall and his wife. As they circumnavigated the university Parks, the Dean was overheard saying, 'And *seventeenthly*, my dear ... '

4 Two American women were observing and admiring the statue of Achilles in Park Lane, London. One was overheard saying to the other, 'No, dear – Big Ben is a clock.'

Anonymous. Quoted by Norman Mitchell of Weybridge in the same book as above. The origins of this are said to lie in a cartoon (by 1965) but, if this is the case, it has not yet been found.

5 A young artist saw an eminent critic and a noble lord standing in front of one of his paintings, so he crept nearer to hear what they were saying about it. The noble lord said to the critic: 'Of the two, I prefer washing up.'

Anonymous. Quoted in the same book as above. Compare T.H. White discussing a comic story current just after the Second World War in *The Age of Scandal* (1950): 'It said that there was some conference or other at Lambeth, thronged with Archbishops, Cardinals, Patriarchs, Moderators and so forth. The Archbishops of Canterbury and York were seen to be in earnest consultation in one corner of the room. Were they discussing a reunion with Rome or a revision of the Prayer Book? Thrilled with the ecclesiastical possibilities of such a meeting, one of the stripling curates managed to edge himself within earshot of these princes of the Church. They were discussing whether it was worse to wash-up or dry-up.'

Overheard at a hospital:

6 I don't mind dying; the trouble is, you feel so bloody stiff the next day.

Anonymous. Quoted on BBC Radio *Quote ... Unquote* (13 September 1979). Compare this exchange from Richard Brinsley Sheridan's farce *St Patrick's Day* (1775):

Justice Credulous: I don't like death.
Mrs Bridget Credulous: Psha! there is nothing in it: a moment, and it is over.
Justice Credulous: Ay, but it leaves a numbness behind that lasts a plaguy long time.

After a performance of Vivat! Vivat Regina! *that he directed at Chichester and which ends with the execution of Mary Queen of Scots, Peter Dews overheard a female member of the audience say:*

1 Do you know, it's extraordinary – exactly the same thing happened to Monica.

Anonymous. In a letter to me dated 10 January 1980, Dews called this remark, 'absolutely true. I heard it with my own ears.'

2 During the First World War, my mother heard someone say, 'My husband has been wounded in the Dardanelles ... and they cannot find his whereabouts.'

Anonymous. Contributed to BBC Radio *Quote ... Unquote* (25 August 1984) by Mrs V. Lewis of Handsworth, Birmingham. However, in BBC TV, *The Dawson Watch* (Christmas 1980), Les Dawson spoke the line 'During the war, I was shot in the Dardanelles' – with similar implications – and in the BBC Radio show *Beyond Our Ken* (15 July 1960) there was the line, 'The Turks pinned the Australians in the Dardanelles.' Compare: '*Granny Growl*: Me tired husband, poor ould Paddins, he was shot in the Dardanelles. *Granny Grunt*: And a most painful part of the body to be shot!' – Brendan Behan, *Brendan Behan's Island* (1962).

3 Alfred Deller, the celebrated counter-tenor, was walking behind two women when he overheard one say to the other, 'Ow's Flo? Ow's 'er feet?' The second woman replied, 'Well, of course, they're not much use to 'er now. Not as *feet*, that is ... '

Anonymous. Contributed to BBC Radio *Quote ... Unquote* (5 June 1979) by Paul Fincham of Suffolk – who heard it from Paul Jennings who had it from Deller. Denis Norden recalled (1996) that he had first heard it from Nancy Spain at a recording of *My Word* in Cambridge in that programme's early years (it began in 1956). The most venerable overheard remark of all – and often re-told by people who claim to have heard it first *themselves* ...

Of a well-meant but rather pretentious play at Brighton:

4 Well, Emily, all I can say is, I hope the dogs haven't been sick in the car.

Anonymous (woman). Quoted by Patrick Garland, the theatre and TV director, on BBC Radio *Quote ... Unquote* (11 September 1979).

Owning up

Asked how many of the Hill's Angels dancing troupe he had been to bed with:

5 Off the record, I haven't made love to one of those girls. I think her name was Sandra.

Benny Hill, English television comedian (1924–92). Quoted in David Lister's obituary of Hill in *The Independent* (22 April 1992).

Oxford

6 I was not unpopular [at school] ... It is Oxford that has made me insufferable.

Sir Max Beerbohm, English writer and caricaturist (1872–1956). *More*, 'Going Back to School' (1899).

7 Very nice sort of place, Oxford, I should think, for people that like that sort of place.

Bernard Shaw, Irish playwright and critic (1856–1950). *Man and Superman*, Act 2 (1903).

P

Paintings and painters

1 Buy old masters. They fetch a better price than old mistresses.

1st Baron Beaverbrook (Maxwell Aitken), Canadian-born English politician and newspaper proprietor (1879–1964). Quoted in *The Bloomsbury Dictionary of Quotations* (1987).

2 Painting is not very difficult when you don't know how; but when you know how – ah, then it's a different matter.

Edgar Degas, French painter (1834–1917). Quoted in Herbert V. Prochnow, Snr & Jnr, *A Treasury of Humorous Quotations* (1969).

3 Every time I paint a portrait I lose a friend.

John Singer Sargent, American painter (1856–1925). Quoted in *The Treasury of Humorous Quotations*, eds Evan Esar & Nicolas Bentley (1951).

4 [Rogers] had candles placed all round the dining room, in order to show off the pictures. 'I asked Smith how he liked the plan.' 'Not at all,' he replied, 'above there is a blaze of light, and below, nothing but darkness and gnashing of teeth.'

(Revd) Sydney Smith, English clergyman, essayist and wit (1771–1845). Quoted in *Rogers's Table Talk*, ed. A. Dyce (1856).

5 A portrait is a picture in which there is something wrong with the mouth.

Eugene Speicher, American portrait painter (1883–1962). Quoted in *The Frank Muir Book* (1976).

6 Painting is saying 'Ta' to God.

(Sir) Stanley Spencer, English painter (1891–1959). Quoted in letter to *The Observer* from his daughter Shirin (7 February 1988).

Pakistan

7 The sort of place everyone should send his mother-in-law for a month, all expenses paid.

Ian Botham, English cricketer (1955–). In BBC Radio interview (March 1984). The following month he was fined £1,000 by the Test and County Cricket Board for making the comment.

Pants

An old Nonconformist minister chose as his text Psalm 42 v.1: 'As the hart panteth after the water-brooks, so panteth my soul after Thee, O God.' His discourse, the minister said, would be divided into three parts:

8 The pants of the hart, the pants of the Psalmist, and, finally, pants in general.

Anonymous (by 1978). Source unrecorded.

Paradox

9 Paradox has been defined as 'Truth standing on her head to get attention.'

G.K. Chesterton, English poet, novelist and critic (1874–1936). *The Paradoxes of Mr Pond*, 'When Doctors Agree' (1937). But who was the definer? In 1999, Denis Conlon of the Chesterton Society recalled that Dean Inge had once described GKC himself as 'a fat clown who crucifies truth upside-down.' Brian Robinson, however, found the most likely original. In *The Romantic Nineties* (1926),

Richard Le Gallienne wrote of Oscar Wilde: 'Paradox with him was only Truth standing on its head to attract attention.' Compare the story told about George Orwell (Eric Blair). When the young Blair was eleven years old, he saw three children playing in a field – one of whom, Jacintha Buddicom, was to have great influence on him. Wanting to get to know them, he used a simple stratagem to gain their attention and when they came across the field to him and asked him why he was standing on his head, he replied, 'You are noticed more if you are standing on your head than if you are the right way up.'

Paranoia

1 I wouldn't be paranoid if people didn't pick on me.

Anonymous (graffito). Quoted in my book *Graffiti Lives OK* (1979).

2 Just because you're paranoid, it doesn't mean they're not out to get you.

Anonymous (graffito). Quoted in my book *Graffiti 2* (1980). In the 1976 biography of Rodgers and Hart written by Clayton and Marx, it is claimed that in preparing the 1943 revival of the musical *A Connecticut Yankee*, the line 'Just because you're paranoid doesn't mean they're not out to get you' became a running joke between Lorenz Hart, the lyricist, and the librettist Herbert Fields. The line is not, however, apparently, spoken in the show. Other formulations of this idea include:

3 Even a paranoid can have enemies.

Henry Kissinger, American Republican politician (1923–). Quoted in *Time* Magazine (24 January 1977). Has also been ascribed to Delmore Schwartz. Compare this parallel: 'Because a person has a monomania she need not be wrong about her facts' – Dorothy L. Sayers, *Murder Must Advertise*, Chap. 16 (1933).

4 Margaret said: 'Has it ever struck you that when people get persecution mania, they usually have a good deal to feel persecuted about?'

C.P. Snow (Lord Snow), English novelist and scientist (1905–80). *The Affair*, Chap. 11 (1960). An early example of this observation.

Parents

5 Never lend your car to anyone to whom you have given birth.

Erma Bombeck, American humorous columnist (1927–96). Attributed remark.

6 Some people seem compelled by unkind fate to parental servitude for life. There is no form of penal servitude much worse than this.

Samuel Butler, English author (1835–1902). Quoted in Herbert V. Prochnow, Snr & Jnr, *A Treasury of Humorous Quotations* (1969).

7 'Why'd you have me if you didn't want me?' 'Who knew it would be you?'

Joseph Heller, American novelist (1923–). *Good As Gold*, Pt 6 (1979). This exchange between father and twelve-year-old daughter closely parallels the one from Samuel Beckett's play *Endgame* (1957):

Hamm: Scoundrel! Why did you engender me?
Nagg: I didn't know.
Hamm: What? What didn't you know?
Nagg: That it'd be you.

Compare also Groucho Marx's remark in *Horse Feathers* (US 1931): 'I married your mother because I wanted children. Imagine my disappointment when you arrived.'

8 Mom and Pop were just a couple of kids when they got married. He was eighteen, she was sixteen, and I was three.

Billie Holiday, American singer (1915–59). *Lady Sings the Blues* (1958). Opening words.

9 The question of who are the best people to take charge of children is a very difficult one; but it is quite certain that the parents are the very worst.

William Morris, English poet and craftsman (1834–96). Quoted in Shaw's *Everybody's Political What's What?*, Chap. 19 (1944). An unverified suggestion that 'Parents are the last people on earth who ought to have children' appears in Samuel Butler's *Notebooks* (according to Laurence J. Peter in *Quotations for Our Time* 1977). Earlier, Jonathan Swift, *Gulliver's Travels*, Chap. 6 (1726) has, of the Lilliputians: 'Their opinion is, that parents are the last of all others to be trusted with the education of their own children: and therefore they have in every town public nurseries, where all parents, except cottagers and labourers, are obliged to send their infants of both sexes to be reared and educated when they come to the age of twenty moons.' Not quite the same as the Morris / Shaw view but an interesting precursor.

1 Before I got married I had six theories about bringing up children; and now I have six children, and no theories.

2nd Earl of Rochester (John Wilmot), English poet (1647–80). Quoted in *The Treasury of Humorous Quotations*, eds Evan Esar & Nicolas Bentley (1951).

2 Parentage is a very important profession, but no test of fitness for it is ever imposed in the interest of the children.

Bernard Shaw, Irish playwright and critic (1856–1950). *Everybody's Political What's What* (1944).

3 I wish either my father or my mother, or indeed both of them, as they were in duty both equally bound to it, had minded what they were about when they begot me.

Laurence Sterne, Irish-born novelist and clergyman (1713–68). *Tristram Shandy*, Bk 1, Chap. 1 (1760–7). Opening sentence.

4 Children begin by loving their parents; after a time they judge them. Rarely, if ever, do they forgive them.

Oscar Wilde, Irish playwright, poet and wit (1854–1900). *A Woman of No Importance*, Act 4 (1893).

5 *Lady Bracknell:*
To lose one parent, Mr Worthing, may be regarded as a misfortune; to lose both looks like carelessness.

Oscar Wilde. *The Importance of Being Earnest*, Act 1 (1895).

6 Few parents nowadays pay any regard to what their children say to them. The old-fashioned respect for the young is fast dying out.

Oscar Wilde. In the same play, Act 1.

7 The thing that impresses me most about America is the way parents obey their children.

Duke of Windsor, British ex-King (1894–1972). Quoted in *Look* Magazine (5 March 1957).

Parking

Alvy to Annie who has just parked the car somewhat eccentrically:

8 That's OK, we can walk to the kerb from here.

Line from film *Annie Hall* (US 1977). Screenwriters: Woody Allen, Marshall Brickman. Spoken by Woody Allen (Alvy) to Annie (Diane Keaton). Also quoted in the form: 'After she's parked the car, it's normally just a short walk to the pavement.'

Parliament

9 The only man who had a proper understanding of Parliament was old Guy Fawkes.

Bernard Shaw, Irish playwright and critic (1856–1950). *On the Rocks*, Act 2 (1933).

Parodies

Of Adam Lindsay Gordon's 'Life is mostly froth and bubble', which was often quoted by Diana, Princess of Wales:

10 Life is mainly toil and labour.
Two things see you through:
Chortling when it hits your neighbour
Whingeing when it's you.

(Sir) Kingsley Amis, English novelist, poet and critic (1922–95). Quoted in *The Observer* (14 November 1999).

Of Lewis Carroll's 'Jabberwocky':

11 'Twas Danzig, and the Swastikoves
Did heil and hittle in the reich,
All nazi were the lindengroves
And the neuraths jewstreich.

Michael Barsley, English writer and broadcaster. *Grabberwocky and other Flights of Fancy* (1939). First published in *Time and Tide* Magazine.

1 *Of Rudyard Kipling's poem 'If':*

If you can keep your girl when all about you
Are losing theirs and blaming it on you ...
If you can meet a new girl every minute
And not be faithful to a single one
Yours is the world and every woman in it
And, what is more, you'll be a cad, my son.

Anonymous. Lord Wavell quoted only the first two lines in *Other Men's Flowers* (1944). A complete text is in *More Rugby Songs* (1968). This is one of the most parodied poems in the language. Compare also: 'As someone pointed out recently, if you can keep your head when all about you are losing theirs, it's just possible you haven't grasped the situation' – Jean Kerr, *Please Don't Eat the Daisies* (1958) (90:8).

Of the Sankey and Moody hymn, 'The Blood of the Lamb':

2 Oh, wash me in the water
That you washed the colonel's daughter in
And I shall be whiter
Than the whitewash on the wall.

Anonymous. Song popular among British troops in France during the First World War. The parodied hymn has the chorus:

Wash me in the Blood of the Lamb
And I shall be whiter than snow!
(Whiter than the snow!)
(Whiter than the snow!)
Wash me in the Blood of the Lamb
And I shall be whiter than snow (the snow!)

Of 'In the Workhouse – Christmas Day' (1879) by George R. Sims:

3 It was Christmas day in the cookhouse,
The happiest day of the year,
Men's hearts were full of gladness
And their bellies full of beer,
When up spoke Private Shorthouse,
His face as bold as brass,
Saying, 'We don't want your Christmas
pudding
You can stick it up your ... '

Anonymous. From the First World War. Included in the stage show *Oh What a Lovely War* (1963). Compare Billy Bennett below.

Of Jane Taylor's 'The Star' ('Twinkle, twinkle, little star ... '):

4 Scintillate, scintillate, globule vivific,
Fain would I fathom thy nature specific.
Loftily poised in the ether capacious,
Strongly resembling a gem carbonaceous.

Anonymous. Current by the mid-1940s.

Of the song 'Mighty Lak' a Rose' (1901):

5 Sweetest little feller,
Wears his mother's clothes.
We don't know what to call him –
But we think he's one of those.

Anonymous (by 1992).

Of John Keats's 'On First Looking Into Chapman's Homer*':*

6 There can't have been an RSPCA
Beside the Pacific on that fatal day
When Cortez, far the stoutest of his men,
Stood silent on a peke in Darien.

Anonymous (by 1991).

Of the Lord's Prayer:

7 Our Farnham which art in Hendon, Harrow be thy Name. Thy Kingston come. Thy Wimbledon, in Erith as it is in Heston. Give us this day our Leatherhead. And forgive us our Westminsters. As we forgive them that Westminster against us. And lead us not into Thames Ditton; But deliver us from Ealing: For thine is the Kingston, The Purley, and the Crawley, For Iver and Iver. Crouch End.

Anonymous. This 'Home Counties' version of the Lord's Prayer was quoted in my book *Say No More!* (1987). Correspondence in the magazine *Oxford Today* (Hilary/Trinity terms 1990) produced a number of variations and a date of composition somewhere in the 1930s, but no author. Peter Hay in *Business Anecdotes* (1988) includes a faintly similar parody written in 1930s America by a Ford motors worker before unionization. It begins:

Our Father, who art in Dearborn, Henry be thine name.

Let payday come. Thy will be done in Fordson as it is in Highland Park …

Of Mrs Hemans's lines from 'Casabianca', 'The boy stood on the burning deck … ':

1 The boy stood in the supper-room
Whence all but he had fled;
He'd eaten seven pots of jam
And he was gorged with bread.

'Oh, one more crust before I bust!'
He cried in accents wild;
He licked his plates, he sucked the spoons –
He was a vulgar child.

There came a hideous thunder-clap –
The boy – oh! where was he?
Ask of the maid who mopped him up,
The bread-crumbs and the tea.

Anonymous. Included in *A Century of Humorous Verse* (1959) – though it is also to be found in the Opie's collection *I Saw Esau* (1947).

Of Rudyard Kipling:

2 The sun like a Bishop's bottom
Rosy and round and hot
Looked down upon us who shot 'em
And down on the devils we shot.

Raymond Asquith, English poet (1878–1916). Quoted by Lord Wavell in a footnote to his famous anthology *Other Men's Flowers* (1944). Prime Minister Asquith's poet son was killed in action in 1916. The full text is to be found in J. Joliffe, *Raymond Asquith, Life and Letters* (1980). The poem was written in about 1900.

Of John Betjeman:

3 Here I sit, alone and sixty,
Bald, and fat, and full of sin,
Cold the seat and loud the cistern,
As I read the Harpic tin.

Alan Bennett, English playwright and actor (1934–). From 'On Going to the Excuse-me', in BBC TV *On the Margin* (30 November 1966). It had previously been broadcast on *BBC-3*, and later came to be anthologized as 'Place Names of China'.

Of 'In the Workhouse – Christmas Day' (1879) by George R. Sims:

4 It was Christmas Day in the cookhouse.
The troops had all gone to bed.
None of them had any Christmas pudding
'Cause the sergeant had done what they
said.

Billy Bennett, English music-hall comedian (1887–1942). Quoted in *The Penguin Dictionary of Modern Quotations*, eds J.M. & M.J. Cohen (1980 edn).

Of W.B. Yeats's 'The Lake Isle of Innisfree':

5 I will arise and go now, and go to Innisfree,
And tell them, at the little Inn,
That there'll be twenty-four for tea.
Twenty-four ladies of the Band of Hope,
United in their hatred of the Pope,
Each one declaring loudly she would rather
Serve the Devil than the Holy Father.
The bee-loud glade may hum with sounds,
I fear,
Other than the murmur of the bee.
I do not fancy they'll be very welcome there
At Innisfree.

Gerald Berners (Lord Berners), English writer, composer, painter and eccentric (1883–1950). Quoted by Philip Lane of Cheltenham (1984).

Of ballads in general:

6 The farmer's daughter hath soft brown hair;
(Butter and eggs and a pound of cheese)
And I met with a ballad, I can't say where,
Which wholly consisted of lines like these.

C.S. Calverley, English poet and parodist (1831–84). 'Ballad' (1872).

Of song, 'Drake Goes West' (1910), written by P.J. O'Reilly to music by Wilfrid Sanderson:

7 In Dublin they're depressed, lads,
Maybe because they're Celts
For Drake is going West, lads,
And so is everyone else.

(Sir) Noël Coward, English entertainer and writer

(1899–1973). Song, 'There Are Bad Times Just Around the Corner' (1952). Compare Milligan below.

Of Time *Magazine style:*

1 Backward ran sentences until reeled the mind.

Wolcott Gibbs, American writer (1902–58). 'Time ... Fortune ... Life ... Luce', in *The New Yorker* (28 November 1936), reprinted in *More in Sorrow* (1958), which concludes with: 'Where it will all end, knows God.'

Of Longfellow's 'Excelsior':

2 The shades of night were falling fast,
And the rain was falling faster,
When through an Alpine village passed
An Alpine village pastor ...

A.E. Housman, English poet (1859–1936). 'The Shades of Night' – attributed.

Of A.E. Housman, A Shropshire Lad, *No. 21 (1896):*

3 'Tis Summer Time on Bredon,
And now the farmers swear;
The cattle rise and listen
In valleys far and near,
And blush at what they hear.

But when the mists in autumn
On Bredon top are thick,
The happy hymns of farmers
Go up from fold and rick,
The cattle then are sick.

Hugh Kingsmill, English writer (1889–1949). One of 'Two Poems after A.E. Housman', *The Table of Truth* (1933).

Of Newdigate Prize poems at Oxford:

4 King Nebuchadnezzar was turned out to grass
With oxen, horses and the savage ass.
The King surveyed the unaccustomed fare
With an inquiring but disdainful air
And murmured as he cropped the unwanted food,
'It may be wholesome but it is not good.'

Goldwin Knox, English historian (1823–1910). So ascribed by *Everyman's Dictionary of Quotations and Proverbs*, ed. D.C. Browning (1951). However: 'Spake as he champed the unaccustomed food, / This may be wholesome but it is not good' – 'Anon. 1852' is the only hint given in *The Making of Verse: A Guide to English Metres* (1934) by Robert Swan and Frank Sidgwick, where this appears among examples of heroic couplets. In *The Dublin Review* (July 1937), J. Lewis May, while discussing 'Flashed from his bed the electric tidings came', says: 'The name of the inventor of these immortal lines has not been handed down, but one may hazard a guess that they proceeded from the same source as those on another prince, also a subject for the Newdigate [prize poem at Oxford] – to wit, Nebuchadnezzar, "Who murmured – as he ate the unaccustomed food – / It may be wholesome, but it is not good".'

Of Rudyard Kipling's 'Recessional':

5 The tumult and the shouting dies,
The captains and the kings depart,
And we are left with large supplies
Of cold blancmange and rhubarb tart.

Ronald Knox, English priest and writer (1888–1957). 'After the Party', included in Laurence Eyres, *In Three Tongues* (1959).

Of poet Ted Hughes and how he would have celebrated the Queen's Silver Jubilee in 1977:

6 The sky split apart in malice
Stars rattled like pans on a shelf.
Crow shat on Buckingham Palace
God pissed Himself ...

Philip Larkin, English poet (1922–85). Included in *Selected Letters of Philip Larkin* (1992).

Of song, 'Drake Goes West' (1910), written by P.J. O'Reilly to music by Wilfrid Sanderson:

7 Drake is going West, lad
Howard is going East
But little Fred just lies in bed
Lazy little beast.

Spike Milligan, Irish entertainer and writer (1918–). Compare Coward above.

Of A.A. Milne's 'Vespers' in When We Were Very Young *(1924):*

1 Hush, hush
Nobody cares!
Christopher Robin
Has
Fallen
Down –
Stairs.

J.B. Morton (Beachcomber), English humorous writer (1893–1979). *By the Way,* 'Now We are Sick' (1931).

Of J.W. Burgon's poem 'Petra' (1845):

2 Broadbosomed, bold, becalm'd, benign
Lies Balham foursquare on the Northern Line.
Matched by no marvel save in Eastern scene,
A rose-red city half as gold as green.

Frank Muir and Denis Norden, English writers (1920–98) and (1922–). Sketch, 'Balham – Gateway to the South' on BBC *Third Programme* comedy show *Third Division* (1948). In 1959, this was re-recorded by Peter Sellers on his album *The Best of Sellers.* Non-Londoners might like to know that there is a place called Golders Green.

Of T.S. Eliot:

3 As we get older we do not get any younger.
Seasons return, and today I am fifty-five,
And this time last year I was fifty-four,
And this time next year I shall be sixty-two.

Henry Reed, English poet and playwright (1914–86). *A Map of Verona,* 'Chard Whitlow' (1946).

Of Wordsworth:

4 I saw them go: one horse was blind,
Tails of both hung down behind.

James Smith, English parodist (1775–1839). *Rejected Addresses,* No. 2 'The Baby's Début' (1812).

Of Longfellow's 'I shot an arrow into the air, / It fell to earth, I knew not where' – from 'The Arrow and the Song' (1845):

5 I shot an arrow into the air:
I don't know how it fell, or where;
But strangely enough, at my journey's end,
I found it again in the neck of a friend.

D.B. Wyndham Lewis, English writer (1894–1969). 'A Shot at Random'. In the film *Kind Hearts and Coronets* (UK 1949), there is another parody of this poem: Mazzini, the villain, referring to Lady Agatha, the suffragette he has shot down in the balloon in which she is riding, says 'I shot an arrow in the air. / She fell to earth in Berkeley Square.'

Parthenon

6 The Parthenon without the [Elgin] marbles is like a smile with a tooth missing.

Neil Kinnock, Welsh Labour politician (1942–). Quoted in *The Observer,* 'Sayings of the Week' (8 January 1984).

Party-goers

On a frequent first-nighter and party-goer:

7 Sylvia Miles would go to the opening of an envelope.

Anonymous. Though sometimes attributed to Andy Warhol. Quoted by Christopher Matthew on BBC Radio *Quote ... Unquote* (12 June 1979).

Passion

8 The only difference between a caprice and a life-long passion is that the caprice lasts a little longer.

Oscar Wilde, Irish playwright, poet and wit (1854–1900). *The Picture of Dorian Gray,* Chap. 17 (1891).

Patience

9 *Con la patciencia et la saliva l'elephante la metio a la formiga* [With patience and saliva, the elephant screws the ant].

Anonymous (proverb). Quoted by Valerie Bornstein in

Proverbium Yearbook of International Proverb Scholarship (1991). The original language may have been Mexican Spanish or Catalan: it does not appear to be regular Spanish or Italian.

1 If you wait by the river long enough, the body of your enemy will float by.

Anonymous (proverb). Described by Julian Critchley MP as Spanish when he quoted it to Sir Edward Heath on the defenestration of Margaret Thatcher in November 1990 (recalled in *The Observer*, 27 June 1993). Heath replied with a broad grin, 'Rejoice, rejoice.' A version of the Spanish proverb is: '*El que se sienta en la puerta de su casa verá pasar el cadáver de su enemigo* [He who sits at the door of his house will watch his enemy's corpse go by].'

Patriotism

2 'My country, right or wrong' is a thing no patriot would ever think of saying except in a desperate case. It is like saying, 'My mother, drunk or sober.'

G.K. Chesterton, English poet, novelist and critic (1874–1936). *The Defendant* (1901).

3 Patriotism is the last refuge of a scoundrel.

(Dr) Samuel Johnson, English writer and lexicographer (1709–84). Quoted in James Boswell, *The Life of Samuel Johnson* (1791) – for 7 April 1775. Boswell adds that, of course, he means 'pretended patriotism which so many, in all ages and countries, have made a cloak for self-interest.'

4 Patriotism is the last refuge of the sculptor.

William Plomer, English writer and poet (1903–73). Quoted in *The Lyttelton Hart-Davis* Letters, Vol. 2 (1979) – for 13 October 1956.

5 Patriotism is your conviction that this country is superior because you were born in it.

Bernard Shaw, Irish playwright and critic (1856–1950). Quoted in *The Treasury of Humorous Quotations*, eds Evan Esar & Nicolas Bentley (1951).

Patrons

6 Is not a Patron, my Lord, one who looks with unconcern on a man struggling for life in the water, and, when he has reached ground, encumbers him with help?

(Dr) Samuel Johnson, English writer and lexicographer (1709–84). Letter to the Earl of Chesterfield (February 1755), reproduced in James Boswell, *The Life of Samuel Johnson* (1791). When Johnson's Dictionary was nearing publication, Chesterfield (who might have fancied it would be dedicated to him) attempted to insinuate himself into the learned Doctor's favour, having done nothing to help until that time. Johnson made it clear to him what the position was in a devastating letter.

7 *Patron*. Commonly a wretch who supports with insolence, and is paid with flattery.

(Dr) Samuel Johnson. *A Dictionary of the English Language* (1755). Definition.

Paunches

8 F.E. Smith, 1st Earl of Birkenhead, taunted Lord Chief Justice Hewart about the size of his stomach. 'What's it to be – a boy or a girl?' Replied Hewart: 'If it's a boy I'll call him John. If it's a girl I'll call her Mary. But if, as I suspect, it's only wind, I'll call it F.E. Smith.'

Gordon Hewart (Viscount Hewart), British lawyer and politician (1870–1943). Quoted in the book *Quote ... Unquote* (1978). The story had come to me the previous year from a *Quote ... Unquote* listener who said it had been told to her brother 'by a stranger in a bus queue in Harrogate in 1923'. Smith died in 1930.

According to Humphrey McQueen in *Social Sketches of Australia* (1978), the Antipodean version has Sir George Houstoun Reid (1845–1918) replying, in answer to the question, apropos his stomach, 'What are you going to call it, George?': 'If it's a boy, I'll call it after myself. If it's a girl, I'll call it Victoria after our Queen. But if, as I strongly suspect, it's nothing but piss and wind, I'll call it after you.'

In *Pass the Port Again* (1981 edn), the exchange occurs between Lord Haldane and Winston Churchill, as also in John Parker, *Father of the House* (1982), in which the exchange is specifically located at the Oxford Union in 1926. *The Faber Book of Anecdotes* (1985) has the US version: President Taft (d. 1930) making the retort to Senator Chauncey Depew (d. 1929)

Pauses

On being telephoned by the Evening News *and asked if he had a comment on Harold Pinter's 50th birthday:*

1 I don't; it's only later I realize I could have suggested two minutes' silence.

Alan Bennett, English playwright and actor (1934–). *Writing Home* (1994) – diary entry for 1 October 1980.

Pavarotti, Luciano

ITALIAN TENOR (1935–)

2 Only slightly smaller than Vermont.

Anonymous (American). Quoted in Norman Lebrecht, *When the Music Stops* (1996).

Pay

3 In his chamber, weak and dying,
While the Norman Baron lay,
Loud, without, his men were crying,
'Shorter hours and better pay' ...

Lives of great men all remind us
We can make as much as they,
Work no more, until they find us
Shorter hours and better pay.

Anonymous. 'A Strike Among the Poets' – included in *The Faber Book of Comic Verse* (1974 edn). Probably from the late 19th century. The second verse parodies Longfellow.

To his agent:

4 Before God I'm worth 35 dollars a week. Before the motion picture industry I'm worth anything you can get.

Ronald Colman, English actor (1891–1958). Quoted in Leslie Halliwell, *The Filmgoer's Book of Quotes* (1973).

Peace

5 Peace: in international affairs, a period of cheating between two periods of fighting.

Ambrose Bierce, American journalist (1842–?1914). *The Cynic's Word Book* (later retitled *The Devil's Dictionary*) (1906).

6 A conqueror is always a lover of peace.

Karl von Clausewitz, Prussian soldier (1780–1831). Attributed remark. Lenin, copying it into his notebook, commented: 'Ah! Ah! Witty.'

Pedantry

7 'Whom are you?' said he, for he had been to night school.

George Ade, American humorist and playwright (1866–1944). 'The Steel Box', in the *Chicago Record* (16 March 1898).

8 'You smell!'
'No, *you* smell, *I* stink.'

Anonymous. It has been attributed, inevitably, to Dr Samuel Johnson because, as a lexicographer, he would be thought fastidious about usage.

9 'Who was the leader of the Pedants' Revolt?' 'Which Tyler.'

Anonymous. Quoted in The '*Quote ... Unquote' Newsletter* (July 1995).

Correcting the proofs of his last parliamentary speech (31 March 1881):

10 I will not go down to posterity talking bad grammar.

Benjamin Disraeli (1st Earl of Beaconsfield), British Conservative Prime Minister and writer (1804–81). Quoted in Robert Blake, *Disraeli* (1966).

11 Noah Webster, the famous lexicographer, was discovered by his wife as he embraced one of the maidservants: 'Why, Noah, I am surprised!' she said. 'No, dear,' replied Webster, 'You are astonished; it is I who am surprised.'

Noah Webster, American lexicographer (1758–1843). Quoted in Ralph L. Marquard, *Jokes and Anecdotes for All Occasions* (1977). A version with 'amazed/surprised' was quoted by William Safire in *The New York Times* (15 October 1973).

Pedestrians

1 [There are] only two classes of pedestrians in these days of reckless motor traffic – the quick, and the dead.

Lord (Thomas Robert) Dewar, Scottish distiller (1864–1930). Quoted in George Robey, *Looking Back on Life* (1933). A *Times* leader in April that same year merely ventured: 'The saying that there are two sorts of pedestrians, the quick and the dead, is well matured.'

Peerages

2 When I want a peerage, I shall buy one like an honest man.

1st Viscount Northcliffe (Alfred Harmsworth), British newspaper proprietor (1865–1922). Quoted in R. Pound & G. Harmsworth, *Northcliffe* (1959), and Tom Driberg, *Swaff* (1974). An unlikely remark, even if meant in jest. Harmsworth was created a Baron in 1905 and a Viscount in 1917. His battles with David Lloyd George, the principal purveyor of pay-as-you-rise ennoblement, raged throughout the First World War.

3 You should study the Peerage, Gerald ... it is the best thing in fiction the English have ever done.

Oscar Wilde, Irish playwright, poet and wit (1854–1900). *A Woman of No Importance*, Act 3 (1893).

Pelicans

4 Oh, a wondrous bird is the pelican!
His beak holds more than his belican.
He takes in his beak
Food enough for a week.
But I'll be darned if I know how the helican.

Dixon Lanier Merritt, American writer (1879–1972). In the *Nashville Banner* (22 April 1913).

Penises

On penis envy:

5 I'm one of the few males who suffers from that.

Line from film *Annie Hall* (US 1977). Screenwriters: Woody Allen, Marshall Brickman. Spoken by Woody Allen (Alvy).

6 A stiff prick hath no conscience.

Anonymous. Ascribed confidently by John Osborne in *Almost a Gentleman* (1991), to St Augustine, but dubiously so. The proverbial status of the remark was, however, evident by the 1880s when 'Walter' in *My Secret Life* (Vol. 1, Chap. 12) wrote: 'I thought how unfair it was to her sister, who was in the family way by me ... but a *standing* prick stifles all conscience.' Indeed, 'a standing prick has no conscience' is an equally well-known variant. Earlier, in his diary (15 May 1663), Samuel Pepys writes of hearing from Sir Thomas Crew that: 'The King [Charles II] doth mind nothing but pleasures and hates the very sight or thoughts of business. That my Lady Castlemayne rules him; who he says hath all the tricks of Aretin [erotic writer Pietro Aretino] that are to be practised to give pleasure – in which he is too able, hav[ing] a large –[Pepys's blank]; but that which is the unhappiness is that, as the Italian proverb says, "*Cazzo dritto non vuolt consiglio*".' This may be translated as 'A stiff prick doesn't want any advice.' Compare: 'Another writer whom [Wilde] did not spare was his old teacher J.P. Mahaffy, two of whose books Wilde reviewed ... [he] might have treated Mahaffy nostalgically, but the erect pen has no conscience' – Richard Ellman, *Oscar Wilde* (1987).

7 I'm sixty-one today,
A year beyond the barrier,
And what was once a Magic Flute
Is now a Water Carrier.

Anonymous. Quoted in *The Penguin Dictionary of Modern Quotations*, eds J.M. & M.J. Cohen (1971).

Little girl to little boy when he dropped his trousers for her to have a look:

8 My, that's a handy little gadget.

Anonymous. Before 1941. Quoted in my book *Babes and Sucklings* (1983).

Fat man with an enormous stomach (or 'corporation') that prevents him from seeing the small boy seated at his feet:

9 Can't see my little Willy.

Donald McGill, English comic postcard artist (1875–1962). Caption to postcard *c.* 1910. *I've Lost My Little Willie!* (which rather obscures the joke) was used as the title of a 'celebration of comic postcards' (1976) by Benny Green.

This book title may have been taken from the caption to a re-drawing of the idea by another cartoonist.

After a streaker disrupted the Academy Awards ceremony (2 April 1974):

1 The only laugh that man will probably ever get is for stripping and showing off his shortcomings.

David Niven, English actor (1910–83). Quoted in F.L. Worth, *Complete Unabridged Super Trivia Encyclopedia* (1979). Just as Niven was about to introduce Elizabeth Taylor, a streaker appeared. Henry Mancini and the orchestra played 'Sunny Side Up' as the streaker was led off by security guards. The streaker was Robert Opal who later reappeared in the news when he was found murdered in his San Francisco sex shop.

2 He's got – I don't mean to be – well, he looks like he's got a cheese danish stuffed down his pants!

Tom Wolfe, American novelist and journalist (1931–). *The Bonfire of the Vanities* (1984).

Pens

3 None of us can have as many virtues as the fountain-pen, or half its cussedness; but we can try.

Mark Twain, American writer (1835–1910). *Following the Equator*, Vol. 2 (1897).

Pensioners

4 Pensioner: a kept patriot.

H.L. Mencken, American journalist and linguist (1880–1956). Quoted in Herbert V. Prochnow, Snr & Jnr, *A Treasury of Humorous Quotations* (1969).

Perfection

5 Bachelors' wives and old maids' children are always perfect.

Nicolas-Sébastien Chamfort, French writer (1741–94). Quoted in *The Treasury of Humorous Quotations*, eds Evan Esar & Nicolas Bentley (1951).

6 The very pink of perfection.

Oliver Goldsmith, Irish-born playwright and writer (1730–74). *She Stoops To Conquer*, Act 1, Sc. 2 (1773). Miss Neville speaking. The first use of this phrase. Mrs Malaprop's abuse of 'the very pinnacle of politeness', three years later, may be related (*see* MALAPROPISMS 268:7).

7 When a beautiful young lady cried out to the Rev. Sydney Smith in his garden that he would 'never bring this pea to perfection', he replied: 'Then allow me to bring perfection to the pea.'

(Revd) Sydney Smith, English clergyman, essayist and wit (1771–1845). Quoted in T.H. White, *The Age of Scandal* (1950).

To 'Daphne' (Jack Lemmon, in drag), who has just confessed that he is not a woman and is thus unable to marry the wealthy Osgood:

8 Well, nobody's perfect.

Line from film *Some Like It Hot* (US 1959). Screenwriters Billy Wilder, I.A.L. Diamond. Spoken by Joe E. Brown (Osgood E. Fielding III). Last line of the film.

9 *Revd Chasuble:*

Charity, dear Miss Prism, charity! None of us are perfect. I myself am peculiarly susceptible to draughts.

Oscar Wilde, Irish playwright, poet and wit (1854–1900). *The Importance of Being Earnest*, Act 2 (1895).

Perseverance

10 When the going gets tough, the tough get going.

Anonymous. Quoted in J.H. Cutler, *Honey Fitz* (1962). On the election of John F. Kennedy as US President in 1961, attention was focused on several axioms said to come from the Boston-Irish political world and more precisely from Joseph P. Kennedy (John F.'s father). At this distance, it would be impossible to say for sure whether this wealthy, ambitious businessman / ambassador / politician originated the expressions, but he certainly instilled them in his sons. In due course, the saying was used as a slogan for the film *The Jewel of the Nile* (US, 1985) and a song with the title sung by Billy Ocean and the stars of the film was a No. 1 hit in 1986. The joke slogan 'When the going gets tough, the tough go shopping' had appeared on T-shirts in the US by 1982.

1 It's dogged as does it. It ain't thinking about it.

Anthony Trollope, English novelist (1815–82). *The Last Chronicle of Barset*, Chap. 61 (1867).

2 By perseverance, the snail reached the Ark.

(Revd) C.H. Spurgeon, English Baptist preacher (1834–92). Quoted in Laurence J. Peter, *Quotations for Our Time* (1977).

Pessimists

3 A pessimist is one who has been intimately acquainted with an optimist.

Elbert Hubbard, American writer and editor (1856–1915). *A Thousand and One Epigrams* (1911).

4 There is no sadder sight than a young pessimist, except an old optimist.

Mark Twain, American writer (1835–1910). *Mark Twain's Notebook*, ed. A.B. Paine (1935).

5 Pessimist: one who, when he has the choice of two evils, chooses both.

Oscar Wilde, Irish playwright, poet and wit (1854–1900). Quoted in Herbert V. Prochnow, Snr & Jnr, *A Treasury of Humorous Quotations* (1969).

See also OPTIMISM.

Pets

Explaining his penchant for taking a lobster for a walk on a long blue leash (pink, in some versions), in the gardens of the Palais Royal, Paris:

6 Well, you see, he doesn't bark and he knows the secrets of the sea.

Gérard de Nerval, French poet (1808–55). Quoted in Théophile Gautier, *Portraits et Souvenirs Littéraires* (1875), which has an elaborate version of Nerval's explanation: 'Why should a lobster be any more ridiculous than a dog? Or any other animal that one chooses to take for a walk? I have a liking for lobsters; they are peaceful, serious creatures; they know the secrets of the sea; they don't bark, and they don't gnaw upon one's *monadic* privacy like dogs do. And Goethe had an aversion to dogs, and he wasn't mad.'

7 I can train any dog in five minutes. It's training the owner that takes longer.

Barbara Woodhouse, English animal trainer (1910–88). Quoted in *Handbook of 20th Century Quotations*, ed. Frank S. Pepper (1984).

See also CATS; DOGS AND DOG-OWNERS.

Philanthropy

8 Philanthropy seems … to have become simply the refuge of people who wish to annoy their fellow creatures.

Oscar Wilde, Irish playwright, poet and wit (1854–1900). *An Ideal Husband*, Act 1 (1895).

Philately

9 I don't know much about philately, but I know what I lick.

Philip French, English film critic (1933–). In *The Observer* Review (20 October 1985).

Philosophers and philosophy

10 Definition of a philosopher: a philosopher is a blind man in a dark cellar at midnight looking for a black cat that isn't there. He is distinguished from a theologian, in that the theologian finds the cat. He is also distinguished from a lawyer, who smuggles in a cat in his overcoat pocket, and emerges to produce it in triumph.

Anonymous. Quoted in *Cornell Law Quarterly*, Nos. 292–5 (1942). *Compare* METAPHYSICS 283:1.

11 I expect to pass through this world but once and therefore if there is anybody that I want to kick in the crutch I had better kick them in the crutch now, for I do not expect to pass this way again.

(Sir) Maurice Bowra, English academic (1898–1971). Quoted in Arthur Marshall, *Life's Rich Pageant* (1984). Bowra was lunching at the Reform Club where there was a bishop sitting at the next table.

1 As I said in another connection: 'An excellent plumber is infinitely more admirable than an incompetent philosopher. The society which scorns excellence in plumbing because plumbing is a humble activity and tolerates shoddiness in philosophy because it is an exalted activity will have neither good plumbing nor good philosophy. Neither its pipes nor its theories will hold water.'

John W. Gardner, American government official (1912–). *Excellence: Can We Be Equal and Excellent Too?* (1961). Quoted by Lyndon Johnson (27 July 1965), when naming Gardner as his Secretary of Health, Education and Welfare. The alliterative comparison between the two professions is fairly commonplace. J.M. Keynes said that 'economists should not be regarded as philosophers, telling us the meaning of life, or even as doctors, laying down rules for healthy living, but as plumbers, who could fix things within their competence' – unverified, but quoted in the *Financial Times* (30 December 1991); 'Of course, this tends to downgrade the ambitions and claims of the advertisers; they are capitalism's plumbers rather than its philosophers' – *The Sunday Times* (17 June 1990).

See also METAPHYSICS.

Photography

2 They used to photograph Shirley Temple through gauze. They should photograph me through linoleum.

Tallulah Bankhead, American actress (1903–68). Quoted in Leslie Halliwell, *The Filmgoer's Book of Quotes* (1973).

3 Most things in life are moments of pleasure and a lifetime of embarrassment; photography is a moment of embarrassment and a lifetime of pleasure.

Tony Benn, English Labour politician (1925–). Quoted in *The Independent* (21 October 1989).

4 As much of an art form as interior decorating.

Gore Vidal, American novelist and critic (1925–). Attributed remark.

5 If you look like your passport photo, in all probability you need the holiday.

Earl Wilson, American journalist (1907–87). In *Ladies' Home Journal* (1961). As 'If I look like this, I need the trip', ascribed to Gloria Swanson in Herbert V. Prochnow, Snr & Jnr, *A Treasury of Humorous Quotations* (1969). Compare: *When You Look Like Your Passport Photo, It's Time To Go Home*, title of book (1991) by Erma Bombeck.

Picasso, Pablo

SPANISH ARTIST (1881–1973)

On being asked what he would do if he saw Picasso walking ahead of him down Piccadilly:

6 I would kick him up the arse, Alfred.

(Sir) Winston S. Churchill, British Conservative Prime Minister and writer (1874–1965). Attributed by Sir Alfred Munnings in a speech at the Royal Academy dinner (1949). Alas, the BBC recording of the event fails to confirm that Munnings ever said this. Not a born speaker, to put it mildly, what he said was, 'Once he said to me, "Alfred, if you met Picasso coming down the street, would you join with me in kicking his something-something?" I said, "Yes, sir, I would!"'

Pie in the sky

7 You don't want no pie in the sky when
you die,
You want something here on the ground
while you're still around.

Muhammad Ali (Cassius Clay), American heavyweight boxing champion (1942–). Quoted on BBC Radio *Quote ... Unquote* (22 January 1979).

Pigeons

8 *Il y avait un jeune homme de Dijon*
Qui n'avait que peu de religion.
Il dit: 'Quant à moi,
Je déteste tous les trois,
Le Père, et le Fils, et le Pigeon.'

[There was a young man of Dijon
Who had only a little religion,
He said, 'As for me,
I detest all the three,
The Father, the Son and the Pigeon.']

Anonymous. Quoted in the introduction to *Some Limericks* (1928), privately printed by Norman Douglas (published 1969 as *The Norman Douglas Limerick Book*). To talk of the Holy Ghost in these terms (deriving from the traditional depiction of the Holy Ghost as a dove) seems to have been nothing new, even in the 1920s. Lord Berners describing his time at Eton in the 1890s in *A Distant Prospect* (1945) tells of a friend called Manston: 'At first I was inclined to be shocked by his irreverence – for instance, when he had said that the Trinity put him in mind of a music-hall turn – the Father, the Son and the Performing Pigeon.'

Pigs

On the qualities that a good pig should have:

1 The shoulders of a parlour maid and the buttocks of a cook.

Anonymous. A saying of her father's, quoted by Celia Haddon on BBC Radio *Quote ... Unquote* (7 September 1999).

Pipe-smoking

2 If you want to be happy for a day, go fishing. If you want to be happy for a week, get married. If you want to be happy for a month, kill a pig. If you want to be happy and contented for all time, smoke a pipe.

Anonymous. Quoted by Lord Mason, convenor of the Lords and Commons Pipesmokers' Club in March 1995, but untraced. On the other hand, the following version, described as a 'Chinese proverb', was heard in 1993: 'If you wish to be happy for an hour, drink wine; if you wish to be happy for three days, get married; if you wish to be happy for eight days, kill your pig and eat it; but if you wish to be happy for ever, *become a gardener*.'

Plagiarism

3 If I should die, think only this of me –
That in some corner of a foreign field
There lies a plagiarist.

Derek Alder (untraced). Quoted in my book *Quote ... Unquote 3* (1983).

4 Plagiarists are always suspicious of being stolen from.

Samuel Taylor Coleridge, English poet, critic and philosopher (1772–1834). Quoted in *The Treasury of Humorous Quotations*, eds Evan Esar & Nicolas Bentley (1951).

5 Originality is undetected plagiarism.

William R. Inge, English clergyman and writer (1860–1954). Quoted in the same collection as above.

6 If you steal from one author, it's plagiarism; if you steal from many, it's research.

Wilson Mizner, American playwright (1876–1933). Quoted in Alva Johnston, *The Legendary Mizners* (1953).

7 The difference between my quotations and those of the next man is that I leave out the inverted commas.

George Moore, Irish novelist (1852–1933). Quoted in Laurence J. Peter, *Quotations for Our Time* (1977).

8 Taking something from one man and making it worse is plagiarism.

George Moore. Quoted in *The Treasury of Humorous Quotations*, eds Evan Esar & Nicolas Bentley (1951).

Of a well-known author:

9 The only 'ism' she believes in is plagiarism.

Dorothy Parker, American writer (1893–1967). Quoted in *Publishers' Weekly* (19 June 1967).

On a quotation thief:

10 He's a cultural Robin Hood. He steals from the witty and gives to the dull.

Line from film *Pete 'n' Tillie* (US 1972). Screenwriter: Julius J. Epstein (from Peter de Vries novella). Spoken by Walter Matthau (Pete Seltzer).

11 Accusations of plagiarism ... proceed either from the thin colourless lips of impotence, or from the grotesque mouths of those who, possessing nothing of their own, fancy that they can gain a reputation for wealth by crying out that they have been robbed.

Oscar Wilde, Irish playwright, poet and wit (1854–1900). 'The Critic As Artist' (1890).

1 Of course I plagiarize. It is the privilege of the appreciative man.

Oscar Wilde. Quoted in Richard Ellman, *Oscar Wilde* (1987).

2 I do borrow from other writers, *shamelessly*! I can only say in my defense, like the woman brought before the judge on a charge of kleptomania, 'I do steal; but, Your Honor, only from the very best stores.'

Thornton Wilder, American novelist and playwright (1897–1975). Quoted in Barbara Rowes, *The Book of Quotes* (1979).

Platitudes

3 Applause is the echo of a platitude.

Ambrose Bierce, American journalist (1842–?1914). Quoted in *The Treasury of Humorous Quotations*, eds Evan Esar & Nicolas Bentley (1951).

4 The art of newspaper paragraphing is to stroke a platitude until it purrs like an epigram.

Don Marquis, American journalist and humorist (1878–1937). Quoted in Edward Anthony, *O Rare Don Marquis* (1962).

5 In modern life nothing produces such an effect as a good platitude. It makes the whole world kin.

Oscar Wilde, Irish playwright, poet and wit (1854–1900). *An Ideal Husband*, Act 1 (1895).

6 Literature is the orchestration of platitudes.

Thornton Wilder, American writer (1897–1975). Quoted in *Time* Magazine (12 January 1953).

7 *Travels* by Edward Heath is a reminder that *Morning Cloud*'s skipper is no stranger to platitude and longitude.

Christopher Wordsworth, English journalist and critic (1914–98). In *The Observer* (18 December 1977). The conjunction had been made earlier by Christopher Fry in his play *The Lady's Not For Burning* (1949): 'Where in this small-talking world can I find / A longitude with no platitude?'

Plays

When it was stated that the most important ingredients of a play were life, death, food, sex and money:

8 But not necessarily in that order.

(Sir) Noël Coward, English entertainer and writer (1899–1973). Quoted in Dick Richards, *The Wit of Noel Coward* (1968).

Plonking

9 If you have nothing to say, or, rather, something extremely stupid and obvious, say it, but in a 'plonking' tone of voice – i.e. roundly, but hollowly and dogmatically.

Stephen Potter, English humorist (1900–69). *Lifemanship* (1950). Although 'plonking' had been used in Yorkshire dialect for 'large', this would appear to be the first appearance of the term, as defined.

Poets and poetry

10 *Witwoud*:

Madam, do you pin up your hair with all your letters?

Millamant:

Only with those in verse, Mr Witwoud. I never pin up my hair with prose.

William Congreve, English playwright (1670–1744). *The Way of the World* (1700).

On 'free' verse:

11 I'd just as soon play tennis with the net down.

Robert Frost, American poet (1874–1963). Quoted in *Newsweek* Magazine (30 January 1956). Compare: 'Writing free verse is like playing tennis with the net down' – the version quoted in *The Treasury of Humorous Quotations*, eds Evan Esar & Nicolas Bentley (1951).

12 The poetic spirit … is capable of flourishing in even the most barren and unpromising soil. Simon, for whom poetry is a closed book in a locked cupboard in a high attic in a lonely house in a remote hamlet in a dis-

tant land, kept saying to his friends, 'This is Uncle Ted. He's a famous poet.'

Stephen Fry, English novelist and actor (1957–). *The Hippopotamus*, Chap. 4 (1995).

1 If there's no money in poetry, neither is there poetry in money.

Robert Graves, English poet (1895–1985). Speech at the London School of Economics (6 December 1963).

2 A year or two ago, in common with others, I received from America a request that I would define poetry. I replied that I could no more define poetry than a terrier can define a rat, but that I thought we both recognised the object by the symptoms which it provokes in us.

A.E. Housman, English poet (1859–1936). Lecture, 'The Name and Nature of Poetry' at Cambridge (9 May 1933).

3 Dr Donne's verses are like the peace of God; they pass all understanding.

James I, English King (1566–1625). Quoted by Archdeacon Plume (1630–1704).

In answer to Boswell's question, 'Then, Sir, what is poetry?':

4 Why, Sir, it is much easier to say what it is not.

(Dr) Samuel Johnson, English writer and lexicographer (1709–84). In James Boswell, *The Life of Samuel Johnson* (1791) – for 11 April 1776.

5 Perhaps no person can be a poet, or even enjoy poetry, without a certain unsoundness of mind.

Thomas Babington Macaulay (Lord Macaulay), English historian and poet (1800–59). *Collected Essays*, 'Milton' (1843).

6 Writing a book of poetry is like dropping a rose petal down the Grand Canyon and waiting for the echo.

Don Marquis, American writer (1878–1937). Quoted in Edward Anthony, *O Rare Don Marquis*, Chap. 6 (1962).

7 Poetry is what Milton saw when he went blind.

Don Marquis. Quoted in the same book as above.

8 Poets are born, not paid.

Wilson Mizner, American playwright (1876–1933). Quoted in *The Treasury of Humorous Quotations*, eds Evan Esar & Nicolas Bentley (1951).

9 I like a man with poetry in him, but not a poet.

Marilyn Monroe, American film actress (1926–62). Attributed, from 1956, in *The Oxford Dictionary of Literary Quotations*, ed. Peter Kemp (1997).

10 Poetry is a form of refrigeration that stops language going bad.

Peter Porter, Australian-born poet (1929–). Attributed remark.

11 Lady Caroline Lamb stabbed herself at Lady Ilchester's ball for the love of Lord Byron. What a charming thing to be a Poet. I preached for many years in London and was rather popular, but never heard of a lady doing herself the smallest mischief on my account.

(Revd) Sydney Smith, English clergyman, essayist and wit (1771–1845). Letter (1813), quoted in *The Sayings of Sydney Smith*, ed. Alan Bell (1993).

Of Ezra Pound:

12 A village explainer, excellent if you were a village, but if you were not, not.

Gertrude Stein, American poet (1874–1946). Quoted in Janet Hobhouse, *Everyone Who Was Anybody* (1975).

13 Anyway, it's not the most important thing in life, is it? Frankly, I'd much rather lie in a hot bath sucking boiled sweets and reading Agatha Christie, which is just exactly what I intend to do as soon as I get home.

Dylan Thomas, Welsh poet (1914–53). Quoted in Joan Wyndham, *Love Is Blue* (1986).

1 Wordsworth went to the Lakes, but he was never a Lake poet. He found in stones the sermons he had already hidden there.

Oscar Wilde, Irish playwright, poet and wit (1854–1900). 'The Decay of Lying', in *Nineteenth Century* (January 1889).

2 All bad poetry springs from genuine feeling.

Oscar Wilde. 'The Critic As Artist' (1891).

When asked who should be the next Poet Laureate:

3 Mr Swinburne is already the Poet Laureate of England. The fact that his appointment to this high post has not been degraded by official confirmation renders his position all the more unassailable.

Oscar Wilde. In *The Idler* (April 1895).

When Lewis Morris asked what he should do about the 'conspiracy of silence' surrounding his name being put forward for the Poet Laureateship at Tennyson's death:

4 Join it.

Oscar Wilde. Quoted in Walter Jerrold, *A Book of Famous Wits* (1912).

5 I was working on the proof of one of my poems all the morning and took out a comma ... In the afternoon – well, I put it back again.

Oscar Wilde. Quoted in R.H. Sherard, *Oscar Wilde: The Story of an Unhappy Friendship* (1902).

6 Longfellow is a great poet for those who never read poetry.

Oscar Wilde. Quoted in E.H. Mikhail, Oscar Wilde: *Interviews and Recollections* (1979).

7 England never appreciates a poet until he is dead.

Oscar Wilde. Quoted in the same book as above.

8 At twilight nature becomes a wonderfully suggestive effect, and is not without loveliness, though perhaps its chief use is to illustrate quotations from the poets.

Oscar Wilde. 'The Decay of Lying', in *Nineteenth Century* (January 1889).

9 One man's poetry is another man's poison.

Oscar Wilde. Quoted in *The Treasury of Humorous Quotations*, eds Evan Esar & Nicolas Bentley (1951).

10 Peotry is sissy stuff that rhymes. Weedy people sa la and fie and swoon when they see a bunch of daffodils.

Geoffrey Willans, English writer (1911–58) and Ronald Searle, English artist (1920–). *Down with Skool!* (1953).

On being told over the telephone that he had been awarded the Nobel Prize for Literature in 1923:

11 Stop babbling, man! How much?

W.B. Yeats, Irish poet (1865–1939). Quoted in *A Dictionary of Literary Quotations* (1990). Another version: on being told how great an honour it was for himself and for the country, he asked, 'How much is it, Smyllie, how much is it?' – attributed in W.R. Rodgers (ed.), *Irish Literary Portraits* (1972).

Poker

12 As elaborate a waste of human intelligence as you could find outside an advertising agency.

Raymond Chandler, American novelist (1888–1959). Quoted in *The Observer* (16 September 1990).

Poles

13 There are few virtues that the Poles do not possess – and there are few mistakes they have ever avoided.

(Sir) Winston S. Churchill, British Conservative Prime Minister and writer (1874–1965). Speech, House of Commons (16 August 1945).

Police

On being awoken at 6.30 a.m. and assuming the men were reporters, Pandora Maxwell told them to 'piss off' and said that she would call the police if they did not leave. The reply came back:

1 Madam, we are the police.

Anonymous. Quoted in *The Independent* (19 June 1992). The police had come to arrest her husband Kevin Maxwell (son of the deceased Robert) on fraud charges.

2 *Moore Marriott (telephoning):*
Help! Help! Help! Police! Police!
Will :
Shut up, you old idiot. We are the police.

Lines from film *Ask a Policeman* (UK 1938). Screenwriters: Marriott Edgar, Val Guest.

3 I never came across a situation so dismal that a policeman couldn't make it worse.

Brendan Behan, Irish playwright (1923–64). On New York's *Open End* TV show (1959) and quoted in *The Sayings of Brendan Behan*, ed. Aubrey Dillon-Malone (1997).

4 Publicity is justly commended as a remedy for social and industrial diseases. Sunlight is said to be the best of disinfectants; electric light the most efficient policeman.

Louis D. Brandeis, American jurist (1856–1941). Quoted in *Harper's Weekly* (20 December 1913). Compare the saying, 'Rain is the best policeman of all', heard from a senior police officer after London's Notting Hill Carnival had been rained off on the Late Summer Bank Holiday in August 1986. Meaning that the incidence of crime falls when the rain does (as it also does in very cold weather).

5 When constabulary's duty's to be done,
The policeman's lot is not a happy one.

(Sir) W.S. Gilbert, English writer and lyricist (1836–1911). *The Pirates of Penzance,* Act 2 (1879).

On the supposed youthfulness of the Irish police force:

6 A thing of duty is a boy forever.

Flann O'Brien, Irish novelist and journalist (1911–66). Quoted in *The Listener* (24 February 1977).

Political correctness

On political correctness in book publishing:

7 'You old scrubber' came back as 'You ex-cleaning woman you'.

Jilly Cooper, English novelist and journalist (1937–). Quoted in *The Observer*, 'Sayings of the Week' (5 March 1995).

Politicians

8 It is a well-known fact that those people who must *want* to rule people are, ipso facto, those least suited to do it ... Anyone who is capable of getting themselves made President should on no account be allowed to do the job.

Douglas Adams, English novelist (1952–2001). *The Restaurant At the End of the Universe*, Chap. 28 (1980).

9 A politician is an animal who can sit on a fence and yet keep both ears to the ground.

Anonymous. Quoted in *H.L. Mencken's Dictionary of Quotations* (1942). A commonly evoked criticism – from *The Observer* (8 September 1996): '[Archbishop Robert Runcie] was once described in a speech in the General Synod by the then Bishop of Leicester as a man who enjoyed "sitting on the fence with both ears to the ground". It helped him to accommodate both sides in every argument, but in the long term had the effect of destroying trust in his own statements.'

10 A politician is a person who approaches every subject with an open mouth.

Anonymous – variously ascribed. Quoted in Leon A. Harris, *The Fine Art of Political Wit* (1966), where it is attributed to Adlai Stevenson. *Compare* DIPLOMACY 120:14.

11 The finest Congress money can buy.

Anonymous. Has been ascribed to Mark Twain, who did once put the following in an undelivered speech: 'I think I can say, and say with pride, that we have some legislatures that bring higher prices than any in the world.'

1 The only way for a newspaperman to look at a politician is *down*.

Anonymous. Has been ascribed to Mark Twain and, by H.L. Mencken, to Frank Simonds, American journalist (1887–1936). Also to Frank Kent, American journalist (1907–78) in T. Crouse, *The Boys on the Bus* (1973).

2 I am on the right wing of the middle of the road and with a strong radical bias.

Tony Benn, English Labour politician (1925–). Remark, from the 1950s, quoted by Robin Day in a radio interview (1977) when asked about his own political position.

3 An honest politician is one who when he is bought will stay bought.

Simon Cameron, American politician (1799–1889). Compare Twain below.

4 I was told when a young man … that the two occupational hazards of the Palace of Varieties [Westminster] were alcohol and adultery. 'The Lords,' [a Knight of the Shires] said severely, 'has the cup for adultery' … The hurroosh that follows the intermittent revelation of the sexual goings-on of an unlucky MP has convinced me that the only safe pleasure for a parliamentarian is a bag of boiled sweets.

(Sir) Julian Critchley, English Conservative politician and writer (1930–2000). In *The Listener* (10 June 1982).

5 a politician is an arse upon
which everyone has sat except a man.

e.e. cummings, American poet (1894–1962). 'a politician', *1 x 1* (1944).

6 I always voted at my party's call,
And I never thought of thinking for myself
at all!

(Sir) W.S. Gilbert, English writer and lyricist (1836–1911). *H.M.S. Pinafore*, Act 1 (1878).

7 I knew that, 'He who wields the knife never wears the crown.'

Michael Heseltine, English Conservative politician (1933–). Interviewed in *New Society* (14 February 1986). He later went on to prove it by standing against Mrs Thatcher, only to see John Major succeed her as Prime Minister. No other instance of this expression has so far been turned up and, at the moment, it would appear to have been an 'instant proverb', coined vividly to illustrate a political fact. David Whayman prefers 'The hand that bears the sword seldom wears the crown' as the original of this putative proverb and traces the *idea* back to the assassination of Julius Caesar – with Brutus doing the wielding and Augustus doing the wearing. He also notes that, post-Heseltine, Andrew Roberts in *Salisbury* (1999) has: 'In denouncing his Party leader for lack of principle in the 1860s, Salisbury had after all only attempted unsuccessfully to do what Disraeli had managed to do to Peel twenty years earlier. They constitute two rare examples of politicians who both wielded the knife and also wore the crown.'

In his autobiography, *Life In the Jungle* (2000), Heseltine wrote: 'I had once over lunch in February 1986 encapsulated my position to the *New Society* journalist David Lipsey … I am amused by my early and uncharacteristic flash of modesty. It turned out to be a prophetic, if injudicious, comment.'

On his brother Robert Kennedy's appointment as Attorney General:

8 I can't see that it's wrong to give him a little legal experience before he goes out to practice law.

John F. Kennedy, American Democratic President (1917–63). Quoted in Victor Lasky, *J.F.K.: The Man and the Myth* (1963).

9 Politicians are the same all over. They promise to build a bridge even when there is no river.

Nikita Khruschev, Soviet Communist Party leader (1894–1971). Remark, Glen Cove, New York (1960).

10 I once said cynically of a politician, 'He'll double-cross that bridge when he comes to it.'

Oscar Levant, American pianist and actor (1906–72). *Memoirs of an Amnesiac* (1965).

1 He was the consummate politician. He didn't lie, neither did he tell the truth.

John Lundberg, political writer (1885–1962). Attributed remark.

Of two members of the US Congress:

2 They never open their mouths without subtracting from the sum of human knowledge.

Thomas B. Reed, American Speaker of the House of Representatives (1839–1902). Quoted in Samuel W. McCall, *The Life of Thomas Brackett Reed*, Chap. 21 (1914).

3 He knows nothing and he thinks he knows everything. That points clearly to a political career.

Bernard Shaw, Irish playwright and critic (1856–1950). *Major Barbara*, Act 3 (1905).

4 The country is going down the drain and they are squabbling about the size of the plughole.

Jeremy Thorpe, English Liberal politician (1929–). Quoted on BBC Radio *Quote … Unquote* (4 January 1976).

5 The only definition of an honest politician is one who once bought stays bought.

Mark Twain, American writer (1835–1910). Quoted in David Rogers, *Politics, Prayer and Parliament* (2000). Compare Cameron above.

6 Reader, suppose you were an idiot. And suppose you were a member of Congress. But I repeat myself.

Mark Twain. A.B. Paine, *Mark Twain:* A Biography (1912).

7 Fleas can be taught nearly anything that a Congressman can.

Mark Twain. Attributed remark.

8 Truth is that politics makes strange bedfellows.

Charles Dudley Warner, American journalist and writer (1829–1900). *My Summer in a Garden* (1870). In 1854, however, Leigh Hunt had written a letter (published in 1862) that included this sentence: 'Politics, like "misery", certainly makes a man acquainted with strange bedfellows.' Both remarks probably allude to Shakespeare, *The Tempest*, II.ii.40: 'Misery acquaints a man with strange bedfellows.'

Referring to President Woodrow Wilson:

9 [I am suspicious of anyone with a handshake] like a ten-cent pickled mackerel in brown paper.

William Allen White, American journalist and writer (1868–1944). Quoted in Walter Lord, *The Good Years* (1960).

Politics

On leaving his post as Secretary of State:

10 I will undoubtedly have to seek what is happily known as gainful employment, which I am glad to say does not describe holding public office.

Dean Acheson, American Democratic politician (1893–1971). Quoted in *Time* Magazine (22 December 1952).

11 There are three kinds of lie: a small lie, a big lie and politics.

Anonymous (Russian). Quoted in *Time* Magazine (25 March 1985). Prefaced by, 'As one of your [i.e. presumably American] writers said … ' Sometimes said to be a Jewish proverb in the form, 'One is a lie, two are lies, but three is politics.'

12 I have noticed that whenever a distinguished politician declares that a particular question is above party, he really means that everybody should vote for him.

(Sir) Winston S. Churchill, British Conservative Prime Minister and writer (1874–1965). Quoted by Anthony Montague Brown (his Private Secretary 1952–65) in speech to the International Churchill Societies (25 September 1986).

13 Politics is too important to be left to the politicians.

Charles de Gaulle, French general and President

(1890–1970). Quoted in Clement Attlee, *A Prime Minister Remembers* (1961).

1 Politics should be fun – politicians have no right to be pompous or po-faced. The moment politics become dull, democracy is in danger.

Quintin Hogg (Lord Hailsham), English Conservative politician (1907–). Quoted in 1966 and re-quoted in *The Observer*, 'Sayings of the Decade' (1970).

2 When we got into office, the thing that surprised me most was to find that things were just as bad as we'd been saying they were.

John F. Kennedy, American Democratic President (1917–63). Speech, Washington DC (27 May 1961).

3 Being in politics is like being a football coach. You have to be smart enough to understand the game, and dumb enough to think it's important.

Eugene McCarthy, American Democratic politician (1916–). In an interview while campaigning for the Presidency (1968).

On the Munich Agreement:

4 A policy of reculer pour mieux reculer.

Christopher Mayhew, English Liberal politician (1915–97). Speech, Oxford Union debating society (1938).

5 Political language ... is designed to make lies sound truthful and murder respectable, and to give an appearance of solidity to pure wind.

George Orwell, English novelist and journalist (1903–50). *Shooting an Elephant*, 'Politics and the English Language' (1950).

Following his defeat in the presidential election:

6 A funny thing happened to me on the way to the White House.

Adlai Stevenson, American Democratic politician (1900–65). Speech, Washington DC (13 December 1952).

7 Politics is perhaps the only profession for which no preparation is thought necessary.

Robert Louis Stevenson, Scottish writer (1850–94). *Familiar Studies of Men and Books* (1882).

'One of the basic rules of American politics':

8 When the water reaches the upper deck, follow the rats.

Claude Swanson. Quoted by Joseph Alsop in *New York Herald Tribune* (5 February 1964).

Polls

9 Opinion polls should be taken but not inhaled.

Adlai Stevenson, American Democratic politician (1900–65). Ascribed by Peter Kellner on BBC Radio *Quote ... Unquote* (20 March 2000).

Pollution

10 Pollution is cirrhosis of the river.

Anonymous (Australian). Quoted in my book *Graffiti 4* (1982).

11 People don't actually swim in Dublin Bay. They're merely going through the motions.

Brendan Behan, Irish playwright (1923–64). Quoted in *The Sayings of Brendan Behan*, ed. Aubrey Dillon-Malone (1997).

Polygamy

12 Mark once argued the question of polygamy with a Mormon who insisted that polygamy was moral and defied him to cite any passage in the Scriptures that forbids the practice. 'Well,' queried the humorist, 'how about the passage that tells us no man can serve two masters?'

Mark Twain, American writer (1835–1910). In *The Mark Twain Jest Book*, ed. Cyril Clemens (1957).

Pomposity

A pompous woman, complaining to Berners that the head waiter of a restaurant had not shown her and her husband immediately to a table, said, 'We had to tell him who we were.' Berners, interested, inquired:

1 And who were you?

Gerald Berners (Lord Berners), English writer and composer (1883–1950) . Quoted in Edith Sitwell, *Taken Care Of* (1965). Also told about John Betjeman. However, Patrick Balfour in *Society Racket* (1933) noted: 'I discovered the other day that [this] remark, attributed to a modern wit (and a true wit), Lord Berners, was in fact made by Lord Charles Beresford.' On 11 January 1933, *Punch* carried a cartoon by Fred Pegram, with the caption: 'They had the cheek to say there wasn't a single room in the whole blasted place. We were simply furious, and so we told 'em who we were.' – 'Really, and who were you?' Even earlier, on 2 May 1885, *Punch* had carried this exchange in a cartoon caption: 'You didn't know who I was this morning.' 'No, who were you?'

Pooterism

2 I left the room with silent dignity, but caught my foot in the mat.

George and Weedon Grossmith, English humorous writers (1847–1912) and (1854–1919). *The Diary of a Nobody*, Chap. 12 (1894). The nobody in question is Charles Pooter, an assistant in a mercantile firm, whose mundane doings and thoughts, described with a total lack of humour, gave rise to the term 'Pooterish' for anyone who displays similar characteristics coupled with a lack of awareness. From Chap. 1: 'When he had gone, I thought of a splendid answer I ought to have given him. However, I will keep it for another occasion.' From Chap. 13: 'I am a poor man, but I would gladly give ten shillings to find out who sent me the insulting Christmas card I received this morning.'

Pope, Alexander

ENGLISH POET (1688–1744)

3 One whom it was easy to hate but still easier to quote.

Augustine Birrell, English Liberal politician and writer (1850–1933). *Obiter Dicta*, 'Alexander Pope' (1884–7).

4 There are two ways of disliking poetry, one way is to dislike it, the other is to read Pope.

Oscar Wilde, Irish playwright, poet and wit (1854–1900). Quoted in Hesketh Pearson, *The Life of Oscar Wilde* (1946).

Popes

On the Pope's attitude to birth control, 1974:

5 He no play-a da game. He no make-a da rules!

Earl Butz, American politician (1909–). A joke of the time. Butz lost his job as President Ford's Secretary of Agriculture after making another similar but racist remark.

6 It often happens that I wake at night and begin to think about a serious problem and decide I must tell the Pope about it. Then I wake up completely and remember I am the Pope.

John XXIII, Italian-born Pope (1881–1963). Quoted in H. Fesquet, *The Wit and Wisdom of Good Pope John* (1964).

7 Anybody can be Pope; the proof of this is that I have become one.

John XXIII. From the same. Said to be in a letter to a boy who had wanted to know if he should be a pope or a policeman.

8 Oho! The Pope! How many divisions has he got?

Joseph Stalin, Soviet leader (1879–1953). Quoted in Winston Churchill, *The Second World War*, Vol. 1 (1948). Pierre Laval, French Foreign minister, asked Stalin in 1935, 'Can't you do something to encourage religion and the Catholics in Russia? It would help me so much with the Pope.' This was Stalin's reply.

Popularity

9 President Reagan frequently used showbiz analogies in his political career. When asked whether he resented the popularity of Mikhail Gorbachev in 1987, he told students in Jacksonville, Florida, 'Good Lord, I co-starred with Errol Flynn once.'

Ronald Reagan, American film actor, Republican governor and President (1911–). Quoted in *Time* Magazine (14 December 1987).

Of the poet W.E. Henley:

1 He has fought a good fight and has had to face every difficulty except popularity.

Oscar Wilde, Irish playwright, poet and wit (1854–1900). In an unpublished sketch, quoted in William Rothenstein, *Men and Memories* (1931). In Wilde's *The Duchess of Padua*, Act 1 (1883), the Duke remarks: 'Popularity / Is the one insult I have never suffered.'

2 To be popular one must be a mediocrity.

Oscar Wilde. *The Picture of Dorian Gray*, Chap. 17 (1891).

Posh

3 L'Avenue Foch
Is for people who are posh,
L'Avenue Victor Hugo
Is where people like me and you go.

Chas Henessey (untraced). Quoted in The *'Quote … Unquote' Newsletter* (January 1995).

Posing

4 Being natural is simply a pose, and the most irritating pose I know.

Oscar Wilde, Irish playwright, poet and wit (1854–1900). *The Picture of Dorian Gray*, Chap. 1 (1891).

5 Perhaps one never seems so much at one's ease as when one has to play a part.

Oscar Wilde. In the same book, Chap. 15.

6 To be natural … is such a very difficult pose to keep up.

Oscar Wilde. *An Ideal Husband*, Act 1 (1895).

Positive thinking

7 *Right Reverend Host:*
I'm afraid you've got a bad egg, Mr Jones!
Nervous young curate:
Oh no, my Lord, I assure you! Parts of it are excellent!

George Du Maurier, French-born British artist, cartoonist and novelist (1834–96). Caption to cartoon in *Punch*, Vol. 109 (9 November 1895).

Posterity

8 After being turned down by numerous publishers, he had decided to write for posterity.

George Ade, American humorist and playwright (1866–1944). *Fables in Slang* (1900).

9 'We are always doing,' says he, 'something for Posterity, but I would fain see Posterity do something for us.'

Joseph Addison, English essayist and politician (1672–1719). In *The Spectator*, No. 583 (20 August 1714). However, *Notes & Queries* (Vol. 152) has it that, in 1723, the Oxford antiquary Thomas Hearne attributed to Dr Thomas Stafford (1641?–1723) the remark, 'Posterity? What good will Posterity do for us?' Which came first?

10 Posterity is capable of infinite vulgarity.

(Sir) Noël Coward, English entertainer and writer (1899–1973). In *The Daily Telegraph* (1969).

11 Why should I write for posterity?
What, if I may be free
To ask a ridiculous question,
Has posterity done for me?

E.Y. Harburg, American lyricist (1898–1981). Song 'Posterity is Right Around the Corner' (1976). See Kaufman/Ryskind below.

12 When my sonnet was rejected, I exclaimed: Damn the age; I will write for antiquity.

Charles Lamb, English essayist (1775–1834). Letter to B.W. Procter (1829).

13 Posterity? Why posterity is just around the corner.

Line from musical *Of Thee I Sing*, Act 2, Sc. 3 (1931). Written by George S. Kaufman and Morrie Ryskind.

14 Why should we put ourselves out of our way to do anything for posterity; for what has posterity done for us? (*Laughter*). I apprehend you gentlemen have entirely mistaken my words, I assure the house that by posterity I do not mean my ancestors but those who came immediately after them.

(Sir) Boyle Roche, Irish politician (1743–1807). Quoted in *A Book of Irish Quotations* (1984). *Benham's Book of Quotations* (1948), claiming that it is 'erroneously attributed' to Roche, notes that the words occur in John Trumbull's poetic work *McFingal* (1775) and that Mrs Elizabeth Montagu had earlier written in a letter (1 January 1742): 'The man was laughed at as a blunderer who said in a public business "We do much for posterity; I would fain see them do something for us".' Stevenson's *Book of Quotations* (1974) has Thomas Gray writing in a letter to Dr Warton (8 March 1758): 'As to posterity, I may ask (with somebody whom I have forgot) what has it ever done to oblige me?' Inevitably, Oscar Wilde is also credited with the words, and Hesketh Pearson in *The Life of Oscar Wilde* (1946) duly quotes one of Oscar's early theatrical revues: 'What our descendants will think of [a certain farce] is an open question. However, posterity has as yet done nothing for us!' All these references obviously allude to the true originator, Addison, above.

Potatoes

Spitting out a hot potato at dinner:

1 Madam, a fool would have swallowed that.

Anonymous – though Dr Samuel Johnson is often credited with the remark. In The '*Quote … Unquote' Newsletter* (July 1996). Leonard Miall, the BBC's first post-war Washington correspondent, recalled attending a Dean Acheson press conference at the State Department when he was asked a very cleverly loaded question. 'None of us could imagine how the Secretary of State could answer it without getting himself into trouble. Acheson stroked his guardsman's moustache for a moment and then replied, "My late law partner, Judge Covington, once attended an oyster roast on the Eastern shore of Maryland. He was given a very hot oyster which he immediately spat on to the floor, remarking, 'A bigger damn fool would have swallowed that one'." There were no supplementaries.'

Poverty

2 No naked man lost anything.

Anonymous (Japanese proverb). Quoted in *Oriental Humour*, ed. R.H. Blyth (1942).

3 She was poor but she was honest,
Victim of a rich man's game.
First he loved her, then he left her,
And she lost her maiden name …
It's the same the whole world over,
It's the poor wot gets the blame,
It's the rich wot gets the gravy.
Ain't it all a bleedin' shame?

Anonymous. Song, 'She Was Poor But She Was Honest' – popular with British soldiers in the First World War. The fifth, sixth and seventh lines here have each achieved near proverbial status.

4 Poverty is an anomaly to rich people; it is very difficult to make out why people who want dinner do not ring the bell.

Walter Bagehot, English political writer (1826–77). *Literary Studies*, Chap. 2 (1879).

5 My children didn't have my advantages: I was born into abject poverty.

Kirk Douglas, American film actor (1916–). Remark, in several interviews, early 1980s. Quoted again in *Sunday Today*, 'Quotes of the Week' (26 April 1987).

6 One of the strangest things about life is that the poor, who need money the most, are the very ones that never have it.

Finley Peter Dunne, American humorist (1867–1936). Quoted in *The Treasury of Humorous Quotations*, eds Evan Esar & Nicolas Bentley (1951).

7 Poverty must have many satisfactions, else there would not be so many poor people.

Don Herold, American humorist and artist (1889–1966). Quoted in the same collection as above.

8 We were so poor that if we woke up on Christmas day without an erection, we had nothing to play with.

Frank McCourt, Irish writer. *Angela's Ashes* (1996).

9 Oh, I realize it's a penny here and a penny there, but look at me: I worked myself up from nothing to a state of extreme poverty.

Line from film *Monkey Business* (US 1931). Screenwriters: S.J. Perelman, Will B. Johnstone, Arthur Sheekman. Spoken by Groucho Marx.

1 Poverty of course is no disgrace, but it is damned annoying.

William Pitt (the younger), British Prime Minister (1759–1806). Quoted in *The Treasury of Humorous Quotations*, eds Evan Esar & Nicolas Bentley (1951). As 'Poverty's no disgrace, but 'tis a great inconvenience', this was said to be 'a common saying among the Lark Rise people' in Flora Thompson, *Lark Rise*, Chap. 1 (1939). G.L. Apperson's *English Proverbs and Proverbial Phrases* (1929) finds it in John Florio, *Second Frutes* (1591), in the form: 'Poverty is no vice but an inconvenience'.

2 I wasn't always rich. There was a time I didn't know where my next husband was coming from.

Line from film *She Done Him Wrong* (US 1933). Screenwriter: Mae West (from her play *Diamond Lil*). Spoken by Mae West (Lady Lou).

3 Men of small incomes have often very acute feelings; and a Curate trod on feels a pang as great as when a Bishop is refuted.

(Revd) Sydney Smith, English clergyman, essayist and wit (1771–1845). In *The Edinburgh Review* (1822).

4 As for the virtuous poor, one can pity them, of course, but one cannot possibly admire them.

Oscar Wilde, Irish playwright, poet and wit (1854–1900). 'The Soul of Man Under Socialism' (1895).

5 I have no money at all: I live, or am supposed to live, on a few francs a day ... Like dear St Francis of Assisi I am wedded to Poverty: but in my case the marriage is not a success.

Oscar Wilde. Letter (June 1899).

Power

6 All power is delightful – and absolute power is absolutely delightful!

Anonymous. Quoted on BBC Radio *Quote ... Unquote* (18 October 1999).

On what it is like not to be President:

7 Well, for one thing, I find I no longer win every golf game I play.

George Bush, American Republican President (1924–). Quoted in *The Independent*, 'Quote Unquote' (15 January 1994).

8 I see nothing wrong with power as long as I am the fellow who has it.

Cecil King, English newspaper proprietor (1901–87). Quoted in *The Observer*, 'Sayings of the Decade' (1970). When Chairman of the *Daily Mirror*.

Pragmatism

9 Alfred Lunt has his head in the clouds and his feet in the box-office.

(Sir) Noël Coward, English entertainer and writer (1899–1973). Quoted in *The Treasury of Humorous Quotations*, eds Evan Esar & Nicolas Bentley (1951).

Praise

10 Fan mail – a sort of hippopotamus that, having pushed one's front door open with his nose, squats with a dripping smile in a pool on one's hearthrug. Its impulse is charming, but one doesn't quite know what the devil to do with him.

John Barrymore, American actor (1882–1942). Quoted in *The Home Book of Humorous Quotations*, ed. A.K. Adams (1969).

11 The advantage of doing one's praising for oneself is that one can lay it on so thick and exactly in the right places.

Samuel Butler, English novelist and writer (1835–1902). *The Way of All Flesh*, Chap. 34 (1903).

12 Among the smaller duties of life, I hardly know one more important than that of not praising where praise is not due.

(Revd) Sydney Smith, English clergyman, essayist and wit (1771–1845). Quoted in Lady Holland, *A Memoir of Sydney Smith* (1855).

1 Praise is the best diet for us, after all.

(Revd) Sydney Smith. Quoted in the same book as above.

Prayers

2 Dear God, as you will undoubtedly have read in the leader column of *The Times* this morning …

Anonymous (Anglican clergyman). Quoted by Anna Ford on BBC Radio *Quote … Unquote* (29 June 1977). Richard Ingrams, *Muggeridge: The Biography* (1995) has, rather: 'A story was current at the time [1930s] of a clergyman who began an impromptu prayer with the words "Oh God, as thou wilt have read in the *Manchester Guardian* this morning …"'

At a village kirk in the Scottish Highlands, the minister was much given to interminable impromptu prayer, but occasionally lost his train of thought, 'Oh Lord,' he entreated, 'Thou that paintest the crocus purple … ' Here, his inspiration failing him, and he rapidly concluded:

3 Paint us purple, too.

Anonymous. Quoted on BBC Radio *Quote … Unquote* (8 June 1984).

4 O God, send me some good actors – cheap.

Lilian Baylis, English theatre manager and producer (1874–1937). Quoted in R. & S. Thorndike, *Lilian Baylis* (1938).

5 Think of what our Nation stands for,
Books from Boots' and country lanes,
Free speech, free passes, class distinction,
Democracy and proper drains.
Lord, put beneath thy special care
One eighty-nine Cadogan Square.

(Sir) John Betjeman, English poet (1906–84). 'Westminster Abbey' (1940).

6 Vouchsafe, O Lord, to keep us this day without being found out.

Samuel Butler, English author (1835–1902). Quoted in *The Treasury of Humorous Quotations*, eds Evan Esar & Nicolas Bentley (1951).

7 O Lord, if there is a Lord, save my soul, if I have a soul.

Ernest Renan, French philologist and philosopher (1823–90). Quoted in the same collection as above.

8 Behold thy votaries submissive beg,
That thou will deign to grant them all
they ask;
Assist them to accomplish all their ends,
And sanctify whatever means they use
To gain them!

Richard Brinsley Sheridan, English dramatist and politician (1751–1816). *The Critic*, Act 2, Sc. 2 (1779).

9 I am just going to pray for you in St Paul's, but with no very lively hope of success.

(Revd) Sydney Smith, English clergyman, essayist and wit (1771–1845). Letter to Richard Monckton Milnes (8 November 1843). Quoted in Hesketh Pearson, *The Smith of Smiths* (1934).

10 Sudden prayers make God jump.

Eric Thacker & Anthony Earnshaw, English writers. *Musrum* (1968).

11 When the Gods wish to punish us they answer our prayers.

Oscar Wilde, Irish playwright, poet and wit (1854–1900). *An Ideal Husband*, Act 2 (1895).

12 Prayer must never be answered: if it is, it ceases to be prayer and becomes correspondence.

Oscar Wilde. Quoted in Hesketh Pearson, *The Life of Oscar Wilde* (1946). A remark made to Laurence Housman.

Precociousness

13 Mr Salteena was an elderly man of 42 and was fond of asking people to stay with him.

Daisy Ashford, English child writer (1881–1972). *The Young Visiters*, Chap. 1 (1919).

1 I am parshial to ladies if they are nice I suppose it is my nature. I am not quite a gentleman but you would hardly notice it but cant be helped anyhow.

Daisy Ashford. From the same book.

2 I am very fond of fresh air and royalties.

Daisy Ashford. From the same book, Chap. 5.

3 Ronald Knox once related how it had been alleged by a friend of the family that when Knox was a mere four years old and suffering from insomnia, he was asked how he managed to occupy his time at night. He answered, apparently, 'I lie awake and think about the past.'

Ronald Knox, English priest and writer (1888–1957). *Literary Distractions* (1941).

Predictions

4 I have determined that there is no market for talking pictures.

Thomas Alva Edison, American inventor (1847–1931). In 1926. Quoted in Stuart Berg Flexner, *Listening to America* (1982).

5 The phonograph is not of any commercial value.

Thomas Alva Edison. Quoted in *Time* Magazine (13 August 1984).

Prefaces

6 Having to write a preface after labouring for five years to produce the book is an unnerving experience and something of an anticlimax; rather like an elephant who has succeeded at long last in giving birth to her calf being then required to balance a bun on her head.

Frank Muir, English writer (1920–98). Preface to *The Frank Muir Book* (1976).

Pregnancy

On going into hospital for an abortion:

7 It serves me right for putting all my eggs in one bastard.

Dorothy Parker, American writer (1893–1967). Quoted in John Keats, *You Might as Well Live* (1970).

Presidency

8 I would rather that the people should wonder why I wasn't President than why I am.

Salmon P. Chase, American lawyer and politician (1808–73). Quoted in *The Home Book of Humorous Quotations*, ed. A.K. Adams (1969).

9 When I was a boy I was told that anybody could become President; I'm beginning to believe it.

Clarence Darrow, American lawyer (1857–1938). Quoted in Irving Stone, *Clarence Darrow for the Defence* (1941).

10 The pay is good and I can walk to work.

John F. Kennedy, American Democratic President (1917–63). Attributed remark.

11 Scrubbing floors and emptying bedpans has as much dignity as the Presidency.

Richard M. Nixon, American Republican President (1913–94). Quoted in Laurence J. Peter, *Quotations for Our Time* (1977).

Press

12 Have you heard? The Prime Minister has resigned and Lord Northcliffe has sent for the King.

Anonymous (member of the *Daily Mail* staff). In 1919. Quoted in Hamilton Fyfe, *Northcliffe: An Intimate Biography* (1930).

13 On the whole I would not say that our Press is obscene. I would say that it trembles on the brink of obscenity.

7th Earl of Longford (Francis Pakenham), English writer and politician (1905–). Quoted in *The Observer*, 'Sayings of the Week' (2 June 1963).

1 Freedom of the press in Britain is freedom to print such of the proprietor's prejudices as the advertisers don't object to.

Hannen Swaffer, English journalist (1879–1962). In conversation with Tom Driberg, *c.* 1928 (recalled in Driberg's *Swaff*, 1974). Driberg suspected that Swaffer began to take this view in *c.* 1902.

2 It is a free press ... There are laws to protect the freedom of the press's speech, but none that are worth anything to protect the people from the press.

Mark Twain, American writer (1835–1910). *Mark Twain's Speeches*, ed. A.B. Paine (1923).

See also JOURNALISM; JOURNALISTS; NEWS AND NEWSPAPERS.

Presumption

3 I and my rhinoceros, said the tick-bird.

Anonymous (Sotho proverb). Quoted in Ruth Finnegan, *Oral Literature in Africa* (1970).

Pretentiousness

4 Two London taxi drivers were having a heated dispute. Said one, 'You know what you are, don't you? – pretentious!' And the other adopted a tone of hurt pride. 'Pretentious?' he replied. '*Moi*?'

Anonymous. Quoted by Anna Ford on BBC Radio *Quote ... Unquote* (recorded 5 December 1978). This joke featured also in the form:

5 So Harry says, 'You don't like me any more. Why not?' And he says, 'Because you've got so terribly pretentious.' And Harry says, 'Pretentious? *Moi?*'

John Cleese, English actor and writer and Connie Booth, American actress and writer, (1939–) and (1941–). 'The Psychiatrists', BBC TV *Fawlty Towers* (1979). Probably repeating an established joke of the time. It may have originally been uttered by Miss Piggy in TV's *The Muppet Show* at some time in the late 1970s.

Priestley, J. B.

ENGLISH NOVELIST AND PLAYWRIGHT (1894–1984)

6 Playing on a fuddled fiddle, somewhere in the muddled middle.

Aneurin Bevan, Welsh Labour politician (1897–1960). Attributed remark, during the Second World War.

Priests

7 A priest is a man who is called Father by everyone except his own children who are obliged to call him Uncle.

Anonymous. Quoted in *The Lyttelton Hart-Davis Letters*, Vol. 1 (1978) – in which Rupert Hart-Davis says he came across this 'Italian saying' in 'a French novel, read in the train', but gives no further information.

Princes of Wales

8 Tell me, Alvanley, who is your fat friend?

Beau Brummell, English dandy (1778–1840). Quoted in Capt. Jesse, *Life of George Brummell* (1844). A famous question to Lord Alvanley about the Prince Regent. Brummell, a dandy almost by profession, had fallen out with the Prince of Wales. He is said to have annoyed the Prince by ridiculing his mistress and also by saying once to his royal guest at dinner, 'Wales, ring the bell, will you?' When they met in London in July 1813, the Prince cut Brummell but greeted his companion. As the Prince walked off, Brummell put his question in ringing tones.

9 To be Prince of Wales is not a position. It is a predicament.

Line from film *The Madness of King George* (UK 1994). Screenwriter: Alan Bennett (from his play). Spoken by Rupert Everett (Prince of Wales). In the play *The Madness of George III*, the line is, 'To be heir to the throne is not a position. It is a predicament. People laugh at me.'

Principles

10 'Would you sleep with me if I gave you £10,000?' he asked her. She thought about it and acknowledged that, theoretically, she would. 'Good,' said Shaw, 'so would you

also sleep with me for sixpence?' The lady became indignant. 'What sort of woman do you think I am?' she exploded. 'We've established what sort of woman you are,' the writer pointed out, 'we're merely haggling over the price.'

Bernard Shaw, Irish playwright and critic (1856–1950). Quoted in *The Sunday Times* (13 May 1990). The origin of this exchange remains untraced. This is the earliest citation found so far, ascribing it to Shaw – except that it was quoted in Epson advertisements (May 1987) – where the figure given was £500. In *The Sayings of Bernard Shaw*, ed. Joseph Spence (1993), the figure is given as £1,000. Compare, from William Rushton, *Superpig* (1976): 'This is from the same stable as a Lord Curzon asking some duchess or other whether she'd bed down with him for a million pounds and saying upon her eager nod, "Having established the principle, now let's get down to the hard bargaining".'

Priorities

1 You mustn't take out a man's appendix while he's moving a grand piano.

Anonymous. Quoted as a 'favourite aphorism' of Denis Healey in Philip Ziegler, *Mountbatten* (1985).

Prison

2 The only thing I really mind about going to prison is the thought of Lord Longford coming to visit me.

Richard Ingrams, English writer and editor (1937–). On the prospect of having to go to gaol (1976) as a result of litigation concerning *Private Eye*, the magazine he then edited. Ingrams had no recollection of having made this remark but was happy to accept authorship, when asked about it on BBC Radio *Quote ... Unquote* (26 December 1976).

Handcuffed, standing in the pouring rain, on his way to prison:

3 If this is the way Queen Victoria treats her convicts, she doesn't deserve to have any.

Oscar Wilde, Irish playwright, poet and wit (1854–1900). Quoted in Hesketh Pearson, *The Life of Oscar Wilde* (1946).

Privacy

4 Everyone heard that I'd written the book and got it in the press. After that, I might have been a gold-fish in a glass bowl for all the privacy I got.

Saki (H.H. Munro), English writer (1870–1916). *Reginald*, 'The Innocence of Reginald' (1904).

Privileges

5 That most delicious of all privileges – spending other people's money.

John Randolph, American writer (1773–1833). In *The Letters of John Randolph* (1834).

On being made Poet Laureate in 1850:

6 In the end I accepted the honour, because during dinner Venables told me, that, if I became Poet Laureate, I should always when I dined out be offered the liver-wing of a fowl.

Alfred Tennyson (Lord Tennyson), English poet (1809–92). Quoted in *Alfred Lord Tennyson: a Memoir by his Son*, Vol. 1 (1897).

Problems

7 When all you have is a hammer, all your problems start to look like nails.

Abraham Maslow, American professor of psychology (1908–70). *The Psychology of Science: a Reconnaissance* (1966). However, in Arthur Bloch's third *Murphy's Law* book (1982), this view is listed as 'Baruch's Observation', with no clue given who Baruch is or was.

8 There is always an easy solution to every human problem – neat, plausible, and wrong.

H.L. Mencken, American journalist and linguist (1880–1956). Attributed remark.

Procrastination

9 Never do today what you can put off till tomorrow.

Line from film *The African Queen* (UK 1951). Screenwriter: James Agee (from C.S. Forester novel). Spoken by Humphrey Bogart (Charlie Allnutt). In James Parton, *The*

Life and Times of Aaron Burr (1858), 'Never do today what you can do as well tomorrow' is ascribed to Burr in *c.* 1835).

1 King Alfonso of Spain – 'So you want to start these reforms at once; not put them off till to-morrow, which is supposed to be our Spanish way with everything?' President of the Directory: 'Yes, sire, we have no mañanas to-day.'

Anonymous. Caption to cartoon in *Punch* (26 September 1923). The song 'Yes, We Have No Bananas' had been published earlier that year and was enormously popular.

2 Never put off till tomorrow what you can do the day after tomorrow just as well.

Mark Twain, American writer (1835–1910). 'The Late Benjamin Franklin'.

3 I never put off till tomorrow what I can possibly do – the day after.

Oscar Wilde, Irish playwright, poet and wit (1854–1900). Quoted in Hesketh Pearson, *The Life of Oscar Wilde* (1946).

Productivity

On the Emperor Gordian:

4 Twenty-two acknowledged concubines, and a library of sixty-two thousand volumes, attested the variety of his inclinations, and from the productions which he left behind him, it appears that the former as well as the latter were designed for use rather than ostentation.

Edward Gibbon, English historian (1737–94). *The Decline and Fall of the Roman Empire*, Chap. 7 (1776–88). An example of Gibbon's stony-faced sense of humour. In a footnote, Gibbon adds: 'By each of his concubines, the younger Gordian left three or four children. His literary productions were by no means contemptible.'

Professionals

5 A professional is a man who can do his job when he doesn't feel like it; an amateur is one who can't [do his job] when he does feel like it.

James Agate, English drama critic (1877–1947). *Ego* (1935) – entry for 17 September 1933. The context was a lunch with the actor Cedric Hardwicke, who said: 'My theory of acting is that it is so minor an art that the only self-respect attaching to it is to be able to reproduce one's performance with mathematical accuracy.' The above was Agate's concurrence. Hardwicke added: 'It shouldn't make a hair's breadth of difference to an actor if he has a dead baby at home and a wife dying.'

6 Professionals built the *Titanic*; amateurs built the Ark.

Anonymous. Quoted by Richard Needham MP in seconding the Loyal Address in the House of Commons (6 November 1984).

7 Amateurs [musicians] practise until they can get it right; professionals practise until they can't get it wrong.

Anonymous. Quoted by Harold Craxton, one-time professor at the Royal Academy of Music, and re-quoted in The *'Quote ... Unquote' Newsletter* (April 1994).

Professions

8 *Kitty*:
The guy said that machinery is going to take the place of every profession?
Carlotta:
That's something you need never worry about.

Line from film *Dinner At Eight* (US 1933). Screenwriters: Frances Marion, Herman J. Mankiewicz. Spoken by Jean Harlow (Kitty), Marie Dressler (Carlotta Vance).

9 As long as they've got sidewalks, you've got a job.

Line from film *Footlight Parade* (US 1933). Screenwriters: Manuel Seff, James Seymour. Spoken by Joan Blondell (Nan Prescott) to Claire Dodd (Vivian Rich).

10 The Actor and the Streetwalker ... the two oldest professions in the world – ruined by amateurs.

Alexander Woollcott, American writer and critic (1887–1943). *Shouts and Murmurs* (1922).

Professors

1 A professor is one who talks in someone else's sleep.

W.H. Auden, Anglo-American poet (1907–73). Quoted in *The Treasury of Humorous Quotations*, eds Evan Esar & Nicolas Bentley (1951).

2 Old professors never die, they merely lose their faculties.

Stephen Fry, English author and actor (1957–). *The Liar*, Chap. 2 (1991). But quoting an established line.

Prohibition

3 Prohibition is an awful flop,
We like it.
It can't stop what it's meant to stop.
We like it.
It's filled our land with vice and crime,
It's left a trail of graft and slime,
It don't prohibit worth a dime,
Nevertheless we're for it.

Anonymous. Quoted in Kenneth Allsop, *The Bootleggers* (1961), as much repeated in the early 1930s. *Compare* TOBACCO 435:2.

Promiscuity

4 What is a promiscuous person? It's usually someone who is getting more sex than you are.

Victor Lownes, American Playboy Club manager (1928–). Quoted in Bob Chieger, *Was It Good For You Too?* (1983).

5 There's a lot of promiscuity around these days and I'm all for it.

Ben Travers, English playwright (1886–1980). Quoted in the *Telegraph Sunday Magazine*, *c.* 1980.

6 So many men, so little time!

Mae West, American vaudeville and film actress (1893–1980). Quoted in *The Observer* (3 September 2000).

7 She's been on more laps than a napkin.

Walter Winchell, American journalist and broadcaster (1897–1972). Quoted in *The Penguin Dictionary of Modern Humorous Quotations*, ed. Fred Metcalf (1987).

Promise

8 Whom the gods wish to destroy they first call promising.

Cyril Connolly, English critic (1903–74). *Enemies of Promise* (1938).

Pronunciation

9 I take it you already know
Of tough and bough and cough and dough?
Others may stumble, but not you,
On hiccough, thorough, laugh and through.
Well done! And now you wish perhaps
To learn of less familiar traps.
Beware of heard, a dreadful word
That looks like beard and sounds like bird.
And dead. It's said like bed, not bead –
For goodness sake don't call it deed.
Watch out for meat and great and threat
(They rhyme with suite and straight and debt).
A moth is not a moth in mother
Nor both in bother, broth in brother.
And here is not a match for there
Nor dear and fear for bear and pear.
And then there's does and rose and lose –
Just look them up – and goose and choose,
And cork and work and card and ward,
And font and front and word and sword
And do and go and thwart and cart –
And yet I've hardly made a start!

Anonymous (by March 1980). This England's Book of Parlour Poetry (1989) adds a final couplet: 'A dreadful language? Man alive, / I'd mastered it when I was five!'

10 If ever you go to Dolgelley,
Don't stay at the —— HOTEL;
There's nothing to put in your belly,
And no-one to answer the bell.

Thomas Hughes, English novelist (1822–96). So ascribed in *The Faber Book of Comic Verse*, ed. Michael Roberts (1974 edn), assuming that this is the Hughes who is better remembered as the author of *Tom Brown's Schooldays*. 'Dolgelley' used to be the official spelling of what is now 'Dolgellau'. The key to the verse is that the place name, however spelt, is pronounced 'Dolgethly' – and so 'belly' must be pronounced 'bethly'. At the time, 'belly' was considered a distasteful word and so this is a way round pronouncing it. Some versions have 'Lion Hotel', and there has indeed been an establishment with this name (on the west side of the market square) but it no longer exists. Thomas Firbank in his book *A Country of Memorable Honour* (1953) states that he saw the verse hanging in the 'Royal Lion Hotel' at Dolgelley (in about 1951) when it was attributed to Wordsworth following his stay there.

To an American actor who returned from London pronouncing 'skedule' in the English way – 'schedule':

1 If you don't mind my saying so, I think you're full of skit.

Dorothy Parker, American writer (1893–1967). Quoted in Ned Sherrin, *Cutting Edge* (1984).

2 They spell it Vinci and pronounce it Vinchy; foreigners always spell better than they pronounce.

Mark Twain, American writer (1835–1910). *The Innocents Abroad* (1869).

Proposals

3 Emily, I have a little confession to make. I really am a horse doctor. But marry me and I'll never look at any other horse.

Last line from film *A Day at the Races* (US 1937). Screenwriters: Robert Pirosh, George Seaton, George Oppenheimer. Spoken by Groucho Marx (Dr Hackenbush) to Margaret Dumont (Mrs Emily Upjohn).

Prose

4 Men will forgive a man anything except bad prose.

(Sir) Winston S. Churchill, British Conservative Prime Minister and writer (1874–1965). Speech, Manchester (1906).

5 *Il y a plus de quarante ans que je dis de la prose sans que j'en susse rien* [Good heavens! For more than forty years I have been speaking prose without knowing it].

Molière, French playwright (1622–73). *Le Bourgeois Gentilhomme*, Act 2, Sc. 4 (1671).

6 Meredith is a prose Browning, and so is Browning. He used poetry as a medium for writing in prose.

Oscar Wilde, Irish playwright, poet and wit (1854–1900). 'The Critic As Artist', (1890).

7 *Acquaintance*:
How are you today?
Yeats:
Not very well. I can only write prose today.

William Butler Yeats, Irish poet (1865–1939). Quoted in *The Oxford Dictionary of Literary Quotations*, ed. Peter Kemp (1997).

Prospects

8 Before undergoing a surgical operation arrange your temporal affairs. You may live.

Rémy de Gourmont, French writer (1858–1915). Quoted in Herbert V. Prochnow, Snr & Jnr, *A Treasury of Humorous Quotations* (1969).

9 'Alf Todd,' said Ukridge, soaring to an impressive burst of imagery, 'has about as much chance as a one-armed blind man in a dark room trying to shove a pound of melted butter into a wild cat's left ear with a red-hot needle.'

(Sir) P(elham) G. Wodehouse, English-born novelist and lyricist (1881–1975). *Ukridge*, Chap. 5 (1924).

Prosperity

10 There is an old time toast which is golden for its beauty. 'When you ascend the hill of prosperity may you not meet a friend.'

Mark Twain, American writer (1835–1910). *Following the Equator* (1897).

11 Prosperity is the best protector of principle.

Mark Twain. In the same book as above.

12 Few of us can stand prosperity. Another man's, I mean.

Mark Twain. In the same book as above.

Proverbs

1 You should never touch your eye but with your elbow.

Anonymous. A genuine proverb, recorded by 1640 as 'Diseases of the eye are to be cured with the elbow.' There is a similar proverb for the ear: 'Never pick your ear but with your elbow.'

2 Better a handful of dry dates and [be] content therewith than to own the Gate of Peacocks and be kicked in the eye by a broody camel.

Anonymous (Arab proverb).

3 Never rub bottoms with a porcupine.

Anonymous (Ashanti proverb). Quoted in *The Guardian* and used as the title of a collection of *New Statesman* competition winners (1979).

4 Do not tie your shoes in a melon field or adjust your hat under a plum tree, if you wish to avoid suspicion.

Anonymous (Chinese proverb). Quoted in Claud Cockburn, *I, Claud*, Chap. 15 (1967).

5 It is useless to go to bed to save the light, if the result be twins.

Anonymous (Chinese proverb). Quoted in *The Home Book of Humorous Quotations*, ed. A.K. Adams (1969).

6 He that would have good luck in horses must kiss the parson's wife.

Anonymous (English proverb). In John Ray, *English Proverbs* (1670).

7 Pissing in his shoe keeps no man warm for long.

Anonymous (Icelandic proverb), at least according to W.H. Auden and Louis MacNeice, *Letters from Iceland* (1937). Also ascribed to Richard Selzer (1928–) in 'In Praise of Senescence', *Confessions of a Knife* (1979).

8 If you cannot catch a bird of paradise, better take a wet hen.

Anonymous (Russian proverb). Quoted as spoken by Nikita Khruschev, the Soviet leader, in *Time* Magazine (6 January 1958). Khruschev became famous for his citing of folksy Russian proverbs (always assuming they were genuine and he had not made them up for himself). Another one:

9 If you start throwing hedgehogs under me, I shall throw two porcupines under you.

Anonymous (Russian proverb). Quoted as spoken by Nikita Khruschev, in *The New York Times* (7 November 1963).

Making tour of castle:

10 This is yet another example of the late neoclassical baroque period and, as I always say, if it's not baroque, don't fix it!

Line from film *Beauty and the Beast* (US 1991). Screenwriter: Linda Woolverton. Spoken by David Ogden Stiers (Cogsworth).

11 A shut mouth will catch no flies.

Brendan Behan, Irish playwright (1923–64). *Hold Your Hour and Have Another* (1963).

12 There is a proverb in our tongue, which I take to contain a great deal of truth, as generally those sorts of sayings do, being short sentences framed upon observation and long experience.

Miguel de Cervantes, Spanish novelist (1547–1616). *Don Quixote*, Pt 1, Chap. 39 (1605).

13 He that hath a head of wax must not walk in the sun.

George Herbert, English divine and poet (1593–1633). Collected in his *Jacula Prudentum* (1640).

14 People who live in glass houses should pull down the blinds.

Oliver Herford, American humorist (1863–1935). Quoted in *The Treasury of Humorous Quotations*, eds Evan Esar & Nicolas Bentley (1951).

1 'The more articulate, the less said' is an old Chinese proverb which I just made up myself.

Don Herold, American humorist and artist (1889–1966). Quoted in the same collection as above.

A dachshund-comforting proverb:

2 No leg is too short to touch the ground.

Lyndon Irving, English writer (1905–). Contributed to a *New Statesman* competition and included in the anthology *Salome, Dear, Not In the Fridge* (1968). Sometimes quoted as 'Even a short leg reaches the ground.'

When a woman says 'I don't like this innuendo':

3 That's what I always say. Love flies out the door when money comes innuendo.

Line from film *Monkey Business* (US 1931). Screenwriters: S.J. Perelman, Will B. Johnstone, Arthur Sheekman. Spoken by Groucho Marx.

4 There's another old saying, Senator. Don't piss down my back and tell me it's raining.

Line from film *The Outlaw Josey Wales* (US 1976). Screenwriters: Phil Kaufman, Sonia Chernus. Spoken by John Vernon (Fletcher) to Frank Schofield (Senator Lane).

5 A proverb is one man's wit and all men's wisdom.

Lord John Russell, British Whig Prime Minister (1792–1878). Quoted in R.J. Mackintosh, *Sir James Mackintosh*, Vol. 2, Chap. 7 (1835). Sometimes rendered as ' … the wisdom of many and the wit of one.'

6 He digs deepest who deepest digs.

Roger Woddis, English poet (1917–93). Submitted for a *New Statesman* competition and collected in *Never Rub Bottoms With a Porcupine*, ed. Arthur Marshall (1979).

7 The older I get, the more I agree with Shakespeare and those poet Johnnies about it always being darkest before the dawn and there's a silver lining and what you lose on the swings you make up on the roundabouts.

(Sir) P(elham) G. Wodehouse, English-born novelist and lyricist (1881–1975). *Carry On Jeeves* (1925). Bertie Wooster speaking.

Providence

8 *Judge*:
What do you suppose I am on the bench for, Mr Smith?
F.E. Smith:
It is not for me, your honour, to attempt to fathom the inscrutable workings of Providence.

F.E. Smith (1st Earl of Birkenhead), English politician and lawyer (1872–1930). Quoted in Winston Churchill, *Great Contemporaries* (1937).

Psychiatrists

9 A psychiatrist is a man who goes to the Folies-Bergère and looks at the audience.

Mervyn Stockwood, English Anglican bishop (1913–95) Quoted in *The Observer* (15 October 1961).

Public relations

10 When business is good it pays to have public relations; when business is bad you've got to have public relations.

Anonymous.

11 Will somebody please explain to me why public relations people are almost invariably 'associates'? Whom do they associate with, and who can stand it?

George Dixon (American). Quoted in Herbert V. Prochnow, Snr & Jnr, *A Treasury of Humorous Quotations* (1969).

12 I don't keep a dog and bark myself.

Elizabeth I, English Queen (1533–1603). Quoted in Frederick Chamberlin, *The Sayings of Queen Elizabeth* (1923), who says: 'High authority vouches for this Saying, but I have not seen the original.'

Public schools

13 Show me the man who has enjoyed his schooldays and I will show you a bully and a bore.

Robert Morley, English actor and writer (1908–92). *Robert Morley: Responsible Gentleman* (1966).

1 Anyone who has been to an English public school will always feel comparatively at home in prison. It is the people brought up in the gay intimacy of the slums, Paul learned, who find prison soul-destroying.

Evelyn Waugh, English novelist (1903–66). *Decline and Fall*, Pt 3, Chap. 4 (1928).

Publicity

2 Publicity is easy to get. Just be so successful you don't need it, and then you'll get it.

Anonymous (American). Quoted in Herbert V. Prochnow, Snr & Jnr, *A Treasury of Humorous Quotations* (1969).

3 There's no such thing as bad publicity except your own obituary.

Brendan Behan, Irish playwright (1923–64). Quoted in the *Sunday Express* (5 January 1964) and in Dominic Behan, *My Brother Brendan* (1965).

4 I don't care what you say about me, as long as you say *something* about me, and as long as you spell my name right.

George M. Cohan, American songwriter and entertainer (1878–1942). Quoted in J. McCabe, *George M. Cohan* (1973).

Of a theatrical manager who was puffing an actress who was also his mistress:

5 The fellow is blowing his own strumpet.

(Sir) W.S. Gilbert, English writer and lyricist (1836–1911). Quoted in Hesketh Pearson, *Gilbert and Sullivan*, Pt 3 (1935).

6 I don't care what is written about me so long as it isn't true.

Katharine Hepburn, American film actress (1909–). Quoted in news summaries (24 May 1954).

7 Our great Dryden has long carried it as far as it would go, and with incredible success. He has often said to me in confidence, that the world would have never suspected him to be so great a poet, if he had not assured them so frequently in his Prefaces that it was impossible they could either doubt or forget it.

Jonathan Swift, Anglo-Irish writer and clergyman (1667–1745). *A Tale of a Tub*, Chap. 5 (1704).

See also PUBLIC RELATIONS.

Publishers

8 Now Barabbas was a publisher.

Lord Byron, English poet (1788–1824). Attributed remark. The story has it that when John Murray, Byron's publisher, sent the poet a copy of the Bible in return for a favour, Byron sent it back with the words 'Now Barabbas was a robber' (St John 18:40) altered to, 'Now Barabbas was a publisher ... ' This story was included in Kazlitt Arvine's *Cyclopedia of Anecdotes of Literature and the Fine Arts*, published in Boston, Massachussetts, in 1851. In 1981, the then head of the firm, John G. (Jock) Murray, told me that those involved were in fact the poet Coleridge and *his* publishers, Longman. But when I asked for evidence in 1988, he could only say that, 'I have satisfied myself that it was not Byron.' The copy of Byron's Bible that exists has no such comment in it. He also drew my attention to the fact that in Byron's day publishers were more usually called booksellers.

H. L. Mencken's Dictionary of Quotations (1942), on the other hand, gives Thomas Campbell (1777–1844) as the probable perpetrator. Certainly, Campbell seems to have taken the required attitude. At a literary dinner he once toasted Napoleon, explaining: 'I agree with you that Napoleon is a tyrant, a monster, the sworn foe of our nation. But, gentlemen – he once shot a publisher!' (quoted in G.O. Trevelyan, *The Life and Letters of Lord Macaulay*, 1876 – diary entry for 12 December 1848). Mark Twain wrote in a letter: 'How often we recall, with regret, that Napoleon once shot at a magazine editor and missed him and killed a publisher. But we remember with charity, that his intentions were good.' The reference is to Napoleon's having personally ordered the execution of Johann Palm, a German publisher of subversive pamphlets.

9 As repressed sadists are supposed to become policemen or butchers, so those with an irrational fear of life become publishers.

Cyril Connolly, English critic (1903–74). *Enemies of Promise* (1938).

1 It is with publishers as with wives: one always wants somebody else's.

Norman Douglas, Scottish writer and novelist (1868–1952). Quoted in *The Frank Muir Book* (1976).

2 I suppose publishers are untrustworthy. They certainly always look it.

Oscar Wilde, Irish playwright, poet and wit (1854–1900). Letter (February 1898).

3 Being published by the Oxford University Press is rather like being married to a duchess: the honour is almost greater than the pleasure.

G.M. Young, English historian (1882–1959). Quoted by Rupert Hart-Davis in letter to George Lyttelton (29 April 1956).

Publishing

Of poems:

4 You shall see them on a beautiful quarto page where a neat rivulet of text shall meander through a meadow of margin.

Richard Brinsley Sheridan, English dramatist and politician (1751–1816). *The School for Scandal*, Act 1, Sc.1 (1777).

Punch Magazine

When asked why his organ wasn't as funny or as good as it used to be:

5 It never was.

(Sir) F(rancis) C. Burnand, English editor (1836–1917). Quoted in R.G.G. Price, *A History of Punch* (1957).

When told by an editor that Punch *was sent over a thousand jokes every week:*

6 Why don't you print any of them?

(Sir) W.S. Gilbert, English writer and lyricist (1836–1911). Quoted by Miles Kington on BBC Radio *Quote ... Unquote* (17 October 2000).

7 Very much like the Church of England. It is doctrinally inexplicable but it goes on.

Malcolm Muggeridge, English writer and broadcaster (1903–90). Quoted in A. Andrews, *Quotations for Speakers and Writers* (1969).

Punctuality and unpunctuality

8 The only way of catching a train I ever discovered is to miss the train before.

G.K. Chesterton, English poet, novelist and critic (1874–1936). Quoted in *The Treasury of Humorous Quotations*, eds Evan Esar & Nicolas Bentley (1951). P. Daninos, *Vacances à tous prix*, 'Le Supplice de l'heure' (1958) has: 'Chesterton taught me this: the only way to be sure of catching a train was to miss the one before it.'

When criticized for continually arriving late for work in the City in 1919:

9 But think how early I go.

Lord Castlerosse, English eccentric (1891–1943). Quoted in Leonard Mosley, *Castlerosse* (1956). Also attributed to Howard Dietz at MGM.

On being told that he was seven minutes late arriving at Dublin Castle on 16 January 1922 for the handing-over ceremony by British forces:

10 We've been waiting seven hundred years. You can have the seven minutes.

Michael Collins, Irish politician (1880–1922). Quoted in Tim Pat Collins, *Michael Collins* (1990).

11 Five minutes! Zounds! I have been five minutes too late all my lifetime!

Hannah Cowley, English playwright (1743–1809). *The Belle's Stratagem*, Act 1, Sc. 1 (1780).

12 I am a believer in punctuality though it makes me very lonely.

E.V. Lucas, English essayist and writer (1868–1938). Quoted in *The Treasury of Humorous Quotations*, eds Evan Esar & Nicolas Bentley (1951).

13 I've been on a calendar, but never on time.

Marilyn Monroe, American film actress (1926–62). Quoted in *Look* Magazine (16 January 1962).

1 Punctuality is a species of constancy, a very unfashionable quality in a lady.

Richard Brinsley Sheridan, English playwright and politician (1751–1816). *The School for Scandal*, Act 4 Sc. 3 (1777). Joseph Surface speaking.

2 Better late than never, as Noah remarked to the Zebra, which had understood that passengers arrived in alphabetical order.

Bert Leston Taylor, American journalist (1866–1921). *The So-Called Human Race* (1922).

3 He was always late on principle, his principle being that punctuality is the thief of time.

Oscar Wilde, Irish playwright, poet and wit (1854–1900). *The Picture of Dorian Gray*, Chap. 4 (1891).

Punishment

When sewing mail-bags in prison and being greeted by a visitor with the words, 'Ah, Bottomley, sewing?':

4 No, reaping.

Horatio Bottomley, English journalist, financier and politician (1860–1933). Quoted in S.T. Felstead, *Horatio Bottomley* (1936). In 1922, Bottomley (an MP) was found guilty of fraudulent conversion and sent to prison.

Punning

5 Hanging is too good for a man who makes puns. He should be drawn and quoted.

Fred Allen, American comedian (1894–1956). Quoted in Laurence J. Peter, *Quotations for Our Time* (1977).

6 A man who would make so vile a pun would not scruple to pick a pocket.

John Dennis, English playwright and critic (1657–1734). Editorial note in *The Gentleman's Magazine* (1781). Possibly said *of* Dennis rather than by him.

7 It [a pun] is a pistol let off at the ear; not a feather to tickle the intellect.

Charles Lamb, English essayist (1775–1834). *Last Essays of Elia*, 'Popular Fallacies No. 9. That the Worst Puns are the Best' (1833).

8 I never knew an enemy to puns who was not an ill-natured man.

Charles Lamb. Attributed remark.

9 May my last breath be drawn through a pipe and exhaled in a pun.

Charles Lamb. Quoted in W. Toynbee, *Diaries of William Charles Macready* 1833–1851 (1912).

10 A pun is the lowest form of humour – when you don't think of it first.

Oscar Levant, American pianist and actor (1906–72). Quoted in *The Treasury of Humorous Quotations*, eds Evan Esar & Nicolas Bentley (1951).

11 I have very little to say about puns; they are in very bad repute, and so they *ought* to be. The wit of language is so miserably inferior to the wit of ideas that it is very deservedly driven out of good company.

(Revd) Sydney Smith, English clergyman, essayist and wit (1771–1845). *Sketches of Moral Philosophy* (1849).

12 Punning is a talent which no man affects to despise but he that is without it.

Jonathan Swift, Anglo-Irish writer and clergyman (1667–1745). Quoted in *The Treasury of Humorous Quotations*, eds Evan Esar & Nicolas Bentley (1951).

Puns

13 Un Oeuf is as Good as a Feast.

Anonymous. Headline in *Punch* (26 January 1861).

14 'Do you know Sir Arthur Evans's reported remark on finding a fragment of pottery in Crete – "an ill-favoured thing, but Minoan"?'

Anonymous. Quoted in *The 'Quote ... Unquote' Newsletter* (April 1995). 'A Small Thing But Minoan' is ascribed as a title to Alan Coren in Frank Muir, *The Oxford Book of Humorous Prose* (1992).

1 *Teacher*:
And who was JOAN OF ARC?
Scholar:
Please, sir, NOAH's wife.

Anonymous. *Punch*, Vol. 122 (29 January 1902). 'Noah's wife was called Joan of Ark' was listed as one of 'British children's answers to church school questions' in a US publication called *Speaker's Idea File* (1993). But how old did the compilers think it to be? About as old as the Ark itself is the fact of the matter.

2 Peccavi – I have Sindh.

Anonymous. *Punch*, Vol. 6 (18 May 1844). *Punch* suggested that Caesar's '*Veni, vidi, vici*' was beaten for brevity by 'Napier's dispatch to Lord Ellenborough, *Peccavi*.' *The Oxford Dictionary of Quotations* credits the joke to Catherine Winkworth (1827–78). She was a young girl, so it was sent into *Punch* on her behalf. Later, she became a noted translator of hymns. It seems, however, that the supposed remark was soon taken as genuine, even at *Punch* itself. On 22 March 1856, the magazine (confusing sender and receiver in the original) included the couplet: '"*Peccavi* – I've Scinde," wrote Lord Ellen, so proud. More briefly Dalhousie wrote – "*Vovi* – I've Oude".' *Peccavi*' is the Latin phrase for 'I've sinned'; *vovi* for 'I vowed'.

3 *Macbull*:
I shall be a gay grass widower for the next two months – wife's gone for a holiday to the West Indies.
O'Bear:
Jamaica?
Macbull:
No, it was her own idea.

Anonymous (cartoonist). Caption to cartoon in *Punch* (25 February 1914).

4 The quality of Mersey is not strained.

Anonymous. *Punch*, Vol. 181 (19 August 1931). Writing to James Agate from Liverpool on 17 April 1942, John Gielgud, the actor, who was touring in *Macbeth*, noted: 'There was a very nice misprint in the *Liverpool Echo* on Wednesday, paying tribute to our broad comedian George Woodbridge, who plays the Porter, as "an engaging Portia". I could not forbear to murmur that the quality of Mersey is not strained.' Well, this was an early appearance of the 'Mersey' joke, in *Ego 5* (1942). It had already appeared, though, in *Punch*, as here, not to mention on 15 January 1859.

5 I'd give my right arm to be ambidextrous.

Anonymous (graffito). Included in my book *Graffiti Lives, OK* (1979).

6 Dada wouldn't buy me a Bauhaus.

Anonymous (graffito). Included in my book *Graffiti 3* (1981). By students at local art college, spotted by Finlay Bates of Norwich (1981).

7 Life's a binge and then you diet.

Anonymous (headline). To an article in *The Observer* (23 September 1990) about frozen food.

Promoting sun-tan products with a window-display under the slogan:

8 Life's a beach – and then you fry.

Anonymous (slogan). For the Body Shop chain in the UK (summer of 1991).

9 Like Webster's Dictionary
We're Morocco bound.

Johnny Burke, American songwriter (1908–64). Song, 'Road to Morocco', with music by Jimmy van Heusen. In film, *Road To Morocco* (US 1942). Performed by Bob Hope and Bing Crosby.

10 [I have made] a consommé devoutly to be wished.

(Sir) Noël Coward, English entertainer and writer (1899–1973). Quoted in Cole Lesley, *The Life of Noël Coward*, Chap. 17 (1976).

11 After two days in hospital, I took a turn for the nurse.

W.C. Fields, American comedian (1879–1946). Attributed remark.

12 *Non Angli sed Angeli* [not Angles but Angels].

Gregory I (the Great), Rome-born Pope and saint (*c.* 540–604). In about AD 590, Gregory supposedly met some slaves in the market-place in Rome who said they were 'Angles' (i.e. Anglo-Saxons) and he said, 'It is well, because they have the faces of angels' – usually remembered as above.

1 He holds the mirror up to Nietzsche.

Philip Guedalla, English biographer and historian (1889–1944). Quoted in *The Treasury of Humorous Quotations*, eds Evan Esar & Nicolas Bentley (1951).

To a waiter at Buckingham Palace who had spilled soup on her new dress:

2 Never darken my Dior again!

Beatrice Lillie, Canadian-born actress (1898–1989). *Every Other Inch a Lady* (1973).

3 A water bison is what yer wash yer face in.

Roger McGough, English poet (1937–). *An Imaginary Menagerie* (1988).

4 A bird in the Strand is worth two in Shepherd's Bush.

Spike Milligan, Irish entertainer and writer (1918–). In BBC Radio *The Goon Show*, 'The Lost Emperor' (4 October 1955).

5 Are you a spy?
Yes.
Then why are you covered in mint?
I'm a mint-spy!

Spike Milligan. In BBC Radio, *The Goon Show*, 'The Jet-Propelled Guided NAAFI' (24 January 1956).

6 It's better to have lost a loft than never to have lost at all.

Line from film *Monkey Business* (US 1931). Screenwriters: S.J. Perelman, Will B. Johnstone, Arthur Sheekman. Spoken by Chico Marx. Compare: 'It is better to have loafed and lost than never to have loafed at all' – the moral to 'The Courtship of Arthur and Al' in James Thurber, *Fables For Our Time* (1940).

7 I remember once having made this observation to Edmund Burke, that it would be no bad definition of one sort of epitaphs, to call them grave epigrams. He repeated the words '*grave* epigrams', and gave me the credit of a pun, which I never intended.

(Sir) Joshua Reynolds, English painter (1723–92). Letter (31 May 1791).

8 *Kenneth Horne:*
Then I stepped into the shower. Suddenly I felt something in the small of my back. I turned. I was looking down the muzzle of a Mauser.
Bill Pertwee (as German):
This pussy cat is loaded. One false move and you get it.

Lines from BBC Radio *Round the Horne* (14 May 1967). Script by Barry Took and Marty Feldman.

9 And I'll stay off Verlaine, too; he was always chasing Rimbauds.

Kenneth Tynan, English critic (1927–80). Quoted in James Agate, *Ego 8* (1945) – for 20 July 1945. Agate commented: To say that "Verlaine was always chasing Rimbauds" is just *common*. Like cheap scent.' Whether the schoolboy Tynan knew it or not, he had been anticipated by Dorothy Parker who wrote the 'chasing Rimbauds' line, in *Here Lies*, 'The Little Hours' (1939).

See also WORDPLAY.

Puritanism

10 We have long passed the Victorian Era when asterisks were followed after a certain interval by a baby.

W. Somerset Maugham, English writer (1874–1965). *The Constant Wife* (1926).

11 Puritanism – The haunting fear that someone, somewhere, may be happy.

H.L. Mencken, American journalist and linguist (1880–1956). *A Book of Burlesques* (1920).

12 That kind of so-called housekeeping where they have six Bibles and no corkscrew.

Mark Twain, American writer (1835–1910). *Mark Twain's Notebook*, ed. A. B. Paine (1935).

1 Cavaliers and Puritans are interesting for their costumes and not for their convictions.

Oscar Wilde, Irish playwright, poet and wit (1854–1900). Quoted in Hesketh Pearson, *The Life of Oscar Wilde* (1946).

Purity

2 I knew a girl who was so pure
She couldn't say the word Manure.

Reginald Arkell, English poet (1882–1959). Poem, 'A Perfect Lady' in *Green Fingers* (1934).

3 I'm as pure as the driven slush.

Tallulah Bankhead, American actress (1903–68). Quoted in the *Saturday Evening Post* (12 April 1947).

4 To the pure, all things are unpure.

Mark Twain, American writer (1835–1910). *Mark Twain's Notebook*, ed. A.B. Paine (1935).

5 I used to be Snow White … but I drifted.

Mae West, American vaudeville and film actress (1893–1980). Quoted in Joseph Weintraub, *Peel Me a Grape* (1975).

Purpose

6 If people want a sense of purpose they should get it from their archbishops. They should not hope to get it from their politicians.

Harold Macmillan (1st Earl of Stockton), British Conservative Prime Minister (1894–1986). Quoted in Henry Fairlie, *The Life of Politics* (1968). Said to Fairlie in 1963.

Push

7 It is most important in this world to be pushing, but it is fatal to seem so.

Benjamin Jowett, English academic (1817–93). Quoted in *The Treasury of Humorous Quotations*, eds Evan Esar & Nicolas Bentley (1951).

Put-downs

Remark addressed to Brendan Bracken (1st Viscount Bracken), Irish journalist and British Conservative politician (1901-58):

8 You're phoney. Everything about you is phoney. Even your hair – which looks false – is real.

Anonymous (American diplomat). However, Charles Edward Lysaght, in *Brendan Bracken* (1979), attributes it to a 'journalist', in the form: 'I don't believe a word you say, Brendan. Everything about you is phoney. Even your hair, which looks like a wig, isn't.' Bracken was Churchill's Minister of Information during the Second World War. In *Crossing the Line* (1958), Claud Cockburn appeared to be commenting on the same phenomenon: 'A wartime Minister of Information is compelled, in the national interest, to such continuous acts of duplicity that even his natural hair must grow to resemble a wig.'

To a man who came up to her at a party and exclaimed, effusively, 'Tallulah! I haven't seen you for 41 years!':

9 I thought I told you to wait in the car.

Tallulah Bankhead, American actress (1903–68). Quoted by Clement Freud on BBC Radio *Quote … Unquote* (15 January 1979).

Katharine Hepburn, sighing with relief after she had completed filming A Bill of Divorcement *with John Barrymore in 1932, said, 'Thank goodness I don't have to act with you any more.' Replied he:*

10 I didn't know you ever had, darling.

John Barrymore, American actor (1882–1942). Quoted in Leslie Halliwell, *The Filmgoer's Book of Quotes* (1973).

To Lady Astor, who had said, 'If you were my husband, I'd poison your coffee' (at Blenheim Palace, c. *1912):*

11 If you were my wife, I'd drink it.

(Sir) Winston S. Churchill, British Conservative Prime Minister and writer (1874–1965). Quoted in Consuelo Vanderbilt Balsan, *Glitter and Gold* (1952).

To Bessie Braddock MP, who had told him he was drunk:

1 And you, madam, are ugly. But I shall be sober in the morning.

(Sir) Winston S. Churchill. Quoted in Sykes & Sproat, *The Wit of Sir Winston* (1965), without naming Braddock. She was named in Leslie Frewin, *Immortal Jester* (1973). Compare this earlier exchange from the film *It's a Gift* (US, 1934): a swindling real estate agent says to W.C. Fields, 'You're drunk!' 'Yeah, and you're crazy,' replies Fields. 'I'll be sober tomorrow, but you'll be crazy the rest of your life.'

When Ned Sherrin claimed that Laugh-In *was a spin-off of* That Was The Week That Was*:*

2 Like Concorde is a spin-off of the Tiger Moth, darling.

Germaine Greer, Australian-born writer and feminist (1939–). On BBC Radio *Quote ... Unquote* (7 March 1976).

To her husband Walter, who had asked a starlet with thick legs how old she was:

3 For God's sake, Walter, why don't you chop off her legs and count the rings?

Carol Matthau, American writer (1932–). Quoted in Truman Capote, *Answered Prayers* (1986). A well-known Hollywood joke by this stage. George Axelrod had told it on BBC Radio *Quote ... Unquote* (11 September 1979).

4 *Squire*:
If I had a son who was an idiot, by Jove, I'd make him a parson.
Smith:
Very probably, but I see that your father was of a different mind.

(Revd) Sydney Smith, English clergyman, essayist and wit (1771–1845). Quoted in *The Sayings of Sydney Smith*, ed. Alan Bell (1993). *Compare* FOOLS 175:4.

Of William F. Buckley Jnr:

5 Looks and sounds not unlike Hitler, but without the charm.

Gore Vidal, American novelist, playwright and critic (1925–). Quoted in *The Observer* (26 April 1981). Which came first, this or the line used by Peter Cook about Dudley Moore ('A power-crazed ego-maniac, a kind of Hitler without the charm') in a newspaper interview of February 1979?

Pyjamas

6 One morning I shot an elephant in my pyjamas. How he got in my pyjamas I dunno ... But that's entirely irrelephant to what I'm talking about.

Line from film *Animal Crackers* (US 1930). Screenwriters: Morrie Ryskind, George S. Kaufman. Spoken by Groucho Marx (Capt. Spaulding).

Quakers

1 Did you say 'a Quaker baby'? Impossible! there is no such thing; there never was; they are always born broad-brimmed and in full quake.

(Revd) Sydney Smith, English clergyman, essayist and wit (1771–1845). Quoted in Lady Holland, *A Memoir of Sydney Smith* (1855).

Qualifications

2 My only qualification for being put at the head of the Navy is that I am very much at sea.

Edward Carson (Lord Carson), Irish-born lawyer and politician (1854–1935). Quoted in Ian Colvin, *Life of Lord Carson* (1936).

Queerness

On breaking up with his business partner, W. Allen, at New Lanark (1828):

3 All the world is queer save thee and me, and even thou art a little queer.

Robert Owen, Welsh-born socialist reformer (1771–1858). Quoted in *The Penguin Dictionary of Quotations*, J.M. & M.J. Cohen (1960).

Questions

4 Long ago, during an interval half-way through a production of Shakespeare's *Antony and Cleopatra* at a London theatre, two well-dressed people went up to the manager and said, 'Tell us, is this, or is this not, *Bunty Pulls the String*?'

Anonymous. Quoted by Tom Stoppard on BBC Radio *Quote ... Unquote* (4 January 1976). *Bunty Pulls the String* was a new comedy in *c.* 1912.

5 There is an old Oxford story, dating from the days when there were several all-female colleges, about a girl announcing loudly in the Junior Common Room that she had just met a man. At Somerville, the other girls asked, 'What is he reading?' At Lady Margaret Hall, 'Who is his father?' At St Hugh's they asked, 'What does he play?' And at St Hilda's they asked, 'Where is he?'

Anonymous. Quoted in Dacre Balsdon, *Oxford Life* (1957). There are many versions of this catechism. In 1999, I was told what *men* would say coming from different cities in Georgia: 'If meeting someone new, a man from Atlanta would ask, "What company are you with?" A man from Macon, "What religion are you?" From Charleston, South Carolina, "What family are you?" And from Savannah, "What are you drinking?" An earlier version is to be found in John Douglas Pringle, *Australian Accent* (1958): 'Australians themselves have a saying that when a stranger arrives in Perth, the first question he is asked is, "Where do you come from?"; in Adelaide, "What church do you belong to?"; in Melbourne, "What school were you at?"; in Sydney, "How much money have you got?"; while in Brisbane they merely say, "Come and have a drink".' Compare all that with this from Mark Twain, *What Paul Bourget Thinks of Us* (1895) (citing a 'familiar American joke'): 'In Boston they ask, How much does he know? In New York, How much is he worth? In Philadelphia. Who were his parents?' And with this from Benjamin Disraeli's novel *Coningsby*, Bk 5, Chap. 11 (1844): 'In England when a new character appears in our circles the first question always is,"Who is he?" In France it is,"What is he?" In England,"How much a year?" In France,"What has he done?"'

On being told, when he was a housemaster at Eton, that a murder had been committed in the College and one of the boys killed:

1 What dangerous clown has done this?

A.C. Benson, English writer (1862–1925). Quoted by Humphrey Lyttelton (an Old Etonian) on BBC Radio *Quote ... Unquote* (1988). Two years earlier it had been told on the show by Steve Race who happened to have the headmaster of Eton sitting next to him (and who did not dispute the tale). However, Kenneth Tynan in a 1948 theatre review (included in *A View of the English Stage*) gives it as an 'Alexander Woollcott story' of merely 'a schoolmaster' who, coming upon a mutilated torso in the Lower Third dormitory, remarked: 'Some dangerous clown has been here.' Humphrey Lyttelton's father, George, apparently resolves the matter in *The Lyttelton Hart-Davis Letters* (for 23 February 1956): 'Woollcott records in one of his books his high appreciation when my colleague [at Eton] Booker was summoned one Sunday afternoon to his kitchen where his cook had been murdered, and on seeing the body, asked "What dangerous clown has done this?"'

2 Ask me no questions, and I'll tell you no fibs.

Oliver Goldsmith, Irish-born playwright and writer (1730–74). *She Stoops to Conquer*, Act 3 (1773).

3 Who, or why, or which, or *what*,
Is the Akond of SWAT?

Edward Lear, English poet and artist (1812–88). 'The Akond of Swat' (1888). This alludes to the real Akhoond (or Sultan) of Swat, now part of Pakistan, in the 1870s, whose death gave rise to this poem.

4 Ah, what is man? Wherefore does he why? Whence did he whence? Whither is he withering?

Dan Leno, English music-hall entertainer (1860–1904). *Dan Leno Hys Booke* (1901).

When an excitable Fellow rushed up to announce that a member of the college had killed himself:

5 Pray don't tell me who. Allow me to guess.

Martin Routh, President of Magdalen College, Oxford (1755–1854). Quoted in Dacre Balsdon, *Oxford Life* (1957).

6 Well, if I Called the Wrong Number, Why Did You Answer the Phone?

James Thurber, American cartoonist and writer (1894–1961). Caption to cartoon in *Men, Women and Dogs* (1943).

7 'Pray, my dear,' quoth my mother, 'have you not forgot to wind up the clock?' – 'Good G–?' cried my father, making an exclamation, but taking care to moderate his voice at the same time, – 'Did ever woman, since the creation of the world, interrupt a man with such a silly question?'

Laurence Sterne, Irish novelist and clergyman (1713–68). *Tristram Shandy*, Bk 1, Chap.6 (1760–7). Accordingly, Walter Shandy attributed most of his son's misfortunes to the fact that at a highly critical moment his wife had asked him if he had wound the clock, a question so irrelevant that he despaired of the child's ever being able to pursue a logical train of thought.

8 Questions are never indiscreet. Answers sometimes are.

Oscar Wilde, Irish playwright, poet and wit (1854–1900). *An Ideal Husband*, Act 1 (1895).

Quiet

In the wilds:

9 It's so quiet up here you can hear a mouse get a hard-on.

Line from film *Continental Divide* (US 1981). Screenwriter Lawrence Kasdan. Spoken by John Belushi (Ernie Souchak).

Quotations and quoting

10 *Jamison (reading from letter Spaulding has dictated):*
Quotes, unquotes, and quotes.
Spaulding:
That's three quotes ... And another quote'll make it a gallon.

Lines from film *Animal Crackers* (US 1930). Screenwriters: Morrie Ryskind, George S. Kaufman. Spoken by Groucho Marx (Capt. Spaulding) and Zeppo Marx (Jamison).

1 When I'm talking to people I like to stop and quote myself. My quotes have a way of spicing up a conversation.

Brendan Behan, Irish playwright (1923–64). *With Brendan Behan* (1981). Compare Shaw below.

2 The surest way to make a monkey of a man is to quote him.

Robert Benchley, American humorist (1889–1945). Quoted in *The Penguin Dictionary of Modern Quotations*, eds J.M. & M.J. Cohen (1971).

3 So copious was the wealth of familiar and stimulating quotations, that one of her subjects had once said that a stroll in Lucia's garden was not only to enjoy her lovely flowers, but to spend a simultaneous half-hour with the best authors.

E.F. Benson, English novelist (1867–1940). *Queen Lucia*, Chap. 1 (1920).

4 Quotation, *n.* The act of repeating erroneously the words of another. The words erroneously repeated.

Ambrose Bierce, American journalist (1842–?1914). *The Cynic's Word Book* (later retitled *The Devil's Dictionary*) (1906).

5 I don't want to be quoted, and don't quote me that I don't want to be quoted.

Winston Burdett, American journalist (20th century). Quoted in Barbara Rowes, *The Book of Quotes* (1979).

6 Ah, yes! I wrote the 'Purple Cow' –
I'm sorry, now, I wrote it!
But I can tell you anyhow,
I'll kill you if you quote it.

Gelett Burgess, American writer (1866–1951). 'Confessional' (1914).

7 It is bad enough to see one's own good things fathered on other people, but it is worse to have other people's rubbish fathered upon oneself.

Samuel Butler, English novelist and writer (1835–1902). Quoted in *The Treasury of Humorous Quotations*, eds Evan Esar & Nicolas Bentley (1951).

8 One original thought is worth a thousand mindless quotings.

Diogenes, Greek philospopher (*c.* 410–*c.* 320 BC). Quoted by William Safire in *The New York Times* (7 April 1996).

9 Sometimes it seems the only accomplishment my education ever bestowed on me, the ability to think in quotations.

Margaret Drabble, English novelist (1939–). *A Summer Bird-Cage* (1963).

When asked for 'a good quote' by a French journalist on a cold night:

10 If I had a good quote, I'd be wearing it.

Bob Dylan, American singer and songwriter (1941–). Quoted in *The Times* (July 1981).

11 Everything I've ever said will be credited to Dorothy Parker.

George S. Kaufman, American playwright (1889–1961). Quoted in Scott Meredith, *George S. Kaufman and the Algonquin Round Table* (1974).

When asked for his favourite quotation:

12 My favourite quotation is eight pounds ten for a second-hand suit.

Spike Milligan, Irish entertainer and writer (1918–). On BBC Radio *Quote … Unquote* (1 January 1979).

13 He liked those literary cooks
Who skim the cream of other's books;
And ruin half an author's graces
By plucking bon-mots from their places.

Hannah More, English writer (1745–1833). *Florio* (1786).

Reviewing a book by Edmund Blunden:

14 Mr Blunden is no more able to resist a quotation than some people are to refuse a drink.

George Orwell, English novelist and journalist (1903–50). In the *Manchester Evening News* (20 April 1944).

1 Misquotation is … the pride and privilege of the learned. A widely-read man never quotes accurately for the rather obvious reason that he has read too widely.

Hesketh Pearson, English biographer and writer (1887–1964). *Common Misquotations* (1937). Pearson was, apparently, the first person to compile a dictionary solely devoted to misquotations. It is a slim volume and slightly muddies its own water by claiming that certain sayings are commonly misquoted when they are not and by condemning variants of proverbs (which surely cannot be said to have a correct form). Pearson truly observed, however, that:

2 Misquotations are the only quotations that are never misquoted.

Hesketh Pearson. In the same book as above.

3 When in doubt, ascribe all quotations to George Bernard Shaw.

Nigel Rees, English writer and broadcaster (1944–). *Quote … Unquote* 3, 'Rees's First Law of Quotations' (1983). Quoted in Des MacHale, *Wit* (1996). The law's first qualification is: 'Except when they obviously derive from Shakespeare, the Bible or Kipling.' The first corollary is: 'In time, all humorous remarks will be ascribed to Shaw whether he said them or not.' To which one might now add that Shaw may on occasions be replaced by Wilde, Chesterton or Churchill. All quotations in translation, on the other hand, should be attributed to Goethe (with 'I think' obligatory).

4 I often quote myself – it adds spice to my conversation.

Bernard Shaw, Irish playwright and critic (1856–1950). Quoted in *Reader's Digest* (1943). Compare Behan above.

5 You see I have the common folly of quoting myself.

Jonathan Swift, Anglo-Irish writer and clergyman (1667–1745). Letter to Charles Ford (9 December 1732).

6 What though his head be empty, provided his commonplace book be full.

Jonathan Swift. *A Tale of a Tub*, 'Digression in Praise of Digressions' (1704).

Talking of a man who dealt in nothing but quotations:

7 That fellow has a mind of inverted commas.

Charles Maurice de Talleyrand, French politician (1754–1838). 'Unpublished Anecdote' in *Punch* (16 July 1853).

8 What a good thing Adam had – when he said a good thing he knew nobody had said it before.

Mark Twain, American writer (1835–1910). *Mark Twain's Notebook*, ed. A.B. Paine (1935). Has also been ascribed to Bernard Shaw.

9 *Oscar Wilde:*
I wish I had said that.
Whistler:
You will, Oscar, you will.

James McNeill Whistler. American painter (1834–1903). Quoted in L.C. Ingleby, *Oscar Wilde* (1907) and Douglas Sladen, *Twenty Years of My Life* (1915). Sladen says that it was of a remark by a woman that Wilde had rather taken a fancy to, but Hesketh Pearson, *The Life of Oscar Wilde* (1946), has it, more convincingly, that it was something said by Whistler himself that Wilde was obviously going to make his own. In Frank Harris, *Oscar Wilde, His Life and Confessions*, Chap. 4 (1930), is this: 'The art critic of *The Times*, Mr Humphry Ward, had come to see an exhibition of Whistler's pictures. Filled with an undue sense of his own importance, he buttonholed the master and pointing to one picture said: "That's good, first-rate, a lovely bit of colour; but that, you know," he went on, jerking his finger over his shoulder at another picture, "that's bad, drawing all wrong … bad!"

'"My dear fellow," cried Whistler, "you must never say that this painting's good or that bad, never! Good and bad are not terms to be used by you; but say, I like this, and I dislike that, and you'll be within your right. And now come and have a whiskey for you're sure to like that."

'Carried away by the witty fling, Oscar cried: "I wish I had said that."

"You will, Oscar, you will," came Whistler's lightning thrust.'

10 Some, for *renown*, on scraps of learning dote,
And think they grow immortal as they *quote*.

Edward Young, English poet and playwright (1683–1765). *The Love of Fame*, Satire 1, l. 89 (1725–8).

R

Rabbits

1 The rabbit has a charming face:
Its private life is a disgrace.
I really dare not name to you
The awful things that rabbits do.

Anonymous. 'The Rabbit'. Quoted in *The Week-End Book* (1925).

Radicals

2 A radical is a man with both feet firmly planted in the air.

Franklin D. Roosevelt, American Democratic President (1882–1945). Radio broadcast (26 October 1939).

Railways

In a letter to the station master at Baker Street station, London, on the Metropolitan Line:

3 Sir, Saturday morning, although recurring at regular and well-foreseen intervals, always seems to take this railway by surprise.

(Sir) W.S. Gilbert, English writer and lyricist (1836–1911). Quoted in John Julius Norwich, *A Christmas Cracker* (1973).

Rain

4 The rain, it raineth on the just
And also on the unjust fella:
But chiefly on the just, because
The unjust steals the just's umbrella.

Lord Bowen, English judge (1835–94). Quoted in Walter Sichel, *The Sands of Time* (1923).

5 If God had intended man to live in England, he'd have given him gills.

David Renwick and Andrew Marshall, English writers (1951–) and (1954 –). In BBC Radio *The Burkiss Way* (11 November 1980).

Rank

Wishing to address the Prime Minister (Harold Macmillan) rather than the Foreign Secretary (Selwyn Lloyd):

6 I am not going to spend any time whatsoever in attacking the Foreign Secretary. Quite honestly I am beginning to feel extremely sorry for him. If we complain about the tune, there is no reason to attack the monkey when the organ grinder is present.

Aneurin Bevan, Welsh Labour politician (1897–1960). In House of Commons post-Suez debate (16 May 1957). However, *Safire's Politics* (1978) has, 'Never hold discussions with the monkey when the organ grinder is in the room.' William Safire, unsourced, puts: 'Attributed to Winston Churchill, replying to a query from the British ambassador in Rome as to whether he should raise a question with Mussolini or Count Ciano, his Foreign Minister.' Evidence that this sort of metaphor did indeed exist before Bevan's use can be found in the caption to a cartoon by Chas. Grave in *Punch* (23 January 1924): '*Tommy (describing his experience of being up before the Colonel).* "I WAS TELLIN' THE C.O. WOT 'APPENED WHEN THE SERGEANT-MAJOR INTERRUPTED ME, SO I TURNED ROUND AN' I SED, 'NOW LOOK 'ERE, SERGEANT-MAJOR,' I SEZ, 'WHEN I'M TALKIN' TO THE ORGAN-GRINDER I DON'T WANT THE BLEEDIN' MONKEY TO CHIP IN.'"'

Rape

Appearing before a military tribunal to put his case as a conscientious objector, he was asked by the chairman what, in view of his beliefs, he would do if he saw a German soldier trying to violate his sister:

1 I would try to get between them.

Lytton Strachey, English biographer (1880–1932). Quoted in Robert Graves, *Goodbye To All That* (1929).

Rats

On puppet Roland Rat's success in reversing the fortunes of TV-am, a rival breakfast television tation (1983):

2 This must be the first time a rat has come to the aid of a sinking ship.

Anonymous (BBC spokesman). Quoted on BBC Radio *Quote ... Unquote* (25 August 1984).

On 'crossing the floor' of the House of Commons (i.e. changing political allegiance) more than once:

3 They say you can rat, but you can't re-rat.

(Sir) Winston S. Churchill, British Conservative Prime Minister and writer (1874–1965). Quoted in John Colville, *The Fringes of Power*, Vol 1 (1985) – entry for 26 January 1941. The remark may date from 1923/4 when Churchill rejoined the Conservatives, having earlier left them to join the Liberals.

On Air Vice-Marshal Bennett, who had joined the Liberals:

4 It [is] the first time that [I have] heard of a rat actually swimming out to join a sinking ship.

(Sir) Winston S. Churchill. Quoted in Malcolm Muggeridge, *Like It Was* (1981) – diary entry for 14 February 1948. Later, Ralph Yarborough said of John B. Connally's 1973 switch from Democratic to Republican Party in pursuit of the presidential nomination: 'It is the only case on record of a *man* swimming toward a sinking ship' (quoted in *The Washington Post*, 18 January 1988).

5 Even if you win the rat-race, you're still a rat.

(Revd) William Sloane Coffin, American clergyman (1924–). When consulted at his home in Vermont (July 1995), the Revd Coffin said that to the best of his knowledge he did originate this statement in the above form. He thought up the quip 'in the 1950s or 1960s' when he was chaplain either at Williams College or at Yale University. He added the caveat that he originated the statement 'as far as I know'. The line is often attributed to the American actress Lily Tomlin, who, in turn, ascribes it to the writer Jane Wagner.

Ravishment

6 I have been more ravished myself than any body since the Trojan war.

Lord Byron, English poet (1788–1824). Letter to Hoppner (1819).

7 Take not the first refusal ill: tho' now she won't, anon she will.

Thomas D'Urfey, English poet and playwright (1653–1723). Quoted in *The Treasury of Humorous Quotations*, eds Evan Esar & Nicolas Bentley (1951).

8 He in a few minutes ravished this fair creature, or at least would have ravished her, if she had not, by a timely compliance, prevented him.

Henry Fielding, English novelist and judge (1707–54). *Jonathan Wild*, Bk 3, Chap.7 (1743).

9 It is impossible to ravish me,
I'm so willing.

John Fletcher, English playwright (1579–1625). *The Faithful Shepherdess*, Act 3, Sc. 1 (1610).

10 Some things can't be ravished. You can't ravish a tin of sardines.

D.H. Lawrence, English novelist and poet (1885–1930). *Lady Chatterley's Lover*, Chap. 8 (1928).

Reading

11 There is a great deal of difference between the eager man who wants to read a book and the tired man who wants a book to read.

G.K. Chesterton, English poet, novelist and critic (1874–1936). Quoted in *The Treasury of Humorous Quotations*, eds Evan Esar & Nicolas Bentley (1951).

To an author who had sent him an unsolicited manuscript:

1 Many thanks; I shall lose no time in reading it.

Benjamin Disraeli (1st Earl of Beaconsfield), British Conservative Prime Minister and writer (1804–81). Quoted in Wilfrid Meynell, *The Man Disraeli* (1903). G.W.E. Russell, *Collections and Recollections*, Chap. 31 (1898), has the remark but merely ascribes it to an eminent man 'on this side of the Atlantic'.

To Melvyn Bragg when no one in the audience admitted to having read any of his novels:

2 You're going to have to slow down. We can't keep up with you!

Barry Humphries, Australian entertainer (1934–). As 'Dame Edna Everage' in LWT TV show *An Audience With Dame Edna Everage* (1980/1). Michael Coveney in an article about Humphries in *The Observer* Magazine (16 March 1997) gave the line as: 'Why do you do it, Melvyn, why go to all that bother for so little recognition?' He also added: 'Bragg had no choice but to crease his face in signs of hysterical laughter, along with everyone else. He might have been weeping inside.'

3 We read to say what we have read.

Charles Lamb, English essayist (1775–1834). Quoted in *The Treasury of Humorous Quotations*, eds Evan Esar & Nicolas Bentley (1951).

4 I've given up reading books; I find it takes my mind off myself.

Oscar Levant, American pianist and actor (1906–72). Quoted in the same collection as above.

5 The chief knowledge that a man gets from reading books is the knowledge that very few of them are worth reading.

H.L. Mencken, American journalist and linguist (1880–1956). Quoted in the same collection as above.

Of Aldous Huxley:

6 You could always tell by his conversation which volume of the *Encyclopedia Brittanica* he'd been reading. One day it would be Alps, Andes and Apennines, and the next it would be the Himalayas and the Hippocratic Oath.

Bertrand Russell (3rd Earl Russell), English philosopher and mathematician (1872–1970). Letter to R.W. Clark (July 1965).

7 The man who does not read good books has no advantage over the man who can't read them.

Anonymous. Has been ascribed to Mark Twain and Abby Van Buren.

Reagan, Ronald

AMERICAN FILM ACTOR AND REPUBLICAN PRESIDENT (1911–)

Doing a microphone test prior to a broadcast:

8 My fellow Americans, I am pleased to tell you that I have signed legislation to outlaw Russia for ever. We begin bombing in five minutes.

Ronald Reagan. Audio recording (13 August 1984).

9 After carefully watching Ronald Reagan, he is attempting a great break-through in political technology – he has been perfecting the Teflon-coated Presidency. He sees to it that nothing sticks to him.

Patricia Schroeder, American Democratic politician (1940–). Speech in the US House of Representatives (2 August 1983).

10 We've got the kind of President who thinks arms control means some kind of deodorant.

Patricia Schroeder. Quoted in *The Observer*, 'Sayings of the Week' (9 August 1987).

11 A triumph of the embalmer's art.

Gore Vidal, American novelist, playwright and critic (1925–). Quoted in *The Observer* (26 April 1981).

12 He does not dye his hair – he bleaches his face.

Gore Vidal. Quoted in my book *A Year of Stings and Squelches* (1985).

When it was announced that Ronald Reagan was going to stand for the governorship of California:

1 All wrong. Jimmy Stewart for governor, Reagan for best friend.

Jack L. Warner, American film producer (1892–1978). Quoted in Max Wilk, *The Wit and Wisdom of Hollywood* (1971) and Edmund G. & Bill Brown, *Reagan: The Political Chameleon* (1976).

Realist

2 In Israel, in order to be a realist you must believe in miracles.

David Ben-Gurion, Polish-born Israeli Prime Minister (1886–1973). Comment on CBS TV (5 October 1956).

Reality

3 Reality is a delusion created by an alcohol deficiency.

Anonymous (graffito). Quoted on BBC Radio *Quote ... Unquote* (7 June 1979).

4 Reality is a crutch for people who can't cope with drugs.

Jane Wagner, American writer, actor, director and producer (1935–). *Appearing Nitely* (1977).

Reason

5 I can stand brute force, but brute reason is quite unbearable. There is something unfair about its use. It is hitting below the intellect.

Oscar Wilde, Irish playwright, poet and wit (1854–1900). *The Picture of Dorian Gray*, Chap. 3 (1891).

Reasons

6 I don't care anything about reasons, but I know what I like.

Henry James, American novelist (1843–1916). *The Portrait of a Lady*, Chap. 24 (1881). *Compare* MUSICAL CRITICISM 297:8.

Referring to his edition of Shakespeare (1763):

7 Sir, I have two very cogent reasons for not printing any list of subscribers; – one that I have lost all the names, – the other, that I have spent all the money.

(Dr) Samuel Johnson, English writer and lexicographer (1709–84). Quoted in James Boswell, *The Life of Samuel Johnson* (1791) – for May 1781.

8 The Spanish fleet thou canst not see – because – It is not yet in sight!

Richard Brinsley Sheridan, English playwright and politician (1751–1816). *The Critic*, Act 2, Sc. 2 (1779).

Recession

9 It's a recession when your neighbour loses his job: it's a depression when you lose yours.

Harry S. Truman, American Democratic President (1884–1972). Quoted in *The Observer* (13 April 1958).

Recordings

10 Phonograph, *n*. An irritating toy that restores life to dead noises.

Ambrose Bierce, American journalist (1842–?1914). *The Cynic's Word Book* (later retitled *The Devil's Dictionary*) (1906).

11 Sir, I have tested your machine [a gramophone]. It adds new terror to life and makes death a long-felt want.

(Sir) Herbert Beerbohm Tree, English actor-manager (1853–1917). Quoted in Hesketh Pearson, *Beerbohm Tree* (1956).

Rectification

12 Once the toothpaste is out of the tube, it is awfully hard to get it back in.

H.R. Haldeman, American government official (1926–93). Remark to John Dean on the Watergate affair (8 April 1973) and reported in *Hearings Before the Select Committee on Presidential Campaign Activities: Watergate and Related Activities*, Vol. 4 (1973). The remark has been wrongly attributed to his colleague, John D. Ehrlichman, and to President Nixon, but it is probably not an original expression in any case. Indeed, according to Lord Baden-Powell's daughter Heather, the founder of the Scout

Movement would reply to those who said that Scouting was impossible for them: 'Nothing is impossible, except putting toothpaste back into the tube' – quoted in Heather King, *Baden-Powell, A Family Album* (1986).

Reform

1 Any reform that does not result in the exact opposite of what it was intended to do must be considered a success.

Anonymous. Quoted by Katharine Whitehorn in letter to the author (21 January 1992).

2 Every reform, however necessary, will by weak minds be carried to an excess which will itself need reforming.

Samuel Taylor Coleridge, English poet and writer (1772–1834). *Biographia Literaria* (1815–16).

3 The attempt of the Lords to stop the progress of Reform reminds me very forcibly of the great storm of Sidmouth, and of the conduct of the excellent Mrs Partington on that occasion. In the winter of 1824 there set in a great flood upon that town – the tide rose to an incredible height, the waves rushed in upon the houses, and everything was threatened with destruction! In the midst of this sublime and terrible storm, Dame Partington, who lived upon the beach, was seen at the door of her house with mop and pattens, trundling her mop, squeezing out the sea-water, and vigorously pushing away the Atlantic Ocean. The Atlantic was roused. Mrs Partington's spirit was up; but I need not tell you that the contest was unequal. The Atlantic Ocean beat Mrs Partington. She was excellent at a slop, or a puddle, but she should not have meddled with a tempest. Gentlemen, be at your ease – be quiet and steady. You will beat Mrs Partington.

(Revd) Sydney Smith, English clergyman, essayist and wit (1771–1845). Speech at Taunton on Parliamentary Reform (1831).

Regrets

When asked if he had any regrets:

4 Yes, I haven't had enough sex.

(Sir) John Betjeman, English poet (1906–84). On BBC TV, *Time With Betjeman* (February 1983).

5 One of my chief regrets during my years in the theater is that I couldn't sit in the audience and watch me.

John Barrymore, American actor (1882–1942). Quoted in *The Treasury of Humorous Quotations*, eds Evan Esar & Nicolas Bentley (1951) and in Eddie Cantor, *The Way I See It*, Chap. 2 (1959).

Rejection

6 Look here, Steward, if this is coffee, I want tea; but if this is tea, then I wish for coffee.

G.D. Armour, English cartoonist. Caption to cartoon in *Punch*, Vol. 123 (23 July 1902). Robert Byrne in *The 637 Best Things Anybody Ever Said* (1982) ascribes the line to Abraham Lincoln, as does *The Treasury of Humorous Quotations*, eds Evan Esar & Nicolas Bentley (1951).

Rejection slip when editor of the American Mercury*:*

7 Mr Mencken has just entered a trappist monastery in Kentucky and left strict instructions that no mail was to be forwarded. The enclosed is returned therefore for your archives.

H.L. Mencken, American journalist and linguist (1880–1956). Quoted on BBC Radio *Quote ... Unquote* (19 January 1982).

8 'I may as well inform you that it is not twenty-four hours since she turned me down.' 'Turned you down?' 'Like a bedspread. In this very garden.'

(Sir) P(elham) G. Wodehouse, English-born novelist and lyricist (1881–1975). *Right Ho, Jeeves*, Chap. 15 (1934).

Relations and relatives

9 Distant relatives are the best kind, and the further the better.

Frank McKinney ('Kin') Hubbard, American humorist and caricaturist (1868–1930). Quoted in *The Treasury of Humorous Quotations*, eds Evan Esar & Nicolas Bentley (1951).

1 Th' richer a relative is th' less he bothers you.

Frank McKinney ('Kin') Hubbard, American humorist and caricaturist (1868–1930). *Abe Martin's Primer* (1914).

To Mrs Thrale, who lamented a first cousin lost in America:

2 Prithee, my dear, have done with canting; how would the world be worse for it, I may ask, if all your relations were at once spitted like larks, and roasted for Presta's [the dog's] supper?

(Dr) Samuel Johnson, English writer and lexicographer (1709–84). Quoted in James Boswell, *The Life of Samuel Johnson* (1791) – for 30 June 1784.

3 [Friends are] God's apology for relations.

Hugh Kingsmill, English writer (1889–1949). Quoted in Michael Holroyd, *The Best of Hugh Kingsmill* (1970). The origin of the saying has been said to lie in a Spanish proverb.

4 Relations are simply a tedious pack of people, who haven't got the remotest knowledge of how to live, nor the smallest instinct about when to die.

Oscar Wilde, Irish playwright, poet and wit (1854–1900). *The Importance of Being Earnest*, Act 1 (1895).

5 Relations never lend one any money, and won't give one credit, even for genius. They are a sort of aggravated form of the public.

Oscar Wilde. Attributed remark.

Relativity

6 When a man sits with a pretty girl for an hour, it seems like a minute. But let him sit on a hot stove for a minute – and it's longer than any hour. That's relativity.

Albert Einstein, German-born physicist (1879–1955). Quoted in *The New York Times* (19 April 1955).

Religion

7 I don't go to church. Kneeling bags my nylons.

Line from film *Ace in the Hole* (US 1951). Screenwriters: Billy Wilder, Lesser Samuels, Walter Newman. Spoken by Jan Sterling (Lorraine).

8 It is the test of a good religion whether you can joke about it.

G.K. Chesterton, English poet, novelist and critic (1874–1936). Quoted in Herbert V. Prochnow, Snr & Jnr, *A Treasury of Humorous Quotations* (1969).

Defining the Calvinist doctrine of 'Particular Election':

9 You can and you can't – You shall and you shan't – You will and you won't – You'll be damned if you do – And you'll be damned if you don't.

Lorenzo Dow, American preacher (1777–1834). *Reflections on the Love of God*, Chap 6. (1836).

On hearing an evangelical sermon:

10 Things have come to a pretty pass when religion is allowed to invade the sphere of private life.

2nd Viscount Melbourne (William Lamb), British Whig Prime Minister (1779–1848). Quoted in G.W.E. Russell, *Collections and Recollections*, Chap. 6 (1898).

11 'Fear God and dread the Sunday School' exactly describes that old feeling I used to have, but I couldn't have formulated it.

Mark Twain, American writer (1835–1910). *Mark Twain's Letters*, ed. A.B. Paine (1917).

12 If I were a cassowary
On the plains of Timbuctoo,
I would eat a missionary,
Cassock, band, and hymn book too.

Samuel Wilberforce, English bishop and author (1805–73). Attributed impromptu verse.

See also CHURCH OF ENGLAND; CHURCH-GOING; GOD.

Repartee

When a woman said to him, 'I could give you tit for tat any time':

1 Tat!

Calvin Coolidge, American Republican President (1872–1933). Quoted on BBC Radio *Quote . . . Unquote* (2 March 1982).

2 Repartee is a duel fought with the points of jokes.

Max Eastman, American writer and editor (1883–1959). Quoted in *The Treasury of Humorous Quotations*, eds Evan Esar & Nicolas Bentley (1951).

3 On one occasion, Wilde claimed that he would discuss any subject put to him, whether he had made any preparations or not. A companion proposed he speak on the subject of the queen. Wilde replied: 'The queen is not a subject.'

Oscar Wilde, Irish playwright, poet and wit (1854–1900). Quoted in Alvin Redman, *The Wit and Humour of Oscar Wilde* (1952).

4 *Sir Edward Carson:*
Do you drink champagne yourself?
Wilde:
Yes; iced champagne is a favourite drink of mine – strongly against my doctor's orders.
Carson:
Never mind your doctor's orders, sir!
Wilde:
I never do.

Oscar Wilde. Exchange during trial (1895). Quoted in same book as above.

Replies

Message telegraphed to the Prince of Wales (presumably the future Edward VII), on receiving a dinner invitation at short notice:

5 VERY SORRY CAN'T COME. LIE FOLLOWS BY POST.

Lord Charles Beresford, English politician (1846–1919). Quoted in Ralph Nevill, *The World of Fashion 1837–1922* (1923). The same joke occurs in Marcel Proust, *Le Temps Retrouvé* (published in 1927 after his death in 1922), in the form: 'One of those telegrams of which M. de Guermantes has wittily fixed the formula: "Can't come, lie follows [*Impossible venir, mensonge suit*]".'

When told (which he was frequently) that he had never written as good a novel as his first one, Catch-22, *its author would reply:*

6 Who has?

Joseph Heller, American novelist (1923–99). Quoted in numerous interviews and profiles, 1980s–1990s, e.g. in *The Times* (9 June 1993).

Reports

7 The report of my death was an exaggeration.

Mark Twain, American writer (1835–1910). Twain's reaction to a false report, quoted in the *New York Journal* (2 June 1897). Frequently over-quoted and paraphrased ever since, this has become the inevitable remark to invoke when someone's death has been wrongly reported (most usually one's own). Twain's own version of the incident appears in A.B. Paine, *Mark Twain: A Biography* (1912): a reporter had called regarding reports of his death with an order to write 5,000 words if very ill, 1,000 if dead; Twain remarked, 'You don't need as much as that. Just say the report of my death has been grossly exaggerated.' Variations include: 'Reports of my death have been greatly exaggerated' or 'are premature'.

Reputation

8 A woman with a past has no future.

Oscar Wilde, Irish playwright, poet and wit (1854–1900). Quoted in *The Treasury of Humorous Quotations*, eds Evan Esar & Nicolas Bentley (1951).

9 One can survive everything nowadays, except death, and live down anything except a good reputation.

Oscar Wilde. *A Woman of No Importance*, Act 1 (1893).

10 When Oscar Wilde was released from prison and went into exile in Dieppe, his friend Ernest Dowson, the poet, urged him to acquire 'a more wholesome taste'. Accordingly, they totted up how much money they

had with them and decided there was enough to support a visit to the nearest brothel (female, that is). When the news of this got out, they were accompanied on their way by a cheering crowd. After the deed was done, Wilde confided to Dowson that it was, 'The first these ten years, and it will be the last. It was like cold mutton.' Then he added, so that the crowd could hear, 'But tell it in England, for it will entirely restore my character.'

Oscar Wilde. Quoted in W.B. Yeats, *Autobiographies* (1926).

Research

1 In that state of resentful coma that they dignified by the name of research.

Harold Laski, English political scientist (1893–1950). In one of his letters to Oliver Wendell Holmes Jnr (published 1953) – dated 10 October 1922.

2 The outcome of any serious research can only be to make two questions grow where one question grew before.

Thorstein Veblen, American economist (1857–1929). 'Evolution of the Scientific Point of View' in the *University of California Chronicle* (1908).

Resemblance

Of Anna Pavlova, Russian ballerina (1885–1931), who was making her last appearance in Edinburgh:

3 She's awfully like Mrs Wishart ...

Anonymous (Scotswoman). Eric Maschwitz in *No Chip on My Shoulder* (1957) pinpoints the originator of the tale as Walford Hyden, a conductor who accompanied Pavlova on her world tours. His version: when she gave a performance of 'The Dying Swan' in *Glasgow* and finally sank to the floor in her feathered costume, Hyden heard a woman in the front row observe to her companion, 'Aye, she *is* awfu' like Mrs Wishart'.

Responsibility

4 'Once the rockets are up, who cares where
they come down,
That's not my department,' says Wernher
von Braun.

Tom Lehrer, American songwriter and entertainer (1928–). Song, 'Wernher von Braun' (1965).

5 Do you realize the responsibility I carry? I'm the only person standing between Nixon and the White House.

John F. Kennedy, American Democratic President (1917–63). Remark (13 October 1960), quoted in Arthur M. Schlesinger Jnr, *A Thousand Days* (1965).

Restaurants

6 Avoid approaching horses and restaurants from the rear.

Anonymous (proverb). Quoted in *The 'Quote ... Unquote' Newsletter* (October 1994).

7 Restaurants have this in common with ladies: the best are often not the most enjoyable, nor the grandest the most friendly, and the pleasures of the evening are frequently spoiled by the writing of an exorbitant cheque.

(Sir) John Mortimer, English lawyer, playwright and novelist (1923). In *The Observer* (1978).

8 Avoid any restaurant where a waiter arrives with a handful of knives and forks just as you reach the punchline of your best story and says 'Which of you is having the fish?'

(Sir) John Mortimer. In the same article as above.

Revelations

Of Earl Haig:

9 With the publication of his Private Papers in 1952, he committed suicide twenty-five years after his death.

1st Lord Beaverbrook (Max Aitken), Canadian-born politician and newspaper proprietor (1879–1964). *Men and Power* (1956).

On seeing soldiers bathing in the First World War:

10 I never knew the lower classes had such white skins.

George Curzon (1st Marquess Curzon), English Viceroy and Conservative politician (1859–1925). Quoted in Lord Ronaldshay, *The Life of Lord Curzon* (1928).

Reviews

1 A bad review may spoil your breakfast but you shouldn't allow it to spoil your lunch.

(Sir) Kingsley Amis, English novelist, poet and critic (1922–95). Quoted in the *Independent on Sunday* (6 September 1992).

2 A bad review is even less important than whether it is raining in Patagonia.

(Dame) Iris Murdoch, English novelist and philosopher (1919–99). Quoted in a profile in *The Times* (6 July 1989).

Revolution

3 Come the revolution, everyone will eat strawberries and cream.
But, Comrade, I don't *like* strawberries and cream.
Come the revolution, *everyone* will eat strawberries and cream!

Willis Howard, American vaudeville comedian (b. 1899). Attributed lines. Also included as an anonymous Jewish joke in Leo Rosten, *The Joys of Yiddish* (1968).

4 One revolution is just like one cocktail; it just gets you organized for the next.

Will Rogers, American humorist (1879–1935). Quoted in Alistair Cooke, *One Man's America* (1952).

Rewrites

Alterations ordered to the script of The Bed-Sitting Room *(1963) by John Antrobus and Spike Milligan:*

5 Omit 'You get all the dirt off the tail of your shirt.' Substitute 'You get all the dirt off the front of your shirt' … Omit the song 'Plastic Mac Man' and substitute 'Oh you dirty young devil, how dare you presume to wet the bed when the po's in the room. I'll wallop your bum with a dirty great broom when I get up in the morning.'

Anonymous. From the Office of the Lord Chamberlain, British theatre censor until 1968. Quoted in Kenneth Tynan, *Tynan Right and Left* (1967).

6 By the shores of Gitchie Gumee
Hiawatha socked it to me.

Anonymous (American cartoonist). Quoted by Denis Norden on BBC Radio *Quote … Unquote* (11 October 1999).

7 Ah, did you once see Shelley plain?
And was he such a frightful pain … ?

Anonymous. With apologies to Browning. Quoted in *The 'Quote … Unquote' Newsletter* (January 1993). Most of the following are 'deflating additions' as they were called in *New Statesman* competitions of yesteryear, from which these are taken:

When forbidden to sing 'She sits among the cabbages and peas,' she substituted:

8 She sits among the cabbages and leaks.

Marie Lloyd, English music-hall entertainer (1870–1922). Quoted by John Trevelyan, the British film censor, in *TV Times* (23 April–9 May 1981), and alluded to in the 'Battle of Spion Kop' episode of BBC Radio's *The Goon Show* (29 December 1958). The reputed song (untraced) was reportedly censored by a local 'watch' committee before being performed by her in a theatre.

9 When you are old and grey and full of sleep
You haven't got to bother counting sheep.

W.B. Yeats, done over by H.A.C. Evans.

10 When lovely woman stoops to folly
The evening can be awfully jolly.

Oliver Goldsmith, done over by Mary Demetriadis.

11 Yet once more, O ye Laurels, and once more,
I deliver the 'Telegraph' under the door.

John Milton, altered by Edward Blishen, English writer (1920–96).

12 Full fathom five thy father lies,
His aqualung was the wrong size.

Shakespeare, seen to by June Mercer Langfield.

1 Birds in their little nests agree
With Chinamen but not with me.

Isaac Watts, revised by Hilaire Belloc, French-born English poet and writer (1870–1953).

2 Earth has not anything to show more fair
Than Auntie Mabel since she bleached her hair.

With apologies to Wordsworth, by Harold Ollerenshaw. Quoted in *The 'Quote … Unquote' Newsletter* (April 1993).

Rhodes, Cecil

ENGLISH-BORN SOUTH AFRICAN COLONIALIST (1853–1902)

3 I admire him, I frankly confess it. When his time comes I shall buy a piece of the rope for a keepsake.

Mark Twain, American writer (1835–1910). *Following the Equator* (1897).

Rich and poor

4 How easy it is for a man to die rich, if he will but be contented to live miserable.

Henry Fielding, English novelist and judge (1707–54). Quoted in *The Treasury of Humorous Quotations*, eds Evan Esar & Nicolas Bentley (1951).

5 A rich man is nothing but a poor man with money.

W.C. Fields, American comedian (1879–1946). Quoted in *The Home Book of Humorous Quotations*, ed. A.K. Adams (1969).

6 *F. Scott Fitzgerald*:
The very rich are different from you and me.
Hemingway:
Yes, they have more money.

Ernest Hemingway, American novelist (1899–1961). In Tom Burnam, *More Misinformation* (1980), the facts are neatly established about this famous exchange. In his short story 'The Rich Boy' (1926) Fitzgerald had written: 'Let me tell you about the very rich. They are different from you and me.' Twelve years later in *his* short story 'The Snows of Kilimanjaro' (1938), Hemingway had the narrator remember 'poor Scott Fitzgerald', his awe of the rich and that 'someone' had said, 'Yes, they have more money.' When Fitzgerald read the story, he protested to Hemingway, who dropped Fitzgerald's name from further printings. In any case, the put-down 'Yes, they have more money' had been administered not to Fitzgerald but to Hemingway himself. In 1936, Hemingway said at a lunch with the critic Mary Colum: 'I am getting to know the rich.' She replied: 'The only difference between the rich and other people is that the rich have more money.' Also discussed in *Scott and Ernest* (1978) by Mathew J. Bruccoli. Compare: 'The Rich aren't like us – they pay less taxes' – Peter de Vries, in *The Washington Post* (30 July 1989).

7 It doesn't matter whether you're rich or whether you're poor – as long as you have money.

Max Miller, English comedian (1895–1963). Attributed remark – or, possibly, in the form, 'Whether you're rich or whether you're poor – it's nice to be rich.'

8 If you have to ask the price you can't afford it.

J.P. Morgan, Jnr, American banker (1867–1943). Morgan succeeded his father as head of the banking house of Morgan. The story has it that a man was thinking of buying a yacht similar to Morgan's and asked him how much it cost in annual upkeep. Morgan replied with words to this effect. Quoted in Bennett A. Cerf, *Laughing Stock* (1945).

9 I'm like Robin Hood. I steal from the rich and give to the poor – us poor.

Line from film *Poppy* (US 1936). Screenwriters: various (from a play). Spoken by W.C. Fields (Prof. Eustace McGargle).

10 I've been rich and I've been poor. Believe me, honey, rich is better.

Sophie Tucker, Russian-born American entertainer (1884–1966). Attributed but unsourced. However, 'I've been rich and I've been poor; believe me rich is better' is definitely spoken by Gloria Grahame in the film *The Big Heat* (US 1953), screenplay by Sydney Boehm from the story by William P. McGivern. In the musical *Minnie's Boys* (1970), the line was incorporated in the song 'Rich Is': 'I've been poor and I've been rich / And if anyone should ask me which / Is better – rich is better – much, much better.'

1 Like all other nations, we worship money and the possessors of it – they being our aristocracy, and we have to have one.

Mark Twain, American writer (1835–1910). In *North American Review* (4 January 1907).

2 The only thing that can console one for being poor is extravagance. The only thing that can console one for being rich is economy.

Oscar Wilde, Irish playwright, poet and wit (1854–1900). In *Saturday Review* (17 November 1894).

3 There is only one class in the community that thinks more about money than the rich, and that is the poor. The poor can think of nothing else. That is the misery of being poor.

Oscar Wilde. 'The Soul of Man Under Socialism' (1895).

4 Don't soak the rich, soak the poor. There's more of them.

Eric Wright (unidentified). Attributed remark.

Riddles

5 Why is a raven like a writing desk?

Lewis Carroll, English writer (1832–98). *Alice's Adventures in Wonderland*, Chap. 7 (1865). The Hatter poses this riddle at the 'Mad Tea-Party', but Carroll stated positively that there was no answer. Nevertheless, various people have tried to supply one: 'a quill' – what a raven and a writing desk would have had in common in the last century (Christopher Brown of Portswood, Southampton); 'they both begin with the letter R' (Leo Harris); 'because it can produce a few notes, tho they are very flat; and it is never put with the wrong end in front' – these were Lewis Carroll's own possible solutions (1896 edition); 'because the notes for which they are noted are not noted for being musical notes' (Sam Loyd); 'Edgar Allan Poe' – he wrote on both a raven and a writing desk (Sam Loyd); 'because bills and tales (tails) are among their characteristics; because they both stand on their legs; conceal their steels (steals); and ought to be made to shut up' (Sam Loyd); 'because it slopes with a flap' (A. Cyril Pearson); 'because there is a "B" in "both"' (Dr E.V. Rieu). Some of these solutions are included in *The Annotated Alice*, ed. Martin Gardner (1960).

6 'How many legs does a dog have, if you call a tail a leg?' After someone said, 'Five', Lincoln would say, 'No, only four. Calling a tail a leg doesn't make it a leg.'

Abraham Lincoln, American Republican President (1809–65). Attributed remark. Another version is told by George W. Julian in *Reminiscences of Abraham Lincoln*, ed. Allen T. Rice (1885): 'The boy who, when asked how many legs his calf would have if he called its tail a leg, replied, "Five", to which the prompt response was made that calling the tail a leg would not make it one.' A version of the riddle occurs in Denis Johnston's play *The Moon in the Yellow River* (1931).

Right

7 Always do right. This will gratify some people, and astonish the rest.

Mark Twain, American writer (1835–1910). Talk to young people, Brooklyn (16 February 1901). Included as 'Frontispiece' in *Mark Twain in Eruption*, ed. Bernard de Vote (1940). President Truman kept this saying on his desk.

Ripostes

One Saturday night, the actor playing the lead in Shakespeare's Richard III *had taken rather too much drink with a fellow cast member prior to the performance. This fact communicated itself to the audience when he came on swaying like a ship at sea. Someone shouted, 'Get off – you're drunk!' At which the actor, steadying himself, replied:*

8 Who, me? Drunk? Just wait till you see Buckingham!

Anonymous. Quoted in Sir Cedric Hardwicke, *A Victorian in Orbit* (1961). Sometimes told as though involving Wilfred Lawson, a noted tippler, though he does not appear to have played either part.

9 Nancy Astor (Lady Astor), who was always preaching against the evils of drink, was doing this in the House of Commons one day when she said to the crowded chamber, 'Well, there's nothing I wouldn't do rather than let a glass of beer cross my lips. I'd do anything. Why, I'd even commit adultery.' A voice from the back benches said, 'And so would I!'

Anonymous. Quoted by Ludovic Kennedy on BBC Radio *Quote … Unquote* (30 July 1983). Walter H. Brown of Weston-super-Mare wrote to me subsequently: 'I was of the opinion that her comment of "I would rather commit adultery" was made at a public political meeting at Plymouth and immediately a reply came from the back of the hall, "Who wouldn't?"'

Pass the Port Again (1980) has the exchange involving a Cambridge academic called E.E. Genner rather than Lady Astor. In *The Lyttelton Hart-Davis Letters*, Vol. 3 (1981), in a letter dated 9 July 1958, George Lyttelton has: 'I prefer the perfectly true comment of – who was it? – who, when some teetotal ass said he would rather commit adultery than drink a glass of port, said, "So would we all, my dear L., so would we all".'

1 Two men who had been rivals since their schooldays eventually ended up as a bishop and an admiral. At the height of this eminence, they met at Paddington station. The bishop, not recognizing his old schoolmate but perceiving from his uniform that he was an official of some sort, addressed him with the words: 'Tell me, my man, which platform is it for Reading?' The admiral, perceiving not only who the bishop was but that he was kitted out in all his finery, replied: 'I don't know, *madam* – and should you be travelling in your condition?'

Anonymous. Quoted in *Pass the Port* (1976) and by Kingsley Amis on BBC Radio *Quote … Unquote* (12 June 1979). Could this by any chance have begun life as a *Punch* cartoon caption?

2 George Bernard Shaw sent Winston Churchill two tickets for the first night of *St Joan* (which was in 1924), with a note explaining, 'One for yourself, the other for a friend – if you have one.' Churchill sent them back, regretting he would be unable to attend the first night, but saying he would like some tickets for the second night – 'If there is one.'

(Sir) Winston S. Churchill, British Conservative Prime Minister and writer (1874–1965). Quoted in *Pass the Port* (1976). Peter Hay in *Theatrical Anecdotes* (1987) says that it was told by his grandfather when Hay was growing up in London (1950s). I have also seen a version involving Churchill and Noël Coward. According to Michael Holroyd, *Bernard Shaw*, Vol. 3 (1991), Shaw's secretary, Blanche Patch, dismissed the story as a journalistic invention.

On being asked if he had ever smoked a marijuana cigarette in the permissive Sixties:

3 Only when committing adultery.

Senator Wyche Fowler, American politician. Quoted in *The Oxford Dictionary of Humorous Quotations*, ed. Ned Sherrin (1995).

A magazine writer preparing a profile of Cary Grant sent a cable to his agent inquiring, 'HOW OLD CARY GRANT?' Grant sent the reply himself:

4 OLD CARY GRANT FINE. HOW YOU?

Cary Grant, English-born American film actor (1904–86). Quoted in Leslie Halliwell, *The Filmgoer's Book of Quotes* (1973).

When interviewing Mae West and encouraged by her PR man to try and sound a bit more 'sexy':

5 If, sir, I possessed the power of conveying unlimited sexual attraction through the potency of my voice, I would not be reduced to accepting a miserable pittance from the BBC for interviewing a faded female in a damp basement.

Gilbert Harding, English radio and TV personality (1907–60). Quoted by Wynford Vaughan-Thomas in *Gilbert Harding By His Friends* (1961).

In answer to a heckler who cried, 'I wouldn't vote for you if you were the Archangel Gabriel':

6 If I were the Archangel Gabriel, madam, I'm afraid you would not be in my constituency.

(Sir) Robert Menzies, Australian Liberal Prime Minister (1894–1978). Quoted in R. Robinson, *The Wit of Sir Robert Menzies* (1966).

Replying to Mr Dundas in the House of Commons:

1 The Right Honourable Gentleman is indebted to his memory for his jests, and to his imagination for his facts.

Richard Brinsley Sheridan, English dramatist and politician (1751–1816). Quoted in T. Moore, *Life of Sheridan* (1825).

Mother at table saying: 'It's broccoli, dear.' Her little girl replies:

2 'I say it's spinach, and I say the hell with it.'

Elwyn Brooks White, American humorist (1899–1985). Caption devised for a cartoon by Carl Rose in *The New Yorker* (8 December 1928).

3 *Earl of Sandwich:*
'Pon my soul, Wilkes, I don't know whether you'll die upon the gallows or of the pox.
Wilkes:
That depends, my Lord, whether I first embrace your Lordship's principles, or your Lordship's mistresses.

John Wilkes, English politician (1727–97). Quoted in Sir Charles Petrie, *The Four Georges* (1935). But it is quite likely apocryphal. Where did Petrie get it from, and where had it been for the intervening two centuries? In *Memoirs of the Life and Writings of Percival Stockdale, Written by Himself* (1809) the exchange is given as between Sandwich and one 'Foote'.

It is frequently misapplied. George E. Allen in *Presidents Who Have Known Me* (1950) has it between Gladstone and Disraeli. It is difficult to imagine the circumstance in which either Disraeli or Gladstone could have made either of the remarks.

Rise and fall

4 [Always] be nice to people on your way up, because you'll meet 'em on your way down.

Wilson Mizner, American playwright (1876–1933). Quoted in Alva Johnston, *The Legendary Mizners* (1953). Also ascribed to Jimmy Durante and others.

Rivalry

5 Every time Mr Macmillan comes back from abroad, Mr Butler goes to the airport and grips him warmly by the throat.

Harold Wilson (Lord Wilson of Rievaulx), British Labour Prime Minister (1916–95). Quoted in Leslie Smith, *Harold Wilson* (1964).

Rivers

6 I have seen the Mississippi. That is muddy water. I have seen the St Lawrence. That is crystal water. But the Thames is liquid history.

John Burns, English Labour politician (1858–1943). Quoted in a *Daily Mail* report (25 January 1943) at Burns's death. This remark was reputedly made to an American who had spoken disparagingly of the River Thames. There are various versions of it. Denis Bridge commented (1994) that he used to live near Burns on North Side, Clapham Common, London. His father's version of the Burns remark went: 'The Mississippi is dirty water. The St Lawrence is cold, dirty water. But the Thames is liquid history.' The version I prefer is the one uttered with Burns's characteristic dropped aitch: 'The Thames is liquid 'istory!'

Roads

7 Before the Roman came to Rye or out to Severn strode,
The rolling English drunkard made the rolling English road.

G.K. Chesterton, English poet, novelist and critic (1874–1936). *The Flying Inn*, 'The Rolling English Road' (1914).

Romance

8 It's the old, old story. Boy meets girl – Romeo and Juliet – Minneapolis and St Paul!

Line from film *A Day at the Races* (US 1937). Screenwriters: Robert Pirosh, George Seaton, George Oppenheimer. Spoken by Groucho Marx (Dr Hackenbush) to Margaret Dumont (Mrs Emily Upjohn).

9 When one is in love, one always begins by deceiving oneself; and one always ends by deceiving others. That is what the world calls a romance.

Oscar Wilde, Irish playwright, poet and wit (1854–1900). *The Picture of Dorian Gray*, Chap. 4 (1891). Compare: *A Woman of No Importance*, Act 3 (1893): 'When one is in love one begins by deceiving oneself. And one ends by deceiving others.'

1 [There is no such thing as romance in our day,] women have become too brilliant; nothing spoils a romance so much as a sense of humour in the woman.

Oscar Wilde. *A Woman of No Importance*, Act 1 (1893).

Rosebery, Archibald Primrose, 5th Earl of

BRITISH LIBERAL PRIME MINISTER (1847–1929)

2 A man who never missed an occasion to let slip an opportunity.

Bernard Shaw, Irish playwright and critic (1856–1950). Quoted in Robert Rhodes James, *Rosebery* (1963), as the 'man who never missed a chance of missing an opportunity.'

Routine

3 The first thing I do in the morning is brush my teeth and sharpen my tongue.

Oscar Levant, American pianist and actor (1906–72). Quoted in *The Treasury of Humorous Quotations*, eds Evan Esar & Nicolas Bentley (1951).

Rowing

Of a rowing eight:

4 Eight minds with but a single thought – if that!

(Sir) Max Beerbohm, English writer and caricaturist (1872–1956). Attributed remark.

5 All rowed fast, but none so fast as stroke.

Desmond Coke, English writer and schoolteacher (1879–1931). In *Sandford of Merton*, Chap. 12 (1903), Coke wrote: 'His blade struck the water a full second before any other: the lad had started well. Nor did he flag as the race wore on: as the others tired, he seemed to grow more fresh, until at length, as the boats began to near the winning-post, his oar was dipping into the water nearly twice as often as any other.' This is deemed to be the original of the modern proverbial saying as above. But that is also sometimes thought to have been a deliberate distortion of something written earlier than Coke, by Ouida, 'designed to demonstrate the lady's ignorance of rowing, or indeed of any male activity' – Peter Farrer in *Oxford Today* (Hilary, 1992). The *Oxford Companion to English Literature* (1985) refers to the ridicule Ouida suffered for 'her inaccuracies in matter's of men's sports and occupations', of which her alleged observation must be one.

Royal jokes

When confronted by a delegation of 18 tailors:

6 Good morrow, gentlemen both.

Elizabeth I, English Queen (1533–1603). Quoted in Frederick Chamberlin, *The Sayings of Queen Elizabeth* (1923), where the sole authority given for her remark is Thomas Carlyle, *Sartor Resartus* (1836). Was this a slur upon the reputation of tailors? Was it justified? Or was this an Elizabethan version of the modern slurs against male flight attendants, hairdressers and ballet dancers? No. In all probability, the Queen was making a royal joke by playing on the expression 'It takes nine tailors to make a man.' This is said to have come originally from the French in about 1600. The meaning of it seems to be that a man should buy his clothes from various sources. Chamberlin notes that the ancient quip about the number of tailors it takes to make a man has 'lately been familiar in the United States through the comic opera, *Robin Hood*, by Reginald de Koven'. G.L. Apperson in his *English Proverbs and Proverbial Phrases* (1929) shows that, until the end of the 17th century, there was some uncertainty about the number of tailors mentioned in the expression. In *Westward Hoe* by John Webster and Thomas Dekker (1605) it appears as three.

When a fishbone lodged in her throat:

7 The salmon are striking back.

Elizabeth the Queen Mother, British Queen (1900–). Attributed in November 1982.

To her daughter, when the Queen accepted a second glass of wine at lunch:

8 Do you think it's wise, darling? You know you've got to rule this afternoon.

Elizabeth the Queen Mother. Quoted in Compton Miller, *Who's Really Who* (1983).

1 No more coals to Newcastle, no more Hoares to Paris.

George V, British King (1865–1936). Quoted in the Earl of Avon, *Facing the Dictators* (1962). This rare example of a royal joke comes from the period just before George V's death. In December 1935, it was revealed that Sir Samuel Hoare, the Foreign Secretary, had come to an arrangement with Pierre Laval, his French counterpart, whereby Abyssinia was virtually to be consigned to the Italians behind the back of the League of Nations. The Hoare-Laval Pact had been concluded in Paris when Sir Samuel was passing through on his way to a holiday in Switzerland. In the furore that followed he had to resign. The King may have been repeating a remark that was current anyway and it is surely unlikely that he made it direct to Hoare himself, despite Lord Avon's recollection of what the King told him.

2 We are not amused.

Victoria, British Queen (1819–1901). Quoted in *Notebooks of a Spinster Lady* (1919) written by Miss Caroline Holland (1878–1903): '[The Queen's] remarks can freeze as well as crystallize ... there is a tale of the unfortunate equerry who ventured during dinner at Windsor to tell a story with a spice of scandal or impropriety in it."We are not amused," said the Queen when he had finished.' The equerry in question appears to have been the Hon. Alexander Yorke. Unfortunately, the German visitor he had told the story to laughed so loud that the Queen's attention was drawn to it. Another contender for the snub is Admiral Maxse, whom she had commanded to give his well-known imitation of her which he did by putting a handkerchief on his head and blowing out his cheeks. Interviewed in 1978, Princess Alice, Countess of Athlone, said she had once questioned her grandmother about the phrase – 'I asked her ... [but] she never said it' – and affirmed what many have held, that Queen Victoria was 'a very cheerful person'.

Rules and regulations

3 Regulations [are] written for the obedience of fools and the guidance of wise men.

Anonymous. Featured in the film *Reach for the Sky* (UK, 1956). It is not clear how the saying originated but it is spoken in this form (prefaced with 'Some') by a man called Harry Day in Paul Brickhill, *Reach for the Sky* (1954), his biography of Douglas Bader. Day apparently made the observation when Bader's squadron was in training for the team aerobatics display in the annual Hendon air show. Day was acting squadron commander. Compare what is attributed to General Douglas MacArthur: 'Rules are mostly made to be broken and are too often for the lazy to hide behind' – William A. Ganoe, *MacArthur Close-Up* (1962).

4 The rule is, jam tomorrow and jam yesterday – but never jam today.

Lewis Carroll, English writer (1832–98). *Through the Looking-Glass and What Alice Found There*, Chap. 5 (1872). The White Queen wants Alice to be her maid and offers her twopence a week and jam every other day, except that she can never actually have any – it's never jam today. An early version of Catch-22. Nowadays, the phrase is quite often used in connection with the unfulfilled promises of politicians. But did Carroll adopt an older phrase? Others recall being taught that this was an academic joke. In Latin there are two words meaning 'now': *nunc* and *iam*. The former is used in the present tense, whereas the latter is the correct word for past and future tenses, i.e., yesterday and tomorrow, so it is correct to say *iam* for tomorrow and *iam* for yesterday but never *iam* for today.

5 Learn all the rules, every one of them, so that you will know how to break them.

Irvin S. Cobb, American humorist and journalist (1876–1944). Quoted in *The Treasury of Humorous Quotations*, eds Evan Esar & Nicolas Bentley (1951).

6 The golden rule is that there are no golden rules.

Bernard Shaw, Irish playwright and critic (1856–1950). *Man and Superman*, 'Maxims for Revolutionists' (1903).

Running

7 *The Red Queen*:
Now, *here*, you see, it takes all the running *you* can do, to keep in the same place. If you want to get somewhere else, you must run at least twice as fast as that.

Lewis Carroll, English writer (1832–98). *Through the Looking-Glass and What Alice Found There*, Chap. 2 (1872).

S

Sack

On being replaced in the Shadow Cabinet by a man four years his senior:

1 There comes a time in every man's life when he must make way for an older man.

Reginald Maudling, English Conservative politician (1917–77). Reported in *The Guardian* (20 November 1976). He also said at that time: 'I have never been sacked before. I was appointed by Winston Churchill and I am now being dismissed by Margaret Thatcher. Life goes on. The world changes.'

Sackville-West, Vita

ENGLISH NOVELIST AND POET (1892–1962)

2 She looked like Lady Chatterley above the waist and the gamekeeper below.

Cyril Connolly, English writer and critic (1903–74). Attributed remark. Alluded to in Peter Quennell, *Customs and Characters* (1982): the poet's appearance was 'strange almost beyond the reach of adjectives ... she resembled a puissant blend of both sexes – Lady Chatterley and her lover rolled into one, I recollect a contemporary humorist observing ... her legs, which reminded [Virginia] Woolf of stalwart tree trunks, were encased in a gamekeeper's breeches and top-boots laced up to the knee.' By 'contemporary humorist' he probably meant Connolly, who indeed went with him on a joint visit to Sackville-West at Sissinghurst in 1936.

Salaries

3 The salary of the chief executive of the large corporation is not a market award for achievement. It is frequently in the nature of a warm personal gesture by the individual to himself.

John Kenneth Galbraith, Canadian-born American economist (1908–). *Annals of an Abiding Liberal* (1979).

4 If you pay peanuts, you get monkeys.

(Sir) James Goldsmith, British businessman (1933–97). This remark – made *c.* 1980 in connection with the pay given to journalists on his short-lived news magazine *Now!* – is not original. The modern proverb was in use by 1966.

Sang-froid

5 By God! I've lost my leg!

1st Marquess of Anglesey, English cavalry officer (1768–1854). At the Battle of Waterloo (1815), Lord Uxbridge (later to become Marquess of Anglesey) said this to the Duke of Wellington, who replied, 'Have you, by God?' and rode on. The partly severed leg was amputated and buried in a garden in the village of Waterloo. He consequently acquired the nickname 'One-Leg'. Quoted in Elizabeth Longford, *Wellington: The Years of the Sword*, Chap. 23 (1969).

On being found drinking a glass of wine in the street, when watching the Drury Lane Theatre, which he owned, burning down (24 February 1809):

6 A man may surely be allowed to take a glass of wine by his own fireside.

Richard Brinsley Sheridan, English dramatist and politician (1751–1816). Quoted in T. Moore, *Life of Sheridan* (1825).

1 Charlotte, having seen his body
Borne before her on a shutter,
Like a well-conducted person,
Went on cutting bread-and-butter.

W.M. Thackeray, English novelist (1811–63). 'The Sorrows of Werther' (1855).

Sarcasm

2 Sarcasm is the lowest form of wit.

Anonymous (proverbial saying). Quoted in Greville Janner, *Janner's Complete Letterwriter* (1989). Origin obscure. Thomas Carlyle remarked in *Sartor Resartus*, Pt 2, Chap. 4 (1834), that 'Sarcasm is the language of the devil.' The more usual observation is that 'Punning is the lowest form of wit', which probably derives from Dryden's comment on Ben Jonson's 'clenches' – 'the lowest and most grovelling kind of wit'.

3 A true sarcasm is like a sword-stick – it appears, at first sight, to be much more innocent than it really is, till, all of a sudden, there leaps something out of it – sharp, deadly and incisive – which makes you tremble and recoil.

(Revd) Sydney Smith, English clergyman, essayist and wit (1771–1845). *Sketches of Moral Philosophy* (1849).

Satire

4 Satire is what closes Saturday night.

George S. Kaufman, American playwright (1889–1961). Quoted in Scott Meredith, *George S. Kaufman and the Algonquin Round Table* (1974).

5 The purpose of satire, it has been rightly said, is to strip off the veneer of comforting illusion and cosy half-truth; and our job, as I see it, is to put it back again.

Michael Flanders, English writer and entertainer (1922–75). *At the Drop of Another Hat* (1963).

6 To hear some people talk, you would think humour was an aspect of satire, instead of the other way round. Satire is simply humour in uniform.

Paul Jennings, English humorist (1918–90). Quoted in his obituary in *The Guardian* (1 January 1990).

7 Satire does not look pretty upon a tombstone.

Charles Lamb, English essayist (1775–1834). Quoted in *The Treasury of Humorous Quotations*, eds Evan Esar & Nicolas Bentley (1951).

8 I never lack material for my humor column when Congress is in session.

Will Rogers, American humorist (1879–1935). Quoted in the same collection as above.

9 Satire is a kind of glass, wherein beholders do generally discover everybody's face but their own.

Jonathan Swift, Anglo-Irish writer and clergyman (1667–1745). *The Battle of the Books*, Preface (1704).

10 Perhaps I may allow the Dean
Had too much satire in his vein;
And seemed determined not to starve it,
Because no age could more deserve it,
Yet, malice never was his aim;
He lashed the vice, but spared the name;
No individual could resent,
Where thousands equally were meant.
His satire points at no defect,
But what all mortals may correct.

He gave the little wealth he had,
To build a house for fools and mad;
And showed by one satiric touch,
No nation wanted it so much.

Jonathan Swift. 'Verses on the Death of Doctor Swift' (1731).

11 Well, it was satire, wasn't it? … You can say bum, you can say po, you can say anything … Well, he said it! The thin one! He said bum one night. I heard him! Satire!

Keith Waterhouse and Willis Hall, English writers (1929–) and (1929–). Sketch, 'Close Down', BBC TV *That Was the Week That Was* (1962–3).

Satisfaction

1 It is better to be a human being dissatisfied than a pig satisfied; better to be Socrates dissatisfied than a fool satisfied.

John Stuart Mill, English philosopher and social reformer (1806–73). *Utilitarianism,* Chap. 2 (1863).

Saving

2 Saving is a very fine thing especially when your parents have done it for you.

(Sir) Winston S. Churchill, British Conservative Prime Minister and writer (1874–1965). Quoted in Fred Metcalf, *The Penguin Dictionary of Modern Humorous Quotations* (1987).

3 It saves a lot of trouble if, instead of having to earn money and save it, you can just go and borrow it.

(Sir) Winston S. Churchill. Quoted in *The Treasury of Humorous Quotations*, eds Evan Esar & Nicolas Bentley (1951).

4 Thrifty! Man, she'd skin a flea for his hide.

James Duffy, Irish playwright (19th century). Quoted in the same collection as above. Possibly just a proverbial expression – of which other reported variants are, 'She is *that* mean she would skin a flea for its hide and tallow' and 'She'd skin a gnat for its hide.'

5 Simple rules for saving money: To save half, when you are fired by an eager impulse to contribute to charity, wait, and count to forty. To save three-quarters, count sixty. To save it all, count sixty-five.

Mark Twain, American writer (1835–1910). *Following the Equator*, Vol. 2 (1897).

6 Save a boyfriend for a rainy day and another in case it doesn't.

Mae West, American vaudeville and film actress (1893–1980). Quoted in the *Daily Mail* (1980).

Scandal

7 Love and scandal are the best sweeteners of tea.

Henry Fielding, English novelist and judge (1707–54). *Love In Several Masques*, Act 4, Sc. 2 (1728).

8 Oh! Gossip is charming! History is merely gossip. But scandal is gossip made tedious by morality.

Oscar Wilde, Irish playwright, poet and wit (1854–1900). *Lady Windermere's Fan*, Act 3 (1892).

Schedule

9 There cannot be a crisis next week. My schedule is already full.

Henry Kissinger, American Republican politician (1923–). Quoted in *The New York Times* Magazine (1 June 1969).

Science and scientists

10 Every great scientific truth goes through three stages. First, people say it conflicts with the Bible. Next, they say it has been discovered before. Lastly, they say they have always believed it.

Louis Agassiz, Swiss-born American naturalist (1807–73). Quoted in Bennett Cerf, *The Laugh's On Me* (1961). *However,* something like this ('All truth passes through three stages. First, it is ridiculed. Second, it is violently opposed. Third, it is accepted as being self-evident.') has also been attributed to Arthur Schopenhauer (frequently), William Whewell, Gustav Le Bon, Elbert Hubbard, William James, Arthur C. Clarke and Adrienne Zihlman, but nothing solid has been found in Agassiz's works (or anywhere else).

11 When I find myself in the company of scientists, I feel like a shabby curate who has strayed by mistake into a drawing room full of dukes.

W.H. Auden, Anglo-American poet (1907–73). *The Dyer's Hand*, 'The Poet and the City' (1962).

12 Research is something that tells you that a jackass has two ears.

Albert D. Lasker, American physician (1880–1952). Quoted in John Gunther, *Taken at the Flood: The Story of Albert D. Lasker* (1960).

See also RELATIVITY.

Scotsmen and Scottishness

Said by a Scotsman who has just been on a visit to London:

1 Mun, a had na' been the-ere abune twa hoours when – *Bang* – went *Saxpence*!

Anonymous (cartoonist). Caption to cartoon in *Punch*, Vol. 54 (5 December 1868).

2 The history of Scotland is one of theology tempered by homicide.

Ivor Brown, English drama critic (1891–1974). Quoted in Wilfred Taylor, *Scot Free: A Book of Gael Warnings* (1953).

3 Sir, let me tell you, the noblest prospect which a Scotsman ever sees, is the high road that leads him to England!

(Dr) Samuel Johnson, English writer and lexicographer (1709–84). In James Boswell, *The Life of Samuel Johnson* (1791) – for 6 July 1763. Johnson no doubt enjoyed baiting the Scotsman Boswell in this fashion, but his biographer records how 'this unexpected and pointed sally produced a roar of applause.'

4 *Boswell*: I do indeed come from Scotland, but I cannot help it …
Johnson: That, Sir, I find, is what a very great many of your countrymen cannot help.

(Dr) Samuel Johnson. Quoted in the same book – for 16 May 1763.

5 Much may be made of a Scotchman, if he be caught young.

(Dr) Samuel Johnson. Quoted in the same book as above – for 1772.

6 I have been trying all my life to like Scotchmen, and am obliged to desist from the experiment in despair.

Charles Lamb, English writer (1775–1834). *Essays of Elia*, 'Imperfect Sympathies' (1823).

7 In all my travels I have never met with any one Scotchman but what was a man of sense … I believe everybody of that country that has any, leaves it as fast as they can.

Francis Lockier, English divine and essayist (1667–1740). Quoted in Joseph Spence, *Anecdotes* (1858).

8 It requires a surgical operation to get a joke well into a Scotch understanding. Their only idea of wit, or rather that inferior variety of the electric talent which prevails occasionally in the North, and which, under the name of WUT, is so infinitely distressing to people of good taste, is laughing immoderately at stated intervals.

(Revd) Sydney Smith, English clergyman, essayist and wit (1771–1845). Quoted in Lady Holland, *A Memoir of Sydney Smith* (1855). In J.M. Barrie's play *What Every Woman Knows* (1908), this remark is built upon further to undermine a humourless Scotsman, John Shand: 'I remember reading of someone that said it needed a surgical operation to get a joke into a Scotsman's head. "Yes, that's been said." What beats me, Maggie, is how you could insert a joke with an operation.'

9 I proposed that we should set up a Review, and I remained long enough in Edinburgh to edit the first number. The motto I proposed for the Review was *Tenui musam meditamur avena* – 'we cultivate literature on a little oatmeal'. But this was too near the truth to be admitted.

(Revd) Sydney Smith. Quoted in the same book as above.

10 That garret of the earth – that knuckle-end of England – that land of Calvin, oatcakes and sulphur.

(Revd) Sydney Smith. Quoted in the same book as above.

11 It is never difficult to distinguish between a Scotsman with a grievance and a ray of sunshine, and Lord Emsworth, gazing upon the dour man, was able to see at once into which category Angus McAllister fell.

(Sir) P(elham) G. Wodehouse, English-born novelist and lyricist (1881–1975). *Blandings Castle and Elsewhere*, 'The Custody of the Pumpkin' (1935).

Screenwriting

1 'Oh, son, I wish you hadn't become a scenario writer!' she sniffed.

'Aw, now, Moms,' I comforted her, 'it's no worse than playing the piano in a call house.'

S.J. Perelman, American humorist (1904–79). 'Strictly from Hunger' – which later became the title of his second book (1937).

Seals

2 All right, have it your way – you heard a seal bark.

James Thurber, American cartoonist and writer (1894–1961). Caption to cartoon 'The Seal in the Bedroom' in *The New Yorker* (1932).

Secrets

3 Three may keep a secret, if two of them are dead.

Benjamin Franklin, American politician and scientist (1706–90). *Poor Richard's Almanack* (July 1735) – a work in which Franklin often revised already existing sayings.

Self-indulgence

4 In the order named, these are the hardest to control: Wine, Women, and Song.

Franklin P. Adams, American journalist, poet and humorist (1881–1960). Quoted in *The Treasury of Humorous Quotations*, eds Evan Esar & Nicolas Bentley (1951).

After Lord Hailsham's comments on John Profumo's frailties in 1963:

5 From Lord Hailsham we have had a virtuoso performance in the art of kicking a fallen friend in the guts … When self-indulgence has reduced a man to the shape of Lord Hailsham, sexual continence requires no more than a sense of the ridiculous.

Reginald Paget (Lord Paget), English lawyer and Labour politician (1908–90). Quoted in Ned Sherrin, *Cutting Edge* (1984).

Self-knowledge

6 On being turned down when he attempted to join an exclusive golf club – the grounds given were that he was an actor – Victor Mature replied: 'I am not an actor – and I have 60 films to prove it.'

Victore Mature, American actor (1915–99). Quoted in Melvyn Bragg, *Rich: The Life of Richard Burton* (1988).

7 At the end of the first night of Oscar Wilde's play *Lady Windermere's Fan* in 1892, the author was called for. Wilde duly appeared before the curtain with a cigarette between his fingers to respond to the audience's cheers. 'I am so glad, ladies and gentlemen, that you like my play,' he said. 'I feel sure you estimate the merits of it almost as highly as I do myself …'

Oscar Wilde, Irish playwright, poet and wit (1854–1900). Quoted in Frank Harris, *Oscar Wilde, His Life and Confessions*, Chap. 9 (1930). Another version of this speech (including the emphases) was taken down in shorthand by George Alexander, a member of the theatre staff. Hesketh Pearson included it in his biography of Wilde (1946): 'Ladies and Gentlemen, I have enjoyed this evening *immensely*. The actors have given us a *charming* rendering of a *delightful* play, and your appreciation has been *most* intelligent. I congratulate you on the *great* success of your performance, which persuades me that you think *almost* as highly of the play as I do myself.' Curiously, there was an even longer and probably more accurate transcript made of the speech for the *Boston Evening Transcript* (10 March 1892).

8 I don't at all like knowing what people say of me behind my back. It makes me far too conceited.

Oscar Wilde. *An Ideal Husband*. Act 4 (1893).

Remark to Arthur Humphreys, about Wilde's own play The Importance of Being Earnest *(February 1895):*

9 It is written by a butterfly for butterflies.

Oscar Wilde. Quoted in *The Home Book of Humorous Quotations*, ed. A.K. Adams (1969).

Self-made men

1 The trouble with self-made men is that they're working with inferior materials.

Anonymous. Quoted in *Picking on Men,* compiled by Judy Allen (1985). In the film *Thanks a Million* (US 1935), a judge says, 'In me you see a self-made man.' Fred Allen replies: 'Showing the horrors of unskilled labour.'

2 Self-made men are most alwus apt tew be a leetle too proud ov the job.

Josh Billings (Henry Wheeler Shaw), American humorist (1818–85). 'Koarse Shot' included in *Everybody's Friend* and in *Josh Billing's Encyclopedia and Proverbial Philosophy of Wit and Humor* (1874).

Of Benjamin Disraeli:

3 He is a self-made man and worships his creator.

John Bright, English Radical politician (1811–89). Attributed remark. *H.L. Mencken's Dictionary of Quotations* (1942) has, rather, Henry Clapp saying this (*c.* 1858) about Horace Greeley, and dates Bright's use of the saying about Benjamin Disraeli ten years later, to *c.* 1868. Leon Harris, in *The Fine Art of Political Wit* (1965), has *Disraeli* saying it about *Bright*. To William Cowper, the poet, has been ascribed the remark, 'A self-made man? Yes – and worships his creator' – quoted in *The Treasury of Humorous Quotations*, eds Evan Esar & Nicolas Bentley (1951).

4 He was a self-made man who owed his lack of success to nobody.

Joseph Heller, American novelist (1923–99). *Catch-22*, Chap. 3 (1961).

5 Self-made men are very apt to usurp the prerogative of the Almighty and overwork themselves.

Edgar Wilson ('Bill') Nye, American humorist (1850–96). Quoted in Herbert V. Prochnow, Snr & Jnr, *A Treasury of Humorous Quotations* (1969).

6 Self-made man, you know. They know how to talk. They do deserve more credit than any other breed of men, yes, that is true, and they are among the very first to find it out, too.

Mark Twain, American writer (1835–1910). *A Connecticut Yankee in King Arthur's Court* (1889).

Self-regard

7 I like to be introduced as America's foremost actor. It saves the necessity of further effort.

John Barrymore, American actor (1882–1942). Quoted in Leslie Halliwell, *The Filmgoer's Book of Quotes* (1973).

8 That favourite subject, Myself.

James Boswell, Scottish lawyer, biographer and diarist (1740–95). Letter to William Temple (26 July 1763), quoted in Boswell's *The Life of Samuel Johnson* (1791).

9 The world has treated me very well – but then I haven't treated it so badly either.

(Sir) Noël Coward, English entertainer and writer (1899–1973). Interviewed by Ed Murrow on US TV *Small World* (1959).

10 Talk to a man about himself and he will listen for hours.

Benjamin Disraeli (1st Earl of Beaconsfield), English politician and writer (1804–81). Quoted in *The Home Book of Humorous Quotations*, ed. A.K. Adams (1969).

To himself in mirror, after spraying himself and smoothing his moustache before meeting girl:

11 Oh, you sexy beast!

Line from film *The Fast Lady* (UK 1962). Screenwriters: Jack Davies, Henry Blyth. Spoken by Leslie Phillips (Freddie Fox).

12 He that falls in love with himself, will have no rivals.

Benjamin Franklin, American politician and scientist (1706–90). *Poor Richard's Almanack* (May 1738) – a work in which Franklin often revised already existing sayings.

13 Sal laughs at every thing you say.
Why? Because she has fine teeth.

Benjamin Franklin. In the same book as above.

Of her former husband, George Sanders:

1 We were both in love with George Sanders.

Zsa Zsa Gabor, Hungarian-born film actress (1919–). Quoted in John Robert Colombo, *Wit and Wisdom of the Moviemakers* (1979).

2 CELEBRITY (after lengthy monopoly of the conversation) 'But enough about me; let's talk about yourself. Tell me – what do you think of my part in the new play?'

D.L. Ghilchik, English cartoonist. Caption to cartoon in *Punch* (date not known). It was reproduced in Vol. ix ('Mr *Punch*'s Theatricals') in *The New Punch Library* (*c.* 1933).

When President Eisenhower's death prevented her from being on the cover of Newsweek *Magazine:*

3 Fourteen heart attacks and he had to die in my week. In MY week.

Janis Joplin, American rock musician (1943–70). In *New Musical Express* (12 April 1969).

To George Gershwin:

4 Tell me, George, if you had to do it all over would you fall in love with yourself again?

Oscar Levant, American pianist and actor (1906–72). Quoted in David Ewen, *The Story of George Gershwin* (1943). In the Gershwin biopic *Rhapsody in Blue* (1945), Levant (playing himself) got to repeat the line. He is also reputed to have told Gershwin once: 'George, why don't you sit down and play us a medley of your hit.'

5 Don't talk about yourself, it will be done when you leave.

Addison Mizner, American architect (1872–1933). Quoted in *The Treasury of Humorous Quotations*, eds Evan Esar & Nicolas Bentley (1951).

6 The affair between Margot Asquith and Margot Asquith will live as one of the prettiest love stories in all literature.

Dorothy Parker, American writer (1893–1967). Reviewing Asquith's *Lay Sermons* in *The New Yorker* (22 October 1927).

On being awarded the Order of Merit in 1977:

7 I've only two things to say about it. First I deserve it. Second, they've been too long about giving me it. There'll be another vacancy very soon.

J.B. Priestley, English playwright, novelist and author (1894–1984). In radio interview (October 1977), quoted in John Braine, *J.B. Priestley* (1978).

8 Faith, that's as well said, as if I had said it myself.

Jonathan Swift, Anglo-Irish writer and clergyman (1667–1745). *Polite Conversation* (1738) – a compendium of traditional conversational expressions.

Of A Tale of a Tub*:*

9 Good God! What a genius I had when I wrote that book.

Jonathan Swift. Quoted in Sir Walter Scott's edition of *The Works of Swift* (1814).

10 To love oneself is the beginning of a lifelong romance.

Oscar Wilde, Irish playwright, poet and wit (1854–1900). *An Ideal Husband*, Act 3 (1895). Earlier this was in 'Phrases and Philosophies for the Use of the Young', in *The Chameleon* (December 1894).

Selfishness

11 Selfishness is not living as one wishes to live, it is asking others to live as one wishes to live.

Oscar Wilde, Irish playwright, poet and wit (1854–1900). 'The Soul of Man Under Socialism' (1895).

Sequels

On the vogue for sequels:

12 It adds a new terror to the death of the novelist.

Peter Ackroyd, English novelist (1949–). *In The Independent on Sunday* (22 September 1996).

Serendipity

1 Serendipity means searching for a needle in a haystack and instead finding a farmer's daughter.

Anonymous. Quoted by the scientist Sir Herman Bondi and reported in *The 'Quote ... Unquote' Newsletter* (July 1995).

Seriousness

2 One should not exaggerate the importance of trifles. Life, for instance, is much too short to be taken seriously.

Nicolas Bentley, English cartoonist and writer (1907–78). Quoted in *The Treasury of Humorous Quotations*, eds Evan Esar & Nicolas Bentley (1951).

3 The one serious conviction that a man should have is that nothing is to be taken seriously.

Samuel Butler, English author (1835–1902). Quoted in the same collection as above.

Of Lincoln Steffens:

4 Everything serious that he says is a joke and everything humorous that he says is dead serious.

Clarence Darrow, American lawyer (1857–1938). Quoted in my book *A Year of Stings and Squelches* (1985).

5 Do not take life too seriously; you will never get out of it alive.

Elbert Hubbard, American writer and editor (1856–1915). Quoted in *The Treasury of Humorous Quotations*, eds Evan Esar & Nicolas Bentley (1951).

6 Life is much too important ever to talk seriously about it.

Oscar Wilde, Irish playwright, poet and wit (1854–1900). *Vera: Or The Nihilists*, Act 2 (1880). Later in *Lady Windermere's Fan*, Act 2 (1892).

7 Seriousness is the only refuge of the shallow.

Oscar Wilde. Quoted in Herbert V. Prochnow, Snr & Jnr, *A Treasury of Humorous Quotations* (1969).

Sermons

8 Preaching to some people is like eating custard with a fork. It goes in one ear and out the other.

Anonymous (curate). Quoted on BBC Radio *Quote ... Unquote* (2 February 1982).

9 A good honest and painful sermon.

Samuel Pepys, English civil servant and diarist (1633–1703). Diary (17 March 1661). Painful here = painstaking. It was preached by 'a stranger', but Pepys does not reveal upon what text.

10 I never sleep comfortably except when I am at a sermon.

François Rabelais, French humorist and satirist (1495?–1553). Quoted in *The Treasury of Humorous Quotations*, eds Evan Esar & Nicolas Bentley (1951).

11 There is not the least use in preaching to anyone, unless you chance to catch them ill.

(Revd) Sydney Smith, English clergyman, essayist and wit (1771–1845). Quoted in *Bon-Mots of Sydney Smith &c.*, ed. Walter Jerrold (1893).

12 When I am in the pulpit, I have the pleasure of seeing my audience nod approbation while they sleep.

(Revd) Sydney Smith. Attributed remark.

13 Few sinners are saved after the first twenty minutes of a sermon.

Mark Twain, American writer (1835–1910). Quoted in the *Hannibal Courier-Post* (6 March 1935).

14 He charged nothing for his preaching, and it was worth it too.

Mark Twain. Quoted in *The Home Book of Humorous Quotations*, ed. A.K. Adams (1969).

Servants

15 *Vivre? les serviteurs feront cela pour nous* [Living? The servants will do that for us].

Philippe-Auguste Villiers de l'Isle Adam, French poet, novelist and playwright (1838–89). *Axël*, Act 4, Sc. 2 (1890).

In the course of a routine house-to-house inquiry in Belgravia, a highly-placed old lady was told of the murder of Sandra Rivett, the nanny it is alleged Lord Lucan mistakenly killed instead of his wife. Said she:

1 Oh dear, what a pity. Nannies are so hard to come by these days.

Anonymous. Quoted in *The Sunday Times* Magazine (8 June 1975).

2 The difference between a man and his valet: they both smoke the same cigars, but only one pays for them.

Robert Frost, American poet (1874–1963). Quoted in *The Treasury of Humorous Quotations*, eds Evan Esar & Nicolas Bentley (1951).

When told that he looked as though he had slept in his clothes, he is said to have replied:

3 Don't be ridiculous. I pay someone to do that for me.

Victor Mature, American film actor (1915–99). Quoted by William Franklyn on BBC Radio *Quote ... Unquote* (20 July 1985).

Sex

4 Sex between a man and a woman can be wonderful – provided you get between the right man and the right woman.

Woody Allen, American film actor, writer and director (1937–). Attributed remark. Compare 'I believe that sex is a beautiful thing between two people. Between *five*, it's fantastic ... ' on Allen's record album *The Nightclub Years 1964–1968* (1972).

5 The psychiatrist asked me if I thought sex was dirty and I said, 'It is if you're doing it right.'

Woody Allen. Line from his film, *Take the Money and Run* (US 1969). Compare: 'Is sex dirty? Only if it's done right' – line from his film, *Everything You Always Wanted to Know About Sex* (1972).

6 Fun? That was the most fun I've ever had without laughing.

Woody Allen. Line from his film, *Annie Hall* (US 1977), written with Marshall Brickman. Woody Allen (Alvy) speaking. Also attributed to Humphrey Bogart In the form 'It was the most fun I ever had without laughing.'

7 Prostitutes for pleasure, concubines for service, wives for breeding ... A melon for ecstasy.

Anonymous. The first part was quoted by Pearl Binder (Lady Elwyn-Jones) when she appeared with octogenarian aplomb on BBC Radio *Quote ... Unquote* in 1984. She claimed that Sir Richard Burton had 'borrowed it from Demosthenes.' Alan Brien, who was in attendance, chimed in with, 'And a melon for ecstasy.' This, a separate saying, was used as the title of a novel (1971) by John Fortune and John Wells. Apparently, the novelist John Masters once ascribed to a 'Pathan tribesman' the saying 'A woman for duty, a boy for pleasure, a goat for ecstasy' whereas Stephen Fry in *Paperweight* (1992) credits this to the Greeks. Apropos the main quotation, compare John Gay, 'The Toilette' (1716): 'A miss for pleasure, and a wife for breed.'

8 Do you think that sex ought to take place before the wedding?
No, not if it delays the ceremony ...

Anonymous. Line from the sketch 'Sex' in the Kenneth Williams revue, *One Over the Eight*, London (1961). David Rogers writes in *Politics, Prayer and Parliament* (2000): 'I have heard this after-dinner [story] used in connection with the last three Archbishops [of Canterbury]. The Archbishop (whichever one) is talking to the Duke of Edinburgh at a reception in St James'. The Duke asks, "I don't know, all this promiscuity nowadays. Tell me, Archbishop, do you believe in sex before marriage?" "No, Sir. Certainly not." "Good," says Edinburgh, "I'm very glad to hear it. But can you tell me why?" "Well, Sir. Sex before marriage? Oh no. It tends to delay the start of the service".'

9 Bed is the poor man's opera.

Anonymous (Italian proverb). Quoted in Aldous Huxley, *Heaven and Hell* (1956). Sometimes given as 'Sex is ... ' Compare Charles Baudelaire, *Journaux intimes* (1887): 'Sexuality is the lyricism of the masses.'

10 Mad men and lame men copulate best.

Anonymous (proverb). Quoted in Walter Redfern, *Clichés and Coinages* (1989). Compare, from the Greek poet

Mimnermus (7th century BC): 'The lame copulate best.' Byron may also have expressed this thought, for understandable reasons.

To an admirer:

1 I'll come and make love to you at five o'clock. If I'm late start without me.

Tallulah Bankhead, American actress (1903–68). Quoted in Ted Morgan, *Somerset Maugham* (1980). In *Crying With Laughter* (1993), Bob Monkhouse claims that he invented this line for Ted Ray to say after a rousing concert performance by Diana Dors in the early 1950s: 'Thank you, Diana, you may go to my room and lie down. And if I'm not there in twenty minutes, start without me.' Monkhouse adds that this was a line that 'subsequently went all round show business to be used by comedians everywhere ... Only two years later I offered the same gag to Bob Hope. "But I know that line," he said, as if I were trying to sell him a stolen watch.' Compare the exchange between Neal (Richard Benjamin) and Brenda (Ali McGraw) as he reaches out for her in the film *Goodbye, Columbus* (US 1969): 'Later.' 'What if I can't wait?' 'Start without me.'

2 The thing that takes the least amount of time and causes the most amount of trouble is sex.

John Barrymore, American actor (1882–1942). Quoted in *The Treasury of Humorous Quotations*, eds Evan Esar & Nicolas Bentley (1951).

3 I met my love in the graveyard
I did her before we were wed
I laid her on top of the tombstone
We did it to cheer up the dead.

Brendan Behan, Irish playwright (1923–64). Attributed verse.

4 *Mrs Swabb:*

Me, I don't bother with sex. I leave that to the experts.

Alan Bennett, English playwright and actor (1934–). *Habeas Corpus*, Act 1 (1973).

Written on a photograph that she gave to her fiancé, Harry Richman:

5 To my gorgeous lover, Harry. I'll trade all my It for your that.

Clara Bow, American film actress (1905–65), known as the 'It Girl' – to describe her vivacious sex appeal – after appearing in the film *It* (1928). Quoted in Bob Chieger, *Was It Good for You, Too?* (1983).

6 A little still she strove, and much repented,
And whispering 'I will ne'er consent' – consented.

Lord Byron, English poet (1788–1824). *Don Juan*, Canto 1, St. 117 (1819–24).

7 It doesn't matter what you do, as long as you don't do it in the street and frighten the horses.

Mrs Patrick Campbell, English actress (1865–1940). Variously worded. Quoted in Daphne Fielding, *The Duchess of Jermyn Street* (1964), as: 'It doesn't matter what you do *in the bedroom* as long as you don't do it in the street and frighten the horses.' The *Oxford Dictionary of Quotations* (1979) had, 'I don't mind where people *make love*, so long as they ... ' Margot Peters, in her otherwise painstakingly footnoted biography *Mrs Pat* (1984), gives no reason for stating her belief that it was 'when told of a *homosexual affair* between actors' that the actress uttered: 'I don't care what people do, as long as they don't do it in the street and frighten the horses.' More precisely, in *Brendan Behan's New York* (1964) is this remark: 'My attitude to homosexuality is rather like that of the woman who, at the time of the trial of Oscar Wilde, said she didn't mind what they did, so long as they didn't do it in the street and frighten the horses.'

8 The pleasure is momentary, the position ridiculous, the expense damnable.

4th Earl of Chesterfield (Philip Dormer Stanhope), English politician and writer (1694–1773). Usually attributed to Chesterfield, as in *Nature*, Vol. 227 (22 August 1970), though it has not been found in his works. An earlier unattached allusion is contained in a letter from Evelyn Waugh to Nancy Mitford (5 May 1954): 'Of children as of procreation – the pleasure momentary, the posture ridiculous, the expense damnable.' Compare D.H. Lawrence, *Lady Chatterley's Lover*, Chap. 12 (1928): 'It was quite true, as some poets said, that the God who created man must have had a sinister sense of humour, creating him a reasonable being, yet forcing him to take this ridiculous posture … Men despised the intercourse act, and yet did it.'

On sex scandal in the newspapers in the age of AIDS:

1 The more you don't do it, the more it's fun to read about.

Caryl Churchill, English playwright (1938–). *Serious Money*, Act 2 (1987).

To Laurence Olivier's five-year-old daughter, Tamsin, when she asked what two dogs were doing together:

2 The doggie in front has suddenly gone blind, and the other one has very kindly offered to push him all the way to St Dunstan's.

(Sir) Noël Coward, English entertainer and writer (1899–1973). Quoted by Kenneth Tynan in *The Observer* (1 April 1973). Tynan probably took this version from David Niven, *The Moon's a Balloon*, Chap. 17 (1971).

3 When Eve said to Adam
'Start calling me Madam'
The world became far more exciting;
Which turns to confusion,
The modern delusion
That sex is a question of lighting.

(Sir) Noël Coward. Introduction on the album 'Marlene Dietrich at the Café de Paris' (a recording of her London cabaret performance, 1954). Misquoted as 'sex is a question of *liking*' in *The Observer* (24 March 1992).

4 The last time I was inside a woman was when I visited the Statue of Liberty.

Line from film *Crimes and Misdemeanors* (US 1989). Screenwriter: Woody Allen. Spoken by Woody Allen (Cliff Stern).

5 At certain times I like sex – like after a cigarette.

Rodney Dangerfield, American comedian (1921–). Quoted in *The Penguin Dictionary of Modern Humorous Quotations*, ed. Fred Metcalf (1987).

6 He had ambitions, at one time, to become a sex maniac, but he failed his practical.

Les Dawson, English comedian (1934–93). Quoted in the same collection as above.

7 I say I don't sleep with married men, but what I mean is that I don't sleep with happily married men.

Britt Ekland, Swedish actress (1942–). Attributed in the *Telegraph Weekend Magazine* (January 1980) as having been said in 1979.

When the Earl of Lichfield dropped her because she was 'no good in the country':

8 And he's no good in bed.

Britt Ekland. Quoted in my book *Nudge Nudge Wink Wink* (1986).

9 There are many things better than sex, but there's nothing quite like it.

W.C. Fields, American comedian (1879–1946). Attributed remark.

10 My dad told me, 'Anything worth having is worth waiting for.' I waited until I was fifteen.

Zsa Zsa Gabor, Hungarian-born film actress (1919–). In 1981 – quoted in Bob Chieger, *Was It Good For You Too?* (1983).

11 I like to wake up feeling a new man.

Jean Harlow, American film actress (1911–37). Quoted in John Robert Colombo, *Wit and Wisdom of the Moviemakers* (1979).

On Henry Kissinger:

12 Henry's idea of sex is to slow down to thirty miles an hour when he drops you off at the door.

Barbara Howar, American one-time companion of Kissinger. Quoted in Barbara Rowes, *The Book of Quotes* (1979).

To David Garrick:

1 I'll come no more behind your scenes, David; for the silk stockings and white bosoms of your actresses excite my amorous propensities.

(Dr) Samuel Johnson, English writer and lexicographer (1709–84). In James Boswell's *The Life of Samuel Johnson* (1791) – for 1750. In Appendix G to the *Life,* John Wilkes recalls this statement in the form: '... the silk stockings and white bosoms of your actresses do make my genitals to quiver.'

2 Sexual intercourse began
In nineteen sixty-three
(Which was rather late for me) –
Between the end of the *Chatterley* ban
And the Beatles' first LP.

Philip Larkin, English poet (1922–85). *High Windows,* 'Annus Mirabilis' (1974).

On reading Lady Chatterley's Lover *by D.H. Lawrence:*

3 Surely the sex business isn't worth all this damned fuss? I've met only a handful of people who cared a biscuit for it.

T.E. Lawrence, English soldier and writer (1888–1935). Quoted in Christopher Hassall, *Edward Marsh* (1959).

4 My own belief is that there is hardly anyone whose sexual life, if it were broadcast, would not fill the whole world at large with surprise and horror.

W. Somerset Maugham, English writer (1874–1965). Quoted in *The Penguin Dictionary of Modern Humorous Quotations,* ed. Fred Metcalf (1987).

On sex in the age of AIDS:

5 These days, you fuck someone, your arm drops off.

Bette Midler, American actress (1944–). Quoted in *The Independent* (12 November 1988).

6 Sex is one of the nine reasons for re-incarnation ... The other eight are unimportant.

Henry Miller, American writer (1891–1980). Quoted in *The Penguin Dictionary of Modern Humorous Quotations,* ed. Fred Metcalf (1987).

7 I am always looking for meaningful one-night stands.

Dudley Moore, English musician and actor (1935–). In 1982. Quoted in Bob Chieger, *Was It Good For You Too?* (1983).

8 It has to be admitted that we English have sex on the brain, which is a very unsatisfactory place to have it.

Malcolm Muggeridge, English writer and broadcaster (1903–90). 'Ideas and Men', in *The New York Times* (11 October 1964).

9 Sex – the poor man's polo.

Clifford Odets, American playwright (1906–63). Quoted in *The Penguin Dictionary of Modern Humorous Quotations,* ed. Fred Metcalf (1987).

10 You were born with your legs apart. They'll send you to the grave in a Y-shaped coffin.

Joe Orton, English playwright (1933–67). *What the Butler Saw,* Act 1 (1967).

11 Cannes is where you lie on the beach and stare at the stars – or vice versa.

Rex Reed, American critic (1938–). Quoted in *Playboy* Magazine (*c.* 1980).

12 As I grow older and older
And totter towards the tomb,
I find that I care less and less
Who goes to bed with whom.

Dorothy L. Sayers, English novelist (1893–1957). 'That's Why I Never Read Modern Novels', quoted in Janet Hitchman, *Such a Strange Lady* (1975).

When asked whether the first person he had experienced sex with was male or female:

13 I was far too polite to ask.

Gore Vidal, American novelist, playwright and critic (1925–). Remark in interview (*c.* 1971), quoted in *Forum* (1987).

1 This sublime age reduces everything to its quintessence; all periphrases and expletives are so much in disuse, that I suppose soon the only way to making love will be to say 'Lie down'.

Horace Walpole (4th Earl of Orford), English writer (1717–97). Letter to H.S. Conway (23 October 1778).

2 All this fuss about sleeping together. For physical pleasure I'd sooner go to the dentist any day.

Evelyn Waugh, English novelist (1903–66). *Vile Bodies*, Chap. 6 (1930).

3 I caught a thin bat's squeak of sexuality, inaudible to any but me.

Evelyn Waugh. *Brideshead Revisited*, Chap. 3 (1945).

Sexes

4 This world consists of men, women and Herveys.

Lady Mary Wortley Montagu, English writer (1689–1762). Quoted by Lord Wharncliffe in *The Letters and Works of Lady Mary Wortley Montagu* (1837). Alluding to John Harvey, Baron Hervey of Ickworth (1696–1743), with whom she had some sort of literary friendship. According to the *Dictionary of National Biography*, Hervey had loose morals, was 'effeminate in appearance as well as in habits', but had eight children. Because of epilepsy, he existed on a diet of ass's milk and biscuits, and coloured his chalk-white face with rouge. Pope attacked him in *The Dunciad* as 'Lord Fanny'.

Sexual orientation

On being asked by Ian McKellen if he was homosexual:

5 [That's] a bit like asking a man crawling across the Sahara whether he would prefer Perrier or Malvern Water.

Alan Bennett, English playwright and actor (1934–). Quoted in *The Observer* (12 June 1988).

6 He was into animal husbandry – until they caught him at it.

Tom Lehrer, American songwriter and entertainer (1928–). On record album *An Evening Wasted with Tom Lehrer* (1953).

When asked, 'Why have you come to America, Mr Thomas?':

7 In pursuit of my life-long quest for naked women in wet mackintoshes.

Dylan Thomas, Welsh poet (1914–53). Quoted in Constantine Fitzgibbon, *Dylan Thomas*, Chap. 8 (1965). Another version from the *Evening Standard* (2 May 1995): 'Asked by the hack pack the reason for his visit to [New York] his succinct reply was: "Naked women in wet macs".'

8 I'm all for bringing back the birch, but only between consenting adults in private.

Gore Vidal, American novelist, playwright and critic (1925–). Interviewed on TV by David Frost and quoted in *The Sunday Times* Magazine (16 September 1973). This refers to an edition of Rediffusion TV's *The Frost Programme* in 1966. In his memoirs (1993), Frost suggests that the line was, 'Yes, I am in favour of birching, but only between consenting adults', and that it was not actually uttered on air: 'In the hospitality room after the programme Gore Vidal was kicking himself for having thought of one rejoinder ten minutes too late.'

See also HOMOSEXUALITY.

Shakespeare, William

ENGLISH PLAYWRIGHT AND POET (1564–1616)

9 There is no mystery about the authorship of Shakespeare's plays. They were not written by Shakespeare at all. They were all written by a total stranger, about whom all we know is that he was called Shakespeare.

Alphonse Allais, French humorist (1854–1905). Attributed by Miles Kington (editor of *The World of Alphonse Allais*), from memory, in 1998. Jerome K. Jerome in *My Life and Times* (1926) took up the theme: 'The Bacon stunt was in full swing about the same time, and again it was [Israel] Zangwill who discovered that Shakespeare's plays had all been written by another gentleman of the same name.'

Edwin Moore suggested that something akin to the observation was to be found in H.N. Gibson, *The Shakespeare Claimants* (1962). I'm not sure that it is. However, in outlining the Baconian theory, Gibson mentions the story that when Bacon felt his supposed authorship of *Richard II* was suspected by Queen Elizabeth I, 'to disarm her suspicions he hastily looked around for someone to use as cover. He had adopted the name "William Shakespeare" as a pseudonym for his secret works, and finding by an extraordinary coincidence an actor with a similar sounding name [*Shakespere*], he engaged him for the purpose.' Barking mad all this, of course, but there you are.

But if anyone can be credited with popularizing this idea, it may have been Robert Manson Myers in *From Beowulf to Virginia Woolf* (1954), a sort of literary *1066 And All That*: 'Until recently the so-called Shakespeare–Bacon Controversy remained a mute question, but it has finally been established, after the perusal of a rare manuscript found in a bottle, that Shakespeare never wrote Shakespeare's plays. Actually they were written by another man of the same name.'

Ultimately, the application to Shakespeare may derive from what a schoolboy may once have solemnly written: 'Homer's writings are Homer's Essays Virgil the Aeneid and Paradise Lost [*sic*] some people say that these poems were not written by Homer but by another man of the same name.' In his essay 'English As She is Taught' in *Century* Magazine (April 1887), Mark Twain largely quotes from howlers, among which is this one, collected by Caroline B. Le Row. Later in the year, the essay appeared as the introduction to Le Row's book entitled *English as She Is Taught*. From there the observation seems to have become well-known, though not as a schoolboy howler. Compare the subsequent Aldous Huxley mention in *Those Barren Leaves*, Chap. 5 (1925): 'It's like the question of the authorship of the Iliad … The author of that poem is either Homer, or if not Homer, somebody else of the same name.'

Cry at first performance of a new Scottish tragedy:

1 Whaur's yer Wullie Shakespeare noo?

Anonymous (audience member). Quoted in David Erskine Baker, *Biographia Dramatica* (1812 edn) – in the form, 'Weel, lads; what think you of Wully Shakespeare now?' In 1756, this (or something like it) was the reported cry at the first Edinburgh (or possibly first London) performance of a tragedy called *Douglas* by the Scottish playwright John Home. There were those who thought the play marked a resurgence of Scots drama and that it was far superior to anything Shakespeare had written.

2 Shake was a dramatist of note;
He lived by writing things to quote.

Henry Cuyler Bunner, American humorous writer (1855–96). 'Shake, Mulleary and Go-ethe'. Quoted in *The Treasury of Humorous Quotations*, eds Evan Esar & Nicolas Bentley (1951).

3 Was there ever such stuff as great part of Shakespeare? Only one must not say so! But what think you? – what? – Is there not sad stuff? what? – what?

George III, British King (1738–1820). Quoted in Fanny Burney, *Diary and Letters of Madame d'Arblay*, Vol. 2 (1842) – entry for 19 December 1785. Remark made to Burney.

4 The remarkable thing about Shakespeare is that he is really very good – in spite of all the people who say he is very good.

Robert Graves, English poet (1895–1985). Quoted in *The Observer* (6 December 1964).

5 Playing Shakespeare is so tiring. You never get a chance to sit down, unless you're a king.

Josephine Hull, American actress (1886–1957). Quoted in *Time* Magazine (16 November 1953). Compare what Laura, a part-time actress, says in the film *The Solid Gold Cadillac* (US 1956): 'Do you like Shakespeare? … Take my advice, don't play it. It's so tiring. They never let you sit down unless you're a king.' Screenwriter: Abe Burrows (based on a play by George S. Kaufman and Howard Teichmann). Spoken by Judy Holliday (Laura Partridge) to Paul Douglas (Edward L. McKeever).

6 I remember the players have often mentioned it as an honour to Shakespeare that in his writing (whatsoever he penned) he never blotted out a line. My answer hath been 'Would he had blotted out a thousand.' Which they thought a malevolent speech.

Ben Jonson, English playwright and poet (1572–1637). *Timber, or Discoveries made upon Men and Matter* (1641).

7 I thought I'd begin with a sonnet by Shakespeare but then I thought why should I? He never reads any of mine.

Spike Milligan, Irish entertainer and writer (1918–). Remark at Poetry and Jazz concert, Hampstead Town Hall (1961), quoted in *The Oxford Dictionary of Literary Quotations*, ed. Peter Kemp (1997). In fact, Milligan used this format about all and sundry. On *The Last Goon Show of All* (1972), he applies it to Cole Porter.

1 Brush up your Shakespeare,
Start quoting him now.
Brush up your Shakespeare
And the women you will wow …
If she says your behaviour is heinous
Kick her right in the 'Coriolanus'.
Brush up your Shakespeare
And they'll all kowtow.

Cole Porter, American composer and lyricist (1891–1964). Song, 'Brush Up Your Shakespeare' from *Kiss Me Kate* (1948).

2 The Devil can quote Shakespeare for his own purposes.

Bernard Shaw, Irish playwright and critic (1856–1950). Quoted in *The Treasury of Humorous Quotations*, eds Evan Esar & Nicolas Bentley (1951).

3 With the single exception of Homer, there is no eminent writer, not even Sir Walter Scott, whom I can despise so entirely as I despise Shakespear when I measure my mind against his … It would positively be a relief to me to dig him up and throw stones at him.

Bernard Shaw. *Dramatic Opinions and Essays*, Vol. 2 (1907).

Contribution to the debate as to whether Shakespeare or Bacon wrote Shakespeare's plays:

4 Beerbohm Tree should play Hamlet. Then they should dig up both Shakespeare and Bacon and see which one had turned over.

Bernard Shaw. Quoted on BBC Radio *Quote … Unquote* (1985), but almost certainly a misattribution. In fact, it was W.S. Gilbert who wrote in a letter: 'Do you know how they are going to decide the Shakespeare–Bacon dispute? They are going to dig up Shakespeare and dig up Bacon; they are going to set their coffins side by side, and they are going to get Tree to recite Hamlet to them. And the one who turns in his coffin will be the author of the play' – quoted in Hesketh Pearson, *Lives of the Wits* (1962). Alexander Woollcott wrote in *While Rome Burns* (1934) of a bad actor's performance of Hamlet: 'Scholars should have kept watch beside the graves of Shakespeare and Bacon to see which one of them turned over.'

5 Now we sit through Shakespeare in order to recognise the quotations.

Orson Welles, American film director, writer and actor (1915–85). Quoted in *The Treasury of Humorous Quotations*, eds Evan Esar & Nicolas Bentley (1951). In Herbert V. Prochnow, Snr & Jnr, *A Treasury of Humorous Quotations* (1969), the remark is ascribed to Oscar Wilde. Easy to confuse the two, of course …

See also BOSTON 62:7.

Shaw, (George) Bernard

IRISH PLAYWRIGHT AND CRITIC (1856–1950)

6 When you were quite a little boy somebody ought to have said 'hush' just once!

Mrs Patrick Campbell, English actress (1865–1940). Letter to Shaw (1 November 1912).

On the grounds that he was a vegetarian:

7 You are a terrible man, Mr Shaw. One day you'll eat a beefsteak and then God help all women.

Mrs Patrick Campbell. Quoted in Arnold Bennett, *The Journals* (18 June 1919). Alexander Woollcott, *While Rome Burns* (1934), has a slightly different version: 'Some day you'll eat a pork chop, Joey, and then God help all women.'

8 Shaw's relations with women have always been gallant, coy even. The number he has surrendered to physically have been few – perhaps not half a dozen in all – the first man to have cut a swathe through the theatre and left it strewn with virgins.

Frank Harris, Irish writer and journalist (1856–1931). *Bernard Shaw* (1931).

9 That Bernadette Shaw? What a chatterbox! Nags away from asshole to breakfast-time

but never sees what's staring her in the face.

Peter Nichols, English playwright (1927–). *Privates on Parade*, Act 1 Sc. 5 (1977).

1 He writes like a Pakistani who has learned English when he was twelve years old in order to become a chartered accountant.

John Osborne, English playwright (1929–94). Letter to *The Guardian* (undated).

2 Bernard Shaw is an excellent man; he has not an enemy in the world, and none of his friends like him.

Oscar Wilde, Irish playwright, poet and wit (1854–1900). Shaw himself quoted this remark in *Sixteen Self Sketches* (1949). An early appearance occurs in Irvin S. Cobb, *A Laugh a Day Keeps the Doctor Away* (1921), in which some-one says of Shaw, 'He's in a fair way to make himself a lot of enemies.' 'Well,' replies Wilde, 'as yet he hasn't become prominent enough to have any enemies. But none of his friends like him.' In fact, long before, Shaw himself had quoted the remark – in a letter to Archibald Henderson (22 February 1911). Hesketh Pearson in *The Life of Oscar Wilde* (1946) wonders whether Shaw did not adapt to himself the following from *Dorian Gray*: 'Ernest Harrowden, one of those middle-aged mediocrities so common in London clubs, who have no enemies, but are thoroughly disliked by their friends.'

3 The way Bernard Shaw believes in himself is very refreshing in these atheistic days when so many people believe in no God at all.

Israel Zangwill, English writer (1864–1926). Quoted in *The Treasury of Humorous Quotations*, eds Evan Esar & Nicolas Bentley (1951).

Shepherd's pie

4 Shepherd's pie and peppered
With genuine shepherds on top.

Stephen Sondheim, American songwriter (1930–). *Sweeney Todd* (1979). Compare this cartoon caption from *Punch* (30 January 1918): '*Bobbie (who is eating shepherd's pie, and has been told not to be wasteful)* "Mummie, *must* I eat this? It's such a *partickerly* nasty bit of the shepherd?"'

Shooting

5 When I take a gun in hand, the safest place for a pheasant is just opposite the muzzle.

(Revd) Sydney Smith, English clergyman, essayist and wit (1771–1845). Quoted in *The Treasury of Humorous Quotations*, eds Evan Esar & Nicolas Bentley (1951).

Shopkeepers

6 *Customer*:
D'you serve lobsters?
Fishmonger:
Yessir, we serve anybody.

Charles Graves, English cartoonist. Caption to cartoon in *Punch* (11 January 1933).

7 All English shop assistants are Miltonists. A Miltonist firmly believes that 'they also serve who only stand and wait.'

George Mikes, Hungarian-born humorist (1912–87). *How To Be Inimitable* (1960).

Show business

8 Every crowd has a silver lining.

P.T. Barnum, American showman (1810–91). Quoted in *The Treasury of Humorous Quotations*, eds Evan Esar & Nicolas Bentley (1951).

9 Why must the show go on?
It can't be all that indispensable,
To me it really isn't sensible
On the whole
To play a leading role
While fighting through tears you can't
control.

(Sir) Noël Coward, English entertainer and writer (1899–1973). Song, 'Why Must the Show Go On?' (1954).

10 Show business is dog eat dog. It's worse than dog eat dog. It's dog doesn't return other dog's phone calls.

Line from film *Crimes and Misdemeanors* (US 1989). Screenwriter: Woody Allen. Spoken by Alan Alda (Lester).

Stopped at the stage door and asked if he was 'with the show':

1 Well, let's say I'm not against it ...

George S. Kaufman, American playwright (1889–1961). Quoted in Scott Meredith, *George S. Kaufman and the Algonquin Round Table* (1974).

2 All you need to be a success in show business is about seventeen good breaks.

Walter Matthau, American actor (1920–2000). Quoted by Peter Jones on BBC Radio *Quote ... Unquote* (5 April 1978).

Sick verse

3 Willie, with a thirst for gore,
Nailed the baby to the door.
Mother said, with humor quaint,
'Willie dear, don't spoil the paint.'

Anonymous. One of the 'Little Willie' quatrains that started around 1900 and ran into the 1930s. Anonymous they seem to be, though Alan Dundes in *Cracking Jokes: Studies of Sick Humor Cycles & Stereotypes* (1987) notes the similarity to:

4 Billy, in one of his nice new sashes,
Fell in the fire and was burnt to ashes;
Now, although the room grows chilly,
I haven't the heart to poke poor Billy.

Harry Graham, English writer and journalist (1874–1936). *Ruthless Rhymes for Heartless Homes*, 'Tender-Heartedness' (1899).

Sickness

When told that his boss, whom he disliked, was off sick:

5 Nothing trivial, I trust?

Irvin S. Cobb, American humorist and writer (1876–1944). Quoted in Ralph L. Marquard, *Jokes and Anecdotes* (1977). When Cobb was a reporter on the New York *World*, he had to work under Charles E. Chapin, whom he found to be a difficult boss. Arriving at the office one day, Cobb was told that Chapin was off sick and made this inquiry. Recalled earlier as 'I've just learned about his illness; let's hope it's nothing trivial' in *The Treasury of Humorous Quotations*, eds Evan Esar & Nicolas Bentley (1951). In Ulick O'Connor's *Oliver St John Gogarty* (1964), John Pentland Mahaffy is quoted as having said of the illness of Traill who had beaten him for the Provostship of Trinity College Dublin (in 1904): 'Nothing trivial, I hope.' Compare the caption to an L. Raven-Hill cartoon in *Punch* (19 September 1896): Doctor. 'Now, what did your father and mother die of?' Applicant. 'Well, Sir, I can't say as I do 'xactly remember; but 'twarn't nothing serious!'

Signs *See* NOTICES AND SIGNS

Silence

6 You ain't learnin' nothing when you're talking.

Anonymous (saying). It hung in the office of Lyndon B. Johnson during his years in the US Senate.

Referring to the taciturn German, Helmuth Graf von Moltke (1800–91):

7 The soldier ... of today is ... a quiet, grave man ... perhaps like Count Moltke, 'silent in seven languages'.

Walter Bagehot, English constitutional historian (1826–77). *The English Constitution*, 'Checks and Balances' (1867). 'Moltke' is, in consequence, a name given to a taciturn, unsmiling person. Michael Wharton ('Peter Simple' columnist in *The Daily Telegraph*) described in *The Missing Will* (1984) how he was so nicknamed, as a child, by his German grandfather after the famous general, 'who seldom spoke and was said to have smiled only twice in his life'. Geoffrey Madan's *Notebooks* (1981) recorded that these two occasions were 'once when his mother-in-law died, and once when a certain fortress was declared to be impregnable'.

8 Silence is the unbearable repartee.

G.K. Chesterton, English poet, novelist and critic (1874–1936). Quoted in *The Treasury of Humorous Quotations*, eds Evan Esar & Nicolas Bentley (1951).

9 Silence – a conversation with an Englishman.

Heinrich Heine, German poet and critic (1797–1856). Quoted in the same collection as above.

10 A man is known by the silence he keeps.

Oliver Herford, American humorist (1863–1935). Quoted in the same collection as above.

1 Blessed are they who have nothing to say, and who cannot be persuaded to say it.

James Russell Lowell, American poet (1819–91). Quoted in the same collection as above.

2 If you keep your mouth shut you will never put your foot in it.

Austin O'Malley, American oculist and humorist (1858–1932). Quoted in the same collection as above.

3 Better to keep your mouth shut and appear stupid than to open it and remove all doubt.

Mark Twain, American writer (1835–1910). Quoted in *The Sayings of Mark Twain*, ed. James Munson (1992). Has also been ascribed to Abraham Lincoln in *The Golden Book* (November 1931). *Compare* FOOLS 174:11.

Similes

4 I mean – your eyes – your eyes, they shine like the pants of a blue serge suit.

Line from film *The Cocoanuts* (US 1929). Screenwriters: George S. Kaufman, Morrie Ryskind. Spoken by Groucho Marx (Hammer) to Margaret Dumont (Mrs Potter).

5 Like using a guillotine to cure dandruff.

Clare Boothe Luce, American writer and diplomat (1903–87). Quoted in Laurence J. Peter, *Quotations for Our Time* (1977).

6 Boswell, on his way back from Corsica, was asked to escort Mlle. Levasseur to England where Rousseau was taking refuge. This was like asking a rabbit to escort a lettuce.

Frank Muir, English writer (1920–98). *The Frank Muir Book*, 'Literature' (1976). Referring to Thérèse Levasseur, Rousseau's servant and mistress. Boswell did indeed make good use of the opportunity his chargeship afforded – thirteen times, in fact.

7 I wish I could shimmy like my sister Kate,
She shivers like the jelly on a plate.

Armand J. Piron and Peter Bocage, American songwriters (1888–1943) and (1887–1967). Song, 'I Wish I Could Shimmy Like My Sister Kate' (1919).

8 I turned to Aunt Agatha, whose demeanour was now rather like that of one who, picking daisies on the railway, has just caught the down express in the small of the back.

(Sir) P(elham) G. Wodehouse English-born novelist and lyricist (1881–1975). *The Inimitable Jeeves*, Chap. 4 (1923).

9 Jeeves coughed one soft, low, gentle cough like a sheep with a blade of grass stuck in its throat, and then stood gazing serenely at the landscape.

(Sir) P(elham) G. Wodehouse. In the same book, Chap. 13.

Sin

10 Dearly beloved brethren: is it not a sin
When we peel potatoes, to throw away the skin?
For the skin feeds the pigs, and the pigs feed us;
Dearly beloved brethren, is it not thus?

Anonymous. Rhyme known by the 1930s and probably by the 1880s. Quoted by Iona & Peter Opie in *The Oxford Dictionary of Nursery Rhymes* (1952), as forming a sequel to the finger-game which is accompanied by the rhyme: 'Here is the church, and here is the steeple; / Open the door and here are the people, / Here is the parson going upstairs, / And here he is a-saying his prayers.' At this point, 'school-children then make the parson deliver an oration on potato peeling.'

When asked what a clergyman had said in his sermon on sin:

11 He was against it.

Calvin Coolidge, American Republican President (1872–1933). Quoted in John Hiram McKee, *Coolidge Wit and Wisdom* (1933). Mrs Coolidge said it was just the sort of thing he would have said. Coolidge himself said it would be funnier if it were true.

12 To err is human – but it feels divine.

Mae West, American vaudeville and film actress (1893–1980). Quoted in *The Penguin Dictionary of Modern Humorous Quotations*, ed. Fred Metcalf (1987).

1 The only difference between a saint and a sinner is that every saint has a past, and every sinner has a future.

Oscar Wilde, Irish playwright, poet and wit (1854–1900). *A Woman of No Importance*, Act 3 (1893).

Sincerity

2 A little sincerity is a dangerous thing, and a great deal of it is absolutely fatal.

Oscar Wilde, Irish playwright, poet and wit (1854–1900). 'The Critic As Artist' (1890).

3 What people call insincerity is simply a method by which we can multiply our personalities.

Oscar Wilde. In the same work as above.

Singers

4 Swans sing before they die; 'twere no bad thing
Should certain persons die before they sing.

Samuel Taylor Coleridge, English poet and writer (1772–1834). 'On a Volunteer Singer' (1834).

5 A German singer! I should as soon expect to get pleasure from the neighing of my horse.

Frederick the Great, Prussian King (1712–86). Quoted in *The Treasury of Humorous Quotations*, eds Evan Esar & Nicolas Bentley (1951).

Of the singing voice of his writing partner Denis Norden:

6 Like a heron with its leg caught.

Frank Muir, English writer, broadcaster and humorist (1920–98). Quoted by Katharine Whitehorn on BBC Radio *Quote … Unquote* (3 March 1992).

7 She's so original, so far-reaching. Of course, we've all *dreamed* of reviving the *castrati*; but it's needed Hilda to take the first practical steps towards making them a reality … There may be difficulties. Singers are very conservative, as you know.

Henry Reed, English poet and playwright (1914–86). Radio play, *The Private Life of Hilda Tablet* (24 May 1954). The Duchess of Mulset on Hilda Tablet.

Of Barry Manilow's singing voice:

8 [It sounds like] a bluebottle caught in the curtains.

Jean Rook, English journalist (1931–91). Quoted in Lynn Barber, *Mostly Men* (1991).

Of Anna Neagle in the stage show The Glorious Days *(1953):*

9 She sings, shaking her voice at the audience like a tiny fist.

Kenneth Tynan, English critic (1927–80). Review collected in *Curtains* (1961). The show was a historical pageant for Coronation year. Neagle reprised roles in it that she had already essayed in the cinema – Nell Gwyn, Queen Victoria and so on.

Singing

10 What is too silly to be said can be sung.

Pierre Augustin Caron de Beaumarchais, French playwright (1732–99). Quoted by Philip Larkin in letter to Barbara Pym (22 July 1975). The original is likely to be this from Beaumarchais's *Le Barbier de Séville*, Act 1 Scene 2 (1775): '*Aujourd'hui ce que ne vaut pas la peine d'être dit, on le chante* [Today, what's not worth saying is sung instead].'

11 I have never met a member of a choir who was depressed.

Yehudi Menuhin (Lord Menuhin), American-born British violinist (1916–99). Quoted in *The Observer* Magazine (26 April 1992).

12 If all the world were music,
Our hearts would often long
For one sweet strain of silence,
To break the endless song.

Henry Van Dyke, American essayist and poet (1852–1933). This is the middle verse of 'If All the Skies'.

Situations

1 The situation in Germany is serious but not hopeless; the situation in Austria is hopeless but not serious.

Anonymous. Described as 'an Austrian proverb collected by Franklin Pierce Adams' in A. Andrews, *Quotations for Speakers and Writers* (1969). Hence, *Situation Hopeless But Not Serious*, the title of a film (US 1965).

2 When John Donne married Anne, the daughter of Sir George More, without her father's knowledge or consent, the couple were thrown out of Sir George's house and Donne lost his job. Taking refuge in a house at Pyrford, Surrey, Donne scratched on a pane of glass:

John Donne
An Donne
Undone.

John Donne, English poet and divine (1572–1631). Quoted in Sir James Prior, *Life of Edmond Malone* … (1860). The words were still visible at the house in 1749. However, in Izaak Walton, *The Life of Dr Donne* (1640), the lines are said to come from a letter from Donne to his wife.

Sitwell, (Dame) Edith

ENGLISH POET (1887–1964)

3 She's genuinely bogus.

Christopher Hassall, English writer (1912–63). Quoted in *The Penguin Dictionary of Modern Quotations*, J.M. & M.J. Cohen (1971).

Sixties, The

4 If you can remember the sixties you weren't really there.

Anonymous. Quoted as said by 'a guy from Jefferson Airplane' in *Today* (2 June 1987); 'The best quote about the period came from a leading American hippie – now, I think, something huge on Wall Street – who said: "If you can remember the sixties, you weren't there." There's a lot of truth in that, though I think he's pointing at certain kinds of substance' – *The Independent* (11 March 1989). This hippie might well have been Jerry Rubin.

Size

Two women were discussing a man, when one of them said:

5 God, he was so small, he had turn-ups in his underpants.

Anonymous. Quoted by Julian Mitchell on BBC Radio *Quote … Unquote* (5 January 1982).

6 Robert Benchley and Dorothy Parker once had to share a small office at *The New Yorker*. When asked precisely how small it was, he said, 'One cubic foot less of space and it would have constituted adultery.'

Robert Benchley, American humorist (1889–1945). Quoted in R. Drennan, *Wit's End* (1973).

On his film Titanic*:*

7 Does this prove once and for all that size does matter?

James Cameron, Canadian-born film director (1954–). Quoted in *The Observer* (25 January 1998).

On the physically unimpressive cast of David Storey's rugby play The Changing Room*:*

8 No, fifteen acorns is hardly worth the price of admission.

(Sir) Noël Coward, English entertainer and writer (1899–1973). Quoted by Kenneth Tynan in *The New York Times* (1970). *See also* NAKEDNESS 299:4.

9 Well, that covers a lot of ground. Say, you cover a lot of ground yourself. You better beat it. I hear they're going to tear you down and put up an office building where you're standing. You can leave in a taxi. If you can't get a taxi you can leave in a huff. If that's too soon, you can leave in a minute and a huff.

Lines from film *Duck Soup* (US 1933). Screenwriters: Bert Kalmar, Harry Ruby, Arthur Sheekman, Nat Perrin. Spoken by Groucho Marx (Rufus T. Firefly) to Margaret Dumont (Mrs Teasdale).

10 Cinemas and theatres are always bigger inside than they are outside.

Miles Kington, English humorist (1941–). In *The Independent* (29 March 1989). One of his 'Albanian proverbs'.

Slang

1 Slang is a language that rolls up its sleeves, spits on its hands and goes to work.

Carl Sandburg, American poet (1878–1967). In *The New York Times* (13 February 1959). But quoted earlier in the film *Ball of Fire* (US 1941).

Sleaze

2 I got fed up with all the sex and sleaze and backhanders of rock'n'roll so I went into politics.

Tony Blair, British Labour Prime Minister (1953–). Quoted in *The Observer*, 'Sayings of the Week' (13 November 1994).

Sleep

3 Insomniacs don't sleep because they worry about it, and they worry about it because they don't sleep.

Franklin P. Adams, American journalist, poet and humorist (1881–1960). Quoted in *The Treasury of Humorous Quotations*, eds Evan Esar & Nicolas Bentley (1951).

4 Up, sluggards, and waste no life; in the grave will be sleeping enough.

Benjamin Franklin, American politician and scientist (1706–90). *Poor Richard's Almanack* (September 1741) – a work in which Franklin often revised already existing sayings.

5 How do people go to sleep? … I might repeat to myself, slowly and soothingly, a list of quotations from minds profound; if I can remember any of the damn things.

Dorothy Parker, American writer (1893–1967). *Here Lies*, 'The Little Hours' (1939).

6 I am writing to you at two o'clock in the morning, having heard of a clergyman who brought himself down from twenty-six to sixteen stone in six months, by lessening his sleep. I shall be so thin when you see me, that you may trundle me about like a mop.

(Revd) Sydney Smith, English clergyman, essayist and wit (1771–1845). Letter (1818), quoted in *The Sayings of Sydney Smith*, ed. Alan Bell (1993).

7 Don't go to sleep, so many people die there.

Mark Twain, American writer (1835–1910). Quoted in *The Sayings of Mark Twain*, ed. James Munson (1992).

See also SNORING.

Slogans

8 Be alert. Your country needs lerts.

Anonymous (graffito). Included in my book *Graffiti Lives, OK* (1979).

9 It's not whether you win or lose. It's how you look playing the game.

Anonymous (T-shirt slogan). Quoted on BBC Radio *Quote … Unquote* (25 July 1987).

10 Bowen's Beer Makes You Drunk.

(Sir) Kingsley Amis, English novelist, poet and critic (1922–95). *I Like It Here* (1958). Barnet Bowen suggests that this is the only type of beer slogan that would really appeal.

Slough, England

11 Come, friendly bombs, and fall on Slough. It isn't fit for humans now.

(Sir) John Betjeman, English poet (1906–84). 'Slough' (1937). In a reply to a correspondent (9 January 1967), published in *John Betjeman Letters: Volume Two 1951 to 1984* (1995), the poet explained the precise nature and cause of his aversion: 'The town of Slough was not, when those verses were written, such a congestion as it is now and I was most certainly not thinking of it but of the Trading Estate … which had originated in a dump that now stretches practically from Reading to London … The chain stores were only then just beginning to deface the High Street, but already the world of "executives" with little moustaches, smooth cars and smooth manners and ruthless methods was planted in my mind along the fronts of those Trading Estate factories.'

Smells

1 If you don't eat garlic, they'll never smell it on your breath.

Sholom Aleichem, Ukrainian-born writer (1859–1916). 'Eternal Life'.

2 How can you stop a dead fish from smelling? Cut off its nose.

Fred Allen, American comedian (1894–1956). *Much Ado About Me* (1956). Compare the traditional music-hall joke: 'My dog has no nose.' 'How does he smell?' 'Awful.'

3 I am the Bishop of Bath and Wells,
I wear the most delicious smells –
Lime at matins, cologne at dusk,
And late at night a trace of musk,
For eau-de-cologne should never trespass
On a well-conducted vespers.

Miles Kington, English humorist (1941–). From poem written *c.* 1975, first published in *The 'Quote ... Unquote' Newsletter* (January 1999).

4 No smells were ever equal to Scotch smells. It is the School of Physic; walk the streets, and you would imagine that every medical man had been administering cathartics to every man, woman and child in the town. Yet the place [Edinburgh] is uncommonly beautiful, and I am in a constant balance between admiration and trepidation: Taste guides my eye, where e'er new beauties spread. While prudence whispers, 'Look before you tread.'

(Revd) Sydney Smith, English clergyman, essayist and wit (1771–1845). Letter (1798), quoted in *The Sayings of Sydney Smith*, ed. Alan Bell (1993).

5 [I] never smelt anything like it. It was an insurrection in a gasometer.

Mark Twain, American writer (1835–1910). *A Connecticut Yankee at King Arthur's Court*, Chap. 20 (1889).

Smiles

6 It takes seventy-two muscles to frown, but only thirteen to smile.

Anonymous. Quoted in Celia Haddon, *The Yearbook of Comfort and Joy* (1991).

Of Sir Robert Peel:

7 [The Right Honourable Gentleman's smile is] like the silver plate on a coffin.

John Philpot Curran, Irish judge (1750–1817). Quoted by Daniel O'Connell in the House of Commons (26 February 1835). Also mistakenly ascribed to Benjamin Disraeli.

8 When you wake up in the morning, smile – and get it over with.

W.C. Fields, American comedian (1879–1946). Attributed line or remark.

Smoking

9 Cancer cures smoking.

Anonymous (graffito). Quoted in *Encyclopedia of Graffiti*, eds Reisner & Wechsler (1974).

10 A straw with a light on one end and a fool on the other, that's what he called a cigarette.

Anonymous. Quoted in Virgil Scott, *The Dead Tree Gives No Shelter*.

11 Thomas Beecham was travelling in the no-smoking carriage of a train when a woman passenger lit a cigarette with the words, 'You won't object if I smoke?' To which Beecham replied, 'Certainly not – and you won't object if I'm sick.' It was in the days when the rail-ways were still privately owned. 'I don't think you know who I am,' the woman angrily pointed out. 'I am one of the directors' wives.' To which Beecham riposted: 'Madam, if you were the director's *only* wife, I should still be sick.'

(Sir) Thomas Beecham, English conductor (1879–1961). *Pass the Port* (1976) ascribes these two barbs to Beecham, but a story about 'Harty-Tarty', the Marquess of Hartington (1833–1908) who became the 8th Duke of

Devonshire, is told in Anita Leslie, *Edwardians in Love* (1972): 'When a man entering his railway carriage put the question, "Do you mind if I smoke a cigar?" Hartington serenely answered: "No, my dear sir, provided you don't mind me being sick".'

Non-smoker to smoker in restaurant:

1 Thank you for not smoking: I hope my food isn't interfering with your cigar.

Mel Calman, English cartoonist (1931–94). Caption to cartoon. Quoted in Nigel Rees, *Best Behaviour* (1992). This may be just an old joke. In 1998, David Rees told me of a venerable exchange that goes: 'Do you mind if I eat while you smoke?' 'Not so long as I can still hear the orchestra.'

2 And a woman is only a woman, but a good Cigar is a Smoke.

Rudyard Kipling, English poet and novelist (1865–1936). Poem, 'The Betrothed' (1886). Lest Kipling, as usual, take more blame than he should for what one of his characters says – now seen as an outrageous example of male chauvinism – it is worth pointing out that the man in question (the poem is in the first person) is choosing between his cigars and his betrothed, a woman called Maggie. The situation arose in an actual breach of promise case, *c.* 1885, in which the woman had said to the man: 'You must choose between me and your cigar.' The poem ends: 'Light me another Cuba – I hold to my first-sworn vows. / If Maggie will have no rival, I'll have no Maggie for Spouse!'

3 A good cigar is as great a comfort to a man as a good cry to a woman.

Edward Bulwer-Lytton (1st Baron Lytton), English novelist and politician (1803–73). Quoted in *The Treasury of Humorous Quotations*, eds Evan Esar & Nicolas Bentley (1951).

4 What this country needs is a really good five-cent cigar.

Thomas R. Marshall, American Democratic Vice President (1854–1925). Said to John Crockett, the chief clerk of the Senate, during a tedious debate in 1917 and quoted in the *New York Tribune* (4 January 1920). Another version is that it was said to Henry M. Rose, assistant Secretary of State. The remark is mentioned in a caption in *Recollections of Thomas R. Marshall* (1925). At about that time, 'Owls' cigars cost six cents and 'White Owls' seven cents. Subsequently, Will Rogers is said to have commented: 'Our country has plenty of good five-cent cigars, but the trouble is they charge fifteen cents for them.'

5 I kissed my first woman and smoked my first cigarette on the same day; I have never had time for tobacco since.

Arturo Toscanini, Italian-born operatic and orchestral conductor (1867–1957). Quoted in Herbert V. Prochnow, Snr & Jnr, *A Treasury of Humorous Quotations* (1969).

6 It has always been my rule never to smoke when asleep and never to refrain when awake.

Mark Twain, American writer (1835–1910). Quoted in *The Treasury of Humorous Quotations*, eds Evan Esar & Nicolas Bentley (1951).

7 To cease smoking is the easiest thing I ever did; I ought to know because I've done it a thousand times.

Mark Twain. Quoted in the same collection as above.

8 More than one cigar at a time is excessive smoking.

Mark Twain. Quoted in *The Home Book of Humorous Quotations*, ed. A.K. Adams (1969).

9 A cigarette is the perfect type of a perfect pleasure. It is exquisite, and it leaves one unsatisfied. What more can one want?

Oscar Wilde, Irish playwright, poet and wit (1854–1900). *The Portrait of Dorian Gray*, Chap. 6 (1891).

See also STATISTICS and TOBACCO.

Smoothness

Of a certain Conservative MP:

10 With him, one just has to learn to take the smooth with the smooth.

Anonymous. Quoted by Susan Hill on BBC Radio *Quote ... Unquote* (29 August 1980).

Snails

1 'The snail,' says the Hindoo, 'sees nothing but his own shell, and thinks it the grandest palace in the universe.'

(Revd) Sydney Smith, English clergyman, essayist and wit (1771–1845). *Peter Plymley Letters*, No. 10 (1807–8).

Snobbery

2 Sapper, Buchan, Dornford Yates, practitioners in that school of Snobbery with Violence that runs like a thread of good-class tweed through twentieth-century literature.

Alan Bennett, English playwright and actor (1934–). *Forty Years On*, Act 2 (1969). In his preface to the published text of *Forty Years On and Other Plays* (1991), Bennett states that he thought he *had* invented the phrase 'snobbery with violence', but was then told it had been used before: it was the title of a pamphlet by the New Zealand eccentric, Count Potocki de Montalk. *Snobbery with Violence: A Poet in Gaol* was published in 1932.

Snoring

3 Laugh and the world laughs with you;
Snore and you sleep alone.

Anthony Burgess, English novelist (1917–93). *Inside Mr Enderby* (1963) – though he did not claim this as original despite its appearance as such in *The Penguin Dictionary of Modern Quotations*, eds J.M. & M.J. Cohen (1971). Based on the earlier anonymous parody of Ella Wheeler Cox, 'Solitude' (1883) ending, '... Weep and you sleep alone'. This last was quoted by the architectural historian James Lees-Milne and recorded by him in his diary on 6 June 1945 (published in *Prophesying Peace*, 1977).

Sobriety

4 I drink little, miss my glass often, put water in my wine, and go away before the rest, which I take to be a good receipt for sobriety. Let us put it into rhyme, and so make a proverb:

Drink little at a time:
Put water with your wine;
Miss your glass when you can;
And go off the first man.

Jonathan Swift, Anglo-Irish writer and clergyman (1667–1745). *Journal to Stella* (1768) – for 21 April 1711.

Socialism and Socialists

Of Paul Johnson, socialist journalist, before his swing to the right:

5 He eats more oysters than the dukes.

Anonymous waiter at London club. Quoted in the 'William Hickey' column of the *Daily Express* (*c.* 1977).

6 Why is it always the intelligent people who are socialists?

Alan Bennett, English playwright and actor (1934–). *Forty Years On*, Act 2 (1969).

7 There is nothing in Socialism that a little age or a little money will not cure.

Will Durant, American writer (1885–1981). Quoted in my *Dictionary of Twentieth Century Quotations* (1987).

8 The trouble with Socialism is that it would take up too many evenings.

Oscar Wilde, Irish playwright, poet and wit (1854–1900). Usually so attributed, but untraced.

Society

9 Mrs So-and-So, a well-known figure in Café. (Pause). Nescafé Society.

(Sir) Noël Coward, English entertainer and writer (1899–1973). Quoted in Alec Guinness, *Blessings in Disguise* (1985). Remark made to Guinness in Jamaica prior to the filming of *Our Man In Havana* (UK 1959).

10 The security of society lies in custom and unconscious instinct, and the basis of the stability of society, as a healthy organism, is the complete absence of any intelligence among its members.

Oscar Wilde, Irish playwright, poet and wit (1854–1900). 'The Critic As Artist' (1890).

11 She tried to found a salon, but only succeeded in opening a restaurant.

Oscar Wilde. *The Picture of Dorian Gray*, Chap. 1 (1891).

1 To get into the best society nowadays, one has either to feed people, amuse people, or shock people.

Oscar Wilde. *A Woman of No Importance*, Act 3 (1893).

2 *Gerald:*
I suppose society is wonderfully delightful!
Lord Illingworth:
To be in it is merely a bore. But to be out of it simply a tragedy.

Oscar Wilde. In the same act of the same play.

3 Never speak disrespectfully of Society … Only people who can't get it into it do that.

Oscar Wilde. *The Importance of Being Earnest*, Act 3 (1895).

4 Other people are quite dreadful. The only possible society is oneself.

Oscar Wilde. *An Ideal Husband*, Act 3 (1895).

Soixante-neuf

5 As for that topsy-turvy tangle known as soixante-neuf, personally I have always felt it to be madly confusing, like trying to pat your head and rub your stomach at the same time.

Helen Lawrenson, American writer. Quoted in *Esquire* (1977) and then in Bob Chleger, *Was It Good For You Too?* (1983).

Songwriting

In answer to the question, 'Which comes first, the music or the words?':

6 First comes the phone call.

Sammy Cahn, American lyricist and librettist (1913–93). Attributed remark. Most songwriters have become expert at heading this question off. Ira Gershwin is supposed to have replied: 'What usually comes first is the contract' – quoted at his death in *The Guardian* (18 August 1983). To Cole Porter is ascribed the similar view: 'All the inspiration I ever needed was a phone call from the producer.' According to the musical entertainment *Cole* (1974), however, when Porter (who wrote both music and lyrics) was asked which came first, he answered, 'Yes!' Having designated it a cliché in my book *The Gift of the Gab* (1985), I found myself interviewing one of the breed on a television show a short while afterwards, and was dreadfully conscious of the clanger I might drop. And so I asked him, 'Which comes first, the words or the lyrics?'

7 Yes, we have no bananas,
We have no bananas today.

Irving Cohn, American songwriter (1898–1961). Song 'Yes, We Have No Bananas' (1923), to music by Frank Silver (1892–1960). According to Ian Whitcomb in *After the Ball* (1972), the title line came from a cartoon strip by Tad Dorgan and not, as the composers were wont to claim, from a Greek fruit-store owner on Long Island. Alternatively, it was a saying picked up by US troops in the Philippines from a Greek pedlar. In Britain, Elders & Fyffes, the banana importers, embraced the song and distributed 10,000 hands of bananas to music-sellers with the slogan: 'Yes! we have no bananas! On sale here'.

8 You write a hit the same way you write a flop.

Alan Jay Lerner, American songwriter and playwright (1918–86). Attributed in my *Dictionary of Twentieth Century Quotations* (1987).

9 I claim that it ['Yes, We Have No Bananas'] is the greatest document that has been penned in the entire history of American literature.

Will Rogers, American humorist (1879–1935). *The Illiterate Digest* (1924).

Soul

10 Said Descartes, 'I extoll
Myself because I have a soul
And beasts do not.' (Of course
He *had* to put Descartes before the horse.)

Clifton Fadiman, American writer (1904–). 'Theological'.

Soviet Union

11 I cannot forecast to you the action of Russia. It is a riddle wrapped in a mystery inside an enigma.

(Sir) Winston S. Churchill, British Conservative Prime Minister and writer (1874–1965). Radio broadcast (1 October 1939). Not, as might appear, a general reflection on the Russian character but a specific response to the Soviet occupation of East Poland, in league with Germany, on 18 September.

1 Miles of cornfields, and ballet in the evening.

Alan Hackney, English comedy writer (1924–). *Private Life* (1958) – filmed as *I'm All Right, Jack* (UK, 1959).

2 Gaiety is the most outstanding feature of the Soviet Union.

Joseph Stalin, Soviet Communist leader (1879–1953). Quoted in *The Observer* (24 November 1935). This comment is said to have been made after Stalin had watched a display of folk dancing by collectivized farm workers to mark his birthday.

Space

3 There is just one thing I can promise you about the outer space program: your tax dollar will go farther.

Wernher von Braun, German-born American rocket scientist (1912–77). Quoted in Laurence J. Peter, *Quotations for Our Time* (1977).

4 To infinity and beyond.

Line from film *Toy Story* (US 1995). Screenwriters: Joss Whedon and others. Spoken by Tim Allen as the astronaut figure Buzz Lightyear. Also in *Toy Story 2* (2000). In the Preface to his book *To Infinity and Beyond: A Cultural History of the Infinite* (1987), Eli Maor states: 'I took the title *To Infinity and Beyond*, from a telescope manual that listed among the many virtues of the instrument the following: "The range of focus of your telescope is from fifteen feet to infinity and beyond".'

Spades

5 *Cecily*:
When I see a spade I call it a spade.
Gwendolen:
I am glad to say that I have never seen a spade.

Oscar Wilde, Irish playwright, poet and wit (1854–1900). *The Importance of Being Earnest*, Act 3 (1895).

Spam

6 I'm pink therefore I'm spam.

Anonymous (graffito). Contributed by J. O'Grady of Longford, Coventry, to Granada TV *Cabbages and Kings* (18 November 1979).

Speculation

7 October. This is one of the peculiarly dangerous months to speculate in stocks in. The others are July, January, September, April, November, May, March, June, December, August, and February.

Mark Twain, American writer (1835–1910). *Puddn'head Wilson* (1894).

8 There are two times in a man's life when he should not speculate: when he can afford it, and when he can't.

Mark Twain. *Following the Equator* (1897).

Speeches and speech-making

9 Accustomed as I am to public speaking, I know the futility of it.

Franklin P. Adams, American journalist, poet and humorist (1881–1960). Quoted in *The Treasury of Humorous Quotations*, eds Evan Esar & Nicolas Bentley (1951).

10 My dear friends – I will not call you ladies and gentlemen, since I know you too well.

Anonymous (curate addressing his congregation). Quoted in William Patten, *Among the Humorists* (c. 1909).

11 Speeches are like babies – easy to conceive but hard to deliver.

Aristotle, Greek philosopher (384–322 BC). Attributed remark.

12 Drawing on my fine command of language, I said nothing.

Robert Benchley, American humorist (1889–1945). Quoted in *The Treasury of Humorous Quotations*, eds Evan Esar & Nicolas Bentley (1951).

Speeches and speech-making

1 I do not object to people looking at their watches when I am speaking. But I strongly object when they start shaking them to make sure they are still going.

Norman Birkett (Lord Birkett), English barrister and judge (1883–1962). Quoted in *The Observer* (30 October 1960). However, in *Joyce Grenfell Requests the Pleasure* (1976), Grenfell writes: 'It made me think of my father's story of Edward Marsh, who said he didn't mind if anyone looked at his watch when he was lecturing, but he didn't much like it when they looked at it a second time and shook it to see if it was still going.' As Eddie Marsh died in 1953 and Joyce Grenfell's father died in 1954, there may be grounds for wondering if Birkett really originated the joke.

2 The head cannot take in more than the seat can endure.

(Sir) Winston S. Churchill, British Conservative Prime Minister and writer (1874–1965). Quoted in Jock Murray, *A Gentleman Publisher's Commonplace Book* (1996).

3 I have always been a bit shy of the really extemporary speech ever since I heard it said that an extemporary speech was not worth the paper it was written on.

(Sir) Winston S. Churchill. Speech in his constituency (18 November 1955).

4 I'm going to make a long speech because I've not had time to prepare a short one.

(Sir) Winston S. Churchill. Quoted by Anthony Montague Brown, his Private Secretary 1952–65, in a speech to the International Churchill Societies (25 September 1986).

Opening a Red Cross bazaar in Oxford:

5 Desperately accustomed as I am to public speaking …

(Sir) Noël Coward, English entertainer and writer (1899– 1973). Quoted in Dick Richards, *The Wit of Noël Coward* (1968).

6 Half the world is composed of people who have something to say and can't, and the other half who have nothing to say and keep on saying it.

Robert Frost, American poet (1874–1963). Quoted in *The Treasury of Humorous Quotations*, eds Evan Esar & Nicolas Bentley (1951).

Of Lord Derby:

7 When he rises to speak, he does not know what he is going to say. When he is speaking he does not know what he is saying, and when he sits down he does not know what he has said.

W.E. Gladstone, British Liberal Prime Minister (1809–98). Quoted in Kenneth Rose, *Superior Person* (1969). Compare Winston Churchill on Lord Charles Beresford: 'He is one of those orators of whom it was well said, 'Before they get up, they do not know what they are going to say; when they are speaking, they do not know what they are saying; and when they have sat down, they do not know what they have said' – speech, House of Commons (20 December 1912).

8 If you haven't struck oil in your first three minutes, *stop boring*!

George Jessel, American entertainer (1898–1981). *Dais Without End* (1969).

9 Why don't th' feller who says, 'I'm not a speechmaker', let it go at that instead o' givin' a demonstration!

Frank McKinney ('Kin') Hubbard, American humorist and caricaturist (1868–1930). *Abe Martin's Primer* (1914).

10 Of all substitutes, a substitute speaker is worst.

Frank McKinney ('Kin') Hubbard. Quoted in Herbert V. Prochnow, Snr & Jnr, *A Treasury of Humorous Quotations* (1969).

11 A speech is a solemn responsibility. The man who makes a bad thirty-minute speech to two hundred people wastes only a half-hour of his own time. But he wastes one hundred hours of the audience's time – more than four days – which should be a hanging offense.

Jenkin Lloyd Jones. Quoted in Laurence J. Peter, *Quotations for Our Time* (1977).

1 A speech is like a love affair. Any fool can start it, but to end it requires considerable skill.

Lord Mancroft, English writer (1914–87). Quoted in *Reader's Digest* (February 1967).

2 No man should presume to stand up and speak in public for longer than he can lie down and make love in private.

Godfrey Smith, English journalist (1926–). In his *Sunday Times* column, late 1990s. Modestly, but falsely, he attributed the saying to Chamfort or La Rochefoucauld, or someone like that.

3 We often say a speaker needs no introduction: what most of them need is a conclusion. In my view, an after-dinner speech – and I've experienced 40,000 of them – needs a good beginning, a good ending, and not much space in between.

Ivor Spencer, English President, Guild of Professional Toastmasters (1924–). Quoted in *The Observer*, 'Sayings of the Week' (24 November 1991).

4 It usually takes me more than three weeks to prepare a good impromptu speech.

Mark Twain, American writer (1835–1910). Quoted in *The Home Book of Humorous Quotations*, ed. A.K. Adams (1969).

5 There is but one pleasure in life equal to that of being called on to make an after-dinner speech, and that is not being called on to make one.

Charles Dudley Warner, American editor and writer (1829–1900). Quoted in *The Treasury of Humorous Quotations*, eds Evan Esar & Nicolas Bentley (1951).

6 [She] talks more and says less than anybody I ever met. She is made to be a public speaker.

Oscar Wilde, Irish playwright, poet and wit (1854–1900). *An Ideal Husband*, Act 2 (1895).

7 If I am to speak for ten minutes, I need a week for preparation; if fifteen minutes, three days; if half an hour, two days; if an hour, I am ready now.

Woodrow Wilson, American Democratic President (1856–1924). Quoted in Josephus Daniels, *The Wilson Era* (1946).

Speechlessness

8 *The Times* is speechless [over Irish Home Rule] and takes three columns to express its speechlessness.

(Sir) Winston S. Churchill, British Conservative Prime Minister and writer (1874–1965). Speech, Dundee (14 May 1908).

Spelling

9 A rose by any other name
As sweet would smell –
A rhododendron, by any other name,
Would be much easier to spell.

Anonymous. Quoted in my book *Quote ... Unquote* (1978).

10 My spelling is Wobbly. It's good spelling but it Wobbles. And letters get in the wrong places.

A.A. Milne, English writer (1882–1956). *Winnie-the-Pooh*, Chap. 6 (1926).

Spoonerisms

Announcing a hymn in New College Chapel (1879):

11 Kinquering congs their titles take.

(Revd) William Spooner, English clergyman and academic (1844–1930). Quoted in the Oxford *Echo* (4 May 1892).

12 Which of us has not felt in his heart a half-warmed fish?

(Revd) William Spooner. Quoted on BBC Radio *Quote ... Unquote* (15 June 1977). According to Willard R. Espy, *An Almanac of Words at Play* (1975), this had been ascribed to Spooner by Bergen Evans. This was being attributed simply to a 'don' by G.K. Chesterton in 'High-Brows and Humbugs' (in *Hearst's Magazine*, December 1913).

13 Sir, you have tasted two whole worms; you have hissed all my mystery lectures and been

caught fighting a liar in the quad; you will leave Oxford by the next town drain.

(Revd) William Spooner. Quoted in *The Oxford University What's What* (1948). Surely apocryphal.

1 Let us drink a toast to the queer old dean.

(Revd) William Spooner. Quoted in *Everyman's Dictionary of Quotations and Proverbs*, ed. D.C. Browning (1951).

The most remarkable sight in Egypt:

2 The Minx by Spoonlight.

(Revd) William Spooner. Quoted in Julian Huxley, *Memories* (1970).

Of a cat falling from a window:

3 It popped on its little drawers.

(Revd) William Spooner. Quoted in William Hayter, *Spooner* (1977).

4 Yes indeed, the Lord is a shoving leopard.

(Revd) William Spooner. Quoted in *Brewer's Dictionary of Phrase & Fable* (1989 edn).

5 Through a dark glassly …

(Revd) William Spooner. Quoted by James Laver, in conversation with the author (5 December 1969).

Introducing radio broadcast by President Herbert Hoover:

6 Ladies and gentlemen – the President of the United States, Hoobert Herver.

Harry Von Zell, American broadcaster and actor (1906–81). Quoted in *Current Biography* (1944).

Spring

7 In the spring a young man's fancy lightly turns to what he's been thinking about all winter.

Line from film *The Awful Truth* (US 1937). Screenwriter: Vina Delmar (from a play). Spoken by Cary Grant (Jerry Warriner). Compare exactly the same line spoken in *Mildred Pierce* (US 1945) by Zachary Scott (Monte Beragon).

Standards

8 Standards are always out of date. That is what makes them standards.

Alan Bennett, English playwright and actor (1934–). *Forty Years On*, Act 2 (1969).

Standing

9 There are seventy stanzas in the Uruguay national anthem, which fact may account for the Uruguay standing army.

Franklin P. Adams, American humorist (1881–1960). Quoted in *The Treasury of Humorous Quotations*, eds Evan Esar & Nicolas Bentley (1951).

Stars

Of the screenwriter's problems over the star system:

10 You can't make a 'Hamlet' without breaking a few egos.

William Goldman, American screenwriter and novelist (1931–). Quoted in *The Observer* (8 April 1984).

11 Being a star has made it possible for me to get insulted in places where the average Negro could never *hope* to go and get insulted.

Sammy Davis Jnr, American entertainer (1925–90). *Yes I Can* (1965).

On swimming film star Esther Williams:

12 Wet, she was a star – dry she ain't.

Joe Pasternak, Hungarian-born film producer (1901–91). Quoted (except for the last three words) in Leslie Halliwell, *The Filmgoer's Book of Quotes* (1973).

Statesmen

13 The first requirement of a statesman is that he be dull. This is not always easy to achieve.

Dean Acheson, American Democratic politician (1893–1971). Quoted in *The Observer* (8 March 1998).

Of David Steel, leader of the Liberal Party:

14 I say this in the utmost affection … he has passed from rising hope to elder statesman without any intervening period whatsoever.

Michael Foot, English journalist and Labour politician (1913–). Speech in the House of Commons (28 March 1979) – taken from a recording rather than *Hansard*. Foot, as Leader of the House, was ending the debate that resulted in the Labour Government's defeat on a motion of no confidence (and led to its General Election defeat the following month). The Liberals, led by the youngish David Steel, had until a few months previously been part of the 'Lib-Lab' pact that had helped keep Labour in office. The Liberals ended the pact in the autumn of 1978.

1 A politician is a person with whose politics you don't agree; if you agree with him he is a statesman.

David Lloyd George (1st Earl Lloyd George of Dwyfor), British Liberal Prime Minister (1863–1945). Speech at Central Hall, Westminster (2 July 1935).

2 A statesman is a successful politician who is dead.

Thomas B(rackett) Reed, American politician (1839–1902). In *c.* 1880. Quoted in Henry Cabot Lodge, *The Democracy of the Constitution* (1915). Reed was a member of the House of Representatives.

3 Statesmen think they make history; but history makes itself and drags the statesmen along.

Will Rogers, American humorist (1879–1935). Quoted in Alistair Cooke, *One Man's America* (1952).

4 A politician is a man who understands government, and it takes a politician to run a government. A statesman is a politician who's been dead ten or fifteen years.

Harry S. Truman, American Democratic President (1884–1972). In the *New York World Telegram and Sun* (12 April 1958).

Statisticians

5 A statistician is someone who is good with figures but who doesn't have the personality to become an accountant.

Anonymous. Known by 1994. Another version: 'An actuary is someone who is too boring to be an accountant.' Also: 'An actuary is someone who finds accountancy too exciting' – quoted by Richard Boston in *The Guardian* (20 July 1987). Compare: '[A] tax lawyer is a person who is good with numbers but does not have enough personality to be an accountant' – James D. Gordon III.

6 A statistician is a person who draws a mathematically precise line from an unwarranted assumption to a foregone conclusion.

Anonymous. Quoted in *The Guinness Dictionary of Jokes* (1995).

Statistics

7 *La statistique est la première des sciences inexactes* [Statistics is the foremost of the inexact sciences].

Edmond & Jules de Goncourt, French novelists (1822–96) and (1830–70). *Journal des Goncourts* (1888–96) – for 14 January 1861).

8 It is now proved beyond doubt that smoking is one of the leading causes of statistics.

Fletcher Knebel, American writer (1911–93). Quoted in *Reader's Digest* (December 1961).

9 There are lies, damn lies – and statistics.

Benjamin Disraeli (1st Earl of Beaconsfield), English politician and writer (1804–81). Although often attributed to Mark Twain – because it appears in his *Autobiography* (1924) – this should more properly be ascribed to Disraeli, as indeed Twain took trouble to do. On the other hand, the remark remains untraced among Disraeli's writings and sayings. It is one of the most frequently cited remarks. Comparable sayings: Dr Halliday Sutherland's autobiographical *A Time to Keep* (1934) has an account of Sir Henry Littlejohn, 'Police Surgeon, Medical Officer of Health and Professor of Forensic Medicine at the University [Edinburgh] … Sir Henry's class at 9 a.m. was always crowded, and he told us of the murder trials of the last century in which he had played his part. It was Lord Young [judge] who said, "There are four classes of witnesses – liars, damned liars, expert witnesses, and Sir Henry Littlejohn"'; 'There are lies, damned lies … and Fianna Fáil party political broadcasts' – Barry Desmond MEP, (Irish) Labour Party director of elections, in November 1992.

1 He uses statistics as a drunken man uses lamp-posts – for support rather than illumination.

Andrew Lang, Scottish poet and scholar (1844–1912). In 1910. Quoted in *The Treasury of Humorous Quotations*, eds Evan Esar & Nicolas Bentley (1951).

Statues

2 I had rather men should ask why no statue has been erected in my honour, than why one has.

Marcus Porcius Cato ('the Censor'), Roman politician (234–149 BC). Quoted in *The Treasury of Humorous Quotations*, eds Evan Esar & Nicolas Bentley (1951).

Stein, Gertrude

AMERICAN POET (1866–1936)

3 Gertrude Stein is the mama of dada.

Clifton Fadiman, American writer (1904–). *Party of One* (1955).

4 Miss Stein was a past master in making nothing happen very slowly.

Clifton Fadiman. In the same book.

See also FAMILIES 164:4.

Steps

5 Aunt Jane observed, the second time
She tumbled off the bus,
The step is short from the Sublime
To the ridiculous.

Harry Graham, English humorous poet and journalist (1874–1936). *Ruthless Rhymes for Heartless Homes*, 'Equanimity' (1899).

6 From the sublime to the ridiculous there is but one step.

Napoleon I, French Emperor (1769–1821). Nowadays most often used as a phrase without the last five words. Napoleon is said to have uttered on one occasion (probably to the Polish ambassador, De Pradt, after the retreat from Moscow in 1812): *'Du sublime au ridicule il n'y a qu'un pas.'* However, Thomas Paine had already written in *The Age of Reason* (1795): 'The sublime and the ridiculous are often so nearly related, that it is difficult to class them separately. One step above the sublime, makes the ridiculous; and one step above the ridiculous, makes the sublime again.' Indeed, the chances are that 'from the sublime to the ridiculous' may have been a standard turn of phrase in the late 18th century. 'Dante, Petrarch, Boccacio, Ariosto, make very sudden transitions from the sublime to the ridiculous' – Joseph Warton, *Essay on the Genius and Writings of Pope*, Vol. 2, 1772.

Stigma

7 Any stigma, as the old saying is, will serve to beat a dogma.

Philip Guedalla, English writer (1889–1944). *Outspoken Essays: First series*, 'Patriotism' (1923).

Strangers

8 Who's 'im, Bill?
A stranger!
'Eave 'arf a brick at 'im.

Anonymous (cartoonist). Caption to cartoon in *Punch*, Vol.26 (25 February 1854).

Streisand, Barbra

AMERICAN SINGER AND ACTRESS (1942–)

In the film What's Up, Doc?:

9 She's playing herself – and it's awfully soon for that.

Pauline Kael, American film critic (1919–). *Deeper into Movies*, 'Collaboration and Resistance' (1973).

10 I am a nice person. I care about my driver having lunch, you know …

Barbra Streisand. Quoted in *The Sunday Times*, 'Words of the Week' (1 April 1984).

Strength

On Lady Desborough:

11 She's as strong as an ox. She'll be turned into Bovril when she dies.

Margot Asquith (Countess of Oxford and Asquith) (1864–1945). Quoted by her stepdaughter Baroness Asquith in BBC TV programme *As I Remember* (30 April 1967).

1 My mother had given me this hint – she's a powerful woman, my mother – she can break a swan's wing with a blow of her nose.

Line from BBC TV series *Not Only ... But Also ...* (9 January 1965). Sketch 'The Ravens' written and performed by Peter Cook and Dudley Moore, with Cook as Sir Arthur Strebe-Grebeling.

Stroking

2 'Why are you stroking the shell?', said my father. 'Oh, to please the turtle.' 'Why, child, you might as well stroke the dome of St Paul's, to please the Dean and Chapter.'

(Revd) Sydney Smith, English clergyman, essayist and wit (1771–1845). Quoted in Lady Holland, *A Memoir of Sydney Smith* (1855).

Struggles

To the actor Victor Spinetti:

3 Ah, Victor, still struggling to keep your head below water?

Emlyn Williams, Welsh actor and playwright (1905–87). Quoted in Ned Sherrin, *Cutting Edge* (1984).

Students

4 Undergraduates owe their happiness chiefly to the consciousness that they are no longer at school. The nonsense which was knocked out of them at school is all put gently back at Oxford or Cambridge.

(Sir) Max Beerbohm, English writer and caricaturist (1872–1956). *More*, 'Going Back to School' (1899).

5 Some men are graduated from college *cum laude*, some are graduated *summa cum laude*, and some are graduated *mirabile dictu*.

William Howard Taft, American Republican President (1857–1930). Quoted in *The Treasury of Humorous Quotations*, eds Evan Esar & Nicolas Bentley (1951).

Stupidity

6 To call you stupid would be an insult to stupid people. I've known sheep that could outwit you. I've worn dresses with higher IQs. But you think you're an intellectual, don't you, ape?

Line from film *A Fish Called Wanda* (UK 1988). Screenwriters: John Cleese, Charles Crichton. Spoken by Jamie Lee Curtis (Wanda Gerschwitz) to Kevin Kline (Otto).

7 Genius may have its limitations, but stupidity is not thus handicapped.

Elbert Hubbard, American writer and editor (1856–1915). Quoted in *The Treasury of Humorous Quotations*, eds Evan Esar & Nicolas Bentley (1951).

Style, literary

8 I affected a combination of the styles of Macaulay and Gibbon, the staccato antithesis of the former, and the rolling sentences and genitival endings of the latter: and I stuck in a bit of my own from time to time.

(Sir) Winston S. Churchill, British Conservative Prime Minister and writer (1874–1965). Quoted in A *Treasury of Humorous Quotations* (1969).

9 As a general rule, run your pen through every other word you have written; you have no idea what vigour it will give your style.

(Revd) Sydney Smith, English clergyman, essayist and wit (1771–1845). Quoted in Lady Holland, *A Memoir of Sydney Smith* (1855).

10 Proper words in proper places, makes the true definition of a style.

Jonathan Swift, Anglo-Irish writer and clergyman (1667–1745). *Letter to a young gentleman lately entered into Holy Orders* (1720).

11 Feather-footed through the plashy fen passes the questing vole.

Evelyn Waugh, English novelist (1903–66). *Scoop*, Bk 1, Chap. 1 (1938). An example of the prose style of the countryman writer William Boot in his column 'Lush Places'.

12 In matters of grave importance, style, not sincerity, is the vital thing.

Oscar Wilde, Irish playwright, poet and wit (1854–1900).

The Importance of Being Earnest, Act 3 (1895). Earlier, in 'Phrases and Philosophies for the Use of the Young', in *The Chameleon* (December 1894).

Suburbs

On the city of Salisbury (now Harare) when capital of Rhodesia (now Zimbabwe):

1 All suburb and no urb.

Alan Coren, English humorist (1938–). Quoted in *The Sunday Times* Magazine (27 November 1977). Earlier, in *Punch* (11 November 1970), Coren had also written of Rhodesia, 'It is a suburb pretending to be a country.'

2 Los Angeles is seventy-two suburbs in search of a city.

James Gleason, American actor (1886–1959). Quoted in Leslie Halliwell, *The Filmgoer's Book of Quotes* (1973).

Subversion

Scrawled on an interminable US immigration questionnaire that had asked, 'Is it your intention to subvert the government of the United States?':

3 Sole purpose of visit!

Gilbert Harding, English radio and TV personality (1907–60). Quoted by Wallace Reyburn, *Gilbert Harding: A Candid Portrayal* (1978) – he sets the story in the American consulate in Toronto.

Success

4 Eighty per cent of success is showing up.

Woody Allen, American film actor, writer and director (1937–). Confirmed by Allen in remarks to William Safire in *The New York Times* Magazine (13 August 1989), though the percentage has been known to vary.

5 To Succeed –
Early to bed, early to rise,
Never get tight, and – advertise.

Anonymous (proverb). In *Life* Magazine, No. 833 (1898). Has also been ascribed to the American entrepreneur, Dr Scholl. Compare this much more recent caption to a *Punch* cartoon (13 January 1989): '[Father to son] Remember this: early to bed, early to rise, work like hell and computerize.'

6 On the door to success it says: push and pull.

Anonymous (Yiddish proverb). Quoted in Herbert V. Prochnow, Snr & Jnr, *A Treasury of Humorous Quotations* (1969).

7 The higher the monkey climbs, the more he shows his tail.

Anonymous (proverbial saying), though Montaigne, in his *Essais*, Bk 2, Chap. 17 (1580), ascribes to Chancelier François Olivier (1487–1560): *'Plus haut monte le singe, plus il montre son cul'.* Earlier, Wyclif's Bible had this gloss to Proverbs 3:35: 'The filthe of her foli aperith more, as the filthe of the hynd partis of an ape aperith more, whanne he stieth [climbs] on high.' Francis Bacon has 'He doth like the ape that the higher he clymbes the more he shows his ars', in *Promus*, No. 924 (about 1594). Discussed in *Notes and Queries* (1887). Applied to anyone in any profession who has achieved high rank, as for example in the version, 'The egotistical surgeon is like a monkey; the higher he climbs the more you see of his less attractive features.' On BBC Radio *Quote ... Unquote* (29 March 1994), John Oaksey recalled that his father, Geoffrey Lawrence (Lord Oaksey) (1880–1971) had said the same sort of thing about judges and other high-ups in the legal profession, drawing a parallel rather with orang-utangs.

8 If at first you don't succeed – failure may be your thing.

George Burns, American comedian (1896–1996). Attributed remark.

9 It takes twenty years to make an overnight success.

Eddie Cantor, American entertainer (1892–1964). Quoted in *The New York Times* Magazine (20 October 1963).

10 I have found some of the best reasons I ever had for remaining at the bottom simply by looking at the men at the top.

Frank Moore Colby, American writer (1865–1925). *Essays*, Vol. 2 (1926).

11 The critical laurels that had been so confidently prophesied for me in the Twenties never graced my brow, and I was forced throughout the Thirties to console myself

with the bitter palliative of commercial success – which I enjoyed very much indeed.

(Sir) Noël Coward, English entertainer and writer (1899–1973). *Play Parade*, Introduction to Vol. 4 (1954).

On becoming Prime Minister in 1868:

1 Yes, I have climbed to the top of the greasy pole.

Benjamin Disraeli (1st Earl of Beaconsfield), English politician and writer (1804–81). Quoted in Fraser, *Disraeli and His Day* (1891).

Referring to Ambrose Bierce:

2 Born in a log cabin, he defied Alger's law and did not become President.

Clifton Fadiman, American writer (1904–). *The Selected Writings of Clifton Fadiman*, 'Portrait of a Misanthrope' (1955).

3 If at first you don't succeed – you're fired.

Lew Grade (Lord Grade), Russian-born British media tycoon (1906–99). Or, at least, a Grade family motto, according to his nephew Michael Grade on BBC *Quote ... Unquote* (28 February 2000).

4 If at first you don't succeed – give up.

Benny Green, English writer and broadcaster (1927–98). Re-stated by him on BBC Radio *Quote ... Unquote* (8 June 1988).

5 A *succès d'estime* is a *succès* that runs out of steam.

George S. Kaufman, American playwright (1889–1961). Quoted in Michael Coveney, *Cats On a Chandelier*, Chap. 9 (1999).

6 There is an old motto that runs, 'If at first you don't succeed, try, try again.' This is nonsense. It ought to read – 'If at first you don't succeed, quit, quit at once.'

Stephen Leacock, Canadian economist and humorist (1869–1944). *Laugh With Leacock* (1930).

7 To succeed pre-eminently in English public life it is necessary to conform either to the popular image of a bookie or of a clergyman; Churchill being a perfect example of the former, Halifax of the latter.

Malcolm Muggeridge, English writer and broadcaster (1903–90). *The Infernal Grove* (1973). To James Callaghan (Lord Callaghan) has, however, been ascribed the view: 'Prime Ministers tend either to be bookmakers or bishops, and they take it in turn.'

8 Success smells like Brighton.

Laurence Olivier (Lord Olivier), English actor (1907–89). Quoted in *Peter Hall's Diaries* (1983) – in an entry for 1977. Unless it was a remark Olivier was fond of making, this quotation comes from a TV interview he gave to Kenneth Tynan in the BBC series *Great Acting* (26 February 1966). Talking of the tumultuous reception of his stage *Richard III* (1944), Olivier said: 'There was something in the atmosphere ... There is a phrase "the sweet smell of success" ... I have had two experiences like that and it just smells like Brighton and oyster bars and things like that.'

9 It is not enough to succeed. Others must fail.

Gore Vidal, American novelist, playwright and critic (1925–). This was quoted as 'the cynical maxim of a clever friend' by the (Revd) Gerard Irvine during his 'anti-panegyric' for Tom Driberg (Lord Bradwell) after a requiem mass in London on 7 December 1976. 'It's not enough that I should succeed – others should fail,' was attributed to David Merrick, the Broadway producer, in Barbara Rowes, *The Book of Quotes* (1979).

At the end of an American lecture tour:

10 A great success! I had two secretaries, one to answer my letters, the other to send locks of hair to my admirers. I have had to let them both go, poor fellows: one is in hospital with writer's cramp, and the other is quite bald.

Oscar Wilde, Irish playwright, poet and wit (1854–1900). Quoted in Frank Harris, *My Life and Loves* (1925).

Suicide

11 The strangest whim has seized me ... After all I think I will not hang myself today.

G.K. Chesterton, English poet, novelist and critic (1874–1936). 'A Ballade of Suicide' (1915). This short poem is about a suicide who finds reasons for putting off the deed. In *Lyrics on Several Occasions* (1959), Ira Gershwin notes that the title of his song *I Don't Think I'll Fall in Love Today* (written in 1928) was inspired by the second line.

On being told that a certain person he knew had just blown his brains out:

1 He must have been an incredibly good shot.

(Sir) Noël Coward, English entertainer and writer (1899–1973). Quoted in Dick Richards, *The Wit of Noël Coward* (1968). Some versions have it that it was Coward's accountant who had shot himself.

On the Labour Party's 1983 General Election manifesto:

2 The longest suicide note in history.

Gerald Kaufman, English Labour politician (1930–). Quoted in Denis Healey, *The Time of My Life* (1989). Kaufman was a member of the Labour Shadow Cabinet at the time.

3 Suicide is a belated acquiescence in the opinion of one's wife's relatives.

H.L. Mencken, American journalist and linguist (1880–1956). *A Mencken Chrestomathy* (1949).

4 Guns aren't lawful;
Nooses give;
Gas smells awful;
You might as well live.

Dorothy Parker, American writer (1893–1967). *Enough Rope*, 'Resumé' (1927). Hence, *You Might As Well Live*, title of a biography of Parker (1970) by John Keats.

Sullivan, Ed

AMERICAN JOURNALIST AND BROADCASTER (1902–74)

5 Ed Sullivan will be around as long as someone else has talent.

Fred Allen, American comedian (1894–1956). Quoted in Laurence J. Peter, *Quotations for Our Time* (1977).

Summer

6 An English summer – three fine days and a thunderstorm.

Anonymous (proverbial saying). Quoted in *The 'Quote ... Unquote' Newsletter* (January 1992). John Aiton's *Manual of Domestic Economy for Clergymen* (1842) has: 'Our [Scotch] summers are said to consist of 3 hot days and a thunder-storm', which would seem to suggest it is a saying by no means restricted to English summers. M.A. Denham, *A Collection of Proverbs ... relating to the Weather* (1846) has, rather, 'An English summer, two fine days and a thunderstorm.'

7 The English winter – ending in July, To recommence in August.

Lord Byron, English poet (1788–1824). *Don Juan*, Canto 13, St. 42 (1819–24).

8 Summer has set in with its usual severity.

Samuel Taylor Coleridge, English poet, critic and philosopher (1772–1834). Letter to Vincent Novello (dated 9 May 1826).

9 The coldest winter I ever spent was a summer in San Francisco.

Mark Twain, American writer (1835–1910). Quoted in *The Sayings of Mark Twain*, ed. James Munson (1992). The origin of this may lie in an 1879 letter in which Twain quoted another who, when asked if he had ever seen such a cold winter, replied, 'Yes. Last summer.' Twain added: 'I judge he spent his summer in Paris.'

Sunshine

10 Thank heavens, the sun has gone in, and I don't have to go out and enjoy it.

Logan Pearsall Smith, American writer (1865–1946). These are sometimes quoted as though they were Logan Pearsall Smith's last (dying) words – as in *A Dictionary of Famous Quotations*, ed. Robin Hyman (1962), for example. They are not, though the misunderstanding is understandable. They appear in 'Last Words' in his *All Trivia* (1933). Smith did not die until 1946 when, according to James Lees-Milne, *Caves of Ice* (1983), his actual last words were, 'I must telephone to the Pope-Hennesseys'.

Superiority

1 He was not brought by the stork; he was delivered by a man from the Audubon Society personally.

Fred Allen, American comedian (1894–1956). Quoted in *The Treasury of Humorous Quotations*, eds Evan Esar & Nicolas Bentley (1951).

When accused by a member of Parliament of harbouring a superiority complex:

2 Considering the company I keep in this place, that is hardly surprising.

(Sir) Robert Menzies, Australian Liberal Prime Minister (1894–1978). Quoted in *Time* Magazine (29 May 1978).

In reply to the comment 'Anyway, she's always very nice to her inferiors':

3 Where does she find them?

Dorothy Parker, American writer (1893–1967). Quoted in *The Lyttelton Hart-Davis Letters*, Vol. 1 (1978). Told sometimes as though referring to Clare Boothe Luce – as in Parker's obituary in *Publishers' Weekly* (19 June 1967). Compare how Boswell in his *Life of Johnson* (1791) – for 1770 – writes of Johnson: ' ... being told that [a certain tradesman's daughter] was remarkable for her humility and condescension to inferiours, he observed, that those were very laudable qualities, but it might not be so easy to discover who the lady's inferiours were.'

4 The only thing that sustains one through life is the consciousness of the immense inferiority of everybody else.

Oscar Wilde, Irish playwright, poet and wit (1854–1900). 'The Remarkable Rocket' (1888).

Support

5 Behind every great woman is a man telling her she's ignoring him.

Anonymous. Quoted in Nan Tucket, *The Dumb Men Joke Book*, Vol. 2 (1994).

6 The road to success is filled with women pushing their husbands along.

Lord (Thomas Robert) Dewar, British distiller (1864–1930). Quoted in Burton Stevenson, *The Home Book of Quotations* (1967).

7 Behind every man with pull is a woman with push.

Robert H. Felix, American academic (1904–). Address at seminar of Metropolitan College, St Louis University. Quoted in *St Louis Post-Dispatch* (23 November 1965).

8 Behind every successful man you'll find a woman who has nothing to wear.

L. Grant Glickman. Quoted in Laurence J. Peter, *Quotations for Our Time* (1977). Also attributed to James Stewart, the film actor (quoted in 1979).

9 Behind every successful man stands a surprised mother-in-law.

Hubert Humphrey, American Democratic Vice President (1911–78). Speech (1964). Quoted in *The Home Book of Humorous Quotations*, ed. A.K. Adams (1969). Also attributed to Brooks Hays in the form 'Back of every achievement is a proud wife and a surprised mother-in-law', in Herbert V. Prochnow, Snr & Jnr, *A Treasury of Humorous Quotations* (1969).

10 As usual there's a great woman behind every idiot.

John Lennon, English singer and songwriter (1940–80). Quoted in 1979.

11 We in the industry know that behind every successful screenwriter stands a woman. And behind her stands his wife.

Groucho Marx, American comedian (1895–1977). Quoted in 1977.

12 And behind every man who is a *failure* there's a woman, too!

John Ruge (untraced). Cartoon caption in *Playboy* (March 1967).

13 Behind every good man is a good woman – I mean an exhausted one.

Sarah, British Duchess of York (1959–). Speech (September 1987).

1 Every great man has a woman behind him … And every great woman has some man or other in front of her, tripping her up.

Dorothy L. Sayers, English novelist and playwright (1893–1957). In *Love All*, a little known-play that opened at the Torch Theatre, Knightsbridge, London (9 April 1940) and closed before the end of the month. Sayers herself had even earlier referred to it as an old saying in *Gaudy Night*, Chap. 3 (1935). Harriet Vane is talking to herself, musing on the problems of the great woman who must either die unwed or find a still greater man to marry her: 'Wherever you find a great man, you will find a great mother or a great wife standing behind him – or so they used to say. It would be interesting to know how many great women have had great fathers and husbands behind them.'

Sureness

2 I wish I was as cocksure of anything as Tom Macaulay is of everything.

2nd Viscount Melbourne (William Lamb), British Whig Prime Minister (1779–1848). Quoted in Lord Cowper's preface to *Lord Melbourne's Papers* (1889). Bennett Cerf, *Try and Stop Me* (1944) transfers this to Benjamin Disraeli on W.E. Gladstone in a parliamentary debate: 'I wish that I could be as sure of anything as my opponent is of everything.'

Survival

When asked what he had done in the Reign of Terror:

3 *J'ai vécu* [I lived = survived].

Emmanuel Joseph Sieyès, French prelate and revolutionary leader (1748–1836). The Abbé Sieyès played an important part in the French Revolution and then lapsed into 'philosophic silence'. He was asked this question in about 1795. Recorded by 1836.

Suspense

4 This suspense is terrible. I hope it will last.

Oscar Wilde, Irish playwright, poet and wit (1854–1900). *The Importance of Being Earnest*, Act 3 (1895).

Suspicions

5 I suspect everyone, and I suspect no one.

Line from film *The Pink Panther Strikes Again* (UK 1976). Screenwriters: Frank Waldman, Blake Edwards. Spoken by Peter Sellers (Inspector Clouseau).

6 *Eliza:*
My aunt died of influenza: so they said … But it's my belief (as how) they done the old woman in.

Bernard Shaw, Irish playwright and critic (1856–1950). *Pygmalion*, Act 3 (1914). The words 'as how' were inserted by Mrs Patrick Campbell in her performances as Eliza Doolittle and were also incorporated in the 1938 film.

Swans

7 What happened when Leda was seduced by that swan in classical mythology?
Well, for one thing, she got down in the dumps.

Anonymous. A version was quoted in BBC Radio *The Burkiss Way* c. 1979. Script by Andrew Marshall and David Renwick.

Swearing

8 Blasphemy is merely the comic verse of belief.

Brendan Behan, Irish playwright (1923–64). Quoted in *The New York Times* (1960).

9 When it comes down to pure ornamental cursing, the native American is gifted above the sons of man.

Mark Twain, American writer (1835–1910). *Roughing It*, Vol. 2 (1872).

Sweat

10 Here's a little proverb that you surely ought to know:
Horses sweat and men perspire, but ladies only glow.

Anonymous. Included in *More Comic and Curious Verse*, ed. J.M. Cohen (1956). It is listed as a nanny's reprimand in *Nanny Says* (1972) in the form: 'Horses sweat, gentlemen perspire, but ladies only gently glow.'

Switzerland

Of a beautiful maiden:

1 She's like Switzerland – beautiful but dumb.

Anonymous. Quoted in my book *A Year of Stings and Squelches* (1985).

2 I look upon Switzerland as an inferior sort of Scotland.

(Revd) Sydney Smith, English clergyman, essayist and wit (1771–1845). Letter to Lord Holland (1815).

3 You know what the fellow said – in Italy, for thirty years under the Borgias, they had warfare, terror, murder and bloodshed, but they produced Michelangelo, Leonardo da Vinci and the Renaissance. In Switzerland, they had brotherly love; they had five hundred years of democracy and peace – and what did that produce? The cuckoo clock.

Line from film *The Third Man* (UK 1949). Screenwriters: Graham Greene and Carol Reed. Spoken by Orson Welles (Harry Lime). It soon got around that Welles had added this speech to the basic script. Indeed, it appears only as a footnote in the published version. In a letter, dated 13 October 1977, Greene confirmed to me that it *had* been written by Welles: 'What happened was that during the shooting of *The Third Man* it was found necessary for the timing to insert another sentence and the speech you mention was put in by Orson Welles.'

Whether the idea was original to Welles is another matter. After all, he introduces the speech with, 'You know what the fellow said ... ' In James McNeill Whistler, *Mr Whistler's 'Ten O'Clock'* (1888), the text of a lecture he gave on art in 1885, he spoke of: 'The Swiss in their mountains ... What more worthy people! ... yet, the perverse and scornful [goddess, Art] will none of it, and the sons of patriots are left with the clock that turns the mill, and the sudden cuckoo, with difficulty restrained in its box! For this was Tell a hero! For this did Gessler die!'

In *This Is Orson Welles* (1993), Welles is quoted as saying: 'When the picture came out, the Swiss very nicely pointed out to me that they've never made any cuckoo clocks – they all come from the Schwarzwald in Bavaria!' Actually the Schwarzwald (Black Forest) is in Baden-Württemberg.

4 I don't like Switzerland: it has produced nothing but theologians and waiters.

Oscar Wilde, Irish playwright, poet and wit (1854–1900). In *The Letters of Oscar Wilde*, ed. Rupert Hart-Davis (1962) – for 20 March 1899.

Sympathy

5 My nose bleeds for you.

(Sir) Herbert Beerbohm Tree, English actor-manager (1853–1917). Quoted in Hesketh Pearson, *Beerbohm Tree* (1956).

T

Taciturnity

1 Women like silent men. They think they are listening.

Marcel Achard, French playwright (1899–1974). Quoted in *Quote* Magazine (4 November 1956).

2 If a man keep his trap shut, the world will beat a path to his door.

Franklin P. Adams, American journalist, poet and humorist (1881–1960). Quoted in *The Treasury of Humorous Quotations*, ed. Evan Esar & Nicolas Bentley (1951).

A woman sat down next to him at a dinner party and said, 'You must talk to me, Mr Coolidge. I made a bet with someone that I could get more than two words out of you.' Coolidge replied:

3 You lose.

Calvin Coolidge, American Republican President (1872–1933). Quoted in Gamaliel Bradford, *The Quick and the Dead* (1931).

When a girl said to Coolidge that her father had bet her she could not get more than two words out of him:

4 Poppa wins.

Calvin Coolidge. Quoted on BBC Radio *Quote ... Unquote* (7 June 1978).

5 If you don't say anything, you won't be called on to repeat it.

Calvin Coolidge. Quoted in *The Treasury of Humorous Quotations*, ed. Evan Esar & Nicolas Bentley (1951).

6 None preaches better than the ant, and she says nothing.

Benjamin Franklin, American politician and scientist (1706–90). *Poor Richard's Almanack* (July 1736) – a work in which Franklin often revised already existing sayings.

7 He knew the psychological moment when to say nothing.

Oscar Wilde, Irish playwright, poet and wit (1854–1900). *The Picture of Dorian Gray*, Chap. 2 (1891).

8 It was one of those ... parties where you cough twice before you speak, and then decide not to say it after all.

(Sir) P(elham) G. Wodehouse, English-born novelist and lyricist (1881–1975). *Carry on Jeeves*, 'The Aunt and the Sluggard' (1925).

Tact

9 Tact consists in knowing how far we may go too far.

Jean Cocteau, French poet and playwright (1889–1963). *Le Coq at l'Arlequin* (1918).

Taj Mahal

10 *Amanda:*

How *was* the Taj Mahal? ... And it didn't look like a biscuit box did it? I've always felt that it might.

(Sir) Noël Coward, English entertainer and writer (1899–1973). *Private Lives*. Act 1 (1930). In an *Observer* interview (1969), Coward himself stated that he had refused to view the Taj Mahal when staying round the corner: 'I'd seen it on biscuit boxes and didn't want to spoil the illusion.'

Talk and talkativeness

1 'The time has come,' the Walrus said,
'To talk of many things;
Of shoes – and ships – and sealing wax –
Of cabbages – and kings –
And why the sea is boiling hot –
And whether pigs have wings.'

Lewis Carroll, English writer (1832–98). *Through the Looking-Glass and What Alice Found There,* 'The Walrus and the Carpenter', Chap. 4 (1872).

2 You know, you haven't stopped talking since I came here. You must have been vaccinated with a phonograph needle.

Line from film *Duck Soup* (US 1933). Screenwriters: Bert Kalmar, Harry Ruby, Arthur Sheekman, Nat Perrin. Spoken by Groucho Marx (Rufus T. Firefly) to Margaret Dumont (Mrs Teasdale).

3 And 'tis remarkable, that they
Talk most who have the least to say.

Matthew Prior, English poet (1664–1721). *Alma; or the Progress of the Mind,* Canto 2 (1718).

4 There are few wild beasts more to be dreaded than a talking man having nothing to say.

Jonathan Swift, Anglo-Irish writer and clergyman (1667–1745). Quoted in *The Treasury of Humorous Quotations*, ed. Evan Esar & Nicolas Bentley (1951).

5 I like to do all the talking myself. It saves time and prevents arguments.

Oscar Wilde, Irish playwright, poet and wit (1854–1900). 'The Remarkable Rocket' (1888).

6 I like hearing myself talk. It is one of my greatest pleasures. I often have long conversations with myself, and I am so clever that sometimes I don't understand a single word of what I am saying.

Oscar Wilde. In the same work as above.

7 I seem to have heard that observation before ... It has all the vitality of error and all the tediousness of an old friend.

Oscar Wilde. 'The Critic As Artist' (1890).

8 If one could only teach the English how to talk and the Irish how to listen, society would be quite civilized.

Oscar Wilde. *An Ideal Husband*. Act 3 (1893).

9 It is very vulgar to talk like a dentist when one isn't a dentist. It produces a false impression.

Oscar Wilde. *The Importance of Being Earnest*, Act 1 (1895).

10 The only possible form of exercise is to talk, not to walk.

Oscar Wilde. Quoted in Alvin Redman, *The Epigrams of Oscar Wilde* (1952).

Tallness

Of Virginia Woolf:

11 Of all the honours that fell upon Virginia's head, none, I think, pleased her more than the *Evening Standard* Award for the Tallest Woman Writer of 1927, an award she took by a neck from Elizabeth Bowen ... She did stand head and shoulders above her contemporaries, and sometimes of course, much more so. Dylan Thomas for instance, a man of great literary stature, only came up to her waist. And sometimes not even to there.

Alan Bennett, English playwright and actor (1934–). *Forty Years On,* Act 2 (1968).

Of Aldous Huxley:

12 He was the tallest English author known to me. He was so tall (and thin, so that he seemed to stretch to infinity) that when, long ago, he lived in Hampstead, ribald little boys in that neighbourhood used to call out to him, 'Cold up there?'

Frank Swinnerton, English novelist and critic (1884–1982). *The Georgian Literary Scene* (1935).

Taste

1 Everyone to his taste, as the woman said when she kissed her cow.

Anonymous (proverbial saying). François Rabelais is said to have this in *Pantagruel* (*c.* 1532). Walter Scott, *Peveril of the Peak*, Chap. 7 (1823) has: '... as the dame said who kissed her cow.'

2 There's no accounting for tastes, as the woman said when somebody told her her son was wanted by the police.

Franklin Pierce Adams, American humorist (1881–1960). Quoted in *The Treasury of Humorous Quotations*, ed. Evan Esar & Nicolas Bentley (1951).

3 He has impeccable bad taste.

Otis Ferguson, American critic (1907–43). Attributed remark.

4 Nowhere probably is there more true feeling, and nowhere worse taste, than in a churchyard.

Benjamin Jowett, English academic (1817–93). Quoted in *The Treasury of Humorous Quotations*, ed. Evan Esar & Nicolas Bentley (1951).

5 What sight is sadder than the sight of a lady we admire admiring a nauseating picture.

Logan Pearsall Smith, American writer (1865–1946). *All Trivia* (1933).

6 I have the simplest tastes. I am always satisfied with the best.

Oscar Wilde, Irish playwright, poet and wit (1854–1900). Quoted in Edgar Saltus, *Oscar Wilde: An Idler's Impression* (1917).

Tautology

7 To create man was a fine and original idea; but to add the sheep was tautology.

Mark Twain, American writer (1835–1910). *Mark Twain's Notebook*, ed. A.B. Paine (1935).

Tax and taxation

8 He's spending a year dead for tax reasons.

Douglas Adams, English novelist (1952–2001). Attributed remark.

9 Count that day won when, turning on its axis, this earth imposes no additional taxes.

Franklin P. Adams, American journalist, poet and humorist (1881–1960). Quoted in *The Treasury of Humorous Quotations*, ed. Evan Esar & Nicolas Bentley (1951).

10 Another difference between death and taxes is that death is frequently painless.

Anonymous.

11 A person doesn't know how much he has to be thankful for until he has to pay taxes on it.

Anonymous. Quoted by Ann Landers.

12 If Patrick Henry thought that taxation without representation was bad, he should see how bad it is with representation.

Anonymous. Quoted in *The Old Farmer's Almanac*.

13 A citizen can hardly distinguish between a tax and a fine, except that the fine is generally much lighter.

G.K. Chesterton, English poet, novelist and critic (1874–1936). Attributed remark.

14 The art of taxation consists in plucking the goose as to obtain the largest possible amount of feathers with the smallest possible amount of hissing.

Jean-Baptiste Colbert, French politician (1619–83). Colbert was minister of finance to Louis XIV. Quoted in *H.L. Mencken's Dictionary of Quotations* (1942). Also attributed to Cardinal Mazarin, under whom Colbert served.

15 The avoidance of tax may be lawful, but it is not yet a virtue.

Lord Denning, English judge (1899–1999). Attributed remark.

1 The one thing that hurts more than paying an income tax is not having to pay an income tax.

Lord (Thomas Robert) Dewar, British distiller (1864–1930). Quoted in *The Treasury of Humorous Quotations*, ed. Evan Esar & Nicolas Bentley (1951).

2 The hardest thing in the world is to understand income tax.

Albert Einstein, German-born physicist (1879–1955). Attributed remark.

3 If you get up early, work late, and pay your taxes, you will get ahead - if you strike oil.

J. Paul Getty, American oil tycoon (1892–1976). Attributed remark.

4 We have long had death and taxes as the two standards of inevitability. But there are those who believe that death is the preferable of the two. 'At least,' as one man said, 'there's one advantage about death; it doesn't get worse every time Congress meets.'

Erwin N. Griswold, American lawyer (1904–). Attributed remark.

5 The avoidance of taxes is the only pursuit that still carries any reward.

John Maynard Keynes (Lord Keynes), English economist (1883–1946). Attributed remark.

6 On my income tax [form] 1040 it says 'Check this box if you are blind.' I wanted to put a check mark about three inches away.

Tom Lehrer, American songwriter and entertainer (1928–). Attributed remark.

7 [A tax loophole is] something that benefits the other guy. If it benefits you, it is tax reform.

Russell B. Long. Attributed remark.

8 Unquestionably, there is progress. The average American now pays out almost as much in taxes alone as he formerly got in wages.

H.L. Mencken, American journalist and linguist (1880–1956). Attributed remark.

9 Death and taxes and childbirth! There's never any convenient time for any of them!

Margaret Mitchell, American novelist (1900–49). *Gone With the Wind*, Chap. 38 (1936).

10 All money nowadays seems to be produced with a natural homing instinct for the Treasury.

Philip, Greek-born British prince and consort of Queen Elizabeth II (1921–). Quoted in *The Observer*, 'Sayings of the Week' (26 May 1963).

11 Next to being shot at and missed, nothing is quite as satisfying as an income tax refund.

F.J. Raymond. Attributed remark.

12 When everybody has got money they cut taxes, and when they're broke they [politicians] raise 'em. That's statesmanship of the highest order.

Will Rogers, American humorist (1879–1935). Attributed remark.

13 A government which robs Peter to pay Paul can always depend on the support of Paul.

Bernard Shaw, Irish playwright and critic (1856–1950). Attributed remark.

14 What is the difference between a taxidermist and a tax collector? The taxidermist takes only your skin.

Mark Twain, American writer (1835–1910). *Mark Twain's Notebook*, ed. A.B. Paine (1935).

Taxis

15 I have done almost every human activity inside a taxi which does not require main drainage.

Alan Brien, English journalist (1925–). In *Punch* (1972).

Tea

1 If I had known there was no Latin word for tea, I would have let the vulgar stuff alone.

Hilaire Belloc, French-born English poet and writer (1870–1953). Quoted in *The Frank Muir Book* (1976).

2 I like a nice cup of tea in the morning,
For to start the day, you see,
And at half-past eleven
Well, my idea of Heaven
Is a nice cup of tea:
I like a nice cup of tea with me dinner
And a nice cup of tea with me tea,
And when it's time for bed
There's a lot to be said
For a nice cup of tea.

(Sir) A(lan) P. Herbert, English writer and politician (1890–1971). Song, 'I Like a Nice Cup of Tea In the Morning', from revue *Home and Beauty* (1937).

3 English afternoon tea is an affront to luncheon and an insult to dinner.

Mark Twain, American writer (1835–1910). Quoted in *Everyone's Mark Twain*, ed. C.T. Harnsberger (1972).

Teachers

4 I've taught you all I know ... and now you know *nothing*!

Anonymous (teacher). However, Mrs B.J. Vines of St Annes-on-Sea quoted it as her husband's exasperated remark to a class when he was a school physics master and contributed this to BBC Radio *Quote ... Unquote* (1 August 1987).

5 He that teaches himself hath a fool for a master.

Benjamin Franklin, American politician and scientist (1706–90). Quoted in *The Treasury of Humorous Quotations*, ed. Evan Esar & Nicolas Bentley (1951).

6 A teacher is one who, in his youth, admires teachers.

H.L. Mencken, American journalist and linguist (1880–1956). Quoted in the same collection as above.

7 No teacher I of boys or smaller fry,
No teacher I of teachers, no, not I.
Mine was the distant aim, the longer reach,
To teach men how to teach men how to
  teach.

A.B. Ramsay, English writer (*fl.* 1930s/40s). 'Epitaph on a Syndic', *Frondes Salicis* (1935).

8 He who can, does. He who cannot, teaches.

Bernard Shaw, Irish playwright and critic (1856–1950). *Man and Superman*, 'Maxims for Revolutionists' (1903). Compare: '... And those who can't teach lecture on the sociology of education degrees' - anonymous (graffito). Quoted in *Graffiti 2* (1980), from Middlesex Polytechnic in 1979.

9 I see everyone who is incapable of learning has taken to teaching.

Oscar Wilde, Irish playwright, poet and wit (1854–1900). 'The Decay of Lying', in *Nineteenth Century* (January 1889).

Tebbit, Norman (Lord Tebbit)

ENGLISH CONSERVATIVE POLITICIAN (1931–)

10 Is it always his desire to give his imitation of a semi-house-trained polecat?

Michael Foot, English journalist and Labour politician (1913–). Speech, Ebbw Vale in 1983. He noted that he had said it first in the House of Commons 'a few years ago' – indeed, on 2 March 1978.

Teenagers

11 The invention of the teenager was a mistake. Once you identify a period of life in which people get to stay out late but don't have to pay taxes – naturally, no one wants to live any other way.

Judith Martin, American journalist (1938–). Attributed remark (writing as 'Miss Manners').

12 The best way to keep children home is to make the home atmosphere pleasant – and let the air out of the tires.

Dorothy Parker, American writer (1893–1967). Quoted in Laurence J. Peter, *Quotations for Our Time* (1977).

Teeth

1 She could eat an apple through a tennis racquet.

(Sir) Noël Coward, English entertainer and writer (1899–1973). *Come Into the Garden, Maud* (1966). Coward's inspiration for this line is apparent from a note in his diary for 10 December 1954: 'Lunched and dined with Darryl Zannuck who, David Niven wickedly said, is the only man who can eat an apple through a tennis racquet!' Compare: 'One of the sayings reported in the *Publications of the American Dialect Society* is that a girl was so buck-toothed that she could eat a pumpkin to the hollow through a crack in a board fence' – James N. Tidewell, quoted in Willard R. Espy, *An Almanac of Words at Play* (1975).

Telegrams

Telegram received by Sir Alec Douglas-Home:

2 TO HELL WITH YOU. OFFENSIVE LETTER FOLLOWS.

Anonymous. Quoted in William Safire, *Safire's Political Dictionary* (1978).

When Cantor heard that Norma Shearer, the actress wife of Irving Thalberg, had produced a son, he sent a telegram of the utmost point to the noted Jewish film producer:

3 CONGRATULATIONS ON YOUR LATEST PRODUCTION. AM SURE IT WILL LOOK BETTER AFTER IT'S BEEN CUT.

Eddie Cantor, American comedian, in vaudeville and films (1892–1964). Quoted by Max Wilk in *The Wit and Wisdom of Hollywood* (1972).

Telegram to Gertrude Lawrence on her marriage to Richard S. Aldrich:

4 Dear Mrs A., hooray hooray,
At last you are deflowered
On this as every other day
I love you. Noël Coward.

(Sir) Noël Coward, English entertainer and writer (1899–1973). Quoted in Sheridan Morley, *A Talent to Amuse* (1969).

First night cable of congratulations to Gertrude Lawrence:

5 A WARM HAND ON YOUR OPENING.

(Sir) Noël Coward. Quoted in *The Sayings of Noël Coward*, ed. Philip Hoare (1997).

Telegram to Cole Lesley after a visit to Turkey:

6 AM BACK FROM ISTANBUL WHERE I WAS KNOWN AS ENGLISH DELIGHT.

(Sir) Noël Coward. Quoted in Cole Lesley, *The Life of Noël Coward* (1976).

While ill in Italy, telegram to Cole Lesley:

7 HAVE MOVED HOTEL EXCELSIOR COUGHING MYSELF INTO A FIRENZE.

(Sir) Noël Coward. Quoted in the same book as above.

Telegram to Mrs Robert Sherwood, when delivered of a baby after a pregnancy that had been long and/or one that she had made much of:

8 GOOD WORK, MARY. WE ALL KNEW YOU HAD IT IN YOU.

Dorothy Parker, American writer (1893–1967). Quoted in Alexander Woollcott, *While Rome Burns* (1934).

Telegram to a couple who were marrying after living together:

9 WHAT'S NEW?

Dorothy Parker. Quoted in *The Sayings of Dorothy Parker*, ed. S. T. Brownlow (1992).

A Marquess of Salisbury once sent a telegram to his heir, Viscount Cranborne, at the family seat in Dorset:

10 CRANBORNE. CRANBORNE. ARRIVING 6.30 SALISBURY. SALISBURY.

Marquess of Salisbury (unidentified). Quoted in a letter to *The Times* (15 April 1985).

Telephones

11 I have often thanked God for the telephone.

G.K. Chesterton, English poet, novelist and critic (1874–1936). *What's Wrong With the World* (1910).

1 Never answer a telephone that rings before breakfast. It is sure to be one of three types of persons that is calling: a strange man in Minneapolis who has been up all night and is phoning collect; a salesman who wants to come over and demonstrate a new, patented combination dictaphone and music box that also cleans rugs; or a woman out of one's past.

James Thurber, American cartoonist and writer (1894–1961). *Lanterns and Lances* (1961).

Television

2 TV ... is our latest medium – we call it a medium because nothing's well done.

Goodman Ace, American writer (1899–1982). In letter (1954) to Groucho Marx, quoted in *The Groucho Letters* (1967). However, Leslie Halliwell, *The Filmgoer's Book of Quotes* (1973) ascribes, 'A medium, so called because it is neither rare nor well done' to Ernie Kovacs, the American entertainer (1919–62).

3 Television – a device that permits people who haven't anything to do to watch people who can't do anything.

Fred Allen, American comedian (1894–1956). Quoted in *The Home Book of Humorous Quotations*, ed. A.K. Adams (1969).

4 The bland leading the bland.

Anonymous. Quoted in Leslie Halliwell, *The Filmgoer's Book of Quotes* (1973). This probably alludes to 'Television is the bland leading the bland' which occurs in Murray Schumach, *The Face on the Cutting Room Floor* (1964).

5 Some television programmes are so much chewing gum for the eyes.

John Mason Brown, American critic (1900–69). In interview (28 July 1955) with James B. Simpson, in *Best Quotes of '54, '55, '56* (1957). This was not his own remark – he was, in fact, quoting a young friend of his son.

6 Television is more interesting than people. If it were not, we should have people standing in the corners of our rooms.

Alan Coren, English humorist (1938–). In *The Times*, quoted in *The Penguin Dictionary of Modern Quotations* (1980 edn).

7 Time has convinced me of one thing. Television is for appearing on, not for looking at.

(Sir) Noël Coward, English entertainer and writer (1899–1973). Interviewed on US TV *The Ed Murrow Show* (1956). Quoted in Wallace Raeburn, *Gilbert Harding* (1978).

8 Television is an invention that permits you to be entertained in your living room by people you wouldn't have in your home.

(Sir) David Frost, English broadcaster (1939–). On CBS TV, *David Frost Revue* (1971).

9 I have had my [TV] aerials removed – it's the moral equivalent of a prostate operation.

Malcolm Muggeridge, English writer and broadcaster (1903–90). Quoted in the *Radio Times* (April 1981).

Of TV chat shows:

10 The kind of show I do consists of two consenting adults performing unnatural acts in public.

Michael Parkinson, English broadcaster and journalist (1935–). Quoted in *Sunday Today*, 'Quotes of the Week' (29 March 1987).

11 Television? No good will come of this device. The word is half Greek and half Latin.

C.P. Scott, English editor (1846–1932). Quoted in *The Penguin Dictionary of Modern Quotations* (1971).

12 An audience doesn't know what it wants; it only knows when it sees it.

William G. Stewart, English TV producer and presenter (1935–). Quoted in *The Observer*, 'Sayings of the Week' (30 September 1990).

13 Never miss a chance to have sex or be on television.

Gore Vidal, American novelist, playwright and critic (1925–). Quoted in Bob Chieger, *Was It Good For You Too?* (1983).

1 Television is now so desperately hungry for material that they're scraping the top of the barrel.

Gore Vidal. In *Comment* (20 July 1955).

Temperance

On a dinner given by President Rutherford B. Hayes, who occupied the White House between 1877–81 and whose wife was a temperance advocate:

2 It was a brilliant affair; the water flowed like champagne.

William Maxwell Evarts, American lawyer and politician (1818–1901). Quoted in George F. Hoar, *Autobiography of Seventy Years* (1906).

Temptation

3 The only way to get rid of a temptation is to yield to it.

Oscar Wilde, Irish playwright, poet and wit (1854–1900). *The Picture of Dorian Gray*, Chap. 2 (1891).

4 I can resist everything except temptation.

Oscar Wilde. *Lady Windermere's Fan*, Act 1 (1892).

5 Fastidiousness is the ability to resist a temptation in the hope that a better one will come along.

Oscar Wilde, Irish playwright, poet and wit (1854–1900). Quoted in Herbert V. Prochnow, Snr & Jnr, *A Treasury of Humorous Quotations* (1969).

Texas

6 [Texas is] the place where there are the most cows and the least milk and the most rivers and the least water in them, and where you can look the furthest and see the least.

Anonymous. Quoted in *H. L. Mencken's Dictionary of Quotations* (1942).

A child asks a stranger where he comes from, whereupon his father rebukes him gently:

7 Never do that, son. If a man's from Texas, he'll tell you. If he's not, why embarrass him by asking.

Anonymous. Quoted in John Gunther, *Inside U.S.A.* (1947). Roy Hattersley reworked this on BBC Radio *Quote ... Unquote* (27 October 1984) as though said by Sydney Smith to the French Ambassador. 'Never asks a man if he comes from Yorkshire. If he does, he'll already have told you. If he does not, why humiliate him?'

8 If I owned Texas and Hell, I would rent out Texas and live in Hell.

Philip Henry Sheridan, American general (1831–88). Remark in officers' mess, Fort Clark, Texas (1855).

Thatcher, Margaret (Baroness Thatcher)

BRITISH CONSERVATIVE PRIME MINISTER (1925–)

9 She cannot see an institution without hitting it with her handbag.

(Sir) Julian Critchley, English Conservative politician (1930–2000). In *The Times* (21 June 1982).

10 Prima donna inter pares.

(Sir) Julian Critchley. Interviewed in *The Guardian* (5 September 1987).

11 Mrs Thatcher is doing for monetarism what the Boston Strangler did for door-to-door salesmen.

Denis Healey (Lord Healey), English Labour politician (1917–). Speech, House of Commons (15 December 1979). It may be instructive to note, however, what happened to this one by way of subsequent use and attribution. From *Today* (24 May 1987): 'Liberal David Steel said earlier this year: "Mrs Thatcher seems to have done for women in politics what the Boston Strangler did for door-to-door salesmen".' From *The Independent* (20 January 1989): 'Mr Healey also had a pithy word for President Reagan: "He has done for monetarism what the Boston Strangler did for door-to-door salesmen".' From *The Washington Post* (16 October 1991): 'Shields introduced Hatch, the starched shirt of the Senate hearings, as "the man who has done for bipartisanship what the Boston Strangler did for door-to-door salesman"." From *The Sunday Times* (9 February 1992): 'Denis Healey ... claimed to have tried to do for economic forecasters what the Boston Strangler did for door-to-door salesmen.'

1 The great she-elephant, she who must be obeyed, the Catherine the Great of Finchley.

Denis Healey. Quoted in *The Observer*, 'Sayings of the Week' (4 March 1984).

Asked if he knew the reason why Baroness Thatcher disapproved of him:

2 I am not a doctor.

(Sir) Edward Heath, British Conservative Prime Minister (1916–). Quoted in *The Independent on Sunday* (30 October 1994).

Theatre

Definition of a stage director:

3 A person engaged by the management to conceal the fact that the players cannot act.

James Agate, English dramatic critic (1877–1947). Quoted in *The Frank Muir Book* (1976).

4 You know, I go to the theatre to be entertained ... I don't want to see plays about rape, sodomy and drug addiction ... I can get all that at home.

Peter Cook, English humorist (1937–95). Caption to cartoon by Roger Law in *The Observer* (8 July 1962). However, the words 'I go to the theatre to be entertained. I want to be taken out of myself. I don't want to see lust and rape, incest and sodomy – I can get all that at home' also occur in the sketch 'Frank Speaking' credited to Cook and Alan Bennett in *Beyond the Fringe*. This sketch is also described as 'Lord Cobbold/The Duke' and credited to Cook and Jonathan Miller. By the time of Leslie Halliwell, *The Filmgoer's Book of Quotes* (1973), this was being quoted as: 'I don't like watching rape and violence at the cinema. I get enough of that at home!'

5 The only link between Literature and Drama left to us in England at the present moment is the bill of the play.

Oscar Wilde, Irish playwright, poet and wit (1854–1900). In *Saturday Review* (17 November 1894).

Theatrical criticism

6 One of Eric Maschwitz's early successes was the play *Goodnight Vienna* in 1929. Three years later it was turned into a musical film. After a substantial run in London's West End, the play went on a tour of the then provincial circuit, gradually making its way to less and less glamorous venues. One night as he was driving back home through the London suburbs, Maschwitz spied that his show was playing at the Hippodrome in Lewisham. Interested to find out what business was like, he popped into the foyer and consulted a dinner-jacketed man he took to be the manager. Without revealing who he was, Maschwitz asked, 'And is *Goodnight Vienna* going down well in Lewisham?' Came the sour reply: 'I'd say, about as well as *Goodnight Lewisham* would go down in Vienna ...'

Anonymous. Variously quoted. Another version is told in Peter Black, *The Biggest Aspidistra in the World* (1972) involving the Theatre Royal, Huddersfield. On the other hand, *Roy Hudd's Book of Music-Hall, Variety and Showbiz Anecdotes* (1993) has an agent phoning the man who booked the attractions for Walthamstow Palace. The agent, desperate to fill in vacant weeks for the tour of a musical comedy he was representing, asked, 'How do you think *Goodnight Vienna* would go in Walthamstow?' Replied the booker, 'About as well as *Goodnight Walthamstow* would go in Vienna!'

The only trouble about all these versions is that they concern themselves with a *stage* production of *Goodnight Vienna*. In fact, it seems to have started life as a radio programme in 1932 and went straight to film in the same year. Only somewhat later did a stage version become a standby of amateur operatic societies. Perhaps Maschwitz was presented with the classic critical upsumming when he asked about the *film* at some suburban cinema?

7 The audience came out whistling the set.

Anonymous (critic) – supposedly commenting on Irving Berlin's musical *Miss Liberty* (1949) – the paradigm of criticisms made when incidentals are more impressive than the songs in a musical.

On the nude revue Oh! Calcutta!*:*

1 Smithfield with songs.

Anonymous. Quoted by Barry Cryer on BBC Radio *Quote ... Unquote* (29 January 1979).

Reviewing a 'modern' production of a Shakespeare play in Sheffield:

2 [It should be titled] Twelfth Night, or What the Hell.

Anonymous (critic). In *The Guardian* (11 February 1987).

Of an off-Broadway revue in the 1920s called A Good Time*:*

3 No.

Anonymous (critic). Quoted in *The Observer* (18 January 1998). Ascribed dubiously to C. A. Lejeune.

Of Oscar Wilde's shortlived play Vera, or The Nihilists *(1882), Punch opined:*

4 It must have been vera, vera bad.

Anonymous. Quoted in Diana Rigg, *No Turn Unstoned* (1982). In fact, *Punch* (1 September 1883) put it like this: 'Mr Oscar Wilde's play, *Vera* ... was, from all accounts, except the Poet's own, Vera Bad.'

On the play Aglavaine and Selysette *by Maurice Maeterlinck on 3 January 1922:*

5 There's less in this than meets the eye.

Tallulah Bankhead, American actress (1903–68). Remark to Alexander Woollcott, quoted by him in *Shouts and Murmurs* (1922). However, in his journal, James Boswell attributed a version to Richard Burke, son of Edmund (1 May 1783): 'I suppose here *less* is meant than meets the ear.'

On Oh! Calcutta!*:*

6 This is the kind of show that gives pornography a dirty name.

Clive Barnes, English-born theatre and ballet critic (1927–) Review in *The New York Times* (18 June 1969).

On a less than adequate performance in King Lear*:*

7 Quite a sweet little Goneril, don't you think?

Lilian Baylis, English theatrical manager (1874–1937). Quoted in *The Guardian* (1 March 1976).

Going backstage after a particularly disastrous opening night, Beerbohm is supposed to have reassured the leading lady with the compliment:

8 My dear, good is not the word.

(Sir) Max Beerbohm, English writer and caricaturist (1872–1956). Quoted on BBC Radio *Quote ... Unquote* (1979), but later also ascribed to Bernard Shaw. Probably earlier is this caption from a cartoon (possibly by Tenniel) of an amateur asking a professional 'if my Hamlet was pretty good': 'Oh, my dear fellow, 'pon my word you know – really I assure you, good's not the word' – *Punch* (26 August 1865).

On a play he disliked:

9 Its impact was like the banging together of two damp dish-cloths.

Brendan Behan, Irish playwright (1923–64). Quoted in *The Sayings of Brendan Behan*, ed. Aubrey Dillon-Malone (1997).

When the play Abie's Irish Rose *ran for so long on Broadway (1922–7), Benchley found that he was incapable of saying anything new about it in the capsule criticisms that he had to supply each week, so he put:*

10 See Hebrews 13:8.

Robert Benchley, American humorist and drama critic for *Life* and *The New Yorker* (1889–1945). Quoted in Diana Rigg, *No Turn Unstoned* (1982). The text he alluded to reads: 'Jesus Christ the same yesterday, and today, and for ever.'

11 It was one of those plays in which all the actors unfortunately enunciated very clearly.

Robert Benchley. Quoted in *The Treasury of Humorous Quotations*, ed. Evan Esar & Nicolas Bentley (1951).

On a revival of the musical Godspell *in 1981:*

12 Heralded by a sprinkling of glitter-dust and much laying on of microphones, *Godspell* is back in London at the Young Vic. For those who missed it the first time, this is your golden opportunity: you can miss it again.

Michael Billington, English theatre critic (1939–). Quoted in Diana Rigg, *No Turn Unstoned* (1982).

On Bankhead as Shakespeare's Cleopatra:

1 Tallulah Bankhead barged down the Nile last night and sank. As the Serpent of the Nile she proves to be no more dangerous than a garter snake.

John Mason Brown, American critic (1900–69). In the *New York Post* (11 November 1937).

When Lady Diana Cooper told Coward that she had not laughed once at his comedy The Young Idea *when it was presented in London in 1922:*

2 How strange, when I saw you acting in *The Glorious Adventure* [a film about the Great Fire of London], I laughed all the time!

(Sir) Noël Coward, English entertainer and writer (1899–1973). This exchange is quoted in *The Noël Coward Diaries* (footnote to entry of 13 March 1946). It appears to be the original of an anecdote that takes several forms. Here it is as told to me by another actress in 1979: 'Diana Wynyard said to Coward, "I saw your *Private Lives* the other night. Not very funny." He replied: "I saw your Lady Macbeth the other night – very funny!"' Compare the story recounted in *Sheridaniana, or Anecdotes of the Life of Richard Brinsley Sheridan* (1826): the playwright Richard Cumberland took his children to see Sheridan's *The School for Scandal* and kept reprimanding them when they laughed at it – 'You should not laugh, my angels; there is nothing to laugh at.' When Sheridan was informed of this long afterwards, he commented: 'It was very ungrateful in Cumberland to have been displeased with his poor children for laughing at my comedy; for I went the other night to see his tragedy, and laughed at it from beginning to end.'

On Lionel Bart's musical Blitz! *(1962) – which was all about London in the Second World War and chiefly notable for the elaborate moving scenery by Sean Kenny:*

3 Just as long as the real thing and twice as noisy.

(Sir) Noël Coward. Quoted in Sheridan Morley, *Spread a Little Happiness* (1987). Bart himself quoted this as 'Almost as bad as the real thing – only twice as long' – according to *The Sayings of Noël Coward*, ed. Philip Hoare (1997).

On the musical Camelot *on Broadway, in December 1960:*

4 It's like *Parsifal* without the jokes. [*Or* 'It's about as long as *Parsifal*, and not as funny'].

(Sir) Noël Coward. Quoted in Dick Richards, *The Wit of Noël Coward* (1968). In *The Noël Coward Diaries* (entry for 16 December 1960) he merely relates how he took Marlene Dietrich to the first night and found the show 'disappointing ... music and lyrics uninspired and story uninteresting'.

On an inadequate portrayal of Queen Victoria in a play:

5 It made me feel that Albert had married beneath his station.

(Sir) Noël Coward. Quoted in Kenneth Tynan, *Tynan on Theatre* (1964) and in *The Wit of Noël Coward* (ed. Dick Richards, 1968). However, James Agate has this in *Ego 6* (for 17 August 1943): 'At a luncheon party to-day I heard two women discussing historical films. One said, "My dear, they have a certain social value. Until I saw Anna Neagle and Anton Walbrook in the film about Queen Victoria [*Sixty Glorious Years*, 1938] I had no idea that the Prince Consort married beneath him!"' This may be no more than Agate purposely obscuring a source which was known to him, if indeed Coward was the originator. Coward makes no comment on the film in his published diaries.

On an American production of Chekhov's The Cherry Orchard *set in the Deep South:*

6 A Month in the Wrong Country.

(Sir) Noël Coward. In *The Noël Coward Diaries* (1982) – entry for 4 September 1950.

Of Creston Clarke as King Lear:

7 He played the King as though under momentary apprehension that someone else was about to play the ace.

Eugene Field, American critic (1850–95). In a review attributed to him in the *Denver Tribune* (c. 1880), quoted in Willard R. Espy, *An Almanac of Words at Play* (1975).

On a 1946 Chekhov production:

1 If you were to ask me what *Uncle Vanya* is about, I would say about as much as I can take.

Robert Garland. In *Journal American* (1946). Quoted in Diana Rigg, *No Turn Unstoned* (1982).

Of David Garrick:

2 On the stage, he was natural, simple,
affecting;
'Twas only that when he was off, he was
acting.

Oliver Goldsmith, Irish-born playwright and writer (1730–74). *Retaliation* (1774).

3 I have knocked everything but the knees of the chorus-girls, and Nature has anticipated me there.

Percy Hammond, American theatre critic (1873–1936). Quoted in *The Frank Muir Book* (1976).

4 I acted so tragic the house rose like magic,
The audience yelled 'You're sublime.'
They made me a present of Mornington
Crescent –
They threw it a brick at a time.

William Hargreaves, English songwriter (1880–1941). Song, 'The Night I Appeared as Macbeth' (1919).

On the first night of J.M. Barrie's play Peter Pan *(1904):*

5 Oh, for an hour of Herod!

Anthony Hope (Sir Anthony Hope Hawkins), English novelist (1863–1933). Quoted in Denis Mackail, *The Story of JMB* (1941). Compare: 'There are moments when one sympathizes with Herod' – Saki, 'Reginald on House-Parties' (1904). An even earlier outing for this remark occurred when 'Master Betty', the child acting prodigy, was all the rage in London theatre. Dorothea Jordan, the actress mistress of the Duke of Clarence, surveying the throng of juvenile would-be imitators of 'Master Betty', exclaimed, 'Oh, for the days of King Herod!' – Anne Matthews, *Anecdotes of Actors* (1844).

Of an actor called Guido Nadzo:

6 Guido Nadzo is nadzo guido.

George S. Kaufman, American playwright (1889–1961). Quoted in Scott Meredith, *George S. Kaufman and the Algonquin Round Table* (1974). Also attributed to Brooks Atkinson.

7 [*Hook 'n' Ladder* is] the sort of play that gives failures a bad name.

Walter Kerr, American critic (1913–). Reviewing short-lived Broadway play in the *New York Herald* (1950s).

8 *On the London production of* The World of Suzie Wong *in 1959:*

It is ... a lot of Chinese junk ... To pay it a visit would be to enter the world of choosy wrong.

Bernard Levin, English journalist and critic (1928–). In the *Daily Express* (November 1959).

Dashing into a colleague's dressing room after a first night:

9 Darling, I don't care what anybody says – I thought you were marvellous.

Beatrice Lillie, Canadian-born actress (1898–1989). Quoted on BBC Radio *Quote ... Unquote* (12 June 1980).

Review of play by Channing Pollock, in The New Yorker *(1933):*

10 *The House Beautiful* is the play lousy.

Dorothy Parker, American writer (1893–1967). Quoted in Alexander Woollcott, *While Rome Burns* (1934).

Reviewing The Lake *(1933):*

11 Go to the Martin Beck Theatre and watch Katharine Hepburn run the whole gamut of emotions from A to B.

Dorothy Parker. Quoted in *Publishers' Weekly* (19 June 1967). G. Carey, *Katharine Hepburn* (1985) has it only as a remark made in the intermission on the first night, not in a written review. Some would say that Parker went on and stated that Hepburn put some distance, 'between herself and a more experienced colleague [Alison Skipworth] lest she catch acting from her.'

On a play called The Nerd *by Larry Shue:*

1 The lesson of the evening is that writing comedy is quite a serious business, and Mr Shue is much too small for his boots.

John Peter, English theatre critic (1938–). In *The Sunday Times*. Quoted in *A Year of Stings and Squelches* (1985).

2 I think one of the deaths of Hollywood is that producers tried to make everybody normal. Nobody would be in this business if he were normal. When you think of the people you knew – all the Barrymores, Errol Flynn, Charles Laughton – they were eccentrics. I don't want to read about some of these actresses who are around today. They sound like my niece in Scarsdale. I love my niece in Scarsdale, but I won't buy tickets to see her act.

Vincent Price, American actor (1911–93). Interviewed by United Press International (28 February 1964).

Reviewing Dustin Hoffman's performance as Willy Loman in Arthur Miller's Death of a Salesman*:*

3 I was overwhelmed by the tragic smallness of Dustin Hoffman's Willy.

Frank Rich, American theatre critic (of *The New York Times*). Quoted in *The Observer* (28 May 1989).

4 A dramatic critic is a man who leaves no turn unstoned.

Bernard Shaw, Irish playwright and critic (1856–1950). Attributed in *The New York Times* (5 November 1950). According to E. Short, *Fifty Years of Vaudeville*, Arthur Wimperis, the songwriter (1874–1953), said of a music-hall show: 'My dear fellow, a unique evening! I wouldn't have left a turn unstoned.'

On costume drama:

5 Audiences don't like plays where people write letters with feathers.

Lee Shubert, American impresario (1875–1953). Attributed remark. Also ascribed to Max Gordon, Broadway producer, by Arthur Miller – in Ned Sherrin, *Theatrical Anecdotes* (1991). On the other hand, it has also been ascribed, regarding *film* costume epics, to a Missouri cinema owner of the mid-1930s – by Robin Bailey on BBC Radio *Quote ... Unquote* (27 July 1985). Simon Rose, *Classic Film Guide* (1995), ascribes the remark to a Kansas City cinema owner in the wake of the 1933 success of *The Private Life of Henry VIII*. He told a Hollywood rep that his audiences wouldn't put up with any more pictures 'in which men wrote with feathers'.

A comedy by Kenneth Horne with the title Yes and No, *featuring Steve Geray and Magda Kun, opened at the Ambassadors Theatre, London, in the autumn of 1938. It occasioned probably the shortest theatrical notice of all time:*

6 *Yes and No* – No!

Hannen Swaffer, English journalist (1879–1962). Quoted in letter from Bill Galley to *The Sunday Telegraph* (24 March 1970).

Overcome by the usual embarrassment over what to say when going backstage after a performance to greet fellow thespians, he settled for:

7 You *couldn't* have been better.

Ernest Thesiger, English actor (1879–1961). Quoted by Peter Jones on BBC Radio *Quote ... Unquote* (17 September 1983).

To Anton Chekhov, after seeing Uncle Vanya*:*

8 Shakespeare's plays are bad enough, but yours are even worse.

Leo Tolstoy, Russian novelist (1828–1910). Quoted in Henri Troyat, *Tolstoy* (1965).

To the theatre manager after the first night of The Importance of Being Earnest*:*

9 My dear Alec, it was charming, quite charming. And, do you know, from time to time I was reminded of a play I once wrote myself called *The Importance of Being Earnest*.

Oscar Wilde, Irish playwright, poet and wit (1854–1900). Quoted in Hesketh Pearson, *The Life of Oscar Wilde* (1946).

1 The best play I ever slept through.

Oscar Wilde. Quoted in E.H. Mikhail, *Oscar Wilde: Interviews and Recollections* (1979).

On being bored with J. M. Barrie's play The Admirable Crichton*:*

2 Well, for Crichton out loud.

Walter Winchell, American journalist and broadcaster (1892–72). Reported by Dorothy Parker and quoted in *The Sayings of Dorothy Parker*, ed. S.T. Brownlow (1992).

On a show starring Earl Carroll:

3 I saw it at a disadvantage – the curtain was up.

Walter Winchell. Quoted in A. Whiteman, *Come To Judgement*. Ascribed to Groucho Marx (about a play) and quoted in Laurence J. Peter, *Quotations for Our Time* (1977).

4 The play left a taste [in the mouth] of lukewarm parsnip juice.

Alexander Woollcott, American writer and critic (1887–1943). Quoted in H. Techman, *Smart Alex* (1976).

5 The scenery was beautiful, but the actors got in front of it.

Alexander Woollcott. Quoted in *The Frank Muir Book* (1976).

Theft

6 Thieves respect property; they merely wish the property to become their property that they may more perfectly respect it.

G.K. Chesterton, English poet, novelist and critic (1874–1936). *The Man Who Was Thursday* (1908).

7 See how the rascals use me! They will not let my play run and yet they steal my thunder!

John Dennis, English playwright (1657–1734). Quoted in William S. Walsh, *A Handy-Book of Literary Curiosities* (1893). Hence the expression 'to steal a person's thunder' meaning 'to get in first and do whatever the other wanted to make a big impression with', particularly with regard to ideas and policies. It is said to derive from an incident involving Dennis who had invented a device for making the sound of thunder in plays and had used it in an unsuccessful one of his own at the Drury Lane Theatre, London (*c.* 1700). Subsequently, at the same theatre, he saw a performance of *Macbeth* and noted that the thunder was being produced in his special way. Another version of his remark is: 'That is *my* thunder, by God; the villains will play my thunder, but not my play.'

8 The people of Zaire are not thieves. It merely happens that they move things, or borrow them.

Sese Seko Mobuto, Zaïrean President (1930–97). Quoted in *The Sunday Times* (28 May 1978).

9 Lady Dorothy Nevill, so Sir Edmund Gosse tells, preserved her library by pasting in each volume the legend: 'This book has been stolen from Lady Dorothy Nevill.'

Lady Dorothy Nevill (untraced). Quoted in *The Week-End Book* (1955).

10 There was an old man of Nantucket
Who kept all his cash in a bucket;
But his daughter named Nan,
Ran away with a man –
And as for the bucket – Nantucket.

Dayton Vorhees. In *The Princeton Tiger* (1902).

Theory

11 It is a good thing not to put confidence in observations until they have been checked against theory.

Anonymous. Quoted in *The 'Quote ... Unquote' Newsletter* (October 1994). Also known in a French form, sarcastically applied by graduates of the Napoleonic *Grandes Écoles* to the graduates of the post-war, Gaullist *École Nationale d'Administration* (ENA): '*Ça marche en pratique, mais en théorie ... ?* [Well, it works in practice, but will it work in theory?]'

12 In making theories always keep a window open so that you can throw one out if necessary.

Béla Schick (1877–1967), Austrian pediatrician. Attributed remark.

Thinness

1 Outside every thin girl there is a fat man trying to get in.

Katharine Whitehorn, English journalist (1928–). Re-stated by her on BBC Radio *Quote ... Unquote* (27 July 1985).

2 You can never be too rich or too thin.

Duchess of Windsor, American-born wife of the Duke of Windsor (1896–1986). Quoted in *The Penguin Dictionary of Modern Quotations* (1980 edn). Has also been ascribed to Gloria Vanderbilt and Barbara 'Babe' Paley.

Thought

3 Thinking is the most unhealthy thing in the world, and people die of it just as they die of any other disease.

Oscar Wilde, Irish playwright, poet and wit (1854–1900). 'The Decay of Lying', in *Nineteenth Century* (January 1889).

4 A Radical is merely a man who has never dined, and a Tory simply a gentleman who has never thought.

Oscar Wilde. Quoted in Herbert V. Prochnow, Snr & Jnr, *A Treasury of Humorous Quotations* (1969).

Threats

5 I'd horsewhip you if I had a horse.

Line from film *Horse Feathers* (US 1932). Screenwriters: Bert Kalmar and others. Spoken by Groucho Marx (Prof. Wagstaff) to Zeppo Marx (Frank Wagstaff).

When asked what was the greatest threat to the Beatles – the H-Bomb or dandruff:

6 The H-Bomb. We've already got dandruff.

Ringo Starr, English pop musician and singer (1940–). Quoted in Michael Braun, *Love Me Do: the Beatles' Progress* (1964).

Time

7 Well, time wounds all heels.

Jane Ace, American (1905–74). Quoted in Goodman Ace, *The Fine Art of Hypochondria* (1966).

8 Fairest to me of all delights
That makes this earth a heaven,
Is the joy of finding it's half past six,
When I thought it was half-past seven.

Anonymous. Quoted by the Revd Clifford Warren in a letter to *The Daily Telegraph* (5 February 1995).

9 *Vladimir*: That passed the time.
Estragon: It would have passed in any case.
Vladimir: Yes, but not so rapidly.

Samuel Beckett, Irish playwright (1906–89). *Waiting for Godot*, Act 1 (1954).

10 The Duke of Newcastle did everything by halves and nothing well. He invariably lost half an hour in the morning and spent the rest of the day trying to find it.

4th Earl of Chesterfield (Philip Dormer Stanhope), English politician and writer (1694–1773). Quoted in *The 'Quote ... Unquote' Newsletter* (October 1992).

11 I spent a year in that town, one Sunday.

Warwick Deeping, English novelist (1877–1950). Quoted in *The Treasury of Humorous Quotations*, ed. Evan Esar & Nicolas Bentley (1951).

12 Time and tide wait for no man, but time always stands still for a woman of thirty.

Robert Frost, American poet (1874–1963). Quoted in the same collection as above.

13 At my back I often hear Time's winged chariot changing gear.

Eric Linklater, Scottish writer (1899–1974). *Juan in China* (1937).

14 It is a commonplace observation that work expands so as to fill the time available for its completion.

C. Northcote Parkinson, English author and historian (1909–93). First promulgated in *The Economist* (19 November 1955), what later became known as 'Parkinson's Law' was concerned with the pyramidal structure of bureacratic organizations. A pre-echo may be found in the eighteenth-century Lord Chesterfield's letters: 'The less one has to do, the less time one finds to do it in.'

1 The Law of Triviality means that the time spent on any item on the agenda will be in inverse proportion to the sum involved.

C. Northcote Parkinson. His second law. *Parkinson's Law* (1958).

2 I have made this letter longer only because I have not had time to make it shorter.

Blaise Pascal, French philosopher and mathematician (1623–62). *Lettres Provinciales*, No. 16 (1657).

Timidity

3 Faint heart never won fair lady or sold any life insurance.

Frank McKinney ('Kin') Hubbard, American humorist and caricaturist (1868–1930). *Abe Martin's Primer* (1914).

Titanic

On the sinking of the Titanic *in 1912:*

4 I am sorry to hear there has been a bad boating accident.

Mrs Edmund Warre, wife of the Headmaster of Eton at that time. Quoted by George Lyttelton in *The Lyttelton Hart-Davis Letters* (for 7 December 1955). He adds, 'She came in, quivering slightly with age and dottiness ... An odd but very characteristic way of describing the sinking of the largest ship in the world and the death of 1400 people.'

Titles (honours)

5 Titles distinguish the mediocre, embarrass the superior, and are disgraced by the inferior.

Bernard Shaw, Irish playwright and critic (1856–1950). *Man and Superman*, 'Maxims for Revolutionaries' (1903).

Titles (literary)

Advice to a young writer who did not know what title to give his work. 'Are there any trumpets in it?' 'No'. 'Are there any drums in it?' 'No.'

6 Then why not call it *Without Drums or Trumpets*?

(Sir) J(ames) M. Barrie, Scottish playwright (1860–1937). Untraced, but when quoted by Ludovic Kennedy (1991), the title suggested was, rather, *No Horses, No Trumpets*. A similar story is told about the French playwright Tristan Bernard (1866–1947) in Cornelia Otis Skinner's *Elegant Wits and Grand Horizontals* (1962). Somebody did take the advice: the English translation of Alec Le Vernoy's Second World War memoir was entitled *No Drums, No Trumpets* (1983).

7 *The Ancient Mariner* would not have taken so well if it had been called *The Old Sailor*.

Samuel Butler, English novelist and writer (1835–1902). *Notebooks* (1912).

Toasts

8 Here's to pure scholarship. May it never be of any use to anyone!

Anonymous. Quoted in *The 'Quote ... Unquote' Newsletter* (July 1993). John Julius Norwich commented that his father, Duff Cooper (1890–1954), used to quote this as a toast specifically to higher mathematics.

9 Here's to the best years of our lives,
Passed in the arms of other men's wives –
our mothers!

Anonymous. Quoted in *The 'Quote ... Unquote' Newsletter* (October 1996). Reportedly a favourite of Sir Edwin Lutyens.

10 To our sweethearts and wives. May they never meet.

Anonymous. In *Toasts for All Occasions*, ed. Lewis C. Henry (1949).

11 'Gentlemen, lift the seat' ... perhaps it's a loyal toast?

Jonathan Miller, English entertainer, writer and director (1934–). *Beyond the Fringe*, 'The Heat-Death of the Universe' (1961).

1 I was the toast of two continents: Greenland and Australia.

Dorothy Parker, American writer (1893–1967). Quoted in *The Sayings of Dorothy Parker*, ed. S.T. Brownlow (1992).

Tobacco

2 Tobacco is a dirty weed: I like it.
It satisfies no normal need: I like it.
It makes you thin, it makes you lean,
It takes the hair right off your bean [= head].
It's the worst darn stuff I've ever seen: I like it.

Graham L. Hemminger. In *Penn State Froth* (November 1915). Another version:

Tobacco is an ugly weed, I like it!
It can fulfil no earthly need, I like it!
Its smell is neither nice nor clean,
It takes the hair hair right off your bean.
It's the foulest weed I've ever seen, I like it!

Compare PROHIBITION 351:3.

When asked by Patrick Campbell where he got his tobacco from:

3 Paddy, even as we speak, Turkish doxies of unimaginable beauty are rolling my baccy between their golden thighs.

S.J. Perelman, American humorist (1904–79). Quoted on BBC Radio *Quote ... Unquote* (15 June 1977).

Tolkien, J. R. R.

ENGLISH SCHOLAR AND NOVELIST (1892–1973)

4 Tolkien is Hobbit-forming.

Anonymous (graffito). In the 1980s. In a letter to Roger Lancelyn Green (8 January 1971) and included in *The Letters of J.R. Tolkien* (1981), Tolkien himself noted: 'A review appeared in *The Observer* 16 Jan[uary] 1938, signed "*Habit*" (incidentally thus long anticipating [Nevill] Coghill's perception of the similarity of the words in his humorous adj. "hobbit-forming" applied to my books).'

Tomorrow

5 Let us have wine and women, mirth and laughter,
Sermons and soda-water the day after.

Lord Byron, English poet (1788–1824). *Don Juan*, Canto 2, St. 178 (1819–24).

Tongue

6 A tart temper mellows with age, and a sharp tongue is the only edge tool that grows keener with constant use.

Washington Irving, American writer (1783–1859). *The Sketch Book*, 'Rip Van Winkle' (1820).

Tongue twisters

7 The curious cream-coloured cat that crept into the crypt, crapped, and crept out again.

Anonymous. Collected by Martin Gardner and quoted in Willard R. Espy, *An Almanac of Words at Play* (1975).

8 Moses supposes his toeses are roses,
But Moses supposes erroneously.
For Moses he knowses his toeses aren't roses
As Moses supposes his toeses to be.

Anonymous. Famously sung by Donald O'Connor in the film *Singin' in the Rain* (1952), this is an old tongue-twister. It appears in the Opies' collection *I Saw Esau* (1947), though curiously not in any of their other ones. Nor is its origin and development recorded. In their 1955 *Oxford Nursery Rhyme Book*, the third line is given as: 'For nobody's toeses are posies of roses.' Pat Guy pointed out that there is a precedent for Moses/noses/supposes rhymes elsewhere in the Opies' collections. *Esau* also has:

Said Aaron to Moses,
Let's cut off our noses,
Said Moses to Aaron,
It's the fashion to wear 'em.

Said Moses to Aaron,
That fellow's a-swearin';
Said Aaron to Moses,
He's drunk I supposes.

Tourists

9 If it's Tuesday it must be Belgium.

Anonymous. The kind of thing fast-moving American tourists would say. Enshrined in the title of a film (US 1969).

Suggestion to tourists visiting Britain for the first time:

1 Have you tried the famous echo in the Reading Room of the British Museum?

Gerard Hoffnung, English cartoonist and musician (1925–59). Speech, Oxford Union debating society (4 December 1958).

2 The vagabond, when rich, is called a tourist.

Paul Richard, French writer (1874–??). *The Scourge of Christ* (1929).

Tragedy

3 The bad ended unhappily, the good unluckily. That is what tragedy means.

(Sir) Tom Stoppard, English playwright (1937–). *Rosencrantz and Guildenstern Are Dead*, Act 2 (1966).

4 Voltaire was asked *why* no woman has ever written even a tolerable tragedy? 'Ah (said the Patriarch) the composition of a tragedy requires *testicles.*'

Voltaire, French writer and philosopher (1694–1778). Quoted by Lord Byron in a letter to John Murray (2 April 1817), but otherwise unverified. Byron goes on: 'If this be true, Lord Knows what Joanna Baillie does: I suppose she borrows them.' Baillie (1762–1851) was a Scottish dramatist and poet.

Translations

5 And Saul went in to cover his feet.

The Bible. 1 Samuel 24:3 in the Authorised Version. David was hiding from Saul in a cave when into the cave came Saul to evacuate his bowels. Most modern versions of the Bible say, 'to relieve himself.' The Revised Authorised Version (1982) has: 'Saul went in to attend to his needs.' *The Living Bible* (Illinois, 1971) has, memorably: 'Saul went in to a cave to *go to the bathroom*.'

6 Translations (like wives) are seldom strictly faithful if they are in the least attractive.

Roy Campbell, South African poet and journalist (1901–57). In *Poetry Review* (June–July 1949).

7 Nothing is improved by translation, except a Bishop.

4th Earl of Chesterfield (Philip Dormer Stanhope), English politician and writer (1694–1773). Quoted in *The 'Quote ... Unquote' Newsletter* (October 1992).

8 *La belle dame sans merci* ... the beautiful lady who never says thank you.

Michael Flanders, English writer and entertainer (1922–75). *At the Drop of Another Hat*, 'By Air' (1963).

9 She has ideas above her station ... How would you say that in French? ... you can't say *au-dessus de sa gare*. It isn't that sort of station.

(Sir) Terence Rattigan, English playwright (1911–77). *French Without Tears*, Act 1 (1937).

10 Edward III had very good manners. One day at a royal dance he noticed some men-about-court mocking a lady whose garter had come off, whereupon to put her at her ease he stopped the dance and made the memorable epitaph: '*Honi soie qui mal y pense*' ('Honey, your silk stocking's hanging down').

W.C. Sellar & R.J. Yeatman, English humorists (1898–1951) and (1897–1968). *1066 and All That* (1930). Byron is said to have re-translated the motto as, 'On his walk he madly puns.'

11 I have a prejudice against people who print things in a foreign language and add no translation. When I am the reader, and the author considers me able to do the translating myself, he pays me quite a nice compliment – but if he would do the translating for me I would try to get along without the compliment.

Mark Twain, American writer (1835–1910). *A Tramp Abroad*, Chap. 16 (1880).

Travel

12 While armchair travellers dream of going places, travelling armchairs dream of staying put.

Line from film *The Accidental Tourist* (US 1988); screenwriters: Frank Galati, Lawrence Kasdan (from Anne Tyler novel). Spoken by Bill Pulman (Julian).

1 Well, you go Uruguay, and I'll go mine.

Line from film *Animal Crackers* (US 1930). Screenwriters: Morrie Ryskind, George S. Kaufman. Spoken by Groucho Marx (Capt. Spaulding).

2 Definition: I am traveller, you are a tourist, *they* are trippers.

Anonymous. Quoted in about 1974 by John Julius Norwich. It may have originated in a *New Statesman* competition.

3 There was a young lady of Spain
Who often got sick on a train,
Not once and again
But again and again
And again and again and again.

Anonymous (limerick). Quoted by Osbert Sitwell as a great favourite of the painter John Singer Sargent.

4 In America there are two classes of travel – first class, and with children.

Robert Benchley, American humorist (1889–1945). *Pluck and Luck*, 'Kiddie-Kar Travel' (1925).

5 It is not travel that narrows the mind but travel writing.

James Buchan, British writer (1916–). In *The Spectator* (11 August 1990).

6 It is no longer difficult to reach Jerusalem; the real difficulty is the one experienced by the crusaders; to know what to do when you have arrived there.

Benjamin Disraeli (1st Earl of Beaconsfield), English politician and writer (1804–81). *Tancred*, Bk 2, Chap. 11 (1847).

7 The Owl and the Pussy-Cat went to sea
In a beautiful pea-green boat.
They took some honey, and plenty of money,
Wrapped up in a five-pound note.

Edward Lear, English poet and artist (1812–88). 'The Owl and the Pussy-Cat' (1871).

8 I have found out that there ain't no surer way to find out whether you like people or hate them than to travel with them.

Mark Twain, American writer (1835–1910). *Tom Sawyer Abroad* (1894).

9 Commuter – one who spends his life
In riding to and from his wife;
A man who shaves and takes a train
And then rides back to shave again.

E(lwyn) B(rooks) White, American humorist (1899–1985). 'The Commuter' (by 1969).

Trivia

10 The great things of life leave one unmoved ... We regret the burden of their memory, and have anodynes against them. But the little things, the things of the moment, remain with us.

Oscar Wilde, Irish playwright, poet and wit (1854–1900). *The Portrait of Mr W.H.* (1889)

11 We should treat all trivial things of life very seriously, and all the serious things of life with sincere and studied triviality.

Oscar Wilde. Quoted in E.H. Mikhail, *Oscar Wilde: Interviews and Recollections* (1979).

Troubles

12 Too often our Washington reflex is to discover a problem and then throw money at it, hoping it will somehow go away.

Kenneth B. Keating, American Senator (1900–75), Quoted in *The New York Times* (24 December 1961).

13 Never trouble trouble
Till trouble troubles you
For if you trouble trouble

You'll only double trouble
And trouble others too.

David Keppel. Song, 'Trouble', known by 1916.

On Leo Durocher, the baseball manager:

1 He can always be counted upon to make an impossible situation infinitely worse.

Branch Rickey, American baseball player (1881–1965). Quoted in *The Home Book of Humorous Quotations*, ed. A.K. Adams (1969).

2 I am an old man and have known a great many troubles, but most of them never happened.

Mark Twain, American writer (1835–1910). Quoted in *The Treasury of Humorous Quotations*, ed. Evan Esar & Nicolas Bentley (1951). In *The Second World War*, Vol. 2 'Their Finest Hour' (1949), Winston Churchill wrote: 'When I look back on all these worries I remember the story of the old man who said on his deathbed that he had had a lot of trouble in his life, most of which had never happened.'

Trousers

In November 1982 when Sir Geoffrey Howe, British Chancellor of the Exchequer, had his trousers stolen when travelling by rail on an overnight sleeper:

3 I am thrilled about the loss of your trousers because it revealed your human face.

Anonymous (colleague). Probably a fellow member of the Cabinet. Quoted by Lady Howe in *The Observer* Magazine (12 January 1984).

4 You should never have your best trousers on when you go out to fight for freedom and truth.

Henrik Ibsen, Norwegian playwright (1828–1906). *An Enemy of the People*, Act 5 (1882).

Trust

5 Trust him no further than you can throw him.

Anonymous (proverbial saying). Quoted in Thomas Fuller, *Gnomologia* (1732).

6 In God we trust, all others [must] pay cash.

Anonymous (American). Quoted by US Secretary of State George Schulz after the Washington summit between Mikhail Gorbachev and Ronald Reagan in December 1987. Listed in *H. L. Mencken's Dictionary of Quotations* (1942) as an 'American saying'. It may have been seen first in the 18th century.

7 Never trust a man who speaks well of everybody.

John Churton Collins, English literary critic (1848–1908). Quoted in *The Home Book of Humorous Quotations*, ed. A.K. Adams (1969).

After being acquitted of drug-dealing:

8 I have aged 600 years and my life as a hard-working industrialist is in tatters. Would you buy a used car from me?

John De Lorean, American businessman. Quoted in *The Observer*, 'Sayings of the Week' (19 August 1984).

Truth

9 How true that is, even today.

Anonymous (saying). A rather plonking remark once thought to have originated in a sketch or satire upon churchy folk? However, in the actor Kenneth Williams's published letters we find: 'I must say I fell about at your line "Age shall not wither her nor iron bars a cage." I thought "How true that is even today".' This is dated 2 October 1971. And the saying has been found in at least three episodes of the BBC radio show *Round the Horne* (in which Williams appeared). Instances of the phrase occur in regular parodies during the 1966 series, of Eamonn Andrews's catastrophically bad TV chat shows. On 20 March, 'Seamus Android' (played by Bill Pertwee) replies to one of his guests: 'How true that is even today.' On 27 March, Williams as 'Claphanger' (a movie star) says, 'You see, I'm illiterate, too.' 'Android' replies: 'Yes. And how true those words are even today.' On 30 March, movie star 'Zsa Zsa Poltergeist' (Betty Marsden) says, 'I'll get around to all of you in time.' 'Android' comments: 'And how true those words are even today.' Clearly a catchphrase in the making at that time. So we may say, rather than stemming from the airy philosophizing of church folk in the 1960s, the expression is really just another example of the plonking style of a chat-show host. The scripts were written by Barry Took and Marty Feldman.

1 It is always the best policy to speak the truth, unless of course you are an exceptionally good liar.

Jerome K. Jerome, English writer (1859–1927). *The Idler* (February 1892).

2 Truth is always duller than fiction.

Piers Paul Read, English writer (1941–). In *The Observer* (1981).

3 My way of joking is to tell the truth; it's the funniest joke in the world.

Bernard Shaw, Irish playwright and critic (1856–1950). *John Bull's Other Island*, Act 2 (1907).

4 If you want to be thought a liar always tell the truth.

Logan Pearsall Smith, American writer (1865–1946). Quoted in *The Home Book of Humorous Quotations*, ed. A.K. Adams (1969).

5 I don't mind what the opposition say of me, so long as they don't tell the truth about me, but when they descend to telling the truth about me, I consider that is taking an unfair advantage.

Mark Twain, American writer (1835–1910). Speech, Hartford, Conn. (26 October 1880).

6 There was things he stretched, but mainly he told the truth.

Mark Twain. *The Adventures of Huckleberry Finn* (1884).

7 Truth is stranger than fiction – to some people, but I am measurably familiar with it. Truth is stranger than fiction, but it is because fiction is obliged to stick to possibilities; truth isn't.

Mark Twain. *Following the Equator*, Vol. 1, Chap. 15 (1897).

8 A thing is not necessarily true because a man dies for it.

Oscar Wilde, Irish playwright, poet and wit (1854–1900). *The Portrait of Mr W.H.* (1889).

9 If one tells the truth, one is sure, sooner or later, to be found out.

Oscar Wilde. 'Phrases and Philosophies for the Use of the Young', in *The Chameleon* (December 1894).

10 It is perfectly monstrous the way people go about nowadays, saying things against one behind one's back that are absolutely true.

Oscar Wilde, *The Picture of Dorian Gray*, Chap. 15 (1891). Later in *A Woman of No Importance*, Act 1 (1893).

11 The truth is rarely pure and never simple. Modern life would be very tedious if it were either, and modern literature a complete impossiblity!

Oscar Wilde. *The Importance of Being Earnest*, Act 1 (1895).

12 Untruthful! My nephew Algernon? Impossible! He is an Oxonian.

Oscar Wilde. In the same play, Act 3. Lady Bracknell speaking.

Turpentine

13 Two farmers met and one said to the other: ''Ere, you remember telling me you gave your 'oss turpentine when 'e 'ad colic.' The other said: 'Ay!' The first farmer went on: 'Well, I gave my 'oss turpentine, an' 'e died.' Said the other: 'Well, *mine died too*!'

L. Raven-Hill, English cartoonist. Caption to cartoon in *Punch* Magazine (24 November 1909). This was later used in an exchange involving Al Jolson in the film *Big Boy* (US 1930).

Tutankhamen

1 Tutankhamen has changed his mind and wants to be buried at sea.

Anonymous (graffito). Included in book *Graffiti Lives, OK* (1979).

Twins

2 In form and feature, face and limb,
I grew so like my brother
That folks got taking me for him,
And each for one another.

And when I died the neighbours came
And buried brother John!

Henry Sambrooke Leigh, English poet (1837–83). 'The Twins'.

Typewriters

3 I wrote all my formal communications to the press in longhand. I have never had the secret knack of typewriters. Typewriters can't spell, you know.

(Sir) Max Beerbohm, English writer and caricaturist (1872–1956). Quoted in S. N. Behrman, *Conversations with Max* (1960).

U

Ugliness

1 I was so ugly when I was born, the doctor slapped my mother.

Henny Youngman, British-born American comedian (1906–98). Quoted in *The Times* (26 February 1998).

Umbrellas

2 All men are equal – all men, that is to say, who possess umbrellas.

E.M. Forster, English novelist (1879–1970). *Howard's End*, Chap. 6 (1910).

3 Envoy: Love me, love my umbrella.

James Joyce, Irish novelist (1882–1941). *Giacomo Joyce* (*c.* 1914). The final fragment in this posthumously published work.

Uniforms

4 He [Benchley] came out of a night club one evening and, tapping a uniformed figure on the shoulder, said, 'Get me a cab.' The uniformed figure turned round furiously and informed him that he was not a doorman but a rear admiral. 'O.K.,' said Benchley, 'Get me a battleship.'

Robert Benchley, American humorist (1889–1945). Quoted in *The New Yorker* (5 January 1946).

Universe

'I accept the universe' was a favourite utterance of the New England transcendentalist, Margaret Fuller:

5 Gad! She'd better.

Thomas Carlyle, Scottish historian and philosopher (1795–1881). Quoted in William James, *The Varieties of Religious Experience* (1902).

6 My suspicion is that the universe is not only queerer than we suppose, but queerer than we *can* suppose.

J.B.S. Haldane, British scientist (1892–1964). *Possible Worlds* (1927).

7 My theology, briefly, is that the universe was dictated but not signed.

Christopher Morley, American writer and editor (1890–1957). Quoted in *The Treasury of Humorous Quotations*, ed. Evan Esar & Nicolas Bentley (1951).

Usefulness

One old woman is reported to have said to another:

8 Yes, I had him cremated and his ashes made into an eggtimer. He never did any work while he was alive, so he might as well do some now he's dead.

Anonymous. In J.B. Priestley's *English Journey* (1934), he recounts attending a lunch club in Manchester where commercial travellers told stories. He repeats one: 'A weaver up Blackburn way had just lost her husband. "Where yer going to bury 'im?" a neighbour asked her. "Ah'm not going to bury 'im," she replied. "Ah'm going to 'ave 'im creamated," she replied. The neighbour was impressed. "But whatever will yer do wi' th'ashes?" she inquired. "Ah'll tell yer what Ah'm going to do wi' th'ashes," said the widow. "Ah'm going to 'ave 'em put into an eggtimer. Th'owd devil wouldn't ever work when 'e wer alive, so 'e can start doing a bit now 'e's deead."' Priestley comments: 'That still seems to me a very good story, even though I am no longer under the influence of beer and Bury Black Puddings. It is a fair sample of Lancashire's grimly ironic humour.' The line was also quoted by Alan Bennett in 'The English Way of Death', *Beyond the Fringe*, Broadway version (1964).

Of Prince Andrew:

1 He's the only one who knows how to work the video.

Elizabeth II, British Queen (1926–). Quoted in *The Observer*, 'Sayings of the Week' (11 August 1985).

Remark by a small boy to his mother about a man carrying a bag of golf clubs:

2 Mummy, what's that man *for*?

F.H. Townsend, English illustrator. Caption to cartoon in *Punch*, Vol. 131 (14 November 1906).

Utopias

3 An acre in Middlesex is better than a principality in Utopia.

Thomas Babington Macaulay (Lord Macaulay), English historian and poet (1800–59). *Essays Contributed to the Edinburgh Review*, 'Lord Bacon' (1843).

4 A map of the world that does not include Utopia is not worth even glancing at, for it leaves out the one country at which Humanity is always landing. And when Humanity lands there, it looks out, and, seeing a better country, sets sail. Progress is the realisation of Utopias.

Oscar Wilde, Irish playwright, poet and wit (1854–1900). 'The Soul of Man Under Socialism' (1895)

V

Van Gogh

To actor Cliff Osmond:

1 You have Van Gogh's ear for music.

Billy Wilder, American film director and writer (1906–). Quoted in Leslie Halliwell, *The Filmgoer's Book of Quotes* (1973). Appearing on BBC Radio *Quote ... Unquote* in 1977, the comic actor Kenneth Williams came up with a rather good showbiz story. He quoted the above as what Orson Welles had reputedly said of the singing of Donny Osmond (then a popular young star). In fact, Orson Welles did not say it, nor was it about Donny Osmond, but the reasons why the joke had been reascribed and redirected are instructive. It was in fact Billy Wilder who made the original remark. He has a notably waspish wit but is, perhaps, not such a household name as Orson Welles. He lacks, too, Welles's Falstaffian stature and his, largely unearned, reputation in the public mind for having said witty things. And Wilder said it about Cliff Osmond, an American comedy actor who had appeared in the film director's *Kiss Me Stupid*, *The Fortune Cookie* and *The Front Page*. As far as one knows, he is not related to Donny Osmond but, apparently, he had to be replaced in the anecdote because he lacked star status. Tom Stoppard included something very similar in *The Real Inspector Hound* (1968): 'An uncanny ear that might [have] belonged to a Van Gogh.'

Vanity

2 You're so vain, you probably think this song is about you.

Carly Simon, American singer and songwriter (1945–). Song, 'You're So Vain' (1972). It is usually assumed that the subject of the song was, in fact, the film actor Warren Beatty.

Vasectomy

3 A vasectomy means never having to say you're sorry.

Anonymous (graffito). Quoted in Reisner & Wechsler, *The Encyclopedia of Graffiti* (1974). Ascribed to Rubin Carson (untraced) in Laurence J. Peter, *Quotations for Our Time* (1977).

Vegetarianism

4 Vegetarianism is harmless enough, though is apt to fill a man with wind and self-righteousness.

(Sir) Robert Hutchinson, English physician. Quoted in *The Wit of Medicine*, ed. L. & M. Cowan (1972).

Vendettas

Of Peter Cook:

5 For a man linked with satire he was without malice to anyone, although he did admit to pursuing an irrational vendetta against the late great Gracie Fields.

Richard Ingrams, English editor and writer (1937–). Quoted in *The Independent* 'Quote Unquote' (6 May 1995).

Venice

6 The most striking thing about the City of Venice is the complete absence of the smell of horse dung.

Alphonse Allais, French humorist (1854–1905). Quoted in *The World of Alphonse Allais*, ed. Miles Kington (1976).

1 We have often heard Cork called the Venice of Ireland, but have never heard Venice called the Cork of Italy.

Anonymous. Quoted by John Betjeman in a letter to Michael Rose (25 September 1955).

Telegram to The New Yorker *on arriving in Venice:*

2 STREETS FLOODED. PLEASE ADVISE.

Robert Benchley, American humorist (1889–1945). Quoted in R.E. Drennan, *Wit's End* (1973).

3 Venice is like eating an entire box of chocolate liqueurs at one go.

Truman Capote, American writer (1924–84). Quoted in *The Observer* (26 November 1961).

The Duke of Plaza-Toro:

4 As a Castilian hidalgo ... I should have preferred to ride through the streets of Venice; but owing, I presume, to an unusually wet season, the streets are in such a condition that equestrian exercise is impracticable.

(Sir) W.S. Gilbert, English writer and lyricist (1836–1911). *The Gondoliers*, Act 1 (1889).

Venus de Milo

5 See what'll happen if you don't stop biting your finger-nails.

Will Rogers, American humorist (1879–1935). Quoted in Bennett Cerf, *Shake Well Before Using* (1948). Has also been ascribed to Noël Coward.

Verbosity

Of Gladstone:

6 A sophistical rhetorician, inebriated with the exuberance of his own verbosity, and gifted with an egotistical imagination that can at all times command an interminable and inconsistent series of arguments to malign an opponent and to glorify himself.

Benjamin Disraeli (1st Earl of Beaconsfield), English politician and writer (1804–81). Speech to banquet in the Knightsbridge Riding School (27 July 1878), quoted in *The Times* (29 July). Commonly rendered in the form: 'Sir, you are intoxicated by the exuberance of your own verbosity'. In *Scouse Mouse* (1984), George Melly tells how this was ascribed to *Dr Johnson* by a headmaster called W.W. Twyne. A common mistake.

7 He has, more than any man, the gift of compressing the largest amount of words into the smallest amount of thought.

(Sir) Winston S. Churchill, British Conservative Prime Minister and writer (1874–1965). Speech, House of Commons (23 March 1933).

8 He can compress the most words into the smallest ideas better than any man I ever met.

Abraham Lincoln, American Republican President (1809–65). Attributed remark.

Vice-Presidency

9 [The Vice-Presidency] isn't worth a pitcher of warm piss.

John Nance Garner, American Democratic Vice-President (1868–1967). Quoted in O. C. Fisher, *Cactus Jack* (1978). Usually bowdlerized to 'warm spit', as apparently it was by the first journalist who reported it and (invariably) by Alistair Cooke. Garner was Vice-President (1933–41) during F.D. Roosevelt's first two terms. Furthermore, Garner said, in 1963, that the job 'didn't amount to a hill of beans' (also in Fisher). Theo Lippman Jr in the *San Francisco Chronicle* (25 December 1992) provided this further Garner story: he was walking down the halls of the Capitol one day when the circus was in Washington. A fellow came up to him and introduced himself. 'I am the head clown in the circus,' he said. Very solemnly, Garner replied, 'And I am the Vice-President of the United States. You'd better stick around here a while. You might pick up some new ideas.'

10 Once there were two brothers: one ran away to sea, the other was elected Vice-President – and nothing was ever heard from either of them again.

Thomas R. Marshall, American Democratic Vice-President (1854–1925). *Recollections* (1925).

Views

1 Oh it really is a wery pretty garden, and
  Chingford to the eastward can be seen;
Wiv a ladder and some glasses
You could see to 'Ackney Marshes,
If it wasn't for the 'ouses in between.

Edgar Bateman, English songwriter (1860–1946). Song, 'The 'Ouses In Between' (1894), to music by George Le Brunn (1862–1905). Popularized by Gus Elen (1862–1940).

Violence

2 Violence is the repartee of the illiterate.

Alan Brien, English writer and journalist (1925–). In *Punch* (7 February 1973). When Brien was asked to source this quotation on BBC Radio *Quote ... Unquote* (10 August 1985) he said: 'I don't think I've heard it before ... modernish? ... it can't be very old. Bernard Shaw would be too good for it ... but it's approaching Bernard Shaw. Perhaps it's Chesterton, is it?'

3 *Amanda*:
I've been brought up to believe that it's beyond the pale, for a man to strike a woman.
Elyot:
A very poor tradition. Certain women should be struck regularly, like gongs.

(Sir) Noël Coward, English entertainer and writer (1899–1973). *Private Lives*, Act 3 (1930).

Virginity

4 *Romance on the High Seas* was Doris Day's first picture; that was before she became a virgin.

Oscar Levant, American pianist and actor (1906–72). *Memoirs of an Amnesiac* (1965).

5 Nature abhors a virgin – a frozen asset.

Clare Boothe Luce, American writer and diplomat (1903–87). In *The Women* (film US, 1939, based on Luce's play), Florence Nash reflects: 'I'm what nature abhors - an old maid. A frozen asset.'

To unsuitable American actresses who had been assembled to play ladies-in-waiting to a queen:

6 Ladies, just a little more virginity, if you don't mind.

(Sir) Herbert Beerbohm Tree, English actor-manager (1853–1917). Quoted in Alexander Woollcott, *Shouts and Murmurs* (1923).

Visits and visitors

7 Fish and visitors smell in three days.

Anonymous. Quoted in Benjamin Franklin, *Poor Richard's Almanack* (1736). The *Concise Oxford Dictionary of Proverbs* (1982) finds the idea (without the fish) in Plautus and the first English reference (with the fish) in Lyly's *Euphues* (1580).

On American troops in Britain during the Second World War:

8 Overpaid, overfed, oversexed and over here.

Anonymous. Sometimes attributed to Tommy Trinder, English comedian (1909–89).

9 It was a delightful visit; – perfect, in being much too short.

Jane Austen, English novelist (1775–1817). *Emma*, Chap. 13 (1816).

Voices

10 What is more enchanting than the voices of young people when you can't hear what they say?

Logan Pearsall Smith, American writer (1865–1946). *All Trivia* (1933).

Of Margaret Thatcher before the 1979 General Election:

11 I cannot bring myself to vote for a woman who has been voice-trained to speak to me as though my dog has just died.

Keith Waterhouse, English journalist, playwright and novelist (1929–). Attributed remark.

Vulgarity

1 Vulgarity is the garlic in the salad of charm.

Cyril Connolly, English writer and critic (1903–74). Epigraph, ascribed to 'St Bumpus', of 'Told in Gath', Connolly's parody of Aldous Huxley, contained in *The Condemned Playground* (1945).

2 No crime is vulgar, but all vulgarity is crime. Vulgarity is the conduct of others.

Oscar Wilde, Irish playwright, poet and wit (1854–1900). 'Phrases and Philosophies for the Use of the Young', in *The Chameleon* (December 1894). Later, in *An Ideal Husband*, Act 3 (1895).

Vultures

3 If there's one thing above all a vulture can't stand, it's a glass eye.

Frank McKinney ('Kin') Hubbard, American humorist (1868–1930). Attributed remark. Possibly from *Abe Martin's Sayings and Sketches* (1915). 'Abe Martin' was a folksy humorous character whose sayings, originally published in the *Indianapolis News* from 1892, were later collected annually.

W

Wagner, Richard

GERMAN COMPOSER (1813–83)

1 Wagner is the Puccini of music.

J.B. Morton (Beachcomber), English humorous writer (1893–1979). Quoted in the *Lyttelton Hart-Davis Letters* (for 5 February 1956). Rupert Hart-Davis comments that the announcement 'summed up the jargon-bosh of art- and music-critics beautifully.' On the other hand, James Agate in *Ego 6* (for 13 October 1943) has: 'I do not doubt the sincerity of the solemn ass who, the other evening, said portentously: "Wagner is the Puccini of music!"' As Agate was addressing a group of 'school-marms' and as he generally had an after-dinner speaker's way with attribution, it may well still have been a Beachcomber coinage.

When asked what you needed to sing the part of Isolde in Wagner's Tristan und Isolde:

2 A comfortable pair of shoes.

Birgit Nilsson, Swedish singer (1918–). Attributed remark. Because the part is an endurance test for the singer (and sometimes for the audience).

3 I have been told that Wagner's music is better than it sounds.

Edgar Wilson 'Bill' Nye, American humorist (1850–96). In Mark Twain's *Autobiography* (published posthumously in 1924) he ascribes this to Nye who had predeceased him. Given the dates involved here, it is curious that Lewis Baumer was providing this caption to a *Punch* cartoon (20 November 1918): (Two women talking) – 'Going to hear some Wagner.' 'What! – do you like the stuff?' 'Frankly, no; but I've heard on the best authority that his music's very much better than it sounds.'

4 *Parsifal* is the kind of opera that starts at six o'clock. After it has been going three hours, you look at your watch and it says 6.20.

David Randolph, American conductor and writer (1914–). Quoted in *The American Treasury*, ed. Clifton Fadiman (1955).

5 Wagner has beautiful moments but awful quarters of an hour.

Gioacchino Rossini, Italian composer (1792–1868). Letter (April 1867), quoted in E. Naumann, *Italiensiche Tondichter* (1883). In his *Reminiscences, Inscriptions & Anecdotes* (1913), the musician Francesco Berger attributed this to the pianist Hans von Bülow: 'Some one observed, "Well, you must admit that he [Wagner] has some heavenly moments." "I don't dispute the *heavenly moments*," said he, "but he has some *devilish ugly half-hours*."'

6 One can't judge Wagner's opera *Lohengrin* after a first hearing, and I certainly don't intend hearing it a second time.

Gioacchino Rossini. Quoted in *The Frank Muir Book* (1976).

On hearing Wagner's Lohengrin:

7 The banging and slamming and booming and crashing were something beyond belief. The racking and pitiless pain of it remains stored up in my memory alongside the memory of the time that I had my teeth fixed.

Mark Twain, American writer (1835–1910). *A Tramp Abroad*, Vol. 1, Chap. 9 (1880).

1 The present opera was *Parsifal*. Madame Wagner does not permit its representation anywhere but in Bayreuth. The first act of the three occupied two hours, and I enjoyed that in spite of the singing.

Mark Twain. *What Is Man? and other essays*, 'At the Shrine of St Wagner' (1917).

Lady Henry commenting on a performance of Lohengrin*:*

2 I like Wagner's music better than anybody's. It is so loud that one can talk the whole time without other people hearing what one says. That is a great advantage.

Oscar Wilde, Irish playwright, poet and wit (1854–1900). *The Picture of Dorian Gray*, Chap. 4 (1891).

Waiters

3 I vividly recall one story [Compton Mackenzie] told. He was sitting in the Café Royal, dining alone. Near him, leaning against a pillar, was a waiter. A second waiter approached the first waiter, looked surreptitiously all round, then whispered confidentially: '*Well* ... He's eaten it.'

Anonymous. Quoted in Michael Pertwee, *Name Dropping* (1974). The real original probably lies in a *Punch* cartoon by G.L. Stampa that appeared on 16 May 1934. 'He's eaten it!' was the caption below a picture of two waiters and a diner.

Diner:

4 I'd complain about the service if I could find a waiter to complain to.

Mel Calman, English cartoonist (1931–94). Caption to cartoon in *How to Survive Abroad* (1971).

Of a dead waiter:

5 God finally caught his eye.

George S. Kaufman, American playwright (1889–1961). Quoted in Scott Meredith, *George S. Kaufman and the Algonquin Round Table* (1974). As 'By and by / God caught his eye' this epitaph is attributed to David McCord (1897–), in 'Remainders' from *Bay Window Ballads* (1935).

Wales and the Welsh

6 Welshmen prize their women so highly that they put a picture of their mother-in-law on the national flag.

Anonymous. Quoted by Canon Don Lewis on BBC Radio *Quote ... Unquote* (16 July 1983).

7 A Welshman is a man who prays on his knees on Sundays and preys on his neighbours all the rest of the week.

Anonymous. Quoted in *The Penguin Dictionary of Modern Humorous Quotations*, ed. Fred Metcalf (1987).

8 The Welsh are the Italians in the rain.

Anonymous. Quoted by the writer Elaine Morgan on BBC Radio *Quote ... Unquote* (25 April 1983). An earlier version spoken, though probably not coined, by the journalist René Cutforth was: 'The Welsh are the Mediterraneans in the rain', which was quoted by Nancy Banks-Smith in *The Guardian* (17 October 1979).

9 The land of my fathers – my fathers can have it.

Dylan Thomas, Welsh poet (1914–53). Quoted in *Adam* Magazine (December 1953). 'Land of My Fathers' (1860) is the Welsh national anthem.

10 There are still parts of Wales where the only concession to gaiety is a striped shroud.

Gwyn Thomas, Welsh novelist, playwright and humorist (1913–81). In *Punch* (18 June 1958).

11 We can trace nearly all the disasters of English history to the influence of Wales.

Evelyn Waugh, English novelist (1903–66). *Decline and Fall* (1928).

Waltz

On the waltz when it was introduced to England from Germany in 1812:

12 [An] outright romp in which the couples not only embrace throughout the dance but, flushed and palpitating, whirl about in the posture of copulation.

Anonymous. Quoted in *The Frank Muir Book* (1976).

War

On how to get out of Vietnam:

1 Claim victory and retreat.

George Aiken, American Republican politician (1892–1984). What he actually said in a speech to the US Senate (19 October 1966) was: 'The United States could well declare unilaterally that this stage of the Vietnam War is over – that we have "won" in the sense that our Armed Forces are in control of most of the field and no potential enemy is in a position to establish its authority over South Vietnam.' Sometimes encapsulated as 'Aiken's Solution' in the form 'Claim victory and retreat', this was an attempt to persuade President Johnson to 'declare the United States the winner and begin de-escalation'. Commenting on the eventual 1973 withdrawal, Aiken said: 'What we got was essentially what I recommended ... we said we had won and we got out.'

2 They are rolling up the maps all over Europe. We shall not see them lit again in our lifetime.

Alan Bennett, English playwright and actor (1934–). *Forty Years On*, Act 1 (1969).

3 Non-combatant, *n*. A dead Quaker.

Ambrose Bierce, American journalist (1842–?1914). *The Cynic's Word Book* (later retitled *The Devil's Dictionary*) (1906).

4 Thc Falklands thing was a fight between two bald men over a comb.

Jorge Luis Borges, Argentinian novelist (1899–1986). Quoted in *Time* Magazine (14 February 1983). The basic expression is proverbial, however. It is quoted in *H. L. Mencken's Dictionary of Quotations* (1942), as 'Two baldheaded men are fighting over a comb' (listed as a 'Russian saying') and in Champion's *Racial Proverbs* (1938).

5 *La guerre, c'est une chose trop grave pour la confier à des militaires* [War is too serious a business to be left to the generals].

Georges Clemenceau, French Prime Minister (1841–1929). In France the National Assembly had suspended its sittings at the outbreak of the First World War and the conduct of the war had been entrusted to the goverment and to Joffre and the General Staff. By 1915, however, opinion was changing. It may have been about this time that Clemenceau, who became French Prime Minister again in 1917, uttered this, his most famous remark. It was, apparently, quoted by Aristide Briand to David Lloyd George. Later it was quoted in Suarez, *Soixante Années d'histoire française: la vie orgueilleuse de Clemenceau* (1932), and Hampden Jackson, *Clemenceau and the Third Republic* (1946). It is also attributed to Clemenceau in the film *Dr Strangelove ...* (US 1963).

The notion has also been attributed to Talleyrand and, indeed, Clemenceau may have said it himself much earlier (in 1886 even). Subsequently, the format of the saying has been applied to many other professions.

Replying to the newspaper artist Frederic Remington's request to be allowed to return home from Cuba because there was no war for him to cover (1898):

6 Please remain. You furnish the pictures and I will furnish the war.

William Randolph Hearst, American newspaper proprietor (1863–1951). Quoted in John K. Winkler, *William Randolph Hearst: An American Phenomenon* (1928). In the film *Citizen Kane* (US 1941), Kane replies to a war correspondent's message, 'Could send you prose poems about scenery but ... there is no war in Cuba', with: 'Dear Wheeler, you provide the prose poems. I'll provide the war.' Hearst was, of course, the model for Kane.

7 The world has turned over many times since I took the oath on the Plain at West Point, and the hopes and dreams have long since vanished. But I still remember the refrain of one of the most popular barrack ballads of that day, which proclaimed, most proudly, that old soldiers never die. They just fade away.

Douglas MacArthur, American general (1880–1964). Speech to Congress (19 April 1951). In fact, the ballad quoted by MacArthur (on his forced retirement) and which he dated as 'turn of the century' was a British Army song of the First World War. It is a parody of the gospel hymn 'Kind Words Can Never Die'. J. Foley copyrighted a version of the parody in 1920. The more usual form of the words is, 'Old soldiers never die – they simply fade away.'

1 The late unpleasantness.

Petroleum V. Nasby (David Ross Locke), American humorist (1833–88). *Ekkoes from Kentucky* (1868). A euphemism for a previous war or recent hostilities. 'Nasby' actually referred to the recently ended Civil War as 'the late onpleasantniss'.

2 Sometime they'll give a war and nobody will come.

Carl Sandburg, American poet (1878–1967). The origin of this light joke appears to lie in Sandburg's epic poem *The People, Yes* (1936). It became popular in the 1960s – especially as a graffito – at the time of protests against the Vietnam War. Charlotte Keyes (1914–) wrote an article in *McCall's* Magazine (October 1966), which was given the title 'Suppose They Gave a War, and No One Came?' A US film (1969) was called *Suppose They Gave a War and Nobody Came?*

It is also well known in German as '*Stell dir vor, es gibt Krieg, und keiner geht hin* [Suppose they gave a war and nobody came]'. Ralf Bülow in the journal *Der Sprachdienst* (No. 27, 1983) traced it back not only to Sandburg but also to Thornton Wilder. They both lived in Chicago in the early 1930s. Bülow recounts a Wilder anecdote which Sandburg may have picked up. In the same edition of *Der Sprachdienst*, Reinhard Roche comments on how German journalists and others have ascribed the remark to Bertolt Brecht because of his poem '*Wer zu Hause bleibt, wenn der Kampf beginnt* [Who will be away from home when the war begins?]' and argues that 'much more philological caution is needed before assigning certain popular expressions to literary figures'. Quite so.

Describing what it was like to be in battle:

3 Oh, my dear fellow, the noise ... and the people!

'Captain Strahan' (unidentified). According to the *Hudson Review* (Winter, 1951), he said it after the Battle of Bastogne in 1944. Various correspondents have suggested it was earlier in the war than this, however. Roy T. Kendall wrote (1986): 'I heard this phrase used, in a humorous manner, during the early part of 1942. It was related to me as having been said by a young Guards officer, newly returned from Dunkirk, who on being asked what it was like used the expression: the inference being, a blasé attitude to the dangers and a disdain of the common soldiery he was forced to mix with.' Tony Bagnall Smith added that the Guards officer was still properly dressed and equipped when he said it, and that his reply was: 'My dear, the noise and the people – how they smelt!'

The *Oxford Dictionary of Quotations* (1992) appeared to have come round to the earlier use regarding Dunkirk and gives a citation. In the form 'The noise, my dear! And the people!', it was already being quoted in Anthony Rhodes, *Sword of Bone*, Chap. 22 (1942).

Another originator is said to be Lord Sefton, a Guards officer at Dunkirk (suggested in correspondence in *The London Review of Books*, beginning 29 October 1998). In the same correspondence, an assertion reappeared that it was something said by the actor Ernest Thesiger at a dinner party in 1919 regarding his experiences as a soldier in the battle of the Somme.

4 I launched the phrase 'the war to end war' and that was not the least of my crimes.

H.G. Wells, English novelist and writer (1866–1946). Quoted in Geoffrey West, *H.G. Wells* (1930).

5 As long as war is regarded as wicked, it will always have its fascination. When it is looked upon as vulgar, it will cease to be popular.

Oscar Wilde, Irish playwright, poet and wit (1854–1900). 'The Critic As Artist' (1890).

6 Retreat? Hell, no! We just got here!

Lloyd S. William, American soldier (early twentieth century). Attributed remark. Made by Captain William when advised by the French to retreat, shortly after his arrival at the Western Front in the First World War. Or, specifically referring to the retreat from Belloar (5 June 1918). Margaret Thatcher quoted it at a Confederation of British Industry dinner in 1980. Compare: 'Retreat, hell! We're just fighting in another direction' - attributed to General Oliver Prince Smith, US Marine Corps, at Changjin Reservoir, North Korea (Fall 1950). When trapped by eight divisions of Chinese Communists in North Korea he led the 20,000-man 1st Division on a bloody, 13-day, 70-mile breakthrough to the sea and rescue (information from Eric Partridge, *A Dictionary of Catch Phrases*, 1985 edn). However, when the title *Retreat, Hell!* was bestowed on a film of this event (US 1952), a different ascription was given by the screenwriters Milton Sperling and Ted Sherdeman. A Colonel says: 'We've been ordered to withdraw.' Soldier: 'You mean retreat?' Colonel: 'Retreat? Hell, we're just attacking in another direction.'

Washington D.C.

1 Too small to be a state but too large to be an asylum for the mentally deranged.

Anne M. Burford, American environmentalist (1942–). Speech, Vail, Colorado (27 July 1984). Compare the remark made by James L. Petigru in Christmas week 1860: 'South Carolina is too small for a republic and too large for an insane asylum' – quoted in Earl Schenck Miers, *The Great Rebellion* (1958).

2 Washington is a city of southern efficiency and northern charm.

John F. Kennedy, American Democratic President (1917–63). Quoted in Arthur M. Schlesinger, *A Thousand Days* (1965).

Waste

3 *Tony (disguised as hotel detective):*
Have you got a woman in here?
Hackenbush:
If I haven't, I've wasted thirty minutes of valuable time.

Lines from film *A Day at the Races* (US 1937). Screenwriters: Robert Pirosh, George Seaton, George Oppenheimer. Spoken by Groucho Marx (Dr Hackenbush) and Chico Marx (Tony).

Watches

4 I am a sundial, and I make a botch
Of what is done far better by a watch.

Hilaire Belloc, French-born English poet and writer (1870–1953). Epigram in *Sonnets and Verse* (1923).

Water

5 Water taken in moderation cannot hurt anybody.

Mark Twain, American writer (1835–1910). *Mark Twain's Notebook*, ed. A. B. Paine (1935).

We

6 Only presidents, editors, and people with tapeworms have the right to use the editorial 'we'.

H.L. Mencken, American journalist and linguist (1880–1956). Attributed remark. Sometimes in the form: 'There are two kinds of people entitled to refer to themselves as "we". One is an editor, the other is a fellow with a tapeworm.' Also attributed to Edgar Wilson 'Bill' Nye and Mark Twain.

7 We have become a grandmother.

Margaret Thatcher (Baroness Thatcher), British Conservative Prime Minister (1925–). Remark to news reporters (3 March 1989). From this use of the royal 'we' stemmed a conviction in some observers that all was not well with Mrs Thatcher. She only remained in office another year and a half.

Wealth

8 A man who has a million dollars is as well off as if he were rich.

John Jacob Astor, American financier (1864–1912). Quoted as told to Julia Ward Howe, in Cleveland Amory, *The Last Resorts* (1952).

9 If you would know what the Lord God thinks of money, you have only to look at those to whom He gave it.

Maurice Baring, English writer (1874–1945). Attributed by Dorothy Parker, according to Malcolm Cowley (ed.), *Writers at Work*, First Series (1958). This has also been described as a New England saying.

10 Money is honey, my little sonny,
A rich man's joke is always funny.

T(homas) E(dward) Brown, English poet and schoolmaster (1830–97). Poem, 'The Doctor' (1887). Compare Goldsmith below.

11 Lord Finchley tried to mend the Electric
Light
Himself. It struck him dead: And serve
him right!
It is the business of the wealthy man
To give employment to the artisan.

Hilaire Belloc, French-born English poet and writer (1870–1953). *More Peers*, 'Lord Finchley' (1911).

1 Mother told me a couple of years ago, 'Sweetheart, settle down and marry a rich man.' I said, 'Mom, I am a rich man.'

Cher, American actress and singer (1946–). Interviewed in *The Observer* Review (November 1995).

2 *Amanda:*

Whose yacht is that?

Elyot:

The Duke of Westminster's, I expect. It always is.

(Sir) Noël Coward, English entertainer and writer (1899–1973). *Private Lives*. Act 1 (1930).

3 He does not possess wealth; it possesses him.

Benjamin Franklin, American politician and scientist (1706–90). *Poor Richard's Almanack* (July 1735) – a work in which Franklin often revised already existing sayings.

4 The jests of the rich are ever successful.

Oliver Goldsmith, Irish-born playwright and writer (1730–74). *The Vicar of Wakefield*, Chap. 7 (1766). Compare Brown above.

5 I don't know how much money I've got ... I did ask the accountant how much it came to. I wrote it down on a bit of paper. But I've lost the bit of paper.

John Lennon, English singer and songwriter (1940–80). Quoted in Hunter Davies, *The Beatles* (1968).

6 God shows his contempt for wealth by the kind of person he selects to receive it.

Austin O'Malley, American oculist and humorist (1858–1932). Quoted in *The Treasury of Humorous Quotations*, ed. Evan Esar & Nicolas Bentley (1951).

Weariness

7 After three days men grow weary, of a wench, a guest and weather rainy.

Benjamin Franklin, American politician and scientist (1706–90). *Poor Richard's Almanack* (June 1733) – a work in which Franklin often revised already existing sayings.

Weather

8 The weather will be cold. There are two reasons for this. One is that the temperatures will be lower.

Anonymous (radio weather forecaster). In 1969. Contributed to BBC Radio *Quote ... Unquote* (15 June 1977).

9 A woman rang to say she'd heard there was a hurricane on the way. Well, don't worry. There isn't.

Michael Fish, English TV weather forecaster (1933–). On BBC TV, on the eve of the Great Storm in which devastation laid waste a swathe of southern England. Quoted in *The Observer*, 'Sayings of the Week' (19 October 1987).

10 Some are weather-wise, some otherwise.

Benjamin Franklin, American politician and scientist (1706–90). *Poor Richard's Almanack* (February 1735) – a work in which Franklin often revised already existing sayings.

11 When two Englishmen meet, their first talk is of the weather.

(Dr) Samuel Johnson, English writer and lexicographer (1709–84). In *The Idler*, No. 11 (27 May 1758).

After heavy rain:

12 I was measured for a cork jacket yesterday. Walking is out of the question just now. We can only get from place to place by swimming.

(Revd) Sydney Smith, English clergyman, essayist and wit (1771–1845). Letter (December 1838), quoted in Saba, Lady Holland, *Memoir* (1855).

13 Heat, ma'am! It was so dreadful here that I found there was nothing left for it but to take off my flesh and sit in my bones.

(Revd) Sydney Smith. Quoted in Saba, Lady Holland, *Memoir*, Vol. 1, Chap. 9 (1855).

14 'Tis very warm weather when one's in bed.

Jonathan Swift, Anglo-Irish writer and clergyman (1667–1745). *Journal to Stella* (1768) – for 8 November 1710.

1 If you don't like the weather in New England now, just wait a few minutes.

Mark Twain, American writer (1835–1910). So ascribed in Herbert V. Prochnow, Snr & Jnr, *A Treasury of Humorous Quotations* (1969), but this does not appear in the text of the speech on 'The Weather' to the New England Society (22 December 1876). On the other hand, Wolfgang Mieder lists 'If you don't like the weather in New England, just wait a minute and it will change' as merely a 'New England saying' in his *Yankee Wisdom: New England Proverbs* (1989). Perhaps this proverbial saying was assigned to Twain on account of its similarity to this passage in his 1876 speech: 'There is a sumptuous variety about the New England weather that compels the stranger's admiration – and regret. The weather is always doing something there; always attending strictly to business; always getting up new designs and trying them on the people to see how they will go. But it gets through more business in spring than in any other season. In the spring I have counted one hundred and thirty-six different kinds of weather inside of four-and-twenty hours ... Yes, one of the brightest gems in the New England weather is the dazzling uncertainty of it.'

2 Everybody talks about the weather but nobody does anything about it.

Charles Dudley Warner, American journalist (1829–1900). It first appeared in an unsigned editorial in the *Hartford Courant* (24 August 1897) in the form – 'A well-known American writer said once that, while everybody talked about the weather, nobody seemed to do anything about it' – but the quip has often been assigned to Mark Twain who lived in Hartford (Connecticut) at the time and was a friend and collaborator of Warner's.

3 Whenever people talk to me about the weather, I always feel certain that they mean something else.

Oscar Wilde, Irish playwright, poet and wit (1854–1900). *The Importance of Being Earnest*, Act 1 (1895). Gwendolen speaking.

Webb, Sidney and Beatrice

ENGLISH SOCIALIST THINKERS (1859–1947) AND (1858–1943)

4 Two of the nicest people if ever there was one.

Alan Bennett, English playwright and actor (1934–). *Forty Years On*, Act 2 (1969). This line does not appear in the published script of Bennett's play, though it was spoken in the original production.

Welcomes

5 *Mrs Teasdale:*
As chairwoman of the reception committee, I welcome you with open arms.
Firefly:
Is that so? How late do you stay open?

Lines from film *Duck Soup* (US 1933). Screenwriters: Bert Kalmar, Harry Ruby, Arthur Sheekman, Nat Perrin. Spoken by Margaret Dumont (Mrs Teasdale) and Groucho Marx (Rufus T. Firefly).

6 I appreciate your welcome. As the cow said to the Maine farmer, 'Thank you for a warm hand on a cold morning.'

John F. Kennedy, American Democratic President (1917–63). Speech, Los Angeles (2 November 1960).

Wellerisms

7 'That's an antelope,' observed the small boy when he heard that his mother's sister had run away with the coachman.

Anonymous. In *The Wasp* (California), Vol 3, No. 144 (1879). Quoted in *A Dictionary of Wellerisms*, ed. Mieder & Kingsbury (1994).

8 'Every little helps,' quoth the wren when she pissed in the sea.

Anonymous. Quoted in William Camden, *Remains Concerning Britaine* (1605).

9 '*Au contraire*', as the man said when asked if he'd dined on the boat.

G.K. Chesterton, English poet, novelist and critic (1874–1936). *The Man Who Was Thursday* (1907/8).

10 *Sam Weller:*
It's over, and can't be helped, and that's one consolation, as they always say in Turkey, ven they cut the wrong man's head off.

Charles Dickens, English novelist (1812–70). *Pickwick*

Papers, Chap. 23 (1837). Hence, the term 'wellerism' for a form of comparison in which a saying or proverbial expression is attributed to an amusingly inapposite source. Mieder & Kingsbury in their *Dictionary of Wellerisms* (1994) note that a wellerism usually consists of three parts: a statement, a speaker who makes this remark, and a phrase or clause that places the utterance in a new light or an incompatible setting. The type was known long before Dickens gave a fondness for uttering these jocular remarks to Sam Weller. Dickens did, however, popularize the form which came to be known as 'wellerism' (the word known by 1839).

1 Anythin' for a quiet life, as the man said wen he took the sitivation at the lighthouse.

Charles Dickens. In the same book as above.

2 Business first, pleasure afterwards, as King Richard said when he stabbed the other king in the Tower, before he smothered the babies.

Charles Dickens. In the same book as above.

3 Far from it, as the private said when he aimed at the bulls-eye and hit the gunnery instructor.

Dorothy L. Sayers, English novelist (1893–1957). *Unnatural Death* (1927).

Wembley

4 Wembley, adj. Suffering from a vague *malaise*. 'I feel a bit w. this morning.'

Paul Jennings, English humorist (1918–89). *The Jenguin Pennings*, 'Ware, Wye, Watford' (1963).

Westerns

5 I wouldn't say when you've seen one Western you've seen the lot: but when you've seen the lot you get the feeling you've seen one.

Katharine Whitehorn, English journalist (1928–). *Sunday Best*, 'Decoding the West' (1976).

Wetness

6 I must get out of these wet clothes and into a dry martini.

Robert Benchley, American humorist (1889–1945).

Variously used line, as in the film, *The Major and the Minor* (US 1942) – spoken by Benchley to Ginger Rogers in the form 'Why don't you get out of that wet coat and into a dry Martini?' Sometimes also attributed to Alexander Woollcott, the line may actually have originated with Benchley's press agent in the 1920s or with his friend Charles Butterworth. In any case, Mae West used the line, as screenwriter, in *Every Day's a Holiday* (1937).

Whims

7 King Barumph has a whim of iron.

Oliver Herford, American humorist (1863–1935). *Excuse It Please*, 'Impossible pudding' (1929). In Frank Crowninshield, *A Wit With a Whim of Iron*, there is also this: 'One morning Oliver arrived at the Club wearing an exaggerated, not to say impossible, hat. Derided for it, he explained that the choice had not been his, "It was a whim of my wife's," he said. "Disregard all that, and throw the hat away," his friends said. "You don't know her," he said, "she has a whim of iron".'

Whistler, James McNeill

AMERICAN PAINTER (1834–1903)

8 As for borrowing Mr Whistler's ideas about art, the only thoroughly original ideas I have ever heard him express have had reference to his own superiority as a painter over painters greater than himself.

Oscar Wilde, Irish playwright, poet and wit (1854–1900). In *Truth* (January 1890).

9 Mr Whistler always spelt art, and we believe still spells it, with a capital 'I'.

Oscar Wilde. Quoted in *The Uncollected Oscar Wilde*, ed. John Wyse Jackson (1995).

10 That he is indeed one of the very greatest masters of painting is my opinion. And I may add that in this opinion Mr Whistler himself entirely concurs.

Oscar Wilde. Quoted in the same book as above.

11 Whistler, with all his faults, was never guilty of writing a line of poetry.

Oscar Wilde. Quoted in *The Treasury of Humorous Quotations*, ed. Evan Esar & Nicolas Bentley (1951).

Wickedness

1 Wickedness is a myth invented by good people to account for the curious attractiveness of others.

Oscar Wilde, Irish playwright, poet and wit (1854–1900). 'Phrases and Philosophies for the Use of the Young', in *The Chameleon* (December 1894).

Widows

2 He had heard that one is permitted a certain latitude with widows, and went in for the whole 180 degrees.

George Ade, American humorist (1866–1944). Quoted in *The Treasury of Humorous Quotations*, ed. Evan Esar & Nicolas Bentley (1951).

3 The rich widow cries with one eye and rejoices with the other.

Miguel de Cervantes, Spanish novelist (1547–1616). Attributed remark.

4 When widows exclaim loudly against second marriages, I would always lay a wager that the man, if not the wedding day, is absolutely fixed-on.

Henry Fielding, English novelist and judge (1707–54). *Amelia*, Chap. 6 (1751).

Letter from a Tyrolean landlord:

5 Standing among savage scenery, the hotel offers stupendous revelations. There is a French widow in every bedroom (affording delightful prospects).

Gerard Hoffnung, English cartoonist and musician (1925–59). Speech, Oxford Union debating society (4 December 1958).

Lady Bracknell (having called on Lady Harbury):

6 I hadn't been there since her poor husband's death. I never saw a woman so altered; she looks quite twenty years younger…

Algernon:

I hear her hair turned quite gold from grief.

Oscar Wilde, Irish playwright, poet and wit (1854–1900). *The Importance of Being Earnest*, Act 1 (1895).

Wilde, Oscar

IRISH PLAYWRIGHT, POET AND WIT (1854–1900)

7 The only crime he ever committed was having three plays running simultaneously in the West End.

Brendan Behan, Irish playwright (1923–64). Quoted in Peter Arthurs, *With Brendan Behan* (1981).

8 He had nothing to say and he said it.

Ambrose Bierce, American journalist (1942–?1914). Attributed remark. In Wilde's own *The Picture of Dorian Gray*, there is: 'Women ... never have anything to say, but they say it charmingly.' Similarly, a review in *The Times* (5 May 1937) of a book by A.A. Milne said: 'When there is nothing whatever to say, no one knows better than Mr Milne how to say it.' Compare also: 'The magic of [Bernard] Shaw's words may still bewitch posterity ... but it will find that he has nothing to say' - A.J.P. Taylor in *The Observer* (22 July 1956). 'Berlioz says nothing in his music but he says it magnificently' – James Gibbons Huneker, *Old Fogy* (1913). And before this from Charles Dickens, *Little Dorrit*, Bk 1, Chap. 10 (1855–1857): 'And although one of two things always happened, namely, either that the Circumlocution Office had nothing to say and said it, or that it had something to say of which the noble lord, or right honourable gentleman, blundered one half and forgot the other; the Circumlocution Office was always voted immaculate by an accommodating majority.'

9 He left behind, as his essential contribution to literature, a large repertoire of jokes which survive because of their sheer neatness, and because of a certain intriguing uncertainty – which extends to Wilde himself – as to whether they really mean anything.

George Orwell, English novelist and journalist (1903–50). Included in *Orwell: The Lost Writings* (1985).

10 If, with the literate, I am
Impelled to try an epigram,

I never seek to take the credit;
We all assume that Oscar said it.

Dorothy Parker, American writer (1893–1967). 'A Pig's Eye View of Literature' (1937).

1 I awoke the imagination of my century so that it created myth and legend around me: I summed up all systems in a phrase, and all existence in an epigram.

Oscar Wilde, Irish playwright, poet and wit (1854–1900). *De Profundis* (1905) – originally in letter from Reading gaol, to Lord Alfred Douglas (January–March 1897).

2 Oscar was NOT a man of bad character: you could have trusted him with a woman anywhere.

Willie Wilde, Oscar's brother. Quoted in George Bernard Shaw, *Pen Portraits and Reviews* (1932).

Wills (1)

3 To be enjoyable, a will must be at one and the same time a practical joke on the heirs and an advertisement of the man that made it.

Finley Peter Dunne, American humorist (1867–1936). *Mr Dooley Remembers* (1963 edn).

4 Where there's a will there's a lawsuit.

Oliver Herford, American humorist (1863–1935), and Addison Mizner, American architect (1872–1933). *The Cynic's Calendar* (1902).

Wills (2)

5 I think it will be a clash between the political will and the administrative won't.

Jonathan Lynn and (Sir) Antony Jay, English writers (1943–) and (1930–). *Yes Prime Minister*, Vol. 2 (1987).

Wilson, Harold (Lord Wilson of Rievaulx)

BRITISH LABOUR PRIME MINISTER (1916–95)

6 If ever he went to school without any boots it was because he was too big for them.

Ivor Bulmer-Thomas (formerly Ivor Thomas), Welsh Labour, then Conservative, MP (1905–93). Speech at Conservative Party Conference (12 October 1949) – a remark often wrongly ascribed to Harold Macmillan. It followed a press dispute involving Wilson the previous year.

Wine

7 The point about white Burgundies is that I hate them myself ... so closely resembling a blend of chalk soup and alum cordial with an additive or two to bring it to the colour of children's pee.

(Sir) Kingsley Amis, English novelist, poet and critic (1922–95). *The Green Man* (1969).

8 *One drinker to another:*
I keep this port only for my best friends.
Other drinker:
I don't blame you.

Anonymous. Quoted in *A Year of Stings and Squelches* (1985).

9 When wine is in the wit is out.

Anonymous (proverb). The idea is expressed as far back as Pliny.

10 And Noah he often said to his wife when
he sat down to dine,
'I don't care where the water goes if it
doesn't get into the wine.'

G.K. Chesterton, English poet, novelist and critic (1874–1936). *The Flying Inn*, 'Wine and Water' (1914).

11 Wine hath drowned more men than the sea.

Thomas Fuller, English writer and physician (1654–1734). *Gnomologia* (1732).

12 God made only water, but man made wine.

Victor Hugo, French poet and writer (1802–85). *Les Contemplations* (1856).

How to promote a Cockburn '97, clearly past its best:

13 Talk of the 'imperial decay' of your invalid port. 'Its gracious withdrawal from perfection, keeping a hint of former majesty,

withal, as it hovers between oblivion and the divine *Untergang* of infinite recession.'

Stephen Potter, English humorist (1900–69). *One-Upmanship* (1952).

1 It's a Naive Domestic Burgundy without Any Breeding, But I Think You'll be amused by its Presumption.

James Thurber, American cartoonist and writer (1894–1961). Caption to cartoon in *Men, Women and Dogs* (1943).

2 A meal without wine is a day without sunshine.

Louis Vaudable, French restaurateur. Quoted in *Life* Magazine (7 January 1966). Vaudable was owner of Maxim's in Paris. He may have been quoting a proverbial saying.

3 Wine gives you liberty, love takes it away.

William Wycherley, English playwright (1640?–1716). *The Country Wife*, Act 1, Sc. 1 (1675).

Winning

4 Anybody can win, unless there happens to be a second entry.

George Ade, American humorist and playwright (1866–1944). Quoted in *The Treasury of Humorous Quotations*, ed. Evan Esar & Nicolas Bentley (1951).

On the tortoise and hare myth:

5 In real life, of course, it is the hare who wins. Every time. Look around you. And in any case it is my contention that Aesop was writing for the tortoise market ... Hares have no time to read. They are too busy winning the game.

Anita Brookner, English art historian and novelist (1928–). *Hotel du Lac*, Chap. 2 (1984).

Wisdom

6 It hath been my opinion, that the French are wiser than they seem, and the Spaniards seem wiser than they are.

Francis Bacon (1st Baron Verulam and Viscount St Albans), English philosopher and politician (1561–1626). *Essays*, 'Of Seeming Wise' (1625).

To a judge who had complained that he was no wiser at the end than when he started hearing one of Smith's cases:

7 Possibly not, My Lord, but far better informed.

F.E. Smith (1st Earl of Birkenhead), English politician and lawyer (1872–1930). Quoted in 2nd Earl of Birkenhead, *The Earl of Birkenhead* (1933).

8 Some folks are wise, and some are otherwise.

Tobias Smollett, Scottish-born novelist (1721–71). *The Adventures of Roderick Random*, Chap. 6 (1748). A popular saying of the time.

Wishes

9 I wish I were a teddy bear
With hairs upon my tummy.
I'd climb into a honey poet
And get my tummy, gummy.

Anonymous. Known by the late 1950s.

Wit

On New York taxi drivers:

10 They try to live up to the reputation all taxi drivers have, of being a wit. As I am in the wit business myself, I object to competition.

Brendan Behan, Irish playwright (1923–64). *Brendan Behan's New York* (1964).

11 A wit should no more be sincere than a woman constant: one argues a decay of parts, as t'other of beauty.

William Congreve, English playwright (1670–1729). *The Way of the World*, Act 1, Sc. 6 (1700).

12 Wit is like caviar – it should be served in small portions, and not spread about like marmalade.

(Sir) Noël Coward, English entertainer and writer (1899–1973). Quoted in *Newsweek* (1965).

1 A dinner of wits is proverbially a palace of silence.

Benjamin Disraeli (1st Earl of Beaconsfield), English politician and writer (1804–81). *Endymion*, Chap. 91 (1880).

On W.S. Gilbert's memorial on the Victoria Embankment, London:

2 His foe was folly & his weapon wit.

Anthony Hope (Sir Anthony Hope Hawkins), English novelist (1863–1933). Hope recalled: 'Whilst on the committee of the Authors' Society I had something to do with the memorial. The words on the memorial are mine, except that I put them first into prose – "Folly was his foe, and wit his weapon", - then somebody (I forget who) pointed out that transposed they would make a line, and this was adopted [in 1915].'

3 Wit sometimes enables us to act rudely with impunity.

François, Duc de La Rochefoucauld, French writer (1613–80). Quoted in *The Treasury of Humorous Quotations*, ed. Evan Esar & Nicolas Bentley (1951).

4 There's a hell of a difference between wise-cracking and wit. Wit has truth in it; wise-cracking is simply callisthenics with words.

Dorothy Parker, American writer (1893–1967). In *The Paris Review* (Summer 1956).

5 You beat your pate, and fancy wit will come:
Knock as you please, there's nobody at home.

Alexander Pope, English poet (1688–1744). 'Epigram: you beat your pate' (1732).

6 Lightning must, I think, be the wit of heaven.

(Revd) Sydney Smith, English clergyman, essayist and wit (1771–1845). Quoted in Saba, Lady Holland, *Memoir* (1855).

7 A very little wit is valued in a woman, as we are pleased with a few words spoken plain by a parrot.

Jonathan Swift, Anglo-Irish writer and clergyman (1667–1745). *Thoughts on Various Subjects* (1711–45).

Wives

8 They say a woman should be a cook in the kitchen and a whore in bed. Unfortunately, my wife is a whore in the kitchen and a cook in bed.

Anonymous. Quoted in Geoffrey Gorer, *Exploring English Character* (1955) – in which readers of the *Sunday People* were invited to take part in a survey about their sex lives. This was collected from a 'working class, Sunderland' man.

Notice outside fried-fish shop:

9 CLEANLINESS, ECONOMY AND CIVILITY. ALWAYS HOT AND ALWAYS READY.

Anonymous. A passer-by remarked that this was the motto for a perfect wife. The passer-by was possibly Edward Thomas and the remark was recorded by E.S.P. Haynes in his *Lawyer's Notebook* (1932).

10 There is a lady, sweet and kind
As any lady you will find.
I've known her nearly all my life;
She is, in fact, my present wife.

Reginald Arkell, English poet (1882–1959). Poem, 'The Lady with the Lamp', which appeared in his *Green Fingers* (1934). 'There is a lady sweet and kind' is also the first line of a poem attributed to Thomas Ford (d. 1648).

11 'Gad, my wife looks terrible tonight!'
'Sir, you are speaking of the woman I love!'

Peter Arno, American cartoonist (1904–68). Caption to cartoon included in *Parade* (1931).

12 A quarrelsome wife is like a dripping tap on a rainy day.

The Bible. Proverbs 27:15.

13 I've never yet met a man who could look after me. I don't need a husband. What I need is a wife.

Joan Collins, English actress (1933–). Quoted in *The Observer* 'Sayings of the Week' (26 July 1987). After her fourth marriage had gone bust.

1 These articles subscribed, if I continue to endure you a little longer, I may by degrees dwindle into a wife.

William Congreve, English playwright (1670–1729). *The Way of the World,* Act 4, Sc. 5 (1700). Millamant to Mirabell.

2 A good wife is good, but the best wife is not so good as no wife at all.

Thomas Hardy, English novelist and poet (1840–1928). Quoted in *The Treasury of Humorous Quotations*, ed. Evan Esar & Nicolas Bentley (1951).

3 I have learned that only two things are necessary to keep one's wife happy. First, let her think she's having her way. And second, let her have it.

Lyndon B. Johnson, American Democratic President (1908–73). Speech at White House reception for Princess Margaret and Lord Snowdon (17 November 1965).

On his wife's joining a national defense program:

4 My only regret is that I have but one wife to give to my country.

Line from film *The Major and the Minor* (US 1942). Screenwriters: Billy Wilder and Charles Brackett. Spoken by Robert Benchley as 'Mr Osborne'.

5 Wife: a former sweetheart.

H.L. Mencken, American journalist and linguist (1880–1956). Quoted in *The Treasury of Humorous Quotations*, ed. Evan Esar & Nicolas Bentley (1951).

6 'Come, come,' said Tom's father, 'at your time of life,
'There's no longer excuse for thus playing the rake -
'It is time you should think, boy, of taking a wife' -
'Why, so it is, father - whose wife should I take?'

Thomas Moore, Irish poet (1779–1852). *Miscellaneous Poems,* 'A Joke Versified' (1840). The joke would appear to have been cracked by the radical politician John Horne Tooke (1736–1812) who, on being told he should take a wife, replied, 'With all my heart. Whose wife shall it be?'

Explaining why he wasn't taking his wife on an official visit to Paris:

7 You don't take a ham sandwich to the Lord Mayor's banquet, do you?

J(ames) H(enry) Thomas, English trade unionist and politician (1874–1949). Quoted in the *Cassell Companion to Quotations* (1997).

8 Take my wife – please!

Henny Youngman, British-born American comedian (1906–98). His most famous joke. According to an obituary in *The Times* (26 February 1998), this 'most-repeated one-liner was, in fact, first delivered by accident. Nervous before a radio appearance, he had begged an usher to seat his wife with the words: "Take my wife – please!" Everyone laughed, and the line became his signature.' He used it as the title of his autobiography in 1973.

Women

9 Women should be obscene and not heard.

Anonymous (graffito). In New York. Quoted in Reisner & Wechsler, *Encyclopedia of Graffiti* (1974).

10 A woman without a man is like a fish without a bicycle.

Anonymous (graffito). Elaine Partnow's *The Quotable Woman 1800–1981* (1982) attributes this saying to the American feminist Gloria Steinem but gives no hint as to why it makes such a very dubious attribution, though it is reasonable to assume that the words must have crossed Ms Steinem's lips at some stage. It is, after all, probably the most famous feminist slogan of recent decades. *Bartlett's Familiar Quotations* (1992) lists it anonymously as a 'feminist slogan of the 1980s'.

So, if not from Steinem, whence came the saying? Mrs C. Raikes of Moseley, Birmingham contributed it to BBC Radio *Quote ... Unquote* (1977), adding: 'I felt you had to share in this pearl of wisdom I found yesterday on a lavatory wall in Birmingham University. Written in German, it translates as ...' Indeed, the chances are that the saying may have originated in West Germany where it was known in the form, '*Eine Frau ohne Mann ist wie ein Fisch ohne Velo!*' Meanwhile, in the US this same year, *Ms.* Magazine was advertising T-shirts with the slogan on them (in English). Perhaps this is the explanation for the Steinem attribution?

Compare, however, what Arthur Bloch in *Murphy's Law*

... (also 1977) calls 'Vique's Law': 'A man without religion is like a fish without a bicycle.' In a 1974 book called *II Cybernetic Frontiers*, Stewart Brand attributed 'A man without a God is like a fish without a bicycle' to the late *San Francisco Chronicle* columnist Herb Caen. All this seemed to suggest that the feminist slogan had merely been grafted on to an already existing phrase format.

In 1999, Charles S. Harris, a psychologist of Middle-town, NJ, presented me with some well-documented research into both facets of the case. For a start, he found an earlier attribution to Steinem in *Life* (December 1979)- [it is also in Barbara Rowes, *The Book of Quotes* (1979)] - and a mention of her specifically not wearing a T-shirt with the slogan on it at the 1976 Democratic Convention in *People* (26 July 1976). But also a denial from an interview with her on National Public Radio (9 February 1992): 'Yeah, I wish I knew who said it, 'cause I think it's quite funny, but it wasn't me.'

In addition, Harris put in a reasonable bid to have (as he thinks) coined the original phrase format: 'I do know where the fish without a bicycle came from: an intro philosophy class at Swarthmore College in 1955. In reaction to our assigned reading of St Augustine, I wrote: "*A man without faith* is like a fish without a bicycle." Later, it was printed along with other quips, in my weekly humor column in the Swarthmore College *Phoenix* (8 April 1958).'

Referring to her books of *Quotations by Women*, Rosalie Maggio stated (1999): 'I talked to Gloria Steinem about that quotation a few years ago - she has always maintained it wasn't original to her. Out of curiosity, she tracked it down to Irina Dunn (Patsi Dunn, 1948– , Australian educator, journalist, politician). I spoke with Dunn on the phone in 1995. She says she wrote it in at least two toilets in 1970, spinning it off from something in one of her textbooks – "Man without God is like a fish without a bicycle".' Which is where we came in.

In 1979, Arthur Marshall contributed the interesting variant: 'A woman without a man is like a moose without a hatrack.' In Haan & Hammerstrom, *Graffiti in the Big Ten* (1981) is 'Behind every successful man is a fish with a bicycle.'

1 Men who do not make advances to women are apt to become victims to women who make advances to them.

Walter Bagehot, English political writer (1826–77). Quoted in *The Treasury of Humorous Quotations*, ed. Evan Esar & Nicolas Bentley (1951).

Of Sir Thomas Beecham:

2 I never heard him refer to religion. To women he referred once, saying that none of them was worth the loss of a night's sleep.

(Sir) Thomas Beecham, English conductor (1879–1961). Quoted in Neville Cardus, *Sir Thomas Beecham* (1961).

3 *Mrs Gamadge (on a politician):*
The women are solidly behind Bill Russell.
Mabel Cantwell:
Under him is their more usual position.

Lines from film *The Best Man* (US 1964). Screenwriter: Gore Vidal (from his play). Spoken by Edie Adams (Mabel Cantwell) and Ann Sothern (Mrs Gamadge).

At an all-women college in Massachussetts:

4 Who knows, somewhere out there in the audience may even be someone who will one day follow in my footsteps and preside over the White House as the President's spouse. I wish him well.

Barbara Bush, American First Lady (1925–). Quoted in *The Independent* 'Quote Unquote' (9 June 1990).

5 Brigands demand your money or your life; women require both.

Samuel Butler, English author (1835–1902). Quoted in *The Treasury of Humorous Quotations*, ed. Evan Esar & Nicolas Bentley (1951).

6 There is a tide in the affairs of women,
Which, taken at the flood, leads – God
knows where.

Lord Byron, English poet (1788–1824). *Don Juan*, Canto 6, St. 2 (1819–24).

7 Do you know why God withheld the sense of humour from women? That we may love you instead of laughing at you.

Mrs Patrick Campbell, English actress (1865–1940). Quoted in Bennett Cerf, *The Laugh's On Me* (1961). Leslie Robert Missen, *Quotable Anecdotes* (1966) has the version: 'Women were born without a sense of humour – so they could love men, not laugh at them'.

1 Individually, men may present a more or less rational appearance, eating, sleeping and scheming. But humanity as a whole is changeful, mystical, fickle and delightful. Men are men, but Man is a woman.

G.K. Chesterton, English poet, novelist and critic (1874–1936). *The Napoleon of Notting Hill*, Chap. 1 (1904).

2 Twenty million young women rose to their feet with the cry *We will not be dictated to*, and promptly became stenographers.

G.K. Chesterton. Quoted Hesketh Pearson, *Lives of the Wits* (1962).

3 But what is woman? – only one of Nature's agreeable blunders.

Hannah Cowley, English playwright (1743–1809). *Who's the Dupe?*, Act 2 (1779).

4 The Bible says that the last thing God made was woman; He must have made her on a Saturday night – it shows fatigue.

Alexandre Dumas fils, French writer (1824–95). Quoted in *The Treasury of Humorous Quotations*, ed. Evan Esar & Nicholas Bentley (1951).

5 The happiest women, like the happiest nations, have no history.

George Eliot, English novelist (1819–80). *The Mill on the Floss*, Bk 6, Chap. 3 (1860). Eliot adapted a proverbial expression to her own ends. In the form, 'Happy the people whose annals are blank in history-books!', the saying was ascribed to Montesquieu by Thomas Carlyle in his *History of Frederick the Great* (1858–65). In *The French Revolution – A History* (1838), Carlyle had written: 'A paradoxical philosopher, carrying to the uttermost length that aphorism of Montesquieu's, "Happy the people whose annals are tiresome," has said, "Happy the people whose annals are vacant".'

Theodore Roosevelt said in a speech (10 April 1899): 'It is a base untruth to say that happy is the nation that has no history. Thrice happy is the nation that has a glorious history. Far better it is to dare mighty things, to win glorious triumphs, even though checkered by failure, than to take rank with those spirits who neither enjoy much nor suffer much because they live in the grey twilight that knows neither victory nor defeat.' The earliest form of the proverb found by *Concise Dictionary of Proverbs* is in Benjamin Franklin, *Poor Richard's Almanack* (1740): 'Happy that Nation, – fortunate that age, whose history is not diverting.'

6 My mother said it was simple to keep a man – you must be a maid in the living room, a cook in the kitchen and a whore in the bedroom. I said I'd hire the other two and take care of the bedroom bit.

Jerry Hall, American model (1956–). Quoted in *The Observer*, 'Sayings of the Week' (6 October 1985).

7 Can you imagine a world without men? No crime and lots of happy, fat women.

Nicole Hollander, American illustrator and cartoonist (late twentieth century). Syndicated comic strip 'Sylvia' (1981). It has also been attributed to Marion Smith.

8 The female sex has no bigger fan than I, and I have the bills to prove it.

Alan Jay, American songwriter and playwright (1918–86). *The Street Where I Live*, 'My Fair Lady' (1978).

9 Sir, a woman's preaching is like a dog's walking on his hinder legs. It is not done well; but you are surprised to find it done at all.

(Dr) Samuel Johnson, English writer and lexicographer (1709–84). In James Boswell, *The Life of Samuel Johnson* (1791) – relating to 31 July 1763, when Boswell mentions that, 'I had been that morning at a meeting of the people called Quakers, where I had heard a woman preach.'

10 If I had no duties, and no reference to futurity, I would spend my life in driving briskly in a post-chaise with a pretty woman; but she should be one who could understand me, and would add something to the conversation.

(Dr) Samuel Johnson. Quoted in the same book – relating to 19 September 1777.

11 When women kiss, it always reminds me of prize-fighters shaking hands.

H.L. Mencken, American journalist and linguist (1880–1956). *A Mencken Chrestomathy* (1949).

1 Women are like elephants to me. I like to look at them, but I wouldn't want to own one.

Line from film *Mississippi* (US 1935). Screenwriters: W.C. Fields and others. Spoken by W.C. Fields (Commodore Orlando Jackson). Has also been attributed to Frank McKinney ('Kin') Hubbard in *Abe Martin's Primer* (1914).

2 She has a Rolls body and a Balham mind.

J.B. Morton (Beachcomber), English humorous writer (1893–1979). *Morton's Folly* (1933).

3 Woman was God's second mistake.

Friedrich Wilhelm Nietzsche, German philosopher (1844–1900). *Der Antichrist*, Aphorism no. 48 (1888).

4 Whether they give or refuse, it delights women to have been asked [*Quod juvat, invitae saepe dedisse volunt*].

Ovid, Roman writer (43 BC–AD c. 17). *Ars Amatoria*, Bk 1, l. 674.

5 A woman is like a teabag. It's only when she's in hot water that you realize how strong she is.

Nancy Reagan, American First Lady (1923–). Quoted in *The Observer*, 'Sayings of the Week' (29 March 1981).

6 Women never look so well as when one comes in wet and dirty from hunting.

R.S. Surtees, English novelist and journalist (1805–64). *Mr Sponge's Sporting Tour*, Chap. 21 (1853). A possibly ambivalent statement, but it is definitely from the point of view of the man who is coming in from hunting.

7 A woman's place is in the wrong.

James Thurber, American cartoonist and writer (1894–1961). Notion discussed but not originated by him.

8 [A husband] was reproached by a friend, who said: 'I think it a shame that you have not spoken to your wife for fifteen years. How do you explain it?' That poor man said: 'I didn't want to interrupt her.'

Mark Twain, American writer (1835–1910). In *North American Review* (15 March 1907).

9 Women represent the triumph of matter over mind, just as men represent the triumph of mind over morals.

Oscar Wilde, Irish playwright, poet and wit (1854–1900). *The Picture of Dorian Gray*, Chap. 4 (1891). Later, in *A Woman of No Importance*, Act 3 (1893).

10 I am on the side of the Trojans. They fought for a woman.

Oscar Wilde. In *Dorian Gray*, Chap. 17.

11 Women have a wonderful instinct about things. They can discover everything except the obvious.

Oscar Wilde. *An Ideal Husband*, Act 2 (1895).

12 Women who have common sense are so curiously plain.

Oscar Wilde. In the same play, Act 3.

13 The three women I have most admired are Queen Victoria, Sarah Bernhardt, and Lillie Langtry. I would have married any one of them with pleasure.

Oscar Wilde. Quoted in Vincent O'Sullivan, *Aspects of Oscar Wilde* (1936).

14 In a world without men, there would be no war – just intense negotations every 28 days.

Robin Williams, American comic and actor (1951–). In *Robin Williams at the Met One-Man Show* (1986).

Wordplay

15 Who's Afraid of Virginia Woolf?

Edward Albee, American playwright (1928–). Title of play (1962), from a graffito seen in Greenwich Village. The character Martha sings it in the play to the tune of 'Who's Afraid of the Big Bad Wolf?' – that is her little joke.

Challenged to compose a sentence including the word 'horticulture':

16 You can a lead a whore to culture but you can't make her think.

Dorothy Parker, American writer (1893–1967). Quoted in John Keats, *You Might as Well Live* (1970).

Words

1 Words fascinate me. They always have. For me, browsing in a dictionary is like being turned loose in a bank.

Eddie Cantor, American entertainer (1892–1964). *The Way I See It* (1959).

2 Short words are best and the old words when short are the best of all.

(Sir) Winston S. Churchill, British Conservative Prime Minister and writer (1874–1965). Speech, London (2 November 1949).

3 Nouns of number, or multitude, such as Mob, Parliament, Rabble, House of Commons, Regiment, Court of King's bench, Den of Thieves, and the like.

William Cobbett, English essayist and politician (1762–1835). *A Grammar of the English Language*, 'Syntax as Relating to Pronouns' (1818).

To two ladies who said they were glad there were no naughty words included in his Dictionary*:*

4 What, my dears! then you have been looking for them.

(Dr) Samuel Johnson, English writer and lexicographer (1709–84). Quoted in *Johnsonian Miscellanies*, ed. Hill (1897).

5 'Well,' said Owl, 'the customary procedure in such cases is as follows.' 'What does Crustimoney Proseedcake mean?' said Pooh. 'For I am a Bear of Very Little Brain, and long words Bother me.'

A.A. Milne, English writer (1882–1956). *Winnie-the-Pooh*, Chap. 4 (1926).

6 In the beginning was the Word. It's about the only sentence on which I find myself in total agreement with God.

(Sir) John Mortimer, English author, playwright and lawyer (1923–). Quoted in *The Observer*, 'Sayings of the Week' (1 July 1984).

7 The trouble with words is that you never know whose mouths they've been in.

Dennis Potter, English playwright (1935–94). Quoted in *The Guardian* (15 February 1993).

8 Man does not live by words alone, despite the fact that sometimes he has to eat them.

Adlai Stevenson, American Democratic politician (1900–65). Speech (5 September 1952).

Wordsworth, William

ENGLISH POET (1770–1850)

9 Two voices are there: one is of the deep;
It learns the storm-cloud's thunderous
  melody,
Now roars, now murmurs with the
  changing sea,
Now bird-like pipes, now closes soft
  in sleep;
And one is of an old half-witted sheep
Which bleats articulate monotony,
And indicates that two and one are three,
That grass is green, lakes damp, and
  mountains steep:
And Wordsworth, both are thine.

J.K. Stephen, English journalist and light versifier (1859–92). *Lapsus Calami*, 'A Sonnet' (1896).

Work

10 You don't have to be mad to work here – but it helps.

Anonymous. An extremely popular slogan on signs made for hanging in offices and workplaces, especially in the 1960s/70s. Preceded by the word 'methinks', it is spoken in Peter Nichols, *The National Health*, Act 1, Sc. 4 (1969).

11 Nothing is really work unless you would rather be doing something else.

(Sir) J(ames) M. Barrie, Scottish playwright (1860–1937). Quoted in Laurence J. Peter, *Quotations for Our Time* (1977).

1 Anyone can do any amount of work provided it isn't the work he is supposed to be doing at that moment.

Robert Benchley, American humorist (1889–1945). Quoted in *The Home Book of Humorous Quotations*, ed. A.K. Adams (1969).

2 The dictionary is the only place where success comes before work.

Arthur Brisbane, American newspaper editor (1864–1936). Attributed remark.

3 The only way to enjoy life is to work. Work is much more fun than fun.

(Sir) Noël Coward, English entertainer and writer (1899–1973). Quoted in Dick Richards, *The Wit of Noel Coward* (1968). This first appeared in *The Observer*, 'Sayings of the Week' (21 June 1963).

4 I like work: it fascinates me. I can sit and look at it for hours. I love to keep it by me: the idea of getting rid of it nearly breaks my heart.

Jerome K. Jerome, English writer (1859–1927). *Three Men In a Boat*, Chap. 3 (1889).

5 And so we plough along, as the fly said to the ox.

Henry Wadsworth Longfellow, American poet (1807–82). Quoted in *The Treasury of Humorous Quotations*, ed. Evan Esar & Nicolas Bentley (1951).

6 I go on working for the same reason that a hen goes on laying eggs.

H.L. Mencken, American writer and editor (1880–1956). Quoted in *The Treasury of Humorous Quotations*, ed. Evan Esar & Nicolas Bentley (1951).

7 It's true hard work never killed anybody, but I figure, why take the chance?

Ronald Reagan, American actor and Republican President (1911–). Speech (28 March 1987).

8 Set me anything to do as a task, and it is inconceivable the desire I have to do something else.

Bernard Shaw, Irish playwright and critic (1856–1950). Quoted in Gamaliel Bradford, *As God Made Them* (1929).

9 Work is the curse of the drinking classes.

Oscar Wilde, Irish playwright, poet and wit (1854–1900). Quoted in Frank Harris, *Oscar Wilde, His Life and Confessions*, Chap. 10 (1930).

10 Hard work is simply the refuge of people who have nothing better to do.

Oscar Wilde. 'The Remarkable Rocket' (1888).

Working life

11 Working for Warner Bros is like fucking a porcupine; it's a hundred pricks against one.

Wilson Mizner, American playwright (1876–1933). Quoted in David Niven, *Bring on the Empty Horses* (1975).

World

12 This world is a comedy to those that think, a tragedy to those that feel.

Horace Walpole (4th Earl of Orford), English writer (1717–97). Letter to the Countess of Upper Ossory (16 August 1776). However, Blaise Pascal (1623–62) is reported to have said earlier: *'La vie, c'est une tragédie pour celui qui sent, mais une comédie pour celui qui pense.'*

Wren, Sir Christopher

ENGLISH ARCHITECT (1632–1723)

13 Sir Christopher Wren
Said, 'I am going to dine with some men.
If anybody calls
Say I am designing St Paul's.'

E. Clerihew Bentley, English novelist, journalist and poet (1875–1956). *Biography for Beginners* (1905).

Wrinkles

14 Wrinkles should only indicate where smiles have been.

Mark Twain, American writer (1835–1910). *Following the Equator*, Vol. 2 (1897).

Writers and writing

To executive who had criticized one of his scripts:

1 Where were you when the page was blank?

Fred Allen, American comedian (1894–1956). Quoted by Denis Norden on BBC Radio *Quote ... Unquote* (11 October 1999).

2 I write in order to find out what I think.

Anonymous. The kind of thing that any writer might say. The British novelist Ian McEwan in *The Times* (27 June 1987): 'Writers divide between those who simply write to find out exactly what it is that they think, and those who have to think of the sentence first, then put it down, and constantly agonize about the gap between the thought and the language that's going to embody the thought.' David Lodge, *The Practice of Writing* (1997): 'You discover what it is you have to say in the process of saying it.'

However, there is also the line, which really says the same thing, in E.M. Forster's *Aspects of the Novel* (1927): 'That old lady in the anecdote ... was not so much angry as contemptuous ..."How can I tell what I think till I see what I say?"' Which may be the same as Graham Wallas, *The Art of Thought* (1926): 'The little girl had the making of a poet in her who, being told to be sure of her meaning before she spoke, said, "How can I know what I think till I see what I say?"'

Some near-misses and allusions: according to *The Treasury of Humorous Quotations*, ed. Bentley & Esar (1951), Horace Walpole wrote: 'I never understand anything until I have written about it.' Alphonse Daudet has a character in *Numa Roumestan* (1881) say: *'Quand je ne parle pas, je ne pense pas.'* To the poet Louis Macneice is attributed: 'How do I know what I think till I hear what I say.' And at the death of the American journalist James Reston in 1995, it was recalled what he said when his newspaper did not appear because of a strike: 'How can I know what I think if I can't read what I write?'

3 To give an accurate and exhaustive account of the period would need a far less brilliant pen than mine.

(Sir) Max Beerbohm, English writer and caricaturist (1872–1956). In *The Yellow Book* (1894).

4 Virginia [Woolf] was never a suffragette, for she subscribed to the theory that the pen was mightier than the sword; and I once saw Evelyn Waugh reel under a savage blow from her Parker 51.

Alan Bennett, English playwright and actor (1934–). *Forty Years On*, Act 2 (1968).

Coral Browne appeared as herself in Alan Bennett's TV play An Englishman Abroad, *based on her actual encounter in Moscow with the exiled spy Guy Burgess. A Hollywood writer told her that although he had enjoyed the play, he didn't think the writing was up to scratch. Aghast at this slight, Browne put the American in his place on the question of writing:*

5 Listen, dear, you couldn't write 'f–' on a dusty venetian blind.

Coral Browne, Australian-born actress (1913–91). Quoted by Alan Bennett in *The Sunday Times* Magazine (18 November 1984). The story was confirmed by Browne in a Channel 4 documentary (December 1990).

On the work of Jack Kerouac:

6 That's not writing, that's typing.

Truman Capote, American writer (1924–84). Attributed remark (1959). In Gerald Clarke, *Capote* (1988), '[It] isn't writing at all – it's typing' is given as his view of Beat Generation writers in general.

7 *Waiter:*

Do you just do your writing now – or are you still working?

Charlie:

No ... I just do the writing.

Lines from film *Charlie Bubbles* (UK 1968). Screenwriter: Shelagh Delaney. Spoken by Albert Finney (Charlie Bubbles) and Joe Gladwin (Waiter).

Of Alexandre Dumas:

8 It requires a great man to write so badly as that.

G.K. Chesterton, English poet, novelist and critic (1874–1936). In *A Handful of Authors*, ed. Dorothy Collins (1953).

1 Writing a book was an adventure. To begin with it was a toy, an amusement; then it became a mistress, and then a master, and then a tyrant.

(Sir) Winston S. Churchill, British Conservative Prime Minister and writer (1874–1965). Speech, London (2 November 1949).

2 When I want to read a novel, I write one.

Benjamin Disraeli (1st Earl of Beaconsfield), English politician and writer (1804–81). Quoted in W. Monypenny and G. Buckle, *The Life of Benjamin Disraeli* (1920). Compare the caption to a George Du Maurier cartoon in *Punch*, Vol.74 (11 May 1878), that has a young unpublished scribbler saying: 'The fact is, I never read books - I *write* them!'

3 The best way to become acquainted with a subject is to write a book about it.

Benjamin Disraeli. Quoted in the same work as above.

4 An author who speaks about his own books is almost as bad as the mother who talks about her own children.

Benjamin Disraeli. Rectorial address, Glasgow (19 November 1873).

5 All good writing is *swimming under water* and holding your breath.

F. Scott Fitzgerald, American novelist (1896–1940). In undated letter to Frances Scott Fitzgerald. Quoted in *The Penguin Dictionary of Modern Quotations* (1971), later printed in his *Notebooks* (1978).

6 If you would not be forgotten,
As soon as you are dead and rotten,
Either write things worth reading
Or do things worth the writing.

Benjamin Franklin, American politician and scientist (1706–90). *Poor Richard's Almanack* (May 1738).

7 There's no greater bliss in life than when the plumber eventually comes to unblock your drains. No writer can give that sort of pleasure.

Victoria Glendinning, English biographer and novelist (1937–). Quoted in *The Observer* (3 January 1993).

Of Ernest Hemingway:

8 He got hold of the red meat of the English language and turned it into hamburgers.

Richard Gordon, English novelist (1921–). Possibly quoting another, on BBC Radio *Quote ... Unquote* (17 May 1978).

9 A bad book is as much of a labour to write as a good one.

Aldous Huxley, English novelist and essayist (1894–1963). *Point Counter Point*, Chap. 3 (1928).

On being asked how he would adjust to writing for the wide screen:

10 Very simple. I'll just put the paper in sideways.

Nunnally Johnson, American screenwriter, director and producer (1897–1977). Quoted in Nora Johnson, *Flashback* (1979).

11 No man but a blockhead ever wrote, except for money.

(Dr) Samuel Johnson, English writer and lexicographer (1709–84). Quoted in James Boswell, *The Life of Samuel Johnson* (1791) – for 5 April 1776.

12 Authors are easy enough to get on with – if you are fond of children.

Michael Joseph, English publisher (1897–1958). Quoted in *The Observer* (29 May 1949).

At a rehearsal of the Marx Brothers film Animal Crackers, *for which he wrote the script:*

13 Excuse me for interrupting but I actually thought I heard a line I wrote.

George S. Kaufman, American playwright (1889–1961). Quoted in Scott Meredith, *George S. Kaufman and the Algonquin Round Table* (1974). In fact, this remark probably dates from the days of the stage version of *The Cocoanuts*. In *Harpo Speaks* (1961), Harpo recalled: 'We were a hit ... But we still didn't know George well enough. He came backstage with his chin on his chest and said that Act One seemed to be all right, but Act Two needed another cut. Somewhere in the middle of Act Two – he wasn't exactly sure where – he could have sworn he heard one of his original lines.' In Arthur Marx, *Son of Groucho* (1973), Kaufman turns to Alexander Woollcott at a stage performance of the show and says, 'Be quiet a minute, Alex – I think I just heard one of the original lines.'

1 When audiences come to see authors lecture, it is largely in the hope that we'll be funnier to look at than to read.

Sinclair Lewis, American novelist (1885–1951). Quoted in Laurence J. Peter, *Quotations for Our Time* (1977).

2 If you want to get rich from writing, write the sort of thing that's read by persons who move their lips when reading.

Don Marquis, American writer (1878–1937). Quoted in *The Oxford Dictionary of Literary Quotations*, ed. Peter Kemp (1997).

3 What does [Upton] Sinclair know about anything? He's just a writer.

Louis B. Mayer, American film producer (1885–1957). Quoted in Philip French, *The Movie Moguls* (1969).

4 It is a good thing when these authors die, for then one gets their works and is done with them.

2nd Viscount Melbourne (William Lamb), British Whig Prime Minister (1779–1848). Quoted in Herbert V. Prochnow, Snr & Jnr, *A Treasury of Humorous Quotations* (1969).

5 An author is a fool who, not content with having bored those who have lived with him, insists on boring future generations.

Baron de Montesquieu, French political philosopher (1689–1755). Quoted in *The Treasury of Humorous Quotations*, ed. Evan Esar & Nicolas Bentley (1951).

6 The shelf life of the modern hardback writer is somewhere between the milk and the yoghurt.

(Sir) John Mortimer, English playwright and lawyer (1923–). Quoted in *The Observer* (28 June 1987). As he had, in fact, said at the time, Mortimer was quoting the American humorous columnist Calvin Trillin (1935–) who had spoken, rather, of 'A shelf life somewhere between butter and yoghurt' in *The New York Times* on the 14 June.

7 Everywhere I go I am asked if university stifles writers. My opinion is that it doesn't stifle enough of them.

Flannery O'Connor, American novelist (1925–64). *Wise Blood* (1952).

8 If a third of all the novelists and maybe two-thirds of all the poets now writing dropped dead suddenly the loss to literature would not be great.

Charles Osborne, Australian-born writer and arts administrator (1927–). Quoted in *The Observer*, 'Sayings of the Week' (3 November 1985) from remarks he had made at a (British) Arts Council press conference. It was only later – as he confirmed in 1991 – that Osborne became aware Rebecca West had uttered a similar sentiment at the 1962 Edinburgh Festival Writers' Conference: 'It would be no loss to the world if most of the writers now writing had been strangled at birth' (a remark recorded, for example, in Stephen Spender, *Journals 1939–83*, 1985).

9 Sure, you make money writing on the coast [i.e. in Hollywood], and God knows you earn it, but that money is like so much compressed snow. It goes so fast it melts in your hand.

Dorothy Parker, American writer (1893–1967). Quoted by John Keats in *You Might As Well Live* (1970). Earlier quoted in Malcolm Cowley, *Writers at Work*, 1st Series (1958) as: 'Hollywood money isn't money. It's congealed snow, melts in your hand, and there you are.'

10 Make 'em laugh, make 'em cry, make 'em wait.

Charles Reade, English novelist (1814–84). A suggested recipe for writing novels to be published in serial form (as done by Charles Dickens and many others in the nineteenth century). Reade who wrote *The Cloister and the Hearth* (1861) came up with it – or at least he did according to the *Penguin Dictionary of Quotations* (1960). Kenneth Robinson in his biography *Wilkie Collins* (1951) attributes the remark to Reade's contemporary, Collins.

1 There are three infallible ways of pleasing an author, and the three form a rising scale of compliment: 1, to tell him you have read one of his books; 2, to tell him you have read all his books; 3, to ask him to let you read the manuscript of his forthcoming book. No. 1 admits you to his respect; No. 2 admits you to his admiration; No. 3 carries you clear into his heart.

Mark Twain, American writer (1835–1910). *Pudd'nhead Wilson*, Chap. 11 (1894).

2 After writing for fifteen years it struck me I had no talent for writing. I couldn't give it up. By that time I was already famous.

Mark Twain. Quoted in *The Twainian* (May–June 1952). Robert Benchley, according to Nathaniel Benchley's *Robert Benchley* (1955), covered much the same ground with the reflection: 'It took me fifteen years to discover that I had no talent for writing, but I couldn't give it up because by that time I was too famous.' Compare also from *Punch* (1924): 'It took me nearly ten years to learn that I couldn't write.' 'I suppose you gave it up then?' 'Oh, no! By that time I had a reputation established.'

3 Some writers take to drink, others take to audiences.

Gore Vidal, American novelist, playwright and critic (1925–). In *The Paris Review* (1981).

4 The art of writing is the art of applying the seat of the pants to the seat of the chair.

Mary Heaton Vorse, American writer and social reformer (1898–1966). Quoted in *The Treasury of Humorous Quotations*, ed. Evan Esar & Nicolas Bentley (1951). Compare: 'Inspiration is the act of drawing up a chair to the writing desk' – Anonymous. Quoted in *Chambers Dictionary of Modern Quotations* (1993).

5 I love being a writer. What I can't stand is the paperwork.

Peter de Vries, American writer (1910–93). Quoted in Laurence J. Peter, *Quotations for Our Time* (1977).

6 There are only two forms of writers in England, the unread and the unreadable.

Oscar Wilde, Irish playwright, poet and wit (1854–1900). Quoted in Hesketh Pearson, *The Life of Oscar Wilde* (1946).

7 I never can understand how two men can write a book together; to me that's like three people getting together to have a baby.

Evelyn Waugh, English novelist (1903–66). Quoted in Laurence J. Peter, *Quotations for Our Time* (1977).

Yes-person

1 That woman speaks eighteen languages, and can't say No in any of them.

Dorothy Parker, American writer (1893–1967). Quoted in Alexander Woollcott, *While Rome Burns* (1934).

Characteristic remark to minions:

2 Don't say yes until I finish talking!

Darryl F. Zanuck, American film producer (1902–79). Hence, the title of Mel Gussow's biography of him (1971).

Youth

3 There's nothing wrong with the younger generation that becoming taxpayers won't cure.

Dan Bennett. Attributed remark.

4 It were a real increase of human happiness, could all young men from the age of nineteen be covered under barrels, or rendered otherwise invisible; and there left to follow their lawful studies and callings; till they emerged, sadder and wiser, at the age of twenty-five.

Thomas Carlyle, Scottish historian and philosopher (1795–1881). *Sartor Resartus* (1838).

5 Only the young die good.

Oliver Herford, American humorist (1863–1935). Quoted in *Quotations for Speakers and Writers*, ed. A. Andrews (1969).

On a youthful presidential candidate:

6 Dewey has thrown his diaper into the ring.

Harold L. Ickes, American lawyer and administrator (1874–1952). Quoted in *The New York Times* (12 December 1939).

On the youthful team that accompanied John F. Kennedy into the White House in 1961:

7 I'd feel a lot better if just one or two of them had ever run for sheriff.

Sam Rayburn, American Democratic politician and Speaker of the House of Representatives (1882–1961). Attributed remark.

8 The secret of staying young is mixing with older people.

Ronnie Scott, English jazz musician (1927–96). Quoted by Miles Kington on BBC Radio *Quote ... Unquote* (11 October 1999).

9 Youth is too important to be wasted on the young.

Bernard Shaw, Irish playwright and critic (1856–1950). Quoted in Copeland, *10,000 Jokes, Toasts, & Stories* (1939) in the form '[Youth is] far too good to waste on children'. Quoted as 'Youth is a wonderful thing; what a crime to waste it on children' – in *The Treasury of Humorous Quotations*, ed. Evan Esar & Nicolas Bentley (1951).

10 No wise man ever wished to be younger.

Jonathan Swift, Anglo-Irish writer and clergyman (1667–1745). *Thoughts on Various Subjects* (1706).

1 I suppose that the high-water mark of my youth in Columbus, Ohio, was the night the bed fell on my father.

James Thurber, American writer and cartoonist (1894–1961). *My Life and Hard Times* (1933). The chapter in which this line occurs is simply called 'The Night the Bed Fell'.

When Somerset Maugham left a dinner party early, saying, 'I must look after my youth':

2 Next time do bring him. We adore those sort of people.

Lady Tree, English aristocrat (1863–1937). Quoted in *The Oxford Dictionary of Humorous Quotations*, ed. Ned Sherrin (1995). In Daphne Fielding, *Emerald and Nancy* (1968), this is ascribed rather to Lady ('Emerald') Cunard, the American-born society figure in Britain: 'Then why didn't you bring him with you? I should be delighted to meet him.'

3 To get back my youth I would do anything in the world, except take exercise, get up early, or be respectable.

Oscar Wilde, Irish playwright, poet and wit (1854–1900). *The Picture of Dorian Gray*, Chap. 19 (1891). Later, there is a variation in *A Woman of No Importance*, Act 3 (1893).

4 Those whom the gods love grow young.

Oscar Wilde. In *Saturday Review* (17 November 1894).

5 The youth of America is their oldest tradition. It has been going on now for three hundred years.

Oscar Wilde. *A Woman of No Importance*, Act 1 (1893).

6 The old believe everything; the middle-aged suspect everything; the young know everything.

Oscar Wilde. 'Phrases and Philosophies for the Use of the Young', in *The Chameleon* (December 1894).

Yugoslavia

7 Never shoot a film in Belgrade, Yugoslavia! The whole town is illuminated by a 20-watt night light and there's nothing to do. You can't even go for a drive. Tito is always using the car.

Mel Brooks, American screenwriter, producer and actor (1926–). Quoted in *Newsweek* Magazine (17 February 1975).

8 The Yugoslav nation is a single people, with three religions and two alphabets.

Nicola Pašic, Serbian politician (*c.*1846–1926). He was the new country's Prime Minister in the early 1920s. The longest version of this numerical description would appear to be: 'Yugoslavia is a country of six republics, five nationalities, four languages, three religions, two alphabets, but is still only one country.'

Z

Zoos

1 Zoo: a place devised for animals to study the habits of human beings.

Oliver Herford, American humorist (1863–1935). Quoted in Herbert V. Prochnow, Snr & Jnr, *A Treasury of Humorous Quotations* (1969).

Index

This Index represents quotations in capsule form under keyword headings drawn from the one or two main or most significant words in the quotation. To keep the Index to a reasonable size, not every occurrence of words like 'man' or 'woman' or 'love' (for example) has been recorded here. The correct form of all the quotations is to be found in the main body of the text and not as here in the Index. References are to page number and quotation number: thus, 287:3 refers to quotation 3 on page 287.

A

Index

Index

C

D

E

F

G

H

I

J

K

L

M

N

O

Q

R

S

U

V

W

Y

Z